THE TEACHINGS OF
JOSEPH
SMITH

THE TEACHINGS OF
JOSEPH
SMITH

—— EDITED BY ——

Larry E. Dahl
Donald Q. Cannon

Bookcraft
Salt Lake City, Utah

Library of Congress Catalog Card Number: 97-70327
ISBN 1-57008-311-8

First Printing, 1997

Printed in the United States of America

Introduction

As the editors of this work, we hope it will be of value to all those who desire to study about the teachings of the Prophet Joseph Smith. The following introduction includes information about the need for such a work; our procedure and philosophy in compiling the materials; editorial matters requiring explanation; and discoveries we have made while engaged in our study.

NEED

Many times over the years, as we have studied about Joseph Smith and his doctrinal teachings, we have asked ourselves, Wouldn't it be wonderful to have a book that would tell us what Joseph Smith taught on any given subject? As we have plowed through what seemed to be acres of material in the existing publications to find a single entry, we have longed for an easier way. This work is the result of that desire to simplify the process of learning about Joseph Smith and what he taught.

PROCEDURE

We have tried to consult all relevant and available sources. A bibliography of source material is included at the back of the work. We have included both sources cited and sources consulted. The principal source has been the *History of the Church*. This seven-volume publication has been a literal gold mine, filled with precious ideas from the Prophet.

In one sense, our work is an encyclopedia. It is arranged alphabetically and chronologically. Thus, the quotations on faith are listed under the letter F and appear in chronological order. One can readily see what Joseph Smith said or wrote on the subject of faith at different times in his prophetic career. At the end of many sections, following the general chronological presentations, we have placed reminiscent accounts of what others said Joseph taught that cannot be clearly dated.

One of the big tasks in this project has been categorization. When we encountered a quote or concept, we had to decide how to categorize it. We had to ask, for example, should it be under "Last Days," "Millennium," "Signs," or somewhere else? Though some duplication has been necessary in order to round out the various categories, we have tried to keep such duplication to a minimum.

To assist the reader in finding what he or she is looking for, a detailed index has been provided. This index should enable one to find any statement included in the volume either by subject or by any one of a number of key words in the quotation.

PHILOSOPHY

In our search of the sources we have tried conscientiously to identify which quotes are from Joseph Smith and which are not. Some that traditionally have been attributed to the Prophet clearly came from William W. Phelps, Sidney Rigdon, Oliver Cowdery, or others. We have made a special effort to include only statements which are Joseph Smith's original ideas or which, if borrowed from others, were clearly stated, written, or endorsed by the Prophet. We have included statements from editorials in the *Times and Seasons* during the time Joseph Smith was listed as editor, even though there is evidence that some of the editorials may have been composed by John Taylor.

Our philosophy has dictated that we include statements that either define or explain a given subject or term rather than statements that simply contain a single use of a term. Each quotation must clarify the concept and add to our understanding.

We have generally avoided Joseph Smith's statements about other people, except for a limited number of key scriptural figures and a few entries about people close to Joseph, such as Emma. Joseph's characterization of others would make an interesting book by itself.

In the interest of space, and because they are already easily accessible and indexed, we did not include scriptural passages that came through the Prophet. We have chosen to concentrate on oral or written statements from Joseph Smith that are not a part of the standard works.

Occasionally during the selection process we encountered statements that do not seem to fit our present historical and cultural context. These ideas were understood and appropriate in their own time and place, but now either are irrelevant to current circumstances or have been superseded by subsequent prophetic teachings; therefore, we chose not to include them.

We have tried to use concise statements that capture the essence of the Prophet's thinking. Since we have provided historical notes, with dates and places, as well as source references, the reader can easily go to the relevant sources and read the quotations in a broader context.

The main thrust of our selection of statements has been doctrinal. We have preferred principle and application over more esoteric or abstract ideas.

EXPLANATIONS

Some of our choices in terms of editorial style, designations, and so on may require some explanation. In the interest of readability, where necessary we have chosen to standardize spelling, capitalization, and punctuation rather than leave all the text in its original and often archaic form (the word *standardized* follows all entries that have been so adjusted).

Sometimes we have standardized or even abbreviated the dating of documents. For example, the letter to the elders of the Church written in September 1835 was published serially in the *Messenger and Advocate* from September through December 1835. For purposes of simplification and brevity, in the footnotes we have chosen to list the date for all quotations from that letter as 1 September 1835.

Generally we have identified a letter by its recipient, with place of authorship and date. In the case of the letter to Nancy Rigdon we have chosen to use B. H. Roberts's designation of "Essay on Happiness," and on the basis of Dean C. Jessee's writings (see *PWJS*, p. 689) we have given the place and date as Nauvoo, 27 August 1842.

Any of our own editorial insertions have been placed within square brackets thus: [the Book of Mormon]. Editorial insertions that are part of the original sources quoted have been placed within braces thus: {co-eternal}.

DISCOVERIES

As we have done the research on this project we have made several significant discoveries. One of the major discoveries, somewhat of a surprise to us, is the realization that the *History of the Church* is a much more comprehensive source of Joseph Smith's teachings than we had supposed. Despite the publication of new collections such as *The Words of Joseph Smith, The Papers of Joseph Smith,* and so on, the *History of the Church* is the single most valuable repository of information about Joseph Smith. It is truly a "documentary" history of the Church because of its valuable collection of all kinds of documents. And because of its general accessibility, we used it as the source whenever the Prophet's teachings were included there.

As our research progressed we found ourselves coming back to certain sources over and over again. The key sources would include Sabbath addresses, funeral sermons, remarks to the Relief Society, and letters to the Church. Recognizing this trend, we asked our research assistant, Robert Bond, to run a computer analysis of the key sources in order to determine the number of hits, or the number of times, we used a particular source. A summary of his evaluation follows:

Source	*Hits*
1. Sabbath addresses	370
2. Editorials in the *Times and Seasons*	136 (total)
Single most often used editorial, 15 July 1842	33
3. Conference addresses	110
4. Remarks to the Relief Society	86
5. King Follett Discourse	74
6. Letter to the brethren scattered from Zion, 22 January 1834	67
7. Liberty Jail letter, 20–25 March 1839	46
8. Letter to the elders of the Church, 1 September 1835	42
9. Discourse on the priesthood, sometime before 8 August 1839	31
10. Funeral of James Adams	26
11. Instructions to the Apostles and Seventies, 2 July 1839	20
12. Essay on happiness	12
13. Funeral of Elias Higbee	11

We found it interesting to establish which subjects Joseph Smith taught the most about. The topics selected which received the greatest amount of attention in this work include the following:

Topic	Number of Entries
1. Revelation	49
2. Abraham, Book of	39
3. Obedience	28
4. Truth	26
5. Devil	25
6. Charity	24
7. God	23
8. Jesus Christ	23
9. Knowledge	23
10. Holy Ghost (and Gift of the Holy Ghost)	22
11. Zion	22

Conversely, we were sometimes amazed to find that the Prophet Joseph Smith apparently taught little or nothing about certain subjects. An excellent example would be the Sabbath day. We do not have a single statement on that subject.

In a certain sense we have produced what might be called "the *best* of Joseph Smith as seen through the eyes of the compilers." That is to say, we have tried to select what seemed to us to be the most meaningful, thought-laden statements from Joseph Smith. It has been our intent to make the ideas of the Prophet easily accessible to anyone who has a desire to know what he taught. We hope we have succeeded in some small measure.

LARRY E. DAHL
DONALD Q. CANNON

Acknowledgments

Many people have assisted us as we have worked on this volume. We wish to acknowledge their collective help and to mention by name a few people who played an especially important role.

Robert Bond, a research assistant, did an excellent job of organizing the material and entering it into the computer. Laura Card's computer skills were invaluable. The entire Bookcraft staff has been helpful, and we extend special thanks to Garry Garff for his editorial skill.

We owe a debt of gratitude to all the authors and compilers of the source material consulted. Of considerable help were Truman Madsen's *Condordance of Doctrinal Statements of Joseph Smith*; Dean Jessee's *The Personal Writings of Joseph Smith* and *The Papers of Joseph Smith* (volumes 1 and 2); Andrew Ehat and Lyndon Cook's *The Words of Joseph Smith*; and Hyrum and Mae Andrus's *They Knew the Prophet*.

Finally, we wish to express appreciation to those who developed computer hardware and software which greatly facilitated searching and organizing information.

Key to Abbreviations

In order to simplify references in the text and the footnotes, the following abbreviations are used. More complete publication details can be found in the bibliography.

APPP	Parley P. Pratt, *Autobiography of Parley P. Pratt*
BYU Library	Harold B. Lee Library, Brigham Young University, Provo, Utah
EJ	*Elders' Journal*
E&MS	*The Evening and the Morning Star*
Family of George A. Smith	Zora Smith Jarvis, comp., *Ancestry, Biography, and Family of George A. Smith*
FV	Milton V. Backman, Jr., *Joseph Smith's First Vision*
FWR	Donald Q. Cannon and Lyndon W. Cook, eds., *Far West Record*
Gospel Doctrine	Joseph F. Smith, *Gospel Doctrine*
HC	Joseph Smith, *History of The Church of Jesus Christ of Latter-day Saints*, 7 vols.
HJS	Lucy Mack Smith, *History of Joseph Smith by His Mother*
JD	*Journal of Discourses*, 26 vols.
JSMS	Hyrum Andrus, *Joseph Smith, the Man and the Seer*
JSP	Truman G. Madsen, *Joseph Smith the Prophet*
LDS Church Archives	Church Library or Archives Division, Church Historical Department, The Church of Jesus Christ of Latter-day Saints, Salt Lake City, Utah
LF	Joseph Smith, *Lectures on Faith*
LHCK	Orson F. Whitney, *Life of Heber C. Kimball*

M&A   *Latter Day Saints' Messenger and Advocate*

MS   *Latter-day Saints' Millennial Star*

PJS   Joseph Smith, *The Papers of Joseph Smith*, 2 vols.

PWJS   Joseph Smith, *The Personal Writings of Joseph Smith*

TK   Hyrum L. Andrus and Helen Mae Andrus, comps., *They Knew the Prophet*

TPJS   Joseph Smith, *Teachings of the Prophet Joseph Smith*

T&S   *Times and Seasons*

TWJS   Donald Q. Cannon, comp. *The Wisdom of Joseph Smith*

WJS   Joseph Smith, *The Words of Joseph Smith*

WWJ   Wilford Woodruff, *Wilford Woodruff's Journal, 1833–1898*, 9 vols.

Aaron

1   No man taketh this honor upon himself except he be called of God as was Aaron, and Aaron was baptised in the cloud and in the sea, together with all Israel, as is related by the Apostle in Corinthians. (*T&S* 3:904)

2   The law was given under Aaron for the purpose of pouring out judgments and destructions. (*HC* 5:554)

3   God made Aaron to be the mouthpiece for the children of Israel, and He will make me be god to you in His stead, and the Elders to be mouth for me. (*HC* 6:319–20)

Aaronic Priesthood
See PRIESTHOOD, AARONIC

Abel

1   By faith in this atonement or plan of redemption, Abel offered to God a sacrifice that was accepted, which was the firstlings of the flock. . . . Abel offered an acceptable sacrifice, by which he obtained witness that he was righteous, God Himself testifying of his gifts. . . . However various may have been, and may be at the present time, the opinions of men respecting the conduct of Abel, and the knowledge which he had on the subject of atonement, it is evident in our minds, that he was instructed more fully in the plan than what the Bible

---

Aaron
1   Editorial in the *Times and Seasons*, 1 September 1842.
2   Sabbath address, Nauvoo, 27 August 1843.
3   General conference address, Nauvoo, 8 April 1844.

Abel
1   Letter to the brethren scattered from Zion, Kirtland, 22 January 1834.

speaks of, for how could he offer a sacrifice in faith, looking to God for a remission of his sins in the power of the great atonement, without having been previously instructed in that plan? And further, if he was accepted of God, what were the ordinances performed further than the offering of the firstlings of the flock?

It is said by Paul in his letter to the Hebrew brethren, that Abel obtained witness that he was righteous, God testifying of his gifts. To whom did God testify of the gifts of Abel, was it to Paul? We have very little on this important subject in the forepart of the Bible. But it is said that Abel himself obtained witness that he was righteous. Then certainly God spoke to him: indeed, it is said that God talked with him; and if He did, would He not, seeing that Abel was righteous, deliver to him the whole plan of the Gospel? And is not the Gospel the news of the redemption? How could Abel offer a sacrifice and look forward with faith on the Son of God for a remission of his sins, and not understand the Gospel? The mere shedding of the blood of beasts or offering anything else in sacrifice, could not procure a remission of sins, except it were performed in faith of something to come; if it could, Cain's offering must have been as good as Abel's. And if Abel was taught of the coming of the Son of God, was he not taught also of His ordinances? We all admit that the Gospel has ordinances, and if so, had it not always ordinances, and were not its ordinances always the same? (*HC* 2:15–16)

2   We read in Genesis, (4th chap., 4th verse), that Abel brought of the firstlings of the flock and the fat thereof, and the Lord had respect to Abel and to his offering. And, again, "By faith Abel offered unto God a more excellent sacrifice than Cain, by which he obtained witness that he was righteous, God testifying of his gifts; and by it he being dead, yet speaketh." (Hebrews xi:4). How doth he yet speak? Why he magnified the Priesthood which was conferred upon him, and died a righteous man, and therefore has become an angel of God by receiving his body from the dead, holding still the keys of his dispensation; and was sent down from heaven unto Paul to minister consoling words, and to commit unto him a knowledge of the mysteries of godliness.

And if this was not the case, I would ask, how did Paul know so much about Abel, and why should he talk about his speaking after he

---

Abel
2   Article on priesthood read at general conference, Nauvoo, 5 October 1840.

was dead? Hence, that he spoke after he was dead must be by being sent down out of heaven to administer. (HC 4:208–9)

3   Abel was slain for his righteousness. . . . Did these afflictions come upon these prophets [Abel, Abraham, Moses, Elijah, and others] of the Lord on account of transgression? No! It was the iron hand of persecution—like the chains of Missouri! And mark—when these old prophets suffered, the vengeance of God, in due time, followed and left the wicked opposers of the Lord's anointed like Sodom and Gomorrah; like the Egyptians; like Jezebel, who was eaten by dogs; and like all Israel, which were led away captive, till the Lord had spent his fury upon them—even to this day. (*T&S* 3:902)

4   If, then Abel was a righteous man he had to become so by keeping the commandments. (*T&S* 3:905)

Abraham
See also TRIALS

1   I must not pass over a notice of the history of Abraham, of whom so much is spoken in the Scripture. If we can credit the account, God conversed with him from time to time, and directed him in the way he should walk, saying, "I am the Almighty; walk before me, and be thou perfect." Paul says the Gospel was preached to this man. And it is further said, that he had sheep and oxen, men-servants and maid-servants, etc. From this I conclude, that if the principle had been an evil one, in the midst of the communications made to this holy man, he would have been instructed to that effect, and if he was instructed against holding men-servants and maid-servants, he never ceased to do it; consequently must have incurred the displeasure of the Lord, and thereby lost His blessings; which was not the fact. (HC 2:439)

Abel
3   Editorial in the *Times and Seasons*, 1 September 1842.
4   Editorial in the *Times and Seasons*, 1 September 1842.

Abraham
1   Letter on abolition published in the *Messenger and Advocate*, April 1836.

2   The learning of the Egyptians, and their knowledge of astronomy was no doubt taught them by Abraham and Joseph, as their records testify, who received it from the Lord. . . .

Abraham was guided in all his family affairs by the Lord; was conversed with by angels, and by the Lord; was told where to go, and when to stop; and prospered exceedingly in all that he put his hand unto; it was because he and his family obeyed the counsel of the Lord. (HC 5:63, 64)

3   If we believe in present revelation, as published in the Times and Seasons last spring, Abraham, the prophet of the Lord, was laid upon the iron bedstead for slaughter; and the book of Jasher, which has not been disproved as a bad author, says he was cast into the fire of the Chaldees. (*T&S* 3:902)

4   The King of Shiloam, (Salem) had power and authority over that of Abraham, holding the key and the power of endless life. Angels desire to look into it, but they have set up too many stakes. . . .

The sacrifice required of Abraham in the offering up of Isaac, shows that if a man would attain to the keys of the kingdom of an endless life, he must sacrifice all things. . . .

Abraham says to Melchizedek, I believe all that thou hast taught me concerning the priesthood and the coming of the Son of Man; so Melchizedek ordained Abraham and sent him away. Abraham rejoiced, saying, Now I have a priesthood. (HC 5:554–55)

Abraham, Book of

1   On the 3rd of July, Michael H. Chandler came to Kirtland to exhibit some Egyptian mummies. There were four human figures, together with some two or more rolls of papyrus covered with hiero-

---

Abraham
   2   Editorial in the *Times and Seasons*, 15 July 1842.
   3   Editorial in the *Times and Seasons*, 1 September 1842.
   4   Sabbath address, Nauvoo, 27 August 1843.

Abraham, Book of
   1   Entry in the *History of the Church* illustrating the involvement of the Prophet with the book of Abraham materials in Kirtland.

glyphic figures and devices. As Mr. Chandler had been told I could translate them, he brought me some of the characters, and I gave him the interpretation, and like a gentleman, he gave me the following certificate:

> Kirtland, July 6, 1835.
>
> This is to make known to all who may be desirous, concerning the knowledge of Mr. Joseph Smith, Jun., in deciphering the ancient Egyptian hieroglyphic characters in my possession, which I have, in many eminent cities, showed to the most learned; and, from the information that I could ever learn, or meet with, I find that of Mr. Joseph Smith, Jun., to correspond in the most minute matters.
>
> Michael H. Chandler,
> Traveling with, and proprietor of, Egyptian mummies. (*HC* 2:235)

2   *Early July 1835.* Soon after this, some of the Saints at Kirtland purchased the mummies and papyrus, a description of which will appear hereafter, and with W. W. Phelps and Oliver Cowdery as scribes, I commenced the translation of some of the characters or hieroglyphics, and much to our joy found that one of the rolls contained the writings of Abraham, another the writings of Joseph of Egypt, etc.,—a more full account of which will appear in its place, as I proceed to examine or unfold them. Truly we can say, the Lord is beginning to reveal the abundance of peace and truth. (*HC* 2:236)

3   *July 1835.* The remainder of this month, I was continually engaged in translating an alphabet to the Book of Abraham, and arranging a grammar of the Egyptian language as practiced by the ancients. (*HC* 2:238)

4   *1 October 1835.* This afternoon I labored on the Egyptian alphabet, in company with Brothers Oliver Cowdery and W. W. Phelps, and during the research, the principles of astronomy as understood by Father Abraham and the ancients unfolded to our understanding, the particulars of which will appear hereafter. (*HC* 2:286)

Abraham, Book of

   2–4 Entries in the *History of the Church* illustrating the involvement of the Prophet with the book of Abraham materials in Kirtland.

5 *3 October 1835*. In the afternoon I waited on most of the Twelve, at my house, and exhibited to them the ancient records, and gave explanations. This day passed off with the blessing of the Lord. (HC 2:287)

6 *7 October 1835*. This afternoon I re-commenced translating the ancient records. (HC 2:289)

7 *19 October 1835*. Exhibited the records of antiquity to a number who called to see them. (HC 2:290)

8 *24 October 1835*. Mr. Goodrich and wife called to see the ancient {Egyptian} records, and also Dr. Frederick G. Williams to see the mummies. (HC 2:291)

9 *29 October 1835*. While at the doctor's, Bishop Edward Partridge came in in company with President Phelps. I was much rejoiced to see him. We examined the mummies, returned home, and my scribe commenced writing in my journal a history of my life. (HC 2:293)

10 *17 November 1835*. Exhibited the alphabet of the ancient records, to Mr. Holmes, and some others. Went with him to Frederick G. Williams', to see the mummies. (HC 2:316)

11 *19 November 1835*. I returned home and spent the day in translating the Egyptian records. (HC 2:318)

12 *20 November 1835*. We spent the day in translating, and made rapid progress. (HC 2:318)

13 *23 November 1835*. Several brethren called to converse with me, and see the records. (HC 2:319)

14 *24 November 1835*. In the afternoon we translated some of the Egyptian records. (HC 2:320)

15 *25 November 1835*. Spent the day in translating. (HC 2:320)

Abraham, Book of

  5–15 Entries in the *History of the Church* illustrating the involvement of the Prophet with the book of Abraham materials in Kirtland.

16 *26 November 1835.* Spent the day in translating Egyptian characters from the papyrus, though severely afflicted with a cold. (HC 2:320–21)

17 *30 November 1835.* Henry Capron, an old acquaintance from Manchester, New York, called on me. I showed him the Egyptian records. (HC 2:322)

18 *7 December 1835.* This evening a number of brethren called to see the records, which I exhibited and explained. (HC 2:326)

19 *10 December 1835.* This morning a number of brethren called to see the records, {Egyptian} which I exhibited to their satisfaction. (HC 2:327–28)

20 *12 December 1835.* Spent the forenoon in reading. About twelve o'clock a number of young persons called to see the Egyptian records. My scribe exhibited them. One of the young ladies who had been examining them, was asked if they had the appearance of antiquity. She observed, with an air of contempt, that they had not. On hearing this, I was surprised at the ignorance she displayed, and I observed to her, that she was an anomaly in creation, for all the wise and learned that had examined them, without hesitation pronounced them ancient. I further remarked, that it was downright wickedness, ignorance, bigotry and superstition had caused her to make the remark; and that I would put it on record. (HC 2:329–30)

21 *14 December 1835.* A number of brethren from New York called to visit me and see the Egyptian records. (HC 2:331)

22 *16 December 1835.* Elders William E. M'Lellin, Brigham Young, and Jared Carter, called and paid me a visit with which I was much gratified. I exhibited and explained the Egyptian records to them, and explained many things concerning the dealing of God with the ancients, and the formation of the planetary system. (HC 2:334)

23 *20 December 1835.* Brothers Palmer and Taylor called to see me. I showed them the sacred records to their joy and satisfaction. (HC 2:344)

Abraham, Book of
   16–23 Entries in the *History of the Church* illustrating the involvement of the Prophet with the book of Abraham materials in Kirtland.

24 *23 December 1835.* [I] also waited upon the brethren who came in, and exhibited to them the papyrus. (*HC* 2:344)

25 The public mind has been excited of late, by reports which have been circulated concerning certain Egyptian mummies and ancient records, which were purchased by certain gentlemen of Kirtland, last July. It has been said that the purchasers of these antiquities pretend they have the bodies of Abraham, Abimelech, (the king of the Philistines,) Joseph, who was sold into Egypt, &c., &c., for the purpose of attracting the attention of the multitude, and gulling the unwary; which is utterly false. Who these ancient inhabitants of Egypt were, I do not at present say. Abraham was buried on his own possession "in the cave of Machpelah, in the field of Ephron, the son of Zohah, the Hittite, which is before Mamre," which he purchased of the sons of Heth. Abimelech lived in the same country, and for aught we know, died there; and the children of Israel carried Joseph's bones from Egypt, when they went out under Moses; consequently, these could not have been found in Egypt, in the nineteenth century. The record of Abraham and Joseph, found with the mummies, is beautifully written on papyrus, with black, and a small part red, ink or paint, in perfect preservation. The characters are such as you find upon the coffins of mummies—hieroglyphics, etc.; with many characters of letters like the present (though probably not quite so square) form of the Hebrew without points. The records were obtained from one of the catacombs in Egypt, near the place where once stood the renowned city of Thebes, by the celebrated French traveler, Antonio Sebolo, in the year 1831. He procured license from Mehemet Ali, then Viceroy of Egypt, under the protection of Chevalier Drovetti, the French Consul, in the year 1828, and employed four hundred and thirty-three men, four months and two days (if I understand correctly)—Egyptian or Turkish soldiers, at from four to six cents per diem, each man. He entered the catacomb June 7, 1831, and obtained eleven mummies. There were several hundred mummies in the same catacomb; about one hundred embalmed after the first order, and placed in niches, and two or three hundred after the second and third orders, and laid upon the floor or bottom of the grand cavity. The two last orders of embalmed were so decayed, that they could not be removed, and only eleven of the first,

---

Abraham, Book of
   24–25 Entries in the *History of the Church* illustrating the involvement of the Prophet with the book of Abraham materials in Kirtland.

found in the niches. On his way from Alexandria to Paris, he put in at Trieste, and, after ten days' illness, expired. This was in the year 1832. Previous to his decease, he made a will of the whole, to Mr. Michael H. Chandler, (then in Philadelphia, Pa.,) his nephew, whom he supposed to be in Ireland. Accordingly, the whole were sent to Dublin, and Mr. Chandler's friends ordered them to New York, where they were received at the Custom House, in the winter or spring of 1833. In April, of the same year, Mr. Chandler paid the duties and took possession of his mummies. Up to this time, they had not been taken out of the coffins, nor the coffins opened. On opening the coffins, he discovered that in connection with two of the bodies, was something rolled up with the same kind of linen, saturated with the same bitumen, which, when examined, proved to be two rolls of papyrus, previously mentioned. Two or three other small pieces of papyrus, with astronomical calculations, epitaphs, &c., were found with others of the mummies. When Mr. Chandler discovered that there was something with the mummies, he supposed or hoped it might be some diamonds or valuable metal, and was no little chagrined when he saw his disappointment. "He was immediately told, while yet in the custom house, that there was no man in that city who could translate his roll; but was referred, by the same gentleman, (a stranger,) to Mr. Joseph Smith, Jun., who, continued he, possesses some kind of power or gifts, by which he had previously translated similar characters." I was then unknown to Mr. Chandler, neither did he know that such a book or work as the record of the Nephites, had been brought before the public. From New York, he took his collection on to Philadelphia, where he obtained the certificate of the learned, and from thence came on to Kirtland, as before related, in July. Thus I have given a brief history of the manner in which the writings of the fathers, Abraham and Joseph, have been preserved, and how I came in possession of the same—a correct translation of which I shall give in its proper place. (HC 2:348–51)

26 *12 January 1836.* This afternoon, a young man called to see the Egyptian manuscripts, which I exhibited. (HC 2:364)

27 *30 January 1836.* Attended school, as usual, and waited upon several visitors, and showed them the record of Abraham. Mr. Seixas, our

---

Abraham, Book of

26–27 Entries in the *History of the Church* illustrating the involvement of the Prophet with the book of Abraham materials in Kirtland.

Hebrew teacher, examined it with deep interest, and pronounced it to be original beyond all doubt. He is a man of excellent understanding, and has a knowledge of many languages which were spoken by the ancients, and he is an honorable man, so far as I can judge yet. (HC 2:388)

28 *3 February 1836.* Received many visitors, and showed them the Records of Abraham. (HC 2:390–91)

29 *11 February 1836.* Spent the afternoon in reading, and in exhibiting the Egyptian records to those who called to see me. (HC 2:394)

30 *16 February 1836.* Many called to see the House of the Lord, and the Egyptian manuscript, and to visit me. (HC 2:396)

31 *17 February 1836.* Elder Coe called to make some arrangements about the Egyptian mummies and records. He proposes to hire a room at John Johnson's Inn, and exhibit them there from day to day, at certain hours, that some benefit may be derived from them. I complied with his request, and only observed that they must be managed with prudence and care, especially the manuscripts. (HC 2:396)

32 *22 February 1836.* Spent the afternoon translating with my scribe, Elder Warren Parrish, at his house. (HC 2:398)

33 *2 November 1837.* The Church in Kirtland voted to sanction the appointment of Brother Phinehas Richards and Reuben Hedlock, by the Presidency, to transact business for the Church in procuring means to translate and print the records taken from the Catacombs of Egypt, then in the Temple. (HC 2:520–21)

34 *23 February 1842.* [I] gave Reuben Hedlock instruction concerning the cut for the altar and gods in the Records of Abraham, as designed for the *Times and Seasons*. (HC 4:518)

Abraham, Book of

28–33   Entries in the *History of the Church* illustrating the involvement of the Prophet with the book of Abraham materials in Kirtland.

34   Entry in the *History of the Church* illustrating the involvement of the Prophet with the book of Abraham materials in Nauvoo.

35 *1 March 1842.* During the forenoon I was at my office and the printing office, correcting the first plate or cut of the records of Father Abraham, prepared by Reuben Hedlock, for the *Times and Seasons.* (HC 4:519)

36 *4 March 1842.* At my office exhibiting the Book of Abraham in the original to Brother Reuben Hedlock, so that he might take the size of the several plates or cuts, and prepare the blocks for the *Times and Seasons;* and also gave instruction concerning the arrangement of the writing on the large cut, illustrating the principles of astronomy, with other general business. (HC 4:543)

37 *8 March 1842.* Recommenced translating from the Records of Abraham for the tenth number of the *Times and Seasons,* and was engaged at my office day and evening. (HC 4:548)

38 *9 March 1842.* In the afternoon [I] continued the translation of the Book of Abraham, called at Bishop Knight's and Mr. Davis', with the recorder, and continued translating and revising. (HC 4:548)

39 *16 May 1842.* I published in this day's *Times and Seasons* the following *fac-simile* [facsimile no. 3] from the Book of Abraham.

Several of the most widely circulated papers are beginning to exhibit "Mormonism" in its true light. The first out of a *fac-simile* from the Book of Abraham, has been republished both in the New York *Herald* and in the *Dollar Week Bostonian,* as well as in the *Boston Daily Ledger,* edited by Mr. Bartlett; together with the translation from the Book of Abraham. (HC 5:11)

Abrahamic Covenant

1 *Report of Don Carlos Smith:* [President Joseph Smith] then spoke on the subject of election, and read the 9th chapter of Romans, from

Abraham, Book of
    35–39 Entries in the *History of the Church* illustrating the involvement of the Prophet with the book of Abraham materials in Nauvoo.

Abrahamic Covenant
    1   Sabbath address, Nauvoo, 16 May 1841.

which it was evident that the election there spoken of was pertaining to the flesh, and had reference to the seed of Abraham, according to the promise God made to Abraham, saying, "In thee, and in thy seed, all the families of the earth shall be blessed." To them belonged the adoption and the covenants, &c. . . . The election of the promised seed still continues, and in the last day, they shall have the Priesthood restored unto them, and they shall be the "saviors on Mount Zion," the ministers of our God; if it were not for the remnant which was left, then might men now be as Sodom and Gomorrah. (HC 4:359–60)

Abundant Life

1   Were the virtues of the inhabitants [of Zion] only equal to the blessings of the Lord which He permits to crown the industry of those inhabitants, there would be a measure of the good things of life for the benefit of the Saints, full, pressed down, and running over, even an hundredfold. (HC 1:198)

2   Agreeable to a notice we gave you, in Brother Whitney's last letter to you with respect to answering your letters, we now commence, after giving thanks to our Heavenly Father for every expression of His goodness in preserving our unprofitable lives to the present time, and for the health and other blessings which we now enjoy through His mercies. (HC 1:340)

3   In our own country, surrounded with blessings innumerable, to which thousands of our fellow men are strangers, enjoying unspeakable benefits and inexpressible comforts, when once our situation is compared with the ancient Saints, as followers of the Lamb of God who has taken away our sins by His own blood, we are bound to rejoice and give thanks to Him always. (HC 2:22)

4   Brother Noah Packard came to my house and loaned the committee one thousand dollars to assist building the house of the Lord. Oh!

Abundant Life
  1   Reflections when the Prophet first arrived in Missouri, August 1831.
  2   Letter to the brethren in Zion, Kirtland, 21 April 1833.
  3   Letter to the brethren scattered from Zion, Kirtland, 22 January 1834.
  4   Kirtland, 23 September 1835.

may God bless him a hundred fold, even of the things of the earth, for this righteous act. My heart is full of desire today, to be blessed of the God of Abraham with prosperity, until I shall be able to pay all my debts, for it is the delight of my soul to be honest. O Lord, that thou knowest right well. Help me, and I will give to the poor. (HC 2:281)

5 We united in prayer, with one voice, before the Lord, for the following blessings: That the Lord would give us means sufficient to deliver us from all our afflictions and difficulties wherein we are placed by reason of our debts; . . . that He would give us blessings of the earth sufficient to carry us to Zion, and that we may purchase inheritances in that land, even enough to carry on and accomplish the work unto which He has appointed us; and also that He would assist all others who desire, according to His commandments, to go up and purchase inheritances, and all this easily and without perplexity and trouble; and finally, that in the end He would save us in His celestial kingdom. Amen. (HC 2:291)

6 The brethren have . . . been very industrious, and supplied me with my winter's wood, for which I am sincerely grateful to each and every one of them, and shall remember, with warm emotions, this expression of their goodness to me. And in the name of Jesus Christ I invoke the rich benediction of heaven to rest upon them and their families; and I ask my heavenly Father to preserve their health, and that of their wives and children, that they may have strength of body to perform their labors in their several occupations in life, and the use and activity of their limbs, also powers of intellect and understanding hearts, that they may treasure up wisdom, understanding and intelligence above measure, and be preserved from plagues, pestilence, and famine, and from the power of the adversary, and the hands of evil-designing men, and have power over all their enemies, and the way be prepared for them that they may journey to the land of Zion, and be established on their inheritances, to enjoy undisturbed peace and happiness forever, and ultimately be crowned with everlasting life in the celestial Kingdom of God, which blessing I ask in the name of Jesus of Nazareth. Amen.

Abundant Life
  5   Kirtland, 23 October 1835.
  6   Kirtland, 10 December 1835.

I would remember Elder Leonard Rich, who was the first one that proposed to the brethren to assist me in obtaining wood for the use of my family, for which I pray my heavenly Father to bless him with all the blessings named above. And I shall ever remember him with much gratitude, for this testimony of benevolence and respect, and thank the great I AM for putting into his heart to do me this kindness. (HC 2:328–29)

7   Let us realize that we are not to live to ourselves, but to God; by so doing the greatest blessings will rest upon us both in time and in eternity. (HC 4:231)

8   After consultation . . . the brethren united in solemn prayer that God . . . would deliver His anointed, His people, from . . . all mobs and evil designing persons, so that His people might continue in peace and build up the city of Nauvoo, and that His chosen might be blessed and live to man's appointed age, and that their households, and the household of faith might continually be blest with the fostering care of heaven, and enjoy the good things of the earth abundantly. (HC 5:45)

9   As God governed Abraham, Isaac and Jacob as families, and the children of Israel as a nation; so we, as a Church, must be under His guidance if we are prospered, preserved and sustained. Our only confidence can be in God; our only wisdom obtained from Him; and He alone must be our protector and safeguard, spiritually and temporally, or we fall. (HC 5:65)

10 You have done great things, and manifested your love towards me in flying to my assistance on this occasion. I bless you, in the name of the Lord, with all the blessings of heaven and earth you are capable of enjoying.
      I have learned that we have no need to suffer as we have heretofore: we can call others to our aid. I know the Almighty will bless all good men: he will bless you. (HC 5:468)

Abundant Life
   7   Letter to the Twelve in England, Nauvoo, 15 December 1840. The placement of this letter in HC implies that it was written in October 1840, but actually it was written on 15 December 1840 (see *PWJS*, p. 480).
   8   Meeting of the high council in the Prophet's home, Nauvoo, 26 June 1842.
   9   Editorial in the *Times and Seasons*, 15 July 1842.
   10 Address regarding his arrest at Dixon, Illinois, Nauvoo, 30 June 1843.

11 God bless good men and good measures! (HC 6:220)

Abuse

1 A man who will whip his wife is a coward. (*WJS*, p. 166)

Accountability

1 Therefore I declare unto you the warning which the Lord has commanded to declare unto this generation, remembering that the eyes of my Maker are upon me, and that to him I am accountable for every word I say. (*HC* 1:315)

2 I have no doubt but that you will agree with me that men will be held accountable for the things which they have and not for the things they have not, or that all the light and intelligence communicated to them from their beneficent creator, whether it is much or little, by the same they in justice will be judged, and that they are required to yield obedience and improve upon that and that only which is given, for man is not to live by bread alone but by every word that proceeds out of the mouth of God. (*PWJS*, p. 298; standardized)

3 Men not unfrequently forget that they are dependent upon heaven for every blessing which they are permitted to enjoy, and that for every opportunity granted them they are to give an account. (*HC* 2:23–24)

Abundant Life
   11 Article entitled "Pacific Innuendo," Nauvoo, 17 February 1844.

Abuse
   1 Address at the temple site in Nauvoo, 21 February 1843.

Accountability
   1 Letter to N. E. Seaton (N. C. Saxton), a newspaper editor in Rochester, N.Y., Kirtland, 4 January 1833.
   2 Letter to Silas Smith, the Prophet's uncle, Kirtland, 26 September 1833.
   3 Letter to the brethren scattered from Zion, Kirtland, 22 January 1834.

4   Before closing this communication, I beg leave to drop a word to the traveling Elders. You know, brethren, that great responsibility rests upon you; and that you are accountable to God, for all you teach the world. (*HC* 2:440)

5   Our heavenly Father is more liberal in His views, and boundless in His mercies and blessings, than we are ready to believe or receive; and, at the same time, is more terrible to the workers of iniquity, more awful in the executions of His punishments, and more ready to detect every false way, than we are apt to suppose Him to be. He will be inquired of by His children. He says: "Ask and ye shall receive, seek and ye shall find;" but, if you will take that which is not your own, or which I have not given you, you shall be rewarded according to your deeds; but no good thing will I withhold from them who walk uprightly before me, and do my will in all things—who will listen to my voice and to the voice of my servant whom I have sent; for I delight in those who seek diligently to know my precepts, and abide by the law of my kingdom; for all things shall be made known unto them in mine own due time, and in the end they shall have joy. (*HC* 5:136)

6   But while one portion of the human race is judging and condemning the other without mercy, the Great Parent of the universe looks upon the whole of the human family with a fatherly care and paternal regard; He views them as His offspring, and without any of those contracted feelings that influence the children of men, causes "His sun to rise on the evil and on the good, and sendeth rain on the just and on the unjust." He holds the reins of judgment in His hands; He is a wise Lawgiver, and will judge all men, not according to the narrow, contracted notions of men, but, "according to the deeds done in the body whether they be good or evil," or whether these deeds were done in England, America, Spain, Turkey, or India. He will judge them, "not according to what they have not, but according to what they have," those who have lived without law, will be judged without law, and those who have a law, will be judged by that law. We need not doubt the wisdom and intelligence of the Great Jehovah; He will award

---

Accountability
   4   Letter on abolition published in the *Messenger and Advocate*, April 1836.
   5   Essay on happiness, Nauvoo, 27 August 1842.
   6   Editorial in the *Times and Seasons*, 15 April 1842.

judgment or mercy to all nations according to their several deserts, their means of obtaining intelligence, the laws by which they are governed, the facilities afforded them of obtaining correct information, and His inscrutable designs in relation to the human family; and when the designs of God shall be made manifest, and the curtain of futurity be withdrawn, we shall all of us eventually have to confess that the Judge of all the earth has done right. . . .

If human laws award to each man his deserts, and punish all delinquents according to their several crimes, surely the Lord will not be more cruel than man, for He is a wise legislator, and His laws are more equitable, His enactments more just, and His decisions more perfect than those of man; and as man judges his fellow man by law, and punishes him according to the penalty of the law, so does God of heaven judge "according to the deeds done in the body." To say that the heathens would be damned because they did not believe the Gospel would be preposterous, and to say that the Jews would all be damned that do not believe in Jesus would be equally absurd; for "how can they believe on him of whom they have not heard, and how can they hear without a preacher, and how can he preach except he be sent;" consequently neither Jew nor heathen can be culpable for rejecting the conflicting opinions of sectarianism, nor for rejecting any testimony but that which is sent of God, for as the preacher cannot preach except he be sent, so the hearer cannot believe without he hear a "sent" preacher, and cannot be condemned for what he has not heard, and being without law, will have to be judged without law. (HC 4: 595–96, 598)

7   After this instruction, you will be responsible for your own sins . . . ; we are all responsible to God for the manner we improve the light and wisdom given by our Lord to enable us to save ourselves. (HC 4:606)

8   God judges men according to the use they make of the light which He gives them. (HC 5:401)

Accountability
7   Remarks to the Relief Society, Nauvoo, 28 April 1842.
8   Sabbath address, Nauvoo, 21 May 1843.

Adam

1   My father . . . shall sit in the general assembly of Patriarchs, even in council with the Ancient of Days when he shall sit and all the Patriarchs with him and shall enjoy his right and authority under the direction of the Ancient of Days. (*TPJS*, p. 39)

2   *Words of Zebedee Coltrin:* Once after returning from a mission to Kirtland, I met Brother Joseph, who asked me if I did not wish to go with him to a conference at New Portage, Ohio. The party consisted of Presidents Joseph Smith, Sidney Rigdon, Oliver Cowdery and me. Next morning at New Portage, I noticed that Joseph seemed to have a far off look in his eyes, or was looking at a distance. Presently he stepped between Brother Cowdery and me, and taking us by the arm said, "Let's take a walk."

We went to a place where there was some beautiful grass, and grapevines and swamp birch interlaced. President Joseph Smith then said, "Let us pray."

We all three prayed in turn—Joseph, Oliver and me. Brother Joseph then said, "Now brethren, we will see some visions."

Joseph lay down on the ground on his back and stretched out his arms, and we laid on them. The heavens gradually opened, and we saw a golden throne, on a circular foundation, and on the throne sat a man and a woman, having white hair and clothed in white garments. Their heads were white as snow, and their faces shone with immortal youth. They were the two most beautiful and perfect specimens of mankind I ever saw. Joseph said, "They are our first parents, Adam and Eve."

Adam was a large broad shouldered man, and Eve, as a woman, was as large in proportion. (*TK*, p. 28)

Adam

  1 The Prophet's blessing upon his father, 18 December 1833.

  2 Vision to Joseph Smith and Zebedee Coltrin as reported by Zebedee Coltrin at a meeting of high priests, Spanish Fork, Utah, 5 February 1878. The vision described took place presumably sometime in April 1834.

3   After man was created, he was not left without intelligence or understanding, to wander in darkness and spend an existence in ignorance and doubt (on the great and important point which effected his happiness) as to the real fact by whom he was created, or unto whom he was amenable for his conduct. God conversed with him face to face. In his presence he was permitted to stand, and from his own mouth he was permitted to receive instruction. He heard his voice, walked before him and gazed upon his glory, while intelligence burst upon his understanding, and enabled him to give names to the vast assemblage of his Maker's works. (*LF* 2:18)

4   The Priesthood was first given to Adam; he obtained the First Presidency, and held the keys of it from generation to generation. He obtained it in the Creation, before the world was formed, as in Gen. i: 26, 27, 28. He had dominion given him over every living creature. He is Michael the Archangel, spoken of in the Scriptures. Then to Noah, who is Gabriel; he stands next in authority to Adam in the Priesthood; he was called of God to this office, and was the father of all living in his day, and to him was given the dominion. These men held keys first on earth, and then in heaven.

The Priesthood is an everlasting principle, and existed with God from eternity, and will to eternity, without beginning of days or end of years. The keys have to be brought from heaven whenever the Gospel is sent. When they are revealed from heaven, it is by Adam's authority.

Daniel in his seventh chapter speaks of the Ancient of Days; he means the oldest man, our Father Adam, Michael, he will call his children together and hold a council with them to prepare them for the coming of the Son of Man. He (Adam) is the father of the human family, and presides over the spirits of all men, and all that have had the keys must stand before him in this grand council. This may take place before some of us leave this stage of action. The Son of Man stands before him, and there is given him glory and dominion. Adam

---

Adam

3   Lectures on Faith, delivered to a school of the elders, Kirtland, December 1834. Although the Lectures on Faith were not written only by Joseph Smith, he reviewed them carefully and prepared them for publication (see Larry E. Dahl and Charles D. Tate, Jr., eds., *The Lectures on Faith in Historical Perspective*, p. 10).

4   Discourse on the priesthood, given sometime before 8 August 1839, Commerce (Nauvoo). For a discussion on the dating of this discourse, see *WJS*, p. 22.

delivers up his stewardship to Christ, that which was delivered to him as holding the keys of the universe, but retains his standing as head of the human family.

. . . The Father called all spirits before Him at the creation of man, and organized them. He (Adam) is the head, and was told to multiply. The keys were first given to him, and by him to others. He will have to give an account of his stewardship, and they to him. . . .

. . . Christ is the Great High Priest; Adam next. . . .

I saw Adam in the valley of Adam-ondi-Ahman. He called together his children and blessed them with a patriarchal blessing. The Lord appeared in their midst, and he (Adam) blessed them all, and foretold what should befall them to the latest generation.

This is why Adam blessed his posterity; he wanted to bring them into the presence of God. (HC 3:385–88)

5 [The Melchizedek Priesthood] is the channel through which the Almighty commenced revealing His glory at the beginning of the creation of this earth, and through which He has continued to reveal Himself to the children of men to the present time, and through which He will make known His purposes to the end of time.

Commencing with Adam, who was the first man, who is spoken of in Daniel as being the "Ancient of Days," or in other words, the first and oldest of all, the great, grand progenitor of whom it is said in another place he is Michael, because he was the first and father of all, not only by progeny, but the first to hold the spiritual blessings, to whom was made known the plan of ordinances for the salvation of his posterity unto the end, and to whom Christ was first revealed, and through whom Christ has been revealed from heaven, and will continue to be revealed from henceforth. Adam holds the keys of the dispensation of the fullness of times; i.e., the dispensation of all the times have been and will be revealed through him from the beginning to Christ, and from Christ to the end of all the dispensations that are to be revealed. "Having made known unto us the mystery of His will, according to His good pleasure which He hath purposed in Himself: that in the dispensation of the fullness of times He might gather together in one all things in Christ, both which are in heaven, and which are on earth; even in him." (Ephesians, 1st chap., 9th and 10th verses). . . .

Adam
5 Article on priesthood read at general conference, Nauvoo, 5 October 1840.

. . . He [God] set the ordinances to be the same forever and ever, and set Adam to watch over them, to reveal them from heaven to man, or to send angels to reveal them. "Are they not all ministering spirits, sent forth to minister for them who shall be heirs of salvation?" (Hebrews i, 14).

These angels are under the direction of Michael or Adam, who acts under the direction of the Lord. From the above quotation we learn that Paul perfectly understood the purposes of God in relation to His connection with man, and that glorious and perfect order which He established in Himself, whereby he sent forth power, revelations, and glory.

God will not acknowledge that which He has not called, ordained, and chosen. In the beginning God called Adam by His own voice. "And the Lord called unto Adam and said unto him, Where art thou? And he said, I heard thy voice in the garden, and I was afraid because I was naked, and hid myself." (See Genesis 3rd chap., 9, 10.) Adam received commandments and instructions from God: this was the order from the beginning.

That he received revelations, commandments and ordinances at the beginning is beyond the power of controversy; else how did they begin to offer sacrifices to God in an acceptable manner? And if they offered sacrifices they must be authorized by ordination. . . .

This, then, is the nature of the Priesthood; every man holding the Presidency of his dispensation, and one man holding the Presidency of them all, even Adam; and Adam receiving his Presidency and authority from the Lord, but cannot receive a fullness until Christ shall present the Kingdom to the Father, which shall be at the end of the last dispensation. (HC 4:207–8, 209)

6   Now, as to Adam, the Lord said, "In the day thou shalt eat thereof thou shalt surely die." Now, the day the Lord has reference to is spoken of by Peter: a thousand of our years is with the Lord as one day, etc. At the time the Lord said this to Adam there was no mode of counting time by man as man now counts time. (*WJS*, pp. 64–65; standardized)

Adam
  6   Instruction to the Nauvoo Lyceum, 9 March 1841, as reported by William P. McIntire.

7   There has been a chain of authority and power from Adam down to the present time. (*HC* 4:425)

8   The spirits of good men cannot interfere with the wicked beyond their prescribed bounds, for Michael, the Archangel, dared not bring a railing accusation against the devil, but said, "The Lord rebuke thee, Satan" [see Jude 1:9]. (*HC* 4:576)

9   The 7th verse of the 2nd chapter of Genesis ought to read—God breathed into Adam his spirit {i.e. Adam's spirit} or breath of life; but when the word "rauch" applies to Eve, it should be translated lives. (*HC* 5:392–93)

10   Adam was created in the very fashion, image and likeness of God, and received instruction from, and walked, talked and conversed with Him, as one man talks and communes with another. (*HC* 6:305)

11   *Words of Heber C. Kimball:* This brings to my mind the vision that Joseph Smith had, when he saw Adam open the gate of the Celestial City and admit the people one by one. He then saw Father Adam conduct them to the throne one by one, when they were crowned Kings and Priests of God. I merely bring this up to impress upon your mind the principles of order, but it will nevertheless apply to every member of the Church. (*JD* 9:41)

Adam-ondi-Ahman

1   *Words of James B. Bracken, Sr.:* In the fall of 1838, we went with David Patten to Adam-ondi-Ahman. When we got to the rock in the valley of Adam-ondi-Ahman, the Prophet Joseph told us it was the altar that Adam built. (*TK*, p. 78)

Adam
7   General conference address, Nauvoo, 3 October 1841.
8   Editorial in the *Times and Seasons*, 1 April 1842.
9   Items of doctrine given at Ramus, Illinois, 17 May 1843.
10   King Follett Discourse, Nauvoo, 7 April 1844.
11   Vision to Joseph Smith as reported by Heber C. Kimball, 17 March 1861.

Adam-ondi-Ahman
1   Statement of James B. Bracken, Sr., 6 November 1881, published in the *Juvenile Instructor*, 1 April 1892.

2   *Words of Edward Stevenson:* I stood with Joseph Smith and others when he pointed out the sacred spot of Adam's altar. Turning to the lovely valley below us, in a large bend of Grand River, he said, "Here is the real valley where Father Adam called his posterity together and blessed them." (*TK*, p. 86)

3   *Words of Orange L. Wight:* We moved to Daviess County, Missouri, and made our principal settlement at Adam-ondi-Ahman. The Prophet Joseph told us that it was the place where Adam offered his holy sacrifices. The altar was not far from our house. (*TK*, p. 104)

Administering to the Sick

Editors' Note: Of the many accounts of healings involving the Prophet Joseph Smith, the compilers have selected but a few, each of which contains important principles concerning administering to the sick.

1   *Words of Oliver B. Huntington:* Soon after Joseph settled in Kirtland, members of the Church began to gather to that place. The name of Joseph Smith and his power with God aroused everybody either for good or for bad. Mrs. John Johnson, who lived at the town of Hiram, forty miles distant from Kirtland, heard of the wonderful man that could receive revelations from God, heal the sick and see angels. She had a stiff arm that she wanted healed and made useful like the other, so she induced her husband to take a journey to Kirtland to see the Prophet.

Joseph asked her if she believed that God could make him instrumental in healing her arm which had been stiff a long time.

She answered that she believed her arm could be healed.

The Prophet only remarked that he would visit her the next day.

Adam-ondi-Ahman
   2   Autobiography of Edward Stevenson, LDS Church Archives.
   3   Letter of Orange L. Wight, son of Lyman Wight, 4 May 1903, BYU Library.

Administering to the Sick
   1   The healing took place in the spring of 1831. Oliver B. Huntington's recollections were first published in the *Young Woman's Journal*, December 1890.

The next day Joseph came to Bishop Newel K. Whitney's home where Mr. Johnson and his wife were staying. There were a Campbellite doctor and a Methodist preacher in the room. He took Mrs. Johnson by the hand and without sitting down or standing on ceremonies, and after a very short mental prayer, pronounced her arm whole in the name of Jesus Christ. He left the house immediately.

When he was gone, the preacher asked if her arm was well. She immediately stretched out her arm straight, remarking at the same time, "It's as well as the other."

The next day the preacher came to the house of Philo Dibble, who lived a little out of town, and related what he saw, and then tried to account for it upon natural principles, saying that when Joseph pronounced that arm whole in the name of Jesus Christ, it frightened her so badly that it threw her in a heavy perspiration and relaxed the cords, and the result was that she could straighten her arm.

When the knowledge of the miracle was had among the Saints, some of the brethren asked the Prophet if the arm would remain sound. Joseph answered, "The arm is as sound as the other and is as liable to accidents or to be hurt as the other." (*TK*, pp. 60–61)

2   This night the cholera burst forth among us, and about midnight it was manifested in its most virulent form. Our ears were saluted with cries and moanings, and lamentations on every hand; even those on guard fell to the earth with their guns in their hands, so sudden and powerful was the attack of this terrible disease. At the commencement, I attempted to lay on hands for their recovery, but I quickly learned by painful experience, that when the great Jehovah decrees destruction upon any people, and makes known His determination, man must not attempt to stay His hand. The moment I attempted to rebuke the disease I was attacked, and had I not desisted in my attempt to save the life of a brother, I would have sacrificed my own. The disease seized upon me like the talons of a hawk, and I said to the brethren: "If my work were done, you would have to put me in the ground without a coffin.". . .

When the cholera made its appearance, Elder John S. Carter was the first man who stepped forward to rebuke it, and upon this, was instantly seized, and became the first victim in the camp. (*HC* 2:114, 115)

Administering to the Sick
  2   Events of Zion's Camp, Rush Creek, Missouri, 24–25 June 1834.

3   Waited on my father again, who was very sick. In secret prayer in the morning, the Lord said, "My servant, thy father shall live." ... We called on the Lord in mighty prayer in the name of Jesus Christ, and laid our hands on him, and rebuked the disease. And God heard and answered our prayers—to the great joy and satisfaction of our souls. Our aged father arose and dressed himself, shouted, and praised the Lord. Called Brother William Smith, who had retired to rest, that he might praise the Lord with us, by joining in songs of praise to the Most High. (HC 2:289)

4   Visited my father, who was very much recovered from his sickness, indeed, which caused us to marvel at the might, power, and condescension of our Heavenly Father, in answering our prayers in his behalf. (HC 2:290)

5   This afternoon I was called, in company with President David Whitmer, to visit Angeline Works. We found her very sick, and so much deranged that she did not recognize her friends and intimate acquaintances. We prayed for her and laid hands on her in the name of Jesus Christ, and commanded her in His name to receive her senses, which were immediately restored. We also prayed that she might be restored to health; and she said she was better. (HC 2:328)

6   Samuel Barnum came to my house, much afflicted with a swollen arm. As he had not sufficient faith to be healed, my wife applied a poultice of herbs, and he tarried over night. (HC 2:332)

7   *Words of Wilford Woodruff:* On the morning of the 22nd of July, 1839, [the Prophet] arose reflecting upon the situation of the Saints of God in their persecutions and afflictions. He called upon the Lord in prayer, and the power of God rested mightily upon him. And as Jesus healed all the sick around Him in His day, so Joseph, the Prophet of God, healed all around on this occasion. He healed all in his house

---

Administering to the Sick

   3   Kirtland, 11 October 1835. The Prophet's father had fallen ill with a fever and continued to worsen.
   4   Kirtland, 13 October 1835.
   5   Kirtland, 10 December 1835.
   6   Kirtland, 14 December 1835.
   7   Wilford Woodruff's account of the Prophet's healing of the sick during the early settlement of Nauvoo, Illinois, and Montrose, Iowa, 22 July 1839.

and dooryard, then, in company with Sidney Rigdon and several of the Twelve, he went through among the sick lying on the bank of the river, and he commanded them in a loud voice, in the name of Jesus Christ, to come up and be made whole, and they were all healed.

When he healed all that were sick on the east side of the river, they crossed the Mississippi River to Montrose, where we were. The first house they went into was President Brigham Young's. He was sick on his bed at the time. The Prophet went into his house and healed him, and they all came out together. As they were passing by my door, Brother Joseph said, "Brother Woodruff, follow me."

These were the only words spoken by any of the company from the time they left Brother Brigham's house till we crossed the public square and entered Brother Elijah Fordham's house. Brother Fordham had been dying for an hour, and we expected each minute would be his last.

I felt the power of God that was overwhelming His prophet. When we entered the house, Brother Joseph walked up to Brother Fordham and took him by the right hand; in his left hand he held his hat.

He saw that Brother Fordham's eyes were glazed, and that he was speechless and unconscious.

After taking hold of his hand, the Prophet looked down into the dying man's face and said, "Brother Fordham, do you not know me?"

At first he made no reply; but we could all see the effect of the Spirit of God resting upon him.

Joseph again said, "Elijah, do you not know me?"

With a low whisper, Brother Fordham answered, "Yes."

The Prophet then said, "Have you not faith to be healed?"

The answer, which was a little plainer than before, was, "I am afraid it is too late. If you had come sooner, I think I might have been."

He had the appearance of a man waking from sleep. It was the sleep of death.

Joseph then said, "Do you believe that Jesus is the Christ?"

"I do, Brother Joseph," was the response.

Then the Prophet of God spoke with a loud voice, as in the majesty of the Godhead, "Elijah, I command you, in the name of Jesus of Nazareth, to arise and be made whole!"

The words of the Prophet were not like the words of man, but like the voice of God. It seemed to me that the house shook from its foundation. Elijah Fordham leaped from his bed like a man raised from the dead. A healthy color came to his face, and life was manifested in every act. His feet were done up in Indian-meal poultices. He kicked them off his feet, scattered the contents, then called for his clothes and put them on. He asked for a bowl of bread and milk and ate it. Then he put on his hat and followed us into the street to visit others who were sick.

As soon as we left Brother Fordham's house, we went into the house of Joseph B. Noble, who was very low and dangerously sick. When we entered the house, Brother Joseph took him by the hand, and commanded him, in the name of Jesus Christ, to arise and be made whole. He did arise and was immediately healed.

While this was going on, the wicked mob in the place, led by one Kilburn, had become alarmed, and followed us into Brother Noble's house. Before they arrived there, Brother Joseph had called upon Brother Fordham to offer prayer. While he was praying, the mob entered, with all the evil spirits accompanying them. As soon as they entered, Brother Fordham, who was praying, fainted and sank to the floor.

When Joseph saw the mob in the house, he arose and had the room cleared of both that class of men and their attendant devils. Then Brother Fordham immediately revived and finished his prayer.

This shows what power evil spirits have upon the tabernacles of men. The Saints are only saved from the devil by the power of God.

This case of Brother Noble's was the last one of healing upon that day. It was the greatest day for the manifestation of the power of God through the gift of healing since the organization of the Church.

When we left Brother Noble, the Prophet Joseph went with those who accompanied him from the other side of the bank of the river, to return home. While waiting for the ferryboat, a man of the world, knowing of the miracles which had been performed, came to him and asked him if he would not go and heal his twin children, about five months old, who were both lying sick nigh unto death. They were some two miles from Montrose.

The Prophet said he could not go, but after pausing some time, he said he would send some one to heal them. He then turned to me and said, "You go with the man and heal his children."

He took a red silk handkerchief out of his pocket and gave it to me, and told me to wipe their faces with the handkerchief when I administered to them, and they should be healed. He also said unto me,

"As long as you will keep that handkerchief, it shall remain a league between you and me."

I went with the man, and did as the Prophet commanded me, and the children were healed.

I have possession of the handkerchief unto this day. (*TK*, pp. 82–84)

8   As a great number of brethren lay sick in the town, on Tuesday, 23rd July, 1839, I told Don Carlos and George A. Smith to go and visit all the sick, exercise mighty faith, and administer to them in the name of Jesus Christ, commanding the destroyer to depart, and the people to arise and walk; and not leave a single person on the bed between my house and Ebenezer Robinson's, two miles distant; they administered to over sixty persons, many of whom thought they would never sit up again; but they were healed, arose from their beds, and gave glory to God; some of them assisted in visiting and administering to others who were sick. (*HC* 4:398–99)

9   I preached to a large congregation at the stand, on the science and practice of medicine, desiring to persuade the Saints to trust in God when sick, and not in an arm of flesh, and live by faith and not by medicine, or poison; and when they were sick, and had called for the Elders to pray for them, and they were not healed, to use herbs and mild food. (*HC* 4:414)

10   In the evening meeting twenty-seven children were blessed, nineteen of whom I blessed myself, with great fervency. Virtue went out of me, and my strength left me, when I gave up the meeting to the brethren. (*HC* 5:303)

Administering to the Sick

   8   The Prophet's recollection of the life of his brother Don Carlos, recorded in the Prophet's history under date of 7 August 1841, the day of Don Carlos's death.

   9   Sabbath address, Nauvoo, 5 September 1841. These comments should be understood in light of the practice of medicine in 1841.

 10   Ramus, Illinois, 13 March 1843.

Adultery

1 I will give you one of the *Keys* of the mysteries of the Kingdom. It is an eternal principle, that has existed with God from all eternity: That man who rises up to condemn others, finding fault with the Church, saying that they are out of the way, while he himself is righteous, then know assuredly, that that man is in the high road to apostasy; and if he does not repent, will apostatize, as God lives. The principle is as correct as the one that Jesus put forth in saying that he who seeketh a sign is an adulterous person; and that principle is eternal, undeviating, and firm as the pillars of heaven; for whenever you see a man seeking after a sign, you may set it down that he is an adulterous man. (HC 3:385)

2 When I was preaching in Philadelphia, a Quaker called out for a sign. I told him to be still. After the sermon, he again asked for a sign. I told the congregation the man was an adulterer; that a wicked and adulterous generation seeketh after a sign; and that the Lord had said to me in a revelation, that any man who wanted a sign was an adulterous person. "It is true," cried one, "for I caught him in the very act," which the man afterwards confessed, when he was baptized. (HC 5:268)

3 In the evening the High Council sat on the case of Harrison Sagers, charged with seduction, and having stated that I had taught it was right. Charge not sustained. I was present with several of the Twelve, and gave an address tending to do away with every evil, and exhorting them to practice virtue and holiness before the Lord; told them that the Church had not received any permission from me to commit fornication, adultery, or any corrupt action; but my every word and action has been to the contrary. If a man commit adultery,

---

Adultery

1   Instructions to the Apostles and Seventies departing for missions to England, Commerce (Nauvoo), 2 July 1839.

2   Nauvoo, 9 February 1843.

3   Nauvoo, 25 November 1843. For commentary and doctrinal clarification, see Spencer W. Kimball, *The Miracle of Forgiveness* (Salt Lake City: Bookcraft, 1969), pp. 347–53; and Bruce R. McConkie, *A New Witness for the Articles of Faith* (Salt Lake City: Deseret Book Co., 1985), pp. 231–32.

he cannot receive the celestial kingdom of God. Even if he is saved in any kingdom, it cannot be the celestial kingdom. I did think that the many examples that have been made manifest, such as John C. Bennett's and others, were sufficient to show the fallacy of such a course of conduct.

I condemned such actions *in toto*, and warned the people present against committing such evils; for it will surely bring a curse upon any person who commits such deeds. (*HC* 6:81)

Adversary
See DEVIL

Adversity
See TRIALS

Affections

1   When we lose a near and dear friend, upon whom we have set our hearts, it should be a caution unto us not to set our affections too firmly upon others, knowing that they may in like manner be taken from us. Our affections should be placed upon God and His work, more intensely than upon our fellow beings. (*HC* 4:587)

Afflictions
See TRIALS

Agency

1   We deem it a just principle, and it is one the force of which we believe ought to be duly considered by every individual, that all men are

---

Affections
1   Remarks at the funeral of Ephraim Marks, Nauvoo, 9 April 1842.

Agency
1   Letter to the brethren scattered from Zion, Kirtland, 22 January 1834.

created equal, and that all have the privilege of thinking for themselves upon all matters relative to conscience. Consequently, then, we are not disposed, had we the power, to deprive any one of exercising that free independence of mind which heaven has so graciously bestowed upon the human family as one of its choicest gifts. (HC 2:6–7)

2 *Report of Mathew L. Davis:* "I believe," said [Joseph], "that a man is a moral, responsible, free agent; that although it was foreordained he should fall, and be redeemed, yet after the redemption it was not foreordained that he should again sin. In the Bible a rule of conduct is laid down for him; in the Old and New Testaments the law by which he is to be governed, may be found. If he violates that law, he is to be punished for the deeds done in the body." (HC 4:78–79)

3 *Report of Don Carlos Smith:* [President Joseph Smith] then observed that Satan was generally blamed for the evils which we did, but if he was the cause of all our wickedness, men could not be condemned. The devil could not compel mankind to do evil; all was voluntary. Those who resisted the Spirit of God, would be liable to be led into temptation, and then the association of heaven would be withdrawn from those who refused to be made partakers of such great glory. God would not exert any compulsory means, and the devil could not; and such ideas as were entertained {on these subjects} by many were absurd. (HC 4:358)

4 After this instruction, you will be responsible for your own sins; it is a desirable honor that you should so walk before our heavenly Father as to save yourselves; we are all responsible to God for the manner we improve the light and wisdom given by our Lord to enable us to save ourselves. (HC 4:606)

5 It is one of the first principles of my life, and one that I have cultivated from my childhood, having been taught it by my father, to allow every one the liberty of conscience. (HC 6:56)

Agency

2   A letter of Mathew L. Davis to his wife describing the Prophet's discourse in Washington, D.C., 6 February 1840.

3   Sabbath address, Nauvoo, 16 May 1841.

4   Remarks to the Relief Society, Nauvoo, 28 April 1842.

5   Sabbath address, Nauvoo, 15 October 1843.

6   I have intended my remarks for all, both rich and poor, bond and free, great and small. I have no enmity against any man. I love you all; but I hate some of your deeds. I am your best friend, and if persons miss their mark it is their own fault. (HC 6:317)

7   *Words of John Taylor:* Concerning government: Some years ago, in Nauvoo, a gentleman in my hearing, a member of the Legislature, asked Joseph Smith how it was that he was enabled to govern so many people, and to preserve such perfect order; remarking at the same time that it was impossible for them to do it anywhere else. Mr. Smith remarked that it was very easy to do that. "How?" responded the gentleman; "to us it is very difficult." Mr. Smith replied, "I teach them correct principles, and they govern themselves." (MS 13:339)

Aggression

1   Be not the aggressor: bear until they strike you on the one cheek; then offer the other, and they will be sure to strike that; then defend yourselves, and God will bear you off. (HC 5:468)

Ahman

1   The Great God has a name by which he will be called, which is Ahman. (WJS, p. 64; standardized)

Agency
   6   King Follett Discourse, Nauvoo, 7 April 1844.
   7   Article on Church organization by John Taylor, published in the *Millennial Star*, 15 November 1851. The incident described apparently took place in Nauvoo, though the exact date is unknown. Howard Coray identified the man with whom the Prophet spoke as Judge Stephen A. Douglas (see Coray Family Papers, BYU Library, Special Collections).

Aggression
   1   Address regarding his arrest at Dixon, Illinois, Nauvoo, 30 June 1843.

Ahman
   1   Instruction to the Nauvoo Lyceum, 9 March 1841, as reported by William P. McIntire.

Angels

1   God was with us, and His angels went before us, and the faith of our little band was unwavering. We know that angels were our companions, for we saw them. (HC 2:73)

2   The harvest and the end of the world [in the parable of the tares] have an allusion directly to the human family in the last days, instead of the earth, as many have imagined; and that which shall precede the coming of the Son of Man, and the restitution of all things spoken of by the mouth of all the holy prophets since the world began; and the angels are to have something to do in this great work, for they are the reapers. (HC 2:271)

3   Angels shall guard his [Bishop Whitney's] house, and shall guard the lives of his posterity. (HC 2:288)

4   *21 January 1836.* Many of my brethren who received the ordinance [of anointing] with me saw glorious visions also. Angels ministered unto them as well as to myself. . . .
. . . Others [high councilors] were ministered unto by holy angels. (HC 2:381, 382)

5   *22 January 1836.* The heavens were opened, and angels ministered unto us. . . .
. . . The gift of tongues fell upon us in mighty power, angels mingled their voices with ours, while their presence was in our midst. (HC 2:383)

6   *28 January 1836.* Elder Roger Orton saw a mighty angel riding upon a horse of fire, with a flaming sword in his hand, followed by five others, encircle the house, and protect the Saints, even the Lord's anointed, from the power of Satan and a host of evil spirits, which were striving to disturb the Saints.

Angels
   1   Events of Zion's Camp, Illinois, 27 May 1834.
   2   Letter to the elders of the Church, Kirtland, 1 September 1835.
   3   Blessing upon Bishop Newel K. Whitney, Kirtland, 7 October 1835.
   4–6 Manifestations in the Kirtland Temple.

President William Smith, one of the Twelve, saw the heavens opened, and the Lord's host protecting the Lord's anointed. (HC 2:386–87)

7   We . . . related the goodness of God to us, in opening our eyes to see the visions of heaven, and in sending His holy angels to minister unto us the word of life. (HC 2:388)

8   I bore record of my mission, and of the ministration of angels. . . .

President Frederick G. Williams arose and testified that while President Rigdon was making his first prayer, an angel entered the window and took his seat between Father Smith and himself, and remained there during the prayer.

President David Whitmer also saw angels in the house. . . .

. . . All the congregation simultaneously arose, being moved upon by an invisible power; many began to speak in tongues and prophesy; others saw glorious visions; and I beheld the Temple was filled with angels, which fact I declared to the congregation. (HC 2:427, 428)

9   *Report of Wilford Woodruff:* Among the vast number of the keys of the kingdom of God, Joseph presented the following one to the Twelve for their benefit in their experience and travels in the flesh, which is as follows. In order to detect the devil when he transforms himself nigh unto an angel of light: When an angel of God appears unto man face-to-face in personage, and reaches out his hand unto the man, and he takes hold of the angel's hand and feels a substance, the same as one man would in shaking hands with another, he may then know that it is an angel of God, and he should place all confidence in him; such personages or angels are Saints with their resurrected bodies. But if a personage appears unto man, and offers him his hand, and the man takes hold of it and he feels nothing or does not sense any substance, he may know it is the devil; for when a Saint whose body is not resurrected appears unto man in the flesh, he will not offer him his hand, for this is against the law given him. And keeping in mind these things, we may detect the devil, that he deceive us not. (WJS, p. 6; standardized)

Angels

   7   A meeting held at the Prophet's home in Kirtland, during which the Prophet's father, the Patriarch to the Church, administered patriarchal blessings, 29 January 1836.

   8   Events during the dedication of the Kirtland Temple, 27 March 1836.

   9   Instructions to the Twelve, Commerce (Nauvoo), 27 June 1839.

10 The Kingdom of Heaven is like a grain of mustard seed. The mustard seed is small, but brings forth a large tree, and the fowls lodge in the branches. The fowls are the angels. Thus angels come down, combine together to gather their children, and gather them. We cannot be made perfect without them, nor they without us; when these things are done, the Son of Man will descend. (HC 3:389)

11 We may look for angels and receive their ministrations, but we are to try the spirits and prove them, for it is often the case that men make a mistake in regard to these things. (HC 3:391)

12 An angel of God never has wings. Some will say that they have seen a spirit; that he offered them his hand, but they did not touch it. This is a lie. First, it is contrary to the plan of God; a spirit cannot come but in glory; an angel has flesh and bones; we see not their glory. The devil may appear as an angel of light. Ask God to reveal it; if it be of the devil, he will flee from you; if of God, He will manifest Himself, or make it manifest. (HC 3:392)

13 [God] set the ordinances to be the same forever and ever, and set Adam to watch over them, to reveal them from heaven to man, or to send angels to reveal them. "Are they not all ministering spirits, sent forth to minister for them who shall be heirs of salvation?" (Hebrews i, 14).

These angels are under the direction of Michael or Adam, who acts under the direction of the Lord. From the above quotation we learn that Paul perfectly understood the purposes of God in relation to His connection with man, and that glorious and perfect order which He established in Himself, whereby he sent forth power, revelations, and glory. (HC 4:208)

Angels
10 Discourse on the priesthood, given sometime before 8 August 1839, Commerce (Nauvoo). For a discussion on the dating of this discourse, see *WJS*, p. 22.
11 Discourse on the priesthood, given sometime before 8 August 1839, Commerce (Nauvoo).
12 Discourse on the priesthood, given sometime before 8 August 1839, Commerce (Nauvoo).
13 Article on priesthood read at general conference, Nauvoo, 5 October 1840.

14 If an Angel or spirit appears offer him your hand; if he is a spirit from God he will stand still and not offer you his hand. If from the Devil he will either shrink back from you or offer his hand, which if he does you will feel nothing, but be deceived.

A good Spirit will not deceive.

Angels are beings who have bodies and appear to men in the form of man. (WJS, p. 44)

15 *Minutes:* [President Joseph Smith] explained the difference between an angel and a ministering spirit; the one a resurrected or translated body, with its spirit ministering to embodied spirits—the other a disembodied spirit, visiting and ministering to disembodied spirits. Jesus Christ became a ministering spirit (while His body was lying in the sepulchre) to the spirits in prison, to fulfill an important part of His mission, without which He could not have perfected His work, or entered into His rest. After His resurrection He appeared as an angel to His disciples. (HC 4:425)

16 A man came to me in Kirtland, and told me he had seen an angel, and described his dress. I told him he had seen no angel, and that there was no such dress in heaven. He grew mad, and went into the street and commanded fire to come down out of heaven to consume me. I laughed at him, and said, You are one of Baal's prophets; your God does not hear you; jump up and cut yourself: and he commanded fire from heaven to consume my house. (HC 5:267–68)

17 Gods have an ascendancy over the angels, who are ministering servants. In the resurrection, some are raised to be angels; others are raised to become Gods. (HC 5:426–27)

18 The Hebrew Church "came unto the spirits of just men made perfect, and unto an innumerable company of angels, unto God the Father of all, and to Jesus Christ, the Mediator of the new covenant." What did they learn by coming to the spirits of just men made perfect?

Angels

   14 Nauvoo, December 1840, as reported by William Clayton.
   15 General conference address, Nauvoo, 3 October 1841.
   16 Nauvoo, 9 February 1843.
   17 Sabbath address, Nauvoo, 11 June 1843.
   18 Remarks upon the death of James Adams, Nauvoo, 9 October 1843.

Is it written? No. What they learned has not been and could not have been written. What object was gained by this communication with the spirits of the just? It was the established order of the kingdom of God: the keys of power and knowledge were with them to communicate to the Saints. Hence the importance of understanding the distinction between the spirits of the just and angels.

Spirits can only be revealed in flaming fire and glory. Angels have advanced further, their light and glory being tabernacled; and hence they appear in bodily shape. The spirits of just men are made ministering servants to those who are sealed unto life eternal, and it is through them that the sealing power comes down.

Patriarch Adams is now one of the spirits of the just men made perfect; and, if revealed now, must be revealed in fire; and the glory could not be endured. Jesus showed Himself to His disciples, and they thought it was His spirit, and they were afraid to approach His spirit. Angels have advanced higher in knowledge and power than spirits. . . .

Flesh and blood cannot go [to the spirit world]; but flesh and bones, quickened by the Spirit of God, can. (HC 6:51, 52)

Anger

1   I think that it is high time for a Christian world to awake out of sleep, and cry mightily to that God, day and night, whose anger we have justly incurred. (HC 1:313)

Animals

1   In pitching my tent we found three massasaugas or prairie rattlesnakes, which the brethren were about to kill, but I said, "Let them alone—don't hurt them! How will the serpent ever lose his venom, while the servants of God possess the same disposition, and continue

---

Anger
  1   Letter to N. E. Seaton (N. C. Saxton), a newspaper editor in Rochester, N.Y., Kirtland, 4 January 1833.

Animals
  1   Events of Zion's Camp, near Paris, Illinois, 26 May 1834.

to make war upon it? Men must become harmless, before the brute creation; and when men lose their vicious dispositions and cease to destroy the animal race, the lion and the lamb can dwell together, and the sucking child can play with the serpent in safety." The brethren took the serpents carefully on sticks and carried them across the creek. I exhorted the brethren not to kill a serpent, bird, or an animal of any kind during our journey unless it became necessary in order to preserve ourselves from hunger. (HC 2:71–72)

2   *Words of Heber C. Kimball:* When we had all got over {the Mississippi}, we camped about one mile back from the little town of Louisiana, in a beautiful oak grove, which is immediately on the bank of the river. At this place there were some feelings of hostility manifested again by Sylvester Smith, in consequence of a dog growling at him while he was marching his company up to the camp, he being the last that came over the river. The next morning Brother Joseph told the camp that he would descend to the spirit that was manifested by some of the brethren, to let them see the folly of their wickedness. He rose up and commenced speaking by saying, "If any man insults me, or abuses me, I will stand in my own defense at the expense of my life; and if a dog growls at me, I will let him know that I am his master." At this moment Sylvester Smith, who had just returned from where he had turned out his horses to feed, came up, and hearing Brother Joseph make those remarks, said, "If that dog bites me, I'll kill him." Brother Joseph turned to Sylvester and said, "If you kill that dog, I'll whip you," and then went on to show the brethren how wicked and unchristianlike such conduct appeared before the eyes of truth and justice. (HC 2:83)

3   [I] moved that an ordinance be passed to protect citizens killing dogs running at large, which were set upon cattle or hogs, or molest individuals. (HC 4:353–54)

4   John learned that God glorified Himself by saving all that His hands had made, whether beasts, fowls, fishes or men; and He will glorify Himself with them.

Animals

  2 Louisiana, Missouri, 5 June 1834, as reported in Heber C. Kimball's journal.
  3 Nauvoo, 1 May 1841.
  4 General conference address, Nauvoo, 8 April 1843.

Says one, "I cannot believe in the salvation of beasts." Any man who would tell you that this could not be, would tell you that the revelations are not true. John heard the words of the beasts giving glory to God, and understood them. God who made the beasts could understand every language spoken by them. The four beasts were four of the most noble animals that had filled the measure of their creation, and had been saved from other worlds, because they were perfect: they were like angels in their sphere. We are not told where they came from, and I do not know; but they were seen and heard by John praising and glorifying God. (*HC* 5:343–44)

5   *Words of Benjamin F. Johnson:* [The Prophet] taught that all the animal kingdoms would be resurrected, and made us understand that they would remain in the dominion of those who, with creative power, reach out for dominion, through the power of eternal lives. (*TK*, p. 95)

Annihilation

1   More painful to me are the thoughts of annihilation than death. If I have no expectation of seeing my father, mother, brothers, sisters and friends again, my heart would burst in a moment, and I should go down to my grave. (*HC* 5:362)

2   All the fools and learned and wise men from the beginning of creation, who say that the spirit of man had a beginning, prove that it must have an end; and if that doctrine is true, then the doctrine of annihilation would be true. (*HC* 6:311)

Animals
   5   Letter of Benjamin F. Johnson to George S. Gibbs, 1903.

Annihilation
   1   Remarks upon the death of Lorenzo D. Barnes, Nauvoo, 16 April 1843.
   2   King Follett Discourse, Nauvoo, 7 April 1844.

Apocrypha

1   *Words of Edward Stevenson:* The Prophet also looked over our large Bible and remarked that much of the Apocrypha was true, but it required the Spirit of God to select the truth out of those writings. (*TK*, p. 86)

Apostasy

1   Christ said to His disciples (Mark xvi:17 and 18), that these signs should follow them that believe:—"In my name shall they cast out devils; they shall speak with new tongues; they shall take up serpents; and if they drink any deadly thing it shall not hurt them; they shall lay hands on the sick, and they shall recover;" and also, in connection with this, read 1st Corinthians, 12th chapter. By the foregoing testimonies we may look at the Christian world and see the apostasy there has been from the apostolic platform; and who can look at this and not exclaim in the language of Isaiah, "The earth also is defiled under the inhabitants thereof; because they have transgressed the laws, changed the ordinances, and broken the everlasting covenant?" (*HC* 1:314)

2   Respecting an apostate, or one who has been cut off from the Church, and who wishes to come in again, the law of our Church expressly says that such shall repent, and be baptized, and be admitted as at the first. (*HC* 1:338)

3   The Messiah's kingdom on earth is of that kind of government, that there has always been numerous apostates, for the reason that it

---

Apocrypha
   1   Autobiography of Edward Stevenson, LDS Church Archives.

Apostasy
   1   Letter to N. E. Seaton (N. C. Saxton), a newspaper editor in Rochester, N.Y., Kirtland, 4 January 1833.
   2   Letter to one of Jared Carter's brothers, written at the request of Jared Carter, Kirtland, 13 April 1833.
   3   Letter to the brethren scattered from Zion, Kirtland, 22 January 1834.

admits of no sins unrepented of without excluding the individual from its fellowship. Our Lord said, "Strive to enter in at the straight gate; for many, I say unto you, will seek to enter in, and shall not be able." And again, many are called, but few are chosen. Paul said to the elders of the Church at Ephesus, after he had labored three years with them, that he knew that some of their own number would turn away from the faith, and seek to lead away disciples after them. None, we presume, in this generation will pretend that he has the experience of Paul in building up the Church of Christ; and yet, after his departure from the Church at Ephesus, many, even of the elders, turned away from the truth; and what is almost always the case, sought to lead away disciples after them. Strange as it may appear at first thought, yet it is no less strange than true, that notwithstanding all the professed determination to live godly, apostates after turning from the faith of Christ, unless they have speed-ily repented, have sooner or later fallen into the snares of the wicked one, and have been left destitute of the Spirit of God, to manifest their wickedness in the eyes of multitudes. From apostates the faithful have received the severest persecutions. Judas was rebuked and immediately betrayed his Lord into the hands of His enemies, because Satan entered into him. There is a superior intelligence bestowed upon such as obeyed the Gospel with full purpose of heart, which, if sinned against, the apostate is left naked and destitute of the Spirit of God, and he is, in truth, nigh unto cursing, and his end is to be burned. When once that light which was in them is taken from them they become as much darkened as they were previously enlightened, and then, no marvel, if all their power should be enlisted against the truth, and they, Judas like, seek the destruction of those who were their greatest benefactors. . . . From what source emanated the principle which has ever been mani-fested by apostates from the true Church to persecute with double dili-gence, and seek with double perseverance, to destroy those whom they once professed to love, with whom they once communed, and with whom they once covenanted to strive with every power in righteous-ness to obtain the rest of God? Perhaps our brethren will say the same that caused Satan to seek to overthrow the kingdom of God, because he himself was evil, and God's kingdom is holy. (HC 2:22–23)

4   At this time the spirit of speculation in lands and property of all kinds, which was so prevalent throughout the whole nation, was taking

---

Apostasy
 4   Kirtland, May 1837.

deep root in the Church. As the fruits of this spirit, evil surmisings, fault-finding, disunion, dissension, and apostasy followed in quick succession, and it seemed as though all the powers of earth and hell were combining their influence in an especial manner to overthrow the Church at once, and make a final end. (HC 2:487)

5 Beware of all disaffected characters, for they come not to build up, but to destroy and scatter abroad. Though we or an angel from heaven preach any other Gospel, or introduce an order of things other than those things which ye have received, and are authorized to receive from the First Presidency, let him be accursed. (HC 2:511)

6 On the morning of the 22nd of December, 1837, Brother Brigham Young left Kirtland in consequence of the fury of the mob spirit that prevailed in the apostates who had threatened to destroy him because he would proclaim publicly and privately that he knew by the power of the Holy Ghost that I was a Prophet of the Most High God, that I had not transgressed and fallen as the apostates declared.

Apostasy, persecution, confusion, and mobocracy strove hard to bear rule at Kirtland, and thus closed the year 1837. (HC 2:529)

7 Thomas B. Marsh, formerly president of the Twelve, having apostatized, repaired to Richmond and made affidavit before Henry Jacobs, justice of the peace, to all the vilest slanders, aspersions, lies and calumnies towards myself and the Church, that his wicked heart could invent. He had been lifted up in pride by his exaltation to office and the revelations of heaven concerning him, until he was ready to be overthrown by the first adverse wind that should cross his track, and now he has fallen, lied and sworn falsely, and is ready to take the lives of his best friends. Let all men take warning by him, and learn that he who exalteth himself, God will abase. (HC 3:166–67)

8 *Words of Daniel Tyler:* When the Prophet had ended telling how he had been treated, Brother Behunnin remarked, "If I should leave

---

Apostasy
5 Announcement concerning certain leaders who had become disaffected from the Church, Kirtland, 3 September 1837.
6 Kirtland, 1837.
7 Far West, Missouri, 24 October 1838.
8 Remembrance of the Prophet's conversation with Isaac Behunnin in Nauvoo soon after Joseph Smith arrived in Nauvoo from Liberty Jail, spring 1839.

this Church, I would not do as those men have done. I would go to some remote place where Mormonism had never been heard of, and no one would ever learn that I knew anything about it."

The great Seer immediately replied: "Brother Behunnin, you don't know what you would do. No doubt these men once thought as you do. Before you joined this Church you stood on neutral ground. When the gospel was preached, good and evil were set before you. You could choose either or neither. There were two opposite masters inviting you to serve them. When you joined this Church you enlisted to serve God. When you did that, you left the neutral ground, and you never can get back on to it. Should you forsake the Master you enlisted to serve, it will be by the instigation of the evil one, and you will follow his dictation and be his servant." (*TK*, p. 54)

9 I will give you one of the *Keys* of the mysteries of the Kingdom. It is an eternal principle, that has existed with God from all eternity: That man who rises up to condemn others, finding fault with the Church, saying that they are out of the way, while he himself is righteous, then know assuredly, that that man is in the high road to apostasy; and if he does not repent, will apostatize, as God lives. (HC 3:385)

10 *Report of Eliza R. Snow:* President Joseph Smith read the 14th chapter of Ezekiel—said the Lord had declared by the Prophet, that the people should each one stand for himself, and depend on no man or men in that state of corruption of the Jewish church—that righteous persons could only deliver their own souls—applied it to the present state of the Church of Jesus Christ of Latter-day Saints—said if the people departed from the Lord, they must fall—that they were depending on the Prophet, hence were darkened in their minds, in consequence of neglecting the duties devolving upon themselves, envious towards the innocent, while they afflict the virtuous with their shafts of envy. (HC 5:19)

11 Of the Twelve Apostles chosen in Kirtland, and ordained under the hands of Oliver Cowdery, David Whitmer and myself, there have

---

Apostasy

9 Instructions to the Apostles and Seventies departing for missions to England, Commerce (Nauvoo), 2 July 1839.

10 Remarks to the Relief Society, Nauvoo, 26 May 1842.

11 Nauvoo, 28 May 1843.

been but two but what have lifted their heel against me—namely Brigham Young and Heber C. Kimball. (*HC* 5:412)

12 By the apostates admitting the testimony of the Doctrine and Covenants, they damn themselves. . . .

I testify again, as the Lord lives, God never will acknowledge any traitors or apostates. Any man who will betray the Catholics will betray you; and if he will betray me, he will betray you. . . .

It is in the order of heavenly things that God should always send a new dispensation into the world when men have apostatized from the truth and lost the priesthood; but when men come out and build upon other men's foundations, they do it on their own responsibility, without authority from God; and when the floods come and the winds blow, their foundations will be found to be sand, and their whole fabric will crumble to dust. (*HC* 6:477, 478–79)

13 *Words of Heber C. Kimball:* I will give you a key which brother Joseph Smith used to give in Nauvoo. He said, that the very step of apostacy commenced with losing confidence in the leaders of this Church and kingdom, and that whenever you discerned that spirit, you might know that it would lead the possessor of it on the road to apostacy. (*JD* 3:270)

Apostles

1 *Minutes:* President Smith then stated that the meeting had been called, because God had commanded it; and it was made known to him by vision and by the Holy Spirit. (*HC* 2:182)

2 *Minutes:* President Smith proposed the following question: What importance is there attached to the calling of these Twelve Apostles, different from the other callings or officers of the Church?

Apostasy
   12 Sabbath address, Nauvoo, 16 June 1844.
   13 Address by Heber C. Kimball, 23 March 1856.

Apostles
   1 Minutes of the meeting at which the members of the first Quorum of the Twelve Apostles in this dispensation were chosen and ordained, Kirtland, 14 February 1835.
   2 Instructions to the Twelve, Kirtland, 27 February 1835.

After the question was discussed by Councilors Patten, Young, Smith, and M'Lellin, President Joseph Smith, Jun., gave the following decision:

They are the Twelve Apostles, who are called to the office of the Traveling High Council, who are to preside over the churches of the Saints, among the Gentiles, where there is a presidency established; and they are to travel and preach among the Gentiles, until the Lord shall command them to go to the Jews. They are to hold the keys of this ministry, to unlock the door of the Kingdom of heaven unto all nations, and to preach the Gospel to every creature. This is the power, authority, and virtue of their apostleship. (HC 2:200)

3   *Minutes:* After the conference was opened, and the Twelve had taken their seats, President Joseph Smith, Jun., said that it would be the duty of the Twelve, when in council, to take their seats together according to age, the oldest to be seated at the head, and preside in the first council, the next oldest in the second, and so on until the youngest had presided; and then begin at the oldest again. (HC 2:219)

4   *Minutes:* President Joseph Smith then stated that . . . [w]hen the Twelve are together, or a quorum of them, in any church, they will have authority to act independently, and make decisions, and those decisions will be valid. . . . When the Twelve pass a decision, it is in the name of the Church, therefore it is valid. . . .

. . . The Twelve and the Seventy have particularly to depend upon their ministry for their support, and that of their families; and they have a right, by virtue of their offices, to call upon the churches to as-sist them. (HC 2:220, 221)

5   *Minutes:* We [the high council at Kirtland] wish you [members of the Twelve] to understand that your duty requires you to seek first the kingdom of heaven and its righteousness; that is, attend to the first things first, and then all things will be added, and that complaint

Apostles
3   Minutes of a general council of the priesthood, Kirtland, 2 May 1835. When the Twelve were first organized, seniority was determined by age. Later, as is the current practice, seniority was determined by date of ordi-nation.
4   Minutes of a general council of the priesthood, Kirtland, 2 May 1835.
5   Minutes of the high council at Kirtland, 4 August 1835.

about your families will be less frequent. Don't preach yourselves crucified for your wives' sake, but remember that Christ was crucified, and you are sent out to be special witnesses of this thing. Men do not wish to hear these little things, for there is no salvation in them, but there is in the other.

Let the hands of the ten [not disfellowshipped] be strengthened, and let them go forth in the name of the Lord, in the power of their mission, giving diligent heed to the direction of the Holy Spirit. We say, be strong in the Lord, and in the power of His might; for great things await you, and great blessings are in store for you. (*HC* 2:240–41)

6 *Minutes*: President Smith next proceeded to explain the duty of the Twelve, and their authority, which is next to the present Presidency. . . . The Twelve are not subject to any other than the first Presidency, viz., "myself," said the Prophet, "Sidney Rigdon, and Frederick G. Williams, who are now my Counselors; and where I am not, there is no First Presidency over the Twelve.". . .

The Prophet also stated to the Twelve . . . , ". . . I will now covenant with you before God, that I will not listen to or credit any derogatory report against any of you, nor condemn you upon any testimony beneath the heavens, short of that testimony which is infallible, until I can see you face to face, and know of a surety; and I do place unremitted confidence in your word, for I believe you to be men of truth. And I ask the same of you, when I tell you anything, that you place equal confidence in my word, for I will not tell you I know anything that I do not know." (*HC* 2:373, 374)

7 I saw the Twelve Apostles of the Lamb, who are now upon the earth, who hold the keys of this last ministry, in foreign lands, standing together in a circle, much fatigued, with their clothes tattered and feet swollen, with their eyes cast downward, and Jesus standing in their midst, and they did not behold Him. The Savior looked upon them and wept.

I also beheld Elder M'Lellin in the south, standing upon a hill, surrounded by a vast multitude, preaching to them, and a lame man

---

Apostles

6   Instructions to the Twelve, Kirtland, 16 January 1836.
7   A vision given to Joseph Smith, 21 January 1836. Part of the vision has been canonized as D&C 137.

standing before him supported by his crutches; he threw them down at his word and leaped as a hart, by the mighty power of God. Also, I saw Elder Brigham Young standing in a strange land, in the far south and west, in a desert place, upon a rock in the midst of about a dozen men of color, who appeared hostile. He was preaching to them in their own tongue, and the angel of God standing above his head, with a drawn sword in his hand, protecting him, but he did not see it. And I finally saw the Twelve in the celestial kingdom of God. I also beheld the re-demption of Zion, and many things which the tongue of man cannot describe in full. (HC 2:381)

8 *Words of Heber C. Kimball:* There Father Adam stood and opened the gate to [the Twelve Apostles of this dispensation], and as they en-tered, he embraced them one by one and kissed them. He then led them to the throne of God, and then the Savior embraced each one of them and kissed them, and crowned each one of them in the presence of God. . . . The impression this vision left on Brother Joseph's mind was of so acute a nature, that he never could refrain from weeping while rehearsing it. (JSMS, p. 95)

9 President William Smith, one of the Twelve, saw a vision of the Twelve, and Seven in council together, in old England, and prophesied that a great work would be done by them in the old countries, and God was already beginning to work in the hearts of the people. (HC 2:392)

10 I then called upon the quorums and congregation of Saints to ac-knowledge the Twelve Apostles, who were present, as Prophets, Seers, Revelators, and special witnesses to all the nations of the earth, hold-ing the keys of the kingdom, to unlock it, or cause it to be done, among them, and uphold them by their prayers, which they assented to by rising. (HC 2:417)

11 The Twelve also are not to serve tables, but to bear the keys of the Kingdom to all nations, and unlock the door of the Gospel to them,

---

Apostles
8 Heber C. Kimball's recollection of a vision given to the Prophet, quoted by Helen Mar Whitney in the *Woman's Exponent*, 1 February 1881.
9 Kirtland, 6 February 1836.
10 Events during the dedication of the Kirtland Temple, 27 March 1836.
11 Solemn assembly in the Kirtland Temple, 30 March 1836.

and call upon the Seventies to follow after them, and assist them. The Twelve are at liberty to go wheresoever they will, and if any one will say, I wish to go to such a place, let all the rest say amen. (HC 2:432)

12 The persecution was so bitter against Elder Brigham Young (on whom devolved the presidency of the Twelve by age, Thomas B. Marsh having apostatized) and his life was so diligently sought for, that he was compelled to flee; and he left Far West on this day for Illinois. (HC 3:261)

13 When the Twelve or any other witnesses stand before the congregations of the earth, and they preach in the power and demonstration of the Spirit of God, and the people are astonished and confounded at the doctrine, and say, "That man has preached a powerful discourse, a great sermon," then let that man or those men take care that they do not ascribe the glory unto themselves, but be careful that they are humble, and ascribe the praise and glory to God and the Lamb; for it is by the power of the Holy Priesthood and the Holy Ghost that they have power thus to speak. What art thou, O man, but dust? And from whom receivest thou thy power and blessings, but from God?

Then, O ye Twelve! notice this *Key*, and be wise for Christ's sake, and your own soul's sake. Ye are not sent out to be taught, but to teach. Let every word be seasoned with grace. Be vigilant; be sober. It is a day of warning, and not of many words. Act honestly before God and man. Beware of Gentile sophistry; such as bowing and scraping unto men in whom you have no confidence. Be honest, open, and frank in all your intercourse with mankind.

O ye Twelve! and all Saints! profit by this important *Key*—that in all your trials, troubles, temptations, afflictions, bonds, imprisonments and death, see to it, that you do not betray heaven; that you do not betray Jesus Christ; that you do not betray the brethren; that you do not betray the revelations of God, whether in the Bible, Book of Mormon, or Doctrine and Covenants, or any other that ever was or ever will be given and revealed unto man in this world or that which is to come. Yea, in all your kicking and flounderings, see to it that you do not this thing, lest innocent blood be found upon your skirts, and you go down

---

Apostles

12 Far West, Missouri, 14 February 1839.

13 Instructions to the Apostles and Seventies departing for missions to England, Commerce (Nauvoo), 2 July 1839.

to hell. All other sins are not to be compared to sinning against the Holy Ghost, and proving a traitor to the brethren. (HC 3:384–85)

14 Be assured, beloved brethren, that I am no disinterested observer of the things which are transpiring on the face of the whole earth; and amidst the general movements which are in progress, none is of more importance than the glorious work in which you are now engaged; consequently I feel some anxiety on your account, that you may by your virtue, faith, diligence and charity commend yourselves to one another, to the Church of Christ, and to your Father who is in heaven; by whose grace you have been called to so holy a calling; and be enabled to perform the great and responsible duties which rest upon you. And I can assure you, that from the information I have received, I feel satisfied that you have not been remiss in your duty; but that your diligence and faithfulness have been such as must secure you the smiles of that God whose servant you are, and also the good will of the Saints throughout the world. . . .

Love is one of the chief characteristics of Deity, and ought to be manifested by those who aspire to be the sons of God. A man filled with the love of God, is not content with blessing his family alone, but ranges through the whole world, anxious to bless the whole human race. This has been your feeling, and caused you to forego the pleasures of home, that you might be a blessing to others, who are candidates for immortality, but strangers to truth; and for so doing, I pray that heaven's choicest blessings may rest upon you. (HC 4:226–27)

15 *Minutes:* President Smith observed that it was necessary that someone should be appointed to fill the Quorum of the Twelve Apostles, in the room of the late Elder David W. Patten; whereupon President Rigdon nominated Elder Lyman Wight to that office; and he was unanimously accepted. (HC 4:341)

16 *Minutes:* President Joseph Smith now arriving, proceeded to state to the conference at considerable length, the object of their present

---

Apostles

14 Letter to the Twelve in England, Nauvoo, 15 December 1840. The placement of this letter in *HC* implies that it was written in October 1840, but actually it was written on 15 December 1840 (see *PWJS*, p. 480).

15 Minutes of a general conference, Nauvoo, 8 April 1841.

16 Special conference, Nauvoo, 16 August 1841.

meeting, and, in addition to what President Young had stated in the morning, said that the time had come when the Twelve should be called upon to stand in their place next to the First Presidency, and attend to the settling of emigrants and the business of the Church at the stakes, and assist to bear off the kingdom victoriously to the nations, and as they had been faithful, and had borne the burden in the heat of the day, that it was right that they should have an opportunity of providing something for themselves and families, and at the same time relieve him, so that he might attend to the business of translating.

Moved, seconded and carried, that the conference approve of the instructions of President Smith in relation to the Twelve, and that they proceed accordingly to attend to the duties of their office. (HC 4:403)

17 This council was called to consider the case of Orson Pratt who had previously been cut off from the Church for disobedience, and Amasa Lyman had been ordained an Apostle in his place. I told the quorum: you may receive Orson back into the quorum of the Twelve and I can take Amasa into the First Presidency. President Young said there were but three present when Amasa was ordained, the rest of the Twelve being either on a mission or sick. I told them that was legal when no more could be had. (HC 5:255)

18 Let the Twelve Apostles keep together. You will do more good to keep together, not travel together all the time, but meet in conference from place to place, and associate together, and not be found long apart from each other. Then travel from here to Maine, till you make a perfect highway for the Saints.

It is better for you to be together; for it is difficult for a man to have strength of lungs and health to be instant in season and out of season, under all circumstances; and you can assist each other. And when you go to spend a day or two in a place, you will find the people will gather together in great companies. If twelve men cannot build that house, they are poor tools.

President Young asked if any of the Twelve should go to England.

I replied—No! I don't want the Twelve to go to England this year. I have sent them to England, and they have broken the ice, and done well. And now I want to send some of the elders and try them. (HC 5:366–67)

Apostles
17 Meeting of the Twelve at Brigham Young's home, Nauvoo, 20 January 1843.
18 Nauvoo, 19 April 1843.

19 Of the Twelve Apostles chosen in Kirtland, and ordained under the hands of Oliver Cowdery, David Whitmer and myself, there have been but two but what have lifted their heel against me—namely Brigham Young and Heber C. Kimball. (HC 5:412)

20 *Words of Heber C. Kimball:* Joseph Smith was a prophet of the Most High, and laid the foundation of this great Work, and established the holy Priesthood upon the earth, and God gave many revelations through him for our guidance. He said many a time while he was living, "I am laying the foundation, and you, Brother Brigham, and your brethren the Twelve Apostles, with those who are connected with you in the holy Priesthood, will rear a great and mighty fabric upon it; you will bear off the kingdom." (JD 11:95)

21 *Words of Orson Hyde:* I will tell you, brethren and sisters, the Apostleship is of some importance to the Saints of God; but I will say, furthermore, that it is very satisfactory to me when I call to mind the remarks of the Prophet Joseph Smith. I will give you my testimony. In one particular place, in the presence of about sixty men, he said, "My work is about done; I am going to step aside awhile. I am going to rest from my labors; for I have borne the burthen and heat of the day, and now I am going to step aside and rest a little. And I roll the burthen off my shoulders on the shoulders of the Twelve Apostles. Now," said he, "round up your shoulders and bear off this kingdom." Has he ever said this to any one else? I do not know; I do not care. It is enough for me to know that he said it to the Quorum of the Twelve Apostles. And since that time we have endeavored to do our duty and perform the work that was given us to do. (JD 13:180)

22 *Words of Wilford Woodruff:* Joseph Smith was what he professed to be, a prophet of God, a seer and revelator. He laid the foundation of this Church and kingdom, and lived long enough to deliver the keys of the kingdom to the Elders of Israel, unto the Twelve Apostles. He spent the last winter of his life, some three or four months, with the Quorum of the Twelve, teaching them. It was not merely a few hours ministering to them the ordinances of the Gospel; but he spent day

---

Apostles

19 Nauvoo, 28 May 1843.
20 Address by Heber C. Kimball, Salt Lake City, April 1859.
21 Address by Orson Hyde, Salt Lake City, 6 October 1869.
22 Address by Wilford Woodruff, Salt Lake City, 12 December 1869.

after day, week after week and month after month, teaching them and a few others the things of the kingdom of God. Said he, during that period, "I now rejoice. I have lived until I have seen this burden, which has rested on my shoulders, rolled on to the shoulders of other men; now the keys of the kingdom are planted on the earth to be taken away no more for ever." But until he had done this, they remained with him; and had he been taken away they would have had to be restored by messengers out of heaven. But he lived until every key, power and principle of the holy Priesthood was sealed on the Twelve and on President Young, as their President. He told us that he was going away to leave us, going away to rest. Said he, "You have to round up your shoulders to bear up the kingdom. No matter what becomes of me. I have desired to see that Temple built, but I shall not live to see it. You will; you are called upon to bear off this kingdom." This language was plain enough, but we did not understand it any more than the disciples of Jesus when he told them he was going away, and that if he went not the Comforter would not come. It was just so with Joseph. He said this time after time to the Twelve and to the Female Relief Societies and in his public discourses; but none of us seemed to understand that he was going to seal his testimony with his blood, but so it was. (JD 13:164)

23 *Words of Wilford Woodruff:* The Prophet Joseph was moved upon by divine inspiration in the establishment of this Church. And before his death he called the Twelve Apostles together, whom he had called to the ministry by revelation, intimating that he was going to leave them, that he would shortly be called home to rest. And he talked with them and instructed them for weeks and months in the ordinances and laws of the Gospel; and he sealed upon their heads all the Priesthood, keys and powers that had been conferred upon him by the angels of God. And then, in addressing them he said, "Brethren, no matter what becomes of me, or what my fate may be, you have got to round up your shoulders and bear off this kingdom; the God of heaven requires it at your hands. I have desired," said he, "to see the Temple completed, but I shall not be spared to see it, but you will." (JD 19:226)

24 *Words of John Taylor:* Before the Prophet Joseph departed, he said, on one occasion, turning to the Twelve, "I roll the burden of this

---

Apostles
  23 Address by Wilford Woodruff, Salt Lake City, 16 September 1877.
  24 Address by John Taylor, Provo, Utah, 14 October 1877.

kingdom on to you," and, on another occasion, he said their place was next to that of the First Presidency, and he wished them to take their place that he might attend to other duties, such as translating, etc. At the time he was taken away he was in the bloom of life and the vigor of health, and although his departure was sudden and unexpected our organization rendered it no difficult matter to decide who should assume the leadership of the Church. There was no difficulty in the matter; it was understood that the duty rested on the Twelve. Why? The revelation stated that the Twelve were to hold the keys of the kingdom in connection with the First Presidency, which were handed down under various circumstances. You will find in the history of the Prophet Joseph Smith, that this matter is made perfectly plain. He said there was no authority or power of presidency over the Twelve except the First Presidency, and where he was not there was no presidency over the Twelve. Hence President Brigham Young said, when the Prophet Joseph was taken away, "Thank God the keys of the kingdom are not taken from us," and being head of the Twelve, he assumed his position and so acted on the authority he held and according to the rules laid down. . . . The Twelve have not assumed the Presidency of the Church to suit themselves, but as a duty which they could not ignore. (*JD* 19:138–39)

25 *Words of William G. Nelson:* I have heard the Prophet speak in public on many occasions. In one meeting I heard him say: "I will give you a key that will never rust—if you will stay with the majority of the Twelve Apostles, and the records of the Church, you will never be led astray." (*TK*, p. 119)

Aspiring

1 We would suggest the propriety of being aware of an aspiring spirit, which spirit has oftentimes urged men forward to make foul speeches, and influence the Church to reject milder counsels, and has eventually been the means of bringing much death and sorrow upon the Church. (*HC* 3:295)

Apostles
 25 Recollection of William G. Nelson, published in the *Young Woman's Journal,* December 1906.

Aspiring
 1 Letter to the Saints from Liberty Jail, 20–25 March 1839.

2   *Report of Eliza R. Snow:* [President Smith] continued to read the chapter [1 Corinthians 12], and give instructions respecting the different offices, and the necessity of every individual acting in the sphere allotted him or her, and filling the several offices to which they are appointed. He spoke of the disposition of many men to consider the lower offices in the Church dishonorable, and to look with jealous eyes upon the standing of others who are called to preside over them; that it was the folly and nonsense of the human heart for a person to be aspiring to other stations than those to which they are appointed of God for them to occupy; that it was better for individuals to magnify their respective callings, and wait patiently till God shall say to them, "Come up higher.". . .

President Smith continued by speaking of the difficulties he had to surmount ever since the commencement of the work, in consequence of aspiring men. "Great big Elders," as he called them, who had caused him much trouble; to whom he had taught the things of the kingdom in private councils, they would then go forth into the world and proclaim the things he had taught them, as their own revelations; said the same aspiring disposition will be in this Society, and must be guarded against; that every person should stand, and act in the place appointed, and thus sanctify the Society and get it pure. He said he had been trampled under foot by aspiring Elders, for all were infected with that spirit; for instance, John E. Page and others had been aspiring; they could not be exalted, but must run away as though the care and authority of the Church were vested with them. He said he had a subtle devil to deal with, and could only curb him by being humble. . . .

. . . Everyone should aspire only to magnify his own office and calling. (*HC* 4:603, 604, 606)

Atonement

1   But notwithstanding the transgression, by which man had cut himself off from an immediate intercourse with his Maker without a

---

Aspiring
  2   Remarks to the Relief Society, Nauvoo, 28 April 1842.

Atonement
  1   Letter to the brethren scattered from Zion, Kirtland, 22 January 1834.

Mediator, it appears that the great and glorious plan of His redemption was previously provided; the sacrifice prepared; the atonement wrought out in the mind and purpose of God, even in the person of the Son, through whom man was now to look for acceptance, and through whose merits he was now taught that he alone could find redemption, since the word had been pronounced, Unto dust thou shalt return.

But that man was not able himself to erect a system, or plan with power sufficient to free him from a destruction which awaited him, is evident from the fact that God, as before remarked, prepared a sacrifice in the gift of His own Son who should be sent in due time, to prepare a way, or open a door through which man might enter into the Lord's presence, whence he had been cast out for disobedience. (HC 2:15)

2   Now I understand by this quotation [Moses 7:62], that God clearly manifested to Enoch the redemption which He prepared, by offering the Messiah as a Lamb slain from before the foundation of the world; and by virtue of the same, the glorious resurrection of the Savior, and the resurrection of all the human family, even a resurrection of their corporeal bodies, is brought to pass. (HC 2:260)

3   "What are the fundamental principles of your religion?"

The fundamental principles of our religion are the testimony of the Apostles and Prophets, concerning Jesus Christ, that He died, was buried, and rose again the third day, and ascended into heaven; and all other things which pertain to our religion are only appendages to it. But in connection with these, we believe in the gift of the Holy Ghost, the power of faith, the enjoyment of the spiritual gifts according to the will of God, the restoration of the house of Israel, and the final triumph of truth. (HC 3:30)

4   [God] foreordained the fall of man; but all merciful as He is, He foreordained at the same time, a plan of redemption for all mankind. I believe in the Divinity of Jesus Christ, and that He died for the sins of all men, who in Adam had fallen. (HC 4:78)

Atonement

2   Letter to the elders of the Church, Kirtland, 1 September 1835.

3   Answers to questions frequently asked the Prophet, Far West, 8 May 1838.

4   A letter of Mathew L. Davis to his wife describing the Prophet's discourse in Washington, D.C., 6 February 1840.

5   Through the atonement of Christ and the resurrection and obedience in the gospel, we shall again be conformed to the image of [God's] Son, Jesus Christ. Then we shall have attained to the image, glory, and character of God. (*WJS*, p. 231; standardized)

6   Salvation could not come to the world without the mediation of Jesus Christ. (*HC* 5:555)

7   The salvation of Jesus Christ was wrought out for all men, in order to triumph over the devil; for if it did not catch him in one place, it would in another. (*HC* 6:314)

Authority

1   I will inform you that it is contrary to the economy of God for any member of the Church, or any one, to receive instructions for those in authority, higher than themselves; therefore you will see the impropriety of giving heed to them; but if any person have a vision or a visitation from a heavenly messenger, it must be for his own benefit and instruction; for the fundamental principles, government, and doctrine of the Church are vested in the keys of the kingdom. (*HC* 1:338)

2   We believe that no man can administer salvation through the gospel, to the souls of men, in the name of Jesus Christ, except he is authorized from God, by revelation, or by being ordained by some one whom God hath sent by revelation, as it is written by Paul, Romans 10:14, "and how shall they believe in him, of whom, they have not heard? and how shall they hear without a preacher? and how shall they preach, except they be sent?" and I will ask, how can they be sent without a revelation, or some other visible display of the manifestation of

Atonement
   5   Sabbath address, Nauvoo, 9 July 1843, as reported by James Burgess.
   6   Sabbath address, Nauvoo, 27 August 1843.
   7   King Follett Discourse, Nauvoo, 7 April 1844.

Authority
   1   Letter to one of Jared Carter's brothers, written at the request of Jared Carter, Kirtland, 13 April 1833.
   2   Letter to Isaac Galland, written while the Prophet was imprisoned in Liberty Jail, 22 March 1839.

God. And again, Hebrews, 5:4, "And no man taketh this honor unto himself, but he that is called of God, as was Aaron."—And I would ask, how was Aaron called, but by revelation? (*PWJS*, p. 421)

3　There has been a chain of authority and power from Adam down to the present time. (HC 4:425)

4　Many objections are urged against the Latter-day Saints for not admitting the validity of sectarian baptism, and for withholding fellowship from sectarian churches. Yet to do otherwise would be like putting new wine into old bottles, and putting old wine into new bottles. What! new revelations in the old churches? New revelations would knock out the bottom of their bottomless pit. New wine into old bottles! The bottles burst and the wine runs out! What! Sadducees in the new church! Old wine in new leathern bottles will leak through the pores and escape. So the Sadducee saints mock at authority, kick out of the traces, and run to the mountains of perdition, leaving the long echo of their braying behind them. (HC 4:426)

5　There was no other name given under heaven, nor no other ordinance admitted, whereby men could be saved. . . . No wonder the angel told good old Cornelius that he must send for Peter to learn how to be saved: Peter could baptise, and angels could not, so long as there were legal officers in the flesh holding the keys of the kingdom, or the authority of the priesthood. There is one evidence still further on this point, and that is that Jesus himself when he appeared to Paul on his way to Damascus, did not inform him how he could be saved. He had set in the church firstly Apostles, and secondly prophets, for the work of the ministry, perfecting of the saints, &c.; and as the grand rule of heaven was that nothing should ever be done on earth without revealing the secret to his servants the prophets, agreeably to Amos 3:7, so Paul could not learn so much from the Lord relative to his duty in the common salvation of man, as he could from one of Christ's ambassadors called with the same heavenly calling of the Lord, and endowed with the same power from on high—so that what they loosed on earth, should be loosed in heaven; and what they bound on earth

---

Authority
　3　General conference address, Nauvoo, 3 October 1841.
　4　General conference address, Nauvoo, 3 October 1841.
　5　Editorial in the *Times and Seasons*, 1 September 1842.

should be bound in heaven: He, the Lord being a priest forever, after the order of Melchisedec, and the anointed son of God, from before the foundation of the world, and they the begotten sons of Jesus through the gospel, to teach all nations—*and lo I am with you always to the end of the world*—that is—by the other comforter which the world cannot receive—for ye are the witnesses—having the testimony of Jesus which is the spirit of prophecy. (*T&S* 3:905)

6 Some say the kingdom of God was not set up on the earth until the day of Pentecost, and that John did not preach the baptism of repentance for the remission of sins; but I say, in the name of the Lord, that the kingdom of God was set up on the earth from the days of Adam to the present time. Whenever there has been a righteous man on earth unto whom God revealed His word and gave power and authority to administer in His name, and where there is a priest of God—a minister who has power and authority from God to administer in the ordinances of the gospel and officiate in the priesthood of God, there is the kingdom of God; and, in consequence of rejecting the Gospel of Jesus Christ and the Prophets whom God hath sent, the judgments of God have rested upon people, cities, and nations, in various ages of the world, which was the case with the cities of Sodom and Gomorrah, that were destroyed for rejecting the Prophets.

Now I will give my testimony. I care not for man. I speak boldly and faithfully and with authority. How is it with the kingdom of God? Where did the kingdom of God begin? Where there is no kingdom of God there is no salvation. What constitutes the kingdom of God? Where there is a prophet, a priest, or a righteous man unto whom God gives His oracles, there is the kingdom of God; and where the oracles of God are not, there the kingdom of God is not. . . .

Whenever men can find out the will of God and find an administrator legally authorized from God, there is the kingdom of God; but where these are not, the kingdom of God is not. All the ordinances, systems, and administrations on the earth are of no use to the children of men, unless they are ordained and authorized of God; for nothing will save a man but a legal administrator; for none others will be acknowledged either by God or angels. (*HC* 5:256–57, 259)

Authority
   6   Sabbath address, Nauvoo, 22 January 1843.

7   The Savior said unto John, I must be baptized by you. Why so? To fulfil all righteousness. John refuses at first, but afterwards obeyed by administering the ordinance of baptism unto him, Jesus having no other legal administrator to apply to.

There is no salvation between the two lids of the Bible without a legal administrator. Jesus was then the legal administrator, and ordained His Apostles. (*TPJS*, p. 319)

8   *Words of Joseph Lee Robinson:* [The Prophet's] instructions to the Quorum of the Twelve before his death: "Though we or an angel from heaven preach any other gospel or introduce any order of things other than those things which ye have received and are authorized to receive from the First Presidency, let him be accursed." (*TK*, p. 164)

Bankruptcy

1   Calvin A. Warren, Esq., lawyer, from Quincy, arrived, and commenced an investigation of the principles of general insolvency in my behalf according to the statutes; for the United States Congress had previously instituted a general bankrupt law by which any individual who was owing to a certain amount more than he was able to pay, could make out a schedule of his property, and of debts due from himself, and by a specified process, pass the same in the hands of a commissioner, government agent, or "assignee," who could make a dividend of all his effects, and pay his creditors whatever percentage his property amounted to, and then the individual was at liberty to start anew in the world, and was not subject to liquidate any claims which were held against him previous to his insolvency, although his property might not have paid but the least percentage, or none at all.

The justice or injustice of such a principle in law, I leave for them who made it, the United States. Suffice it to say, the law was as good for the Saints as for the Gentiles, and whether I would or not, I was

---

Authority
7   Sabbath address, Nauvoo, 23 July 1843.
8   Journal of Joseph Lee Robinson.

Bankruptcy
1   The Prophet is pressed to consider bankruptcy because of loss of property by mob action, 14 April 1842.

forced into the measure by having been robbed, mobbed, plundered, and wasted of all my property, time after time, in various places, by the very ones who made the law, namely, the people of the United States, thereby having been obliged to contract heavy debts to prevent the utter destruction of myself, family and friends, and by those who were justly and legally owing me, taking the advantage of the same act of bankruptcy, so that I could not collect my just dues, thus leaving me no alternative but to become subject again to stripping, wasting, and destitution, by vexatious writs, and law suits, and imprisonments, or take that course to extricate myself, which the law had pointed out. (HC 4:594–95)

2   I continued busily engaged in making out a list of debtors and an invoice of my property to be passed into the hands of the assignee. (HC 4:599–600)

3   In consequence of the utter annihilation of our property by mob violence in the state of Missouri, and the immense expenses which we were compelled to incur, to defend ourselves from the cruel persecutions of that state, we were reduced to the necessity of availing ourselves of the privileges of the general bankrupt law; therefore I went to Carthage with my brothers Hyrum and Samuel H. Smith, and severally testified to our list of insolvency before the clerk of the county commissioners' court. Sidney Rigdon and many more brethren were at Carthage the same day on business. My clerk, Dr. Richards, went with us. (HC 4:600)

4   I proceed without delay to give a hasty reply to yours of the 12th ultimo, just received. My engagements will not admit of a lengthy detail of events and circumstances which have transpired to bring about that state of things which now exists in this place, as before you receive this you will probably be apprised of the failure of myself and brethren to execute our designs in paying off our contracts, or in other words, that we have been compelled to pay our debts by the most popular method; that is by petitioning for the privilege of general bankruptcy, a principle so popular at the present moment throughout the Union.

Bankruptcy

2–3   The Prophet is pressed to consider bankruptcy because of loss of property by mob action, 15 and 18 April 1842.

4   Letter to Horace R. Hotchkiss, Nauvoo, 13 May 1842.

A pressure of business has been sufficient excuse for not giving you earlier notice, although it could have been of no real use to you, yet I wish you to understand our intentions to you and your company, and why we have taken the course we have. You are aware, sir, in some measure of the embarrassment under which we have labored through the influence of mobs and designing men, and the disadvantageous circumstances under which we have been compelled to contract debts in order to [continue] our existence, both as individuals and as a society, and it is on account of this as well as a pressure on us for debts absolutely unjust in themselves, that we have been compelled to resort to the course we have {taken} to make a general settlement, and this we deferred to the last moment, hoping that something would turn in our favor, so that we might be saved the painful necessity of resorting to such measures, to accomplish which, justice demanded a very different course from those who are justly our debtors, but demanded in vain.

We have been compelled to the course we have pursued, and you are aware, sir, that all have to fare alike in such cases. But, sir, you have one, yea, two things to comfort you; our faith, intention and good feeling remain the same to all our creditors, and to none more than yourself; and secondly, there is property sufficient in the inventory to pay every debt, and some to spare, according to the testimony of our solicitors, and the good judgment of others; and if the court will allow us some one for assignee, who will do justice to the cause, we confidently believe that yourself and all others will get their compensation in full, and we have enough left for one loaf more for each of our families. Yes, and I have no doubt you will yet, and in a short time, be enabled to have your pay in full, in the way I have before proposed, or some other equally advantageous, but money is out of sight, it might as well be out of mind, for it cannot be had.

Rest assured, dear sir, that no influence or exertion I can yet make shall be wanting to give you satisfaction, and liquidate your claims, but for a little season you are aware that all proceedings are staid; but I will seek the earliest moment to acquaint you with anything new in this matter.

I remain, sir, with sentiments of respect, your friend and well-wisher. (HC 5:6–7)

5 Yours of the 27th [of] May has been received, which I shall now briefly answer. In regard to my application for the benefit of the bankrupt act, there was no other course for me to pursue than the one I have already taken; and, as I have said before, all my creditors will have to fare alike. Your papers are inventoried along with all the other property.

The influence this step may have upon our society, either commercially or religiously, is a matter we cannot stop to consult, as we had no alternative left. We have been compelled to pursue this course on account of the extreme pressure of the times, which continued to bear harder upon us, until we took the step we have.

A great pressure of business prevents writing more at the present, you will, therefore, excuse a short communication. (HC 5:52)

6 In the morning, attended in council with Brother Hyrum and others on bankruptcy, making an inventory of our property, and schedule of our liabilities, that we might be prepared to avail ourselves of the laws of the land as did others. (HC 5:200)

Baptism

1 "Do the Mormons baptize in the name of 'Joe' Smith?"

No, but if they did, it would be as valid as the baptism administered by the sectarian priests. (HC 3:29)

2 Baptism is a holy ordinance preparatory to the reception of the Holy Ghost; it is the channel and key by which the Holy Ghost will be administered. (HC 3:379)

3 Being born again, comes by the Spirit of God through ordinances. (HC 3:392)

Bankruptcy
   5   Letter to Horace R. Hotchkiss, Nauvoo, 30 June 1842.
   6   Nauvoo, 5 December 1842.

Baptism
   1   Answers to questions frequently asked the Prophet, Far West, 8 May 1838.
   2   Instructions to the Twelve, Commerce (Nauvoo), 27 June 1839.
   3   Instructions to the Apostles and Seventies departing for missions to England, Commerce (Nauvoo), 2 July 1839.

4 *Report of Mathew L. Davis:* He [Joseph Smith] does not believe in infant baptism, sprinkling, but in immersion, after eight years of age. (HC 4:80)

5 *Report of Wilford Woodruff:* [President Smith said:] The doctrine of baptizing children, or sprinkling them, or they must welter in hell, is a doctrine not true, not supported in Holy Writ, and is not consistent with the character of God. All children are redeemed by the blood of Jesus Christ, and the moment that children leave this world, they are taken to the bosom of Abraham. . . .

My intention was to have spoken on the subject of baptism, but having a case of death before us, I thought proper to refer to that subject. I will now, however, say a few words upon baptism, as I intended.

God has made certain decrees which are fixed and immovable; for instance,—God set the sun, the moon, and the stars in the heavens, and gave them their laws, conditions and bounds, which they cannot pass, except by His commandments; they all move in perfect harmony in their sphere and order, and are as lights, wonders and signs unto us. The sea also has its bounds which it cannot pass. God has set many signs on the earth, as well as in the heavens; for instance, the oak of the forest, the fruit of the tree, the herb of the field—all bear a sign that seed hath been planted there; for it is a decree of the Lord that every tree, plant, and herb bearing seed should bring forth of its kind, and cannot come forth after any other law or principle. Upon the same principle do I contend that baptism is a sign ordained of God, for the believer in Christ to take upon himself in order to enter into the kingdom of God, "for except ye are born of water and of the Spirit ye cannot enter into the kingdom of God," said the Savior. It is a sign and a commandment which God has set for man to enter into His kingdom. Those who seek to enter in any other way will seek in vain; for God will not receive them, neither will the angels acknowledge their works as accepted, for they have not obeyed the ordinances, nor attended to the signs which God ordained for the salvation of man, to prepare him for, and give him title to, a celestial glory; and God had decreed that all who will not obey His voice shall not escape the damnation of hell. . . .

Baptism

4 A letter of Mathew L. Davis to his wife describing the Prophet's discourse in Washington, D.C., 6 February 1840.

5 Sabbath address, Nauvoo, 20 March 1842.

Baptism is a sign to God, to angels, and to heaven that we do the will of God, and there is no other way beneath the heavens whereby God hath ordained for man to come to Him to be saved, and enter into the kingdom of God, except faith in Jesus Christ, repentance, and baptism for the remission of sins, and any other course is in vain; then you have the promise of the gift of the Holy Ghost. . . .

At the close of the meeting, President Smith said he should attend to the ordinance of baptism in the river, near his house, at two o'clock, and at the appointed hour, the bank of the Mississippi was lined with a multitude of people, and President Joseph Smith went into the river and baptized eighty persons for the remission of their sins, and what added joy to the scene was, that the first person baptized was M.L.D. Wasson, a nephew of Mrs. Emma Smith—the first of her kindred that has embraced the fullness of the Gospel.

At the close of this interesting scene, the administrator lifted up his hands towards heaven, and implored the blessing of God to rest upon the people; and truly the Spirit of God did rest upon the multitude, to the joy and consolation of our hearts. (HC 4:554–55, 557)

6   Upon looking over the sacred pages of the Bible, searching into the prophets and sayings of the apostles, we find no subject so nearly connected with salvation, as that of baptism. In the first place, however, let us understand that the word *baptise* is derived from the Greek verb *baptiso*, and means to immerse or overwhelm, and that sprinkle is from the Greek verb *rantiso*, and means to scatter on by particles; then we can treat the subject as one inseparably connected with our eternal welfare; and always bear in mind that it is one of the only methods by which we can obtain a remission of sins in this world, and be prepared to enter into the joys of our Lord in the world to come.

As it is well known that various opinions govern a large portion of the sectarian world as to this important ordinance of the gospel, it may not be amiss to introduce the commissions and commands of Jesus himself on the subject.—He said to the twelve, or rather eleven at the time: Go ye therefore, and teach all nations, baptising them in the name of the Father, and of the Son, and of the Holy Ghost; teaching them to observe all things whatsoever I have commanded you: Thus it is recorded by Matthew. In Mark we have these important words: Go ye into all the world, and preach the gospel to every creature. He that believeth and is baptised shall be saved, and he that believeth not shall be damned. And to show how the believers are to be known from the unbelievers, he continues and says: And these signs shall follow them that believe: in my name shall they cast out devils: they shall speak with new tongues: they shall take up serpents: and if they drink any deadly thing it shall not hurt them: they shall lay hands on the sick and they shall recover. And in Luke we find the finishing clause like this,—that it was necessary that Christ should die and rise the third day—that remission of sins should be preached in his name among all nations, beginning at Jerusalem. *And ye are witnesses of these things.*

We will now examine the witnesses. As it will be recollected, they were to wait at Jerusalem till they were endowed with power from on high and then go and teach all nations whatsoever the Lord had commanded them. As Peter held the keys of the kingdom, we will examine him first.

Now on the day of Pentecost, when there was a marvelous display of the gifts, according to the promise in Mark, many were pricked in the heart, and said unto Peter, and to the rest of the Apostles, men and brethren what shall we do? Peter said unto them: Repent, and be baptised every one of you in the name of Jesus Christ, for the remission of sins, and ye shall receive the gift of the Holy Ghost, &c.—Here one of the witnesses says in so many words, repent and be baptised. And we are of the opinion that Peter having been taught by the Lord, would be about as correct a counselor, or ambassador as we or they could enquire of to know the right way to enter into the kingdom.

Again, Luke in his record of the acts of the Apostles, says:—And it came to pass, that while Apollos was at Corinth, Paul having passed through the upper coasts, came to Ephesus; and finding certain disciples, he said unto them, have ye received the Holy Ghost since ye believed? And they said unto him, We have not so much as heard whether there be any Holy Ghost. And he said unto them, Unto what then were ye baptised? And they said, unto John's baptism. Then said Paul, John verily baptised with the baptism of repentance, saying unto the people, That they should believe on him which should come after him, that is on Christ Jesus. When they heard this, they were baptised in the name of the Lord Jesus.—And when Paul had laid his hands upon them, the Holy Ghost came on them; and they spake with tongues, and prophesied.

From the above witnesses we are informed that baptism was the essential point on which they could receive the gift of the Holy

Ghost. It seems from the reasoning above that some sectarian Jew had been baptising like John, but had forgotten to inform them that there was one to follow by the name of Jesus Christ, to baptise with fire and the Holy Ghost:—which showed these converts that their first baptism was illegal, and when they heard this they were gladly baptised, and after hands were laid on them, they received the gifts, according to promise, and spake with tongues and prophesied. . . .

. . . Nicodemus . . . came to Jesus by night, and said unto him, Rabbi, we know that thou art a teacher come from God: for no man can do these miracles that thou doest, except God be with him. Jesus answered and said unto him, Verily, verily, I say unto thee, except a man be born again he cannot see the kingdom of God. Nicodemus saith unto him, How can a man be born when he is old? can he enter the second time into his mother's womb, and be born?—Jesus answered, Verily, verily, I say unto thee, Except a man be born of water, and of the Spirit, he cannot enter into the kingdom of God. This strong and positive answer of Jesus, as to water baptism, settles the question: If God is the same yesterday, today, and forever; it is no wonder he is so positive in the great declaration: He that believes and is baptised shall be saved, and he that believes not shall be damned! There was no other name given under heaven, nor no other ordinance admitted, whereby men could be saved: No wonder the Apostle said, being "buried with him in baptism," ye shall rise from the dead! No wonder Paul had to arise and be baptised and wash away his sins: No wonder the angel told good old Cornelius that he must send for Peter to learn how to be saved: Peter could baptise, and angels could not, so long as there were legal officers in the flesh holding the keys of the kingdom, or the authority of the priesthood. . . .

. . . No man can be saved without baptism. . . . Jesus Christ himself, who had no need of repentance, having . . . no sin, [gave the] declaration to John:—now let me be baptised: for no man can enter the kingdom without obeying this ordinance: for thus it becometh us to fulfil *all righteousness*. Surely, then, if it became John and Jesus Christ, the Saviour, to fulfil all righteousness to be baptised—so surely, then, it will become every other person that seeks the kingdom of heaven to go and do likewise; for he is the door, and if any person climbs up any other way, the same is a thief and a robber!

In the former ages of the world, before the Saviour came in the flesh, "the saints" were baptised in the name of Jesus Christ to come, because there never was any other name whereby men could be saved;

and after he came in the flesh and was crucified, then the saints were baptised in the name of Jesus Christ, crucified, risen from the dead and ascended into heaven, that they might be buried in baptism like him, and be raised in glory like him, that as there was but one Lord, one faith, one baptism, and one God and father of us all, even so there was but one door to the mansions of bliss. Amen. (*T&S* 3:903–5)

7   "Do you believe in the baptism of infants?" asks the Presbyterian. No. "Why?" Because it is nowhere written in the Bible. Circumcision is not baptism, neither was baptism instituted in the place of circumcision. Baptism is for remission of sins. Children have no sins. Jesus blessed them and said, "Do what you have seen me do." Children are all made alive in Christ, and those of riper years through faith and repentance.

So far we are agreed with other Christian denominations. They all preach faith and repentance. The gospel requires baptism by immersion for the remission of sins, which is the meaning of the word in the original language—namely, to bury or immerse.

We ask the sects, Do you believe this? They answer, No. I believe in being converted. I believe in this tenaciously. So did the Apostle Peter and the disciples of Jesus. But I further believe in the gift of the Holy Ghost by the laying on of hands. Evidence by Peter's preaching on the day of Pentecost, Acts 2:38. You might as well baptize a bag of sand as a man, if not done in view of the remission of sins and getting of the Holy Ghost. Baptism by water is but half a baptism, and is good for nothing without the other half—that is, the baptism of the Holy Ghost.

The Savior says, "Except a man be born of water and of the Spirit, he cannot enter into the kingdom of God." "Though we or an angel from heaven, preach any other gospel unto you than that which we have preached unto you, let him be accursed," according to Galatians 1:8. (*HC* 5:499–500)

8   The Savior said unto John, I must be baptized by you. Why so? To fulfil all righteousness. John refuses at first, but afterwards obeyed by administering the ordinance of baptism unto him, Jesus having no other legal administrator to apply to. (*TPJS*, p. 319)

Baptism

7   Sabbath address, Nauvoo, 9 July 1843.

8   Sabbath address, Nauvoo, 23 July 1843.

9   I will leave this subject here, and make a few remarks on the subject of baptism. The baptism of water, without the baptism of fire and
the Holy Ghost attending it, is of no use; they are necessarily and inseparably connected. An individual must be born of water and the
spirit in order to get into the kingdom of God. In the German, the
text bears me out the same as the revelations which I have given and
taught for the past fourteen years on that subject. I have the testimony
to put in their teeth. My testimony has been true all the time. You will
find it in the declaration of John the Baptist. (Reads from the German.) John says, "I baptize you with water, but when Jesus comes, who
has the power (or keys) He shall administer the baptism of fire and
the Holy Ghost." Great God! Where is now all the sectarian world?
And if this testimony is true, they are all damned as clearly as anathema
can do it. I know the text is true. I call upon all you Germans who
know that it is true to say, Aye. (Loud shouts of "Aye.")

Alexander Campbell, how are you going to save people with
water alone? For John said his baptism was good for nothing without
the baptism of Jesus Christ. . . .

There is one God, one Father, one Jesus, one hope of our calling,
one baptism. All these three baptisms only make one. Many talk of
baptism not being essential to salvation; but this kind of teaching
would lay the foundation of their damnation. (*HC* 6:316, 317)

10 *Words of Edward Stevenson:* [The Prophet] explained several passages of scripture. . . . The epistle to the Hebrew saints should say,
"Therefore not leaving the principles of the doctrine of Christ, let us
go unto perfection"—not, "Therefore leaving the principles of the
doctrine of Christ." He said that the plural term "baptisms" in this
passage had reference to baptism for the living, baptism for the dead,
and rebaptism. (Hebrews 6:1–2.) (*TK*, p. 87)

11 *Words of Daniel Tyler:* The Prophet Joseph Smith was a great rec-
onciler of discrepancies in passages of scripture which were or seemed
to be in conflict with each other. Until I heard the great expounder of
Bible doctrines explain the following passages I concluded there must

Baptism
   9   King Follett Discourse, Nauvoo, 7 April 1844.
  10   Autobiography of Edward Stevenson, LDS Church Archives.
  11   Daniel Tyler's recollection, published in the *Juvenile Instructor*, 15 May 1893.

be a wrong translation in one verse or the other. One verse read: "I indeed baptize you with water unto repentance, but he that cometh after me is mightier than I, whose shoes I am not worthy to bear; he shall baptize you with the Holy Ghost and with fire."—Matthew iii, 11.

Here we have baptism with water, baptism with the Holy Ghost, and baptism with fire, three in number. The question naturally arises, how can this passage be reconciled with the following: "There is one . . . Lord, one faith, *one baptism*."—Ephesians iv., 4–6.

Joseph Smith reconciled these two scriptural passages. He said: "There is but one baptism; it takes the baptism of water, of the Holy Ghost, and of fire to constitute one full baptism." (*TK*, p. 51)

Baptism for the Dead

1   I presume the doctrine of "baptism for the dead" has ere this reached your ears, and may have raised some inquiries in your minds respecting the same. I cannot in this letter give you all the information you may desire on the subject; but aside from knowledge independent of the Bible, I would say that it was certainly practiced by the ancient churches; and St. Paul endeavors to prove the doctrine of the resurrection from the same, and says, "Else what shall they do which are baptized for the dead, if the dead rise not at all? Why are they then baptized for the dead?"

I first mentioned the doctrine in public when preaching the funeral of Brother Seymour Brunson; and have since then given general instructions in the Church on the subject. The Saints have the privilege of being baptized for those of their relatives who are dead, whom they believe would have embraced the Gospel, if they had been privileged with hearing it, and who have received the Gospel in the spirit, through the instrumentality of those who have been commissioned to preach to them while in prison. (HC 4:231)

2   *Minutes:* President Joseph Smith, by request of the Twelve Apostles, gave instructions on the doctrine of baptism for the dead, which were

---

Baptism for the Dead
1   Letter to the Twelve in England, 15 December 1840. The placement of this letter in *HC* implies that it was written in October 1840, but actually it was written on 15 December 1840 (see *PWJS*, p. 480).
2   General conference address, Nauvoo, 3 October 1841.

listened to with intense interest by the large assembly. He presented baptism for the dead as the only way that men can appear as saviors on Mount Zion.

The proclamation of the first principles of the Gospel was a means of salvation to men individually; and it was the truth, not men, that saved them; but men, by actively engaging in rites of salvation substitutionally became instrumental in bringing multitudes of their kindred into the kingdom of God. (HC 4:424–25)

3   *Report of Wilford Woodruff:* He [Amasa Lyman] was followed by Joseph, the Seer, who made some highly edifying and instructive remarks concerning baptism for the dead. He said the Bible supported the doctrine, quoting 1 Cor., xv; 29: "Else what shall they do which are baptized for the dead, if the dead rise not at all, why are they then baptized for the dead?" If there is one word of the Lord that supports the doctrine of baptism for the dead, it is enough to establish it as a true doctrine. Again; if we can, by the authority of the Priesthood of the Son of God, baptize a man in the name of the Father, of the Son, and of the Holy Ghost, for the remission of sins, it is just as much our privilege to act as an agent, and be baptized for the remission of sins for and in behalf of our dead kindred, who have not heard the Gospel, or the fullness of it. (HC 4:569)

4   Living friends were baptized for their dead friends, and thus fulfilled the requirement of God, which says, "Except a man be born of water and of the Spirit, he cannot enter into the kingdom of God;" they were baptized of course, not for themselves, but for their dead. (HC 4:599)

5   And now as the great purposes of God are hastening to their accomplishment and the things spoken of in the prophets are fulfilling, as the kingdom of God is established on the earth, and the ancient order of things restored, the Lord has manifested to us this duty and privilege, and we are commanded to be baptized for our dead, thus fulfilling the words of Obadiah when speaking of the glory of the Latter Day. "And saviours shall come up upon mount Zion to judge the remnant of Esau; and the kingdom shall be the Lord's." (*T&S* 3:761)

Baptism for the Dead

  3   Sabbath address, Nauvoo, 27 March 1842.
  4   Editorial in the *Times and Seasons*, 15 April 1842.
  5   Editorial in the *Times and Seasons*, 15 April 1842.

6 Ordinances instituted in the heavens before the foundation of the world, in the priesthood, for the salvation of men, are not to be altered or changed. All must be saved on the same principles.

It is for the same purpose that God gathers together His people in the last days, to build unto the Lord a house to prepare them for the ordinances and endowments, washings and anointings, etc. One of the ordinances of the house of the Lord is baptism for the dead. God decreed before the foundation of the world that that ordinance should be administered in a font prepared for that purpose in the house of the Lord. (HC 5:423–24)

7 There is baptism . . . for those to exercise who are alive, and baptism for the dead who die without the knowledge of the Gospel. (HC 6:365)

Baptism of Fire
See BORN AGAIN

Beasts

1 What John saw and speaks of were things which he saw in heaven; those which Daniel saw were on and pertaining to the earth.

I am now going to take exceptions to the present translation of the Bible in relation to these matters. Our latitude and longitude can be determined in the original Hebrew with far greater accuracy than in the English version. There is a grand distinction between the actual meaning of the prophets and the present translation. The prophets do not declare that they saw a beast or beasts, but that they saw the *image* or *figure* of a beast. Daniel did not see an actual bear or a lion, but the images or figures of those beasts. The translation should have been rendered "image" instead of "beast," in every instance where beasts are mentioned by the prophets. But John saw the actual beast in heaven,

---

Baptism for the Dead
6 Sabbath address, Nauvoo, 11 June 1843.
7 Sabbath address, Nauvoo, 12 May 1844.

Beasts
1 General conference address, Nauvoo, 8 April 1843.

showing to John that beasts did actually exist there, and not to represent figures of things on the earth. When the prophets speak of seeing beasts in their visions, they mean that they saw the images, they being types to represent certain things. At the same time they received the interpretation as to what those images or types were designed to represent.

I make this broad declaration, that whenever God gives a vision of an image, or beast, or figure of any kind, He always holds Himself responsible to give a revelation or interpretation of the meaning thereof, otherwise we are not responsible or accountable for our belief in it. Don't be afraid of being damned for not knowing the meaning of a vision or figure, if God has not given a revelation or interpretation of the subject. (HC 5:342–43)

Belief

1   I believe all that God ever revealed, and I never hear of a man being damned for believing too much; but they are damned for unbelief. (HC 6:477)

Bible

1   He that can mark the power of Omnipotence, inscribed upon the heavens, can also see God's own handwriting in the sacred volume: and he who reads it oftenest will like it best, and he who is acquainted with it, will know the hand wherever he can see it; and when once discovered, it will not only receive an acknowledgment, but an obedience to all its heavenly precepts. (HC 2:14)

2   From what we can draw from the Scriptures relative to the teachings of heaven, we are induced to think that much instruction has been given to man since the beginning which we do not possess now. This may not agree with the opinions of some of our friends who are

---

Belief
  1   Sabbath address, Nauvoo, 16 June 1844.

Bible
  1   Letter to the brethren scattered from Zion, Kirtland, 22 January 1834.
  2   Letter to the brethren scattered from Zion, Kirtland, 22 January 1834.

bold to say that we have everything written in the Bible which God ever spoke to man since the world began, and that if he had ever said anything more we should certainly have received it. But we ask, does it remain for a people who never had faith enough to call down one scrap of revelation from heaven, and for all they have now are indebted to the faith of another people who lived hundreds and thousands of years before them, does it remain for them to say how much God has spoken and how much he has not spoken? We have what we have, and the Bible contains what it does contain: but to say that God never said anything more to man than is there recorded, would be saying at once that we have at last received a revelation: for it must require one to advance thus far, because it is nowhere said in that volume by the mouth of God, that He would not, after giving what is there contained, speak again; and if any man has found out for a fact that the Bible contains all that God ever revealed to man he has ascertained it by an immediate revelation, other than has been previously written by the prophets and apostles. But through the kind providence of our Father a portion of His word which He delivered to His ancient saints, has fallen into our hands, is presented to us with a promise of a reward if obeyed, and with a penalty if disobeyed. That all are deeply interested in these laws or teachings, must be admitted by all who acknowledge their divine authenticity. (HC 2:18)

3   You may hug up to yourselves the Bible, but, except through faith in it you get revelation for yourself, the Bible will profit you but little. (TK, p. 101)

4   "Is there anything in the Bible which licenses you to believe in revelation now-a-days?"

Is there anything that does not authorize us to believe so? If there is, we have, as yet, not been able to find it.

. . . "Is not the canon of the Scriptures full?"

If it is, there is a great defect in the book, or else it would have said so. (HC 3:30)

Bible
3   David Osborn's recollection of an 1837 statement, published in the *Juvenile Instructor*, 15 March 1892.
4   Answers to questions frequently asked the Prophet, Far West, 8 May 1838.

5   *Report of Mathew L. Davis:* He [Joseph Smith] then took up the Bible. "I believe," said he, "in this sacred volume. In it the 'Mormon' faith is to be found. We teach nothing but what the Bible teaches. We believe nothing, but what is to be found in this book." (*HC* 4:78)

6   I will now turn linguist. There are many things in the Bible which do not, as they now stand, accord with the revelations of the Holy Ghost to me.

I will criticize a little further. There has been much said about the word hell, and the sectarian world have preached much about it, describing it to be a burning lake of fire and brimstone. But what is hell? It is another modern term, and is taken from hades. I'll hunt after hades as Pat did for the woodchuck. (*HC* 5:425)

7   There is no salvation between the two lids of the Bible without a legal administrator. (*TPJS*, p. 319)

8   I believe the Bible as it read when it came from the pen of the original writers. Ignorant translators, careless transcribers, or designing and corrupt priests have committed many errors. As it read, Gen. vi. 6, "It repented the Lord that he had made man on the earth;" also, Num. xxiii. 19, "God is not a man, that he should lie; neither the Son of man, that he should repent;" which I do not believe. But it ought to read, "It repented *Noah* that God made man." This I believe, and then the other quotation stands fair. If any man will prove to me, by one passage of Holy Writ, one item I believe to be false, I will renounce and disclaim it as far as I promulgated it.

The first principles of the Gospel, as I believe, are, faith, repentance, baptism for the remission of sins, with the promise of the Holy Ghost.

Look at Heb. vi. 1 for contradictions—"Therefore leaving the principles of the doctrine of Christ, let us go on unto perfection." If a man leaves the principles of the doctrine of Christ, how can he be

---

Bible

5   A letter of Mathew L. Davis to his wife describing the Prophet's discourse in Washington, D.C., 6 February 1840.

6   Sabbath address, Nauvoo, 11 June 1843.

7   Sabbath address, Nauvoo, 23 July 1843.

8   Sabbath address, Nauvoo, 15 October 1843.

saved in the principles? This is a contradiction. I don't believe it. I will render it as it should be—"Therefore *not* leaving the principles of the doctrine of Christ, let us go on unto perfection, not laying again the foundation of repentance from dead works, and of faith toward God, of the doctrine of baptisms, and of laying on of hands, and of resurrection of the dead, and of eternal judgment." (*HC* 6:57–58)

9   I have an old edition of the New Testament in the Latin, Hebrew, German and Greek languages. I have been reading the German, and find it to be the most {nearly} correct translation, and to correspond nearest to the revelations which God has given to me for the last fourteen years. (*HC* 6:307)

10   I thank God that I have got this old book; but I thank him more for the gift of the Holy Ghost. I have got the oldest book in the world; but I have got the oldest book in my heart, even the gift of the Holy Ghost. (*HC* 6:308)

Bible, Joseph Smith Translation of the

1   The Lord greatly encouraged and strengthened the faith of His little flock . . . by giving some more extended information upon the Scriptures, a translation of which had already commenced. (*HC* 1:131, 132)

2   The early part of September was spent in making preparations to remove to the town of Hiram, and renew our work on the translation of the Bible. The brethren who were commanded to go up to Zion were earnestly engaged in getting ready to start in the coming October. . . .
    On the 12th of September, I removed with my family to the township of Hiram, and commenced living with John Johnson. Hiram was

---

Bible
   9   King Follett Discourse, Nauvoo, 7 April 1844.
   10   King Follett Discourse, Nauvoo, 7 April 1844.

Bible, Joseph Smith Translation of the
   1   Joseph Smith, with Sidney Rigdon as scribe, was engaged in a translation of the Bible at Fayette, New York, December 1830.
   2   After moving to Kirtland, Joseph made preparations to move to Hiram and recommence translation of the Bible, September 1831.

in Portage county, and about thirty miles southeasterly from Kirtland. From this time until the forepart of October, I did little more than prepare to re-commence the translation of the Bible. (*HC* 1:211, 215)

3   Soon after the above revelation was received [D&C 65, October 1831], I renewed my work on the translation of the Scriptures, in company with Elder Rigdon, who had removed to Hiram, to act in his office of scribe to me.

. . . A committee of six was appointed to instruct the several branches of the Church. Elders David Whitmer and Reynolds Cahoon were appointed as two of the said committee; with the further duty on their mission of setting forth the condition of Brothers Joseph Smith, Jun., and Sidney Rigdon, that they might obtain means to continue the translation. (*HC* 1:219)

4   *Minutes:* [Joseph Smith] said . . . except the Church receive the fulness of the scriptures that they would yet fall. (*FWR*, p. 23; standardized)

5   After Oliver Cowdery and John Whitmer had departed for Jackson county, Missouri, I resumed the translation of the Scriptures, and continued to labor in this branch of my calling with Elder Sidney Rigdon as my scribe, until I received the following: [D&C 71]. (*HC* 1:238)

6   Upon the reception of the foregoing word of the Lord [D&C 73], I recommenced the translation of the Scriptures, and labored diligently until just before the conference, which was to convene on the 25th of January. During this period, I also received the following, as an explanation of the First Epistle to the Corinthians, 7th chapter, 14th verse: [D&C 74]. (*HC* 1:242)

7   Upon my return from Amherst conference, I resumed the translation of the Scriptures. From sundry revelations which had been re-

---

Bible, Joseph Smith Translation of the
3   Hiram, Ohio, October 1831.
4   Minutes of a conference held at Orange, Ohio, 25 October 1831. D&C 42:15 and 104:58–59 show that "fulness of the scriptures" refers to the Joseph Smith Translation of the Bible.
5   Hiram, Ohio, latter part of November 1831.
6   Hiram, Ohio, January 1832.
7   Hiram, Ohio, first half of February 1832.

ceived, it was apparent that many important points, touching the salvation of man, had been taken from the Bible, or lost before it was compiled. (HC 1:245)

8 About the first of March, in connection with the translation of the Scriptures, I received the following explanation of the Revelation of St. John: [D&C 77]. (HC 1:253)

9 Besides the work of translating, previous to the 20th of March, I received the four following revelations: [D&C 78–81]. (HC 1:255)

10 As soon as I could arrange my affairs, I recommenced the translation of the Scriptures, and thus I spent most of the summer. (HC 1:273)

11 I continued the translation of the Bible and ministering to the Church, through the fall, excepting a hurried journey to Albany, New York and Boston, in company with Bishop Whitney, from which I returned on the 6th of November, immediately after the birth of my son Joseph Smith, the third. (HC 1:295)

12 This winter {1832–33} was spent in translating the Scriptures; in the School of the Prophets; and sitting in conferences. (HC 1:322)

13 I completed the translation and review of the New Testament, on the 2nd of February, 1833 and sealed it up, no more to be opened till it arrived in Zion. (HC 1:324)

Bible, Joseph Smith Translation of the
- **8** Hiram, Ohio, March 1832.
- **9** Hiram, Ohio, March 1832.
- **10** Hiram, Ohio, summer 1832.
- **11** Kirtland, November 1832.
- **12** Kirtland, winter 1832–1833.
- **13** Kirtland, 2 February 1833. In a footnote keyed to this entry in *HC*, B. H. Roberts explains: "It was the intention of the Prophet to have this revised version of the Scriptures, which he had made with such laborious care, published in Zion, at the printing establishment of the Church in that place, (New Testament and Book of Mormon to be published together; see [HC 1] p. 341), but before the work could even be commenced, the persecution arose which made the undertaking impracticable. And such was the unsettled state of the Church throughout the remaining years of the Prophet's life that he found no opportunity to publish the revised Scriptures."

14 Having come to that portion of the ancient writings called the Apocrypha, I received the following: [D&C 91]. (*HC* 1:331)

15 It is not the will of the Lord to print any of the New Translation in the *Star*; but when it is published, it will all go to the world together, in a volume by itself; and the New Testament and the Book of Mormon will be printed together. (*HC* 1:341)

16 In regard to the printing of the New Translation: It cannot be done until we can attend to it ourselves, and this we will do as soon as the Lord permits. (*HC* 1:365)

17 We this day finished the translating of the Scriptures, for which we returned gratitude to our Heavenly Father. . . .
   . . . [We] finished the translation of the Bible, a few hours since. . . . (*HC* 1:368, 369)

Bishops

1 The matter of consecration must be done by the mutual consent of both parties; for to give the Bishop power to say how much every man shall have, and he be obliged to comply with the Bishop's judgment, is giving the Bishop more power than a king has; and upon the other hand, to let every man say how much he needs, and the Bishop be obliged to comply with his judgment, is to throw Zion into confusion, and make a slave of the Bishop. The fact is, there must be a balance or equilibrium of power, between the bishop and the people, and thus harmony and good will may be preserved among you. . . .
   . . . In relation to the poor: When the Bishops are appointed according to our recommendation, it will devolve upon them to see to the poor, according to the laws of the Church. (*HC* 1:364, 365)

Bible, Joseph Smith Translation of the
  14 Kirtland, 9 March 1833.
  15 Letter to the brethren in Zion, Kirtland, 21 April 1833.
  16 Letter to the brethren in Zion, Kirtland, 25 June 1833.
  17 Letter to the brethren in Zion, Kirtland, 2 July 1833.

Bishops
  1 Letter to the brethren in Zion, Kirtland, 25 June 1833.

2   The Bishop is a High Priest, and necessarily so, because he is to preside over that particular branch of Church affairs, that is denominated the Lesser Priesthood, and because we have no direct lineal descendant of Aaron, to whom it would of right belong. This is the same, or a branch of the same, Priesthood, which may be illustrated by the figure of the human body, which has different members, which have different offices to perform; all are necessary in their place, and the body is not complete without all the members. (HC 2:477–78)

3   I spent the day in counseling the Bishops, and assisting them to expose iniquity. (HC 5:18)

Bitterness

1   I advise all of you to be careful what you do, or you may by-and-by find out that you have been deceived. Stay yourselves; do not give way; don't make any hasty moves, you may be saved. If a spirit of bitterness is in you, don't be in haste. You may say, that man is a sinner. Well, if he repents, he shall be forgiven. Be cautious: await. When you find a spirit that wants bloodshed,—murder, the same is not of God, but is of the devil. (HC 6:315)

Blessings

1   *Now*, the Lord wants the wheat and tares to grow together; for Zion must be redeemed with judgment, and her converts with righteousness. Every Elder that can, after providing for his family (if he has any) and paying his debts, must go forth and clear his skirts from the blood of this generation. While they are in that region {Missouri},

---

Bishops
2   Solemn assembly in the Kirtland Temple, 6 April 1837.
3   Nauvoo, 25 May 1842.

Bitterness
1   King Follett Discourse, Nauvoo, 7 April 1844.

Blessings
1   Letter to the Saints in Missouri published in the *Messenger and Advocate*, June 1835.

instead of trying members for transgression, or offenses, let every one labor to prepare himself for the vineyard, sparing a little time to comfort the mourners, to bind up the broken-hearted, to reclaim the backslider, to bring back the wanderer, to re-invite into the kingdom such as have been cut off, by encouraging them to lay to while the day lasts, and work righteousness, and, with one heart and one mind, prepare to help to redeem Zion, that goodly land of promise, where the willing and obedient shall be blessed. (HC 2:228–29)

2   I labored in obtaining blessings, which were written by Oliver Cowdery. We were thronged with company, so that our labor in this thing was hindered; but we obtained many precious things, and our souls were blessed. (HC 2:281)

3   And it shall come to pass, that according to the measure that he meteth out with a liberal hand to the poor, so shall it be measured to him again by the hand of his God, even an hundred fold. Angels shall guard his house, and shall guard the lives of his posterity, and they shall become very great and very numerous on the earth. Whomsoever he blesseth, they shall be blessed; and whomsoever he curseth, they shall be cursed. (HC 2:288)

4   In the evening meeting [13 March 1843] twenty-seven children were blessed, nineteen of whom I blessed myself, with great fervency. Virtue went out of me, and my strength left me, when I gave up the meeting to the brethren. . . .
    Elder Jedediah M. Grant enquired of me [14 March 1843] the cause of my turning pale and losing strength last night while blessing children. I told him that I saw that Lucifer would exert his influence to destroy the children that I was blessing, and I strove with all the faith and spirit that I had to seal upon them a blessing that would secure their lives upon the earth; and so much virtue went out of me into the children, that I became weak, from which I have not yet recovered; and I referred to the case of the woman touching the hem of the garment of Jesus. (Luke, 8th chapter). The virtue here referred to is the spirit of life; and a man who exercises great faith in administering to

---

Blessings
2   Kirtland, 16 September 1835.
3   Blessing upon Bishop Newel K. Whitney, Kirtland, 7 October 1835.
4   Ramus, Illinois, 13 and 14 March 1843.

the sick, blessing little children, or confirming, is liable to become weakened. (*HC* 5:303)

5   However indignant you may feel about the high handed oppression which has been raised against me by these men, use not the hand of violence against them, for they could not be prevailed upon to come here till I pledged my honor and my life that a hair of their heads should not be hurt. Will you all support my pledge, and thus preserve my honor? {One universal "Yes!" burst from the assembled thousands.} This is another proof of your attachment to me. I know how ready you are to do right. You have done great things, and manifested your love towards me in flying to my assistance on this occasion. I bless you, in the name of the Lord, with all the blessings of heaven and earth you are capable of enjoying.

I have learned that we have no need to suffer as we have heretofore; we can call others to our aid. I know the Almighty will bless all good men. (*HC* 5:468)

6   When God offers a blessing or knowledge to a man, and he refuses to receive it, he will be damned. (*HC* 5:555)

Blood

1   As concerning the resurrection, . . . all will be raised by the power of God, having spirit in their bodies, and not blood. (*HC* 4:555)

2   Concerning resurrection, flesh and blood cannot inherit the kingdom of God, or the kingdom that God inherits or inhabits, but the flesh without the blood and the Spirit of God flowing in the veins instead of the blood, for blood is the part of the body that causes corruption. Therefore we must be changed in the twinkle of an eye or have to lay down these tabernacles and leave the blood vanish away. . . . Blood is the corruptible part of the tabernacles. (*WJS*, pp. 370–71; standardized)

Blessings
   5   Address regarding his arrest at Dixon, Illinois, Nauvoo, 30 June 1843.
   6   Sabbath address, Nauvoo, 27 August 1843.

Blood
   1   Sabbath address, Nauvoo, 20 March 1842.
   2   Sabbath address, Nauvoo, 12 May 1844.

3   God Almighty Himself dwells in eternal fire; flesh and blood cannot go there, for all corruption is devoured by the fire. "Our God is a consuming fire." When our flesh is quickened by the Spirit, there will be no blood in this tabernacle. (*HC* 6:366)

Blood of Abraham

1   This first Comforter or Holy Ghost has no other effect than pure intelligence. It is more powerful in expanding the mind, enlightening the understanding, and storing the intellect with present knowledge, of a man who is of the literal seed of Abraham, than one that is a Gentile, though it may not have half as much visible effect upon the body; for as the Holy Ghost falls upon one of the literal seed of Abraham, it is calm and serene; and his whole soul and body are only exercised by the pure spirit of intelligence; while the effect of the Holy Ghost upon a Gentile is to purge out the old blood, and make him actually the seed of Abraham. That man that has none of the blood of Abraham (naturally) must have a new creation by the Holy Ghost. In such cases, there may be more of a powerful effect upon the body, and visible to the eye, than upon an Israelite, while the Israelite at first might be far before the Gentile in pure intelligence. (*HC* 3:380)

Blood, Shedding of

1   There needs be no difficulty in relation to the revelations; for they show plainly from the face of them, that no blood is to be shed except in self-defense; and that the law of God as well as man gives us a privilege. If you make yourselves acquainted with the revelations, you will see that this is the case. (*PWJS*, p. 319)

Blood
   3   Sabbath address, Nauvoo, 12 May 1844.

Blood of Abraham
   1   Instruction to the Twelve, Commerce (Nauvoo), 27 June 1839.

Blood, Shedding of
   1   Letter to Edward Partridge and others in Missouri, Kirtland, 30 March 1834.

2 About nine o'clock, while I was riding in a wagon with Brother Hyrum, Ezra Thayer and George A. Smith, we came into a piece of thick woods of recent growth, where I told them that I felt much depressed in spirit and lonesome, and that there had been a great deal of bloodshed in that place, remarking that whenever a man of God is in a place where many have been killed, he will feel lonesome and unpleasant, and his spirits will sink. (HC 2:66)

3 We do not wish to settle down in a body, except where we can purchase the land with money; for to take possession by conquest or the shedding of blood is entirely foreign to our feelings. The shedding of blood we shall not be guilty of, until all just and honorable means among men prove insufficient to restore peace. (HC 2:122)

4 I do not regard my own life. I am ready to be offered a sacrifice for this people; for what can our enemies do? Only kill the body, and their power is then at an end. Stand firm, my friends; never flinch. Do not seek to save your lives, for he that is afraid to die for the truth, will lose eternal life. Hold out to the end, and we shall be resurrected and become like Gods, and reign in celestial kingdoms, principalities, and eternal dominions, while this cursed mob will sink to hell, the portion of all those who shed innocent blood. (HC 6:500)

Bodies

1 We came to this earth that we might have a body and present it pure before God in the celestial kingdom. The great principle of happiness consists in having a body. The devil has no body, and herein is his punishment. He is pleased when he can obtain the tabernacle of man, and when cast out by the Savior he asked to go into the herd of swine, showing that he would prefer a swine's body to having none.

Blood, Shedding of
2 Events of Zion's Camp while near Dayton, Ohio, 16 May 1834.
3 Statement of the intent of Zion's Camp, Clay County, Missouri, 22 June 1834.
4 Address to the Nauvoo Legion, 18 June 1844.

Bodies
1 Lecture given at the Nauvoo Lyceum, 5 January 1841, as reported by William Clayton. (The lyceum met weekly at different locations in Nauvoo for several months, beginning 5 January 1841.)

All beings who have bodies have power over those who have not. (*WJS*, p. 60; standardized)

2   There are three independent principles—the spirit of God, the spirit of man, and the spirit of the devil. All men have power to resist the devil. They who have tabernacles have power over those who have not. (*WJS*, p. 74)

3   *Minutes:* To a remark of Elder Orson Pratt's, that a man's body changes every seven years, President Joseph Smith replied: There is no fundamental principle belonging to a human system that ever goes into another in this world or in the world to come; I care not what the theories of men are. We have the testimony that God will raise us up, and he has the power to do it. If any one supposes that any part of our bodies, that is, the fundamental parts thereof, ever goes into another body, he is mistaken. (*HC* 5:339)

4   No person can have . . . salvation except through a tabernacle. (*HC* 5:388)

5   The spirits in the eternal world are like the spirits in this world. When those have come into this world and received tabernacles, then died and again have risen and received glorified bodies, they will have an ascendency over the spirits who have received no bodies, or kept not their first estate, like the devil. The punishment of the devil was that he should not have a habitation like men. The devil's retaliation is, he comes into this world, binds up men's bodies, and occupies them himself. When the authorities come along, they eject him from a stolen habitation. (*HC* 5:403)

Book of Abraham
   See ABRAHAM, BOOK OF

Bodies
   2   Sabbath address, Nauvoo, 16 May 1841, as reported by William Clayton.
   3   Minutes of a general conference, Nauvoo, 7 April 1843.
   4   Sabbath address at Yelrome (Morley's Settlement), Illinois, 14 May 1843.
   5   Sabbath address, Nauvoo, 21 May 1843.

Book of Life
See LAMB'S BOOK OF LIFE

Book of Mormon

1   In the course of the work of translation, we ascertained that three special witnesses were to be provided by the Lord, to whom He would grant that they should see the plates from which this work (the Book of Mormon) should be translated; and that these witnesses should bear record of the same, as will be found recorded, Book of Mormon, page 581 [book of Ether, chapter 5, verses 2, 3, and 4, p. 496, edition 1981], also page 86 [2 Nephi, chapter 11, verse 3, p. 80, edition 1981]. Almost immediately after we had made this discovery, it occurred to Oliver Cowdery, David Whitmer and the aforementioned Martin Harris (who had come to inquire after our progress in the work) that they would have me inquire of the Lord to know if they might not obtain of him the privilege to be these three special witnesses; and finally they became so very solicitous, and urged me so much to inquire that at length I complied; and through the Urim and Thummim, I obtained of the Lord for them the following: [D&C 17]. (HC 1:52–53)

2   I wish to mention here that the title-page of the Book of Mormon is a literal translation, taken from the very last leaf, on the left hand side of the collection or book of plates, which contained the record which has been translated, the language of the whole running the same as all Hebrew writing in general; and that said title-page is not by any means a modern composition, either of mine or of any other man who has lived or does live in this generation. Therefore, in order to correct an error which generally exists concerning it, I give below that part of the title-page of the English version of the Book of Mormon, which is a genuine and literal translation of the title-page of the original Book of Mormon, as recorded on the plates. (HC 1:71)

3   *Minutes:* Brother Hyrum Smith said that he thought best that the

---

Book of Mormon
1   Fayette, New York, June 1829.
2   Palmyra, New York, June 1829.
3   Minutes of a conference held at Orange, Ohio, 25 October 1831.

information of the coming forth of the Book of Mormon be related by Joseph himself to the Elders present, that all might know for themselves.

Brother Joseph Smith, Jun., said that it was not intended to tell the world all the particulars of the coming forth of the Book of Mormon; and also said that it was not expedient for him to relate these things. (HC 1:220)

4   The Book of Mormon is a record of the forefathers of our western tribes of Indians; having been found through the ministration of an holy angel, and translated into our own language by the gift and power of God, after having been hid up in the earth for the last fourteen hundred years, containing the word of God which was delivered unto them. By it we learn that our western tribes of Indians are descendants from that Joseph who was sold into Egypt, and that the land of America is a promised land unto them, and unto it all the tribes of Israel will come, with as many of the Gentiles as shall comply with the requisitions of the new covenant. (HC 1:315)

5   Take away the Book of Mormon and the revelations, and where is our religion? We have none. (HC 2:52)

6   Let us take the Book of Mormon, which a man took and hid in his field, securing it by his faith, to spring up in the last days, or in due time; let us behold it coming forth out of the ground, which is indeed accounted the least of all seeds, but behold it branching forth, yea, even towering, with lofty branches, and God-like majesty, until it, like the mustard seed, becomes the greatest of all herbs. And it is truth, and it has sprouted and come forth out of the earth, and righteousness begins to look down from heaven, and God is sending down His powers, gifts and angels, to lodge in the branches thereof. (HC 2:268)

7   The Book of Mormon is true, just what it purports to be, and for this testimony I expect to give an account in the day of judgment. If I

Book of Mormon

4   Letter to N. E. Seaton (N. C. Saxton), a newspaper editor in Rochester, N.Y., Kirtland, 4 January 1833.

5   Conference of the elders of the Church, Norton, Ohio, 21 April 1834.

6   Letter to the elders of the Church, Kirtland, 1 September 1835.

7   David Osborn's recollection of an 1837 statement, published in the *Juvenile Instructor*, 15 March 1892.

obtain the glory which I have in view, I expect to wade through much tribulation. (*TK*, p. 101)

8 "How and where did you obtain the Book of Mormon?"

Moroni, who deposited the plates in a hill in Manchester, Ontario county, New York, being dead and raised again therefrom, appeared unto me, and told me where they were, and gave me directions how to obtain them. I obtained them, and the Urim and Thummim with them, by the means of which I translated the plates; and thus came the Book of Mormon. (*HC* 3:28)

9 *Words of Parley P. Pratt:* Brother Rigdon spoke first, and dwelt on the Gospel, illustrating his doctrine by the Bible. When he was through, brother Joseph arose like a lion about to roar; and being full of the Holy Ghost, spoke in great power, bearing testimony of the visions he had seen, the ministering of angels which he had enjoyed; and how he had found the plates of the Book of Mormon, and translated them by the gift and power of God. He commenced by saying: "If nobody else had the courage to testify of so glorious a message from Heaven, and of the finding of so glorious a record, he felt to do it in justice to the people, and leave the event with God." (*APPP*, p. 260)

10 *Report of Mathew L. Davis:* He [Joseph Smith] closed by referring to the Mormon Bible, which he said, contained nothing inconsistent or conflicting with the Christian Bible. . . .

. . . The Mormon Bible, he said, was communicated to him, *direct from heaven.* If there was such a thing on earth, as the author of it, then he (Smith) was the author; but the idea that he wished to impress was, that he had penned it as dictated by God. (*HC* 4:79)

11 I told the brethren that the Book of Mormon was the most correct of any book on earth, and the keystone of our religion, and a man would get nearer to God by abiding by its precepts, than by any other book. (*HC* 4:461)

Book of Mormon
8   Answers to questions frequently asked the Prophet, Far West, 8 May 1838.
9   Address in Philadelphia, January 1840.
10 A letter of Mathew L. Davis to his wife describing the Prophet's discourse in Washington, D.C., 6 February 1840.
11 Meeting with the Twelve in the home of Brigham Young, Nauvoo, 28 November 1841.

12 I was also informed concerning the aboriginal inhabitants of this country and shown who they were, and from whence they came; a brief sketch of their origin, progress, civilization, laws, governments, of their righteousness and iniquity, and the blessings of God being finally withdrawn from them as a people, was made known unto me; I was also told where were deposited some plates on which were engraven an abridgment of the records of the ancient Prophets that had existed on this continent. The angel appeared to me three times the same night and unfolded the same things. After having received many visits from the angels of God unfolding the majesty and glory of the events that should transpire in the last days, on the morning of the 22nd of September, A.D. 1827, the angel of the Lord delivered the records into my hands.

These records were engraven on plates which had the appearance of gold, each plate was six inches wide and eight inches long, and not quite so thick as common tin. They were filled with engravings, in Egyptian characters, and bound together in a volume as the leaves of a book, with three rings running through the whole. The volume was something near six inches in thickness, a part of which was sealed. The characters on the unsealed part were small, and beautifully engraved. The whole book exhibited many marks of antiquity in its construction, and much skill in the art of engraving. With the records was found a curious instrument, which the ancients called the "Urim and Thummim," which consisted of two transparent stones set in the rim of a bow fastened to a breast plate. Through the medium of the Urim and Thummim I translated the record by the gift and power of God.

In this important and interesting book the history of ancient America is unfolded, from its first settlement by a colony that came from the Tower of Babel, at the confusion of languages, to the beginning of the fifth century of the Christian Era. We are informed by these records that America in ancient times has been inhabited by two distinct races of people. The first were called Jaredites, and came directly from the Tower of Babel. The second race came directly from the city of Jerusalem, about six hundred years before Christ. They were principally Israelites, of the descendants of Joseph. The Jaredites were destroyed about the time that the Israelites came from Jerusalem, who succeeded them in the inheritance of the country. The principal

---

Book of Mormon
   12 Letter to John Wentworth, editor of the *Chicago Democrat*, Nauvoo, 1 March 1842.

nation of the second race fell in battle towards the close of the fourth century. The remnant are the Indians that now inhabit this country. This book also tells us that our Savior made His appearance upon this continent after His resurrection; that He planted the Gospel here in all its fulness, and richness, and power, and blessing; that they had Apostles, Prophets, Pastors, Teachers, and Evangelists; the same order, the same priesthood, the same ordinances, gifts, powers, and blessings, as were enjoyed on the eastern continent, that the people were cut off in consequence of their transgressions, that the last of their prophets who existed among them was commanded to write an abridgment of their prophecies, history, &c, and to hide it up in the earth, and that it should come forth and be united with the Bible for the accomplishment of the purposes of God in the last days. (HC 4:537–38)

13 From an extract from "Stephens' Incidents of Travel in Central America," it will be seen that the proof of the Nephites and Lamanites dwelling on this continent, according to the account in the Book of Mormon, is developing itself in a more satisfactory way than the most sanguine believer in that revelation could have anticipated. It certainly affords us a gratification that the world of mankind does not enjoy, to give publicity to such important developments of the remains and ruins of those mighty people.

When we read in the Book of Mormon that Jared and his brother came on to this continent from the confusion and scattering at the Tower, and lived here more than a thousand years, and covered the whole continent from sea to sea, with towns and cities; and that Lehi went down by the Red Sea to the great Southern Ocean, and crossed over to this land, and landed a little south of the Isthmus of Darien, and improved the country according to the word of the Lord, as a branch of the house of Israel, and then read such a goodly traditionary account as the one below, we can not but think the Lord has a hand in bringing to pass his strange act, and proving the Book of Mormon true in the eyes of all the people. The extract below, comes as near the real fact, as the four Evangelists do to the crucifixion of Jesus.—Surely "facts are stubborn things." It will be as it ever has been, the world will prove Joseph Smith a true prophet by circumstantial evidence, in experiments, as they did Moses and Elijah. Now read Stephens' story:

Book of Mormon
13 Editorial in the *Times and Seasons*, 15 September 1842.

"According to Fuentes, the chronicler of the kingdom of Guatemala, the kings of Quiche and Cachiquel were descended from the Toltecan Indians, who, when they came into this country, *found it already inhabited by people of different nations*. According to the manuscripts of Don Juan Torres, the grandson of the last king of the Quiches, which was in the possession of the lieutenant general appointed by Pedro de Alvarado, and which Fuentes says he obtained by means of Father Francis Vasques, the historian of the order of San Francis, *the Toltecas themselves descended from the house of Israel*, who were released by Moses from the tyranny of Pharaoh, and after crossing the Red Sea, fell into idolatry. To avoid the reproofs of Moses, or from fear of his inflicting upon them some chastisement, they separated from him and his brethren, and under the guidance of Tanub, their chief, passed from one continent to the other, to a place which they called the seven caverns, a part of the kingdom of Mexico, where they founded the celebrated city of Tula." (*T&S* 3:921–22)

14 Sir:—Through the medium of your paper, I wish to correct an error among men that profess to be learned, liberal and wise; and I do it the more cheerfully, because I hope sober-thinking and sound-reasoning people will sooner listen to the voice of truth, than be led astray by the vain pretensions of the self-wise. The error I speak of, is the definition of the word "Mormon." It has been stated that this word was derived from the Greek word *mormo*. This is not the case. There was no Greek or Latin upon the plates from which I, through the grace of God, translated the Book of Mormon. Let the language of that book speak for itself. On the 523d page, of the fourth edition, it reads: "And now behold we have written this record according to our knowledge in the characters, which are called among us the *Reformed Egyptian*, being handed down and altered by us, according to our manner of speech; and if our plates had been sufficiently large, we should have written in Hebrew: but the Hebrew hath been altered by us, also; and if we could have written in Hebrew, behold ye would have had no imperfection in our record, but the Lord knoweth the things which we have written, and also, that none other people knoweth our language; therefore he hath prepared means for the interpretation thereof." (*T&S* 4:194)

Book of Mormon
14 Letter to the editor of the *Times and Seasons*, 15 May 1843.

15 Every day adds fresh testimony to the already accumulated evidence on the authenticity of the Book of Mormon. At the time that book was translated, there was very little known about ruined cities and dilapidated buildings. The general presumption was that no people possessing more intelligence than our present race of Indians had ever inhabited this continent; and the accounts given in the Book of Mormon concerning large cities and civilized people having inhabited this land were generally disbelieved and pronounced a humbug. Priest, since then, has thrown some light on this interesting subject. Stephens, in his "Incidents of Travels in Central America," has thrown in a flood of testimony, and from the following statements it is evident that the Book of Mormon does not give a more extensive account of large and populous cities than those discoveries demonstrate to be even now in existence.—Ed.

(*Article from the* Texas Telegraph, *October 11.*)

We have been informed by a gentleman who has traversed a large portion of the Indian country of Northern Texas, and the country lying between Santa Fe and the Pacific, that there are vestiges of ancient cities and ruined castles or temples on the Rio Puerco, and on the Colorado of the West.

He says that on one of the branches of the Rio Puerco, a few days' travel from Santa Fe, there is an immense pile of ruins that appear to belong to an ancient temple. Portions of the walls are still standing, consisting of huge blocks of limestone regularly hewn and laid in cement. The building occupies an extent of more than an acre. It is two or three stories high, has no roof, but contains many rooms, generally of a square form, without windows; and the lower rooms are so dark and gloomy that they resemble caverns rather than the apartments of an edifice built for human habitation.

Our informant did not give the style of architecture, but he believes it could not be erected by Spaniards or Europeans, as the stones are much worn by the rains, and indicate that the building has stood many hundred years. From his description, we are induced to believe that it resembles the ruins of Palenque or Otulum.

He says there are many similar ruins on the Colorado of the West, which empties in the Californian sea. In one of the valleys of the Cordilleras traversed by this river, and about four hundred miles

---

Book of Mormon
15 Editorial in the *Times and Seasons*, 11 October 1843.

from its mouth, there is a large temple still standing, its walls and spires presenting scarcely any traces of dilapidation; and were it not for the want of a roof, it might still be rendered habitable. Near it, scattered along the declivity of a mountain, are the ruins of what must have been once a large city.

The traces of a large aqueduct, part of which is, however, in the solid rock, are still visible. Neither the Indians residing in the vicinity nor the oldest Spanish settlers of the nearest settlements can give any account of the origin of these buildings. They merely know that they have stood there from the earliest periods to which their traditions extend.

The antiquarian who is desirous to trace the Aztec or Toltec races in their migrations from the northern regions of America may find in their ancient edifices many subjects of curious speculation. (HC 6:53–54)

16 The *boldness of my plans and measures* can readily be tested by the touchstone of all schemes, systems, projects, and adventures—*truth;* for truth is a matter of fact; and the fact is, that by the power of God I translated the Book of Mormon from hieroglyphics, the knowledge of which was lost to the world, in which wonderful event I stood alone, an unlearned youth, to combat the worldly wisdom and multiplied ignorance of eighteen centuries, with new revelation, which (if they would receive the everlasting Gospel,) would open the eyes of more than eight hundred millions of people, and make "plain the old paths," wherein if a man walk in all the ordinances of God blameless, he shall inherit eternal life; and Jesus Christ, who was, and is, and is to come, has borne me safely over every snare and plan laid in secret or openly, through priestly hypocrisy, sectarian prejudice, popular philosophy, executive power, or law-defying mobocracy, to destroy me. (HC 6:74)

17 I did translate the Book of Mormon by the gift and power of God, and it is before the world; and all the powers of earth and hell can never rob me of the honor of it. (*TK,* p. 155)

Book of Mormon

> **16** Letter to James Arlington Bennett, Nauvoo, 13 November 1843.
>
> **17** Statement of Joseph Smith as reported in Reminiscence and journal of James Palmer, LDS Church Archives.

Born Again

1   Being born again, comes by the Spirit of God through ordinances. (HC 3:392)

2   Nicodemus . . . came to Jesus by night, and said unto him, Rabbi, we know that thou art a teacher come from God: for no man can do these miracles that thou doest, except God be with him. Jesus answered and said unto him, Verily, verily, I say unto thee, except a man be born again he cannot see the kingdom of God. Nicodemus saith unto him, How can a man be born when he is old? can he enter the second time into his mother's womb, and be born?—Jesus answered, Verily, verily, I say unto thee, Except a man be born of water, and of the Spirit, he cannot enter into the kingdom of God. (*T&S* 3:904–5)

3   If a man is born of water and of the Spirit, he can get into the kingdom of God. (HC 5:258)

4   It is one thing to see the kingdom of God, and another thing to enter into it. We must have a change of heart to see the kingdom of God, and subscribe the articles of adoption to enter therein. (HC 6:58)

Borrowing

1   *Words of Jesse W. Crosby:* One day when the Prophet carried to my house a sack of flour he had borrowed, my wife remarked that he had returned more than he had received. He answered that it should be so; that anything borrowed should be returned always with interest to the lender. "Thus," he said, "the borrower, if he be honest, is a slave to the lender." (*TK*, p. 145)

Born Again
  1   Instructions to the Apostles and Seventies departing for missions to England, Commerce (Nauvoo), 2 July 1839.
  2   Editorial in the *Times and Seasons*, 1 September 1842.
  3   Sabbath address, Nauvoo, 22 January 1843.
  4   Sabbath address, Nauvoo, 15 October 1843.

Borrowing
  1   Reminiscence of Jesse W. Crosby, reported in "Stories from the Notebook of Martha Cox, Grandmother of Fern Cox Anderson," LDS Church Archives.

Buffetings of Satan

1   By the power of the Holy Ghost I pronounced them [the assembled elders] all clean from the blood of this generation; but if any of them should sin wilfully after they were thus cleansed, and sealed up unto eternal life, they should be given over unto the buffetings of Satan until the day of redemption. (HC 1:323–24)

2   Went to meeting at the usual hour. Gideon Carter preached a splendid discourse. In the afternoon we had an exhortation and communion service. Some two or three weeks since, Brother Draper insisted on leaving the meeting before communion, and could not be prevailed on to tarry a few moments, although we invited him to do so, as we did not wish to have the house thrown into confusion. He observed that he "would not," if we excluded him from the Church. Today he attempted to make a confession, but it was not satisfactory to me, and I was constrained by the Spirit to deliver him over to the buffetings of Satan, until he should humble himself and repent of his sins, and make satisfactory confession before the Church. (HC 2:326)

3   The unpardonable sin is to shed innocent blood, or be accessory thereto. All other sins will be visited with judgment in the flesh, and the spirit being delivered to the buffetings of Satan until the day of the Lord Jesus. (HC 5:391–92)

4   This spirit of Elijah was manifest in the days of the apostles, in delivering certain ones to the buffetings of Satan, that they might be saved in the day of the Lord Jesus. They were sealed by the spirit of Elijah unto the damnation of hell until the day of the Lord, or revelation of Jesus Christ. (HC 6:252)

Buffetings of Satan
  1   Instruction to the elders of the Church at a conference, Kirtland, 23 January 1833.
  2   Kirtland, 6 December 1835.
  3   Instruction given to a few Saints at the home of Benjamin F. Johnson, Ramus, Illinois, 16 May 1843.
  4   Sabbath address, Nauvoo, 10 March 1844.

Burial

1 The place where a man is buried is sacred to me. . . .

It has always been considered a great calamity not to obtain an honorable burial: and one of the greatest curses the ancient prophets could put on any man, was that he should go without burial.

I have said, Father, I desire to die here among the Saints. But if this is not Thy will, and I go hence and die, wilt thou find some kind friend to bring my body back, and gather my friends who have fallen in foreign lands, and bring them up hither, that we may all lie together.

I will tell you what I want. If tomorrow I shall be called to lie in yonder tomb, in the morning of the resurrection let me strike hands with my father, and cry, "My father," and he will say, "My son, my son," as soon as the rock rends and before we come out of our graves. (HC 5:361)

Burnings

1 Although the earthly tabernacle is laid down and dissolved, they shall rise again to dwell in everlasting burnings in immortal glory, not to sorrow, suffer, or die any more, but they shall be heirs of God and joint heirs with Jesus Christ. What is it? To inherit the same power, the same glory and the same exaltation, until you arrive at the station of a god, and ascend the throne of eternal power, the same as those who have gone before. . . .

. . . Some shall rise to the everlasting burnings of God; for God dwells in everlasting burnings and some shall rise to the damnation of their own filthiness, which is as exquisite a torment as the lake of fire and brimstone. (HC 6:306, 317)

Burial
1 Remarks upon the death of Lorenzo D. Barnes, Nauvoo, 16 April 1843.

Burnings
1 King Follett Discourse, Nauvoo, 7 April 1844.

Cain

1   Cain offered of the fruit of the ground, and was not accepted, because he could not do it in faith, he could have no faith, or could not
exercise faith contrary to the plan of heaven. It must be shedding the
blood of the Only Begotten to atone for man; for this was the plan of
redemption, and without the shedding of blood was no remission; and
as the sacrifice was instituted for a type, by which man was to discern
the great Sacrifice which God had prepared; to offer a sacrifice contrary to that, no faith could be exercised, because redemption was not
purchased in that way, nor the power of atonement instituted after
that order; consequently Cain could have no faith; and whatsoever is
not of faith, is sin. . . .

. . . The mere shedding of the blood of beasts or offering anything
else in sacrifice, could not procure a remission of sins, except it were
performed in faith of something to come; if it could, Cain's offering
must have been as good as Abel's. (HC 2:15–16)

2   The power, glory and blessings of the Priesthood could not continue with those who received ordination only as their righteousness
continued; for Cain also being authorized to offer sacrifice, but not offering it in righteousness, was cursed. It signifies, then, that the ordinances must be kept in the very way God has appointed; otherwise
their Priesthood will prove a cursing instead of a blessing.

If Cain had fulfilled the law of righteousness as did Enoch, he
could have walked with God all the days of his life, and never failed of
a blessing. (HC 4:209)

Calling and Election

1   The Doctrine of Election. St. Paul exhorts us to make our calling
and election sure. This is the sealing power spoken of by Paul in other
places. . . .

Cain
  1   Letter to the brethren scattered from Zion, Kirtland, 22 January 1834.
  2   Article on priesthood read at general conference, Nauvoo, 5 October 1840.

Calling and Election
  1   Instructions to the Twelve, Commerce (Nauvoo), 27 June 1839.

This principle ought (in its proper place) to be taught, for God hath not revealed anything to Joseph, but what He will make known unto the Twelve, and even the least Saint may know all things as fast as he is able to bear them, for the day must come when no man need say to his neighbor, Know ye the Lord; for all shall know Him (*who remain*) from the least to the greatest. How is this to be done? It is to be done by this sealing power, and the other Comforter spoken of, which will be manifest by revelation.

There are two Comforters spoken of. One is the Holy Ghost, the same as given on the day of Pentecost, and that all Saints receive after faith, repentance, and baptism. . . .

The other Comforter spoken of is a subject of great interest, and perhaps understood by few of this generation. After a person has faith in Christ, repents of his sins, and is baptized for the remission of his sins and receives the Holy Ghost, (by the laying on of hands), which is the first Comforter, then let him continue to humble himself before God, hungering and thirsting after righteousness, and living by every word of God, and the Lord will soon say unto him, Son, thou shalt be exalted. When the Lord has thoroughly proved him, and finds that the man is determined to serve Him at all hazards, then the man will find his calling and his election made sure, then it will be his privilege to receive the other Comforter, which the Lord hath promised the Saints, as is recorded in the testimony of St. John, in the 14th chapter, from the 12th to the 27th verses. (HC 3:379, 380)

2   *Report of Don Carlos Smith:* He [Joseph] then spoke on the subject of election, and read the 9th chapter of Romans, from which it was evident that the election there spoken of was pertaining to the flesh, and had reference to the seed of Abraham, according to the promise God made to Abraham, saying, "In thee, and in thy seed, all the families of the earth shall be blessed." To them belonged the adoption and the covenants, &c. Paul said, when he saw their unbelief, "I wish myself accursed"—according to the flesh—not according to the spirit. . . . The election of the promised seed still continues, and in the last day, they shall have the Priesthood restored unto them, and they shall be the "saviors on Mount Zion," the ministers of our God; if it were not for the remnant which was left, then might men now be as Sodom and

Gomorrah. The whole of the chapter had reference to the Priesthood and the house of Israel; and unconditional election of individuals to eternal life was not taught by the Apostles. God did elect or predestinate, that all those who would be saved, should be saved in Christ Jesus, and through obedience to the Gospel; but He passes over no man's sins, but visits them with correction, and if His children will not repent of their sins He will discard them. (HC 4:359–60)

3   Now, there is some grand secret here, and keys to unlock the subject. Notwithstanding the apostle exhorts them to add to their faith, virtue, knowledge, temperance, &c., yet he exhorts them to make their calling and election sure. And though they had heard an audible voice from heaven bearing testimony that Jesus was the Son of God, yet he says we have a more sure word of prophecy, whereunto ye do well that ye take heed as unto a light shining in a dark place. Now, wherein could they have a more sure word of prophecy than to hear the voice of God saying, This is my beloved Son, &c.

Now for the secret and grand key. Though they might hear the voice of God and know that Jesus was the Son of God, this would be no evidence that their election and calling was made sure, that they had part with Christ, and were joint heirs with Him. They then would want that more sure word of prophecy, that they were sealed in the heavens and had the promise of eternal life in the kingdom of God. Then, having this promise sealed unto them, it was an anchor to the soul, sure and steadfast. Though the thunders might roll and lightnings flash, and earthquakes bellow, and war gather thick around, yet this hope and knowledge would support the soul in every hour of trial, trouble and tribulation. Then knowledge through our Lord and Savior Jesus Christ is the grand key that unlocks the glories and mysteries of the kingdom of heaven.

. . . Then I would exhort you to go on and continue to call upon God until you make your calling and election sure for yourselves, by obtaining this more sure word of prophecy, and wait patiently for the promise until you obtain it, &c. (HC 5:388–89)

4   The more sure word of prophecy means a man's knowing that he is sealed up into eternal life by revelation and the spirit of prophecy,

---

Calling and Election

3   Sabbath address at Yelrome (Morley's settlement), Illinois, 14 May 1843.

4   Items of doctrine given at Ramus, Illinois, 17 May 1843.

through the power of the holy priesthood. It is impossible for a man to be saved in ignorance. (HC 5:392)

5   "We have a more sure word of prophecy, whereunto you do well to take heed, as unto a light that shineth in a dark place. We were eyewitnesses of his majesty and heard the voice of his excellent glory." [See 2 Peter 1.] And what could be more sure? When He was transfigured on the mount, what could be more sure to them? . . .

Contend earnestly for the like precious faith with the Apostle Peter, "and add to your faith virtue," knowledge, temperance, patience, godliness, brotherly kindness, charity; "for if these things be in you, and abound, they make you that ye shall neither be barren nor unfruitful in the knowledge of our Lord Jesus Christ." Another point, after having all these qualifications, he lays this injunction upon the people "to make your calling and election sure." He is emphatic upon this subject—after adding all this virtue, knowledge, &c., "Make your calling and election sure." What is the secret—the starting point? "According as His divine power hath given unto us all things that pertain unto life and godliness." How did he obtain all things? Through the knowledge of Him who hath called him. There could not anything be given, pertaining to life and godliness, without knowledge. . . .

We have no claim in our eternal compact, in relation to eternal things, unless our actions and contracts and all things tend to this. But after all this, you have got to make your calling and election sure. If this injunction would lie largely on those to whom it was spoken, how much more those of the present generation!

1st key: Knowledge is the power of salvation. 2nd key: Make your calling and election sure. 3rd key: It is one thing to be on the mount and hear the excellent voice, &c., &c., and another to hear the voice declare to you, You have a part and lot in that kingdom. (HC 5:401, 402–3)

6   *Report of Willard Richards:* Four destroying angels holding power over the four quarters of the earth until the servants of God are sealed in their foreheads, which signifies sealing the blessing upon their heads, meaning the everlasting covenant, thereby making their calling and election sure. When a seal is put upon the father and mother,

---

Calling and Election
   5   Sabbath address, Nauvoo, 21 May 1843.
   6   Remarks at the funeral of Judge Elias Higbee, Nauvoo, 13 August 1843.

it secures their posterity, so that they cannot be lost, but will be saved by virtue of the covenant of their father and mother.

To the mourners [of the late Judge Higbee] I would say—Do as the husband and the father would instruct you, and you shall be reunited.

The speaker [Joseph Smith] continued to teach the doctrine of election and the sealing powers and principles, and spoke of the doctrine of election with the seed of Abraham, and the sealing of blessings upon his posterity, and the sealing of the fathers and children, according to the declarations of the prophets. He then spoke of Judge Higbee in the world of spirits, and the blessings which he would obtain, and of the kind spirit and disposition of Judge Higbee while living; none of which was reported. (HC 5:530–31)

7   How shall God come to the rescue of this generation? He will send Elijah the prophet. The law revealed to Moses in Horeb never was revealed to the children of Israel as a nation.

Elijah shall reveal the covenants to seal the hearts of the fathers to the children, and the children to the fathers.

The anointing and sealing is to be called, elected and made sure. (HC 5:555)

8   Then what you seal on earth, by the keys of Elijah, is sealed in heaven; and this is the power of Elijah, and this is the difference between the spirit and power of Elias and Elijah; for while the spirit of Elias is a forerunner, the power of Elijah is sufficient to make our calling and election sure; and the same doctrine, where we are exhorted to go on to perfection, not laying again the foundation of repentance from dead works, and of laying on of hands, resurrection of the dead, &c. . . .

Here is the doctrine of election that the world has quarreled so much about; but they do not know anything about it.

The doctrine that the Presbyterians and Methodists have quarreled so much about—once in grace, always in grace, or falling away from grace, I will say a word about. They are both wrong. Truth takes a road between them both, for while the Presbyterian says "once in grace, you cannot fall"; the Methodist says: "You can have grace today,

---

Calling and Election

7   Sabbath address, Nauvoo, 27 August 1843.
8   Sabbath address, Nauvoo, 10 March 1844.

fall from it to-morrow, next day have grace again; and so follow on, changing continually." But the doctrine of the Scriptures and the spirit of Elijah would show them both false, and take a road between them both; for, according to the Scripture, if men have received the good word of God, and tasted of the powers of the world to come, if they shall fall away, it is impossible to renew them again, seeing they have crucified the Son of God afresh, and put Him to an open shame; so there is a possibility of falling away; you could not be renewed again, and the power of Elijah cannot seal against this sin, for this is a reserve made in the seals and power of the Priesthood. (HC 6:252–53)

9   Oh! I beseech you to go forward, go forward and make your calling and your election sure; and if any man preach any other Gospel than that which I have preached, he shall be cursed; and some of you who now hear me shall see it, and know that I testify the truth concerning them. (HC 6:365)

Callings

1   A council of High Priests assembled to investigate the proceedings of Brother Burr Riggs, who was accused of failing to magnify his calling as High Priest, and had been guilty of neglect of duty. (HC 1:327)

2   We feel to rebuke the Elders of that branch of the Church of Christ [in Eugene, Ohio], for not magnifying their office, and letting the transgressor go unpunished. (HC 1:371)

3   [Brother Frederick G. Williams] is perfectly honest and upright, and seeks with all his heart to magnify his Presidency in the Church of Christ, but fails in many instances, in consequence of a want of confidence in himself. (HC 1:444)

Calling and Election
9   Sabbath address, Nauvoo, 12 May 1844.

Callings
1   Kirtland, 13 February 1833.
2   Letter written to the branch of the Church at Eugene, Ohio, from the First Presidency, Kirtland, 2 July 1833.
3   Kirtland, 19 November 1833.

4   The many thoughts which occupy our minds . . . press with continued weight upon our hearts, as we reflect upon the vast importance and responsibility of your callings, in the sight of the Master of the vineyard. (HC 2:4–5)

5   Oliver Cowdery has been in transgression, but as he is now chosen as one of the presidents or counselors, I trust that he will yet humble himself and magnify his calling, but if he should not, the Church will soon be under the necessity of raising their hands against him; therefore pray for him. (HC 2:511)

6   Dear sir, I wish you to stand in your lot, and keep the station which was given you by revelation and the authorities of the Church. Attend to the affairs of the Church with diligence, and then rest assured of the blessings of heaven. It is binding on you to act as president of the Church in Kirtland, until you are removed by the same authority which put you in; and I do hope there will be no cause for opposition, but that good feeling will be manifested in [the] future by all the brethren. (HC 4:167)

7   *Report of Eliza R. Snow:* President Smith continued by speaking of the difficulties he had to surmount ever since the commencement of the work, in consequence of aspiring men. "Great big Elders," as he called them, who had caused him much trouble; to whom he had taught the things of the kingdom in private councils, they would then go forth into the world and proclaim the things he had taught them, as their own revelations; said the same aspiring disposition will be in this Society, and must be guarded against; that every person should stand, and act in the place appointed, and thus sanctify the Society and get it pure. (HC 4:604)

8   *Report of Eliza R. Snow:* [President Smith] continued to read the chapter [1 Corinthians 12], and give instructions respecting the different offices, and the necessity of every individual acting in the sphere

---

Callings

   4   Letter to the brethren scattered from Zion, Kirtland, 22 January 1834.
   5   Announcement concerning certain leaders who had become disaffected from the Church, Kirtland, 3 September 1837.
   6   Letter to Oliver Granger in Kirtland, sent from Nauvoo, July 1840.
   7   Remarks to the Relief Society, Nauvoo, 28 April 1842.
   8   Remarks to the Relief Society, Nauvoo, 28 April 1842.

allotted him or her, and filling the several offices to which they are appointed. He spoke of the disposition of many men to consider the lower offices in the Church dishonorable, and to look with jealous eyes upon the standing of others who are called to preside over them; that it was the folly and nonsense of the human heart for a person to be aspiring to other stations than those to which they are appointed of God for them to occupy; that it was better for individuals to magnify their respective callings, and wait patiently till God shall say to them, "Come up higher.". . .

President Smith continued reading from the above-mentioned chapter [1 Corinthians 12], and to give instructions respecting the order of God, as established in the Church, saying everyone should aspire only to magnify his own office and calling. (HC 4:603, 606)

9   We believe in the gift of the Holy Ghost being enjoyed now, as much as it was in the Apostles' days; we believe that it {the gift of the Holy Ghost} is necessary to make and to organize the Priesthood, that no man can be called to fill any office in the ministry without it. (HC 5:27)

Celestial Kingdom

1   I will proceed to tell you what the Lord requires of all people, high and low, rich and poor, male and female, ministers and people, professors of religion and non-professors, in order that they may enjoy the Holy Spirit of God to a fulness and escape the judgments of God, which are almost ready to burst upon the nations of the earth. Repent of all your sins, and be baptized in water for the remission of them, in the name of the Father, and of the Son, and of the Holy Ghost, and receive the ordinance of the laying on of the hands of him who is ordained and sealed unto this power, that ye may receive the Holy Spirit of God; and this is according to the Holy Scriptures, and the Book of

Callings
9   Editorial in the *Times and Seasons*, 15 June 1842.

Celestial Kingdom
1   Letter to N. E. Seaton (N. C. Saxton), a newspaper editor in Rochester, N.Y., Kirtland, 4 January 1833.

Mormon; and the only way that man can enter into the celestial kingdom. (*HC* 1:314–15)

2   Here, then, we have this part of our subject immediately before us for consideration: God has in reserve a time, or period appointed in His own bosom, when He will bring all His subjects, who have obeyed His voice and kept His commandments, into His celestial rest. This rest is of such perfection and glory, that man has need of a preparation before he can, according to the laws of that kingdom, enter it and enjoy its blessings. This being the fact, God has given certain laws to the human family, which, if observed, are sufficient to prepare them to inherit this rest. This, then, we conclude, was the purpose of God in giving His laws to us: if not, why, or for what were they given? If the whole family of man were as well off without them as they might be with them, for what purpose or intent were they ever given? Was it that God wanted to merely show that He could talk? It would be nonsense to suppose that He would condescend to talk in vain: for it would be in vain, and to no purpose whatever {if the law of God were of no benefit to man}: because, all the commandments contained in the law of the Lord, have the sure promise annexed of a reward to all who obey, predicated upon the fact that they are really the promises of a Being who cannot lie, One who is abundantly able to fulfill every tittle of His word: and if man were as well prepared, or could be as well prepared, to meet God without their ever having been given in the first instance, why were they ever given? for certainly, in that case they can now do him no good. (*HC* 2:11–12)

3   All men who become heirs of God and joint-heirs with Jesus Christ will have to receive the fulness of the ordinances of his kingdom; and those who will not receive all the ordinances will come short of the fullness of that glory, if they do not lose the whole. (*HC* 5:424)

4   The question is frequently asked "Can we not be saved without going through with all those ordinances, &c.?" I would answer, No,

---

Celestial Kingdom
  2   Letter to the brethren scattered from Zion, Kirtland, 22 January 1834.
  3   Sabbath address, Nauvoo, 11 June 1843.
  4   Sabbath address, Nauvoo, 21 January 1844.

not the fullness of salvation. Jesus said, "There are many mansions in my Father's house, and I will go and prepare a place for you." *House* here named should have been translated kingdom; and any person who is exalted to the highest mansion has to abide a celestial law, and the whole law too.

But there has been a great difficulty in getting anything into the heads of this generation. It has been like splitting hemlock knots with a corn-dodger for a wedge, and a pumpkin for a beetle. Even the Saints are slow to understand.

I have tried for a number of years to get the minds of the Saints prepared to receive the things of God; but we frequently see some of them, after suffering all they have for the work of God, will fly to pieces like glass as soon as anything comes that is contrary to their traditions: they cannot stand the fire at all. How many will be able to abide a celestial law, and go through and receive their exaltation, I am unable to say, as many are called, but few are chosen. (HC 6:184–85)

5   Go and read the vision in the Book of Covenants. There is clearly illustrated glory upon glory—one glory of the sun, another glory of the moon, and a glory of the stars; and as one star differeth from another star in glory, even so do they of the telestial world differ in glory, and every man who reigns in celestial glory is a God to his dominions. . . .

. . . They who obtain a glorious resurrection from the dead, are exalted far above principalities, powers, thrones, dominions and angels, and are expressly declared to be heirs of God and joint heirs with Jesus Christ, all having eternal power. (HC 6:477, 478)

Charity

1   Until we have perfect love we are liable to fall; and when we have a testimony that our names are sealed in the Lamb's book of life, we have perfect love, and then it is impossible for false Christs to deceive us. (FWR, p. 23; standardized)

Celestial Kingdom
  5   Sabbath address, Nauvoo, 16 June 1844.

Charity
  1   Minutes of a conference held at Orange, Ohio, 25 October 1831.

2   To be justified before God we must love one another. (HC 2:229)

3   Attended a sumptuous feast at Bishop Newel K. Whitney's. This feast was after the order of the Son of God—the lame, the halt, and the blind were invited, according to the instructions of the Savior. Our meeting was opened by singing, and prayer by Father Smith; after which Bishop Whitney's father and mother, and a number of others, were blessed with a patriarchal blessing. We then received a bountiful refreshment, furnished by the liberality of the Bishop. The company was large, and before we partook we had some of the songs of Zion sung; and our hearts were made glad by a foretaste of those joys that will be poured upon the heads of the Saints when they are gathered together on Mount Zion, to enjoy one another's society for evermore, even all the blessings of heaven, when there will be none to molest or make us afraid. (HC 2:362–63)

4   We ought at all times to be very careful that . . . high-mindedness shall never have place in our hearts; but condescend to men of low estate, and with all long-suffering bear the infirmities of the weak. (HC 3:299)

5   There is a love from God that should be exercised toward those of our faith, who walk uprightly, which is peculiar to itself, but it is without prejudice; it also gives scope to the mind, which enables us to conduct ourselves with greater liberality towards all that are not of our faith, than what they exercise towards one another. These principles approximate nearer to the mind of God, because it is like God, or Godlike. (HC 3:304)

6   I then addressed them [the Twelve and other missionaries] and gave much instruction calculated to guard them against self-sufficiency, self-righteousness, and self-importance; touching upon many subjects of importance and value to all who wish to walk humbly before the

---

Charity

  2   Letter to the Saints in Missouri published in the *Messenger and Advocate*, June 1835.
  3   Kirtland, 7 January 1836.
  4   Letter to the Saints from Liberty Jail, 20–25 March 1839.
  5   Letter to the Saints from Liberty Jail, 20–25 March 1839.
  6   Instructions to the Apostles and Seventies departing for missions to England, Commerce (Nauvoo), 2 July 1839.

Lord, and especially teaching them to observe charity, wisdom and fellow-feeling, with love one towards another in all things, and under all circumstances. (HC 3:383)

7   In order to conduct the affairs of the Kingdom in righteousness, it is all important that the most perfect harmony, kind feeling, good understanding, and confidence should exist in the hearts of all the brethren; and that true charity, love one towards another, should characterize all their proceedings. If there are any uncharitable feelings, any lack of confidence, then pride, arrogance and envy will soon be manifested; confusion must inevitably prevail, and the authorities of the Church set at naught; and under such circumstances, Kirtland cannot rise and free herself from the captivity in which she is held, and become a place of safety for the Saints, nor can the blessings of Jehovah rest upon her. (HC 4:165)

8   Love is one of the chief characteristics of Deity, and ought to be manifested by those who aspire to be the sons of God. A man filled with the love of God, is not content with blessing his family alone, but ranges through the whole world, anxious to bless the whole human race. (HC 4:227)

9   *Words of Mosiah L. Hancock:* The summer of 1841 I played my first game of ball with the Prophet. We took turns knocking and chasing the ball, and when the game was over the Prophet said, "Brethren, hitch up your teams."

We did, and we all drove to the woods. I drove our one-horse wagon, standing on the front bolster, and Brother Joseph and Father rode on the hounds behind. There were thirty-nine teams in the group and we gathered wood until our wagons were loaded. When our wagon was loaded, Brother Joseph offered to pull sticks with anyone who wanted to compete with him—and he pulled them all up one at a time. Afterwards the Prophet sent the wagons out to different places where people needed help; and he told them to cut the wood for the Saints who needed it. Everybody loved to do as the Prophet said, and

---

Charity

7   Letter to Oliver Granger in Kirtland, sent from Nauvoo, July 1840.

8   Letter to the Twelve in England, Nauvoo, 15 December 1840. The placement of this letter in *HC* implies that it was written in October 1840, but actually it was written on 15 December 1840 (see *PWJS*, p. 480).

9   Recollection of Mosiah Hancock, Autobiography, BYU Library.

even though we were sickly, and death was all around us, folks smiled and tried to cheer everyone up. (*TK*, p. 103)

10 I charged the Saints not to follow the example of the adversary in accusing the brethren, and said, "If you do not accuse each other, God will not accuse you. If you have no accuser you will enter heaven, and if you will follow the revelations and instructions which God gives you through me, I will take you into heaven as my back load. If you will not accuse me, I will not accuse you. If you will throw a cloak of charity over my sins, I will over yours—for charity covereth a multitude of sins. (*HC* 4:445)

11 We are well assured from a knowledge of those pure principles of benevolence that flow spontaneously from [the] humane and philanthropic bosoms [of the Relief Society women], that with the resources they will have at command, they will fly to the relief of the stranger; they will pour in oil and wine to the wounded heart of the distressed; they will dry up the tears of the orphan and make the widow's heart to rejoice.

Our women have always been signalized for their acts of benevolence and kindness. (*HC* 4:567)

12 This [the Relief Society] is a charitable Society, and according to your natures; it is natural for females to have feelings of charity and benevolence. You are now placed in a situation in which you can act according to those sympathies which God has planted in your bosoms. (*HC* 4:605)

13 *Report of Eliza R. Snow:* He [Joseph Smith] then commenced reading the 13th chapter [of 1 Corinthians]—"Though I speak with the tongues of men and angels, and have no charity, I am become as sounding brass, or a tinkling cymbal;" and said, don't be limited in your views with regard to your neighbor's virtue, but beware of self-righteousness, and be limited in the estimate of your own virtues, and not think yourselves more righteous than others; you must enlarge

---

Charity
   10 Sabbath address, Nauvoo, 7 November 1841.
   11 Remarks to the Relief Society, Nauvoo, 24 March 1842.
   12 Remarks to the Relief Society, Nauvoo, 28 April 1842.
   13 Remarks to the Relief Society, Nauvoo, 28 April 1842.

your souls towards each other, if you would do like Jesus, and carry your fellow-creatures to Abraham's bosom. He said he had manifested long-suffering, forbearance and patience towards the Church, and also to his enemies; and we must bear with each other's failings, as an indulgent parent bears with the foibles of his children.

. . . As you increase in innocence and virtue, as you increase in goodness, let your hearts expand, let them be enlarged towards others; you must be long-suffering, and bear with the faults and errors of mankind.

How precious are the souls of men! . . .

Let your labors be mostly confined to those around you, in the circle of your own acquaintance, as far as knowledge is concerned, it may extend to all the world; but your administering should be confined to the circle of your immediate acquaintance, and more especially to the members of the Relief Society. (HC 4:606, 607)

14 *Words of Andrew Workman:* I first saw the Prophet Joseph in May, 1842. He was with about a dozen others on the stand in a meeting. I knew him as soon as I saw him.

A few days after this I was at Joseph's house. Several men were sitting on the fence. Joseph came out and spoke to us all. A man came and said that a poor brother who lived out some distance from town had had his house burned down the night before. Nearly all of the men said they felt sorry for the man. Joseph put his hand in his pocket, took out five dollars and said: "I feel sorry for this brother to the amount of five dollars. How much do you all feel sorry?" (*TK*, p. 150)

15 Nothing is so much calculated to lead people to forsake sin as to take them by the hand, and watch over them with tenderness. When persons manifest the least kindness and love to me, O what power it has over my mind, while the opposite course has a tendency to harrow up all the harsh feelings and depress the human mind.

It is one evidence that men are unacquainted with the principles of godliness to behold the contraction of affectionate feelings and lack of charity in the world. The power and glory of godliness is spread out on a broad principle to throw out the mantle of charity. God does not

---

Charity
14 Recollection of Andrew Workman, published in the *Juvenile Instructor*, 15 October 1892.
15 Remarks to the Relief Society, Nauvoo, 9 June 1842.

look on sin with allowance, but when men have sinned, there must be allowance made for them.

... The nearer we get to our heavenly Father, the more we are disposed to look with compassion on perishing souls; we feel that we want to take them upon our shoulders, and cast their sins behind our backs. My talk is intended for all this society [the Relief Society]; if you would have God have mercy on you, have mercy on one another. (HC 5:23–24)

16 Almost all who have fallen in these last days in the Church have fallen in a strange land. This is a strange land to those who have come from a distance.

We should cultivate sympathy for the afflicted among us. If there is a place on earth where men should cultivate the spirit and pour in the oil and wine in the bosoms of the afflicted, it is in this place; and this spirit is manifest here; and although a stranger and afflicted when he arrives, he finds a brother and a friend ready to administer to his necessities.

I would esteem it one of the greatest blessings, if I am to be afflicted in this world to have my lot cast where I can find brothers and friends all around me. (HC 5:360–61)

17 If we would secure and cultivate the love of others, we must love others, even our enemies as well as friends. (HC 5:498)

18 I do not dwell upon your faults, and you shall not upon mine. Charity, which is love, covereth a multitude of sins, and I have often covered up all the faults among you; but the prettiest thing is to have no faults at all. We should cultivate a meek, quiet and peaceable spirit. (HC 5:517)

19 In my feelings I am always ready to die for the protection of the weak and oppressed in their just rights. (HC 6:57)

20 That friendship which intelligent beings would accept as sincere

Charity
16 Remarks upon the death of Lorenzo D. Barnes, Nauvoo, 16 April 1843.
17 Sabbath address, Nauvoo, 9 July 1843.
18 Sabbath address, Nauvoo, 23 July 1843.
19 Sabbath address, Nauvoo, 15 October 1843.
20 Letter to James Arlington Bennett, Nauvoo, 13 November 1843.

must arise from love, and that love grow out of virtue, which is as much a part of religion as light is a part of Jehovah. Hence the saying of Jesus, "Greater love hath no man than this, that a man lay down his life for his friends." (HC 6:73)

21 Wise men ought to have understanding enough to conquer men with kindness.

"A soft answer turneth away wrath," says the wise man; and it will be greatly to the credit of the Latter-day Saints to show the love of God, by now kindly treating those who may have, in an unconscious moment, done wrong; for truly said Jesus, Pray for thine enemies.

Humanity towards all, reason and refinement to enforce virtue, and good for evil are so eminently designed to cure more disorders of society than an appeal to arms, or even argument untempered with friendship, and the one thing needful that no vision for the future, guideboard for the distant, or expositor for the present, need trouble any one with what he ought to do. (HC 6:219–20)

22 I wish to say to you [the editor of the *Nauvoo Neighbor*], as there seems to be a prospect of peace, that it will be more love-like, more God-like, and man-like, to say nothing about the *Warsaw Signal*.

If the editor breathes out that old sulphurous blast, let him go and besmear his reputation and the reputation of those that uphold him with soot and dirt, but as for us and all honest men, we will act well our part, for there the honor lies.

We will honor the advice of Governor Ford, cultivate peace and friendship with all, mind our own business, and come off with flying colors, respected, because, in respecting others, we respect ourselves. (HC 6:221)

23 I have no enmity against any man. I love you all; but I hate some of your deeds. (HC 6:317)

24 My heart is large enough for all men. (HC 6:459)

Charity
21 Article entitled "Pacific Innuendo," Nauvoo, 17 February 1844.
22 Letter to the editor of the *Nauvoo Neighbor*, an LDS newspaper, 19 February 1844.
23 King Follett Discourse, Nauvoo, 7 April 1844.
24 Letter to Washington Tucker, Nauvoo, 12 June 1844.

Chastening

1   The scourge must come; repentance and humility may mitigate the chastisement, but cannot altogether avert it. (HC 2:107)

2   I frequently rebuke and admonish my brethren, and that because I love them, not because I wish to incur their displeasure, or mar their happiness. Such a course of conduct is not calculated to gain the good will of all, but rather the ill will of many; therefore, the situation in which I stand is an important one; so, you see, brethren, the higher the authority, the greater the difficulty of the station; but these rebukes and admonitions become necessary, from the perverseness of the brethren, for their temporal as well as spiritual welfare. They actually constitute a part of the duties of my station and calling. (HC 2:478)

3   *Report of Wilford Woodruff:* President Joseph arose and said—. . . "Some people say I am a fallen Prophet, because I do not bring forth more of the word of the Lord. Why do I not do it? Are we able to receive it? No! not one in this room." He then chastened the congregation for their wickedness and unbelief, " 'for whom the Lord loveth he chasteneth, and scourgeth every son and daughter whom he receiveth,' and if we do not receive chastisements then we are bastards and not sons."

. . . "Because we will not receive chastisement at the hand of the Prophet and Apostles, the Lord chastiseth us with sickness and death. . . . When a corrupt man is chastised he gets angry and will not endure it." (HC 4:478–79)

4   We have been chastened by the hand of God heretofore for not obeying His commands, although we never violated any human law, or transgressed any human precept; yet we have treated lightly His commands, and departed from His ordinances, and the Lord has chastened us sore, and we have felt His arm and kissed the rod; let us be

---

Chastening
1   Events of Zion's Camp, Missouri, June 1834.
2   Instructions to priesthood quorums, Kirtland Temple, April 1837.
3   Meeting of the Twelve at the Prophet's home, Nauvoo, 19 December 1841.
4   Editorial on the government of God published in the *Times and Seasons,* 15 July 1842.

wise in time to come and ever remember that "to obey is better than sacrifice, and to hearken than the fat of rams." The Lord has told us to build the Temple and the Nauvoo House; and that command is as binding upon us as any other; and that man who engages not in these things is as much a transgressor as though he broke any other commandment; he is not a doer of God's will, not a fulfiller of His laws. (HC 5:65)

5   I am your best friend, and if persons miss their mark it is their own fault. If I reprove a man, and he hates me, he is a fool; for I love all men, especially these my brethren and sisters. (HC 6:317)

Chastity

1   I preached in the Grove, and pronounced a curse upon all adulterers, and fornicators, and unvirtuous persons. (HC 4:587)

2   I attended city council in the morning, and advocated strongly the necessity of some active measures being taken to suppress houses and acts of infamy in the city; for the protection of the innocent and virtuous, and the good of public morals; showing clearly that there were certain characters in the place, who were disposed to corrupt the morals and chastity of our citizens, and that houses of infamy did exist, upon which a city ordinance concerning brothels and disorderly characters was passed, to prohibit such things. It was published in this day's *Wasp*. (HC 5:8)

Chastening
   5   King Follett Discourse, Nauvoo, 7 April 1844.

Chastity
   1   Sabbath address, Nauvoo, 10 April 1842.
   2   Meeting of the Nauvoo City Council, 14 May 1842.

Children

1 *Report of Mathew L. Davis:* [Joseph] then entered into some details, the result of which tended to show his total unbelief of what is termed *original sin*. He believes that it is washed away by the blood of Christ, and that it no longer exists. As a necessary consequence, he believes that we are all born pure and undefiled. That *all* children dying at an early age (say *eight* years) not knowing good from evil, were incapable of sinning; and that all such assuredly go to heaven. (HC 4:78)

2 In my leisure moments I have meditated upon the subject, and asked the question, why it is that infants, innocent children, are taken away from us, especially those that seem to be the most intelligent and interesting. The strongest reasons that present themselves to my mind are these: This world is a very wicked world; and it is a proverb that the "world grows weaker and wiser;" if that is the case, the world grows more wicked and corrupt. In the earlier ages of the world a righteous man, and a man of God and of intelligence, had a better chance to do good, to be believed and received than at the present day: but in these days such a man is much opposed and persecuted by most of the inhabitants of the earth, and he has much sorrow to pass through here. The Lord takes many away, even in infancy, that they may escape the envy of man, and the sorrows and evils of this present world; they were too pure, too lovely, to live on earth; therefore, if rightly considered, instead of mourning we have reason to rejoice as they are delivered from evil, and we shall soon have them again. (HC 4:553)

3 That which hath been hid from before the foundation of the world is revealed to babes and sucklings in the last days.

The world is reserved unto burning in the last days. He shall send Elijah the prophet, and he shall reveal the covenants of the fathers in relation to the children, and the covenants of the children in relation to the fathers.

Children
1   A letter of Mathew L. Davis to his wife describing the Prophet's discourse in Washington, D.C., 6 February 1840.
2   Sabbath address, Nauvoo, 20 March 1842.
3   Remarks at the funeral of Judge Elias Higbee, Nauvoo, 13 August 1843.

Four destroying angels holding power over the four quarters of the earth until the servants of God are sealed in their foreheads, which signifies sealing the blessing upon their heads, meaning the everlasting covenant, thereby making their calling and election sure. When a seal is put upon the father and mother, it secures their posterity, so that they cannot be lost, but will be saved by virtue of the covenant of their father and mother. (HC 5:530)

4   *Words of Joseph F. Smith:* Joseph Smith taught the doctrine that the infant child that was laid away in death would come up in the resurrection as a child; and, pointing to the mother of a lifeless child, he said to her: "You will have the joy, the pleasure, and satisfaction of nurturing this child, after its resurrection, until it reaches the full stature of its spirit." (*Gospel Doctrine*, pp. 455–56)

5   *Words of Bathsheba W. Smith:* In Nauvoo, at his home, while playing with my baby boy, he [Joseph Smith] said that children were the "honor, glory, and royal diadem of women." (*TK*, p. 123)

Children of Israel

1   Paul told about Moses' proceedings; spoke of the children of Israel being baptized. (I Cor. x:1–4). He knew this, and that all the ordinances and blessings were in the Church. (HC 3:389)

2   When the children of Israel were chosen with Moses at their head, they were to be a peculiar people, among whom God should

---

Children
  4   Remarks of Joseph F. Smith, reporting the recollection of Agnes Smith, wife of Don Carlos Smith and mother of Sophronia, the deceased child at whose funeral the promise was made. Sophronia died in October 1843.
  5   Recollection of Bathsheba W. Smith, wife of George A. Smith, published in the *Juvenile Instructor*, 1 June 1892.

Children of Israel
  1   Discourse on the priesthood, given sometime before 8 August 1839, Commerce (Nauvoo). For a discussion on the dating of this discourse, see *WJS*, p. 22.
  2   Editorial in the *Times and Seasons*, 15 July 1842.

place His name; their motto was: "The Lord is our lawgiver; the Lord is our Judge; the Lord is our King, and He shall reign over us." While in this state they might truly say, "Happy is that people, whose God is the Lord." Their government was a theocracy; they had God to make their laws, and men chosen by Him to administer them; He was their God, and they were His people. Moses received the word of the Lord from God Himself; he was the mouth of God to Aaron, and Aaron taught the people, in both civil and ecclesiastical affairs; they were both one, there was no distinction; so will it be when the purposes of God shall be accomplished: when "the Lord shall be King over the whole earth," and "Jerusalem His throne." "The law shall go forth from Zion, and the word of the Lord from Jerusalem."

This is the only thing that can bring about the "restitution of all things spoken of by all the holy Prophets since the world was"—"the dispensation of the fullness of times, when God shall gather together all things in one." (HC 5:64)

3   God cursed the children of Israel because they would not receive the last law from Moses. . . .

. . . The Israelites prayed that God would speak to Moses and not to them; in consequence of which he cursed them with a carnal law. . . .

How shall God come to the rescue of this generation? He will send Elijah the prophet. The law revealed to Moses in Horeb never was revealed to the children of Israel as a nation.

Elijah shall reveal the covenants to seal the hearts of the fathers to the children, and the children to the fathers. (HC 5:555)

Church Councils

1   No man is capable of judging a matter, in council, unless his own heart is pure; and that we are frequently so filled with prejudice, or have a beam in our own eye, that we are not capable of passing right decisions.

Children of Israel
   3   Sabbath address, Nauvoo, 27 August 1843.

Church Councils
   1   A council of high priests and elders at the Prophet's home in Kirtland, 12 February 1834.

But to return to the subject of order; in ancient days councils were conducted with such strict propriety, that no one was allowed to whisper, be weary, leave the room, or get uneasy in the least, until the voice of the Lord, by revelation, or the voice of the council by the Spirit, was obtained, which has not been observed in this Church to the present time. It was understood in ancient days, that if one man could stay in council, another could; and if the president could spend his time, the members could also; but in our councils, generally, one will be uneasy, another asleep; one praying, another not; one's mind on the business of the council, and another thinking on something else.

Our acts are recorded, and at a future day they will be laid before us, and if we should fail to judge right and injure our fellow-beings, they may there, perhaps, condemn us; there they are of great consequence, and to me the consequence appears to be of force, beyond anything which I am able to express. Ask yourselves, brethren, how much you have exercised yourselves in prayer since you heard of this council; and if you are now prepared to sit in council upon the soul of your brother. (HC 2:25–26)

2   I then made some observations respecting the order of the day, and the great responsibility we were under to transact all our business in righteousness before God, inasmuch as our decisions will have a bearing upon all mankind, and upon all generations to come. (HC 2:370)

3   *Minutes:* In the investigation of the subject [the government of the house of the Lord], it was found that many who had deliberated upon it, were darkened in their minds, which drew forth some remarks from President Smith respecting the privileges of the authorities of the Church, that each should speak in his turn and in his place, and in his time and season, that there may be perfect order in all things; and that every man, before he makes an objection to any item that is brought before a council for consideration, should be sure that he can throw light upon the subject rather than spread darkness, and that his objection be founded in righteousness, which may be done by men applying themselves closely to study the mind and will of the Lord,

Church Councils
2   Priesthood meeting, Kirtland, 15 January 1836.
3   Minutes of a priesthood meeting, Kirtland, 15 January 1836.

whose Spirit always makes manifest and demonstrates the truth to the understanding of all who are in possession of the Spirit. (*HC* 2:370)

4   *Minutes:* President Joseph Smith, Jun., made remarks by way of charge to the presidents and counselors, instructing them in the duties of their callings, and the responsibility of their stations, exhorting them to be cautious and deliberate in all their councils, and be careful and act in righteousness in all things. (*HC* 3:39)

Church Disciplinary Councils

1   James Blanchard and Alonzo Rider were cut off from the Church by a council of Elders, in Kirtland, for repeated transgressions, and promising to reform, and never fulfilling. Nelson Acre was also cut off, on account of his absenting himself from the meetings, and saying that he wanted no more of the Church, and that he desired to be cut off. None of these being present, the council notified them of their expulsion by letters. This evening a Bishop's court was called to investigate the case of Elder Ezekiel Rider, who had said many hard things against Bishop Whitney: that Brother Whitney was not fit for a Bishop; that he treated the brethren who came into the store with disrespect; that he was overbearing, and fain would walk on the necks of the brethren. Brother Story was also in a similar transgression. I rebuked them sharply, and told them that the Church must feel the wrath of God except they repent of their sins and cast away their murmurings and complainings one of another. Elder Rigdon also lectured them on the same principles. Brothers Rider and Story confessed their wrongs, and all forgave one another. (*HC* 1:469–70)

2   On the evening of the 2nd of January, a Bishop's court assembled in Kirtland to investigate the case of Wesley Hurlburt, against whom charges had been preferred by Harriet Howe and others to the effect

---

Church Councils
  4   Minutes of a meeting in which the stake of Adam-ondi-Ahman was organized, 28 June 1838.

Church Disciplinary Councils
  1   Kirtland, 26 December 1833.
  2   Kirtland, 2 January 1834.

"that Hurlburt had denied the faith, spoken reproachfully of the Church, did not believe Joseph was a true Prophet," etc. Hurlburt was in the place, but did not appear before the court, consequently was cut off. (HC 2:2)

3 When a serious offense is committed, and indignity offered to the High Council, then it is the privilege of the Presidency of the High Council to stamp it with indignation under foot, and cut off the offender as in the case just decided. (HC 2:276)

4 Another, a woman near the same place [in Upper Canada], professed to have the discerning of spirits, and began to *accuse* another sister of things that she was not guilty of, which she said she knew was so by the spirit, but was afterwards proven to be false; she placed herself in the capacity of the "*accuser* of the brethren," and no person through the discerning of spirits can bring a charge against another, they must be proven guilty by positive evidence, or they stand clear. (HC 4:581)

5 If one member becomes corrupt, and you know it, you must immediately put it away, or it will either injure or destroy the whole body. The sympathies of the heads of the Church have induced them to bear a long time with those who were corrupt until they are obliged to cut them off, lest all become contaminated; you must put down iniquity. (HC 4:605)

6 [One of the objects of the conference is] to give a chance to those elders who have been disfellowshipped or had their licenses taken away in the branches to have a rehearing and settle their difficulties. (*WJS*, p. 177; standardized)

7 The question has been asked, can a person not belonging to the Church bring a member before the high council for trial? I answer, No. (HC 5:336)

Church Disciplinary Councils
3   Minutes of a high council meeting, Kirtland, 16 September 1835. The "case just decided" refers to the excommunication of Henry Green.
4   Editorial in the *Times and Seasons*, 1 April 1842.
5   Remarks to the Relief Society, Nauvoo, 28 April 1842.
6   Stated purpose of a general conference, Nauvoo, 6 April 1843.
7   General conference address, Nauvoo, 6 April 1843.

8   *Report of Wilford Woodruff:* Brother Joseph then addressed the Twelve, and said that in all our counsels, especially while on trial of any one, we should see and observe all things appertaining to the subject, and discern the spirit by which either party was governed. We should be in a situation to understand every spirit and judge righteous judgment and not be asleep. We should keep order and not let the council be imposed upon by unruly conduct. The Saints need not think because I am familiar with them and am playful and cheerful, that I am ignorant of what is going on. Iniquity of any kind cannot be sustained in the Church, and it will not fare well where I am; for I am determined while I do lead the Church, to lead it right. (HC 5:411)

Church History

1   [I] told Brother Phelps a dream that the history must go ahead before anything else. (HC 5:394)

2   The history must continue and not be disturbed, as there are but few subjects that I have felt a greater anxiety about than my history, which has been a very difficult task, on account of the death of my best clerks and the apostasy of others, and the stealing of records by John Whitmer, Cyrus Smalling and others. (HC 6:66)

3   For the last three years I have a record of all my acts and proceedings, for I have kept several good, faithful, and efficient clerks in constant employ: they have accompanied me everywhere, and carefully kept my history, and they have written down what I have done, where I have been, and what I have said; therefore my enemies cannot charge me with any day, time, or place, but what I have written testimony to prove my actions; and my enemies cannot prove anything against me. (HC 6:409)

Church Disciplinary Councils
   8   Instructions to the Twelve, 27 May 1843.

Church History
   1   Nauvoo, 19 May 1843.
   2   Nauvoo, 7 November 1843.
   3   Sabbath address, Nauvoo, 26 May 1844.

Church of Jesus Christ

1   [We] made known to our brethren that we had received a commandment to organize the Church; and accordingly we met together
for that purpose, at the house of Mr. Peter Whitmer, Sen., (being six in
number,) on Tuesday, the sixth day of April, A.D., one thousand eight
hundred and thirty. Having opened the meeting by solemn prayer to
our Heavenly Father, we proceeded, according to previous commandment, to call on our brethren to know whether they accepted us as
their teachers in the things of the Kingdom of God, and whether they
were satisfied that we should proceed and be organized as a Church according to said commandment which we had received. To these several
propositions they consented by a unanimous vote. I then laid my hands
upon Oliver Cowdery, and ordained him an Elder of the "Church of
Jesus Christ of Latter-day Saints;" after which, he ordained me also to
the office of an Elder of said Church. We then took bread, blessed it,
and brake it with them; also wine, blessed it, and drank it with them.
We then laid our hands on each individual member of the Church
present, that they might receive the gift of the Holy Ghost, and be
confirmed members of the Church of Christ. The Holy Ghost was
poured out upon us to a very great degree—some prophesied, whilst we
all praised the Lord, and rejoiced exceedingly. Whilst yet together, I received the following commandment: [D&C 21].

We now proceeded to call out and ordain some others of the
brethren to different offices of the Priesthood, according as the Spirit
manifested unto us: and after a happy time spent in witnessing and
feeling for ourselves the powers and blessings of the Holy Ghost,
through the grace of God bestowed upon us, we dismissed with the
pleasing knowledge that we were now individually members of, and
acknowledged of God, "The Church of Jesus Christ," organized in accordance with commandments and revelations given by Him to ourselves in these last days, as well as according to the order of the
Church as recorded in the New Testament. Several persons who had
attended the above meeting, became convinced of the truth and came
forward shortly after, and were received into the Church; among the
rest, my own father and mother were baptized, to my great joy and

---

Church of Jesus Christ
   1   Organization of the Church at the home of Peter Whitmer, Sr., at Fayette,
        New York, 6 April 1830.

consolation; and about the same time, Martin Harris and Orrin Porter Rockwell. (HC 1:75–78, 79)

2   My time was occupied closely in reviewing the commandments and sitting in conference, for nearly two weeks; for from the first to the twelfth of November we held four special conferences. In the last which was held at Brother Johnson's in Hiram, after deliberate consideration, in consequence of the book of revelations, now to be printed, being the foundation of the Church in these last days, and a benefit to the world, showing that the keys of the mysteries of the kingdom of our Savior are again entrusted to man; and the riches of eternity within the compass of those who are willing to live by every word that proceedeth out of the mouth of God—therefore the conference voted that they prize the revelations to be worth to the Church the riches of the whole earth, speaking temporally. (HC 1:235)

3   It was my endeavor to so organize the Church, that the brethren might eventually be independent of every incumbrance beneath the celestial kingdom, by bonds and covenants of mutual friendship, and mutual love. (HC 1:269)

4   The churches seem to be in a cold, languid and disconsolate state; and as the revolution of the earth is once in twenty-four hours, so we may look for frequent revolutions among this wicked and perverse generation, and also in the Church of Christ. When the head is sick, the whole body is faint; and when the Church lifts up the head, the angel will bring us good tidings. Even so. Amen. (HC 2:146)

5   And again, another parable put He [the Savior] forth unto them, having an allusion to the Kingdom that should be set up, just previous to or at the time of the harvest, which reads as follows—"The Kingdom of Heaven is like a grain of mustard seed, which a man took and sowed in his field: which indeed is the least of all seeds: but, when it is grown, it is the greatest among herbs, and becometh a tree, so that the birds of the air come and lodge in the branches thereof." Now we can

---

Church of Jesus Christ

2   Hiram, Ohio, November 1831.
3   Jackson County, Missouri, 27 April 1832.
4   Letter written from Kirtland to the high council in Zion, 16 August 1834.
5   Letter to the elders of the Church, Kirtland, 1 September 1835.

discover plainly that this figure is given to represent the Church as it shall come forth in the last days. Behold, the Kingdom of Heaven is likened unto it. Now, what is like unto it?

Let us take the Book of Mormon, which a man took and hid in his field, securing it by his faith, to spring up in the last days, or in due time; let us behold it coming forth out of the ground, which is indeed accounted the least of all seeds, but behold it branching forth, yea, even towering, with lofty branches, and God-like majesty, until it, like the mustard seed, becomes the greatest of all herbs. And it is truth, and it has sprouted and come forth out of the earth, and righteousness begins to look down from heaven, and God is sending down His powers, gifts and angels, to lodge in the branches thereof.

The Kingdom of heaven is like unto a mustard seed. Behold, then is not this the Kingdom of heaven that is raising its head in the last days in the majesty of its God, even the Church of the Latter-day Saints, like an impenetrable, immovable rock in the midst of the mighty deep, exposed to the storms and tempests of Satan, but has, thus far, remained steadfast, and is still braving the mountain waves of opposition, which are driven by the tempestuous winds of sinking crafts, which have {dashed} and are still dashing with tremendous foam across its triumphant brow; urged onward with redoubled fury by the enemy of righteousness, with his pitchfork of lies, as you will see fairly represented in a cut contained in Mr. Howe's *Mormonism Unveiled?* And we hope that this adversary of truth will continue to stir up the sink of iniquity, that the people may the more readily discern between the righteous and the wicked. (HC 2:268)

6   Our Church organization was converted, by the testimony of the apostates [in court], into a temporal kingdom, which was to fill the whole earth, and subdue all other kingdoms. (HC 3:211)

7   But I beg leave to say unto you, brethren, that ignorance, superstition and bigotry placing itself where it ought not, is oftentimes in the way of the prosperity of this Church; like the torrent of rain from the mountains, that floods the most pure and crystal stream with mire, and dirt, and filthiness, and obscures everything that was clear before,

---

Church of Jesus Christ
   6   Richmond, Missouri, November 1838.
   7   Letter to the Saints from Liberty Jail, 20–25 March 1839.

and all rushes along in one general deluge; but time weathers tide; and notwithstanding we are rolled in the mire of the flood for the time being, the next surge peradventure, as time rolls on, may bring to us the fountain as clear as crystal, and as pure as snow; while the filthiness, floodwood and rubbish is left and purged out by the way. . . .

. . . Hell may pour forth its rage like the burning lava of mount Vesuvius, or of Etna, or of the most terrible of the burning mountains; and yet shall "Mormonism" stand. Water, fire, truth and God are all realities. Truth is "Mormonism." God is the author of it. He is our shield. It is by Him we received our birth. It was by His voice that we were called to a dispensation of His Gospel in the beginning of the fullness of times. It was by Him we received the Book of Mormon; and it is by Him that we remain unto this day; and by Him we shall remain, if it shall be for our glory; and in His Almighty name we are determined to endure tribulation as good soldiers unto the end. (*HC* 3:296–97)

8   The name Mormon, and Mormonism, was given to us by our enemies, but Latter Day Saints was the real name by which the church was organized. (*PWJS*, p. 420)

9   On the 6th of April, 1830, the "Church of Jesus Christ of Latter-day Saints" was first organized in the town of Fayette, Seneca county, state of New York. Some few were called and ordained by the Spirit of revelation and prophecy, and began to preach as the Spirit gave them utterance, and though weak, yet were they strengthened by the power of God, and many were brought to repentance, were immersed in the water, and were filled with the Holy Ghost by the laying on of hands. They saw visions and prophesied, devils were cast out, and the sick healed by the laying on of hands. (*HC* 4:538)

10   And how were apostles, prophets, pastors, teachers, and evangelists chosen? by "prophesy (revelation) and by laying on of hands:"— by a divine communication, and a divinely appointed ordinance—

Church of Jesus Christ

8   Letter to Isaac Galland, written while the Prophet was imprisoned in Liberty Jail, 22 March 1839.

9   Letter to John Wentworth, editor of the *Chicago Democrat*, Nauvoo, 1 March 1842.

10   Editorial in the *Times and Seasons*, 1 April 1842.

through the medium of the priesthood, organized according to the order of God, by divine appointment. (*T&S* 3:744–45)

11 The Church is not fully organized, in its proper order, and cannot be, until the Temple is completed, where places will be provided for the administration of the ordinances of the Priesthood. (*HC* 4:603)

12 The Church is a compact body composed of different members, and is strictly analogous to the human system, and Paul, after speaking of the different gifts, says, "Now ye are the body of Christ and members in particular; and God hath set some in the Church, first Apostles, secondarily Prophets, thirdly Teachers, after that miracles, then gifts of healing, helps, governments, diversities of tongues. Are all Teachers? Are all workers of miracles? Do all speak with tongues? Do all interpret?" It is evident that they do not; yet are they all members of one body. All members of the natural body are not the eye, the ear, the head or the hand—yet the eye cannot say to the ear I have no need of thee, nor the head to the foot, I have no need of thee; they are all so many component parts in the perfect machine—the one body; and if one member suffer, the whole of the members suffer with it: and if one member rejoice, all the rest are honored with it. (*HC* 5:28–29)

13 As God governed Abraham, Isaac and Jacob as families, and the children of Israel as a nation; so we, as a Church, must be under His guidance if we are prospered, preserved and sustained. Our only confidence can be in God; our only wisdom obtained from Him; and He alone must be our protector and safeguard, spiritually and temporally, or we fall. (*HC* 5:65)

14 The servants of the Lord are required to guard against those things that are calculated to do the most evil. The little foxes spoil the vines—little evils do the most injury to the Church. If you have evil feelings, and speak of them to one another, it has a tendency to do mischief. These things result in those evils which are calculated to cut the throats of the heads of the Church. (*HC* 5:140)

Church of Jesus Christ
   11 Remarks to the Relief Society, Nauvoo, 28 April 1842.
   12 Editorial in the *Times and Seasons*, 15 June 1842.
   13 Editorial in the *Times and Seasons*, 15 July 1842.
   14 Remarks to the Relief Society, Nauvoo, 31 August 1842.

15 I see no faults in the Church, and therefore let me be resurrected with the Saints, whether I ascend to heaven or descend to hell, or go to any other place. And if we go to hell, we will turn the devils out of doors and make a heaven of it. Where this people are, there is good society. What do we care where we are, if the society be good? (*HC* 5:517)

16 Christ was the head of the Church, the chief corner stone, the spiritual rock upon which the church was built, and the gates of hell shall not prevail against it. He built up the Kingdom, chose Apostles, and ordained them to the Melchizedek Priesthood, giving them power to administer in the ordinances of the Gospel. (*TPJS*, p. 318)

17 The Church of Jesus Christ of Latter-day Saints was founded upon direct revelation, as the true Church of God has ever been, according to the Scriptures (Amos iii:7, and Acts i:2); and through the will and blessings of God, I have been an instrument in His hands, thus far, to move forward the cause of Zion. (*HC* 6:9)

18 *Words of James Palmer:* In a public meeting of the Saints near the Temple he [Joseph Smith] said that he had accomplished that which the world could never rob him of. The Church of Christ was established, never more to be cast down or overcome, or given to another people. (*TK*, p. 155)

Churches, Other

1 Rail not against the sects, neither talk against their tenets. But preach Christ and him crucified, love to God, and love to man. (*PWJS*, p. 347)

Church of Jesus Christ
  15 Sabbath address, Nauvoo, 23 July 1843.
  16 Sabbath address, Nauvoo, 23 July 1843.
  17 Letter to Daniel Rupp, Nauvoo, 7 September 1843.
  18 Reminiscence and journal of James Palmer, LDS Church Archives.

Churches, Other
  1 Letter to Hezekiah Peck, a Church leader in Missouri, Kirtland, 31 August 1835.

2   We ought always to be aware of those prejudices which sometimes so strangely present themselves, and are so congenial to human nature, against our friends, neighbors, and brethren of the world, who choose to differ from us in opinion and in matters of faith. Our religion is between us and our God. Their religion is between them and their God. (HC 3:303–4)

3   Many objections are urged against the Latter-day Saints for not admitting the validity of sectarian baptism, and for withholding fellowship from sectarian churches. Yet to do otherwise would be like putting new wine into old bottles, and putting old wine into new bottles. What! new revelations in the old churches? New revelations would knock out the bottom of their bottomless pit. New wine into old bottles! The bottles burst and the wine runs out! What! Sadducees in the new church! Old wine in new leathern bottles will leak through the pores and escape. (HC 4:426)

4   Here is a principle of logic that most men have no more sense than to adopt. I will illustrate it by an old apple tree. Here jumps off a branch and says, I am the true tree, and you are corrupt. If the whole tree is corrupt, are not its branches corrupt? If the Catholic religion is a false religion, how can any true religion come out of it? If the Catholic church is bad, how can any good thing come out of it? The character of the old churches have always been slandered by all apostates since the world began. (HC 6:478)

Circumcision

1   The covenant of circumcision made with Abraham, and practiced steadily up to the departing of Israel out of Egypt, was abandoned in the wilderness, forty years—and renewed by Joshua after he passed over Jordan, and encamped at Gilgal, where he made sharp knives and circumcised the whole male portion of the church. (*T&S* 3:904)

Churches, Other
2   Letter to the Saints from Liberty Jail, 20–25 March 1839.
3   General conference address, Nauvoo, 3 October 1841.
4   Sabbath address, Nauvoo, 16 June 1844.

Circumcision
1   Editorial in the *Times and Seasons*, 1 September 1842.

2   "Do you believe in the baptism of infants?" asks the Presbyterian. No. "Why?" Because it is nowhere written in the Bible. Circumcision is not baptism, neither was baptism instituted in the place of circumcision. (*HC* 5:499)

Cleanliness

1   *Words of a Visitor to Nauvoo:* It never occurred to me that clean hands, in administering before the Lord, as mentioned in the scripture, meant anything more than a good conscience; and I had never supposed but that a man could worship God just as acceptably all covered with dirt, and filth and slime, as though he had bathed in Siloam every hour, until I heard the Mormon prophet lecturing his people on the subject of neatness and cleanliness, teaching them that all was clean in heaven, and that Jesus was going to make the place of His feet glorious; and if the Mormons did not keep their feet out of the ashes, they could not stand with Him on Mount Zion. (*HC* 5:407)

Comfort

1   I will try to be contented with my lot knowing that God is my friend. In him I shall find comfort. (*PWJS*, p. 239; standardized)

2   Let us not sorrow as "those without hope." The time is fast approaching when we shall see them [the martyred Saints] again, and rejoice together, without being afraid of wicked men. Yes, those who have slept in Christ shall he bring with him, when he shall come to be

---

Circumcision
    2   Sabbath address, Nauvoo, 9 July 1843.

Cleanliness
    1   A character sketch on the Prophet from a Boston paper, the *Boston Bee*, 24 May 1843.

Comfort
    1   Letter to Emma Smith from Greenville, Indiana, 6 June 1832.
    2   Excerpts from the private journal of Joseph Smith, published in the *Times and Seasons*, Commerce (Nauvoo), November 1839.

glorified in his saints, and admired by all those who believe; but to take vengeance upon his enemies, and all those who obey not the gospel. At that time, the hearts of the widow and fatherless shall be comforted, and every tear shall be wiped from off their faces. (*PWJS*, p. 444; standardized)

Comforter
See HOLY GHOST

Commandments

1   Make yourselves acquainted with the commandments of the Lord, and the laws of the state, and govern yourselves accordingly. (*HC* 1:341)

2   If the Church knew all the commandments, one half they would condemn through prejudice and ignorance. (*HC* 2:477)

3   *Report of Wilford Woodruff:* President Joseph arose and said—. . . "Some people say I am a fallen Prophet, because I do not bring forth more of the word of the Lord. Why do I not do it? Are we able to receive it? No! not one in this room." He then chastened the congregation for their wickedness and unbelief, " 'for whom the Lord loveth he chasteneth, and scourgeth every son and daughter whom he receiveth,' and if we do not receive chastisements then we are bastards and not sons."
. . . "The reason we do not have the secrets of the Lord revealed unto us, is because we do not keep them but reveal them; we do not keep our own secrets, but reveal our difficulties to the world, even to our enemies, then how would we keep the secrets of the Lord? I can keep a secret till Doomsday." (*HC* 4:478, 479)

4   We cannot keep all the commandments without first knowing them, and we cannot expect to know all, or more than we now know

---

Commandments
1   Letter to the brethren in Zion, Kirtland, 21 April 1833.
2   Solemn assembly in the Kirtland Temple, 6 April 1837.
3   Meeting of the Twelve at the Prophet's home, Nauvoo, 19 December 1841.
4   Essay on happiness, Nauvoo, 27 August 1842.

unless we comply with or keep those we have already received. (*HC* 5:135)

5   Any man may believe Jesus Christ is good and be happy in it, and yet not obey his commands, and at last be cut down by his righteous commandments. (*WJS*, p. 214; standardized)

6   When His commandments teach us, it is in view of eternity; for we are looked upon by God as though we were in eternity; God dwells in eternity, and does not view things as we do. (*HC* 6:313)

Common Consent

1   The word of the Lord came unto us in the chamber, commanding us that I should ordain Oliver Cowdery to be an Elder in the Church of Jesus Christ; and that he also should ordain me to the same office; and then to ordain others, as it should be made known unto us from time to time. We were, however, commanded to defer this our ordination until such times as it should be practicable to have our brethren, who had been and who should be baptized, assembled together, when we must have their sanction to our thus proceeding to ordain each other, and have them decide by vote whether they were willing to accept us as spiritual teachers or not. (*HC* 1:60–61)

2   Having opened the meeting by solemn prayer to our Heavenly Father, we proceeded, according to previous commandment, to call on our brethren to know whether they accepted us as their teachers in the things of the Kingdom of God, and whether they were satisfied that we should proceed and be organized as a Church according to said commandment which we had received. To these several propositions they consented by a unanimous vote. (*HC* 1:77)

Commandments
5   Sabbath address, Nauvoo, 11 June 1843, as reported by Wilford Woodruff.
6   King Follett Discourse, Nauvoo, 7 April 1844.

Common Consent
1   Fayette, New York, May–June 1829.
2   Organization of the Church at the home of Peter Whitmer, Sr., at Fayette, New York, 6 April 1830.

3   These seven men [high priests sent from Kirtland to build up Zion], with the common consent of the branches comprising the Church were to appoint presiding Elders, to take the watchcare of the several branches, as they were appointed. (HC 1:336)

4   At a council of High Priests in Zion, Elder Christian Whitmer was ordained to the High Priesthood. And on the 28th, the council resolved, that no High Priest, Elder, or Priest, shall ordain any Priest, Elder, or High Priest in the land of Zion, without the consent of a conference of High Priests. (HC 1:407)

5   The High Priests, Elders, Priests, Teachers, Deacons and members present, then covenanted with hands uplifted to heaven, that they would uphold Brother David Whitmer, as president in Zion, in my absence; and John Whitmer and William W. Phelps, as assistant presidents or counselors; and myself as First President of the Church; and to uphold one another by faith and prayer. (HC 2:125–26)

6   No official member of the church has authority to go into any branch thereof, and ordain any minister for that church, unless it is by the voice of that branch. No Elder has authority to go into any branch of the Church, and appoint meetings, or attempt to regulate the affairs of the Church, without the advice and consent of the presiding Elder of that branch. (HC 2:220–21)

7   After closing his discourse he [Elder Rigdon] called upon the several quorums, commencing with the Presidency, to manifest, by rising, their willingness to acknowledge me as a Prophet and Seer, and uphold me as such, by their prayers of faith. All the quorums, in turn, cheerfully complied with this request. He then called upon all the congregation of Saints, also, to give their assent by rising on their feet, which they did unanimously. (HC 2:416)

Common Consent

3   A council of high priests assembled in Jackson County, Missouri, 26 March 1833.

4   Minutes of a council of high priests in Zion, 21 and 28 August 1833.

5   Meeting at Lyman Wight's home in which the high council and presidency of the Church in Zion were sustained, Missouri, 7 July 1834.

6   Minutes of a general council of the Priesthood, Kirtland, 2 May 1835.

7   Events during the dedication of the Kirtland Temple, 27 March 1836.

8   *Minutes:* The minutes of said meeting at Kirtland were read by the moderator who also nominated Joseph Smith, Jun., the first President of the whole Church, to preside over the same.

All were requested (male and female) to vote; and he was unanimously chosen. (HC 2:522)

9   *Report of William Clayton:* He [Joseph Smith] next presented himself and was unanimously voted President of the whole Church. Next his counselors, Elders Rigdon and William Law, and afterwards Elder Hyrum, who was voted with a hearty aye. (*WJS*, p. 177; standardized)

Common Sense

1   The idea that some men form of the justice, judgment, and mercy of God, is too foolish for an intelligent man to think of: for instance, it is common for many of our orthodox preachers to suppose that if a man is not what they call converted, if he dies in that state he must remain eternally in hell without any hope. Infinite years in torment must he spend, and never, never, never have an end; and yet this eternal misery is made frequently to rest upon the merest casualty. The breaking of a shoe-string, the tearing of a coat of those officiating, or the peculiar location in which a person lives, may be the means, indirectly of his damnation, or the cause of his not being saved. I will suppose a case which is not extraordinary: Two men, who have been equally wicked, who have neglected religion, are both of them taken sick at the same time; one of them has the good fortune to be visited by a praying man, and he gets converted a few minutes before he dies; the other sends for three different praying men, a tailor, a shoemaker, and a tinman; the tinman has a handle to solder to a can, the tailor has a button-hole to work on some coat that he needed in a hurry, and the shoemaker has a patch to put on somebody's boot; they none of them can go in time, the man dies, and goes to hell: one of these is ex-

---

Common Consent
  8   Minutes of a conference held at Far West, 7 November 1837.
  9   General conference address, Nauvoo, 6 April 1843, as reported by William Clayton.

Common Sense
  1   Editorial in the *Times and Seasons*, 15 April 1842.

alted to Abraham's bosom, he sits down in the presence of God and enjoys eternal, uninterrupted happiness, while the other, equally as good as he, sinks to eternal damnation, irretrievable misery and hopeless despair, because a man had a boot to mend, the button-hole of a coat to work, or a handle to solder on to a saucepan.

The plans of Jehovah are not so unjust, the statements of holy writ so visionary, nor the plan of salvation for the human family so incompatible with common sense; at such proceedings God would frown with indignance, angels would hide their heads in shame, and every virtuous, intelligent man would recoil. (HC 4:597–98)

Communication

1   Every subject written upon by the brethren should be plain to the understanding of all, that no jealousy may be raised. . . .

Now I would say to Brother Gilbert, that I do not write this by way of chastisement, but to show him the absolute necessity of having all his communications written in a manner to be clearly understood. (HC 1:341)

2   You remember the testimony which I bore in the name of the Lord Jesus, concerning the great work which He has brought forth in the last days. You know my manner of communication, how that in weakness and simplicity, I declared to you what the Lord had brought forth by the ministering of His holy angels to me for this generation. I pray that the Lord may enable you to treasure these things in your mind, for I know that His Spirit will bear testimony to all who seek diligently after knowledge from Him. (HC 1:442)

Compassion

1   You may in some measure realize what my feelings, as well as Elder Rigdon's and Brother Hyrum's were, when we read your letter—truly

---

Communication
1   Letter to the brethren in Zion, Kirtland, 21 April 1833.
2   Letter to Moses C. Nickerson, written from Kirtland, 19 November 1833.

Compassion
1   Letter to William W. Phelps, Nauvoo, 22 July 1840.

our hearts were melted into tenderness and compassion when we ascertained your resolves, &c. I can assure you I feel a disposition to act on your case in a manner that will meet the approbation of Jehovah, (whose servant I am), and agreeable to the principles of truth and righteousness which have been revealed; and inasmuch as long-suffering, patience, and mercy have ever characterized the dealings of our heavenly Father towards the humble and penitent, I feel disposed to copy the example, cherish the same principles, and by so doing be a savior of my fellow men. (HC 4:163)

2   The nearer we get to our heavenly Father, the more we are disposed to look with compassion on perishing souls; we feel that we want to take them upon our shoulders, and cast their sins behind our backs. My talk is intended for all this society [Relief Society]; if you would have God have mercy on you, have mercy on one another. (HC 5:24)

Compulsion

1   *Report of Don Carlos Smith:* He [Joseph Smith] then observed that Satan was generally blamed for the evils which we did, but if he was the cause of all our wickedness, men could not be condemned. The devil could not compel mankind to do evil; all was voluntary. . . . God would not exert any compulsory means, and the devil could not; and such ideas as were entertained {on these subjects} by many were absurd. (HC 4:358)

2   How oft have wise men and women sought to dictate Brother Joseph by saying, "O, if I were Brother Joseph, I would do this and that;" but if they were in Brother Joseph's shoes they would find that men or women could not be compelled into the kingdom of God, but must be dealt with in long-suffering, and at last we shall save them. (HC 5:24)

Compassion
  2   Remarks to the Relief Society, Nauvoo, 9 June 1842.

Compulsion
  1   Sabbath address, Nauvoo, 16 May 1841.
  2   Remarks to the Relief Society, Nauvoo, 9 June 1842.

3   In relation to the power over the minds of mankind which I hold, I would say, It is in consequence of the power of truth in the doctrines which I have been an instrument in the hands of God of presenting unto them, and not because of any compulsion on my part. I wish to ask if ever I got any of it unfairly? if I have not reproved you in the gate? I ask, Did I ever exercise any compulsion over any man? Did I not give him the liberty of disbelieving any doctrine I have preached, if he saw fit? (HC 6:273)

Condemnation

1   Many of the Elders have come under great condemnation, in endeavoring to steady the ark of God, in a place where they have not been sent. (*PWJS*, p. 346)

2   We again make remark here—for we find that the very principle upon which the disciples were accounted blessed, was because they were permitted to see with their eyes and hear with their ears—that the condemnation which rested upon the multitude that received not His saying, was because they were not willing to see with their eyes, and hear with their ears; not because they could not, and were not privileged to see and hear, but because their hearts were full of iniquity and abominations; "as your fathers did, so do ye." The prophet, foreseeing that they would thus harden their hearts, plainly declared it; and herein is the condemnation of the world; that light hath come into the world, and men choose darkness rather than light, because their deeds are evil. This is so plainly taught by the Savior, that a wayfaring man need not mistake it. (HC 2:266)

3   Thus came the word of the Lord unto me concerning the Twelve, saying—

Compulsion
   3   Sabbath address, Nauvoo, 24 March 1844.

Condemnation
   1   Letter to Hezekiah Peck, a Church leader in Missouri, Kirtland, 31 August 1835.
   2   Letter to the elders of the Church, Kirtland, 1 September 1835.
   3   Kirtland, Ohio, 3 November 1835.

Behold they are under condemnation, because they have not been sufficiently humble in my sight, and in consequence of their covetous desires, in that they have not dealt equally with each other in the division of the monies which came into their hands, nevertheless, some of them dealt equally, therefore they shall be rewarded; but verily I say unto you, they must all humble themselves before me, before they will be accounted worthy to receive an endowment, to go forth in my name unto all nations. (*HC* 2:300)

4   There is no pain so awful as the pain of suspense. This is the condemnation of the wicked; their doubt and anxiety and suspense causes weeping, wailing, and gnashing of teeth. (*WJS*, p. 183; standardized)

5   A man is his own tormentor and his own condemner. Hence the saying, They shall go into the lake that burns with fire and brimstone. The torment of disappointment in the mind of man is as exquisite as a lake burning with fire and brimstone. I say, so is the torment of man. (*HC* 6:314)

Confidence

1   In order to conduct the affairs of the Kingdom in righteousness, it is all important that the most perfect harmony, kind feeling, good understanding, and confidence should exist in the hearts of all the brethren; and that true charity, love one towards another, should characterize all their proceedings. If there are any uncharitable feelings, any lack of confidence, then pride, arrogance and envy will soon be manifested; confusion must inevitably prevail, and the authorities of the Church set at naught. . . .
      . . . When confidence is restored, when pride shall fall, and every aspiring mind be clothed with humility as with a garment, and selfishness give place to benevolence and charity, and a united determina-

---

Condemnation
   4   General conference address, Nauvoo, 8 April 1843, as reported by William Clayton.
   5   King Follett Discourse, Nauvoo, 7 April 1844.

Confidence
   1   Letter to Oliver Granger in Kirtland, sent from Nauvoo, July 1840.

tion to live by every word which proceedeth out of the mouth of the Lord is observable, then, and not till then, can peace, order and love prevail. (HC 4:165, 166)

2   As God governed Abraham, Isaac and Jacob as families, and the children of Israel as a nation; so we, as a Church, must be under His guidance if we are prospered, preserved and sustained. Our only confidence can be in God; our only wisdom obtained from Him: and He alone must be our protector and safeguard, spiritually and temporally, or we fall. (HC 5:65)

3   The way I know in whom to confide—God tells me in whom I may place confidence. (HC 5:392)

Conscience

1   We know not what we shall be called to pass through before Zion is delivered and established; therefore, we have great need to live near to God, and always to be in strict obedience to all His commandments, that we may have a conscience void of offense toward God and man. (HC 1:450)

2   We deem it a just principle, and it is one the force of which we believe ought to be duly considered by every individual, that all men are created equal, and that all have the privilege of thinking for themselves upon all matters relative to conscience. Consequently, then, we are not disposed, had we the power, to deprive any one of exercising that free independence of mind which heaven has so graciously bestowed upon the human family as one of its choicest gifts. (HC 2:6–7)

Confidence
    2   Editorial in the *Times and Seasons*, 15 July 1842.
    3   Instruction given to a few Saints at the home of Benjamin F. Johnson, Ramus, Illinois, 16 May 1843.

Conscience
    1   Letter to Bishop Edward Partridge, Kirtland, 5 December 1833.
    2   Letter to the brethren scattered from Zion, Kirtland, 22 January 1834.

3   I do not believe that human law has a right to interfere in prescribing rules of worship to bind the consciences of men, nor dictate forms for public or private devotion. . . . The civil magistrate should restrain crime, but never control conscience; should punish guilt, but never suppress the freedom of the soul. (*PWJS*, p. 455; standardized)

4   It is one of the first principles of my life, and one that I have cultivated from my childhood, having been taught it by my father, to allow every one the liberty of conscience. (*HC* 6:56)

5   Those who have done wrong always have that wrong gnawing them. . . . You cannot go anywhere but where God can find you out. (*HC* 6:366)

6   I am going like a lamb to the slaughter, but I am calm as a summer's morning. I have a conscience void of offense toward God and toward all men. If they take my life I shall die an innocent man, and my blood shall cry from the ground for vengeance, and it shall be said of me "He was murdered in cold blood!" (*HC* 6:555)

Consecration

1   *Minutes:* Brother Joseph Smith, Jun., said that he had nothing to consecrate to the Lord of the things of the earth, yet he felt to consecrate himself and family. Was thankful that God had given him a place among His Saints; felt willing to labor for their good. (*HC* 1:220)

2   Sir:—I proceed to answer your questions, concerning the consecration of property:—First, it is not right to condescend to very great

---

Conscience
   3   Letter to the editor of a Pennsylvania paper, the *Chester County Register and Examiner,* Brandywine, Pennsylvania, 22 January 1840.
   4   Sabbath address, Nauvoo, 15 October 1843.
   5   Sabbath address, Nauvoo, 12 May 1844.
   6   Statement as Joseph Smith left Nauvoo for Carthage, 24 June 1844.

Consecration
   1   Minutes of a conference held at Orange, Ohio, 25 October 1831.
   2   Letter to the brethren in Zion, Kirtland, 25 June 1833. The section that appears here is addressed to Edward Partridge.

particulars in taking inventories. The fact is this, a man is bound by the law of the Church, to consecrate to the Bishop, before he can be considered a legal heir to the kingdom of Zion; and this, too, without constraint; and unless he does this, he cannot be acknowledged before the Lord on the Church Book; therefore, to condescend to particulars, I will tell you that every man must be his own judge how much he should receive and how much he should suffer to remain in the hands of the Bishop. I speak of those who consecrate more than they need for the support of themselves and their families.

The matter of consecration must be done by the mutual consent of both parties; for to give the Bishop power to say how much every man shall have, and he be obliged to comply with the Bishop's judgment, is giving to the Bishop more power than a king has; and upon the other hand, to let every man say how much he needs, and the Bishop be obliged to comply with his judgment, is to throw Zion into confusion, and make a slave of the Bishop. The fact is, there must be a balance or equilibrium of power, between the Bishop and the people, and thus harmony and good will may be preserved among you.

Therefore, those persons consecrating property to the Bishop in Zion, and then receiving an inheritance back, must reasonably show to the Bishop that they need as much as they claim. But in case the two parties cannot come to a mutual agreement, the Bishop is to have nothing to do about receiving such consecrations; and the case must be laid before a council of twelve High Priests, the Bishop not being one of the council, but he is to lay the case before them. (HC 1:364–65)

3   Oh, brethren, give up all to God; forsake all for Christ's sake. (*PWJS*, p. 283; standardized)

4   Let those who can freely make a sacrifice of their time, their talents, and their property, for the prosperity of the kingdom, and for the love they have to the cause of truth, bid adieu to their homes and pleasant places of abode, and unite with us in the great work of the last days, and share in the tribulation, that they may ultimately share in the glory and triumph. (HC 4:273)

Consecration
3   The Prophet's postscript in a letter from Oliver Cowdery to the leaders of the Church in Missouri, 10 August 1833.
4   Proclamation of the First Presidency, Nauvoo, 15 January 1841.

5   While the busy multitudes have thus been engaged in their several vocations performing their daily labor, and working one-tenth of their time, others have not been less forward in bringing in their tithings and consecrations for the same great object [building the temple]. Never since the foundation of this Church was laid, have we seen manifested a greater willingness to comply with the requisitions of Jehovah, a more ardent desire to do the will of God, more strenuous exertions used, or greater sacrifices made than there have been since the Lord said, "Let the Temple be built by the tithing of my people." It seemed as though the spirit of enterprise, philanthropy and obedience rested simultaneously upon old and young, and brethren and sisters, boys and girls, and even strangers, who were not in the Church, united with an unprecedented liberality in the accomplishment of this great work; nor could the widow, in many instances, be prevented, out of her scanty pittance from throwing in her two mites. (HC 4:609)

6   *Clerk's Report:* This day President Joseph Smith rode over to Brother John Wilkie's at his special request, to give him some instructions relative to his duty in regard to tithing and consecration.

Brother Wilkie has for a long time back been struggling with his feelings, designing to do right, but laboring under many fears and prejudices, in consequence of having in some degree given way to believe the base reports circulated by individuals for the purpose of injuring the authorities of the Church, and also from various other causes. His faithful companion has persevered diligently, and with fervent prayer has called upon God in his behalf, until she has realized her utmost wishes.

Brother Wilkie now feels anxious to do right in all things, and especially to pay his tithing to the full. President Joseph showed him the principles of consecration and the means whereby he might realize the fullness of the blessings of the celestial kingdom; and as an evidence that he desired to do right, he paid over to the Trustee-in-Trust the sum of three hundred dollars in gold and silver for the benefit of the Temple, and which is now recorded on consecration.

He also signified his intention of paying more as soon as he could get matters properly arranged. The president then pronounced a bless-

---

Consecration
   5   Editorial in the *Times and Seasons*, Nauvoo, 2 May 1842.
   6   Instruction and blessing for John Wilkie, Nauvoo, 15 March 1844.

ing upon him and his companion, that they should have the blessing of God to attend them in their basket and in their store—that they should have the blessing of health and salvation and long life, inasmuch as they would continue to walk in obedience to the commandments of God.

May the Lord grant his Spirit and peace to abide upon Brother Wilkie and his companion through the remainder of their days; may their hearts expand and become enlarged to receive the fullness of the blessings of the kingdom of heaven; may they have the light of eternal truth continually springing up in them like a well of living water; may they be shielded from the powers of Satan and the influence of designing men, and their faith increase from day to day until they shall have power to lay hold on the blessings of God and the gifts of the Spirit until they are satisfied; and, finally, may they live to a good old age; and when they have lived while they desire life, may they die in peace and be received into the mansions of eternal life, and enjoy a celestial glory forever and ever! Even so, amen. (HC 6:264–65)

7   *Report of John M. Bernhisel's Recollection:* "Our present system," said the Prophet, "will eventually resolve itself into a 'united order' in which every member will work not purely for his individual aggrandizement, but with an earnest desire to promote the interests of the kingdom of God on the earth." (*TK*, p. 178)

Consolation

1   Notwithstanding the corruptions and abominations of the times, and the evil spirit manifested towards us on account of our belief in the Book of Mormon, at many places and among various persons, yet the Lord continued His watchful care and loving kindness to us day by day; and we made it a rule wherever there was an opportunity, to read a chapter in the Bible, and pray; and these seasons of worship gave us great consolation. (HC 1:188–89)

Consecration
   7   Recollection of John M. Bernhisel, reported in Washington Franklin Anderson, "Reminiscences of John M. Bernhisel," LDS Church Archives.

Consolation
   1   Observation while en route from Kirtland to Missouri, June–July 1831.

2 It is a duty which every Saint ought to render to his brethren freely—to always love them, and ever succor them. To be justified before God we must love one another: we must overcome evil; we must visit the fatherless and the widow in their affliction, and we must keep ourselves unspotted from the world: for such virtues flow from the great fountain of pure religion. Strengthening our faith by adding every good quality that adorns the children of the blessed Jesus, we can pray in the season of prayer; we can love our neighbor as ourselves, and be faithful in tribulation, knowing that the reward of such is greater in the kingdom of heaven. What a consolation! What a joy! Let me live the life of the righteous, and let my reward be like this! (HC 2:229)

3 We say that God is true; that the Constitution of the United States is true; that the Bible is true; that the Book of Mormon is true; that the Book of Covenants is true; that Christ is true; that the ministering angels sent forth from God are true, and that we know that we have an house not made with hands eternal in the heavens, whose builder and maker is God; a consolation which our oppressors cannot feel, when fortune, or fate, shall lay its iron hand on them as it has on us. (HC 3:304–5)

4 Notwithstanding that every avenue of escape seemed to be entirely closed, and death stared me in the face, and that my destruction was determined upon, as far as man was concerned, yet, from my first entrance into the camp, I felt an assurance that I, with my brethren and our families, should be delivered. Yes, that still small voice, which has so often whispered consolation to my soul, in the depths of sorrow and distress, bade me be of good cheer, and promised deliverance, which gave me great comfort. And although the heathen raged, and the people imagined vain things, yet the Lord of Hosts, the God of Jacob was my refuge; and when I cried unto Him in the day of trouble, He delivered me; for which I call upon my soul, and all that is within me, to bless and praise His holy name. For although I was "troubled on

---

Consolation

  2 Letter to the Saints in Missouri published in the *Messenger and Advocate*, June 1835.
  3 Letter to the Saints from Liberty Jail, 20–25 March 1839.
  4 Reflections on Missouri persecutions and confinement in Liberty Jail, Quincy, Illinois, 22 April 1839.

every side, yet not distressed; perplexed, but not in despair; persecuted, but not forsaken; cast down, but not destroyed" [see 2 Corinthians 4:8–9]. (HC 3:329)

5   These are the first principles of consolation. How consoling to the mourners when they are called to part with a husband, wife, father, mother, child, or dear relative, to know that, although the earthly tabernacle is laid down and dissolved, they shall rise again to dwell in everlasting burnings in immortal glory, not to sorrow, suffer, or die any more, but they shall be heirs of God and joint heirs with Jesus Christ. (HC 6:306)

Constitution of the United States

1   Stand by the Constitution of your country; observe its principles. (HC 2:455)

2   *The Political Motto of the Church of Latter-day Saints:* The Constitution of our country formed by the Fathers of liberty. Peace and good order in society. Love to God, and good will to man. All good and wholesome laws, virtue and truth above all things, and aristarchy, live for ever! But woe to tyrants, mobs, aristocracy, anarchy, and toryism, and all those who invent or seek out unrighteous and vexatious law suits, under the pretext and color of law, or office, either religious or political. Exalt the standard of Democracy! Down with that of priest-craft, and let all the people say Amen! that the blood of our fathers may not cry from the ground against us. Sacred is the memory of that blood which bought for us our liberty. (HC 3:9)

3   Hence we say, that the Constitution of the United States is a glorious standard; it is founded in the wisdom of God. It is a heavenly

---

Consolation
   5   King Follett Discourse, Nauvoo, 7 April 1844.

Constitution of the United States
   1   Letter to the brethren in Missouri, Kirtland, 25 July 1836.
   2   Far West, Missouri, March 1838. The word *aristarchy* in this entry means "the rule of those who actually *are* the best" (see *BYU Studies* 5 [Spring and Summer 1964]: 192).
   3   Letter to the Saints from Liberty Jail, 20–25 March 1839.

banner; it is to all those who are privileged with the sweets of its liberty, like the cooling shades and refreshing waters of a great rock in a thirsty and weary land. It is like a great tree under whose branches men from every clime can be shielded from the burning rays of the sun. (HC 3:304)

4 Your constitution guarantees to every citizen, even the humblest, the enjoyment of life, liberty, and property. It promises to all, religious freedom, the right to all to worship God beneath their own vine and fig tree, according to the dictates of their conscience. It guarantees to all the citizens of the several states the right to become citizens of any one of the states, and to enjoy all the rights and immunities of the citizens of the state of his adoption. (HC 4:37)

5 *Words of James Burgess:* In the month of May 1843, several miles east of Nauvoo, the Nauvoo Legion was on parade and review, at the close of which Joseph Smith made some remarks upon our condition as a people and upon our future prospects, contrasting our present condition with our past trials and persecutions by the hands of our enemies; also upon the Constitution and government of the United States, stating that the time would come when the Constitution and government would hang by a brittle thread and would be ready to fall into other hands, but this people, the Latter-day Saints, will step forth and save it. . . .

I, James Burgess, was present and testify to the above. (*WJS*, p. 279; standardized)

6 I am the greatest advocate of the Constitution of the United States there is on the earth. In my feelings I am always ready to die for the protection of the weak and oppressed in their just rights. The only fault I find with the Constitution is, it is not broad enough to cover the whole ground.

Although it provides that all men shall enjoy religious freedom, yet it does not provide the manner by which that freedom can be preserved, nor for the punishment of Government officers who refuse to

---

Constitution of the United States

4 Saints' petition to Congress delivered to government officials in Washington, D.C., November 1839.
5 From James Burgess Notebook, LDS Church Archives.
6 Sabbath address, Nauvoo, 15 October 1843.

protect the people in their religious rights, or punish those mobs, states, or communities who interfere with the rights of the people on account of their religion. Its sentiments are good, but it provides no means of enforcing them. It has but this one fault. Under its provision, a man or a people who are able to protect themselves can get along well enough; but those who have the misfortune to be weak or unpopular are left to the merciless rage of popular fury. (HC 6:56–57)

7 Our common country presents to all men the same advantages, the facilities, the same prospects, the same honors, and the same rewards; and without hypocrisy, the Constitution, when it says, "We, the people of the United States, in order to form a more perfect union, establish justice, ensure domestic tranquility, provide for the common defense, promote the general welfare, and secure the blessings of liberty to ourselves and our posterity, do ordain and establish this Constitution for the United States of America," meant just what it said without reference to color or condition, *ad infinitum*.

The aspirations and expectations of a virtuous people, environed with so wise, so liberal, so deep, so broad, and so high a charter of *equal rights* as appears in said Constitution, ought to be treated by those to whom the administration of the laws is entrusted with as much sanctity as the prayers of the Saints are treated in heaven. (HC 6:198)

8 *Words of Brigham Young:* Will the Constitution be destroyed? No: it will be held inviolate by this people; and, as Joseph Smith said, "The time will come when the destiny of the nation will hang upon a single thread. At that critical juncture, this people will step forth and save it from the threatened destruction." (JD 7:15)

9 *Words of Orson Hyde:* It is said that brother Joseph in his lifetime declared that the Elders of this Church should step forth at a particular time when the Constitution should be in danger, and rescue it, and save it. This may be so; but I do not recollect that he said exactly so. I

Constitution of the United States

7 A pamphlet containing the Prophet's political platform, entitled *Views of the Powers and Policy of the Government of the United States*, Nauvoo, 7 February 1844.

8 Address by Brigham Young, Salt Lake City, 4 July 1854.

9 Address by Orson Hyde, Salt Lake City, 3 January 1858.

believe he said something like this—that the time would come when the Constitution and the country would be in danger of an overthrow; and said he, If the Constitution be saved at all, it will be by the Elders of this Church. I believe this is about the language, as nearly as I can recollect it. (*JD* 6:152)

10 *Words of Eliza R. Snow:* I heard the prophet Joseph Smith say if the people rose up and mobbed us and the authorities countenanced it, they would have mobs to their hearts' content. I heard him say that the time would come when this nation would so far depart from its original purity, its glory, and its love for freedom and its protection of civil and religious rights, that the Constitution of our country would hang as it were by a thread. He said, also, that this people, the sons of Zion, would rise up and save the Constitution and bear it off triumphantly. (*Deseret News Weekly*, 19 January 1870)

Contention

1 Elder Boynton observed that long debates were bad. I replied that it was generally the case that too much altercation was indulged in on both sides, and their debates protracted to an unprofitable length. (*HC* 2:294)

2 When we arrived, some of the young Elders were about engaging in a debate on the subject of miracles. The question—"Was it, or was it not, the design of Christ to establish His Gospel by miracles?" After an interesting debate of three hours or more, during which time much talent was displayed, it was decided, by the President of the debate, in the negative, which was a righteous decision.

I discovered in this debate, much warmth displayed, too much zeal for mastery, too much of that enthusiasm that characterizes a

---

Constitution of the United States
   10 Address by Eliza R. Snow, Salt Lake City, 13 January 1870.

Contention
   1 Joseph's feelings concerning the "debates" in council meetings, Kirtland, 29 October 1835.
   2 Counsel given to a few Saints in Father Smith's home, Kirtland, 18 November 1835.

lawyer at the bar, who is determined to defend his cause, right or wrong. I therefore availed myself of this favorable opportunity to drop a few words upon this subject, by way of advice, that they might improve their minds and cultivate their powers of intellect in a proper manner, that they might not incur the displeasure of heaven; that they should handle sacred things very sacredly, and with due deference to the opinions of others, and with an eye single to the glory of God. (HC 2:317–18)

3 The powers of earth and hell seem combined to overthrow us and the Church, by causing a division in the family; and indeed the adversary is bringing into requisition all his subtlety to prevent the Saints from being endowed, by causing a division among the Twelve, also among the Seventy, and bickering and jealousies among the Elders and the official members of the Church; and so the leaven of iniquity ferments and spreads among the members of the Church. (HC 2:352–53)

4 [Do not] contend with others on account of their faith, or systems of religion, but pursue a steady course. This I delivered by way of commandment; and all who observe it not, will pull down persecution upon their heads, while those who do, shall always be filled with the Holy Ghost; this I pronounced as a prophecy, and sealed with hosanna and amen. (HC 2:431)

5 There are many that creep in unawares, and endeavor to sow discord, strife, and animosity in our midst, and by so doing, bring evil upon the Saints. These things we have to bear with, and these things will prevail either to a greater or less extent until "the floor be thoroughly purged," and "the chaff be burnt up." (HC 4:272–73)

6 Attended a council with the Twelve Apostles. Benjamin Winchester being present, complained that he had been neglected and misrepresented by the Elders, and manifested a contentious spirit. I gave him a severe reproof, telling him of his folly and vanity, and

---

Contention
3 Kirtland, 1 January 1836.
4 Solemn assembly in the Kirtland Temple, 30 March 1836.
5 Proclamation of the First Presidency, Nauvoo, 15 January 1841.
6 Meeting of the Council of the Twelve Apostles, Nauvoo, 31 October 1841.

showing him that the principles which he suffered to control him would lead him to destruction. I counseled him to change his course, govern his disposition, and quit his tale-bearing and slandering his brethren. (HC 4:443)

7   It is no use living among hogs without a snout. This biting and de- vouring each other I cannot endure. Away with it. For God's sake, stop it. (HC 5:286)

8   If we get puffed up by thinking that we have much knowledge, we are apt to get a contentious spirit, and correct knowledge is necessary to cast out that spirit.

    The evil of being puffed up with correct (though useless) knowl- edge is not so great as the evil of contention. (HC 5:340)

9   *Words of Mercy R. Thompson:* I have seen him [Joseph Smith] in the lyceum and heard him reprove the brethren for giving way to too much excitement and warmth in debate. (*TK*, p. 120)

Councils
See also CHURCH COUNCILS

1   The way to get along in any important matter is to gather unto yourselves wise men, experienced and aged men, to assist in council in all times of trouble. (HC 5:389)

Contention
  7   Address at the temple site in Nauvoo, 21 February 1843.
  8   General conference address, Nauvoo, 8 April 1843.
  9   Recollection of Mercy R. Thompson, published in the *Juvenile Instructor*, 1 July 1892.

Councils
  1   Sabbath address at Yelrome (Morley's Settlement), Illinois, 14 May 1843.

Counsel

1   I also laid my hands upon the twelve Councilors, and commanded a blessing to rest upon them, that they might have wisdom and power to counsel in righteousness, upon all subjects that might be laid before them. (HC 2:32)

2   Be wise; let prudence dictate all your counsels. (HC 2:455)

3   About January 16, 1838, being destitute of money to pursue my journey, I said to Brother Brigham Young: "You are one of the Twelve who have charge of the kingdom in all the world; I believe I shall throw myself upon you, and look to you for counsel in this case." Brother Young thought I was not earnest, but I told him I was. Brother Brigham then said, "If you will take my counsel it will be that you rest yourself, and be assured you shall have money in plenty to pursue your journey." (HC 3:2)

4   In the multitude of counsel there is safety. (HC 5:106)

5   Up to this day God had given me wisdom to save the people who took counsel. None had ever been killed who abode by my counsel. At Haun's Mill the brethren went contrary to my counsel; if they had not, their lives would have been spared. (HC 5:137)

6   I showed them that it was generally in consequence of the brethren disregarding or disobeying counsel that they became dissatisfied and murmured. (HC 5:181)

Counsel
1   Meeting of the high council, Kirtland, 19 February 1834.
2   Letter to the brethren in Missouri, Kirtland, 25 July 1836.
3   Dublin, Indiana, 16 January 1838, while fleeing Kirtland en route to Missouri.
4   Letter to Wilson Law, Nauvoo, 16 August 1842.
5   Conference address, Nauvoo, 29 August 1842.
6   Instructions to a group of Saints who had newly arrived in Nauvoo, 29 October 1842.

Countenance

1   Great joy and satisfaction continually beamed in the countenances of the School of the Prophets, and the Saints, on account of the things revealed, and our progress in the knowledge of God. (HC 1:334)

2   We all ought to be thankful for the privilege we enjoy this day of meeting so many of the Saints, and for the warmth and brightness of the heavens over our heads; and it truly makes the countenances of this great multitude to look cheerful and gladdens the hearts of all present. (HC 5:327)

3   Handsome men are not apt to be wise and strong-minded men; but the strength of a strong-minded man will generally create coarse features, like the rough, strong bough of the oak. You will always discover in the first glance of a man, in the outlines of his features something of his mind. (HC 5:389)

Covenants

1   I despise a hypocrite or a covenant breaker. (PWJS, p. 246; standardized)

2   And may God enable us to perform our vows and covenants with each other, in all fidelity and righteousness before Him, that our influence may be felt among the nations of the earth, in mighty power, even to rend the kingdoms of darkness asunder, and triumph over priestcraft and spiritual wickedness in high places, and break in pieces all kingdoms that are opposed to the kingdom of Christ, and spread the light and truth of the everlasting Gospel from the rivers to the ends of the earth. (HC 2:375)

Countenance
1   Kirtland, 18 March 1833.
2   General conference address, Nauvoo, 6 April 1843.
3   Sabbath address at Yelrome (Morley's Settlement), Illinois, 14 May 1843.

Covenants
1   Letter to William W. Phelps in Zion, 31 July 1832, written from Hiram, Ohio.
2   Instructions to the Twelve, Kirtland, 16 January 1836.

3 Everlasting covenant was made between three personages before the organization of this earth, and relates to their dispensation of things to men on the earth; these personages, according to Abraham's record, are called God the first, the Creator; God the second, the Redeemer; and God the third, the witness or Testator. (*TPJS*, p. 190)

4 Our covenants here are of no force one with another except made in view of eternity. (*WJS*, p. 208)

Covetousness

1 *Minutes:* [Joseph Smith] said that God had often sealed up the heavens because of covetousness in the Church. (*FWR*, p. 23)

Creation

1 In the translation [referring to Genesis 1:1–2], "without form and void" it should read, "empty and desolate." The word "created" should be formed or organized. (*WJS*, p. 60)

2 In the beginning, the head of the Gods called a council of the Gods; and they came together and concocted {prepared} a plan to create the world and people it. . . .

Now, I ask all who hear me, why the learned men who are preaching salvation, say that God created the heavens and the earth out of

---

Covenants
  3 Nauvoo, 1841. Manuscript history, LDS Church Archives.
  4 Sabbath address, Nauvoo, 21 May 1843, as reported by Franklin D. Richards.

Covetousness
  1 Minutes of a conference held at Orange, Ohio, 25 October 1831.

Creation
  1 Lecture given at the Nauvoo Lyceum, 5 January 1841, as reported by William Clayton. (The lyceum met weekly at different locations in Nauvoo for several months, beginning 5 January 1841.)
  2 King Follett Discourse, Nauvoo, 7 April 1844.

nothing? The reason is, that they are unlearned in the things of God, and have not the gift of the Holy Ghost; they account it blasphemy in any one to contradict their idea. If you tell them that God made the world out of something, they will call you a fool. But I am learned, and know more than all the world put together. The Holy Ghost does, anyhow, and he is within me, and comprehends more than all the world; and I will associate myself with him.

You ask the learned doctors why they say the world was made out of nothing, and they will answer, "Doesn't the Bible say He *created* the world?" And they infer, from the word create, that it must have been made out of nothing. Now, the word create came from the word *baurau*, which does not mean to create out of nothing; it means to organize; the same as a man would organize materials and build a ship. Hence we infer that God had materials to organize the world out of chaos— chaotic matter, which is element, and in which dwells all the glory. Element had an existence from the time He had. The pure principles of element are principles which can never be destroyed; they may be organized and re-organized, but not destroyed. They had no beginning and can have no end. (HC 6:308–9)

3   I want to analyze the word *Berosheit* [in Genesis 1:1]. *Rosh,* the head; *Sheit,* a grammatical termination. The *Baith* was not originally put there when the inspired man wrote it, but it has been since added by an old Jew. *Baurau* signifies to bring forth; *Eloheim* is from the word *Eloi,* God, in the singular number; and by adding the word *heim,* it renders it Gods. It read first, "In the beginning the head of the Gods brought forth the Gods," or, as others have translated it, "The head of the Gods called the Gods together." . . .

The head God organized the heavens and the earth. I defy all the world to refute me. In the beginning the heads of the Gods organized the heavens and the earth. (HC 6:475)

Creation
3   Sabbath address, Nauvoo, 16 June 1844.

Damnation

1 "Will everybody be damned, but Mormons?"

Yes, and a great portion of them, unless they repent, and work righteousness. (HC 3:28)

2 God had decreed that all who will not obey His voice shall not escape the damnation of hell. What is the damnation of hell? To go with that society who have not obeyed His commands. . . .

. . . I know that all men will be damned if they do not come in the way which He hath opened, and this is the way marked out by the word of the Lord. (HC 4:554–55)

3 What will become of the world, or the various professors of religion who do not believe in revelation and the oracles of God as continued to His Church in all ages of the world, when He has a people on earth? I tell you, in the name of Jesus Christ, they will be damned; and when you get into the eternal world, you will find it will be so, they cannot escape the damnation of hell. (HC 5:257)

4 Compare this principle [the possibility of having one's calling and election made sure] once with Christendom at the present day, and where are they, with all their boasted religion, piety and sacredness while at the same time they are crying out against prophets, apostles, angels, revelations, prophesying and visions &c. Why, they are just ripening for the damnation of hell. They will be damned, for they reject the most glorious principle of the Gospel of Jesus Christ and treat with disdain and trample under foot the key that unlocks the heavens and puts in our possession the glories of the celestial world. Yes, I say, such will be damned, with all their professed godliness. (HC 5:389)

5 All spirits who have not obeyed the Gospel in the flesh must either obey it in the spirit or be damned. (HC 6:312–13)

Damnation
1 Answers to questions frequently asked the Prophet, Far West, 8 May 1838.
2 Sabbath address, Nauvoo, 20 March 1842.
3 Sabbath address, Nauvoo, 22 January 1843.
4 Sabbath address at Yelrome (Morley's Settlement), Illinois, 14 May 1843.
5 King Follett Discourse, Nauvoo, 7 April 1844.

6   Hear it, all ye ends of the earth—all ye priests, all ye sinners, and all men. Repent! Repent! Obey the gospel. Turn to God; for your religion won't save you, and you will be damned. (HC 6:317)

7   I believe all that God ever revealed, and I never hear of a man being damned for believing too much; but they are damned for unbelief. (HC 6:477)

Daniel, Prophecies and Visions of

1   *Words of Henry William Bigler:* The first Sunday after I reached Far West, I went to meeting with the hopes of hearing the Prophet. How disappointed I was when he called to the stand a beardless boy (Erastus Snow). But I soon found there was preach in him. When he finished, the Prophet got up and complimented the young man, but said: "I will correct the idea in regard to the little stone rolling forth, as foretold in Daniel, chapter 2. This is not so. It is stationary, like a grind stone, and revolves. (He made a motion with his hands showing how it turned.) When the Elders go abroad to preach the gospel, and the people become believers in the Book of Mormon and are baptized, they are added to the little stone. Thus, they are gathered around it so that it grows larger and larger until it begins to pinch the toes of the image, and finally breaks it into pieces to be carried away like the chaff of a summer's threshing, while the stone will keep growing until its fills the whole earth." (TK, p. 100)

2   When God made use of the figure of a beast in visions to the prophets He did it to represent those kingdoms which had degenerated and become corrupt, savage and beast-like in their dispositions, even the degenerate kingdoms of the wicked world; but He never made use of the figure of a beast nor any of the brute kind to represent His kingdom.

Damnation
  6   King Follett Discourse, Nauvoo, 7 April 1844.
  7   Sabbath address, Nauvoo, 16 June 1844.

Daniel, Prophecies and Visions of
  1   "Life Sketch of Henry William Bigler," LDS Church Archives.
  2   General conference address, Nauvoo, 8 April 1843.

Daniel says (ch. 7, v. 16) when he saw the vision of the four beasts, "I came near unto one of them that stood by, and asked him the truth of all this," the angel interpreted the vision to Daniel; but we find, by the interpretation that the figures of beasts had no allusion to the kingdom of God. You there see that the beasts are spoken of to represent the kingdoms of the world, the inhabitants whereof were beastly and abominable characters; they were murderers, corrupt, carnivorous, and brutal in their dispositions. The lion, the bear, the leopard, and the ten-horned beast represented the kingdoms of the world, says Daniel; for I refer to the prophets to qualify my observations which I make, so that the young elders who know so much, may not rise up like a flock of hornets and sting me. I want to keep out of such a wasp-nest. . . .

. . . What John saw and speaks of were things which he saw in heaven; those which Daniel saw were on and pertaining to the earth.

I am now going to take exceptions to the present translation of the Bible in relation to these matters. Our latitude and longitude can be determined in the original Hebrew with far greater accuracy than in the English version. There is a grand distinction between the actual meaning of the prophets and the present translation. The prophets do not declare that they saw a beast or beasts, but that they saw the *image* or *figure* of a beast. Daniel did not see an actual bear or a lion, but the images or figures of those beasts. The translation should have been rendered "image" instead of "beast," in every instance where beasts are mentioned by the prophets. But John saw the actual beast in heaven, showing to John that beasts did actually exist there, and not to represent figures of things on the earth. When the prophets speak of seeing beasts in their visions, they mean that they saw the images, they being types to represent certain things. At the same time they received the interpretation as to what those images or types were designed to represent. (HC 5:341, 342–43)

Darkness

1 Consider for a moment, brethren, the fulfillment of the words of the prophet; for we behold that darkness covers the earth, and gross

---

Darkness

1 Letter to the brethren scattered from Zion, Kirtland, 22 January 1834.

darkness the minds of the inhabitants thereof—that crimes of every description are increasing among men—vices of great enormity are practiced—the rising generation growing up in the fullness of pride and arrogance—the aged losing every sense of conviction, and seemingly banishing every thought of a day of retribution—intemperance, immorality, extravagance, pride, blindness of heart, idolatry, the loss of natural affection; the love of this world, and indifference toward the things of eternity increasing among those who profess a belief in the religion of heaven, and infidelity spreading itself in consequence of the same—men giving themselves up to commit acts of the foulest kind, and deeds of the blackest dye, blaspheming, defrauding, blasting the reputation of neighbors, stealing, robbing, murdering; advocating error and opposing the truth, forsaking the covenant of heaven, and denying the faith of Jesus—and in the midst of all this, the day of the Lord fast approaching when none except those who have won the wedding garment will be permitted to eat and drink in the presence of the Bridegroom, the Prince of Peace! (HC 2:5)

2   The condemnation which rested upon the multitude that received not His [Jesus'] saying, was because they were not willing to see with their eyes, and hear with their ears; not because they could not, and were not privileged to see and hear, but because their hearts were full of iniquity and abominations; "as your fathers did, so do ye." The prophet [Isaiah], foreseeing that they would thus harden their hearts, plainly declared it; and herein is the condemnation of the world; that light hath come into the world, and men choose darkness rather than light, because their deeds are evil. This is so plainly taught by the Savior that a wayfaring man need not mistake it. (HC 2:266)

3   Darkness prevails at this time as it did at the time Jesus Christ was about to be crucified. The powers of darkness strove to obscure the glorious Sun of righteousness, that began to dawn upon the world. (HC 2:308)

4   But behold the words of the Savior: "If the light which is in you become darkness, behold how great is that darkness." Look at the dissenters. (HC 3:228)

Darkness
  2   Letter to the elders of the Church, Kirtland, 1 September 1835.
  3   Instructions to the Twelve, Kirtland, 12 November 1835.
  4   Letter to the Church from Liberty Jail, 16 December 1838.

5 Mr. Olney has also been tried by the High Council and disfellowshipped, because he would not have his writings tested by the word of God; evidently proving that he loves darkness rather than light, because his deeds are evil. (*HC* 4:581)

6 Knowledge does away with darkness, suspense and doubt; for these cannot exist where knowledge is. . . .
 In knowledge there is power. (*HC* 5:340)

7 Concerning Brother James Adams, it should appear strange that so good and so great a man was hated. The deceased ought never to have had an enemy. But so it was. Wherever light shone, it stirred up darkness. Truth and error, good and evil cannot be reconciled. Judge Adams had some enemies, but such a man ought not to have had one. (*HC* 6:51)

David

1 The time of redemption here [Acts 3:19–20] had reference to the time when Christ should come; then, and not till then, would their sins be blotted out. Why? Because they were murderers, and no murderer hath eternal life. Even David must wait for those times of refreshing, before he can come forth and his sins be blotted out. For Peter, speaking of him says, "David hath not yet ascended into heaven, for his sepulchre is with us to this day." His remains were then in the tomb. Now, we read that many bodies of the Saints arose at Christ's resurrection, probably all the Saints, but it seems that David did not. Why? Because he had been a murderer. If the ministers of religion had a proper understanding of the doctrine of eternal judgment, they would not be found attending the man who forfeited his life to the injured laws of his country, by shedding innocent blood; for such

---

Darkness
 5 Editorial in the *Times and Seasons*, 1 April 1842. Oliver Olney claimed to be a prophet in Nauvoo.
 6 General conference address, Nauvoo, 8 April 1843.
 7 Remarks upon the death of James Adams, Nauvoo, 9 October 1843.

David
 1 Sabbath address, Nauvoo, 16 May 1841.

characters cannot be forgiven, until they have paid the last farthing. The prayers of all the ministers in the world can never close the gates of hell against a murderer. (HC 4:359)

2   A murderer, for instance, one that sheds innocent blood, cannot have forgiveness. David sought repentance at the hand of God carefully with tears, for the murder of Uriah; but he could only get it through hell: he got a promise that his soul should not be left in hell.

Although David was a king, he never did obtain the spirit and power of Elijah and the fullness of the Priesthood; and the Priesthood that he received, and the throne and kingdom of David is to be taken from him and given to another by the name of David in the last days, raised up out of his lineage. (HC 6:253)

Dead, Salvation of the
See SALVATION OF THE DEAD

Death

1   With respect to the deaths in Zion, we feel to mourn with those that mourn, but remember that the God of all the earth will do right. (HC 1:341)

2   About nine o'clock, while I was riding in a wagon with Brother Hyrum, Ezra Thayer and George A. Smith, we came into a piece of thick woods of recent growth, where I told them that I felt much depressed in spirit and lonesome, and that there had been a great deal of bloodshed in that place, remarking that whenever a man of God is in a place where many have been killed, he will feel lonesome and unpleasant, and his spirits will sink.

In about forty rods from where I made this observation we came

David
   2   Sabbath address, Nauvoo, 10 March 1844.

Death
   1   Letter to the brethren in Zion, Kirtland, 21 April 1833.
   2   Events of Zion's Camp while near Dayton, Ohio, 16 May 1834.

through the woods, and saw a large farm, and there near the road on our left, was a mound sixty feet high, containing human bones. This mound was covered with apple trees, and surrounded with oat fields, the ground being level for some distance around. (*HC* 2:66)

3   *Words of George A. Smith:* When several men died, Joseph said to me, "If your work had been finished, you would have had to tumble into the ground without a coffin."

I told him it did seem as if it would have been better for me to have died than my Cousin Jesse, as he had a good education, and many other qualifications to benefit the Church which I did not possess.

The Prophet replied, "You do not know the mind of the Lord in these things." (*TK*, p. 48)

4   My brother Hyrum's wife, Jerusha Barden Smith, died on the 13th of October while I was at Terre Haute, and her husband at Far West. She left five small children and numerous relatives to mourn her loss; her demise was severely felt by all. She said to one of her tender offspring when on her dying bed, "Tell your father when he comes that the Lord has taken your mother home and left you for him to take care of." She died in full assurance of a part in the first resurrection. (*HC* 2:519)

5   This day President Brigham Young's father, John Young, Sen., died at Quincy, Adams County, Illinois. He was in his seventy-seventh year, and a soldier of the Revolution. He was also a firm believer in the everlasting Gospel of Jesus Christ; and fell asleep under the influence of that faith that buoyed up his soul, in the pangs of death, to a glorious hope of immortality; fully testifying to all, that the religion he enjoyed in life was able to support him in death. He was driven from Missouri with the Saints in the latter part of last year. He died a martyr to the religion of Jesus, for his death was caused by his sufferings in the cruel persecution. (*HC* 4:14–15)

Death

3   Reminiscence of George A. Smith regarding deaths from cholera on the march of Zion's Camp, early summer 1834, contained in *Family of George A. Smith.*

4   Kirtland, 13 October 1837.

5   Nauvoo, 12 October 1839.

6   As to the growth of our place, it is very rapid, and it would be more so, were it not for sickness and death. There have been many deaths, which leaves a melancholy reflection, but we cannot help it. When God speaks from the heavens to call us hence, we must submit to His mandates. (HC 4:432)

7   The only difference between the old and young dying is, one lives longer in heaven and eternal light and glory than the other, and is freed a little sooner from this miserable, wicked world. Notwithstanding all this glory, we for a moment lose sight of it, and mourn the loss, but we do not mourn as those without hope. . . .

. . . It mattereth not whether we live long or short on the earth after we come to a knowledge of these principles [the principles of the gospel] and obey them unto the end. (HC 4:554, 555)

8   *Report of Wilford Woodruff:* President Joseph Smith spoke upon the occasion with much feeling and interest. Among his remarks he said, "It is a very solemn and awful time. I never felt more solemn; it calls to mind the death of my oldest brother, Alvin, who died in New York, and my youngest brother, Don Carlos Smith, who died in Nauvoo. It has been hard for me to live on earth and see these young men upon whom we have leaned for support and comfort taken from us in the midst of their youth. Yes, it has been hard to be reconciled to these things. I have sometimes thought that I should have felt more reconciled to have been called away myself if it had been the will of God; yet I know we ought to be still and know it is of God, and be reconciled to His will; all is right. It will be but a short time before we shall all in like manner be called: it may be the case with me as well as you. Some have supposed that Brother Joseph could not die; but this is a mistake: it is true there have been times when I have had the promise of my life to accomplish such and such things, but, having now accomplished those things, I have not at present any lease of my life, I am as liable to die as other men." (HC 4:587)

9   More painful to me are the thoughts of annihilation than death. If

Death
   6   Letter to Smith Tuttle, Nauvoo, 9 October 1841.
   7   Sabbath address, Nauvoo, 20 March 1842.
   8   Remarks at the funeral of Ephraim Marks, Nauvoo, 9 April 1842.
   9   Remarks upon the death of Lorenzo D. Barnes, Nauvoo, 16 April 1843.

I have no expectation of seeing my father, mother, brothers, sisters and friends again, my heart would burst in a moment, and I should go down to my grave. . . .

. . . This [the death of Lorenzo Barnes] has been a warning voice to us all to be sober and diligent and lay aside mirth, vanity and folly, and to be prepared to die tomorrow. (HC 5:362, 363)

10 When men are prepared, they are better off to go hence. Brother Adams has gone to open up a more effectual door for the dead. (HC 6:52)

11 These are the first principles of consolation. How consoling to the mourners when they are called to part with a husband, wife, father, mother, child, or dear relative, to know that, although the earthly tabernacle is laid down and dissolved, they shall rise again to dwell in everlasting burnings in immortal glory, not to sorrow, suffer, or die any more, but they shall be heirs of God and joint heirs with Jesus Christ. . . .

. . . When I talk to these mourners, what have they lost? Their relatives and friends are only separated from their bodies for a short season: their spirits which existed with God have left the tabernacle of clay only for a little moment, as it were; and they now exist in a place where they converse together the same as we do on the earth. (HC 6:306, 311)

Death of Infants

1 I have meditated upon the subject, and asked the question, why it is that infants, innocent children, are taken away from us, especially those that seem to be the most intelligent and interesting. . . . The Lord takes many away, even in infancy, that they may escape the envy of man, and the sorrows and evils of this present world; they were too pure, too lovely, to live on earth; therefore, if rightly considered, instead of mourning we have reason to rejoice as they are delivered from evil, and we shall soon have them again. (HC 4:553)

Death
10 Remarks upon the death of James Adams, Nauvoo, 9 October 1843.
11 King Follett Discourse, Nauvoo, 7 April 1844.

Death of Infants
1 Sabbath address, Nauvoo, 20 March 1842.

Debt

1   And again, those in debt, should in all cases pay their debts. (HC 1:339)

2   We . . . hope that the brethren who feel interested in the cause of truth, and desire to see the work of the gathering of Israel roll forth with power, will aid us in liquidating the debts which are now owing, so that the inheritances may be secured to the Church, and which eventually will be of great value.

The good spirit which is manifested on this occasion, the desire to do good, and the zeal for the honor of the Church, inspires us with confidence that we shall not appeal in vain, but that funds will be forthcoming on this occasion, sufficient to meet the necessities of the case. (HC 4:214)

Deceit

1   The devil has great power to deceive; he will so transform things as to make one gape at those who are doing the will of God. (HC 4:605)

2   In relation to the kingdom of God, the devil always sets up his kingdom at the very same time in opposition to God. (HC 6:364)

Debt
1   Letter to one of Jared Carter's brothers, written at the request of Jared Carter, Kirtland, 13 April 1833.
2   Report of the First Presidency at general conference, Nauvoo, 5 October 1840.

Deceit
1   Remarks to the Relief Society, Nauvoo, 28 April 1842.
2   Sabbath address, Nauvoo, 12 May 1844.

Decision

1   Though the soul be tried, the heart faint, and the hands hang down, we must not retrace our steps; there must be decision of character, aside from sympathy. (HC 4:570)

Decrees of God

1   God has made certain decrees which are fixed and immovable; for instance,—God set the sun, the moon, and the stars in the heavens, and gave them their laws, conditions and bounds, which they cannot pass, except by His commandments; they all move in perfect harmony in their sphere and order, and are as lights, wonders and signs unto us. The sea also has its bounds which it cannot pass. God has set many signs on the earth, as well as in the heavens; for instance, the oak of the forest, the fruit of the tree, the herb of the field—all bear a sign that seed hath been planted there; for it is a decree of the Lord that every tree, plant, and herb bearing seed should bring forth of its kind, and cannot come forth after any other law or principle. Upon the same principle do I contend that baptism is a sign ordained of God, for the believer in Christ to take upon himself in order to enter into the kingdom of God, "for except ye are born of water and of the Spirit ye cannot enter into the kingdom of God," said the Savior. It is a sign and a commandment which God has set for man to enter into His kingdom. Those who seek to enter in any other way will seek in vain; for God will not receive them, neither will the angels acknowledge their works as accepted, for they have not obeyed the ordinances, nor attended to the signs which God ordained for the salvation of man, to prepare him for, and give him a title to, a celestial glory; and God had decreed that all who will not obey His voice shall not escape the damnation of hell. What is the damnation of hell? To go with that society who have not obeyed His commands. (HC 4:554–55)

Decision
   1   Remarks to the Relief Society, Nauvoo, 30 March 1842.

Decrees of God
   1   Sabbath address, Nauvoo, 20 March 1842.

Defense

See SELF-DEFENSE

Degrees of Glory

1   Nothing could be more pleasing to the Saints upon the order of the kingdom of the Lord, than the light which burst upon the world through the foregoing vision [D&C 76]. Every law, every commandment, every promise, every truth, and every point touching the destiny of man, from Genesis to Revelation, where the purity of the scriptures remains unsullied by the folly of men, go to show the perfection of the theory {of different degrees of glory in the future life} and witnesses the fact that that document is a transcript from the records of the eternal world. The sublimity of the ideas; the purity of the language; the scope for action; the continued duration for completion, in order that the heirs of salvation may confess the Lord and bow the knee; the rewards for faithfulness, and the punishments for sins, are so much beyond the narrow-mindedness of men, that every honest man is constrained to exclaim: "*It came from God.*" (HC 1:252–53)

2   FROM W. W. PHELPS TO JOSEPH SMITH: THE PROPHET.
        VADE MECUM, (TRANSLATED,) GO WITH ME.

> Go with me, will you go to the saints that have died,—
> To the next, better world, where the righteous reside;
> Where the angels and spirits in harmony be
> In the joys of a vast paradise? Go with me.
>
> Go with me where the truth and the virtues prevail;
> Where the union is one, and the years never fail;
> Not a heart can conceive, nor a nat'ral eye see
> What the Lord has prepar'd for the just. Go with me.

Degrees of Glory

1   The Prophet's view of the vision of the glories (D&C 76), Hiram, Ohio, 16 February 1832.

2   A short poem by William W. Phelps addressed to Joseph Smith, followed by a much longer poetic response by the Prophet, published in the *Times and Seasons*, 1 February 1843. The Prophet's piece is a poetic rephrasing of D&C 76, with some interpretive commentary.

Go with me where there is no destruction or war;
Neither tyrants, or sland'rers, or nations ajar;
Where the system is perfect, and happiness free,
And the life is eternal with God. Go with me.

Go with me, will you go to the mansions above,
Where the bliss, and the knowledge, the light, and the love,
And the glory of God do eternally be?—
Death, the wages of sin, is not there. Go with me.

Nauvoo, January, 1843.

THE ANSWER.
TO W. W. PHELPS, ESQ.
A Vision.

1. I will go, I will go, to the home of the Saints,
Where the virtue's the value, and life the reward;
But before I return to my former estate
I must fulfil the mission I had from the Lord.

2. Wherefore, hear, O ye heavens, and give ear O ye earth;
   And rejoice ye inhabitants truly again;
For the Lord he is God, and his life never ends,
   And besides him there ne'er was a Saviour of men.

3. His ways are a wonder; his wisdom is great;
   The extent of his doings, there's none can unveil;
His purposes fail not; from age unto age
   He still is the same, and his years never fail.

4. His throne is the heavens, his life time is all
   Of eternity *now*, and eternity *then*;
His union is power, and none stays his hand,—
   The Alpha, Omega, for ever: Amen.

5. For thus saith the Lord, in the spirit of truth,
   I am merciful, gracious, and good unto those
That fear me, and live for the life that's to come;
   My delight is to honor the saints with repose;

6. That serve me in righteousness true to the end;
   Eternal's their glory, and great their reward;

I'll surely reveal all my myst'ries to them,—
    The great hidden myst'ries in my kingdom stor'd—

7.   From the council in Kolob, to time on the earth.
    And for ages to come unto them I will show
My pleasure & will, what my kingdom will do:
    Eternity's wonders they truly shall know.

8.   Great things of the future I'll show unto them,
    Yea, things of the vast generations to rise;
For their wisdom and glory shall be very great,
    And their pure understanding extend to the skies:

9.   And before them the wisdom of wise men shall cease,
    And the nice understanding of prudent ones fail!
For the light of my spirit shall light mine elect,
    And the truth is so mighty 't will ever prevail.

10.   And the secrets and plans of my will I'll reveal;
    The sanctified pleasures when earth is renew'd,
What the eye hath not seen, nor the earth hath yet heard;
    Nor the heart of the natural man ever hath view'd.

11. I, Joseph, the prophet, in spirit beheld,
    And the eyes of the inner man truly did see
Eternity sketch'd in a vision from God,
    Of what was, and now is, and yet is to be.

12.   Those things which the Father ordained of old,
    Before the world was, or a system had run,—
Through Jesus the Maker and Savior of all;
    The only begotten, (Messiah) his son.

13.   Of whom I bear record, as all prophets have,
    And the record I bear is the fulness,—yea even
The truth of the gospel of Jesus—*the Christ*,
    With whom I convers'd, in the vision of heav'n.

14.   For while in the act of translating his word,
    Which the Lord in his grace had appointed to me,
I came to the gospel recorded by John,
    Chapter fifth and the twenty ninth verse, which you'll see.

    Which was given as follows:

"Speaking of the resurrection of the dead,—

"Concerning those who shall hear the voice of the son of man—
"And shall come forth:—
"They who have done good in the resurrection of the just.
"And they who have done evil in the resurrection of the unjust."

15. I marvel'd at these resurrections, indeed!
   For it came unto me by the spirit direct:—
And while I did meditate what it all meant,
   The Lord touch'd the eyes of my own intellect:—

16. Hosanna forever! they open'd anon,
   And the glory of God shone around where I was;
And there was the Son, at the Father's right hand,
   In a fulness of glory, and holy applause.

17. I beheld round the throne, holy angels and hosts,
   And sanctified beings from worlds that have been,
In holiness worshipping God and the Lamb,
   Forever and ever, amen and amen!

18. And now after all of the proofs made of him,
   By witnesses truly, by whom he was known,
This is mine, last of all, that he lives; yea he lives!
   And sits at the right hand of God, on his throne.

19. And I heard a great voice, bearing record from heav'n,
   He's the Saviour, and only begotten of God—
By him, of him, and through him, the worlds were all made,
   Even all that career in the heavens so broad,

20. Whose inhabitants, too, from the first to the last,
   Are sav'd by the very same Saviour of ours;
And, of course, are begotten God's daughters and sons,
   By the very same truths, and the very same pow'rs.

21. And I saw and bear record of warfare in heav'n;
   For an angel of light, in authority great,
Rebell'd against Jesus, and sought for his pow'r,
   But was thrust down to woe from his Godified state.

22. And the heavens all wept, and the tears drop'd like dew,
   That Lucifer, son of the morning had fell!
Yea, is fallen! is fall'n, and become, Oh, alas!
   The sons of Perdition; the devil of hell!

23. And while I was yet in the spirit of truth,
    The commandment was: write ye the vision all out;
For Satan, old serpent, the devil's for war,—
    And yet will encompass the saints round about.

24. And I saw, too, the suff'ring and mis'ry of those,
    (Overcome by the devil, in warfare and fight,)
In hell-fire, and vengeance, the doom of the damn'd;
    For the Lord said, the vision is further: so write.

25. For thus saith the Lord, now concerning all those
    Who know of my power and partake of the same;
And suffer themselves, that they be overcome
    By the power of Satan; despising my name:—

26. Defying my power, and denying the truth;—
    They are they—of the world, or of men, most forlorn,
The Sons of Perdition, of whom, ah! I say,
    'T were better for them had they never been born!

27. They're vessels of wrath, and dishonor to God,
    Doom'd to suffer his wrath, in the regions of woe,
Through the terrific night of eternity's round,
    With the devil and all of his angels below:

28. Of whom it is said, no forgiveness is giv'n,
    In this world, alas! nor the world that's to come;
For they have denied the spirit of God,
    After having receiv'd it: and mis'ry's their doom.

29. And denying the only begotten of God,—
    And crucify him to themselves, as they do,
And openly put him to shame in their flesh,
    By gospel they cannot repentance renew.

30. They are they, who must go to the great lake of fire,
    Which burneth with brimstone, yet never consumes,
And dwell with the devil, and angels of his,
    While eternity goes and eternity comes.

31. They are they, who must groan through the great second death,
    And are not redeemed in the time of the Lord;
While all the rest are, through the triumph of Christ,
    Made partakers of grace, by the power of his word.

32. The myst'ry of Godliness truly is great;—
    The past, and the present, and what is to be;
And this is the gospel—glad tidings to all,
    Which the voice from the heavens bore record to me:

33. That he came to the world in the middle of time,
    To lay down his life for his friends and his foes,
And bear away sin as a mission of love;
    And sanctify earth for a blessed repose.

34. 'Tis decreed, that he'll save all the work of his hands,
    And sanctify them by his own precious blood;
And purify earth for the Sabbath of rest,
    By the agent of fire, as it was by the flood.

35. The Savior will save all his Father did give,
    Even all that he gave in the regions abroad,
Save the Sons of Perdition: They're lost; ever lost,
    And can never return to the presence of God.

36. They are they, who must reign with the devil in hell,
    In eternity now, and eternity then,
Where the worm dieth not, and the fire is not quench'd;—
    And the punishment still, is eternal. Amen.

37. And which is the torment apostates receive,
    But the end, or the place where the torment began,
Save to them who are made to partake of the same,
    Was never, nor will be, revealed unto man.

38. Yet God shows by vision a glimpse of their fate,
    And straightway he closes the scene that was shown:
So the width, or the depth, or the misery thereof,
    Save to those that partake, is forever unknown.

39. And while I was pondering, the vision was closed;
    And the voice said to me, write the vision: for lo!
'Tis the end of the scene of the sufferings of those,
    Who remain filthy still in their anguish and woe.

40. And again I bear record of heavenly things,
    Where virtue's the value, above all that's pric'd—
Of the truth of the gospel concerning the just,
    That rise in the first resurrection of Christ.

41. Who receiv'd and believ'd, and repented likewise,
     And then were baptis'd, as a man always was,
Who ask'd and receiv'd a remission of sin,
     And honored the kingdom by keeping its laws.

42. Being buried in water, as Jesus had been,
     And keeping the whole of his holy commands,
They received the gift of the spirit of truth,
     By the ordinance truly of laying on hands.

43. For these overcome, by their faith and their works,
     Being tried in their life-time, as purified gold,
And seal'd by the spirit of promise, to life,
     By men called of God, as was Aaron of old.

44. They are they, of the church of the first born of God,—
     And unto whose hands he committeth all things;
For they hold the keys of the kingdom of heav'n,
     And reign with the Savior, as priests, and as kings.

45. They're priests of the order of Melchisedek,
     Like Jesus, (from whom is this highest reward,)
Receiving a fulness of glory and light;
     As written: They're Gods; even sons of the Lord.

46. So all things are theirs; yea, of life, or of death;
     Yea, whether things now, or to come, all are theirs,
And they are the Savior's, and he is the Lord's,
     Having overcome all, as eternity's heirs.

47. 'Tis wisdom that man never glory in man,
     But give God the glory for all that he hath;
For the righteous will walk in the presence of God,
     While the wicked are trod under foot in his wrath.

48. Yea, the righteous shall dwell in the presence of God,
     And of Jesus, forever, from earth's second birth—
For when he comes down in the splendor of heav'n,
     All these he'll bring with him, to reign on the earth.

49. These are they that arise in their bodies of flesh,
     When the trump of the first resurrection shall sound;
These are they that come up to Mount Zion, in life,
     Where the blessings and gifts of the spirit abound.

50. These are they that have come to the heavenly place;
    To the numberless courses of angels above:
To the city of God; e'en the holiest of all,
    And the home of the blessed, the fountain of love:

51. To the church of old Enoch, and of the first born:
    And gen'ral assembly of ancient renown'd,
Whose names are all kept in the archives of heav'n,
    As chosen and faithful, and fit to be crown'd.

52. These are they that are perfect through Jesus' own blood,
    Whose bodies celestial are mention'd by Paul,
Where the sun is the typical glory thereof,
    And God, and his Christ, are the true judge of all.

53. Again I beheld the terrestrial world,
    In the order and glory of Jesus, go on;
'Twas not as the church of the first born of God,
    But shone in its place, as the moon to the sun.

54. Behold, these are they that have died without law;
    The heathen of ages that never had hope,
And those of the region and shadow of death,
    The spirits in prison, that light has brought up.

55. To spirits in prison the Savior once preach'd,
    And taught them the gospel, with powers afresh;
And then were the living baptiz'd for their dead,
    That they might be judg'd as if men in the flesh.

56. These are they that are hon'rable men of the earth;
    Who were blinded and dup'd by the cunning of men:
They receiv'd not the truth of the Savior at first;
    But did, when they heard it in prison, again.

57. Not valiant for truth, they obtain'd not the crown,
    But are of that glory that's typ'd by the moon:
They are they, that come into the presence of Christ,
    But not to the fulness of God, on his throne.

58. Again I beheld the telestial, as third,
    The lesser, or starry world, next in its place,
For the leaven must leaven three measures of meal,
    And every knee bow that is subject to grace.

59. These are they that receiv'd not the gospel of Christ,
    Or evidence, either, that he ever was;
As the stars are all diff'rent in glory and light,
    So differs the glory of these by the laws.

60. These are they that deny not the spirit of God,
    But are thrust down to hell, with the devil, for sins,
As hypocrites, liars, whoremongers, and thieves,
    And stay 'till the last resurrection begins.

61. 'Till the Lamb shall have finish'd the work he begun;
    Shall have trodden the wine press, in fury alone,
And overcome all by the pow'r of his might:
    He conquers to conquer, and save all his own.

62. These are they that receive not a fulness of light,
    From Christ, in eternity's world, where they are,
The terrestrial sends them the Comforter, though;
    And minist'ring angels, to happify there.

63. And so the telestial is minister'd to,
    By ministers from the terrestrial one,
As terrestrial is, from the celestial throne;
    And the great, greater, greatest, seem's stars, moon, and sun.

64. And thus I beheld, in the vision of heav'n,
    The telestial glory, dominion and bliss,
Surpassing the great understanding of men,—
    Unknown, save reveal'd, in a world vain as this.

65. And lo, I beheld the terrestrial, too,
    Which excels the telestial in glory and light,
In splendor, and knowledge, and wisdom, and joy,
    In blessings, and graces, dominion and might.

66. I beheld the celestial, in glory sublime;
    Which is the most excellent kingdom that is,—
Where God, e'en the Father, in harmony reigns;
    Almighty, supreme, and eternal, in bliss.

67. Where the church of the first born in union reside,
    And they see as they're seen, and they know as they're known;
Being equal in power, dominion and might,
    With a fulness of glory and grace, round his throne.

68. The glory celestial is one like the sun;
    The glory terrestr'al is one like the moon;
The glory telestial is one like the stars,
    And all harmonize like the parts of a tune.

69. As the stars are all different in lustre and size,
    So the telestial region, is mingled in bliss;
From least unto greatest, and greatest to least,
    The reward is exactly as promis'd in this.

70. These are they that came out for Apollos and Paul;
    For Cephas and Jesus, in all kinds of hope;
For Enoch and Moses, and Peter, and John;
    For Luther and Calvin, and even the Pope.

71. For they never received the gospel of Christ,
    Nor the prophetic spirit that came from the Lord;
Nor the covenant neither, which Jacob once had;
    They went their own way, and they have their reward.

72. By the order of God, last of all, these are they,
    That will not be gather'd with saints here below,
To be caught up to Jesus, and meet in the cloud:—
    In darkness they worshipp'd; to darkness they go.

73. These are they that are sinful, the wicked at large,
    That glutted their passion by meanness or worth;
All liars, adulterers, sorc'rers, and proud;
    And suffer, as promis'd, God's wrath on the earth.

74. These are they that must suffer the vengeance of hell,
    'Till Christ shall have trodden all enemies down,
And perfected his work, in the fulness of times:
    And is crown'd on his throne with his glorious crown.

75. The vast multitude of the telestial world—
    As the stars of the skies, or the sands of the sea;—
The voice of Jehovah echo'd far and wide,
    Ev'ry tongue shall confess, and they all bow the knee.

76. Ev'ry man shall be judg'd by the works of his life,
    And receive a reward in the mansions prepar'd;
For his judgments are just, and his works never end,
    As his prophets and servants have always declar'd.

77. But the great things of God, which he show'd unto me,
 Unlawful to utter, I dare not declare;
They surpass all the wisdom and greatness of men,
 And only are seen, as has Paul, where they are.

78. I will go, I will go, while the secret of life,
 Is blooming in heaven, and blasting in hell;
Is leaving on earth, and a budding in space:—
 I will go, I will go, with you, brother, farewell.

JOSEPH SMITH.
Nauvoo, Feb. 1843. (*T&S* 4:81–85)

3   Paul ascended into the third heavens, and he could understand the three principal rounds of Jacob's ladder—the telestial, the terrestrial, and the celestial glories or kingdoms, where Paul saw and heard things which were not lawful for him to utter. I could explain a hundred fold more than I ever have of the glories of the kingdoms manifested to me in the vision, were I permitted, and were the people prepared to receive them.

The Lord deals with this people as a tender parent with a child, communicating light and intelligence and the knowledge of his ways as they can bear it. (*HC* 5:402)

4   The great misery of departed spirits in the world of spirits, where they go after death, is to know that they come short of the glory that others enjoy and that they might have enjoyed themselves, and they are their own accusers. "But," says one, "I believe in one universal heaven and hell, where all go, and are all alike, and equally miserable or equally happy."

What! where all are huddled together—the honorable, virtuous, and murderers, and whoremongers, when it is written that they shall be judged according to the deeds done in the body? But St. Paul informs us of three glories and three heavens. He knew a man that was caught up to the third heavens. Now, if the doctrine of the sectarian world, that there is but one heaven, is true, Paul, what do you tell that lie for, and say there are three? Jesus said unto His disciples, "In my Fa-

---

Degrees of Glory
 3   Sabbath address, Nauvoo, 21 May 1843.
 4   Sabbath address, Nauvoo, 11 June 1843.

ther's house are many mansions, if it were not so, I would have told you. I go to prepare a place for you, and I will come and receive you to myself, that where I am ye may be also." (HC 5:425–26)

5   I know a man that has been caught up to the third heavens, and can say, with Paul, that we have seen and heard things that are not lawful to utter. (HC 5:556)

6   My text is on the resurrection of the dead, which you will find in the 14th chapter of John—"In my Father's house are many mansions." It should be—"In my Father's kingdom are many kingdoms," in order that ye may be heirs of God and joint-heirs with me. I do not believe the Methodist doctrine of sending honest men and noble-minded men to hell, along with the murderer and the adulterer. They may hurl all their hell and fiery billows upon me, for they will roll off me as fast as they come on. But I have an order of things to save the poor fellows at any rate, and get them saved; for I will send men to preach to them in prison and save them if I can.

There are mansions for those who obey a celestial law, and there are other mansions for those who come short of the law, every man in his own order. (HC 6:365)

7   Go and read the vision in the Book of Covenants [D&C 76]. There is clearly illustrated glory upon glory—one glory of the sun, another glory of the moon, and a glory of the stars; and as one star differeth from another star in glory, even so do they of the telestial world differ in glory, and every man who reigns in celestial glory is a God to his dominions. (HC 6:477)

Desires

1   The nearer man approaches perfection, the clearer are his views, and the greater his enjoyments, till he has overcome the evils of his

---

Degrees of Glory
   5   Sabbath address, Nauvoo, 27 August 1843.
   6   Sabbath address, Nauvoo, 12 May 1844.
   7   Sabbath address, Nauvoo, 16 June 1844.

Desires
   1   Letter to the brethren scattered from Zion, Kirtland, 22 January 1834.

life and lost every desire for sin. . . . But we consider that this is a station to which no man ever arrived in a moment: he must have been instructed in the government and laws of that kingdom by proper degrees, until his mind is capable in some measure of comprehending the propriety, justice, equality, and consistency of the same. (HC 2:8)

2   Men who have no principle of righteousness in themselves, and whose hearts are full of iniquity, and have no desire for the principles of truth, do not understand the word of truth when they hear it. The devil taketh away the word of truth out of their hearts, because there is no desire for righteousness in them. (HC 2:266)

3   I desire the learning and wisdom of heaven alone. (HC 5:423)

Despair

1   *Words of George A. Smith:* Later, while on a mission to England, I went with Elder Richards to visit Elder Theodore Turley, in Stafford jail. We shook hands with him through a large iron grating, which forcibly brought to mind a circumstance which occurred when Elder Turley and myself parted with the Prophet Joseph Smith in Nauvoo. Joseph had blessed us and said: "Keep up good courage, boys. Some of you will look through grates before you come back!" (*TK*, p. 49)

2   When a man is borne down with trouble, when he is perplexed with care and difficulty, if he can meet a smile instead of an argument or a murmur—if he can meet with mildness, it will calm down his soul and soothe his feelings; when the mind is going to despair, it needs a solace of affection and kindness. (HC 4:606–7)

Desires
2   Letter to the elders of the Church, Kirtland, 1 September 1835.
3   Sabbath address, Nauvoo, 11 June 1843.

Despair
1   Recollection of George A. Smith contained in *Family of George A. Smith*. George A. Smith was in England from April 1840 to April 1841.
2   Remarks to the Relief Society, Nauvoo, 28 April 1842.

Destroying Angels

1 Such experiences [persecution, false accusations] may be necessary to perfect the Church, and render our traducers mete for the devourer, and the shaft of the destroying angel. (HC 2:144)

2 The servants of God will not have gone over the nations of the Gentiles, with a warning voice, until the destroying angel will commence to waste the inhabitants of the earth, and as the prophet hath said, "It shall be a vexation to hear the report." (HC 2:263)

3 When you are endowed and prepared to preach the Gospel to all nations, kindred, and tongues, in their own languages, you must faithfully warn all, and bind up the testimony, and seal up the law, and the destroying angel will follow close at your heels, and exercise his tremendous mission upon the children of disobedience; and destroy the workers of iniquity, while the Saints will be gathered out from among them, and stand in holy places ready to meet the Bridegroom when he comes. (HC 2:309)

4 The world is reserved unto burning in the last days. He shall send Elijah the prophet, and he shall reveal the covenants of the fathers in relation to the children, and the covenants of the children in relation to the fathers.
  Four destroying angels holding power over the four quarters of the earth until the servants of God are sealed in their foreheads, which signifies sealing the blessing upon their heads, meaning the everlasting covenant, thereby making their calling and election sure. (HC 5:530)

5 I would advise all the Saints to go to with their might and gather together all their living relatives to this place, that they may be sealed and saved, that they may be prepared against the day that the destroying angel goes forth. (HC 6:184)

Destroying Angels
  1 Letter written from Kirtland to the high council in Zion, 16 August 1834.
  2 Letter to the elders of the Church, Kirtland, 1 September 1835.
  3 Instructions to the Twelve, Kirtland, 12 November 1835.
  4 Remarks at the funeral of Judge Elias Higbee, Nauvoo, 13 August 1843.
  5 Sabbath discourse, Nauvoo, 21 January 1844.

Destructions

1   *Words of Elizabeth Ann Whitney*: My husband traveled with Joseph the Prophet through many of the Eastern cities [in the fall of 1832], bearing testimony and collecting means toward building a temple in Kirtland, and also toward purchasing lands in Missouri. During this journey the Prophet Joseph often prophesied of the destruction that ultimately would come upon the cities of the Eastern States, and especially New York, that in that city there would not be left a vestige of its grandeur. He said that wars would soon commence in our own land, which last has since transpired. He said to my husband, "If they reject us they shall have our testimony, for we will write it and leave it upon their doorsteps and window sills."

He prophesied of the desolation by fire, by storms, by pestilence and by earthquakes. (*TK*, p. 39)

2   A fine morning. I started to ride to Painesville with my family and scribe. When we were passing through Mentor Street, we overtook a team, with two men in the sleigh; I politely asked them to let me pass. They granted my request, and as we passed them they bawled out, "Do you get any revelations lately?" with an addition of blackguard language that I did not understand. This is a fair sample of the character of Mentor Street inhabitants, who are ready to abuse and scandalize men who never laid a straw in their way; and, in fact, those whose faces they never saw, and {whom they} cannot bring an accusation against, either of a temporal or spiritual nature, except their firm belief in the fullness of the Gospel. I was led to marvel at the longsuffering and condescension of our heavenly Father in permitting these ungodly wretches to possess this goodly land, which is indeed as beautifully situated, and its soil is as fertile, as any in this region of country, and its inhabitants are wealthy, even blessed above measure in temporal things; and fain would God bless them with spiritual blessings, even eternal life, were it not for their evil hearts of unbelief. And we are led to mingle our prayers with those of the Saints that have suffered the like treatment before us, whose souls are under the altar, crying to the Lord

---

Destructions

1   Recollection of Elizabeth Ann Whitney, wife of Newel K. Whitney, published in the *Woman's Exponent*, 1 October 1878.
2   Kirtland, 2 December 1835.

for vengeance upon those that dwell upon the earth. And we rejoice that the time is at hand, when the wicked who will not repent will be swept from the earth as with a besom of destruction, and the earth become an inheritance of the poor and the meek. (HC 2:323–24)

3   Men profess to prophesy. I will prophesy that the signs of the coming of the Son of Man are already commenced. One pestilence will desolate after another. We shall soon have war and bloodshed. The moon will be turned into blood. I testify of these things, and that the coming of the Son of Man is nigh, even at your doors. If our souls and our bodies are not looking forth for the coming of the Son of Man; and after we are dead, if we are not looking forth, we shall be among those who are calling for the rocks to fall upon them. (HC 3:390)

4   The time is soon coming, when no man will have any peace but in Zion and her stakes.
    I saw men hunting the lives of their own sons, and brother murdering brother, women killing their own daughters, and daughters seeking the lives of their mothers. I saw armies arrayed against armies. I saw blood, desolation, fires. The Son of Man has said that the mother shall be against the daughter, and the daughter against the mother. These things are at our doors. They will follow the Saints of God from city to city. Satan will rage, and the spirit of the devil is now enraged. I know not how soon these things will take place; but with a view of them, shall I cry peace? No! I will lift up my voice and testify of them. How long you will have good crops, and the famine be kept off, I do not know; when the fig tree leaves, know then that the summer is nigh at hand. (HC 3:391)

5   Oft he [God] takes man to scourge his fellow man, or water to destroy man—or fire to destroy man, or angels; for instance, the angel

---

Destructions

3   Discourse on the priesthood, given sometime before 8 August 1839, Commerce (Nauvoo). For a discussion on the dating of this discourse, see *WJS*, p. 22.

4   Discourse on the priesthood, given sometime before 8 August 1839, Commerce (Nauvoo).

5   Lecture given at the Nauvoo Lyceum, 5 January 1841. (The lyceum met weekly at different locations in Nauvoo for several months, beginning 5 January 1841.) Recorded in William P. McIntire's Minute Book, LDS Church Archives.

that went forth and destroyed a hundred thousand. (*WJS*, p. 61; standardized)

6   The earth is groaning under corruption, oppression, tyranny and
bloodshed; and God is coming out of His hiding place, as He said He
would do, to vex the nations of the earth. Daniel, in his vision, saw
convulsion upon convulsion. (*HC* 5:65)

7   In consequence of rejecting the Gospel of Jesus Christ and the
Prophets whom God hath sent, the judgments of God have rested
upon people, cities, and nations, in various ages of the world, which
was the case with the cities of Sodom and Gomorrah, that were destroyed for rejecting the Prophets. (*HC* 5:256–57)

8   I prophesy, in the name of the Lord God of Israel, anguish and
wrath and tribulation and the withdrawing of the Spirit of God from
the earth await this generation, until they are visited with utter desolation. This generation is as corrupt as the generation of the Jews that
crucified Christ; and if He were here to-day, and should preach the
same doctrine He did then, they would put Him to death. (*HC* 6:58)

9   The Saints have not too much time to save and redeem their
dead, and gather together their living relatives, that they may be
saved also, before the earth will be smitten, and the consumption decreed falls upon the world.

   . . . If the whole Church should go to with all their might to save
their dead, seal their posterity, and gather their living friends, and
spend none of their time in behalf of the world, they would hardly get
through before night would come, when no man can work; and my
only trouble at the present time is concerning ourselves, that the
Saints *will be divided, broken up, and scattered,* before we get our salvation secure. (*HC* 6:184)

10   In the days of Noah, God destroyed the world by a flood, and He
has promised to destroy it by fire in the last days: but before it should

Destructions

   6   Editorial in the *Times and Seasons*, 15 July 1842.
   7   Sabbath address, Nauvoo, 22 January 1843.
   8   Sabbath address, Nauvoo, 15 October 1843.
   9   Sabbath address, Nauvoo, 21 January 1844.
   10 Sabbath address, Nauvoo, 10 March 1844.

take place, Elijah should first come and turn the hearts of the fathers to the children, &c. (*HC* 6:251)

11 *Words of Jedediah M. Grant:* The Prophet stood in his own house when he told several of us of the night the visions of heaven were opened to him, in which he saw the American continent drenched in blood, and he saw nation rising up against nation. He also saw the father shed the blood of the son, and the son the blood of the father; the mother put to death the daughter, and the daughter the mother; and natural affection forsook the hearts of the wicked; for he saw that the Spirit of God should be withdrawn from the inhabitants of the earth, in consequence of which there should be blood upon the face of the whole earth, except among the people of the Most High. The Prophet gazed upon the scene his vision presented, until his heart sickened, and he besought the Lord to close it up again. (*JD* 2:147)

12 *Report of John M. Bernhisel's Recollection:* "It is only a question of time," said the Prophet, "a few years, or a few hundred, perhaps, according to our reckoning; but time and space being without limit in the estimation of our Father, the course will be determined in accordance with the 'eternal fitness of things' through His will only. Lucifer's reign of anarchy prevails at present, and the nations are even now arming for the conflict which even they foresee must necessarily ensue. In the cruel desolation of war, men will be slain by hundreds, thousands, and perhaps millions. Their widows and orphans will be compelled to flee to Zion for safety, and it will become the bounden duty of the Elders of Israel to provide for their sustenance and welfare." (*TK*, p. 178)

Devil

1 *Words of Philo Dibble:* I saw Joseph Smith the Prophet when he first came to Kirtland [in February 1831]. There was a branch of the

---

Destructions

    11 Address by Jedediah M. Grant, Salt Lake City, 2 April 1854.

    12 Recollection of John M. Bernhisel, reported in Washington Franklin Anderson, "Reminiscences of John M. Bernhisel," LDS Church Archives.

Devil

    1 Recollection of Philo Dibble, published in the *Juvenile Instructor*, 1 January 1892.

Church raised up in Kirtland before he came, and at the time he arrived a variety of false spirits were manifested, such as caused jumping, shouting, falling down, etc. Joseph said, as soon as he came, "God has sent me here, and the devil must leave here, or I will."

Those delusive spirits were not seen nor heard any more at that time. (*TK*, pp. 66–67)

2   After we had encamped upon the bank of the river, at McIlwaine's Bend, Brother Phelps, in open vision by daylight, saw the destroyer in his most horrible power, ride upon the face of the waters; others heard the noise, but saw not the vision.

The next morning after prayer, I received the following: [D&C 61]. . . .

. . . We could not help beholding the exertions of Satan to blind the eyes of the people, so as to hide the true light that lights every man that comes into the world. (*HC* 1:203, 206)

3   You are aware, no doubt, dear brother, that anxieties inexpressible crowd themselves continually upon my mind for the Saints, when I consider the many temptations to which we are subject, from the cunning and flattery of the great adversary of our souls. (*HC* 1:442)

4   I have learned by experience that the enemy of truth does not slumber, nor cease his exertions to bias the minds of communities against the servants of the Lord, by stirring up the indignation of men upon all matters of importance or interest. (*HC* 2:437)

5   And here I would state, that while the evil spirits were raging up and down in the state to raise mobs against the "Mormons," Satan himself was no less busy in striving to stir up mischief in the camp of the Saints: and among the most conspicuous of his willing devotees was one Doctor Sampson Avard. (*HC* 3:178)

Devil
  2   McIlwaine's Bend, Missouri, 11–12 August 1831.
  3   Letter to Moses C. Nickerson, written from Kirtland, 19 November 1833.
  4   Letter on abolition published in the *Messenger and Advocate*, April 1836.
  5   Far West, Missouri, October 1838.

6   While the persecutions were progressing against us in Missouri, the enemy of all righteousness was no less busy with the Saints in England, according to the length of time the Gospel had been preached in that kingdom. Temptation followed temptation, and being young in the cause, the Saints suffered themselves to be buffeted by their adversary. From the time that Elder Willard Richards was called to the apostleship, in July, 1838, the devil seemed to take a great dislike to him, and strove to stir up the minds of many against him. (HC 3:276)

7   It has been the plan of the devil to hamper me and distress me from the beginning, to keep me from explaining myself to them [Church members]; and I never have had opportunity to give them the plan that God has revealed to me; for many have run without being sent, crying "Tidings, my Lord," and have done much injury to the Church, giving the devil more power over those that walk by sight and not by faith. (HC 3:286)

8   There will be here and there a Stake {of Zion} for the gathering of the Saints. . . .

I prophesy, that that man who tarries after he has an opportunity of going, will be afflicted by the devil. . . .

. . . The devil will use his greatest efforts to trap the Saints. . . .

We may look for angels and receive their ministrations, but we are to try the spirits and prove them, for it is often the case that men make a mistake in regard to these things. . . . Lying spirits are going forth in the earth. There will be great manifestations of spirits, both false and true. . . .

. . . The devil may appear as an angel of light. . . .

. . . The devil can speak in tongues; the adversary will come with his work; he can tempt all classes; can speak in English or Dutch. (HC 3:390, 391–92)

Devil
6   Events in England surrounding the missionary labors there, entered into the *History of the Church* under date of 9 March 1839.
7   Letter from Liberty Jail to Mrs. Norman Bull (Buell), 15 March 1839.
8   Discourse on the priesthood, given sometime before 8 August 1839, Commerce (Nauvoo). For a discussion on the dating of this discourse, see *WJS*, p. 22.

9   All beings who have bodies have power over those who have not. The devil has no power over us only as we permit him; the moment we revolt at anything which comes from God, the devil takes power. (*WJS*, p. 60; standardized)

10 *Report of Don Carlos Smith:* [President Joseph Smith] then observed that Satan was generally blamed for the evils which we did, but if he was the cause of all our wickedness, men could not be condemned. The devil could not compel mankind to do evil; all was voluntary. Those who resisted the Spirit of God, would be liable to be led into temptation, and then the association of heaven would be withdrawn from those who refused to be made partakers of such great glory. God would not exert any compulsory means, and the devil could not; and such ideas as were entertained {on these subjects} by many were absurd. (*HC* 4:358)

11 There are three independent principles—the spirit of God, the spirit of man, and the spirit of the devil. All men have power to resist the devil. They who have tabernacles have power over those who have not. (*WJS*, p. 74)

12 *Report of Wilford Woodruff:* The speaker [Joseph Smith], before closing, called upon the assembly before him to humble themselves in faith before God, and in mighty prayer and fasting to call upon the name of the Lord, until the elements were purified over our heads, and the earth sanctified under our feet, that the inhabitants of this city may escape the power of disease and pestilence, and the destroyer that rideth upon the face of the earth, and that the Holy Spirit of God may rest upon this vast multitude. (*HC* 4:556–57)

13 As "no man knows the things of God, but by the Spirit of God," so no man knows the spirit of the devil, and his power and influence,

---

Devil
9 Lecture given at the Nauvoo Lyceum, 5 January 1841, as reported by William Clayton. (The lyceum met weekly at different locations in Nauvoo for several months, beginning 5 January 1841.)
10 Sabbath address, Nauvoo, 16 May 1841.
11 Sabbath address, Nauvoo, 16 May 1841, as reported by William Clayton.
12 Sabbath address, Nauvoo, 20 March 1842.
13 Editorial in the *Times and Seasons*, 1 April 1842.

but by possessing intelligence which is more than human, and having unfolded through the medium of the Priesthood the mysterious operations of his devices; without knowing the angelic form, the sanctified look and gesture, and the zeal that is frequently manifested by him for the glory of God, together with the prophetic spirit, the gracious influence, the godly appearance, and the holy garb, which are so characteristic of his proceedings and his mysterious windings. . . .

As we have noticed before, the great difficulty lies in the ignorance of the nature of spirits, of the laws by which they are governed, and the signs by which they may be known; if it requires the Spirit of God to know the things of God; and the spirit of the devil can only be unmasked through that medium, then it follows as a natural consequence that unless some person or persons have a communication, or revelation from God, unfolding to them the operation of the spirit, they must eternally remain ignorant of these principles. . . . We shall at last have to come to this conclusion, whatever we may think of revelation, that without it we can neither know nor understand anything of God, or the devil. . . .

. . . The spirits of good men cannot interfere with the wicked beyond their prescribed bounds, for Michael, the Archangel, dared not bring a railing accusation against the devil, but said, "The Lord rebuke thee, Satan."

It would seem also, that wicked spirits have their bounds, limits, and laws by which they are governed or controlled, and know their future destiny; hence, those that were in the maniac said to our Savior, "Art thou come to torment us before the time," and when Satan presented himself before the Lord, among the sons of God, he said that he came "from going to and fro in the earth, and from wandering up and down in it;" and he is emphatically called the prince of the power of the air; and, it is very evident that they possess a power that none but those who have the Priesthood can control, as we have before adverted to, in the case of the sons of Sceva. . . .

Again it may be asked, how it was that they [the Irvingites] could speak in tongues if they were of the devil! We would answer that they could be made to speak in another tongue, as well as their own, as they were under the control of that spirit, and the devil can tempt the Hottentot, the Turk, the Jew, or any other nation; and if these men were under the influence of his spirit, they of course could speak Hebrew, Latin, Greek, Italian, Dutch, or any other language that the devil knew. . . .

. . . We have also had brethren and sisters who have had the gift of tongues falsely; they would speak in a muttering, unnatural voice, and their bodies be distorted like the Irvingites before alluded to; whereas, there is nothing unnatural in the Spirit of God. . . .

There have also been ministering angels in the Church which were of Satan appearing as an angel of light. A sister in the state of New York had a vision, who said it was told her that if she would go to a certain place in the woods, an angel would appear to her. She went at the appointed time, and saw a glorious personage descending, arrayed in white, with sandy colored hair; he commenced and told her to fear God, and said that her husband was called to do great things, but that he must not go more than one hundred miles from home, or he would not return; whereas God had called him to go to the ends of the earth, and he has since been more than one thousand miles from home, and is yet alive. Many true things were spoken by this personage, and many things that were false. How, it may be asked, was this known to be a bad angel? By the color of his hair; that is one of the signs that he can be known by, and by his contradicting a former revelation. (HC 4:573–74, 576, 579, 580, 581)

14 God, men, and angels will not condemn those that resist everything that is evil, and devils cannot; as well might the devil seek to dethrone Jehovah, as overthrow an innocent soul that resists everything which is evil. . . .

The devil has great power to deceive; he will so transform things as to make one gape at those who are doing the will of God. (HC 4:605)

15 All the religious world is boasting of righteousness: it is the doctrine of the devil to retard the human mind, and hinder our progress, by filling us with self-righteousness. . . .

. . . We are full of selfishness; the devil flatters us that we are very righteous, when we are feeding on the faults of others. (HC 5:24)

16 Is it not enough to put down all the infernal influences of the

---

Devil
14 Remarks to the Relief Society, Nauvoo, 28 April 1842.
15 Remarks to the Relief Society, Nauvoo, 9 June 1842.
16 Conference address, Nauvoo, 29 August 1842.

devil, what we have felt and seen, handled and evidenced, of this work of God? But the devil had influence among the Jews, after all the great things they had witnessed, to cause the death of Jesus Christ, by hanging Him between heaven and earth. They would deliver me up, Judas like; but a small band of us shall overcome. (HC 5:138)

17 The enemies of this people will never get weary of their persecution against the Church, until they are overcome. I expect they will array everything against me that is in their power to control, and that we shall have a long and tremendous warfare. He that will war the true Christian warfare against the corruptions of these last days will have wicked men and angels of devils, and all the infernal powers of darkness continually arrayed against him. When wicked and corrupt men oppose, it is a criterion to judge if a man is warring the Christian warfare. When all men speak evil of you falsely, blessed are ye, &c. Shall a man be considered bad, when men speak evil of him? No. If a man stands and opposes the world of sin, he may expect to have all wicked and corrupt spirits arrayed against him. But it will be but a little season, and all these afflictions will be turned away from us, inasmuch as we are faithful, and are not overcome by these evils. (HC 5:141)

18 I will venture to say that when God allows the old devil to give power to the beast to destroy the inhabitants of the earth, all will wonder. [See Revelation 13:1–8.] (HC 5:345)

19 Now, in this world, mankind are naturally selfish, ambitious and striving to excel one above another; yet some are willing to build up others as well as themselves. So in the other world there are a variety of spirits. Some seek to excel. And this was the case with Lucifer when he fell. He sought for things which were unlawful. Hence he was sent down, and it is said he drew many away with him; and the greatness of his punishment is that he shall not have a tabernacle. This is his punishment. So the devil, thinking to thwart the decree of God, by going up and down in the earth, seeking whom he may destroy—any person that he can find that will yield to him, he will bind

---

Devil

17 Remarks to the Relief Society, Nauvoo, 31 August 1842.

18 General conference address, Nauvoo, 8 April 1843.

19 Sabbath address at Yelrome (Morley's Settlement), Illinois, 14 May 1843.

him, and take possession of the body and reign there, glorying in it mightily, not caring that he had got merely a stolen body; and by-and-by some one having authority will come along and cast him out and restore the tabernacle to its rightful owner. The devil steals a tabernacle because he has not one of his own: but if he steals one, he is always liable to be turned out of doors. (HC 5:388)

20 The spirits in the eternal world are like the spirits in this world. When those have come into this world and received tabernacles, then died and again have risen and received glorified bodies, they will have an ascendency over the spirits who have received no bodies, or kept not their first estate, like the devil. The punishment of the devil was that he should not have a habitation like men. The devil's retaliation is, he comes into this world, binds up men's bodies, and occupies them himself. When the authorities come along, they eject him from a stolen habitation. (HC 5:403)

21 There are so many fools in the world for the devil to operate upon, it gives him the advantage oftentimes. (HC 6:184)

22 The contention in heaven was—Jesus said there would be certain souls that would not be saved; and the devil said he would save them all, and laid his plans before the grand council, who gave their vote in favor of Jesus Christ. So the devil rose up in rebellion against God, and was cast down, with all who put up their heads for him. (Book of Moses—Pearl of Great Price, Ch. 4:1–4; Book of Abraham, Ch. 3:23–28.) . . .

When a man begins to be an enemy to this work, he hunts me, he seeks to kill me, and never ceases to thirst for my blood. He gets the spirit of the devil—the same spirit that they had who crucified the Lord of Life—the same spirit that sins against the Holy Ghost. You cannot save such persons; you cannot bring them to repentance; they make open war, like the devil, and awful is the consequence.

I advise all of you to be careful what you do, or you may by-and-by find out that you have been deceived. Stay yourselves; do not give

---

Devil
   20 Sabbath address, Nauvoo, 21 May 1843.
   21 Sabbath address, Nauvoo, 21 January 1844.
   22 King Follett Discourse, Nauvoo, 7 April 1844.

way; don't make any hasty moves, you may be saved. If a spirit of bitterness is in you, don't be in haste. You may say, that man is a sinner. Well, if he repents, he shall be forgiven. Be cautious: await. When you find a spirit that wants bloodshed,—murder, the same is not of God, but is of the devil. (HC 6:314–15)

23 False prophets always arise to oppose the true prophets and they will prophesy so very near the truth that they will deceive almost the very chosen ones.

. . . In relation to the kingdom of God, the devil always sets up his kingdom at the very same time in opposition to God. (HC 6:364)

24 It is thought by some that our enemies would be satisfied with my destruction; but I tell you that as soon as they have shed my blood they will thirst for the blood of every man in whose heart dwells a single spark of the spirit of the fullness of the Gospel. The opposition of these men is moved by the spirit of the adversary of all righteousness. It is not only to destroy me, but every man and woman who dares believe the doctrines that God hath inspired me to teach to this generation. (HC 6:498)

25 *Words of Helen Mar Whitney:* We had struggles with evil spirits at Winter Quarters, which were something similar to what the Prophet Joseph Smith experienced in Far West, Missouri. He said the devil contended with him face to face, after he had afflicted his little child, claiming that he had the best right to a house which Joseph had purchased, it having been previously occupied by some wicked people. But the Prophet rebuked the devil in the name of the Lord, and he had to leave the house.

My father [Heber C. Kimball] also had some contests with the evil spirits when young in years and inexperienced. The Prophet once requested him to relate those occurrences and the vision of evil spirits which he had in England on the opening of the gospel to that people. After doing so, he asked Joseph what all those things meant, fearing there might be something wrong in him. Joseph's answer was, "No,

---

Devil

23 Sabbath address, Nauvoo, 12 May 1844.
24 Address to the Nauvoo Legion, 18 June 1844.
25 Recollection of Helen Mar Whitney, published in the *Woman's Exponent*, 15 December 1885.

Brother Heber. At that time, when you were in England, you were
nigh unto the Lord. There was only a veil between you and Him.
When I heard of it, it gave me great joy, for I then knew the work of
God had taken root in that land. It was this that caused the devil to
make a struggle to kill you."

Joseph then said the nearer a person approached to the Lord, the
greater power would be manifest by the devil to prevent the accomplishment of the purposes of God. (*TK*, p. 176)

Diligence

1   We consider that God has created man with a mind capable of instruction, and a faculty which may be enlarged in proportion to the
heed and diligence given to the light communicated from heaven to
the intellect; and that the nearer man approaches perfection, the
clearer are his views, and the greater his enjoyments, till he has overcome the evils of his life and lost every desire for sin; and like the ancients, arrives at that point of faith where he is wrapped in the power
and glory of his Maker, and is caught up to dwell with Him. But we
consider that this is a station to which no man ever arrived in a moment: he must have been instructed in the government and laws of
that kingdom by proper degrees, until his mind is capable in some
measure of comprehending the propriety, justice, equality, and consistency of the same. (*HC* 2:8)

2   [Quoting Paul] "Without faith, it is impossible to please Him, for
he that cometh to God must believe that He is, and that he is a revealer to those who diligently seek him." [Hebrews 11:6.] (*HC* 4:209)

3   In conclusion we would say, brethren and sisters, be faithful, be
diligent, contend earnestly for the faith once delivered to the Saints;
let every man, woman and child realize the importance of the work,

---

Diligence

1   Letter to the brethren scattered from Zion, Kirtland, 22 January 1834.

2   Article on priesthood read at general conference, Nauvoo, 5 October
     1840. Note that the word *revealer* is used here rather than *rewarder* as is
     found in Hebrews 11:6 (KJV and JST).

3   Report of the First Presidency at general conference, Nauvoo, 5 October
     1840.

and act as if success depended on his individual exertion alone; let all feel an interest in it. (HC 4:214)

4   Elias Higbee, of the temple committee, came into my office, and I said unto him: The Lord is not well pleased with you; and you must straighten up your loins and do better, and your family also; for you have not been as diligent as you ought to have been, and as spring is approaching, you must arise and shake yourself, and be active, and make your children industrious, and help build the Temple. (HC 4:503)

5   This [the death of Lorenzo D. Barnes] has been a warning voice to us all to be sober and diligent and lay aside mirth, vanity and folly, and to be prepared to die tomorrow. (HC 5:363)

6   Finally, as one that greatly desires the salvation of men, let me remind you all to strive with godly zeal for virtue, holiness, and the commandments of the Lord. Be good, be wise, be just, be liberal. (HC 5:417)

Disappointment

1   The disappointment of hopes and expectations at the resurrection would be indescribably dreadful [for those who have ignored or rejected revealed truths]. (HC 6:51)

2   A man is his own tormentor and his own condemner. Hence the saying, They shall go into the lake that burns with fire and brimstone. The torment of disappointment in the mind of man is as exquisite as a lake burning with fire and brimstone. I say, so is the torment of man. (HC 6:314)

Diligence
   4   Counsel to Elias Higbee, Nauvoo, 28 January 1842.
   5   Remarks upon the death of Lorenzo D. Barnes, Nauvoo, 16 April 1843.
   6   Authorization given to Brigham Young to collect funds, addressed to "all Saints and honorable men of the earth," Nauvoo, 1 June 1843.

Disappointment
   1   Remarks upon the death of James Adams, Nauvoo, 9 October 1843.
   2   King Follett Discourse, Nauvoo, 7 April 1844.

Discerning of Spirits

1   It is in vain to try to hide a bad spirit from the eyes of them who are spiritual, for it will show itself in speaking and in writing, as well as in all our other conduct. It is also needless to make great pretensions when the heart is not right; the Lord will expose it to the view of His faithful Saints. (HC 1:317)

2   I urged the necessity of prayer, that the Spirit might be given, that the things of the Spirit might be judged thereby, because the carnal mind cannot discern the things of God. (HC 2:31)

3   Every spirit, or vision, or singing, is not of God. . . . The gift of discerning spirits will be given to the Presiding Elder. Pray for him that he may have this gift. (HC 3:392)

4   It is evident from the Apostles' writings, that many false spirits existed in their day, and had "gone forth into the world," and that it needed intelligence which God alone could impart to detect false spirits, and to prove what spirits were of God. The world in general have been grossly ignorant in regard to this one thing, and why should they be otherwise—"for no man knows the things of God, but by the Spirit of God." . . .

There always did, in every age, seem to be a lack of intelligence pertaining to this subject. Spirits of all kinds have been manifested, in every age, and almost amongst all people. . . . Who shall solve the mystery? "Try the spirits," says John, but who is to do it? The learned, the eloquent, the philosopher, the sage, the divine—all are ignorant. . . .

"Try the spirits," but what by? Are we to try them by the creeds of

---

Discerning of Spirits
1   Letter to William W. Phelps in Missouri, written from Kirtland, 14 January 1833. According to Dean Jessee this letter was dated 11 January (see *PWJS*, p. 262).
2   Meeting of the high council, Kirtland, 19 February 1834.
3   Discourse on the priesthood, given sometime before 8 August 1839, Commerce (Nauvoo). For a discussion on the dating of this discourse, see *WJS*, p. 22.
4   Editorial in the *Times and Seasons*, 1 April 1842.

men? What preposterous folly—what sheer ignorance—what mad-ness! Try the motions and actions of an eternal being (for I contend that all spirits are such) by a thing that was conceived in ignorance, and brought forth in folly—a cobweb of yesterday! Angels would hide their faces, and devils would be ashamed and insulted, and would say, "Paul we know, and Jesus we know, but who are ye?" Let each man of society make a creed and try evil spirits by it, and the devil would shake his sides; it is all that he would ask—all that he would desire. Yet many of them do this, and hence "many spirits are abroad in the world."...

Every one of these [sectarians] professes to be competent to try his neighbor's spirit, but no one can try his own, and what is the reason? Because they have not a key to unlock, no rule wherewith to measure, and no criterion whereby they can test it. Could any one tell the length, breadth or height of a building without a rule? test the quality of metals without a criterion, or point out the movements of the plan-etary systems, without a knowledge of astronomy? Certainly not; and if such ignorance as this is manifested about a spirit of this kind, who can describe an angel of light?... We answer that no man can do this without the Priesthood, and having a knowledge of the laws by which spirits are governed; for as "no man knows the things of God, but by the Spirit of God," so no man knows the spirit of the devil, and his power and influence, but by possessing intelligence which is more than human, and having unfolded through the medium of the Priest-hood the mysterious operations of his devices; without knowing the angelic form, the sanctified look and gesture, and the zeal that is fre-quently manifested by him for the glory of God, together with the prophetic spirit, the gracious influence, the godly appearance, and the holy garb, which are so characteristic of his proceedings and his mys-terious windings.

A man must have the discerning of spirits before he can drag into daylight this hellish influence and unfold it unto the world in all its soul-destroying, diabolical, and horrid colors; for nothing is a greater injury to the children of men than to be under the influence of a false spirit when they think they have the Spirit of God. Thousands have felt the influence of its terrible power and baneful effects. Long pil-grimages have been undertaken, penances endured, and pain, misery and ruin have followed in their train; nations have been convulsed, kingdoms overthrown, provinces laid waste, and blood, carnage and desolation are habiliments in which it has been clothed....

A man must have the discerning of spirits, as we before stated, to understand these things, and how is he to obtain this gift if there are no gifts of the Spirit? And how can these gifts be obtained without revelation? . . .

It would seem also, that wicked spirits have their bounds, limits, and laws by which they are governed or controlled, and know their future destiny; . . . it is very evident that they possess a power that none but those who have the Priesthood can control, as we have before adverted to, in the case of the sons of Sceva. . . .

Again it may be asked, how it was that they [the Irvingites] could speak in tongues if they were of the devil! We would answer that they could be made to speak in another tongue, as well as their own, as they were under the control of that spirit, and the devil can tempt the Hottentot, the Turk, the Jew, or any other nation; and if these men were under the influence of his spirit, they of course could speak Hebrew, Latin, Greek, Italian, Dutch, or any other language that the devil knew. . . .

The Church of Jesus Christ of Latter-day Saints has also had its false spirits; and as it is made up of all those different sects professing every variety of opinion, and having been under the influence of so many kinds of spirits, it is not to be wondered at if there should be found among us false spirits. (HC 4:571–72, 573, 574, 576, 579, 580)

Discouragement

1   We truly had a good time, and covenanted to struggle for this thing [the redemption of Zion], until death shall dissolve the union; and if one falls, that the remainder be not discouraged, but pursue this object until it be accomplished; which may God grant unto us in the name of Jesus Christ our Lord. (HC 2:282)

2   *Words of George A. Smith:* I was attacked with inflammatory rheumatism, which swelled my legs, right arm, and shoulder, so that I could not help myself for several weeks except with my left hand. I

Discouragement
1   Meeting of the high council at Joseph's home, Kirtland, 24 September 1835.
2   Recollection of George A. Smith of events in late 1835 and early 1836.

suffered the most excruciating pain, and although the winter was very cold, I could suffer no clothes on me except a very light blanket.

Cousin Joseph came to see me. I told him I was almost discouraged, being afraid that my joints would be drawn out. He told me I should never get discouraged, whatever difficulties might surround me. If I were sunk into the lowest pit of Nova Scotia and all the Rocky Mountains piled on top of me, I ought not to be discouraged, but hang on, exercise faith, and keep up good courage, and I should come out on the top of the heap. January 1, 1836, he laid hands on me in company with several of the Elders. My pain instantly left me and I gradually recovered my strength and the use of my limbs. (*Family of George A. Smith*, p. 54)

3   Brethren, you are in the pathway to eternal fame, and immortal glory: and inasmuch as you feel interested for the covenant people of the Lord, the God of their fathers shall bless you. Do not be discouraged on account of the greatness of the work; only be humble and faithful, and then you can say, "What art thou, O great mountain! Before Zerubbabel shalt thou be brought down." He who scattered Israel has promised to gather them; therefore inasmuch as you are to be instrumental in this great work, He will endow you with power, wisdom, might, and intelligence, and every qualification necessary; while your minds will expand wider and wider, until you can circumscribe the earth and the heavens, reach forth into eternity, and contemplate the mighty acts of Jehovah in all their variety and glory. (HC 4:128–29)

Disease

1   *Report of Wilford Woodruff:* [President Joseph said that] because we will not receive chastisement at the hand of the Prophet and Apostles, the Lord chastiseth us with sickness and death. (HC 4:478–79)

Discouragement
3   Letter to Orson Hyde and John E. Page, Nauvoo, 14 May 1840.

Disease
1   Meeting of the Twelve at the Prophet's home, Nauvoo, 19 December 1841.

Dispensations
See also ADAM

1   Now the purpose in Himself in the winding up scene of the last dispensation is that all things pertaining to that dispensation should be conducted precisely in accordance with the preceding dispensations.

And again. God purposed in Himself that there should not be an eternal fullness until every dispensation should be fulfilled and gathered together in one, and that all things whatsoever, that should be gathered together in one in those dispensations unto the same fullness and eternal glory, should be in Christ Jesus.

. . . All the ordinances and duties that ever have been required by the Priesthood, under the directions and commandments of the Almighty in any of the dispensations, shall all be had in the last dispensation, therefore all things had under the authority of the Priesthood at any former period, shall be had again, bringing to pass the restoration spoken of by the mouth of all the Holy Prophets. (*HC* 4:208, 210–11)

2   The dispensation of the fullness of times will bring to light the things that have been revealed in all former dispensations; also other things that have not been before revealed. (*HC* 4:426)

3   It is left for us to see, participate in and help to roll forward the Latter-day glory, "the dispensation of the fullness of times, when God will gather together all things that are in heaven, and all things that are upon the earth, even in one," when the Saints of God will be gathered in one from every nation, and kindred, and people, and tongue, when the Jews will be gathered together into one, the wicked will also be gathered together to be destroyed, as spoken of by the prophets; the Spirit of God will also dwell with His people, and be withdrawn from the rest of the nations, and all things whether in heaven or on earth will be in one, even in Christ. The heavenly Priesthood will unite with the earthly, to bring about those great pur-

---

Dispensations

1   Article on priesthood read at general conference, Nauvoo, 5 October 1840.
2   General conference address, Nauvoo, 3 October 1841.
3   Editorial in the *Times and Seasons*, 2 May 1842.

poses; and whilst we are thus united in the one common cause, to roll forth the kingdom of God, the heavenly Priesthood are not idle spectators, the Spirit of God will be showered down from above, and it will dwell in our midst. The blessings of the Most High will rest upon our tabernacles, and our name will be handed down to future ages; our children will rise up and call us blessed; and generations yet unborn will dwell with peculiar delight upon the scenes that we have passed through, the privations that we have endured; the untiring zeal that we have manifested; the all but insurmountable difficulties that we have overcome in laying the foundation of a work that brought about the glory and blessing which they will realize; a work that God and angels have contemplated with delight for generations past; that fired the souls of the ancient patriarchs and prophets; a work that is destined to bring about the destruction of the powers of darkness, the renovation of the earth, the glory of God, and the salvation of the human family. (HC 4:610)

4   It is in the order of heavenly things that God should always send a new dispensation into the world when men have apostatized from the truth and lost the priesthood; but when men come out and build upon other men's foundations, they do it on their own responsibility, without authority from God; and when the floods come and the winds blow, their foundations will be found to be sand, and their whole fabric will crumble to dust. (HC 6:478–79)

Doctrine

1   I did not like the old man [Elder Pelatiah Brown] being called up for erring in doctrine. It looks too much like the Methodist, and not like the Latter-day Saints. Methodists have creeds which a man must believe or be asked out of their church. I want the liberty of thinking and believing as I please. It feels so good not to be trammelled. It does not prove that a man is not a good man because he errs in doctrine. (HC 5:340)

Dispensations
   4   Sabbath address, Nauvoo, 16 June 1844.

Doctrine
   1   General conference address, Nauvoo, 8 April 1843.

2   This [the doctrine that people may become exalted as God is exalted] is good doctrine. It tastes good. I can taste the principles of eternal life, and so can you. They are given to me by the revelations of Jesus Christ; and I know that when I tell you these words of eternal life as they are given to me, you taste them, and I know that you believe them. You say honey is sweet, and so do I. I can also taste the spirit of eternal life. I know that it is good; and when I tell you of these things which were given me by inspiration of the Holy Spirit, you are bound to receive them as sweet, and rejoice more and more. (*HC* 6:312)

Doctrine and Covenants

1   *Minutes:* [1 November 1831] Brother Joseph Smith, Jun., said that inasmuch as the Lord had bestowed a great blessing upon us in giving commandments and revelations, he asked the conference what testimony they were willing to attach to these commandments which would shortly be sent to the world. A number of the brethren arose and said that they were willing to testify to the world that they knew that they were of the Lord. . . .

[2 November 1831] . . . The brethren then arose in turn and bore witness to the truth of the Book of Commandments; after which Brother Joseph Smith, Jun., arose and expressed his feelings and gratitude concerning the commandments and preface received yesterday. (*HC* 1:222)

2   After this revelation [D&C 1] was received, some conversation was had concerning revelations and language. I received the following: [D&C 67].

After the foregoing [D&C 67] was received, William E. M'Lellin, as the wisest man, in his own estimation, having more learning than sense, endeavored to write a commandment like unto one of the least of the Lord's, but failed; it was an awful responsibility to write in the name of the Lord. The Elders and all present that witnessed this vain

---

Doctrine
   2   King Follett Discourse, Nauvoo, 7 April 1844.

Doctrine and Covenants
   1   Hiram, Ohio, 1 and 2 November 1831.
   2   Hiram, Ohio, November 1831.

attempt of a man to imitate the language of Jesus Christ, renewed their faith in the fulness of the Gospel, and in the truth of the commandments and revelations which the Lord had given to the Church through my instrumentality; and the Elders signified a willingness to bear testimony of their truth to all the world. (HC 1:224–26)

3 The testimony of the witnesses to the book of the Lord's commandments, which He gave to His Church through Joseph Smith, Jun., who was appointed by the voice of the Church for this purpose; we therefore feel willing to bear testimony to all the world of mankind, to every creature upon the face of all the earth and upon the islands of the sea, that the Lord has borne record to our souls, through the Holy Ghost, shed forth upon us, that these commandments were given by inspiration of God, and are profitable for all men, and are verily true. We give this testimony unto the world, the Lord being our helper; and it is through the grace of God, the Father, and His Son, Jesus Christ, that we are permitted to have this privilege of bearing this testimony unto the world, that the children of men may be profited thereby. (HC 1:226)

4 The Book of Commandments and Revelations was to be dedicated by prayer to the service of Almighty God by me; and after I had done this, I inquired of the Lord concerning these things, and received the following: [D&C 69]. (HC 1:234)

5 My time was occupied closely in reviewing the commandments and sitting in conference, for nearly two weeks; for from the first to the twelfth of November we held four special conferences. In the last which was held at Brother Johnson's, in Hiram, after deliberate

---

Doctrine and Covenants

   3 The testimony concerning the revelations was given by revelation to Joseph Smith. It seems clear that the intention was to include that testimony in the Book of Commandments, signed by the ten elders present at the November 1831 conference (see HC 1:226). With the destruction of the press in Missouri in July 1833, that intent was not realized. A slightly modified version of the testimony, signed by the Twelve Apostles, was included in the 1835 edition of the Doctrine and Covenants and appears in the front of current editions.

   4 Hiram, Ohio, November 1831.

   5 Summary of conferences concerning the printing of the revelations, held in Hiram, Ohio, 1–12 November 1831.

consideration, in consequence of the book of revelations, now to be printed, being the foundation of the Church in these last days, and a benefit to the world, showing that the keys of the mysteries of the kingdom of our Savior are again entrusted to man; and the riches of eternity within the compass of those who are willing to live by every word that proceedeth out of the mouth of God—therefore the conference voted that they prize the revelations to be worth to the Church the riches of the whole earth, speaking temporally. The great benefits to the world which result from the Book of Mormon and the revelations which the Lord has seen fit in His infinite wisdom to grant unto us for our salvation, and for the salvation of all that will believe, were duly appreciated. (*HC* 1:235–36)

6   Nothing could be more pleasing to the Saints upon the order of the kingdom of the Lord, than the light which burst upon the world through the foregoing vision [D&C 76]. Every law, every commandment, every promise, every truth, and every point touching the destiny of man, from Genesis to Revelation, where the purity of the scriptures remains unsullied by the folly of men, go to show the perfection of the theory {of different degrees of glory in the future life} and witnesses the fact that that document is a transcript from the records of the eternal world. The sublimity of the ideas; the purity of the language; the scope for action; the continued duration for completion, in order that the heirs of salvation may confess the Lord and bow the knee; the rewards for faithfulness, and the punishments for sins, are so much beyond the narrow-mindedness of men, that every honest man is constrained to exclaim: "*It came from God.*" (*HC* 1:252–53)

7   Take away the Book of Mormon and the revelations, and where is our religion? We have none. (*HC* 2:52)

8   The second part [of the first edition of the Doctrine and Covenants] contains items or principles for the regulation of the Church as

---

Doctrine and Covenants

6   The Prophet's view of the vision of the glories (D&C 76), Hiram, Ohio, 16 February 1832.

7   Conference of the elders of the Church, Norton, Ohio, 21 April 1834.

8   Preface to the first edition of the Doctrine and Covenants, signed by Joseph Smith, Oliver Cowdery, Sidney Rigdon, and Frederick G. Williams, Kirtland, dated 17 February 1835.

taken from the revelations which have been given since its organization, as well as from former ones.

There may be an aversion in the minds of some against receiving anything purporting to be articles of religious faith, in consequence of there being so many now extant; but if men believe a system, and profess that it was given by inspiration, certainly the more intelligibly they can present it, the better. It does not make a principle untrue to print it, neither does it make it true not to print it.

The Church, viewing this subject to be of importance, appointed, through their servants and delegates the High Council, your servants to select and compile this work. Several reasons might be adduced in favor of this move of the Council, but we only add a few words. They knew that the Church was evil spoken of in many places, its faith and belief misrepresented, and the way of truth thus subverted. By some it was represented as disbelieving the Bible; by others as being an enemy to all good order and uprightness; and by others as being injurious to the peace of all governments, civil and political.

We have, therefore, endeavored to present, though in few words, our belief, and when we say this, humbly trust, the faith and principles of this society as a body.

We do not present this little volume with any other expectation than that we are to be called to answer to every principle advanced, in that day when the secrets of all hearts will be revealed, and the reward of every man's labor be given him. (HC 2:251)

Dove

1   The question arose from the saying of Jesus—"Among those that are born of women there is not a greater prophet than John the Baptist; but he that is least in the kingdom of God is greater then he." How is it that John was considered one of the greatest of prophets? His miracles could not have constituted his greatness.

First. He was entrusted with a divine mission of preparing the way before the face of the Lord. Whoever had such a trust committed to him before or since? No man.

Secondly. He was entrusted with the important mission, and it

Dove
1   Sabbath address, Nauvoo, 29 January 1843.

was required at his hands, to baptize the Son of Man. Whoever had the honor of doing that? Whoever had so great a privilege and glory? Whoever led the Son of God into the waters of baptism, and had the privilege of beholding the Holy Ghost descend in the form of a dove, or rather in the *sign* of the dove, in witness of that administration? The sign of the dove was instituted before the creation of the world, a witness for the Holy Ghost, and the devil cannot come in the sign of a dove. The Holy Ghost is a personage, and is in the form of a personage. It does not confine itself to the *form* of the dove, but in *sign* of the dove. The Holy Ghost cannot be transformed into a dove; but the sign of a dove was given to John to signify the truth of the deed, as the dove is an emblem or token of truth and innocence. (HC 5:260–61)

Dreams

1   *Words of Levi W. Hancock:* The Prophet called me to go on a mission with Evan Green. The snow came and it began to get cold to travel, but we went as far as we could get, and returned back. Joseph talked plain to me for not pressing forward into Pennsylvania. I told him that I was to blame, for I had had a dream that troubled me.

He said, "Don't let that trouble you. I have had dreams as bad as you ever had. You do as I now tell you to and you will come out all right."

He gave me to understand how the Comforter would comfort the mind of man when asleep. He said, "Go again," and we started forthwith for Pennsylvania. (*TK*, p. 19)

2   We believe that we have a right to revelations, visions, and dreams from God, our heavenly Father; and light and intelligence, through the gift of the Holy Ghost, in the name of Jesus Christ, on all subjects pertaining to our spiritual welfare; if it so be that we keep his commandments, so as to render ourselves worthy in his sight. (*PWJS*, p. 421)

Dreams

1   Reminiscence of Levi W. Hancock concerning events that took place probably in early 1832, found in "Life Story of Levi W. Hancock," BYU Library.

2   Letter to Isaac Galland, written while the Prophet was imprisoned in Liberty Jail, 22 March 1839.

3   I . . . spent the evening in the office with Elders Taylor and Richards, interpreting dreams, &c. (HC 4:501)

Earth

1   The time is near when desolation is to cover the earth, and then God will have a place of deliverance in His remnant, and in Zion. (HC 2:52)

2   Righteousness and truth are to sweep the earth as with a flood. And now, I ask, how righteousness and truth are going to sweep the earth as with a flood? I will answer. Men and angels are to be co-workers in bringing to pass this great work, and Zion is to be prepared, even a new Jerusalem, for the elect that are to be gathered from the four quarters of the earth, and to be established an holy city, for the tabernacle of the Lord shall be with them. (HC 2:260)

3   The world and earth are not synonymous terms. The world is the human family. This earth was organized or formed out of other planets which were broken up and remodelled and made into the one on which we live. The elements are eternal. (WJS, p. 60; standardized)

4   This earth will be rolled back into the presence of God and crowned with Celestial Glory. (WJS, p. 60)

5   "The earth shall yield its increase, resume its paradisean glory, and become as the garden of the Lord." . . .

Dreams
   3   Nauvoo, 21 January 1842.

Earth
   1   Conference of the elders of the Church, Norton, Ohio, 21 April 1834.
   2   Letter to the elders of the Church, Kirtland, 1 September 1835.
   3   Lecture given at the Nauvoo Lyceum, 5 January 1841, as reported by William Clayton. (The lyceum met weekly at different locations in Nauvoo for several months, beginning 5 January 1841.)
   4   Lecture given at the Nauvoo Lyceum, 5 January 1841, as reported by William Clayton. (The lyceum met weekly at different locations in Nauvoo for several months, beginning 5 January 1841.)
   5   Editorial in the *Times and Seasons*, 15 July 1842.

... To bring about this state of things, there must of necessity be great confusion among the nations of the earth; "distress of nations with perplexity." Am I asked what is the cause of the present distress? I would answer, "Shall there be evil in a city and the Lord hath not done it?"

The earth is groaning under corruption, oppression, tyranny and bloodshed; and God is coming out of His hiding place, as He said He would do, to vex the nations of the earth. (*HC* 5:61, 65)

6   While at dinner, I remarked to my family and friends present, that when the earth was sanctified and became like a sea of glass, it would be one great urim and thummim, and the Saints could look in it and see as they are seen. (*HC* 5:279)

7   In the days of Noah, God destroyed the world by a flood, and He has promised to destroy it by fire in the last days. (*HC* 6:251)

Edification

1   I do not calculate or intend to please your ears with superfluity of words or oratory, or with much learning; but I calculate {intend} to edify you with the simple truths from heaven. (*HC* 6:303)

Education

1   We consider that God has created man with a mind capable of instruction, and a faculty which may be enlarged in proportion to the heed and diligence given to the light communicated from heaven to the intellect; and that the nearer man approaches perfection, the

---

Earth
6   Nauvoo, 18 February 1843.
7   Sabbath address, Nauvoo, 10 March 1844.

Edification
1   King Follett Discourse, Nauvoo, 7 April 1844.

Education
1   Letter to the brethren scattered from Zion, Kirtland, 22 January 1834.

clearer are his views, and the greater his enjoyments, till he has overcome the evils of his life and lost every desire for sin; and like the ancients, arrives at that point of faith where he is wrapped in the power and glory of his Maker, and is caught up to dwell with Him. But we consider that this is a station to which no man ever arrived in a moment: he must have been instructed in the government and laws of that kingdom by proper degrees, until his mind is capable in some measure of comprehending the propriety, justice, equality, and consistency of the same. (HC 2:8)

2   I then went to assist in organizing the Elders' school. I called it to order and made some remarks upon the object of this school, and the great necessity of our rightly improving our time and reining up our minds to the sense of the great object that lies before us, viz—the glorious endowment that God has in store for the faithful. (HC 2:301)

3   I want you should not let those little fellows [Joseph and Emma's children] forget me. Tell them Father loves them with a perfect love, and he is doing all he can to get away from the mob to come to them. Do teach them all you can, that they may have good minds. (PWJS, p. 426; standardized)

4   I hope you will watch over those tender offsprings [Joseph and Emma's children] in a manner that is becoming a mother and a Saint, and try to cultivate their minds and learn them to read and be sober. (PWJS, p. 448; standardized)

5   The "University of the City of Nauvoo" will enable us to teach our children wisdom, to instruct them in all the knowledge and learning, in the arts, sciences, and learned professions. We hope to make this institution one of the great lights of the world, and by and through it to diffuse that kind of knowledge which will be of practicable utility, and for the public good, and also for private and individual happiness. The

---

Education
2   Kirtland, Ohio, 3 November 1835.
3   Letter to Emma Smith from Liberty Jail, 4 April 1839. Original copy at Yale University library.
4   Letter to Emma Smith from Springfield, Illinois, 9 November 1839.
5   Proclamation of the First Presidency, Nauvoo, 15 January 1841.

Regents of the University will take the general supervision of all matters appertaining to education, from common schools up to the highest
branches of a most liberal collegiate course. (*HC* 4:269)

6   In consequence of the impoverished condition of the Saints, the
buildings which are in course of erection do not progress as fast as
could be desired; but from the interest which is generally manifested
by the Saints at large, we hope to accomplish much by a combination
of effort, and a concentration of action, and erect the Temple and
other public buildings, which we so much need for our mutual instruction and the education of our children. (*HC* 4:338)

7   I am a rough stone. The sound of the hammer and chisel was
never heard on me until the Lord took me in hand. I desire the learning and wisdom of heaven alone. (*HC* 5:423)

8   All the minds and spirits that God ever sent into the world are
susceptible of enlargement. (*HC* 6:311)

Elders

1   It is the privilege of every elder to speak of the things of God, &c.;
and could we all come together with one heart and one mind in perfect faith the veil might as well be rent today as next week, or any
other time, and if we will but cleanse ourselves and covenant before
God, to serve him, it is our privilege to have an assurance that God
will protect us at all times. (*FWR*, p. 20; standardized)

Education
   6   Report of the First Presidency at general conference, Nauvoo, 7 April
        1841.
   7   Sabbath address, Nauvoo, 11 June 1843.
   8   King Follett Discourse, Nauvoo, 7 April 1844.

Elders
   1   Minutes of a conference held at Orange, Ohio, 25 October 1831.

Elect Lady

1   I assisted in commencing the organization of "The Female Relief Society of Nauvoo" in the Lodge Room. Sister Emma Smith, President, and Sister Elizabeth Ann Whitney and Sarah M. Cleveland, Counselors. I gave much instruction, read in the New Testament, and Book of Doctrine and Covenants, concerning the Elect Lady, and showed that the elect meant to be elected to a certain work, &c., and that the revelation was then fulfilled by Sister Emma's election to the Presidency of the Society, she having previously been ordained to expound the Scriptures. Emma was blessed, and her counselors were ordained by Elder John Taylor. (HC 4:552–53)

Election

See CALLING AND ELECTION

Elements

1   The elements are eternal. That which has a beginning will surely have an end. Take a ring, it is without beginning or end; cut it for a beginning place, and at the same time you have an ending place. (*WJS*, p. 60)

2   *Report of Wilford Woodruff:* The speaker [Joseph Smith], before closing, called upon the assembly before him to humble themselves in faith before God, and in mighty prayer and fasting to call upon the name of the Lord, until the elements were purified over our heads, and the earth sanctified under our feet, that the inhabitants of this city may escape the power of disease and pestilence, and the destroyer

---

Elect Lady
  1   Nauvoo, 17 March 1842.

Elements
  1   Lecture given at the Nauvoo Lyceum, 5 January 1841, as reported by William Clayton. (The lyceum met weekly at different locations in Nauvoo for several months, beginning 5 January 1841.)
  2   Sabbath address, Nauvoo, 20 March 1842.

that rideth upon the face of the earth, and that the Holy Spirit of God may rest upon this vast multitude. (*HC* 4:556–57)

3   God had materials to organize the world out of chaos—chaotic matter, which is element, and in which dwells all the glory. Element had an existence from the time He had. The pure principles of element are principles which can never be destroyed; they may be organized and re-organized, but not destroyed. They had no beginning and can have no end. (*HC* 6:308–9)

Elias and Elijah

1   There is a difference between the spirit and office of Elias and Elijah. . . .

The spirit of Elias is to prepare the way for a greater revelation of God, which is the Priesthood of Elias, or the Priesthood that Aaron was ordained unto. And when God sends a man into the world to prepare for a greater work, holding the keys of the power of Elias, it was called the doctrine of Elias, even from the early ages of the world. . . .

We find the apostles endowed with greater power than John: their office was more under the spirit and power of Elijah than Elias. . . .

That person who holds the keys of Elias hath a preparatory work. . . .

. . . What you seal on earth, by the keys of Elijah, is sealed in heaven; and this is the power of Elijah, and this is the difference between the spirit and power of Elias and Elijah; for while the spirit of Elias is a forerunner, the power of Elijah is sufficient to make our calling and election sure. . . .

The spirit of Elias is first, Elijah second, and Messiah last. Elias is a forerunner to prepare the way, and the spirit and power of Elijah is to come after, holding the keys of power, building the Temple to the capstone, placing the seals of the Melchisedec Priesthood upon the house of Israel, and making all things ready; then Messiah comes to His Temple, which is last of all.

Elements
    3   King Follett Discourse, Nauvoo, 7 April 1844.

Elias and Elijah
    1   Sabbath address, Nauvoo, 10 March 1844.

Messiah is above the spirit and power of Elijah, for He made the world, and was that spiritual rock unto Moses in the wilderness. Elijah was to come and prepare the way and build up the kingdom before the coming of the great day of the Lord, although the spirit of Elias might begin it. (HC 6:249, 250, 251, 252, 254)

Elijah

1 Elijah was the last Prophet that held the keys of the Priesthood, and who will, before the last dispensation, restore the authority and deliver the keys of the Priesthood, in order that all the ordinances may be attended to in righteousness. It is true that the Savior had authority and power to bestow this blessing; but the sons of Levi were too prejudiced. "And I will send Elijah the Prophet before the great and terrible day of the Lord," etc., etc. Why send Elijah? Because he holds the keys of the authority to administer in all the ordinances of the Priesthood; and without the authority is given, the ordinances could not be administered in righteousness. (HC 4:211)

2 Elijah had to flee his country, for they [his country and kindred] sought his life,—and he was fed by ravens. . . . Did these afflictions come upon these prophets of the Lord on account of transgression? No! It was the iron hand of persecution—like the chains of Missouri! And mark—when these old prophets suffered, the vengeance of God, in due time, followed and left the wicked opposers of the Lord's anointed like Sodom and Gomorrah; like the Egyptians; like Jezebel, who was eaten by dogs; and like all Israel, which were led away captive, till the Lord had spent his fury upon them—even to this day. (T&S 3:902)

3 He shall send Elijah the prophet, and he shall reveal the covenants of the fathers in relation to the children, and the covenants of the children in relation to the fathers. (HC 5:530)

Elijah
1 Article on priesthood read at general conference, Nauvoo, 5 October 1840.
2 Editorial in the *Times and Seasons*, 1 September 1842.
3 Remarks at the funeral of Judge Elias Higbee, Nauvoo, 13 August 1843.

4   *Report of William Clayton:* Went to meeting, heard J[oseph] preach
on 2 Peter 3. 10 & 11—being a funeral sermon on the death of E. Higbee. When speaking of the passage "I will send Elijah the prophet,
&c.," he said it should read, "And he shall turn the hearts of the children to the covenant made with their fathers." (*WJS*, pp. 241–42;
standardized)

5   The Bible says, "I will send you Elijah the Prophet before the
coming of the great and dreadful day of the Lord; and he shall turn the
hearts of the fathers to the children, and the hearts of the children to
the fathers, lest I come and smite the earth with a curse."

Now, the word *turn* here should be translated *bind*, or *seal*. But
what is the object of this important mission? or how is it to be fulfilled? The keys are to be delivered, the spirit of Elijah is to come, the
Gospel to be established, the Saints of God gathered, Zion built up,
and the Saints to come up as saviors on Mount Zion.

But how are they to become saviors on Mount Zion? By building
their temples, erecting their baptismal fonts, and going forth and receiving all the ordinances, baptisms, confirmations, washings, anointings, ordinations and sealing powers upon their heads, in behalf of all
their progenitors who are dead, and redeem them that they may come
forth in the first resurrection and be exalted to thrones of glory with
them; and herein is the chain that binds the hearts of the fathers to
the children, and the children to the fathers, which fulfills the mission
of Elijah. And I would to God that this temple [the Nauvoo Temple]
was now done, that we might go into it, and go to work and improve
our time, and make use of the seals while they are on earth.

The Saints have not too much time to save and redeem their
dead, and gather together their living relatives, that they may be
saved also, before the earth will be smitten, and the consumption decreed falls upon the world.

I would advise all the Saints to go to with their might and gather
together all their living relatives to this place, that they may be sealed
and saved, that they may be prepared against the day that the destroying angel goes forth; and if the whole Church should go to with all

---

Elijah

   4   Remarks at the funeral of Judge Elias Higbee, Nauvoo, 13 August 1843, as
      reported by William Clayton.
   5   Sabbath address, Nauvoo, 21 January 1844.

their might to save their dead, seal their posterity, and gather their living friends, and spend none of their time in behalf of the world, they would hardly get through before night would come, when no man can work; and my only trouble at the present time is concerning ourselves, that the Saints *will be divided, broken up, and scattered,* before we get our salvation secure; for there are so many fools in the world for the devil to operate upon, it gives him the advantage oftentimes. (*HC* 6:183–84)

6   Now for Elijah. The spirit, power, and calling of Elijah is, that ye have power to hold the key of the revelation, ordinances, oracles, powers and endowments of the fullness of the Melchisedeck Priesthood and of the kingdom of God on the earth; and to receive, obtain, and perform all the ordinances belonging to the kingdom of God, even unto the turning of the hearts of the fathers unto the children, and the hearts of the children unto the fathers, even those who are in heaven. . . .

Now comes the point. What is this office and work of Elijah? It is one of the greatest and most important subjects that God has revealed. He should send Elijah to seal the children to the fathers, and the fathers to the children.

Now was this merely confined to the living, to settle difficulties with families on earth? By no means. It was a far greater work. Elijah! what would you do if you were here? Would you confine your work to the living alone? No; I would refer you to the Scriptures, where the subject is manifest: that is, without us, they could not be made perfect, nor we without them; the fathers without the children, nor the children without the fathers.

I wish you to understand this subject, for it is important; and if you will receive it, this is the spirit of Elijah, that we redeem our dead, and connect ourselves with our fathers which are in heaven, and seal up our dead to come forth in the first resurrection; and here we want the power of Elijah to seal those who dwell on earth to those who dwell in heaven. This is the power of Elijah and the keys of the kingdom of Jehovah.

. . . Then what you seal on earth, by the keys of Elijah, is sealed in heaven. . . .

Elijah
 6   Sabbath address, Nauvoo, 10 March 1844.

This spirit of Elijah was manifest in the days of the apostles, in delivering certain ones to the buffetings of Satan, that they might be saved in the day of the Lord Jesus. They were sealed by the spirit of Elijah unto the damnation of hell until the day of the Lord, or revelation of Jesus Christ. (HC 6:251–52)

7   According to the Scripture, if men have received the good word of God, and tasted of the powers of the world to come, if they shall fall away, it is impossible to renew them again, seeing they have crucified the Son of God afresh, and put Him to an open shame; so there is a possibility of falling away; you could not be renewed again, and the power of Elijah cannot seal against this sin, for this is a reserve made in the seals and power of the Priesthood. (HC 6:253)

8   Again: The doctrine or sealing power of Elijah is as follows:—If you have power to seal on earth and in heaven, then we should be wise. The first thing you do, go and seal on earth your sons and daughters unto yourself, and yourself unto your fathers in eternal glory, and go ahead, and not go back, but use a little wisdom, and seal all you can, and when you get to heaven tell your Father that what you seal on earth should be sealed in heaven, according to his promise. I will walk through the gate of heaven and claim what I seal, and those that follow me and my counsel. (*TPJS*, p. 340)

Elohim (Eloheim)

1   Paul says there are Gods many and Lords many; and that makes a plurality of Gods, in spite of the whims of all men. Without a revelation, I am not going to give them the knowledge of the God of heaven. You know and I testify that Paul had no allusion to the heathen gods. I have it from God, and get over it if you can. I have a witness of the Holy Ghost, and a testimony that Paul had no allusion to the heathen gods in the text. I will show from the Hebrew Bible that I

Elijah
   7   Sabbath address, Nauvoo, 10 March 1844.
   8   Sabbath address, Nauvoo, 10 March 1844.

Elohim (Eloheim)
   1   Sabbath address, Nauvoo, 16 June 1844.

am correct, and the first word shows a plurality of Gods; and I want the apostates and learned men to come here and prove to the contrary, if they can. An unlearned boy must give you a little Hebrew. *Berosheit baurau Eloheim ait aushamayeen vehau auraits*, rendered by King James' translators, "In the beginning God created the heaven and the earth." I want to analyze the word *Berosheit*. *Rosh*, the head; *Sheit*, a grammatical termination; the *Baith* was not originally put there when the inspired man wrote it, but it has been since added by an old Jew. *Baurau* signifies to bring forth; *Eloheim* is from the word *Eloi*, God, in the singular number; and by adding the word *heim*, it renders it Gods. It read first, "In the beginning the head of the Gods brought forth the Gods," or, as others have translated it, "The head of the Gods called the Gods together." I want to show a little learning as well as other fools—

> A little learning is a dangerous thing.
> Drink deep, or taste not the Pierian spring,
> There shallow draughts intoxicate the brain,
> And drinking largely sobers us up again.

All this confusion among professed translators is for want of drinking another draught.

The head God organized the heavens and the earth. I defy all the world to refute me. In the beginning the heads of the Gods organized the heavens and the earth. Now the learned priests and the people rage, and the heathen imagine a vain thing. If we pursue the Hebrew text further, it reads, "*Berosheit baurau Eloheim ait aashamayeen vehau auraits*"— "The head one of the Gods said, Let us make a man in our own image." I once asked a learned Jew, "If the Hebrew language compels us to render all words ending in *heim* in the plural, why not render the first *Eloheim* plural?" He replied, "That is the rule with few exceptions; but in this case it would ruin the Bible." He acknowledged I was right. I came here to investigate these things precisely as I believe them. Hear and judge for yourselves; and if you go away satisfied, well and good.

In the very beginning the Bible shows there is a plurality of Gods beyond the power of refutation. It is a great subject I am dwelling on. The word *Eloheim* ought to be in the plural all the way through— Gods. The heads of the Gods appointed one God for us; and when you take {that} view of the subject, it sets one free to see all the beauty, holiness and perfection of the Gods. All I want is to get the simple, naked truth, and the whole truth. (HC 6:475–76)

Emma

1   Oh, Emma, for God['s] sake do not forsake me nor the truth, but
remember me. If I do not meet you again in this life, may God grant
that we may meet in heaven. I cannot express my feelings, my heart is
full. Farewell, oh my kind and affectionate Emma. I am yours forever,
your hu[s]band and true friend. (*PWJS*, pp. 362–63; standardized)

2   With what unspeakable delight, and what transports of joy
swelled my bosom, when I took by the hand, on that night, my
beloved Emma—she that was my wife, even the wife of my youth, and
the choice of my heart. Many were the reverberations of my mind
when I contemplated for a moment the many scenes we had been
called to pass through, the fatigues and the toils, the sorrows and sufferings, and the joys and consolations, from time to time, which had
strewed our paths and crowned our board. Oh what a commingling of
thought filled my mind for the moment, again she is here, even in the
seventh trouble—undaunted, firm, and unwavering—unchangeable,
affectionate Emma! (*HC* 5:107)

Endowment

1   You will recollect that the first Elders are to receive their endowment in Kirtland, before the redemption of Zion. (*HC* 2:144)

2   I then went to assist in organizing the Elders' school. I called it to
order and made some remarks upon the object of this school, and the
great necessity of our rightly improving our time and reining up our

---

Emma
  1   Letter sent from Independence, Missouri, to the Prophet's wife, Emma, in
      Far West, 4 November 1838. Joseph Smith and other Church leaders were
      in the custody of General Samuel D. Lucas of the Missouri state militia.
  2   The Prophet's sentiments concerning his wife, Emma, 16 August 1842. At
      this time Joseph Smith was in hiding to avoid vexatious lawsuits. In his
      history he expresses kind feelings toward trusted friends, including Emma.

Endowment
  1   Letter written from Kirtland to the high council in Zion, 16 August 1834.
  2   Kirtland, Ohio, 3 November 1835.

minds to the sense of the great object that lies before us, viz—the glorious endowment that God has in store for the faithful. (HC 2:301)

3   The endowment you are so anxious about, you cannot comprehend now, nor could Gabriel explain it to the understanding of your
dark minds; but strive to be prepared in your hearts, be faithful in all
things, that when we meet in the solemn assembly, that is, when such
as God shall name out of all the official members shall meet, we must
be clean every whit. Let us be faithful and silent, brethren, and if God
gives you a manifestation, keep it to yourselves; be watchful and
prayerful, and you shall have a prelude of those joys that God will pour
out on that day. Do not watch for iniquity in each other, if you do you
will not get an endowment, for God will not bestow it on such. But if
we are faithful, and live by every word that proceeds forth from the
mouth of God, I will venture to prophesy that we shall get a blessing
that will be worth remembering, if we should live as long as John the
Revelator; our blessings will be such as we have not realized before, nor
received in this generation. The order of the house of God has been,
and ever will be, the same, even after Christ comes; and after the termination of the thousand years it will be the same; and we shall finally
enter into the celestial Kingdom of God, and enjoy it forever.

   You need an endowment, brethren, in order that you may be prepared and able to overcome all things; and those that reject your testimony will be damned. The sick will be healed, the lame made to walk,
the deaf to hear, and the blind to see, through your instrumentality.
But let me tell you, that you will not have power, after the endowment to heal those that have not faith, nor to benefit them, for you
might as well expect to benefit a devil in hell as such as are possessed
of his spirit, and are willing to keep it; for they are habitations for devils, and only fit for his society. But when you are endowed and prepared to preach the Gospel to all nations, kindred, and tongues, in
their own languages, you must faithfully warn all, and bind up the testimony, and seal up the law, and the destroying angel will follow close
at your heels, and exercise his tremendous mission upon the children
of disobedience; and destroy the workers of iniquity, while the Saints
will be gathered out from among them, and stand in holy places ready
to meet the Bridegroom when he comes. (HC 2:309)

Endowment
3   Instructions to the Twelve, Kirtland, 12 November 1835.

4 I left the meeting in the charge of the Twelve, and retired about nine o'clock in the evening. The brethren continued exhorting, prophesying, and speaking in tongues until five o'clock in the morning. The Savior made His appearance to some, while angels ministered to others, and it was a Pentecost and an endowment indeed, long to be remembered, for the sound shall go forth from this place into all the world, and the occurrences of this day shall be handed down upon the pages of sacred history, to all generations; as the day of Pentecost, so shall this day be numbered and celebrated as a year of jubilee, and time of rejoicing to the Saints of the Most High God. (HC 2:432–33)

5 I spent the day in the upper part of the store, that is in my private office (so called because in that room I keep my sacred writings, translate ancient records, and receive revelations) and in my general business office, or lodge room (that is where the Masonic fraternity meet occasionally, for want of a better place) in council with General James Adams, of Springfield, Patriarch Hyrum Smith, Bishops Newel K. Whitney and George Miller, and President Brigham Young and Elders Heber C. Kimball and Willard Richards, instructing them in the principles and order of the Priesthood, attending to washings, anointings, endowments and the communication of keys pertaining to the Aaronic Priesthood, and so on to the highest order of the Melchisedek Priesthood, setting forth the order pertaining to the Ancient of Days, and all those plans and principles by which any one is enabled to secure the fullness of those blessings which have been prepared for the Church of the First Born, and come up and abide in the presence of the Eloheim in the eternal worlds. In this council was instituted the ancient order of things for the first time in these last days. And the communications I made to this council were of things spiritual, and to be received only by the spiritual minded: and there was nothing made known to these men but what will be made known to all the Saints of the last days, so soon as they are prepared to receive, and a proper place is prepared to communicate them, even to the weakest of the Saints; therefore let the Saints be diligent in building the Temple, and all houses which they have been, or shall hereafter be, commanded of God to build; and wait their time with patience in all meekness, faith,

---

Endowment
   4   Solemn assembly in the Kirtland Temple, 30 March 1836.
   5   First temple endowment given in this dispensation, Nauvoo, 4 May 1842.

perseverance unto the end, knowing assuredly that all these things referred to in this council are always governed by the principle of revelation. (HC 5:1–2)

6 And when the apostles were raised up, they worked in Jerusalem,
and Jesus commanded them to tarry there until they were endowed with
power from on high. Had they not work to do in Jerusalem? They did
work, and prepared a people for the Pentecost. The kingdom of God
was with them before the day of Pentecost, as well as afterwards; and it
was also with John, and he preached the same Gospel and baptism that
Jesus and the apostles preached after him. The endowment was to prepare the disciples for their missions unto the world. (HC 5:259)

7 As soon as the [Nauvoo] Temple and baptismal font are prepared,
we calculate to give the Elders of Israel their washings and anointings,
and attend to those last and more impressive ordinances, without
which we cannot obtain celestial thrones. But there must be a holy
place prepared for that purpose. There was a proclamation made during
the time that the foundation of the Temple was laid to that effect, and
there are provisions made until the work is completed, so that men
may receive their endowments and be made kings and priests unto the
Most High God, having nothing to do with temporal things, but their
whole time will be taken up with things pertaining to the house of
God. There must, however, be a place built expressly for that purpose,
and for men to be baptized for their dead. It must be built in this the
central place; for every man who wishes to save his father, mother,
brothers, sisters and friends, must go through all the ordinances for
each one of them separately, the same as for himself, from baptism to
ordination, washings and anointings, and receive all the keys and powers of the Priesthood, the same as for himself. (HC 6:319)

8 *Words of Mercy R. Thompson:* I received my endowments by the
directions of the Prophet Joseph, his wife Emma officiating in my
case. In his instructions to me at that time, he said, "This will bring
you out of darkness into marvelous light." (*TK*, p. 120)

Endowment
6 Sabbath address, Nauvoo, 22 January 1843.
7 General conference address, Nauvoo, 8 April 1844.
8 Recollection of Mercy R. Thompson, published in the *Juvenile Instructor*, 1
   July 1892.

Enduring to the End

1 I believe I shall be let out of their [the persecutors'] hands some way or another, and shall see good days. We cannot do anything only stand still and see the salvation of God. He must do His own work, or it must fall to the ground. We must not take it in our hands to avenge our wrongs. Vengeance is mine, saith the Lord, and I will repay. I have no fears. I shall stand unto death, God being my helper. (HC 3:286)

2 Calculating as we do, upon the mercy and power of God in our behalf, we hope to persevere on in every good and useful work, even unto the end, that when we come to be tried in the balance we may not be found wanting. (HC 4:9)

3 It mattereth not whether we live long or short on the earth after we come to a knowledge of these principles and obey them unto the end. (HC 4:555)

4 All your losses will be made up to you in the resurrection, provided you continue faithful. By the vision of the Almighty I have seen it. (HC 5:362)

5 He that holds out faithful to the end shall in no wise lose his reward. A good man will endure all things to honor Christ, and even dispose of the whole world, and all in it, to save his soul. (HC 6:427)

6 *History Entry:* He [Joseph Smith] then took Hodge by the hand and said, "Now, Brother Hodge, let what will come, don't deny the faith, and all will be well." (HC 6:546)

Enduring to the End
1 Letter from Liberty Jail to Mrs. Norman Bull (Buell), 15 March 1839.
2 A letter to Isaac Galland, Commerce (Nauvoo), 11 September 1839.
3 Sabbath address, Nauvoo, 20 March 1842.
4 Remarks upon the death of Lorenzo D. Barnes, Nauvoo, 16 April 1843.
5 Letter of the Prophet and Hyrum Smith to Mr. Tewkesbury (Abijah R. Tewksbury), Nauvoo, 4 June 1844, seeking to restore him to fellowship.
6 Statement to Abraham C. Hodge as the Prophet was leaving Nauvoo, intending to go west, 22 June 1844.

Enemies

1   We do not rejoice in the affliction of our enemies but we shall be glad to have truth prevail. (*PWJS*, p. 227)

2   I am a lover of the cause of Christ and of virtue, chastity, and an upright, steady course of conduct and a holy walk. I despise a hypocrite or a covenant breaker. I judge them not; God shall judge them according to their works. I am a lover even of mine enemies, for an enemy seeketh to destroy openly. I can pray for those who despitefully use and persecute me, but for all I cannot hope. (*PWJS*, p. 246; standardized)

3   Cursed shall every man be that lifts his arm to hinder this great work. And God is my witness of this truth; it shall be done, and let all the Saints say amen. (*PWJS*, p. 286; standardized)

4   May every weapon formed against us fall upon the head of him who shall form it. (*HC* 2:175)

5   Those who have associated with us and made the greatest professions of friendship, have frequently been our greatest enemies and our most determined foes, if they became unpopular, if their interest or dignity was touched, or if they were detected in their iniquity; they were always the first to raise the hand of persecution, to calumniate and vilify their brethren, and to seek the downfall and destruction of their friends. (*T&S* 3:868)

6   The enemies of this people will never get weary of their persecution against the Church, until they are overcome. I expect they will

Enemies
1   Letter to Oliver Cowdery from Harmony, Pennsylvania, 22 October 1829.
2   Letter to William W. Phelps in Zion, 31 July 1832, written from Hiram, Ohio.
3   Letter to William W. Phelps and others following mob destruction of the Saints' property in Missouri, Kirtland, 18 August 1833.
4   A prayer, Kirtland, 29 November 1834.
5   Editorial in the *Times and Seasons*, 1 August 1842.
6   Remarks to the Relief Society, Nauvoo, 31 August 1842.

array everything against me that is in their power to control, and that we shall have a long and tremendous warfare. He that will war the true Christian warfare against the corruptions of these last days will have wicked men and angels of devils, and all the infernal powers of darkness continually arrayed against him. When wicked and corrupt men oppose, it is a criterion to judge if a man is warring the Christian warfare. When all men speak evil of you falsely, blessed are ye, &c. Shall a man be considered bad, when men speak evil of him? No. If a man stands and opposes the world of sin, he may expect to have all wicked and corrupt spirits arrayed against him. But it will be but a little season, and all these afflictions will be turned away from us, inasmuch as we are faithful, and are not overcome by these evils. (HC 5:141)

7   Salvation is nothing more nor less than to triumph over all our enemies. (HC 5:387)

8   If we would secure and cultivate the love of others, we must love others, even our enemies as well as friends. (HC 5:498)

9   The Lord once told me that what I asked for I should have. I have been afraid to ask God to kill my enemies, lest some of them should, peradventure, repent.

I asked a short time since for the Lord to deliver me out of the hands of the Governor of Missouri, and if it needs must be to accomplish it, to take him away; and the next news that came pouring down from there was, that *Governor Reynolds had shot himself*. And I would now say, Beware, O earth, how you fight against the Saints of God and shed innocent blood; for in the days of Elijah, his enemies came upon him, and fire was called down from heaven and destroyed them. (HC 6:253–54)

Enemies

7   Sabbath address at Yelrome (Morley's Settlement), Illinois, 14 May 1843.

8   Sabbath address, Nauvoo, 9 July 1843.

9   Sabbath address, Nauvoo, 10 March 1844.

England

1 *Words of Edward Stevenson:* Finally, in speaking of the latter-day work, he [Joseph Smith] said, "There are thousands of good people in England and those old countries who are waiting for the fulness of the gospel, and it will not be long before they will flock to Zion, for Ephraim dwells largely in those parts." (*TK*, p. 86)

Enoch

1 Now this Enoch God reserved unto Himself, that he should not die at that time, and appointed unto him a ministry unto terrestrial bodies, of whom there has been but little revealed. He is reserved also unto the Presidency of a dispensation, and more shall be said of him and terrestrial bodies in another treatise. He is a ministering angel, to minister to those who shall be heirs of salvation, and appeared unto Jude as Abel did unto Paul; therefore Jude spoke of him (14, 15 verses). And Enoch, the seventh from Adam, revealed these sayings: "Behold, the Lord cometh with ten thousand of His Saints."

Paul was also acquainted with this character, and received instructions from him. "By faith Enoch was translated, that he should not see death, and was not found, because God had translated him; for before his translation he had this testimony, that he pleased God; but without faith, it is impossible to please Him, for he that cometh to God must believe that He is, and that he is a revealer to those who diligently seek him." [Hebrews 11:5–6.] (*HC* 4:209)

2 He [the Lord] selected Enoch, whom He directed, and gave His law unto, and to the people who were with him; and when the world in general would not obey the commands of God, after walking with God, he translated Enoch and his church, and the Priesthood or government of heaven was taken away. (*HC* 5:64)

England
1 Autobiography of Edward Stevenson, LDS Church Archives.

Enoch
1 Article on priesthood read at general conference, Nauvoo, 5 October 1840.
2 Editorial in the *Times and Seasons*, 15 July 1842.

3   If Enoch was righteous enough to come into the presence of God, and walk with him, he must have become so by keeping his commandments. (*T&S* 3:905)

Equality

1   Equal rights and privileges is my motto; and one man is as good as another, if he behaves as well; and that all men should be esteemed alike, without regard to distinctions of an official nature. (*HC* 2:403)

Eternal Life
See also EXALTATION

1   He [Newel Knight] saw heaven opened, and beheld the Lord Jesus Christ, seated at the right hand of the majesty on high, and had it made plain to his understanding that the time would come when he would be admitted into His presence to enjoy His society for ever and ever. (*HC* 1:85)

2   If you wish to go where God is, you must be like God, or possess the principles which God possesses, for if we are not drawing towards God in principle, we are going from Him and drawing towards the devil. (*HC* 4:588)

3   Let the lamp of eternal life be lit up in his [Thy servant Joseph's] heart, never to be taken away; and let the words of eternal life be poured upon the soul of Thy servant, that he may know Thy will, Thy

---

Enoch
    3   Editorial in the *Times and Seasons*, 1 September 1842.

Equality
    1   Instructions to priesthood quorums, Kirtland, 3 March 1836.

Eternal Life
    1   First conference of the Church, Fayette, New York, 9 June 1830.
    2   Sabbath address, Nauvoo, 10 April 1842.
    3   A prayer, Nauvoo, 22 August 1842.

statutes, and Thy commandments, and Thy judgments, to do them. (HC 5:127–28)

4   Your life [speaking to William Clayton] is hid with Christ in God, and so are many others. Nothing but the unpardonable sin can pre-vent you from inheriting eternal life for you are sealed up by the power of the Priesthood unto eternal life, having taken the step neces-sary for that purpose. (HC 5:391)

5   Eternal life is to *know* the only true God and his Son Jesus, with-out which there is no salvation. (WJS, p. 241; standardized)

6   The organization of the spiritual and heavenly worlds, and of spir-itual and heavenly beings, was agreeable to the most perfect order and harmony: their limits and bounds were fixed irrevocably, and volun-tarily subscribed to in their heavenly estate by themselves, and were by our first parents subscribed to upon the earth. Hence the impor-tance of embracing and subscribing to principles of eternal truth by all men upon the earth that expect eternal life. (HC 6:51)

7   It is one thing to see the kingdom of God, and another thing to enter into it. We must have a change of heart to see the kingdom of God, and subscribe the articles of adoption to enter therein. (HC 6:58)

8   The scriptures inform us that "This is life eternal that they might know thee, the only true God, and Jesus Christ whom thou hast sent."
If any man does not know God, and inquires what kind of a being He is,—if he will search diligently his own heart—if the declaration of Jesus and the apostles be true, he will realize that he has not eternal life; for there can be eternal life on no other principle. . . .

Eternal Life
   4   Instruction given to a few Saints at the home of Benjamin F. Johnson, Ramus, Illinois, 16 May 1843.
   5   Remarks at the funeral of Judge Elias Higbee, Nauvoo, 13 August 1843. Reported by Howard Coray, Howard and Martha Coray Notebook, LDS Church Archives.
   6   Remarks upon the death of James Adams, Nauvoo, 9 October 1843.
   7   Sabbath address, Nauvoo, 15 October 1843.
   8   King Follett Discourse, Nauvoo, 7 April 1844.

. . . Here, then, is eternal life—to know the only wise and true God; and you have got to learn how to be gods yourselves, and to be kings and priests to God, the same as all gods have done before you, namely, by going from one small degree to another, and from a small capacity to a great one; from grace to grace, from exaltation to exaltation, until you attain to the resurrection of the dead, and are able to dwell in everlasting burnings, and to sit in glory, as do those who sit enthroned in everlasting power. And I want you to know that God, in the last days, while certain individuals are proclaiming His name, is not trifling with you or me.

These are the first principles of consolation. How consoling to the mourners when they are called to part with a husband, wife, father, mother, child, or dear relative, to know that, although the earthly tabernacle is laid down and dissolved, they shall rise again to dwell in everlasting burnings in immortal glory, not to sorrow, suffer, or die any more, but they shall be heirs of God and joint heirs with Jesus Christ. What is it? To inherit the same power, the same glory and the same exaltation, until you arrive at the station of a god, and ascend the throne of eternal power, the same as those who have gone before. . . .

. . . The relationship we have with God places us in a situation to advance in knowledge. He has power to institute laws to instruct the weaker intelligences, that they may be exalted with Himself, so that they might have one glory upon another, and all that knowledge, power, glory, and intelligence, which is requisite in order to save them in the world of spirits.

This is good doctrine. It tastes good. I can taste the principles of eternal life, and so can you. They are given to me by the revelations of Jesus Christ; and I know that when I tell you these words of eternal life as they are given to me, you taste them, and I know that you believe them. You say honey is sweet, and so do I. I can also taste the spirit of eternal life. I know that it is good; and when I tell you of these things which were given me by inspiration of the Holy Spirit, you are bound to receive them as sweet, and rejoice more and more. . . .

. . . What have we to console us in relation to the dead? We have reason to have the greatest hope and consolation for our dead of any people on the earth; for we have seen them walk worthily in our midst, and seen them sink asleep in the arms of Jesus; and those who have died in the faith are now in the celestial kingdom of God. And hence is the glory of the sun. . . .

I have a father, brothers, children, and friends who have gone to a world of spirits. They are only absent for a moment. They are in the spirit, and we shall soon meet again. The time will soon arrive when the trumpet shall sound. When we depart, we shall hail our mothers, fathers, friends, and all whom we love, who have fallen asleep in Jesus. There will be no fear of mobs, persecutions, or malicious lawsuits and arrests; but it will be an eternity of felicity. (HC 6:304, 306, 312, 315, 316)

9 The Savior has the words of eternal life. Nothing else can profit us. (HC 6:363)

10 I do not regard my own life. I am ready to be offered a sacrifice for this people; for what can our enemies do? Only kill the body, and their power is then at an end. Stand firm, my friends; never flinch. Do not seek to save your lives, for he that is afraid to die for the truth, will lose eternal life. Hold out to the end, and we shall be resurrected and become like Gods, and reign in celestial kingdoms, principalities, and eternal dominions. (HC 6:500)

11 *Words of Joseph Lee Robinson:* I will mention several of his [Joseph Smith's] sayings: "There is not one key or one power to be bestowed on this church to lead the people into the celestial kingdom but I have given you, shown you and talked it over with you; the kingdom is set up and you have the perfect pattern and you can go and build up the kingdom, go in at the celestial gate, taking your train with you." (*TK*, p. 164)

Evil

1 In order to do this [serve the Lord effectively], he [a man] and all his house must be virtuous, and must shun the very appearance of evil. (HC 3:231)

Eternal Life
9 Sabbath address, Nauvoo, 12 May 1844.
10 Address to the Nauvoo Legion, 18 June 1844.
11 Journal of Joseph Lee Robinson.

Evil
1 Letter to the Church from Liberty Jail, 16 December 1838.

2 *Report of Eliza R. Snow:* He [Joseph Smith] said if one member becomes corrupt, and you know it, you must immediately put it away, or it will either injure or destroy the whole body. The sympathies of the heads of the Church have induced them to bear a long time with those who were corrupt until they are obliged to cut them off, lest all become contaminated; you must put down iniquity, and by your good examples, stimulate the Elders to good works; if you do right, there is no danger of your going too fast.

He said he did not care how fast we run in the path of virtue; resist evil, and there is no danger; God, men, and angels will not condemn those that resist everything that is evil, and devils cannot; as well might the devil seek to dethrone Jehovah, as overthrow an innocent soul that resists everything which is evil. (HC 4:605)

3 The servants of the Lord are required to guard against those things that are calculated to do the most evil. The little foxes spoil the vines—little evils do the most injury to the Church. If you have evil feelings, and speak of them to one another, it has a tendency to do mischief. These things result in those evils which are calculated to cut the throats of the heads of the Church.

When I do the best I can—when I am accomplishing the greatest good, then the most evils and wicked surmisings are got up against me. I would to God that you would be wise. I now counsel you, that if you know anything calculated to disturb the peace or injure the feelings of your brother or sister, hold your tongues, and the least harm will be done. (HC 5:140)

4 I visited Sister Morey, who was severely afflicted. We [Dr. Willard Richards and Joseph Smith, Jr.] prescribed *lobelia* for her, among other things, which is excellent in its place. I have learned the value of it by my own experience. It is one of the works of God, but, like the power of God, or any other good, it becomes an evil when improperly used. (HC 5:209)

5 Truth and error, good and evil cannot be reconciled. (HC 6:51)

Evil
 2 Remarks to the Relief Society, Nauvoo, 28 April 1842.
 3 Remarks to the Relief Society, Nauvoo, 31 August 1842.
 4 Nauvoo, 26 December 1842.
 5 Remarks upon the death of James Adams, Nauvoo, 9 October 1843.

Evil Spirits

See also DEVIL, FALSE SPIRITS

1   Amongst those who attended our meetings regularly, was Newel Knight, son of Joseph Knight. He and I had many serious conversations on the important subject of man's eternal salvation. We had got into the habit of praying much at our meetings, and Newel had said that he would try and take up his cross, and pray vocally during meeting; but when we again met together, he rather excused himself. I tried to prevail upon him, making use of the figure, supposing that he should get into a mud-hole, would he not try to help himself out? And I further said that we were willing now to help him out of the mud-hole. He replied, that provided he had got into a mud-hole through carelessness, he would rather wait and get out himself, than to have others help him; and so he would wait until he could get into the woods by himself, and there he would pray. Accordingly, he deferred praying until next morning, when he retired into the woods; where, according to his own account afterwards, he made several attempts to pray, but could scarcely do so, feeling that he had not done his duty, in refusing to pray in the presence of others. He began to feel uneasy, and continued to feel worse both in mind and body, until, upon reaching his own house, his appearance was such as to alarm his wife very much. He requested her to go and bring me to him. I went and found him suffering very much in his mind, and his body acted upon in a very strange manner; his visage and limbs distorted and twisted in every shape and appearance possible to imagine; and finally he was caught up off the floor of the apartment, and tossed about most fearfully.

His situation was soon made known to his neighbors and relatives, and in a short time as many as eight or nine grown persons had got together to witness the scene. After he had thus suffered for a time, I succeeded in getting hold of him by the hand, when almost immediately he spoke to me, and with great earnestness requested me to cast the devil out of him, saying that he knew he was in him, and that he also knew that I could cast him out.

I replied, "If you know that I can, it shall be done;" and then almost unconsciously I rebuked the devil, and commanded him in the

---

Evil Spirits
1   Colesville, New York, April 1830.

name of Jesus Christ to depart from him; when immediately Newel spoke out and said that he saw the devil leave him and vanish from his sight. This was the first miracle which was done in the Church, or by any member of it; and it was done not by man, nor by the power of man, but it was done by God, and by the power of godliness; therefore, let the honor and the praise, the dominion and the glory, be ascribed to the Father, Son, and Holy Spirit, for ever and ever. Amen.

This scene was now entirely changed, for as soon as the devil had departed from our friend, his countenance became natural, his distortions of body ceased, and almost immediately the Spirit of the Lord descended upon him, and the visions of eternity were opened to his view. So soon as consciousness returned, his bodily weakness was such that we were obliged to lay him upon his bed, and wait upon him for some time. (HC 1:82–83)

2   Mr. Knight was sworn, and Mr. Seymour interrogated him as follows:

"Did the prisoner, Joseph Smith, Jun., cast the devil out of you?"
"No, sir."
"Why, have not you had the devil cast out of you?"
"Yes, sir."
"And had not Joe Smith some hand in its being done?"
"Yes, sir."
"And did not he cast him out of you?"
"No, sir; it was done by the power of God, and Joseph Smith was the instrument in the hands of God, on the occasion. He commanded him to come out of me in the name of Jesus Christ." (HC 1:92)

Exaltation
See also ETERNAL LIFE

1   God brings low before He exalts. (HC 1:216)

Evil Spirits
   2   Proceedings of a trial held at Colesville, New York, June 1830.

Exaltation
   1   Observation about Ezra Booth, Hiram, Ohio, September 1831.

2   You, who do the will of the Lord and keep His commandments, have need to rejoice with unspeakable joy, for such shall be exalted very high, and shall be lifted up in triumph above all the kingdoms of this world. (HC 1:299)

3   Therefore let your heart be comforted; live in strict obedience to the commandments of God, and walk humbly before Him, and He will exalt thee in His own due time. (HC 1:408)

4   God exalts the humble, and debases the haughty. (HC 6:74)

5   The question is frequently asked "Can we not be saved without going through with all those ordinances [of the temple], &c.?" I would answer, No, not the fullness of salvation. Jesus said, "There are many mansions in my Father's house, and I will go and prepare a place for you." *House* here named should have been translated kingdom; and any person who is exalted to the highest mansion has to abide a celestial law, and the whole law too. . . .

I have tried for a number of years to get the minds of the Saints prepared to receive the things of God; but we frequently see some of them, after suffering all they have for the work of God, will fly to pieces like glass as soon as anything comes that is contrary to their traditions: they cannot stand the fire at all. How many will be able to abide a celestial law, and go through and receive their exaltation, I am unable to say, as many are called, but few are chosen. (HC 6:184, 185)

6   How consoling to the mourners when they are called to part with a husband, wife, father, mother, child, or dear relative, to know that, although the earthly tabernacle is laid down and dissolved, they shall rise again to dwell in everlasting burnings in immortal glory, not to sorrow, suffer, or die any more, but they shall be heirs of God and joint heirs with Jesus Christ. What is it? To inherit the same power, the same glory and the same exaltation, until you arrive at the station of a

Exaltation
  2   Letter to William W. Phelps in Missouri, written from Kirtland, 27 November 1832.
  3   Letter to Vienna Jacques, Kirtland, 4 September 1833.
  4   Letter to James Arlington Bennett, Nauvoo, 13 November 1843.
  5   Sabbath address, Nauvoo, 21 January 1844.
  6   King Follett Discourse, Nauvoo, 7 April 1844.

god, and ascend the throne of eternal power, the same as those who have gone before. What did Jesus do? Why, I do the things I saw my Father do when worlds came rolling into existence. My father worked out His kingdom with fear and trembling, and I must do the same; and when I get my kingdom, I shall present it to My Father, so that He may obtain kingdom upon kingdom, and it will exalt Him in glory. He will then take a higher exaltation, and I will take His place, and thereby become exalted myself. So that Jesus treads in the tracks of His Father, and inherits what God did before; and God is thus glorified and exalted in the salvation and exaltation of all His children. It is plain beyond disputation, and you thus learn some of the first principles of the gospel, about which so much hath been said.

When you climb up a ladder, you must begin at the bottom, and ascend step by step, until you arrive at the top; and so it is with the principles of the gospel—you must begin with the first, and go on until you learn all the principles of exaltation. But it will be a great while after you have passed through the veil before you will have learned them. It is not all to be comprehended in this world; it will be a great work to learn our salvation and exaltation even beyond the grave. . . .

. . . Knowledge saves a man; and in the world of spirits no man can be exalted but by knowledge. So long as a man will not give heed to the commandments, he must abide without salvation. If a man has knowledge, he can be saved; although, if he has been guilty of great sins, he will be punished for them. But when he consents to obey the gospel, whether here or in the world of spirits, he is saved. . . .

. . . All will suffer until they obey Christ himself. (HC 6:306–7, 314)

7 Truth, virtue, and honor, combined with energy and industry, pave the way to exaltation, glory and bliss. (HC 6:425)

Exaltation
  7 Letter to Joel H. Walker, Nauvoo, 1 June 1844.

Example

1 Awake to righteousness, and sin not; let your light shine, and show yourselves workmen that need not be ashamed, rightly dividing the word of truth. Apply yourselves diligently to study, that your minds may be stored with all necessary information. (HC 1:468–69)

2 My dear Emma, there is great responsibility resting upon you, in preserving yourself in honor and sobriety before them [Joseph and Emma's children], and teaching them right things to form their young and tender minds, that they begin in right paths, and not get contaminated when young by seeing ungodly examples. (PWJS, p. 427; standardized)

Excommunication
See CHURCH DISCIPLINARY COUNCILS

Faith

1 When he [Ezra Booth] actually learned that faith, humility, patience, and tribulation go before blessing, . . . then he was disappointed. . . . And when he was disappointed by his own evil heart, he turned away. (HC 1:216)

2 I verily know that he [the Lord] will speedily deliver Zion, for I have his immutable covenant that this shall be the case, but God is pleased to keep it hid from mine eyes the means how exactly the thing will be done. (PWJS, p. 285; standardized)

Example
1 Letter to the elders of the Church, published in *The Evening and the Morning Star*, Kirtland, December 1833.
2 Letter to Emma Smith from Liberty Jail, 4 April 1839. Original copy at Yale University library.

Faith
1 Explanation of Ezra Booth's apostasy, Hiram, Ohio, September 1831.
2 Letter to William W. Phelps and others following mob destruction of the Saints' property in Missouri, Kirtland, 18 August 1833.

3   But we trust in the Lord, and leave the event with Him to govern in his own wise providence. (HC 1:442)

4   Faith [is] the first principle in revealed religion, and the foundation of all righteousness. . . .

. . . Faith is the moving cause of all action in temporal concerns, so it is in spiritual. . . .

. . . Faith is not only the principle of action, but of power also, in all intelligent beings, whether in heaven or on earth. . . .

. . . The principle of power which existed in the bosom of God, by which the worlds were framed, was faith. . . .

. . . [Faith] is the principle by which Jehovah works, and through which he exercises power over all temporal as well as eternal things. Take this principle or attribute—for it is an attribute from the Deity, and he would cease to exist. . . .

Faith, then, is the first great governing principle which has power, dominion, and authority over all things; by it they exist, by it they are upheld, by it they are changed, or by it they remain, agreeable to the will of God. Without it there is no power, and without power there could be no creation nor existence! (LF 1:1, 12, 13, 15, 16, 24)

5   For faith could not center in a Being of whose existence we have no idea, because the idea of his existence in the first instance is essential to the exercise of faith in him. . . .

Let us here observe, that three things are necessary in order that any rational and intelligent being may exercise faith in God unto life and salvation.

First, the idea that he actually exists.

Secondly, a *correct* idea of his character, perfections, and attributes.

Thirdly, an actual knowledge that the course of life which he is pursuing is according to his will. For without an acquaintance with these three important facts, the faith of every rational being must be imperfect and unproductive. . . .

Faith
  3   Letter to Moses C. Nickerson, written from Kirtland, 19 November 1833.
  4–5 Lectures on Faith, delivered to a school of the elders, Kirtland, December 1834. Although the Lectures on Faith were not written only by Joseph Smith, he reviewed them carefully and prepared them for publication (see Larry E. Dahl and Charles D. Tate, Jr., eds., *The Lectures on Faith in Historical Perspective*, p. 10).

. . . Unless [God] was merciful and gracious, slow to anger, long-suffering and full of goodness, such is the weakness of human nature, and so great the frailties and imperfections of men, that unless they believed that these excellencies existed in the divine character, the faith necessary to salvation could not exist; for doubt would take the place of faith, and those who know their weakness and liability to sin would be in constant doubt of salvation if it were not for the idea which they have of the excellency of the character of God, that he is slow to anger and long-suffering, and of a forgiving disposition, and does forgive iniquity, transgression, and sin. An idea of these facts does away doubt, and makes faith exceedingly strong.

But it is equally as necessary that men should have the idea that he is a God who changes not, in order to have faith in him, as it is to have the idea that he is gracious and long-suffering. . . .

. . . The idea that he is a God of truth and cannot lie, is equally as necessary to the exercise of faith in him as the idea of his unchangeableness. . . .

. . . It is also necessary that men should have an idea that [God] is no respecter of persons. . . .

And lastly, but not less important to the exercise of faith in God, is the idea that he is love. (*LF* 3:1, 2–5, 20–21, 22, 23, 24)

6   Having shown . . . that without correct ideas of his [God's] character the minds of men could not have sufficient power with God to the exercise of faith necessary to the enjoyment of eternal life; . . . we shall now proceed to show the connection there is between correct ideas of the attributes of God, and the exercise of faith in him unto eternal life.

. . . Without the idea of the existence of the attributes which belong to God the minds of men could not have power to exercise faith in him so as to lay hold upon eternal life. . . .

Having said so much, we shall proceed to examine the attributes of God, as set forth in his revelations to the human family and to show how necessary correct ideas of his attributes are to enable men

---

Faith

6   Lectures on Faith, delivered to a school of the elders, Kirtland, December 1834. Although the Lectures on Faith were not written only by Joseph Smith, he reviewed them carefully and prepared them for publication (see Larry E. Dahl and Charles D. Tate, Jr., eds., *The Lectures on Faith in Historical Perspective*, p. 10).

to exercise faith in him; for without these ideas being planted in the minds of men it would be out of the power of any person or persons to exercise faith in God so as to obtain eternal life. . . .

We have, in the revelations which he has given to the human family, the following account of his attributes:

First—Knowledge. . . .

Secondly—Faith or power. . . .

Thirdly—Justice. . . .

Fourthly—Judgment. . . .

Fifthly—Mercy. . . .

And sixthly—Truth. . . .

By a little reflection it will be seen that the idea of the existence of these attributes in the Deity is necessary to enable any rational being to exercise faith in him; for without the idea of the existence of these attributes in the Deity men could not exercise faith in him for life and salvation. . . .

It is . . . necessary, in order to the exercise of faith in God unto life and salvation, that men should have the idea of the existence of the attribute justice in him; for without the idea of the existence of the attribute justice in the Deity men could not have confidence sufficient to place themselves under his guidance and direction; for they would be filled with fear and doubt lest the judge of all the earth would not do right, and thus fear or doubt, existing in the mind, would preclude the possibility of the exercise of faith in him for life and salvation. . . .

And again, it is equally important that men should have the idea of the existence of the attribute mercy in the Deity, in order to exercise faith in him for life and salvation; for without the idea of the existence of this attribute in the Deity, the spirits of the saints would faint in the midst of the tribulations, afflictions, and persecutions which they have to endure for righteousness' sake. . . .

And lastly, but not less important to the exercise of faith in God, is the idea of the existence of the attribute truth in him; for without the idea of the existence of this attribute the mind of man could have nothing upon which it could rest with certainty—all would be confusion and doubt. . . .

In view, then, of the existence of these attributes, the faith of the saints can become exceedingly strong, abounding in righteousness unto the praise and glory of God, and can exert its mighty influence in searching after wisdom and understanding, until it has obtained a knowledge of all things that pertain to life and salvation. (*LF* 4:1, 2, 3, 4–5, 6, 7, 8, 9, 10, 11, 13, 15, 16, 18)

7   An actual knowledge to any person, that the course of life which he pursues is according to the will of God, is essentially necessary to enable him to have that confidence in God without which no person can obtain eternal life. . . .

. . . A religion that does not require the sacrifice of all things never has power sufficient to produce the faith necessary unto life and salvation; for, from the first existence of man, the faith necessary unto the enjoyment of life and salvation never could be obtained without the sacrifice of all earthly things. It was through this sacrifice, and this only, that God has ordained that men should enjoy eternal life; and it is through the medium of the sacrifice of all earthly things that men do actually know that they are doing the things that are well pleasing in the sight of God. (*LF* 6:2, 7)

8   When a man works by faith he works by mental exertion instead of physical force. . . .

. . . Salvation is the effect of faith. . . .

. . . It was by obtaining a knowledge of God that men got the knowledge of all things which pertain to life and godliness, and this knowledge was the effect of faith; so that all things which pertain to life and godliness are the effects of faith.

. . . When faith comes it brings its train of attendants with it— apostles, prophets, evangelists, pastors, teachers, gifts, wisdom, knowledge, miracles, healings, tongues, interpretation of tongues, etc. All these appear when faith appears on the earth, and disappear when it disappears from the earth; for these are the effects of faith, and always have attended, and always will, attend it. (*LF* 7:3, 17, 19, 20)

Faith
7–8 Lectures on Faith, delivered to a school of the elders, Kirtland, December 1834. Although the Lectures on Faith were not written only by Joseph Smith, he reviewed them carefully and prepared them for publication (see Larry E. Dahl and Charles D. Tate, Jr., eds., *The Lectures on Faith in Historical Perspective*, p. 10).

9 What God may do for us I do not know, but I hope for the best always in all circumstances. Although I go unto death, I will trust in God. What outrages may be committed by the mob I know not, but expect there will be but little or no restraint. (*PWJS*, p. 362; standardized)

10 Faith comes by hearing the word of God, through the testimony of the servants of God; that testimony is always attended by the Spirit of prophecy and revelation. . . .

. . . Faith comes not by signs, but by hearing the word of God. (*HC* 3:379)

11 Whatever God requires is right, no matter what it is, although we may not see the reason thereof till long after the events transpire. (*HC* 5:135)

12 Because faith is wanting, the fruits are. No man since the world was had faith without having something along with it. The ancients quenched the violence of fire, escaped the edge of the sword, women received their dead, &c. By faith the worlds were made. A man who has none of the gifts has no faith; and he deceives himself, if he supposes he has. Faith has been wanting, not only among the heathen, but in professed Christendom also, so that tongues, healings, prophecy, and prophets and apostles, and all the gifts and blessings have been wanting. (*HC* 5:218)

13 If you have any darkness, you have only to ask, and the darkness is removed. It is not necessary that miracles should be wrought to remove darkness. Miracles are the fruits of faith.

"How then shall they call on Him in whom they have not believed? And how shall they hear without a preacher? And how shall they preach except they be sent?"

Faith
  9 Letter sent from Independence, Missouri, to the Prophet's wife, Emma, in Far West, 4 November 1838. Joseph Smith and other Church leaders were in the custody of General Samuel D. Lucas of the Missouri state militia.
 10 Instructions to the Twelve, Commerce (Nauvoo), 27 June 1839.
 11 Essay on happiness, Nauvoo, 27 August 1842.
 12 Springfield, Illinois, at the home of a Mr. Sollars, 2 January 1843.
 13 Remarks to Saints newly arrived from England, Nauvoo, 13 April 1843.

God may translate the scriptures by me if He chooses. Faith comes by hearing the word of God. If a man has not faith enough to do one thing, he may have faith to do another: if he cannot remove a mountain, he may heal the sick. Where faith is there will be some of the fruits: all gifts and power which were sent from heaven, were poured out on the heads of those who had faith. (HC 5:355)

Faithfulness

1   O ye Twelve! and all Saints! profit by this important Key—that in all your trials, troubles, temptations, afflictions, bonds, imprisonments and death, see to it, that you do not betray heaven; that you do not betray Jesus Christ; that you do not betray the brethren; that you do not betray the revelations of God, whether in the Bible, Book of Mormon, or Doctrine and Covenants, or any other that ever was or ever will be given and revealed unto man in this world or that which is to come. Yea, in all your kicking and flounderings, see to it that you do not this thing, lest innocent blood be found upon your skirts, and you go down to hell. All other sins are not to be compared to sinning against the Holy Ghost, and proving a traitor to the brethren. (HC 3:385)

Fall of Adam

1   There has been no change in the constitution of man since he fell. (HC 2:17)

2   Though our first parents were driven out of the garden of Eden, and were even separated from the presence of God by a veil, they still

---

Faithfulness
  1   Instructions to the Apostles and Seventies departing for missions to England, Commerce (Nauvoo), 2 July 1839.

Fall of Adam
  1   Letter to the brethren scattered from Zion, Kirtland, 22 January 1834.
  2   Lectures on Faith, delivered to a school of the elders, Kirtland, December 1834. Although the Lectures on Faith were not written only by Joseph Smith, he reviewed them carefully and prepared them for publication (see Larry E. Dahl and Charles D. Tate, Jr., eds., *The Lectures on Faith in Historical Perspective*, p. 10).

retained a knowledge of his existence, and that sufficiently to move them to call upon him. And further, . . . no sooner was the plan of redemption revealed to man, and he began to call upon God, than the Holy Spirit was given, bearing record of the Father and Son. (*LF* 2:25)

3   I believe in the fall of man, as recorded in the Bible; I believe that God foreknew everything, but did not foreordain everything; I deny that foreordain and foreknow is the same thing. He foreordained the fall of man; but all merciful as He is, He foreordained at the same time, a plan of redemption for all mankind. (*HC* 4:78)

4   *Minutes:* Joseph said in answer to Mr. [Hosea] Stout that Adam did not commit sin in eating the fruits, for God had decreed that he should eat and fall. . . . [That] he should die was the saying of the Lord; therefore, the Lord appointed us to fall and also redeemed us— for where sin abounded grace did much more abound. (*WJS*, p. 63; standardized)

5   The great Jehovah contemplated the whole of the events connected with the earth, pertaining to the plan of salvation, before it rolled into existence . . . ; He knew of the fall of Adam, the iniquities of the antediluvians . . . ; He comprehended the fall of man, and his redemption. (*HC* 4:597)

Falsehoods

1   Time and experience will teach us more and more how easily falsehood gains credence with mankind in general, rather than the truth. (*HC* 4:8)

Fall of Adam
  3   Statement of Joseph Smith as quoted in a letter of Mathew L. Davis to his wife, Mary, describing the Prophet's discourse in Washington, D.C., 6 February 1840.
  4   Instruction to the Nauvoo Lyceum, 9 February 1841, as reported by William P. McIntire.
  5   Editorial in the *Times and Seasons*, 15 April 1842.

Falsehoods
  1   A letter to Isaac Galland, Commerce (Nauvoo), 11 September 1839.

2   I gave some important instructions upon the situation of the Church, showing that it was necessary that the officers who could should go abroad through the states; and inasmuch as a great excitement had been raised, through the community at large, by the falsehoods put in circulation by John C. Bennett and others, it was wisdom in God that the Elders should go forth and deluge the state with a flood of truth. (HC 5:131–32)

False Spirits
See also DEVIL, EVIL SPIRITS

1   Lying spirits are going forth in the earth. There will be great manifestations of spirits, both false and true. (HC 3:391–92)

2   Recent occurrences that have transpired amongst us render it an imperative duty devolving upon me to say something in relation to the spirits by which men are actuated.

It is evident from the Apostles' writings, that many false spirits existed in their day, and had "gone forth into the world," and that it needed intelligence which God alone could impart to detect false spirits, and to prove what spirits were of God. The world in general have been grossly ignorant in regard to this one thing, and why should they be otherwise—"for no man knows the things of God, but by the Spirit of God." . . .

There always did, in every age, seem to be a lack of intelligence pertaining to this subject. Spirits of all kinds have been manifested, in every age, and almost amongst all people. If we go among the pagans, they have their spirits; the Mohammedans, the Jews, the Christians, the Indians—all have their spirits, all have a supernatural agency, and all contend that their spirits are of God. Who shall solve the mystery?

Falsehoods
  2   Instructions to some of the Twelve Apostles and others, Nauvoo, 26 August 1842.

False Spirits
  1   Discourse on the priesthood, given sometime before 8 August 1839, Commerce (Nauvoo). For a discussion on the dating of this discourse, see *WJS*, p. 22.
  2   Editorial in the *Times and Seasons*, 1 April 1842.

"Try the spirits," says John, but who is to do it? The learned, the eloquent, the philosopher, the sage, the divine—all are ignorant. . . .

"Try the spirits," but what by? Are we to try them by the creeds of men? What preposterous folly—what sheer ignorance—what madness! Try the motions and actions of an eternal being (for I contend that all spirits are such) by a thing that was conceived in ignorance, and brought forth in folly—a cobweb of yesterday! Angels would hide their faces, and devils would be ashamed and insulted, and would say, "Paul we know, and Jesus we know, but who are ye?" Let each man of society make a creed and try evil spirits by it, and the devil would shake his sides; it is all that he would ask—all that he would desire. Yet many of them do this, and hence "many spirits are abroad in the world."

One great evil is, that men are ignorant of the nature of spirits; their power, laws, government, intelligence, &c., and imagine that when there is anything like power, revelation, or vision manifested, that it must be of God. . . .

. . . No man knows the spirit of the devil, and his power and influence, but by possessing intelligence which is more than human, and having unfolded through the medium of the Priesthood the mysterious operations of his devices. . . .

A man must have the discerning of spirits before he can drag into daylight this hellish influence and unfold it unto the world in all its soul-destroying, diabolical, and horrid colors; for nothing is a greater injury to the children of men than to be under the influence of a false spirit when they think they have the Spirit of God. Thousands have felt the influence of its terrible power and baneful effects. Long pilgrimages have been undertaken, penances endured, and pain, misery and ruin have followed in their train; nations have been convulsed, kingdoms overthrown, provinces laid waste, and blood, carnage and desolation are habiliments in which it has been clothed. . . .

It would seem also, that wicked spirits have their bounds, limits, and laws by which they are governed or controlled. . . .

. . . No man nor set of men without the regular constituted authorities, the Priesthood and discerning of spirits, can tell true from false spirits. This power they possessed in the Apostles' day, but it has departed from the world for ages.

The Church of Jesus Christ of Latter-day Saints has also had its false spirits; and as it is made up of all those different sects professing every variety of opinion, and having been under the influence of so many kinds of spirits, it is not to be wondered at if there should be found among us false spirits.

Soon after the Gospel was established in Kirtland, and during the absence of the authorities of the Church, many false spirits were introduced, many strange visions were seen, and wild, enthusiastic notions were entertained; men ran out of doors under the influence of this spirit, and some of them got upon the stumps of trees and shouted, and all kinds of extravagances were entered into by them; one man pursued a ball that he said he saw flying in the air, until he came to a precipice, when he jumped into the top of a tree, which saved his life; and many ridiculous things were entered into, calculated to bring disgrace upon the Church of God, to cause the Spirit of God to be withdrawn, and to uproot and destroy those glorious principles which had been developed for the salvation of the human family. But when the authorities returned, the spirit was made manifest, those members that were exercised with it were tried for their fellowship, and those that would not repent and forsake it were cut off. (HC 4:571–72, 573, 576, 580)

3   *Words of Orson F. Whitney:* Years later, narrating the experience of that awful morning to the Prophet Joseph, Heber asked him what it all meant, and whether there was anything wrong with him that he should have such a manifestation.

"No, Brother Heber," he replied, "at that time you were nigh unto the Lord; there was only a veil between you and Him, but you could not see Him. When I heard of it, it gave me great joy, for I then knew that the work of God had taken root in that land. It was this that caused the devil to make a struggle to kill you."

Joseph then related some of his own experience, in many contests he had had with the evil one, and said: "The nearer a person approaches the Lord, a greater power will be manifested by the adversary to prevent the accomplishment of His purposes." (LHCK, pp. 131–32)

False Spirits
3   Response to Heber C. Kimball's question about the meaning of his frightful experience with evil spirits in Preston, England, 30 July 1837. (See HC 2:503 for a brief account of the incident.)

Family

1   But we pause here, and offer a remark upon the saying which we learn has gone abroad, and has been handled in a manner detrimental to the cause of truth, by saying, "that in preaching the doctrine of gathering, we break up families, and give license for men to leave their families, women their husbands, children their parents and slaves their masters, thereby deranging the order and breaking up the harmony and peace of society." We shall here show our faith, and thereby, as we humbly trust, put an end to these false and wicked misrepresentations, which have caused, we have every reason to believe, thousands to think they were doing God's service, when they were persecuting the children of God; whereas, if they could have enjoyed the true light, and had a just understanding of our principles, they would have embraced them with all their hearts, and been rejoicing in the love of the truth. And now to show our doctrine on this subject, we shall commence with the first principles of the Gospel, which are faith, repentance, and baptism for the remission of sins, and the gift of the Holy Ghost by the laying on of the hands. This we believe to be our duty— to teach to all mankind the doctrine of repentance. . . .

Therefore we believe in preaching the doctrine of repentance in all the world, both to old and young, rich and poor, bond and free, as we shall endeavor to show hereafter how, and in what manner, and how far, it is binding on the consciences of mankind, making proper distinctions between old and young, men, women, children and servants. But we discover, in order to be benefitted by the doctrine of repentance, we must believe in obtaining the remission of sins. (HC 2:255, 256)

2   Fathers should be kind to their children, husbands to their wives, masters to their slaves or servants, children obedient to their parents, wives to their husbands, and slaves or servants to their masters. (HC 2:263–64)

3   God grant that I may have the privilege of seeing once more my lovely family in the enjoyment of the sweets of liberty and social life; to press them to my bosom and kiss their lovely cheeks would fill my

---

Family
1   Letter to the elders of the Church, Kirtland, 1 September 1835.
2   Letter to the elders of the Church, Kirtland, 1 September 1835.
3   Letter to Emma Smith, Richmond, Missouri, 12 November 1838. The Prophet was in a Richmond jail, having been taken into custody two weeks earlier, 31 October 1838.

heart with unspeakable gratitude. . . . Tell little Joseph he must be a good boy. Father loves him with a perfect love. He is the eldest [and] must not hurt those that are smaller than him, but comfort them. Tell little Frederick Father loves him with all his heart. He is a lovely boy. Julia is a lovely little girl. I love her also. She is a promising child. Tell her Father wants her to remember him and be a good girl. Tell all the rest that I think of them and pray for them all. . . . Little Alexander is on my mind continually. Oh my affectionate Emma, I want you to remember that I am a true and faithful friend to you and the children forever. My heart is entwined around yours forever and ever. Oh may God bless you all, amen. (*PWJS*, pp. 367–68; standardized)

4   I think of you and the children continually. . . . I want to see little Frederick, Joseph, Julia, and Alexander, Joanna, and old Major [their horse]. . . . I want you should not let those little fellows forget me. Tell them Father loves them with a perfect love, and he is doing all he can to get away from the mob to come to them. Do teach them all you can, that they may have good minds. Be tender and kind to them. Don't be fractious to them, but listen to their wants. Tell them Father says they must be good children and mind their mother. My dear Emma, there is great responsibility resting upon you, in preserving yourself in honor and sobriety before them, and teaching them right things to form their young and tender minds, that they begin in right paths, and not get contaminated when young by seeing ungodly examples. (*PWJS*, pp. 426–27; standardized)

5   When you go home, never give a cross or unkind word to your husbands, but let kindness, charity and love crown your works henceforward. (HC 4:607)

6   Opened court to try Field for drunkenness and abusing his wife. I fined him $10 and costs, and required him to find bail of $50 to keep the peace for six months. (HC 5:316)

7   It is the duty of all men to protect their lives and the lives of the household, whenever necessity requires. (HC 6:605)

Family

4   Letter to Emma Smith from Liberty Jail, 4 April 1839. Original copy at Yale University library.
5   Remarks to the Relief Society, Nauvoo, 28 April 1842.
6   Nauvoo, 27 March 1843.
7   Letter to Emma from Carthage Jail, 27 June 1844.

8 *Words of Benjamin F. Johnson:* As a son, he [Joseph Smith] was nobility itself, in love and honor of his parents; as a brother he was loving and true, even unto death; as a husband and father, his devotion to wives and children stopped only at idolatry. His life's greatest motto, after "God and His Kingdom," was that of "wives, children and friends." On one Sunday morning while sitting with him in the Mansion dining room, in private converse, two of Emma's children came to him as just from their mother, all so nice, bright and sweet. Calling them to my attention, he said, "Benjamin, look at these children. How could I help loving their mother?" (*TK*, p. 88)

Family Prayer

1 *Words of William Holmes Walker:* My father sent me to Nauvoo on some business with the Prophet. I arrived at his house just as his family was singing, before the accustomed evening prayer. His wife, Emma, was leading the singing. I thought I had never heard such sweet, heavenly music before. I was equally interested in the prayer offered by the Prophet. Much pleased with my visit, and my business accomplished satisfactorily, I returned home in a few days. (*TK*, p. 147)

Fasting

1 If the Saints are sick, or have sickness in their families, and the elders do not prevail, every family should get power by fasting and prayer and anointing with oil, and continue so to do. Their sick shall be healed. This also is the voice of the Spirit. (*WJS*, p. 37; standardized)

Family
  8   Letter of Benjamin F. Johnson to George S. Gibbs, 1903.

Family Prayer
  1   Diary of William Holmes Walker, BYU Library.

Fasting
  1   Instruction at a Thursday fast meeting, Nauvoo, Illinois, 30 July 1840.

2 *Words of Wilford Woodruff:* This was an interesting day—a day that was appointed by general proclamation for humiliation, fasting and prayer, and thanksgiving for the release and delivery we had received. (*WWJ* 2:212; standardized)

3 *Words of James Palmer:* There were great threats of mob violence by the anti-Mormons who lived in adjoining counties. They wished to drive us from the state because we outnumbered them at the ballot box. On election days, we could elect our county officers. They despised us also because of our religion. They would muster and parade and call it a wolf hunt. Some of our brethren were shot at while quietly at home inside their own houses. At this time, the Prophet proclaimed a day of fasting and prayer through all the wards of the city, praying Almighty God to turn away the anger of our enemies and allow us to live in peace. At the same time he advised us to prepare to protect ourselves if they came upon us. (*TK*, p. 154)

Fathers

1 Fathers should be kind to their children. (HC 2:263)

2 There are many teachers, but, perhaps, not many fathers. (HC 3:301)

Faults

1 The man who willeth to do well, we should extol his virtues, and speak not of his faults behind his back. (HC 1:444)

Fasting
2 Wilford Woodruff journal entry, 17 January 1843. An Illinois court had ruled that removing Joseph Smith from Illinois to Missouri to stand trial on earlier charges was illegal, and Joseph was freed.
3 Reminiscence and journal of James Palmer, LDS Church Archives.

Fathers
1 Letter to the elders of the Church, Kirtland, 1 September 1835.
2 Letter to the Saints from Liberty Jail, 20–25 March 1839.

Faults
1 Kirtland, 19 November 1833.

2   As you increase in innocence and virtue, as you increase in goodness, let your hearts expand, let them be enlarged towards others; you must be long-suffering, and bear with the faults and errors of mankind. (HC 4:606)

3   We are full of selfishness; the devil flatters us that we are very righteous, when we are feeding on the faults of others. (HC 5:24)

4   No man lives without fault. Do you think that even Jesus, if He were here, would be without fault in your eyes? His enemies said all manner of evil against Him—they all watched for iniquity in Him. . . .
. . . If you have evil feelings, and speak of them to one another, it has a tendency to do mischief. . . .
. . . If you know anything calculated to disturb the peace or injure the feelings of your brother or sister, hold your tongues, and the least harm will be done. (HC 5:140)

5   I do not dwell upon your faults, and you shall not upon mine. Charity, which is love, covereth a multitude of sins, and I have often covered up all the faults among you; but the prettiest thing is to have no faults at all. We should cultivate a meek, quiet and peaceable spirit. (HC 5:517)

Fear

1   We have nothing to fear if we are faithful. (*PWJS*, p. 319)

Faults
  2   Remarks to the Relief Society, Nauvoo, 28 April 1842.
  3   Remarks to the Relief Society, Nauvoo, 9 June 1842.
  4   Remarks to the Relief Society, Nauvoo, 31 August 1842.
  5   Sabbath address, Nauvoo, 23 July 1843.

Fear
  1   Letter to Edward Partridge and others in Missouri, Kirtland, 30 March 1834.

Feelings

1 We say so much, hoping it will be received in kindness, and our brethren will be careful of one another's feelings, and walk in love, honoring one another more than themselves, as is required by the Lord. (HC 1:368)

2 I have sometimes spoken too harshly from the impulse of the moment, and inasmuch as I have wounded your feelings, brethren, I ask your forgiveness, for I love you and will hold you up with all my heart in all righteousness, before the Lord, and before all men. . . . I will now covenant with you before God, that I will not listen to or credit any derogatory report against any of you, nor condemn you upon any testimony beneath the heavens, short of that testimony which is infallible, until I can see you face to face, and know of a surety; and I do place unremitted confidence in your word, for I believe you to be men of truth. And I ask the same of you, when I tell you anything, that you place equal confidence in my word, for I will not tell you I know anything that I do not know. (HC 2:374)

3 Nothing is so much calculated to lead people to forsake sin as to take them by the hand, and watch over them with tenderness. When persons manifest the least kindness and love to me, O what power it has over my mind, while the opposite course has a tendency to harrow up all the harsh feelings and depress the human mind. . . .
. . . It is the doctrine of the devil to retard the human mind, and hinder our progress, by filling us with self-righteousness. The nearer we get to our heavenly Father, the more we are disposed to look with compassion on perishing souls; we feel that we want to take them upon our shoulders, and cast their sins behind our backs. My talk is intended for all this society [the Relief Society]; if you would have God have mercy on you, have mercy on one another. (HC 5:23–24)

Feelings
1 Letter to the brethren in Zion, Kirtland, 25 June 1833.
2 Instructions to the Twelve, Kirtland, 16 January 1836.
3 Remarks to the Relief Society, Nauvoo, 9 June 1842.

First Presidency

1 "Doctor" Hurlburt was ordained an Elder; after which Elder Rigdon expressed a desire that himself and Brother Frederick G. Williams should be ordained to the offices to which they had been called, viz., those of Presidents of the High Priesthood, and to be equal in holding the keys of the kingdom with Brother Joseph Smith, Jun., according to the revelation given on the 8th of March, 1833. Accordingly I laid my hands on Brothers Sidney and Frederick, and ordained them to take part with me in holding the keys of this last kingdom, and to assist in the Presidency of the High Priesthood, as my Counselors; after which I exhorted the brethren to faithfulness and diligence in keeping the commandments of God. (*HC* 1:334)

2 *Minutes:* President Smith next proceeded to explain the duty of the Twelve, and their authority, which is next to the present Presidency, and that the arrangement of the assembly in this place, on the 15th instant, in placing the High Councils of Kirtland next [to] the Presidency, was because the business to be transacted, was business relating to that body in particular, which was to fill the several quorums in Kirtland, not because they were first in office, and that the arrangements were the most judicious that could be made on the occasion; also the Twelve are not subject to any other than the first Presidency, viz., "myself," said the Prophet, "Sidney Rigdon, and Frederick G. Williams, who are now my Counselors; and where I am not, there is no First Presidency over the Twelve." (*HC* 2:373–74)

3 I then made a short address, and called upon the several quorums, and all the congregation of Saints, to acknowledge the Presidency as Prophets and Seers, and uphold them by their prayers. They all covenanted to do so, by rising. (*HC* 2:417)

First Presidency
1 Kirtland, 18 March 1833.
2 Instructions to the Twelve, Kirtland, 16 January 1836. It has been pointed out that the last eighteen words of this quotation were not part of the original minutes but were added later. It should be remembered, however, that the words were added by those who were the Apostles in the meeting and who had firsthand knowledge of what was said.
3 Events during the dedication of the Kirtland Temple, 27 March 1836.

4 *Minutes:* President Joseph Smith, Jun., addressed the assembly and said, the Melchizedek High Priesthood was no other than the Priesthood of the Son of God; that there are certain ordinances which belong to the Priesthood, from which flow certain results; and the Presidents or Presidency are over the Church; and revelations of the mind and will of God to the Church, are to come through the Presidency. (HC 2:477)

5 Whatever you may hear about me or Kirtland, take no notice of it; for if it be a place of refuge, the devil will use his greatest efforts to trap the Saints. You must make yourselves acquainted with those men who like Daniel pray three times a day toward the House of the Lord. Look to the Presidency and receive instruction. (HC 3:391)

First Principles

1 And now what remains to be done, under circumstances like these? I will proceed to tell you what the Lord requires of all people, high and low, rich and poor, male and female, ministers and people, professors of religion and non-professors, in order that they may enjoy the Holy Spirit of God to a fulness and escape the judgments of God, which are almost ready to burst upon the nations of the earth. Repent of all your sins, and be baptized in water for the remission of them, in the name of the Father, and of the Son, and of the Holy Ghost, and receive the ordinance of the laying on of the hands of him who is ordained and sealed unto this power, that ye may receive the Holy Spirit of God; and this is according to the Holy Scriptures, and the Book of Mormon; and the only way that man can enter into the celestial kingdom. These are the requirements of the new covenant, or first principles of the Gospel of Christ; then "Add to your faith, virtue; and to

---

First Presidency
4   Solemn assembly in the Kirtland Temple, 6 April 1837.
5   Discourse on the priesthood, given sometime before 8 August 1839, Commerce (Nauvoo). For a discussion on the dating of this discourse, see *WJS*, p. 22.

First Principles
1   Letter to N. E. Seaton (N. C. Saxton), a newspaper editor in Rochester, N.Y., Kirtland, 4 January 1833.

virtue, knowledge; and to knowledge, temperance; and to temperance, patience; and to patience, godliness; and to godliness, brotherly kindness; and to brotherly kindness, charity {or love}; for if these things be in you, and abound, they make you that ye shall neither be barren nor unfruitful, in the knowledge of our Lord Jesus Christ." (HC 1:314–15)

2   "What are the fundamental principles of your religion?"

The fundamental principles of our religion are the testimony of the Apostles and Prophets, concerning Jesus Christ, that He died, was buried, and rose again the third day, and ascended into heaven; and all other things which pertain to our religion are only appendages to it. But in connection with these, we believe in the gift of the Holy Ghost, the power of faith, the enjoyment of the spiritual gifts according to the will of God, the restoration of the house of Israel, and the final triumph of truth. (HC 3:30)

3   And again, we believe in the doctrine of faith, and of repentance, and of baptism for the remission of sins, and the gift of the Holy Ghost by the laying on of hands, and of resurrection of the dead, and of eternal judgment. (PWJS, p. 421; standardized)

4   The doctrine of the resurrection of the dead and the eternal judgment are necessary to preach among the first principles of the Gospel of Jesus Christ. (HC 3:379)

5   Report of Don Carlos Smith: [President Joseph Smith] then made some observations on the first principles of the Gospel, observing, that many of the Saints who had come from different states and nations had only a very superficial knowledge of these principles, not having heard them fully investigated.

He then briefly stated the principles of faith, repentance, and baptism for the remission of sins, these were believed by some of the righteous societies of the day, but the doctrine of laying on of hands for the gift of the Holy Ghost was discarded by them. (HC 4:359)

First Principles
2   Answers to questions frequently asked the Prophet, Far West, 8 May 1838.
3   Letter to Isaac Galland, written while the Prophet was imprisoned in Liberty Jail, 22 March 1839.
4   Instructions to the Twelve, Commerce (Nauvoo), 27 June 1839.
5   Sabbath address, Nauvoo, 16 May 1841.

6 Baptism is a sign to God, to angels, and to heaven that we do the will of God, and there is no other way beneath the heavens whereby God hath ordained for man to come to Him to be saved, and enter into the kingdom of God, except faith in Jesus Christ, repentance, and baptism for the remission of sins, and any other course is in vain; then you have the promise of the gift of the Holy Ghost. (HC 4:555)

7 So far we are agreed with other Christian denominations. They all preach faith and repentance. The gospel requires baptism by immersion for the remission of sins, which is the meaning of the word in the original language—namely, to bury or immerse.

We ask the sects, Do you believe this? They answer, No. I believe in being converted. I believe in this tenaciously. So did the Apostle Peter and the disciples of Jesus. But I further believe in the gift of the Holy Ghost by the laying on of hands. Evidence by Peter's preaching on the day of Pentecost, Acts 2:38. You might as well baptize a bag of sand as a man, if not done in view of the remission of sins and getting of the Holy Ghost. Baptism by water is but half a baptism, and is good for nothing without the other half—that is, the baptism of the Holy Ghost.

The Savior says, "Except a man be born of water and of the Spirit, he cannot enter into the kingdom of God." "Though we or an angel from heaven, preach any other gospel unto you than that which we have preached unto you, let him be accursed," according to Galatians 1:8. (HC 5:499–500)

8 The first principles of the Gospel, as I believe, are, faith, repentance, baptism for the remission of sins, with the promise of the Holy Ghost.

Look at Heb. vi. 1 for contradictions—"Therefore leaving the principles of the doctrine of Christ, let us go on unto perfection." If a man leaves the principles of the doctrine of Christ, how can he be saved in the principles? This is a contradiction. I don't believe it. I will render it as it should be—"Therefore *not* leaving the principles of the doctrine of Christ, let us go on unto perfection, not laying again the foundation of repentance from dead works, and of faith toward God, of the doctrine of baptisms, and of laying on of hands, and of resurrection of the dead, and of eternal judgment." (HC 6:57–58)

First Principles
6   Sabbath address, Nauvoo, 20 March 1842.
7   Sabbath address, Nauvoo, 9 July 1843.
8   Sabbath address, Nauvoo, 15 October 1843.

First Vision

Editors' Note: Following are the known accounts of the First Vision that were written during the lifetime of the Prophet Joseph Smith. Joseph Smith wrote or dictated to a scribe the 1832, 1835, 1838, and 1842 (Wentworth Letter) accounts. The Orson Pratt and Orson Hyde accounts were written by them and published in missionary tracts in Great Britain and Germany. The other three accounts (Levi Richards, David Nye White, and Alexander Neibaur) were written by their authors upon hearing Joseph Smith describe the vision in a sermon or private interview. The nine accounts printed here appear in chronological order and retain the spelling, capitalization, and punctuation of the original documents as reproduced in the sources cited.

1   *1832 Recital:* A History of the life of Joseph Smith Jr an account of his marvilous experience and of all the mighty acts which he doeth in the name of Jesus Christ the son of the living God of whom he beareth record and also an account of the rise of the church of Christ in the eve of time according as the Lord brought forth and established by his hand firstly he receiving the testamony from on high secondly the ministering of Angels thirdly the reception of the holy Priesthood by the ministring of Aangels to adminster the letter of the Gospel—the Law and commandments as they were given unto him—and the ordinencs, forthly a confirmation and reception of the high Priesthood after the holy order of the son of the living God power and ordinence from on high to preach the Gospel in the administration and demonstration of the spirit the Kees of the Kingdom of God confered upon him and the continuation of the blessings of God to him &c——— I was born in the town of Charon in the State of Vermont North America on the twenty third day of December A D 1805 of goodly Parents who spared no pains to instructing me in the christian religion at the age of about ten years my Father Joseph Smith Siegnior moved to Palmyra Ontario County in the State of New York and being in indigent circumstances were obliged to labour hard for the Support of a large Family having nine children and as it required the exertions of all that were able to render any assistance for the Support of the Family therefore we were

---

First Vision
1   History partly written by the Prophet and partly dictated by him to Frederick G. Williams between summer and late November 1832.

deprived of the bennifit of an education Suffice it to Say I was mearly instructed in reading ~~and~~ writing and the ground rules of Arithmatic which constuted my whole literary acquirements. At about the age of twelve years my mind became seriously imprest with regard to the all important concerns for the wellfare of my immortal Soul which led me to Searching the Scriptures believeing as I was taught, that they contained the word of God thus applying myself to them and my intimate acquaintance with those of differant denominations led me to marvel excedingly for I discovered that they did not ~~adorn instead~~ of adorn~~ing~~ their profession by a holy walk and Godly conversation agreeable to what I found contained in that Sacred depository this was a grief to my Soul thus from the age of twelve years to fifteen I pondered many things in my heart concerning the sittuation of the world of mankind the contentions and divions the wickeness and abominations and the darkness which pervaded the ~~of the~~ minds of mankind my mind become excedingly distressed for I became convicted of my Sins and by Searching the Scriptures I found that ~~mand~~ mankind did not come unto the Lord but that they had apostatised from the true and liveing faith and there was no society or denomination that built upon the Gospel of Jesus Christ as recorded in the new testament and I felt to mourn for my own Sins and for the Sins of the world for I learned in the Scriptures that God was the same yesterday to day and forever that he was no respecter to persons for he was God for I looked upon the sun the glorious luminary of the earth and also the moon rolling in their magesty through the heavens and also the Stars Shining in their courses and the earth also upon which I stood and the beast of the field and the fowls of heaven and the fish of the waters and also man walking forth upon the face of the earth in magesty and in the Strength of beauty whose power and intiligence in governing the things which are so exceding great and marvilous even in the likeness of him who created ~~him~~ them and when I considered upon these things my heart exclaimed well hath the wise man Said ~~the~~ it is a fool that Saith in his heart there is no God my heart exclained all all these bear testimony and bespeak an omnipotent and omnipreasant power a being who makith Laws and decreeeth and bindeth all things in their bounds who filleth Eternity who was and is and will be fron all Eternity to Eternity and when I considered all these things and that that being Seeketh such to worship him as worship him in spirit and in truth therefore I cried unto the Lord for mercy for there was none else to whom I could go and ~~to~~ obtain mercy and the Lord heard my cry in the wilderness and while in the attitude of calling upon the Lord in the 16th year of my age a pillar of ~~fire~~ light above the brightness of the Sun at noon day come down from above and rested upon me and I was filld with the Spirit of God and the Lord opened the heavens upon me and I Saw the Lord and he Spake unto me Saying Joseph my Son thy Sins are forgiven thee. go thy way walk in my Statutes and keep my commandments behold I am the Lord of glory I was crucifyed for the world that all those who believe on my name may have Eternal life behold the world lieth in sin ~~and~~ at this time and none doeth good no not one they have turned asside from the Gospel and keep not my commandments they draw near to me with their lips while their hearts are far from me and mine anger is kindling against the inhabi- tants of the earth to visit them according to this ungodliness and to bring to pass that which hath been spoken by the mouth of the prophets and Apostles behold and lo I come quickly as it written of me in the cloud clothed in the glory of my Father and my Soul was filled with love and for many days I could rejoice with great joy and the Lord was with me but could find none that would believe the hevenly vision nevertheless I pondered these things in my heart ~~about that time my mother and~~ but after many days I fell into transgression and sinned in many things which brought wound upon my Soul and there were many things which transpired that cannot be writen and my Fathers family have suffered many persecutions and afflictions. (FV, pp. 155–57; also *PJS* 1:7)

2   *1835 Recital:* Monday Nov. 9th. . . . While sitting in his [Joseph Smith's] house this morning between the hours of ten and eleven a man came in and introduced himself to him calling himself Joshua the Jewish Minister. His appearance was something singular, having a beard about three inches in length which is quite grey, his hair was also long and considerably silvered with age. He had the appearance of a man about 50 or 55 years old. He was tall and straight, slender frame, blue eyes, thin visage, and fair complexion. He wore a green

---

First Vision

   2   History kept by various scribes between 1834 and 1836. This particular entry of 9 November 1835, which is in the handwriting of Warren A. Cowdery, describes the Prophet's conversation with a visitor to Kirtland who called himself Joshua the Jewish minister (this was Robert Matthews, alias Robert Matthias, a man with curious religious ideas).

frock coat and pantaloons of the same color. He had on a black fur hat with a narrow brim. When speaking he frequently shuts his eyes and exhibits a kind of scowl upon his countenance. He (Joseph) made some inquiry after his name, but received no definite answer. The conversation soon turned upon the subject of Religion, and after the subject of this narrative had made some remarks concerning the bible, he commenced giving him a relation of the circumstances, connected with the coming forth of the Book of Mormon, which were nearly as follows. Being wrought up in my mind respecting the subject of Religion, and looking at the different systems taught the children of men, I knew not who was right or who was wrong, but considered it of the first importance to me that I should be right, in matters of so much moment, matter[s] involving eternal consequences. Being thus perplexed in mind I retired to the silent grove and there bowed down before the Lord, under a realizing sense (if the bible be true) ask and you shall receive, knock and it shall be opened, seek and you shall find, and again, if any man lack wisdom, let [him ask] of God who giveth to all men liberally & upbraideth not. Information was what I most desired at this time, and with a fixed determination to obtain it, I called on the Lord for the first time in the place above stated, or in other words, I made a fruitless attempt to pray My tongue seemed to be swoolen in my mouth, so that I could not utter, I heard a noise behind me like some one walking towards me. I strove again to pray, but could not; the noise of walking seemed to draw nearer, I sprang upon my feet and looked round, but saw no person or thing that was calculated to produce the noise of walking. I kneeled again, my mouth was opened and my tongue loosed; I called on the Lord in mighty prayer. A pillar of fire appeared above my head; which presently rested down upon me, and filled me with unspeakable joy. A personage appeared in the midst of this pillar of flame, which was spread all around and yet nothing consumed. Another personage soon appeared like unto the first: he said unto me thy sins are forgiven thee. He testified also unto me that Jesus Christ is the son of God. I saw many angels in this vision. I was about 14 years old when I received this first communication. (FV, pp. 158–59)

3   *1838 Recital:* Owing to the many reports which have been put in circulation by evil disposed and designing persons in relation to the rise and progress of the Church of Jesus Christ of Latter day Saints, all of which have been designed by the authors thereof to militate against its Character as a Church, and its progress in the world I have been induced to write this history so as to disabuse the publick mind, and put all enquirers after truth into possession of the facts as they have transpired in relation both to myself and the Church as far as I have such facts in possession.

In this history I will present the various events in relation to this Church in truth and righteousness as they have transpired, or as they at present exist, being now the eighth year since the organisation of said Church. I was born in the year of our Lord One thousand Eight hundred and five, on the twenty third day of December, in the town of Sharon, Windsor County, State of Vermont. <Note A 131> My father Joseph Smith Senior <see Note E page 2. adenda. My Father> left the State of Vermont and moved to Palmyra, Ontario, (now Wayne) County, in the State of New York when I was in my tenth year. or thereabout.

In about four years after my father's arrival at Palmyra, he moved with his family into Manchester in the same County of Ontario. His family consisting of eleven souls, namely, My Father Joseph Smith, My Mother Lucy Smith whose name previous to her marriage was Mack, daughter of Solomon Mack, my brothers Alvin (who ~~is now dead~~ died Nov 19th 1823 in the 25 year of his age) Hyrum, Myself, Samuel-Harrison, William, Don Carloss, and my Sisters Soph[r]onia, Cathrine and Lucy. Sometime in the second year after our removal to Manchester, there was in the place where we lived an unusual excite-

---

First Vision

3   History begun in 1838, sometimes referred to as the 1839 history because the earliest manuscript version in existence was produced during the later year. This is the account that appears in Joseph Smith—History in the Pearl of Great Price. The text printed here comes from the 1839 manuscript, which is in the handwriting of scribe James Mulholland. Three insertions made in the manuscript in December 1842 by Willard Richards, acting as the Prophet's secretary, appear in angle brackets (e.g., <Note A 131>). The texts to which two of these insertions refer are found here under the headings "Note A" and "Note B." The text for the third insertion (referred to as Note E) is not included here. It simply gives a listing of Joseph Smith's paternal ancestors.

ment on the subject of religion. It commenced with the Methodists, but soon became general among all the sects in that region of country, indeed the whole district of Country seemed affected by it and great multitudes united themselves to the different religious parties, which Created no Small stir and division among the people, Some Crying, "Lo here" and some Lo there. Some were contending for the Methodist faith, Some for the Presbyterian, and some for the Baptist, for notwithstanding the great love which the Converts to these different faiths expressed at the time of their conversion, and the great Zeal manifested by the respective Clergy who were active in getting up and promoting this extraordinary scene of religious feeling, in order to have everybody converted as they were pleased to Call it, let them join what sect they pleased. Yet when the Converts began to file off some to one party and some to another, it was seen that the seemingly good feelings of both the Priests and the Converts were ~~more pretended~~ more pretended than real, for a scene of great confusion and bad feeling ensued, Priest contending against priest, and convert against convert So that all their good feelings one for another (if they ever had any) were entirely lost in a strife of words and a contest about opinions.

I was at this time in my fifteenth year. My Fathers family ~~was~~ were proselyted to the Presbyterian faith and four of them joined that Church, Namely, My Mother Lucy, My Brothers Hyrum, Samuel Harrison, and my Sister Soph[r]onia.

During this time of great excitement my mind was called up to serious reflection and great uneasiness, but though my feelings were deep and often pungent, still I kept myself aloof from all these parties though I attended their several meetings as often as occasion would permit. But in process of time my mind became somewhat partial to the Methodist sect, and I felt some desire to be united with them, but so great was the confusion and strife amongst the different denominations that it was impossible for a person young as I was and so unacquainted with men and things to come to any certain conclusion who was right and who was wrong. My mind at different times was greatly excited ~~for~~ the cry and tumult were so great and incessant. The Presbyterians were most decided against the Baptists and Methodists and used all their powers of either reason or sophistry to prove their errors, or at least to make the people think they were in error. On the other hand the Baptists and Methodists in their turn were equally Zealous in endeavoring to establish their own tenets and disprove all others.

In the midst of this war of words, and tumult of opinions, I often said to myself, what is to be done? Who of all these parties are right? Or are they all wrong together? And if any one of them be right which is it? And how shall I know it? While I was laboring under the extreme difficulties caused by the contests of these parties of religionists, I was one day reading the Epistle of James, First Chapter and fifth verse which reads, "If any of you lack wisdom, let him ask of God, that giveth to all men liberally and upbraideth not, and it shall be given him. Never did any passage of scripture come with more power to the heart of man tha[n] this did at this time to mine. It seemed to enter with great force into every feeling of my heart. I reflected on it again and again, knowing that if any person needed wisdom from God, I did, for how to act I did not know and unless I could get more wisdom than I then had, would never know, for the teachers of religion of the different sects understood the same passage of Scripture so differently as to destroy all confidence in settling the question by an appeal to the Bible. At length I came to the conclusion that I must either remain in darkness and confusion or else I must do as James directs, that is, Ask of God. I at last came to the determination to ask of God, Concluding that if he gave wisdom to them that lacked wisdom, and would give liberally and not upbraid, I might venture. So in accordance with this my determination to ask of God, I retired to the woods to make the attempt. It was on the morning of a beautiful clear day early in the spring of Eighteen hundred and twenty. It was the first time in my life that I had made such an attempt, for amidst all my anxieties I had never as yet made the attempt to pray vocally.

After I had retired into the place where I had previously designed to go, having looked around me and finding myself alone, I kneeled down and began to offer up the desires of my heart to God, I had scarcely done so, when immediately I was siezed upon by some power which entirely overcame me and had such astonishing influence over me as to bind my tongue So that I could not speak. Thick darkness gathered around me and it seemed to me for a time as if I were doomed to sudden destruction. But exerting all my powers to call upon God to deliver me out of the power of this enemy which had siezed upon me, and at the very moment when I was ready to sink into despair and abandon myself to destruction, not to an imaginary ruin but to the power of some actual being from the unseen world who had such a marvelous power as I had never before felt in any being. Just at this moment of great alarm I saw a pillar of light exactly over my head above the brightness of the sun, which descended ~~gracefully~~ gradually untill it fell upon me. It no sooner appeared than I found myself delivered from the enemy which held me bound. When the light rested upon me I saw two personages (whose brightness and glory defy all description) standing above me in the air. One of them spake unto me calling me by name and said (pointing to the other) "This is my beloved Son, Hear him." My object in going to enquire of the Lord was to know which of all the sects was right, that I might know which to join. No sooner therefore did I get possession of myself so as to be able to speak, than I asked the personages who stood above me in the light, which of all the sects was right, (for at this time it had never entered into my heart that all were wrong) and which I should join. I was answered that I must join none of them, for they were all wrong, and the Personage who addressed me said that all their Creeds were an abomination in his sight, that those professors were all corrupt, that "they draw near to me with their lips but their hearts are far from me; They teach for doctrines the commandments of men, having a form of Godliness but they deny the power thereof." He again forbade me to join with any of them and many other things did he say unto me which I cannot write at this time. When I came to myself again I found myself lying on my back looking up into Heaven. <B Note P 132> Some few days after I had this vision I happened to be in company with one of the Methodist Preachers who was very active in the before mentioned religious excitement and conversing with him on the subject of religion I took occasion to give him an account of the vision which I had had. I was greatly surprised at his behavior, he treated my communication not only lightly but with great contempt, Saying it was all of the Devil, that there was no such thing as visions or revelations in these days, that all such things had ceased with the Apostles and that there never would be any more of them. I soon found however that my telling the story had excited a great deal of prejudice against me among professors of religion and was the Cause of great persecution which continued to increase and though I was an obscure boy only between fourteen and fifteen years of age or thereabouts and my circumstances in life such as to make a boy of no consequence in the world, Yet men of high standing would take notice ~~sufficiently~~ to excite the public mind against me and create a hot persecution, and this was common among all the Sects: all united to persecute me. It has often caused me serious reflection both then and since, how very strange it was that an obscure boy of a little over fourteen years of age and one too who was doomed to the necessity of obtaining a scanty maintainance by his daily labor should be thought a character of sufficient importance to attract the attention of the great ones of the most popular sects of the day so as to create in them a spirit of the bitterest persecution and reviling. But strange or not, so it was, and was often cause of great sorrow to myself. However it was nevertheless a fact, that I had had a Vision. I have thought since that I felt much like Paul did when he made his defence before King Aggrippa and related the account of the vision he had when he saw a light and heard a voice, but still there were but few who beleived him, Some Said he was dishonest, others said he was mad, and he was ridiculed and reviled, But all this did not destroy the reality of his vision. He had seen a vision he knew he had, and all the persecution under Heaven could not make it otherwise, and though they should persecute him unto death Yet he knew and would know to his latest breath that he had both seen a light and heard a voice speaking unto him and all the world could not make him think or believe otherwise. So it was with me, I had actually seen a light and in the midst of that light I saw two personages, and they did in reality speak unto me, or one of them did, And though I was hated and persecuted for saying that I had seen a vision, Yet it was true and while they were persecuting me reviling me and speaking all manner of evil against me falsely for so saying, I was led to say in my heart why persecute me for telling the truth? I have actually seen a vision, "and who am I that I can withstand God" or why does the world think to make me deny what I have actually seen, for I had seen a vision, I knew it, and I knew that God knew it, and I could not deny it, neither dare I do it, at least I knew that by so doing I would offend God and come under condemnation. I had now got my mind satisfied so far as the Sectarian world was concerned, that it was not my duty to join with any of them, but continue as I was untill further directed, for I had found the testimony of James to be true, that a man who lacked wisdom might ask of God, and obtain and not be upbraided. (FV, pp. 160–65)

Note A

When I was 5 years old or thereabouts I was attacked with the Typhus Fever, and at one time, during my sickness, my father despaired of my life. The Doctors broke the fever, after which it settled under my shoulder and The Dr. Dr. Parker called it a sprained shoulder and anointed it with bone ointment, and freely applied the hot shovel, when it proved to be a swelling under the arm which opened, and discharged freely, after which the disease removed and descended into my left Leg and ancle and terminated in a fever Sore of the worst kind, and I endured the most acute suffering for a long time under the care of Drs. Smith, Stone and Perkins, of Hanover.

At one time eleven doctors came from Dartmouth Medical College, at Hanover, New Hampshire, for the purpose of amputation, but young as I was, I utterly refused to give my assent to the operation, but I consented to their Trying an experiment by removing a large portion of the bone from my left leg, which they did. & fourteen additional peices of bone afterwards worked out before my leg healed, during which time I was reduced so very low that my mother could carry me with ease. & after I began to get about, I went on crutches till I started for the state of New York where ~~he~~ my father had gone for the purpose of preparing a place for the removal of his family, which he affected by sending a man after us by the name of Caleb Howard, who, after he had ~~got~~ started on the Journey with my mother and family spent the money he had received of my father by drinking and Gambling etc.— We fell in with a family by the name of Gates who were travelling west, and Howard drove me from the waggon and made me travel in my weak state through the snow 40 miles per day for several days, during which time I suffered the most excruciating weariness and pain, and all this that Mr. Howard might enjoy the Society of two of Mr. Gates Daughters which he took in the waggon where I should have Rode, and thus he continued to do day day {sic} after day through the Journey and when my brothers remonstrated with Mr. Howard for his treatment to me, he would knock them down with the but of his whip.—When we arrived at Utica, N. York, Howard threw the goods out of the waggon into the Street and attempted to run away with the Horses and waggon, but my mother seized the horses by the reign, and calling witnesses forbid his taking them away as they were her property. On our way from Utica, I was left to ride on the last Sleigh in the company, (the Gates family were in sleighs) but when that came up I was knocked down by the driver, one of Gate's Sons, and left to wollow in my blood until a stranger came along, picked me up, and carried me to the Town of Palmyra.—Howard having spent all our funds My Mother was compelled to pay our landlords bills from Utica to Palmyra, in bits of cloth, clothing etc., the last payment being made with the drops {earrings} taken from Sister Sophronia's ears for that purpose. Although the snow was generally deep through the country during this Journey we performed the whole on wheels, except the first two days when we were accompanied by my mother's mother, grand-mother, Lydia Mack who was injured by the upsetting of the sleigh. & not wishing to accompany her friends west, tarried by the way with her friends in Vermont, and we soon after heard of her death supposing that she never recovered from the injury received by the overturn of the Sleigh. (FV, pp. 165–66)

Note B

When the light had departed I had no strength, but soon recover-ing in some degree, I went home. & as I leaned up to the fire piece, Mother enquired what the matter was. I replied never mind all is well.—I am well enough off. I then told my Mother I have learned for myself that Presbyterranism is not True. It seems as though the adver-sary was aware at a very early period of my Life that I was destined to prove a disturbance & annoyer of his kingdom, or else why should the powers of Darkness combine against me, why the oppression & perse-cution that arose against me, almost in my infancy? (FV, p. 166)

4   *Orson Pratt's Account:* Mr. Joseph Smith, jun., who made the fol-lowing important discovery, was born in the town of Sharon, Windsor county, Vermont, on the 23d of December, A.D. 1805. When ten years old, his parents, with their family, moved to Palmyra, New York; in the vicinity of which he resided for about eleven years, the latter part in the town of Manchester. Cultivating the earth for a livelihood was his occupation, in which he employed the most of his time. His ad-vantages for acquiring literary knowledge, were exceedingly small; hence, his education was limited to a slight acquaintance, with two or three of the common branches of learning. He could read without much difficulty, and write a very imperfect hand; and had a very lim-ited understanding of the ground rules of arithmetic. These were his highest and only attainments; while the rest of those branches, so uni-versally taught in the common schools, throughout the United States, were entirely unknown to him. When somewhere about fourteen or

---

First Vision

   4   Excerpt from Orson Pratt's *Interesting Account of Several Remarkable Vi-sions, and of the Late Discovery of Ancient American Records* . . . , a thirty-one-page pamphlet published in Edinburgh, Scotland, in 1840. This pam-phlet contains the first known publication of the Prophet's first vision.

fifteen years old, he began seriously to reflect upon the necessity of being prepared for a future state of existence; but how, or in what way, to prepare himself, was a question, as yet, undetermined in his own mind. He perceived that it was a question of infinite importance, and that the salvation of his soul depended upon a correct understanding of the same. He saw, that if he understood not the way, it would be impossible to walk in it, except by chance; and the thought of resting his hopes of eternal life upon chance, or uncertainties, was more than he could endure. If he went to the religious denominations to seek information, each one pointed to its particular tenets, saying—"This is the way, walk ye in it;" while, at the same time, the doctrines of each were in many respects, in direct opposition to one another. It also occurred to his mind that God was the author of but one doctrine, and therefore could acknowledge but one denomination as his church, and that such denomination must be a people who believe and teach that one doctrine, (whatever it may be,) and build upon the same. He then reflected upon the immense number of doctrines, now in the world, which had given rise to many hundreds of different denominations. The great question to be decided in his mind, was—if any one of these denominations be the Church of Christ, which one is it? Until he could become satisfied in relation to this question, he could not rest contented. To trust to the decisions of fallible man, and build his hopes upon the same, without any certainty, and knowledge of his own, would not satisfy the anxious desires that pervaded his breast. To decide, without any positive and definite evidence, on which he could rely, upon a subject involving the future welfare of his soul, was revolting to his feelings. The only alternative, that seemed to be left him was to read the Scriptures, and endeavor to follow their directions. He, accordingly commenced perusing the sacred pages of the Bible, with sincerity, believing the things that he read. His mind soon caught hold of the following passage:—"If any of you lack wisdom let him ask of God, that giveth to all men liberally, and upbraideth not; and it shall be given him."—James 1:5. From this promise he learned, that it was the privilege of all men to ask God for wisdom, with the sure and certain expectation of receiving liberally; without being upbraided for so doing. This was cheering information to him; tidings that gave him great joy. It was like a light shining forth in a dark place, to guide him to the path in which he should walk. He now saw that if he inquired of God, there was not only a possibility, but a probability; yea, more, a certainty, that he should obtain a knowledge, which, of all the doctrines, was the doctrine of Christ; and, which, of all the churches, was the church of Christ. He therefore, retired to a secret place in a grove, but a short distance from his father's house, and knelt down, and began to call upon the Lord. At first, he was severely tempted by the powers of darkness, which endeavored to overcome him; but he continued to seek for deliverance, until darkness gave way from his mind, and he was enabled to pray in fervency of the spirit, and in faith. And while thus pouring out his soul, anxiously desiring an answer from God, he at length, saw a very bright and glorious light in the heavens above; which, at first, seemed to be a considerable distance. He continued praying, while the light appeared to be gradually descending towards him; and as it drew nearer, it increased in brightness and magnitude, so that, by the time that it reached the tops of the trees, the whole wilderness, for some distance around was illuminated in a most glorious and brilliant manner. He expected to have seen the leaves and boughs of the trees consumed, as soon as the light came in contact with them; but perceiving that it did not produce that effect, he was encouraged with the hope of being able to endure its presence. It continued descending slowly, until it rested upon the earth, and he was enveloped in the midst of it. When it first came upon him, it produced a peculiar sensation throughout his whole system; and immediately, his mind was caught away, from the natural objects with which he was surrounded; and he was enwrapped in a heavenly vision, and saw two glorious personages, who exactly resembled each other in their features or likeness. He was informed that his sins were forgiven. He was also informed upon the subjects, which had for some time previously agitated his mind, viz.—that all the religious denominations were believing in incorrect doctrines; and consequently, that none of them was acknowledged of God, as his church and kingdom. And he was expressly commanded, to go not after them; and he received a promise that the true doctrine—the fullness of the gospel, should, at some future time, be made known to him; after which, the vision withdrew, leaving his mind in a state of calmness and peace, indescribable. (*FV*, pp. 170–72)

5   Orson Hyde's Account: Joseph Smith, Jr., to whom the angel of the Lord was sent first, was born in the town of Sharon, Windsor County, Vermont, on the 23rd of December, 1805.

When ten years old, his parents with their family, moved to Palmyra, New York, in the vicinity of which he resided for about eleven years, the latter part in the town of Manchester. His only activity was to plow and cultivate the fields. As his parents were poor and had to take care of a large family, his education was very limited. He could read without much difficulty, and write a very imperfect hand; and had a very limited understanding of the elementary rules of arithmetic. These were his highest and only attainments; while the rest of those branches, so universally taught in the common schools throughout the United States, were entirely unknown to him.

When somewhere about fourteen or fifteen years old, he began seriously to reflect upon the necessity of being prepared for a future state of existence; but how, or in what way to prepare himself, was a question, as yet, undetermined in his own mind; he perceived that it was a question of infinite importance. He saw, that if he understood not the way, it would be impossible to walk in it, except by chance; and the thought of resting his hopes of eternal life upon chance or uncertainties, was more than he could endure.

He discovered a religious world working under numerous errors, which through their contradicting nature and principles, gave cause to the organization of so many different sects and parties, and whose feelings against each other were poisoned through hate, envy, malice and rage. He felt that there should be only one truth, and that those who would understand it correctly, would understand it in the same manner. Nature had gifted him with a strong, discerning mind and so he looked through the glass of soberness and good sense upon these religious systems which all were so different; but nevertheless all drawn from the scripture of truth.

First Vision

5   Excerpt from Orson Hyde's *A Cry from the Wilderness, a Voice from the Dust of the Earth*, a book modeled after Orson Pratt's *Interesting Account of Several Remarkable Visions* and published in Frankfurt, Germany, in 1842. Having fulfilled his mission in late 1841 of dedicating the Holy Land for the return of the Jews, Orson Hyde traveled to Germany, where he published in the German language the above-named book. It explains the rise of the Church and its beliefs, and includes an account of the First Vision, the first foreign-language rendition of the Prophet's experience. The translation presented here, located in the LDS Church Archives, was made by Justus Ernst in 1960.

After he had sufficiently assured himself to his own satisfaction that darkness was covering the earth, and gross darkness the minds of the people, he gave up hope ever to find a sect or party that was in the possession of the pure and unadulterated truth.

He accordingly commenced perusing the sacred pages of the Bible with sincerity, believing the things that he read. His mind soon caught hold of the following passage—"If any of you lack wisdom, let him ask of God, that giveth to all men liberally and upbraideth not; and it shall be given him."—James 1:5. From this promise he learned that it was the privilege of all men to ask God for wisdom, with the sure and certain expectation of receiving liberally, without being upbraided for so doing. And thus he started to send the burning desires of his soul with a faithful determination. He, therefore, retired to a secret place, in a grove, but a short distance from his father's house, and knelt down and began to call upon the Lord. At first, he was severely tempted by the powers of darkness, which endeavored to overcome him. The adversary benighted his mind with doubts, and brought to his soul all kinds of improper pictures and tried to hinder him in his efforts and the accomplishment of his goal. However, the overflowing mercy of God came to buoy him up, and gave new impulse and momentum to his dwindling strength. Soon the dark clouds disappeared, and light and peace filled his troubled heart. And again he called upon the Lord with renewed faith and spiritual strength. At this sacred moment his mind was caught away from the natural objects with which he was surrounded, and he was enwrapped in a heavenly vision, and saw two glorious personages, who exactly resembled each other in their features or likeness. They told him that his prayers had been answered, and that the Lord had decided to grant him a special blessing.

He was told not to join any of the religious sects or any party, as they were all wrong in their doctrines and none of them was recognized by God as His Church and kingdom. He received a promise that the true doctrine—the fulness of the gospel—should, at some future time, be made known to him; after which, the vision withdrew, leaving his mind in a state of calmness and peace indescribable. (*FV*, pp. 173–75)

6   *Extract from the Wentworth Letter:* At the request of Mr. John Wentworth, Editor and Proprietor of the *Chicago Democrat*, I have

---

First Vision

6   Letter to John Wentworth, editor of the *Chicago Democrat*, Nauvoo, 1 March 1842.

written the following sketch of the rise, progress, persecution, and faith of the Latter-day Saints, of which I have the honor, under God, of being the founder. Mr. Wentworth says that he wishes to furnish Mr. Bastow [George Barstow], a friend of his, who is writing the history of New Hampshire, with this document. As Mr. Bastow has taken the proper steps to obtain correct information, all that I shall ask at his hands, is, that he publish the account entire, ungarnished, and without misrepresentation.

I was born in the town of Sharon, Windsor County, Vermont, on the 23rd of December, A.D. 1805. When ten years old, my parents removed to Palmyra, New York, where we resided about four years, and from thence we removed to the town of Manchester. My father was a farmer and taught me the art of husbandry. When about fourteen years of age, I began to reflect upon the importance of being prepared for a future state, and upon inquiring {about} the plan of salvation, I found that there was a great clash in religious sentiment; if I went to one society they referred me to one plan, and another to another; each one pointing to his own particular creed as the *summum bonum* of perfection. Considering that all could not be right, and that God could not be the author of so much confusion, I determined to investigate the subject more fully, believing that if God had a Church it would not be split up into factions, and that if He taught one society to worship one way, and administer in one set of ordinances, He would not teach another, principles which were diametrically opposed.

Believing the word of God, I had confidence in the declaration of James—"If any of you lack wisdom, let him ask of God, that giveth to all men liberally, and upbraideth not; and it shall be given him." I retired to a secret place in a grove, and began to call upon the Lord; while fervently engaged in supplication, my mind was taken away from the objects with which I was surrounded, and I was enwrapped in a heavenly vision, and saw two glorious personages, who exactly resembled each other in features and likeness, surrounded with a brilliant light which eclipsed the sun at noon day. They told me that all religious denominations were believing in incorrect doctrines, and that none of them was acknowledged of God as His Church and kingdom: and I was expressly commanded "to go not after them," at the same time receiving a promise that the fullness of the Gospel should at some future time be made known unto me. (HC 4:535–36)

7   *Levi Richards's Account:* attended Meeting at the Temple weather vary fine moderately warm. heard J. Smith preach from Math "Oh Jerusalem Jerusalem &c, how oft would I have gathered you, as a hen gathereth her chickens under her wings & Ye would not, behold your house is left unto you desolate &c

Pres. J. Smith bore testimony to the same saying that when he was a youth he began to think about these things but could not find out which of all the sects were right he went into the grove & enquired of the Lord which of all the sects were right he received for answer that none of them were right, that they were all wrong, & that the Everlasting Covenant was broken= =he said he understood the fulness of the Gospel from beginning to end—& could Teach it & also the order of the priesthood in all its ramifications= =Earth & hell had opposed him & tryed to destroy him, but they had not done it= =& they never would. (*WJS*, p. 215)

8   *David Nye White's Account:* He [Joseph Smith] said: ". . . The Lord does reveal himself to me. I know it. He revealed himself first to me when I was about fourteen years old, a mere boy. I will tell you about it. There was a reformation among the different religious denominations in the neighborhood where I lived, and I became serious, and was desirous to know what Church to join. While thinking of this matter, I opened the Testament promiscuously on these words, in James, 'Ask of the Lord who giveth to all men liberally and upbraideth not.' I just determined I'd ask him. I immediately went out into the woods where my father had a clearing, and went to the stump where I had stuck my axe when I had quit work, and I kneeled down, and prayed, saying, 'O Lord, what Church shall I join?' Directly I saw a light, and then a glorious personage in the light, and then another personage, and the first personage said to the second, 'Behold my beloved Son, hear him.' I then, addressed this second person, saying, 'O Lord, what Church shall I join.' He replied, 'don't join any of them, they are all corrupt.' The vision then vanished, and when I came to myself, I was sprawling on my back; and it was some time before my strength returned. When I went home and told the people that I had a revelation, and that all the

---

First Vision

7   Diary of Levi Richards, 11 June 1843.

8   Newspaper article by David Nye White, senior editor of the *Pittsburgh Weekly Gazette,* based on his interview with the Prophet in August 1843. The article appeared in the 15 September 1843 issue of the *Gazette.*

churches were corrupt, they persecuted me, and they have persecuted me ever since." (*PJS* 1:443, 444)

9 *Alexander Neibaur's Account:* After Dinner . . . called at BR. J.S. met Mr. Bonnie. Br. Joseph tolt us the first call he had a Revival Meeting, his Mother, Br. and Sisters got Religion. He wanted to get Religion too, wanted to feel and shout like the rest but could feel nothing, opened his Bible of the first Passage that struck him was if any man lack wisdom let him ask of God who giveth to all men liberallity & upbraideth not. Went into the Wood to pray, kneels himself Down, his tongue was closet cleaveh to his roof—could utter not a word, felt easier after awhile—saw a fire toward heaven came near and nearer; saw a personage in the fire, light complexion, blue eyes, a piece of white cloth Drawn over his shoulders his right arm bear after a while a other person came to the side of the first. Mr. Smith then asked, must I join the Methodist Church. No, they are not my People, have gone astray There is none that Doeth good, not one, but this is my Beloved Son harken ye him, the fire drew nigher, Rested upon the tree, enveloped him comforted I endeavored to arise but felt uncomen feeble—got into the house told the Methodist priest, said this was not a age for God to Reveal himself in Vision Revelation has ceased with the New Testament. (*FV*, p. 177)

Flattery

1 Flattery also is a deadly poison. (HC 3:295)

Fools

1 None but fools will trifle with the souls of men. (HC 3:295)

First Vision
    9 Journal of Alexander Neibaur, 24 May 1844.

Flattery
    1 Letter to the Saints from Liberty Jail, 20–25 March 1839.

Fools
    1 Letter to the Saints from Liberty Jail, 20–25 March 1839.

2   There are so many fools in the world for the devil to operate upon, it gives him the advantage oftentimes. (HC 6:184)

Foreordination

1   I believe in the fall of man, as recorded in the Bible; I believe that God foreknew everything, but did not foreordain everything; I deny that foreordain and foreknow is the same thing. He foreordained the fall of man; but all merciful as He is, He foreordained at the same time, a plan of redemption for all mankind. (HC 4:78)

2   Every man who has a calling to minister to the inhabitants of the world was ordained to that very purpose in the Grand Council of heaven before this world was. I suppose that I was ordained to this very office in that Grand Council. (HC 6:364)

3   At the general and Grand Council of heaven, all those to whom a dispensation was to be committed were set apart and ordained at that time, to that calling. (WJS, p. 371; standardized)

Forgiveness

1   Thus you see, my dear brother, the willingness of our heavenly Father to forgive sins, and restore to favor all those who are willing to humble themselves before Him, and confess their sins, and forsake them, and return to Him with full purpose of heart, acting no hypocrisy, to serve Him to the end. (HC 2:315)

Fools
   2   Sabbath address, Nauvoo, 21 January 1844.

Foreordination
   1   Statement of Joseph Smith as quoted in a letter of Mathew L. Davis to his wife, Mary, describing the Prophet's discourse in Washington, D.C., 6 February 1840.
   2   Sabbath address, Nauvoo, 12 May 1844.
   3   Sabbath address, Nauvoo, 12 May 1844, as reported by Samuel W. Richards.

Forgiveness
   1   Letter to Harvey Whitlock encouraging him to return to the Church, Kirtland, 16 November 1835.

2 *Words of Daniel Tyler:* Those who testified against him [Joseph Smith] through fear subsequently returned to the Church, some of them weeping and expressing a willingness that the Lord would remove them by death if that would remove the stain they had brought upon themselves by swearing falsely to shield themselves from the threatened death if they said aught in the Prophet's favor.

One scene was particularly touching, and showed the goodness of the Prophet's heart. A man who had stood high in the Church while in Far West was taken down with chills or ague and fever. While his mind as well as body was weak, disaffected parties soured his mind and persuaded him to leave the Saints and go with them. He gave some testimony against the Prophet. While the Saints were settling in Commerce, having recovered from his illness, he removed from Missouri to Quincy, Illinois. There he went to work chopping cordwood to obtain means to take himself and family to Nauvoo, and provide a present to the injured man of God if, peradventure, he would forgive and permit him to return to the fold as a private member. He felt that there was salvation nowhere else for him, and if that was denied him, all was lost as far as he was concerned. He started with a sorrowful heart and downcast look.

While on the way, the Lord told Brother Joseph he was coming. The Prophet looked out of the window and saw him coming up the street. As soon as he turned to open the gate, the Prophet sprang up from his chair and ran and met him in the yard, exclaiming, "O Brother, how glad I am to see you!"

He caught him around the neck, and both wept like children.

Suffice it to say that proper restitution was made, and the fallen man again entered the Church by the door, received his priesthood again, went upon several important missions, gathered with the Saints in Zion, and died in full faith. (*TK*, pp. 53–54)

3 Ever keep in exercise the principle of mercy, and be ready to forgive our brother on the first intimations of repentance, and asking forgiveness; and should we even forgive our brother, or even our enemy, before he repent or ask forgiveness, our heavenly Father would be equally as merciful unto us. (*HC* 3:383)

Forgiveness

  2 Daniel Tyler's recollection of apostates in Missouri, published in the *Juvenile Instructor*, 15 August 1892.

  3 Instructions to the Apostles and Seventies departing for missions to England, Commerce (Nauvoo), 2 July 1839.

4 You may in some measure realize what my feelings, as well as Elder Rigdon's and Brother Hyrum's were, when we read your letter— truly our hearts were melted into tenderness and compassion when we ascertained your resolves, &c. I can assure you I feel a disposition to act on your case in a manner that will meet the approbation of Jehovah, (whose servant I am), and agreeable to the principles of truth and righteousness which have been revealed; and inasmuch as long-suffering, patience, and mercy have ever characterized the dealings of our heavenly Father towards the humble and penitent, I feel disposed to copy the example, cherish the same principles, and by so doing be a savior of my fellow men. . . .

Believing your confession to be real, and your repentance genuine, I shall be happy once again to give you the right hand of fellowship, and rejoice over the returning prodigal. . . .

> "Come on, dear brother, since the war is past,
> For friends at first, are friends again at last."

(HC 4:163–64)

5 *Report of Eliza R. Snow:* [President Joseph Smith] said he had been instrumental in bringing iniquity to light—it was a melancholy thought and awful that so many should place themselves under the condemnation of the devil, and going to perdition. With deep feeling he said that they are fellow mortals, we loved them once, shall we not encourage them to reformation? We have not {yet} forgiven them seventy times seven, as our Savior directed; perhaps we have not forgiven them once. There is now a day of salvation to such as repent and reform;—and they who repent not should be cast out from this society; yet we should woo them to return to God, lest they escape not the damnation of hell! Where there is a mountain top, there is also a valley—we should act in all things on a proper medium to every immortal spirit. Notwithstanding the unworthy are among us, the virtuous should not, from self-importance, grieve and oppress needlessly, those unfortunate ones—even these should be encouraged to hereafter live to be honored by this society, who are the best portions of the community. Said he had two things to recommend to the members of this society, to put a double watch over the tongue: no organized body can exist without this at all. All organized bodies have their peculiar evils,

Forgiveness
4   Letter to William W. Phelps, Nauvoo, 22 July 1840.
5   Remarks to the Relief Society, Nauvoo, 26 May 1842.

weaknesses and difficulties, the object is to make those not so good reform and return to the path of virtue that they may be numbered with the good, and even hold the keys of power, which will influence to virtue and goodness—should chasten and reprove, and keep it all in silence, not even mention them again; then you will be established in power, virtue, and holiness, and the wrath of God will be turned away. . . . To the iniquitous show yourselves merciful. (HC 5:19–20)

6 *Report of Willard Richards:* Joseph remarked that all was well between him and the heavens; that he had no enmity against any one; and as the prayer of Jesus, or his pattern, so prayed Joseph—"Father, forgive me my trespasses as I forgive those who trespass against me," for I freely forgive all men. If we would secure and cultivate the love of others, we must love others, even our enemies as well as friends. (HC 5:498)

7 It is one of the first principles of my life, and one that I have cultivated from my childhood, having been taught it by my father, to allow every one the liberty of conscience. (HC 6:56)

8 One of the most pleasing scenes that can occur on earth, when a sin has been committed by one person against another, is, to forgive that sin; and then according to the sublime and perfect pattern of the Savior, pray to our Father in heaven to forgive him also. (HC 6:245)

Freedom

1 All men are, or ought to be free, possessing unalienable rights, and the high and noble qualifications of the laws of nature and of self-preservation, to think, and act, and say as they please, while they maintain a due respect to the rights and privileges of all other creatures, infringing upon none. (HC 5:156)

Forgiveness
   6 Sabbath address, Nauvoo, 9 July 1843.
   7 Sabbath address, Nauvoo, 15 October 1843.
   8 An appeal for peace and goodwill, addressed to the people of Missouri, Nauvoo, 8 March 1844.

Freedom
   1 Letter to James A. Bennett, Nauvoo, 8 September 1842.

2   Freedom is a sweet blessing. Men have a right to take and read what papers they please; "but do men gather grapes of thorns, or figs of thistles?" It certainly is no more than just to suppose that *charity begins at home*; and if so, what must such as profess to be Saints think, when they patronize the splendor of Babylon and leave the virtue of Zion to linger for want of bread? (HC 6:69)

Friendship

1   Those who have not been enclosed in the walls of prison without cause or provocation, can have but little idea how sweet the voice of a friend is; one token of friendship from any source whatever awakens and calls into action every sympathetic feeling; it brings up in an instant everything that is passed; it seizes the present with the avidity of lightning; it grasps after the future with the fierceness of a tiger; it moves the mind backward and forward, from one thing to another, until finally all enmity, malice and hatred, and past differences, misunderstandings and mismanagements are slain victorious at the feet of hope. (HC 3:293)

2   Pure friendship always becomes weakened the very moment you undertake to make it stronger by penal oaths and secrecy. (HC 3:303)

3   All this day I spent in greeting and receiving visits from my brethren and friends, and truly it was a joyful time. (HC 3:334)

4   From our long acquaintance with these our beloved brethren, their long, tried friendship under circumstances the most trying and

---

Freedom
   2   Letter to the Saints encouraging them to patronize the Church newspaper, published in the *Times and Seasons*, 1 November 1843.

Friendship
   1   Letter to the Saints from Liberty Jail, 20–25 March 1839.
   2   Letter to the Saints from Liberty Jail, 20–25 March 1839.
   3   Quincy, Illinois, 23 April 1839. The Prophet arrived in Quincy from Liberty Jail on 22 April 1839.
   4   Credentials of Elders Samuel Bent and George W. Harris to be agents for the Church, Nauvoo, July 1840.

painful, their zeal for the cause of truth, and their strict morality and honesty, we most cheerfully recommend them to the Saints of the Most High. (HC 4:164)

5   It is an old and trite maxim, that short reckonings [settling business accounts] make long friends. (HC 4:500)

6   Beloved Brother and Friend:—Those few lines which I received from you, written on the 15th, were to me like apples of gold in pictures of silver. I rejoice with exceeding great joy to be associated in the high and responsible stations which we hold, {with one} whose mind and feelings and heart are so congenial with my own. I love that soul that is so nobly entabernacled in that clay of yours. . . .

I add no more, but subscribe myself your faithful and most obedient servant, friend, and brother. (HC 5:105–6)

7   How good and glorious it has seemed unto me, to find pure and holy friends, who are faithful, just, and true, and whose hearts fail not; and whose knees are confirmed and do not falter, while they wait upon the Lord, in administering to my necessities, in the day when the wrath of mine enemies was poured out upon me.

In the name of the Lord, I feel in my heart to bless them, and to say in the name of Jesus Christ of Nazareth, that these are the ones that shall inherit eternal life. I say it by virtue of the Holy Priesthood, and by the ministering of holy angels, and by the gift and power of the Holy Ghost. (HC 5:107)

8   The names of the faithful are what I wish to record in this place. These I have met in prosperity, and they were my friends; and I now meet them in adversity, and they are still my warmer friends. These love the God that I serve; they love the truths that I promulgate; they love those virtuous, and those holy doctrines that I cherish in my bosom with the warmest feelings of my heart, and with that zeal which cannot be denied. I love friendship and truth; I love virtue and law. . . .

Friendship
5   Letter to Isaac Galland, Nauvoo, 19 January 1842.
6   Letter to Wilson Law, Nauvoo, 16 August 1842.
7   Blessing upon Erastus H. Derby, Nauvoo, 16 August 1842.
8   The Prophet's reflections on those who had been faithful to him in Nauvoo, 16 August 1842.

. . . I hope I shall see them again, that I may toil for them, and administer to their comfort also. They shall not want a friend while I live; my heart shall love those, and my hands shall toil for those, who love and toil for me, and shall ever be found faithful to my friends. Shall I be ungrateful? Verily no! God forbid! (*HC* 5:108, 109)

9 Never exact of a friend in adversity what you would require in prosperity. (*TPJS*, p. 317)

10 I would esteem it one of the greatest blessings, if I am to be afflicted in this world, to have my lot cast where I can find brothers and friends all around me. (*HC* 5:361)

11 I don't care what a man's character is; if he's my friend—a true friend, I will be a friend to him. . . .

Friendship is one of the grand fundamental principles of "Mormonism"; {it is designed} to revolutionize and civilize the world, and cause wars and contentions to cease and men to become friends and brothers. . . .

It is a time-honored adage that love begets love. . . . Friendship is like Brother [Theodore] Turley in his blacksmith shop welding iron to iron; it unites the human family with its happy influence. (*HC* 5:517)

12 When you support my friends, you support me. (*HC* 6:70)

13 I want to retain your friendship on holy grounds. (*HC* 6:410)

14 If my life is of no value to my friends it is of none to myself. (*HC* 6:549)

Friendship

   9 Proverbs of the Prophet Joseph Smith, 1843. Manuscript history, LDS Church Archives.
  10 Remarks upon the death of Lorenzo D. Barnes, Nauvoo, 16 April 1843.
  11 Sabbath address, Nauvoo, 23 July 1843.
  12 Letter to the Saints encouraging them to patronize the Church newspaper, published in the *Times and Seasons*, 1 November 1843.
  13 Sabbath address, Nauvoo, 26 May 1844.
  14 Response to accusations of cowardice in the Prophet's leaving Nauvoo to escape his enemies, 23 June 1844.

Garden of Eden

1   *Words of Edward Stevenson:* He [Joseph Smith] also stated that the Garden of Eden was in Jackson County—the Center Place of Zion where a great temple will be reared. (*TK*, p. 86)

2   *Words of Wilford Woodruff:* President Young said, "Joseph the Prophet told me that the Garden of Eden was in Jackson Co., Missouri." (*WWJ* 7:129; standardized)

Gathering

1   The time has at last arrived when the God of Abraham, of Isaac, and of Jacob, has set His hand again the second time to recover the remnants of his people, which have been left from Assyria, and from Egypt, and from Pathros, and from Cush, and from Elam, and from Shinar, and from Hamath, and from the islands of the sea, and with them to bring in the fulness of the Gentiles, and establish that covenant with them, which was promised when their sins should be taken away. . . .
     . . . Unto it [America] all the tribes of Israel will come, with as many of the Gentiles as shall comply with the requisitions of the new covenant. But the tribe of Judah will return to old Jerusalem. The city of Zion spoken of by David, in the one hundred and second Psalm, will be built upon the land of America, "And the ransomed of the Lord shall return, and come to Zion with songs and everlasting joy upon their heads" (Isaiah xxxv:10); and then they will be delivered from the overflowing scourge that shall pass through the land. But Judah shall obtain deliverance at Jerusalem. (*HC* 1:313, 315)

Garden of Eden
   1   Autobiography of Edward Stevenson, LDS Church Archives.
   2   Report by Wilford Woodruff of a conversation in the Church historian's office, 30 March 1873.

Gathering
   1   Letter to N. E. Seaton (N. C. Saxton), a newspaper editor in Rochester, N.Y., Kirtland, 4 January 1833.

2 Being prepared to commence our labors in the printing business, I ask God in the name of Jesus, to . . . cause that His word may speedily go forth to the nations of the earth, to the accomplishing of His great work in bringing about the restoration of the house of Israel. (*HC* 1:451)

3 Without Zion, and a place of deliverance, we must fall; because the time is near when the sun will be darkened, and the moon turn to blood, and the stars fall from heaven, and the earth reel to and fro. Then, if this is the case, and if we are not sanctified and gathered to the places God has appointed, with all our former professions and our great love for the Bible, we must fall; we cannot stand; we cannot be saved; for God will gather out His Saints from the Gentiles, and then comes desolation and destruction, and none can escape except the pure in heart who are gathered. (*HC* 2:52)

4 [The] subject of the gathering . . . is a principle I esteem to be of the greatest importance to those who are looking for salvation in this generation, or in these, that may be called, "the latter times." All that the prophets that have written, from the days of righteous Abel, down to the last man that has left any testimony on record for our consideration, in speaking of the salvation of Israel in the last days, goes directly to show that it consists in the work of the gathering. (*HC* 2:260)

5 And to show further upon this subject of the gathering, Moses, after having pronounced the blessing and cursing upon the children of Israel, for their obedience or disobedience, says thus:
"And it shall come to pass, when all these things are come upon thee, the blessing and the curse which I have set before thee, and thou shalt call them to mind, among all the nations whither the Lord thy God hath driven thee, and shalt return unto the Lord thy God, and shalt obey His voice, according to all that I command thee, this day, thou and thy children, with all thine heart, and with all thy soul, then the Lord thy God will turn thy captivity, and have compassion

Gathering
  2   Dedication of a printing establishment in Kirtland, 6 December 1833.
  3   Conference of the elders of the Church, Norton, Ohio, 21 April 1834.
  4   Letter to the elders of the Church, Kirtland, 1 September 1835.
  5   Letter to the elders of the Church, Kirtland, 1 September 1835.

upon thee, and will return and gather thee from all the nations whither the Lord thy God hath scattered thee. If any of thine be driven out unto the outmost parts of heaven, from thence will the Lord thy God gather thee, and from thence will He fetch thee" (Deut. xxx:1–4). (HC 2:261)

6   I shall now proceed to make some remarks from the sayings of the Savior, recorded in the 13th chapter of His Gospel according to St. Matthew, which, in my mind, afford us as clear an understanding upon the important subject of the gathering, as anything recorded in the Bible. . . .

. . . The angels are to have something to do in this great work, for they are the reapers. As, therefore, the tares are gathered and burned in the fire, so shall it be in the end of the world; that is, as the servants of God go forth warning the nations, both priests and people, and as they harden their hearts and reject the light of truth, these first being delivered over to the buffetings of Satan, and the law and the testimony being closed up, as it was in the case of the Jews, they are left in darkness, and delivered over unto the day of burning; thus being bound up by their creeds, and their bands being made strong by their priests, are prepared for the fulfillment of the saying of the Savior— "The Son of Man shall send forth His angels, and gather out of His Kingdom all things that offend, and them which do iniquity, and shall cast them into a furnace of fire, there shall be wailing and gnashing of teeth." We understand that the work of gathering together of the wheat into barns, or garners, is to take place while the tares are being bound over, and preparing for the day of burning; that after the day of burnings, the righteous shall shine forth like the sun, in the Kingdom of their Father. Who hath ears to hear, let him hear. (HC 2:264, 271)

7   Much has been said and done of late by the general government in relation to the Indians (Lamanites) within the territorial limits of the United States. One of the most important points in the faith of the Church of the Latter-day Saints, through the fullness of the everlasting Gospel, is the gathering of Israel (of whom the Lamanites constitute a part)—that happy time when Jacob shall go up to the house of the Lord, to worship Him in spirit and in truth, to live in holiness; when

---

Gathering
6   Letter to the elders of the Church, Kirtland, 1 September 1835.
7   Meeting of the high council at Kirtland, 6 January 1836.

the Lord will restore His judges as at the first, and His counselors as at the beginning; when every man may sit under his own vine and fig tree, and there will be none to molest or make afraid; when He will turn to them a pure language, and the earth will be filled with sacred knowledge, as the waters cover the great deep; when it shall no longer be said, the Lord lives that brought up the children of Israel out of the land of Egypt, but the Lord lives that brought up the children of Israel from the land of the north, and from all the lands whither He has driven them. That day is one, all important to all men.

In view of its importance, together with all that the prophets have said about it before us, we feel like dropping a few ideas in connection with the official statements from the government concerning the Indians. In speaking of the gathering, we mean to be understood as speaking of it according to scripture, the gathering of the elect of the Lord out of every nation on earth, and bringing them to the place of the Lord of Hosts, when the city of righteousness shall be built, and where the people shall be of one heart and one mind, when the Savior comes; yea, where the people shall walk with God like Enoch, and be free from sin. The word of the Lord is precious; and when we read that the veil spread over all nations will be destroyed, and the pure in heart see God, and reign with Him a thousand years on earth, we want all honest men to have a chance to gather and build up a city of righteousness, where even upon the bells of the horses shall be written *Holiness to the Lord*.

The Book of Mormon has made known who Israel is, upon this continent. And while we behold the government of the United States gathering the Indians, and locating them upon lands to be their own, how sweet it is to think that they may one day be gathered by the Gospel! (HC 2:357–58)

8   The same evening the Elders assembled in conference in the House of the Lord when I addressed them on the subject of the gathering of the Saints in the last days, and the duties of the different quorums in relation thereto.

It appeared manifest to the conference that the places appointed for the gathering of the Saints were at this time crowded to overflowing, and that it was necessary that there be more stakes of Zion appointed in order that the poor might have a place to gather to,

---

Gathering
  8 A conference of the Church, Kirtland, 17 September 1837.

"wherefore it was moved, seconded and voted unanimously that President Joseph Smith, Jun., and Sidney Rigdon be requested by this conference to go and appoint other stakes, or places of gathering, and that they receive a certificate of their appointment, signed by the clerk of the Church." (HC 2:513–14)

9   The word of the Lord was given several months since, for the Saints to gather into the cities, but they have been slow to obey until the judgments were upon them, and now they are gathering by flight and haste, leaving all their effects, and are glad to get off at that. The city of Far West is literally crowded, and the brethren are gathering from all quarters. (HC 3:166)

10   There will be here and there a Stake {of Zion} for the gathering of the Saints. Some may have cried peace, but the Saints and the world will have little peace from henceforth. Let this not hinder us from going to the Stakes; for God has told us to flee, not dallying, or we shall be scattered, one here, and another there. There your children shall be blessed, and you in the midst of friends where you may be blessed. The Gospel net gathers of every kind.

I prophesy, that that man who tarries after he has an opportunity of going, will be afflicted by the devil. Wars are at hand; we must not delay; but are not required to sacrifice. We ought to have the building up of Zion as our greatest object. When wars come, we shall have to flee to Zion. The cry is to make haste. The last revelation says, Ye shall not have time to have gone over the earth, until these things come. It will come as did the cholera, war, fires, and earthquakes; one pestilence after another, until the Ancient of Days comes, then judgment will be given to the Saints. (HC 3:390–91)

11   *Minutes:* He [Joseph Smith] then spoke to the Elders respecting their mission, and advised those who went into the world to preach the Gospel . . . and to teach the gathering as set forth in the Holy Scripture. (HC 4:109)

Gathering

9   History entry. Mob activity forced the Saints to flee to Far West, 23 October 1838. They had not followed earlier counsel to gather.

10   Discourse on the priesthood, given sometime before 8 August 1839, Commerce (Nauvoo). For a discussion on the dating of this discourse, see *WJS*, p. 22.

11   General conference address, Nauvoo, 8 April 1840.

12 The Jewish nations have been scattered abroad among the Gentiles for a long period; and in our estimation, the time of the commencement of their return to the Holy Land has already arrived. (HC 4:112–13)

13 By a concentration of action, and a unity of effort, we can only accomplish the great work of the last days which we could not do in our remote and scattered condition, while our interests, both temporal and spiritual, will be greatly enhanced, and the blessings of heaven must flow unto us in an uninterrupted stream; of this, we think there can be no question.

The greatest temporal and spiritual blessings which always flow from faithfulness and concerted effort, never attended individual exertion or enterprise. The history of all past ages abundantly attests this fact. In addition to all temporal blessings, there is no other way for the Saints to be saved in these last days, {than by the gathering} as the concurrent testimony of all the holy Prophets clearly proves, for it is written—"They shall come from the east, and be gathered from the west; the north shall give up, and the south shall keep not back." "The sons of God shall be gathered from far, and His daughters from the ends of the earth."

It is also the concurrent testimony of all the Prophets, that this gathering together of all the Saints, must take place before the Lord comes to "take vengeance upon the ungodly," and "to be glorified and admired by all those who obey the Gospel." (HC 4:272)

14 It is left for us to see, participate in and help to roll forward the Latter-day glory, "the dispensation of the fullness of times, when God will gather together all things that are in heaven, and all things that are upon the earth, even in one," when the Saints of God will be gathered in one from every nation, and kindred, and people, and tongue, when the Jews will be gathered together into one, the wicked will also be gathered together to be destroyed, as spoken of by the prophets; the Spirit of God will also dwell with His people, and be withdrawn from the rest of the nations, and all things whether in

---

Gathering

12 Credentials given to Orson Hyde as a missionary to Palestine, Nauvoo, April 1840.

13 Proclamation of the First Presidency, Nauvoo, 15 January 1841.

14 Editorial in the *Times and Seasons*, 2 May 1842.

heaven or on earth will be in one, even in Christ. The heavenly Priesthood will unite with the earthly, to bring about those great purposes. (HC 4:610)

15 The main object [of gathering] was to build unto the Lord a house whereby He could reveal unto His people the ordinances of His house and the glories of His kingdom, and teach the people the way of salvation; for there are certain ordinances and principles that, when they are taught and practiced, must be done in a place or house built for that purpose.

It was the design of the councils of heaven before the world was, that the principles and laws of the priesthood should be predicated upon the gathering of the people in every age of the world. Jesus did everything to gather the people, and they would not be gathered, and He therefore poured out curses upon them. . . .

It is for the same purpose that God gathers together His people in the last days, to build unto the Lord a house to prepare them for the ordinances and endowments, washings and anointings, etc. . . .

. . . Jesus said unto the Jews, "How oft would I have gathered thy children together, even as a hen gathereth her chickens under her wings, and ye would not!"—that they might attend to the ordinances of baptism for the dead as well as other ordinances of the priesthood, and receive revelations from heaven, and be perfected in the things of the kingdom of God—but they would not. This was the case on the day of Pentecost: those blessings were poured out on the disciples on that occasion. God ordained that He would save the dead, and would do it by gathering His people together. . . .

. . . Why gather the people together in this place? For the same purpose that Jesus wanted to gather the Jews—to receive the ordinances, the blessings, and glories that God has in store for His Saints. (HC 5:423, 424, 425, 427)

16 The Bible says, "I will send you Elijah the Prophet before the coming of the great and dreadful day of the Lord; and he shall turn the hearts of the fathers to the children, and the hearts of the children to the fathers, lest I come and smite the earth with a curse."

Gathering
  15 Sabbath address, Nauvoo, 11 June 1843.
  16 Sabbath address, Nauvoo, 21 January 1844.

Now, the word *turn* here should be translated *bind*, or seal. But what is the object of this important mission? or how is it to be fulfilled? The keys are to be delivered, the spirit of Elijah is to come, the Gospel to be established, the Saints of God gathered, Zion built up, and the Saints to come up as saviors on Mount Zion. (HC 6:183–84)

General Conference

1   We have a fervent desire that in your general conferences everything should be discussed with a great deal of care and propriety, lest you grieve the Holy Spirit, which shall be poured out at all times upon your heads, when you are exercised with those principles of righteousness that are agreeable to the mind of God, and are properly affected one toward another. (HC 3:299)

2   *Minutes:* President Joseph Smith rose to state to the congregation the nature of the business which would have to come before them. He stated that it had been expected by some that the little petty difficulties which have existed would be brought up and investigated before this conference, but it will not be the case: these things are of too trivial a nature to occupy the attention of so large a body. I intend to give you some instruction on the principles of eternal truth, but will defer it until others have spoken, in consequence of the weakness of my lungs. The Elders will give you instruction; and then, if necessary, I will offer such corrections as may be proper to fill up the interstices. Those who feel desirous of sowing the seeds of discord will be disappointed on this occasion. It is our purpose to build up and establish the principles of righteousness, and not to break down and destroy. (HC 6:287–88)

General Conference

1   Letter to the Saints from Liberty Jail, 20–25 March 1839.
2   General conference address, Nauvoo, 5 April 1844.

Gentiles

1   God will gather out His Saints from the Gentiles, and then comes desolation and destruction, and none can escape except the pure in heart who are gathered. (HC 2:52)

2   The Twelve Apostles . . . are to travel and preach among the Gentiles, until the Lord shall command them to go to the Jews. (HC 2:200)

3   The servants of God will not have gone over the nations of the Gentiles, with a warning voice, until the destroying angel will commence to waste the inhabitants of the earth. (HC 2:263)

Gift of the Holy Ghost
See also HOLY GHOST

1   We then laid our hands on each individual member of the Church present, that they might receive the gift of the Holy Ghost, and be confirmed members of the Church of Christ. The Holy Ghost was poured out upon us to a very great degree—some prophesied, whilst we all praised the Lord, and rejoiced exceedingly. (HC 1:78)

2   Baptism is a holy ordinance preparatory to the reception of the Holy Ghost; it is the channel and key by which the Holy Ghost will be administered.
    The Gift of the Holy Ghost by the laying on of hands, cannot be received through the medium of any other principle than the principle of righteousness, for if the proposals are not complied with, it is of no use, but withdraws. (HC 3:379)

Gentiles
1   Conference of the elders of the Church, Norton, Ohio, 21 April 1834.
2   Instructions to the Twelve, Kirtland, 27 February 1835.
3   Letter to the elders of the Church, Kirtland, 1 September 1835.

Gift of the Holy Ghost
1   Organization of the Church at the home of Peter Whitmer, Sr., at Fayette, New York, 6 April 1830.
2   Instructions to the Twelve, Commerce (Nauvoo), 27 June 1839.

3   In our interview with the President [Martin Van Buren], he interrogated us wherein we differed in our religion from the other religions
of the day. Brother Joseph said we differed in mode of baptism, and
the gift of the Holy Ghost by the laying on of hands. We considered
that all other considerations were contained in the gift of the Holy
Ghost, and we deemed it unnecessary to make many words in preaching the Gospel to him. Suffice it to say he has got our testimony. (*HC*
4:42)

4   What if we should attempt to get the gift of the Holy Ghost
through any other means except the signs or way which God hath appointed—would we obtain it? Certainly not; all other means would
fail. . . .

. . . The sign of Peter was to repent and be baptized for the remission of sins, with the promise of the gift of the Holy Ghost; and in no
other way is the gift of the Holy Ghost obtained. (*HC* 4:555)

5   There is a difference between the Holy Ghost and the gift of the
Holy Ghost. Cornelius received the Holy Ghost before he was baptized, which was the convincing power of God unto him of the truth
of the Gospel, but he could not receive the gift of the Holy Ghost
until after he was baptized. Had he not taken this sign or ordinance
upon him, the Holy Ghost which convinced him of the truth of God,
would have left him. (*HC* 4:555)

6   Various and conflicting are the opinions of men in regard to the
gift of the Holy Ghost. Some people have been in the habit of calling
every supernatural manifestation the effects of the Spirit of God,
whilst there are others that think there is no manifestation connected
with it at all; and that it is nothing but a mere impulse of the mind, or
an inward feeling, impression, or secret testimony or evidence, which
men possess, and that there is no such thing as an outward manifestation. . . .

Gift of the Holy Ghost
   3   Letter to Hyrum Smith reporting on the Prophet's affairs in Washington,
       D.C., 5 December 1839.
   4   Sabbath address, Nauvoo, 20 March 1842.
   5   Sabbath address, Nauvoo, 20 March 1842.
   6   Editorial in the *Times and Seasons*, 15 June 1842.

We believe in the gift of the Holy Ghost being enjoyed now, as much as it was in the Apostles' days; we believe that it {the gift of the Holy Ghost} is necessary to make and to organize the Priesthood, that no man can be called to fill any office in the ministry without it; we also believe in prophecy, in tongues, in visions, and in revelations, in gifts, and in healings; and that these things cannot be enjoyed without the gift of the Holy Ghost. . . . We believe in it {this gift of the Holy Ghost} in all its fullness, and power, and greatness, and glory; but whilst we do this, we believe in it rationally, consistently, and scripturally, and not according to the wild vagaries, foolish notions and traditions of men. (HC 5:26, 27)

7   Again, Luke in his record of the acts of the Apostles, says:—And it came to pass, that while Apollos was at Corinth, Paul having passed through the upper coasts, came to Ephesus; and finding certain disciples, he said unto them, have ye received the Holy Ghost since ye believed? And they said unto him, We have not so much as heard whether there be any Holy Ghost. And he said unto them, Unto what then were ye baptised? And they said, unto John's baptism. Then said Paul, John verily baptised with the baptism of repentance, saying unto the people, That they should believe on him which should come after him, that is on Christ Jesus. When they heard this, they were baptised in the name of the Lord Jesus.—And when Paul had laid his hands upon them, the Holy Ghost came on them; and they spake with tongues, and prophesied.

From the above witnesses we are informed that baptism was the essential point on which they could receive the gift of the Holy Ghost. It seems from the reasoning above that some sectarian Jew had been baptising like John, but had forgotten to inform them that there was one to follow by the name of Jesus Christ, to baptise with fire and the Holy Ghost:—which showed these converts that their first baptism was illegal, and when they heard this they were gladly baptised, and after hands were laid on them, they received the gifts, according to promise, and spake with tongues and prophesied. (*T&S* 3:904)

8   You might as well baptize a bag of sand as a man, if not done in view of the remission of sins and getting of the Holy Ghost. Baptism

---

Gift of the Holy Ghost

7   Editorial in the *Times and Seasons*, 1 September 1842.

8   Sabbath address, Nauvoo, 9 July 1843.

by water is but half a baptism, and is good for nothing without the other half—that is, the baptism of the Holy Ghost. (HC 5:499)

9   I want your prayers and faith that I may have the instruction of Almighty God and the gift of the Holy Ghost, so that I may set forth things that are true and which can be easily comprehended by you, and that the testimony may carry conviction to your hearts and minds of the truth of what I shall say. . . .

. . . I am learned, and know more than all the worlds put together. The Holy Ghost does, anyhow, and he is within me, and comprehends more than all the world; and I will associate myself with him. . . .

This is good doctrine. It tastes good. I can taste the principles of eternal life, and so can you. They are given to me by the revelations of Jesus Christ; and I know that when I tell you these words of eternal life as they are given to me, you taste them, and I know that you believe them. You say honey is sweet, and so do I. I can also taste the spirit of eternal life. I know that it is good; and when I tell you of these things which were given me by inspiration of the Holy Spirit, you are bound to receive them as sweet, and rejoice more and more. . . .

. . . The baptism of water, without the baptism of fire and the Holy Ghost attending it, is of no use; they are necessarily and inseparably connected. An individual must be born of water and the spirit in order to get into the kingdom of God. (HC 6:302–3, 308, 312, 316)

10   I thank God that I have got this old book; but I thank him more for the gift of the Holy Ghost. I have got the oldest book in the world; but I have got the oldest book in my heart, even the gift of the Holy Ghost. (HC 6:308)

Gift of Tongues
See TONGUES, GIFT OF

Gift of the Holy Ghost
  9   King Follett Discourse, Nauvoo, 7 April 1844.
 10   King Follett Discourse, Nauvoo, 7 April 1844.

Gifts of the Spirit

1   The Holy Ghost was poured out upon us in a miraculous manner—many of our number prophesied, whilst others had the heavens
opened to their view, and were so overcome that we had to lay them
on beds or other convenient places. . . .

. . . To witness and feel with our own natural senses, the like glorious manifestations of the powers of the Priesthood, the gifts and blessings of the Holy Ghost, and the goodness and condescension of a
merciful God unto such as obey the everlasting Gospel of our Lord
Jesus Christ, combined to create within us sensations of rapturous
gratitude, and inspire us with fresh zeal and energy in the cause of
truth. (HC 1:85–86)

2   Sister Knight, wife of Newel Knight, had a dream, which enabled
her to say that we would visit them that day, which really came to
pass, for a few hours afterwards we arrived; and thus was our faith
much strengthened concerning dreams and visions in the last days,
foretold by the ancient Prophet Joel. (HC 1:101)

3   The gifts which follow them that believe and obey the Gospel, as
tokens that the Lord is ever the same in His dealings with the humble
lovers and followers of truth, began to be poured out among us, as in
ancient days. (HC 1:322)

4   A man must have the discerning of spirits, as we before stated, to
understand these things, and how is he to obtain this gift if there are
no gifts of the Spirit? And how can these gifts be obtained without
revelation? (HC 4:574)

5   We believe that the Holy Ghost is imparted by the laying on of
hands of those in authority, and that the gift of tongues, and also the
gift of prophecy are gifts of the Spirit, and are obtained through that

---

Gifts of the Spirit
1   First conference of the Church, Fayette, New York, 9 June 1830.
2   Amid the persecutions of the Saints at Colesville, New York, the Lord
comforted the Saints and strengthened their faith, June 1830.
3   Reflections regarding the winter of 1832–33, Kirtland.
4   Editorial in the *Times and Seasons*, 1 April 1842.
5   Editorial in the *Times and Seasons*, 15 June 1842.

medium; but then to say that men always prophesied and spoke in tongues when they had the imposition of hands, would be to state that which is untrue, contrary to the practice of the Apostles, and at variance with holy writ. . . .

But suppose the gifts of the Spirit were immediately, upon the imposition of hands, enjoyed by all, in all their fullness and power; the skeptic would still be as far from receiving any testimony except upon a mere casualty as before, for all the gifts of the Spirit are not visible to the natural vision, or understanding of man; indeed very few of them are. . . .

The greatest, the best, and the most useful gifts would be known nothing about by an observer. . . .

. . . The gifts of God are all useful in their place, but when they are applied to that which God does not intend, they prove an injury, a snare and a curse instead of a blessing. (HC 5:27–28, 30, 31–32)

6   A man who has none of the gifts has no faith; and he deceives himself, if he supposes he has. Faith has been wanting, not only among the heathen, but in professed Christendom also, so that tongues, healings, prophecy, and prophets and apostles, and all the gifts and blessings have been wanting. (HC 5:218)

7   *Words of Edward Stevenson:* A prediction made by the Prophet was afterwards literally fulfilled. Joseph said, "If you will obey the gospel with honest hearts, I promise you in the name of the Lord that the gifts as promised by our Savior will follow you, and by this you may prove me to be a true servant of God."

I both saw and heard the gifts follow those who believed and obeyed the gospel. (TK, p. 85)

God

1   Remember God sees the secret springs of human action, and knows the hearts of all living.

Gifts of the Spirit
   6   Springfield, Illinois, at the home of a Mr. Sollars, 2 January 1843.
   7   Autobiography of Edward Stevenson, LDS Church Archives.

God
   1   Letter to William W. Phelps in Missouri, written from Kirtland, 14 January 1833. According to Dean Jessee this letter was dated 11 January (see PWJS, p. 262).

Brother, suffer us to speak plainly, for God has respect to the feelings of His Saints, and He will not suffer them to be tantalized with impunity. (HC 1:317)

2 The destinies of all people are in the hands of a just God, and He will do no injustice to any one. (HC 1:449)

3 We admit that God is the great source and fountain from whence proceeds all good; that He is perfect intelligence, and that His wisdom is alone sufficient to govern and regulate the mighty creations and worlds which shine and blaze with such magnificence and splendor over our heads, as though touched with His finger and moved by His Almighty word. And if so, it is done and regulated by law; for without law all must certainly fall into chaos. If, then, we admit that God is the source of all wisdom and understanding, we must admit that by His direct inspiration He has taught man that law is necessary in order to govern and regulate His own immediate interest and welfare. (HC 2:12–13)

4 The heavens declare the glory of a God, and the firmament showeth His handiwork; and a moment's reflection is sufficient to teach every man of common intelligence, that all these are not the mere productions of *chance*, nor could they be supported by any power less than an Almighty hand; and He that can mark the power of Omnipotence, inscribed upon the heavens, can also see God's own handwriting in the sacred volume. (HC 2:14)

5 We here observe that God is the only supreme governor and independent being in whom all fullness and perfection dwell; who is omnipotent, omnipresent, and omniscient; without beginning of days or end of life; and that in him every good gift and every good principle dwell; and that he is the Father of lights; in him the principle of faith

God

2   Letter to the brethren in Missouri, Kirtland, 5 December 1833.

3   Letter to the brethren scattered from Zion, Kirtland, 22 January 1834.

4   Letter to the brethren scattered from Zion, Kirtland, 22 January 1834.

5   Lectures on Faith, delivered to a school of the elders, Kirtland, December 1834. Although the Lectures on Faith were not written only by Joseph Smith, he reviewed them carefully and prepared them for publication (see Larry E. Dahl and Charles D. Tate, Jr., eds., *The Lectures on Faith in Historical Perspective*, p. 10).

dwells independently, and he is the object in whom the faith of all other rational and accountable beings centers for life and salvation. (*LF* 2:2)

6   After any portion of the human family are made acquainted with the important fact that there is a God, who has created and does uphold all things, the extent of their knowledge respecting his character and glory will depend upon their diligence and faithfulness in seeking after him, until, like Enoch, the brother of Jared, and Moses, they shall obtain faith in God, and power with him to behold him face to face. (*LF* 2:55)

7   Thus you see, my dear brother, the willingness of our heavenly Father to forgive sins, and restore to favor all those who are willing to humble themselves before Him, and confess their sins, and forsake them, and return to Him with full purpose of heart, acting no hypocrisy, to serve him to the end. (*HC* 2:315)

8   God can do His own work, without the aid of those who are not dictated by His counsel. (*HC* 2:438)

9   The things of God are of deep import; and time, and experience, and careful and ponderous and solemn thoughts can only find them out. Thy mind, O man! if thou wilt lead a soul unto salvation, must stretch as high as the utmost heavens, and search into and contemplate the darkest abyss, and the broad expanse of eternity—thou must commune with God. (*HC* 3:295)

God

   6   Lectures on Faith, delivered to a school of the elders, Kirtland, December 1834. Although the Lectures on Faith were not written only by Joseph Smith, he reviewed them carefully and prepared them for publication (see Larry E. Dahl and Charles D. Tate, Jr., eds., *The Lectures on Faith in Historical Perspective*, p. 10).

   7   Letter to Harvey Whitlock encouraging him to return to the Church, Kirtland, 16 November 1835.

   8   Letter on abolition published in the *Messenger and Advocate*, April 1836.

   9   Letter to the Saints from Liberty Jail, 20–25 March 1839.

10 Love is one of the chief characteristics of Deity, and ought to be manifested by those who aspire to be the sons of God. (HC 4:227)

11 That which is without body or parts is nothing. There is no other God in heaven but that God who has flesh and bones. John 5:26, "As the Father hath life in himself, even so hath he given the Son to have life in himself." God the Father took life unto himself precisely as Jesus did. (WJS, p. 60; standardized)

12 If you wish to go where God is, you must be like God, or possess the principles which God possesses, for if we are not drawing towards God in principle, we are going from Him and drawing towards the devil. (HC 4:588)

13 But while one portion of the human race is judging and condemning the other without mercy, the Great Parent of the universe looks upon the whole of the human family with a fatherly care and paternal regard; He views them as His offspring, and without any of those contracted feelings that influence the children of men, causes "His sun to rise on the evil and on the good, and sendeth rain on the just and on the unjust." (HC 4:595)

14 If human laws award to each man his deserts, and punish all delinquents according to their several crimes, surely the Lord will not be more cruel than man, for He is a wise legislator, and His laws are more equitable, His enactments more just, and His decisions more perfect than those of man; and as man judges his fellow man by law, and punishes him according to the penalty of the law, so does God of heaven judge "according to the deeds done in the body." (HC 4:598)

God
10 Letter to the Twelve in England, Nauvoo, 15 December 1840. The placement of this letter in HC implies that it was written in October 1840, but actually it was written on 15 December 1840 (see PWJS, p. 480).
11 Lecture given at the Nauvoo Lyceum, 5 January 1841, as reported by William Clayton. (The lyceum met weekly at different locations in Nauvoo for several months, beginning 5 January 1841.)
12 Sabbath address, Nauvoo, 10 April 1842.
13 Editorial in the *Times and Seasons*, 15 April 1842.
14 Editorial in the *Times and Seasons*, 15 April 1842.

15 As God governed Abraham, Isaac and Jacob as families, and the children of Israel as a nation; so we, as a Church, must be under His guidance if we are prospered, preserved and sustained. Our only confidence can be in God; our only wisdom obtained from Him; and He alone must be our protector and safeguard, spiritually and temporally, or we fall. (*HC* 5:65)

16 In obedience there is joy and peace unspotted, unalloyed; and as God has designed our happiness—and the happiness of all His creatures, he never has—He never will institute an ordinance or give a commandment to His people that is not calculated in its nature to promote that happiness which He has designed, and which will not end in the greatest amount of good and glory to those who become the recipients of his law and ordinances. . . .

Our heavenly Father is more liberal in His views, and boundless in His mercies and blessings, than we are ready to believe or receive; and, at the same time, is more terrible to the workers of iniquity, more awful in the executions of His punishments, and more ready to detect every false way, than we are apt to suppose Him to be. (*HC* 5:135, 136)

17 In knowledge there is power. God has more power than all other beings, because he has greater knowledge; and hence he knows how to subject all other beings to Him. He has power over all. (*HC* 5:340)

18 It is the constitutional disposition of mankind to set up stakes and set bounds to the works and ways of the Almighty. (*HC* 5:529)

19 When God offers a blessing or knowledge to a man, and he refuses to receive it, he will be damned. (*HC* 5:555)

20 If men do not comprehend the character of God, they do not comprehend themselves. I want to go back to the beginning, and so lift your minds into more lofty spheres and a more exalted understanding than what the human mind generally aspires to.

God
    15 Editorial in the *Times and Seasons*, 15 July 1842.
    16 Essay on happiness, Nauvoo, 27 August 1842.
    17 General conference address, Nauvoo, 8 April 1843.
    18 Remarks at the funeral of Judge Elias Higbee, Nauvoo, 13 August 1843.
    19 Sabbath address, Nauvoo, 27 August 1843.
    20 King Follett Discourse, Nauvoo, 7 April 1844.

. . . What kind of a being is God? . . .

God himself was once as we are now, and is an exalted man, and sits enthroned in yonder heavens! That is the great secret. If the veil were rent today, and the great God who holds this world in its orbit, and who upholds all worlds and all things by His power, was to make himself visible,—I say, if you were to see him today, you would see him like a man in form—like yourselves in all the person, image, and very form as a man; for Adam was created in the very fashion, image and likeness of God, and received instruction from, and walked, talked and conversed with Him, as one man talks and communes with another.

. . . It is necessary we should understand the character and being of God and how He came to be so; for I am going to tell you how God came to be God. We have imagined and supposed that God was God from all eternity. I will refute that idea, and take away the veil, so that you may see.

These are incomprehensible ideas to some, but they are simple. It is the first principle of the gospel to know for a certainty the character of God, and to know that we may converse with Him as one man converses with another, and that He was once a man like us; yea, that God himself, the Father of us all, dwelt on an earth, the same as Jesus Christ Himself did; and I will show it from the Bible.

. . . The scriptures inform us that Jesus said, as the Father hath power in himself, even so hath the Son power—to do what? Why, what the Father did. The answer is obvious—in a manner to lay down his body and take it up again. Jesus, what are you going to do? To lay down my life as my Father did, and take it up again. Do you believe it? If you do not believe it you do not believe the Bible. The scriptures say it, and I defy all the learning and wisdom and all the combined powers of earth and hell together to refute it. Here, then, is eternal life—to know the only wise and true God; and you have got to learn how to be gods yourselves, and to be kings and priests to God, the same as all gods have done before you, namely, by going from one small degree to another, and from a small capacity to a great one; from grace to grace, from exaltation to exaltation, until you attain to the resurrection of the dead, and are able to dwell in everlasting burnings, and to sit in glory, as do those who sit enthroned in everlasting power. And I want you to know that God, in the last days, while certain individuals are proclaiming His name, is not trifling with you or me.

. . . What did Jesus do? Why, I do the things I saw my Father do when worlds came rolling into existence. My Father worked out His kingdom with fear and trembling, and I must do the same; and when I get my kingdom, I shall present it to My Father, so that He may obtain kingdom upon kingdom, and it will exalt Him in glory. He will then take a higher exaltation, and I will take His place, and thereby become exalted myself. So that Jesus treads in the tracks of His Father, and inherits what God did before; and God is thus glorified and exalted in the salvation and exaltation of all His children. . . .

When you climb up a ladder, you must begin at the bottom, and ascend step by step, until you arrive at the top; and so it is with the principles of the gospel—you must begin with the first, and go on until you learn all the principles of exaltation. But it will be a great while after you have passed through the veil before you will have learned them. It is not all to be comprehended in this world; it will be a great work to learn our salvation and exaltation even beyond the grave. . . .

In the beginning, the head of the Gods called a council of the Gods; and they came together and concocted {prepared} a plan to create the world and people it. When we begin to learn this way, we begin to learn the only true God, and what kind of a being we have got to worship. Having a knowledge of God, we begin to know how to approach Him, and how to ask so as to receive an answer.

When we understand the character of God, and know how to come to Him, he begins to unfold the heavens to us, and to tell us all about it. When we are ready to come to him, he is ready to come to us. (HC 6:303, 305–7, 308)

21 God Almighty Himself dwells in eternal fire; flesh and blood cannot go there, for all corruption is devoured by the fire. "Our God is a consuming fire." When our flesh is quickened by the Spirit, there will be no blood in this tabernacle. Some dwell in higher glory than others.

. . . You cannot go anywhere but where God can find you out. (HC 6:366)

22 I will preach on the plurality of Gods. I have selected this text for that express purpose. I wish to declare I have always and in all congre-

---

God
21 Sabbath address, Nauvoo, 12 May 1844.
22 Sabbath address, Nauvoo, 16 June 1844.

gations when I have preached on the subject of the Deity, it has been the plurality of Gods. It has been preached by the Elders for fifteen years.

I have always declared God to be a distinct personage, Jesus Christ a separate and distinct personage from God the Father, and that the Holy Ghost was a distinct personage and a Spirit: and these three constitute three distinct personages and three Gods. If this is in accordance with the New Testament, lo and behold! we have three Gods anyhow, and they are plural: and who can contradict it? (HC 6:474)

23 *Words of Benjamin F. Johnson:* In [Joseph Smith's] teaching us the "Fatherhood of God, and the brotherhood of man," we could begin to see why we should "love God supremely, and our brothers as ourselves."

He taught us that God was the great head of human procreation, was really and truly the father of both our spirits and our bodies; that we were but parts of a great whole, mutually and equally dependent upon each other, according to conditions. (*TK*, p. 95)

Godhead

1   From the foregoing account of the Godhead, which is given in his revelations, the saints have a sure foundation laid for the exercise of faith unto life and salvation, through the atonement and mediation of Jesus Christ; by whose blood they have a forgiveness of sins, and also a sure reward laid up for them in heaven, even that of partaking of the fullness of the Father and the Son through the Spirit. As the Son partakes of the fullness of the Father through the Spirit, so the saints are, by the same Spirit, to be partakers of the same fullness, to enjoy the

---

God
   23 Letter of Benjamin F. Johnson to George S. Gibbs, 1903.

Godhead
   1   Lectures on Faith, delivered to a school of the elders, Kirtland, December 1834. Although the Lectures on Faith were not written only by Joseph Smith, he reviewed them carefully and prepared them for publication (see Larry E. Dahl and Charles D. Tate, Jr., eds., *The Lectures on Faith in Historical Perspective*, p. 10).

same glory; for as the Father and the Son are one, so, in like manner, the saints are to be one in them. Through the love of the Father, the mediation of Jesus Christ, and the gift of the Holy Spirit, they are to be heirs of God, and joint heirs with Jesus Christ. (*LF* 5:3)

2 *Minutes:* Joseph said concerning the Godhead [that] it was not as many imagined—three heads and but one body. He said the three were separate bodies—God the first, and Jesus the Mediator the second, and the Holy Ghost. And these three agree in one; and this is the manner [in which] we should approach God in order to get his blessings. (*WJS*, p. 63; standardized)

3 *Minutes:* [President Joseph Smith] said [it] was the province of the Father to preside as the Chief or President, Jesus as the Mediator, and [the] Holy Ghost as the testator or witness. The Son had a tabernacle and so had the Father, but the Holy Ghost is a personage of spirit without tabernacle. The Great God has a name by which he will be called, which is Ahman. (*WJS*, p. 64; standardized)

4 Everlasting covenant was made between three personages before the organization of this earth, and relates to their dispensation of things to men on the earth; these personages, according to Abraham's record, are called God the first, the Creator; God the second, the Redeemer; and God the third, the witness or Testator. (*TPJS*, p. 190)

5 Any person that had seen the heavens opened knows that there are three personages in the heavens who hold the keys of power, and one presides over all. (*HC* 5:426)

Godhead
  2 Instruction to the Nauvoo Lyceum, 16 February 1841, as recorded in William P. McIntire's Minute Book, LDS Church Archives.
  3 Instruction to the Nauvoo Lyceum, 9 March 1841, as recorded in William P. McIntire's Minute Book, LDS Church Archives.
  4 Nauvoo, 1841. Manuscript history, LDS Church Archives.
  5 Sabbath address, Nauvoo, 11 June 1843.

Gog and Magog

1   The battle of Gog and Magog will be after the millennium. The remnant of all the nations that fight against Jerusalem were commanded to go up to Jerusalem to worship in the millennium. (HC 5:298)

Goodness

1   As you increase in innocence and virtue, as you increase in goodness, let your hearts expand, let them be enlarged towards others, you must be long-suffering, and bear with the faults and errors of mankind. (HC 4:606)

2   If there was anything great or good in the world, it came from God. (HC 5:63)

3   To do good is what I always delight in. (TWJS, p. 33)

Gospel

1   It is said by Paul in his letter to the Hebrew brethren, that Abel obtained witness that he was righteous, God testifying of his gifts. To whom did God testify of the gifts of Abel, was it to Paul? We have very little on this important subject in the forepart of the Bible. But it is said that Abel himself obtained witness that he was righteous. Then

---

Gog and Magog
    1   Observation to Willard Richards in the Prophet's office, Nauvoo, 4 March 1843.

Goodness
    1   Remarks to the Relief Society, Nauvoo, 28 April 1842.
    2   Editorial in the Times and Seasons, 15 July 1842.
    3   The Prophet's remarks to the Potawatomi Indians, 28 August 1843. Joseph Smith Collection, LDS Church Archives.

Gospel
    1   Letter to the brethren scattered from Zion, Kirtland, 22 January 1834.

certainly God spoke to him: indeed, it is said that God talked with him; and if He did, would He not, seeing that Abel was righteous, deliver to him the whole plan of the Gospel. And is not the Gospel the news of the redemption? How could Abel offer a sacrifice and look forward with faith on the Son of God for a remission of his sins, and not understand the Gospel? The mere shedding of the blood of beasts or offering anything else in sacrifice, could not procure a remission of sins, except it were performed in faith of something to come; if it could, Cain's offering must have been as good as Abel's. And if Abel was taught of the coming of the Son of God, was he not taught also of His ordinances? We all admit that the Gospel has ordinances, and if so, had it not always ordinances, and were not its ordinances always the same? Perhaps our friends will say that the Gospel and its ordinances were not known till the days of John, the son of Zacharias, in the days of Herod, the king of Judea. But we will here look at this point: For our own part we cannot believe that the ancients in all ages were so ignorant of the system of heaven as many suppose, since all that were ever saved, were saved through the power of this great plan of redemption, as much before the coming of Christ as since; if not, God has had different plans in operation (if we may so express it), to bring men back to dwell with Himself; and this we cannot believe, since there has been no change in the constitution of man since he fell; and the ordinance or institution of offering blood in sacrifice, was only designed to be performed till Christ was offered up and shed His blood—as said before—that man might look forward in faith to that time. It will be noticed that, according to Paul, (see Gal. iii:8) the Gospel was preached to Abraham. We would like to be informed in what name the Gospel was then preached, whether it was in the name of Christ or some other name. If in any other name, was it the Gospel? And if it was the Gospel, and that preached in the name of Christ, had it any ordinances? If not, was it the Gospel? And if it had ordinances what were they? Our friends may say, perhaps, that there were never any ordinances except those of offering sacrifices before the coming of Christ, and that it could not be possible before the Gospel to have been administered while the law of sacrifices of blood was in force. But we will recollect that Abraham offered sacrifice, and notwithstanding this, had the Gospel preached to him. That the offering of sacrifice was only to point the mind forward to Christ, we infer from these remarkable words of Jesus to the Jews: "Your Father

Abraham rejoiced to see my day: and he saw it, and was glad" (John viii:56.) So, then, because the ancients offered sacrifice it did not hinder their hearing the Gospel; but served, as we said before, to open their eyes, and enable them to look forward to the time of the coming of the Savior, and rejoice in His redemption. We find also, that when the Israelites came out of Egypt they had the Gospel preached to them, according to Paul in his letter to the Hebrews, which says: "For unto us was the Gospel preached, as well as unto them: but the word preached did not profit them, not being mixed with faith in them that heard it" (see Heb. iv:2). It is said again, in Gal. iii:19, that the law (of Moses, or the Levitical law) was "added" because of transgression. What, we ask, was this law added to, if it was not added to the Gospel? It must be plain that it was added to the Gospel, since we learn that they had the Gospel preached to them. From these few facts, we conclude that whenever the Lord revealed Himself to men in ancient days, and commanded them to offer sacrifice to Him, that it was done that they might look forward in faith to the time of His coming, and rely upon the power of that atonement for a remission of their sins. And this they have done, thousands who have gone before us, whose garments are spotless, and who are, like Job, waiting with an assurance like his, that they will see Him in the *latter day* upon the earth, even in their flesh.

We may conclude, that though there were different dispensations, yet all things which God communicated to His people were calculated to draw their minds to the great object, and to teach them to rely upon God alone as the author of their salvation, as contained in His law.

From what we can draw from the Scriptures relative to the teachings of heaven, we are induced to think that much instruction has been given to man since the beginning which we do not possess now. This may not agree with the opinions of some of our friends who are bold to say that we have everything written in the Bible which God ever spoke to man since the world began, and that if he had ever said anything more we should certainly have received it. But we ask, does it remain for a people who never had faith enough to call down one scrap of revelation from heaven, and for all they have now are indebted to the faith of another people who lived hundreds and thousands of years before them, does it remain for them to say how much God has spoken and how much he has not spoken? (HC 2:16–18)

2   This book [the Book of Mormon] also tells us that our Savior made His appearance upon this continent after His resurrection; that He planted the Gospel here in all its fulness, and richness, and power, and blessing; that they had Apostles, Prophets, Pastors, Teachers, and Evangelists; the same order, the same priesthood, the same ordinances, gifts, powers, and blessings, as were enjoyed on the eastern continent. (HC 4:538)

3   The Apostle says the gospel is the power of God unto salvation unto them that believe; and also informs us that life and immortality were brought to light through the gospel; that the scripture, as Paul said to the Galatians, foreseeing that God would justify the heathen through faith, preached before the gospel unto Abraham: saying, In thee shall all nations be blessed.

Now taking it for granted that the scriptures say what they mean, and mean what they say, we have sufficient grounds to go on and prove from the bible that the gospel has always been the same; the ordinances to fulfil its requirements, the same; and the officers to officiate, the same; and the signs and fruits resulting from the promises, the same: therefore, as Noah was a preacher of righteousness he must have been baptised and ordained to the priesthood by the laying on of the hands, &c. For no man taketh this honor unto himself except he be called of God as was Aaron, and Aaron was baptised in the cloud and in the sea, together with all Israel, as is related by the Apostle in Corinthians. (*T&S* 3:904)

4   Some say the kingdom of God was not set up on the earth until the day of Pentecost, and that John did not preach the baptism of repentance for the remission of sins; but I say, in the name of the Lord, that the kingdom of God was set up on the earth from the days of Adam to the present time. Whenever there has been a righteous man on earth unto whom God revealed His word and gave power and authority to administer in His name, and where there is a priest of God— a minister who has power and authority from God to administer in the

---

Gospel

  2   Letter to John Wentworth, editor of the *Chicago Democrat*, Nauvoo, 1 March 1842.
  3   Editorial in the *Times and Seasons*, 1 September 1842.
  4   Sabbath address, Nauvoo, 22 January 1843.

ordinances of the gospel and officiate in the priesthood of God, there is the kingdom of God; and, in consequence of rejecting the Gospel of Jesus Christ and the Prophets whom God hath sent, the judgments of God have rested upon people, cities, and nations, in various ages of the world, which was the case with the cities of Sodom and Gomorrah, that were destroyed for rejecting the Prophets. (HC 5:256–57)

5   The first principles of the Gospel, as I believe, are, faith, repen-tance, baptism for the remission of sins, with the promise of the Holy Ghost.

Look at Heb. vi. 1 for contradictions—"Therefore leaving the principles of the doctrine of Christ, let us go on unto perfection." If a man leaves the principles of the doctrine of Christ, how can he be saved in the principles? This is a contradiction. I don't believe it. I will render it as it should be—"Therefore *not* leaving the principles of the doctrine of Christ, let us go on unto perfection, not laying again the foundation of repentance from dead works, and of faith toward God, of the doctrine of baptisms, and of laying on of hands, and of resurrection of the dead, and of eternal judgment." (HC 6:57–58)

6   All the spirits who have not obeyed the Gospel in the flesh must either obey it in the spirit or be damned. Solemn thought!—dreadful thought! Is there nothing to be done?—no preparation—no salvation for our fathers and friends who have died without having had the op-portunity to obey the decrees of the Son of Man? Would to God that I had forty days and nights in which to tell you all! I would let you know that I am not a "fallen prophet." (HC 6:312–13)

Gossip

1   Search yourselves—the tongue is an unruly member—hold your tongues about things of no moment—a little tale will set the world on fire. (HC 5:20)

Gospel
  5   Sabbath address, Nauvoo, 15 October 1843.
  6   King Follett Discourse, Nauvoo, 7 April 1844.

Gossip
  1   Remarks to the Relief Society, Nauvoo, 26 May 1842.

2 There is no salvation in believing an evil report against our neighbor. (HC 6:363)

Government

1 Every government, from the creation to the present, when it ceased to be virtuous, and failed to execute justice, sooner or later has been overthrown. And without virtuous principles to actuate a government all care for justice is soon lost, and the only motive which prompts it to act is ambition and selfishness. (HC 2:11)

2 Governments were instituted of God for the benefit of man and . . . he holds men accountable for their acts in relation to them, either in making laws or administering them for the good and safety of society. (PWJS, p. 455; standardized)

3 The Almighty is a lover of order and good government. (HC 4:339)

4 The government of the Almighty has always been very dissimilar to the governments of men, whether we refer to His religious government, or to the government of nations. The government of God has always tended to promote peace, unity, harmony, strength, and happiness; while that of man has been productive of confusion, disorder, weakness, and misery.

The greatest acts of the mighty men have been to depopulate nations and to overthrow kingdoms; and whilst they have exalted themselves and become glorious, it has been at the expense of the lives of the innocent, the blood of the oppressed, the moans of the widow, and the tears of the orphan. . . .

Gossip
2 Sabbath address, Nauvoo, 12 May 1844.

Government
1 Letter to the brethren scattered from Zion, Kirtland, 22 January 1834.
2 Letter to the editor of a Pennsylvania paper, the *Chester County Register and Examiner*, Brandywine, Pennsylvania, 22 January 1840.
3 Minutes of a general conference, Nauvoo, 7 April 1841.
4 Editorial in the *Times and Seasons*, 15 July 1842.

The great and wise of ancient days have failed in all their attempts to promote eternal power, peace and happiness. Their nations have crumbled to pieces; their thrones have been cast down in their turn, and their cities, and their mightiest works of art have been annihilated; or their dilapidated towers, of time-worn monuments have left us but feeble traces of their former magnificence and ancient grandeur. They proclaim as with a voice of thunder, those imperishable truths—that man's strength is weakness, his wisdom is folly, his glory is his shame. . . .

. . . Man is not able to govern himself, to legislate for himself, to protect himself, to promote his own good, nor the good of the world.

It has been the design of Jehovah, from the commencement of the world, and is His purpose now, to regulate the affairs of the world in His own time, to stand as a head of the universe, and take the reins of government in His own hand. When that is done, judgment will be administered in righteousness; anarchy and confusion will be destroyed, and "nations will learn war no more." It is for want of this great governing principle, that all this confusion has existed; "for it is not in man that walketh, to direct his steps;" this we have fully shown.

If there was anything great or good in the world, it came from God. . . .

The Lord has at various times commenced this kind of government, and tendered His services to the human family. He selected Enoch, whom He directed, and gave His law unto, and to the people who were with him; and when the world in general would not obey the commands of God, after walking with God, he translated Enoch and his church, and the Priesthood or government of heaven was taken away.

Abraham was guided in all his family affairs by the Lord; was conversed with by angels, and by the Lord; was told where to go, and when to stop; and prospered exceedingly in all that he put his hand unto; it was because he and his family obeyed the counsel of the Lord.

When Egypt was under the superintendence of Joseph it prospered, because he was taught of God. . . .

This is the only thing that can bring about the "restitution of all things spoken of by all the holy Prophets since the world was"—"the dispensation of the fullness of times, when God shall gather together all things in one." Other attempts to promote universal peace and happiness in the human family have proved abortive; every effort has failed; every plan and design has fallen to the ground; it needs the wisdom of

God, the intelligence of God, and the power of God to accomplish this. The world has had a fair trial for six thousand years; the Lord will try the seventh thousand Himself; "He whose right it is, will possess the kingdom, and reign until He has put all things under His feet;" iniquity will hide its hoary head, Satan will be bound, and the works of darkness destroyed; righteousness will be put to the line, and judgment to the plummet, and "he that fears the Lord will alone be exalted in that day." To bring about this state of things, there must of necessity be great confusion among the nations of the earth; "distress of nations with perplexity." . . .

As a Church and a people it behooves us to be wise, and to seek to know the will of God, and then be willing to do it. . . . Our only confidence can be in God; our only wisdom obtained from Him; and He alone must be our protector and safeguard, spiritually and temporally, or we fall. (HC 5:61, 62, 63, 64–65)

5   But meddle not with any man for his religion: all governments ought to permit every man to enjoy his religion unmolested. No man is authorized to take away life in consequence of difference of religion, which all laws and governments ought to tolerate and protect, right or wrong. Every man has a natural, and, in our country, a constitutional right to be a false prophet, as well as a true prophet. (HC 6:304)

Grace

1   I pray that my heavenly Father will pour out His choicest blessings in this world, and enable you by His grace to overcome the evils which are in the world, that you may secure a blissful immortality in the world that is to come. (HC 4:179)

2   The doctrine that the Presbyterians and Methodists have quarreled so much about—once in grace, always in grace, or falling away

---

Government
5   King Follett Discourse, Nauvoo, 7 April 1844.

Grace
1   Letter to John C. Bennett, 8 August 1840, bidding him welcome to Nauvoo.
2   Sabbath address, Nauvoo, 10 March 1844.

from grace, I will say a word about. They are both wrong. Truth takes a road between them both, for while the Presbyterian says "once in grace, you cannot fall;" the Methodist says: "You can have grace today, fall from it to-morrow, next day have grace again; and so follow on, changing continually." But the doctrine of the Scriptures and the spirit of Elijah would show them both false, and take a road between them both; for, according to the Scripture, if men have received the good word of God, and tasted of the powers of the world to come, if they shall fall away, it is impossible to renew them again, seeing they have crucified the Son of God afresh, and put Him to an open shame; so there is a possibility of falling away; you could not be renewed again, and the power of Elijah cannot seal against this sin, for this a reserve made in the seals and power of the Priesthood. (HC 6:252–53)

3   Grace for grace is a heavenly decree. (HC 6:427)

Gratitude

1   When once our situation is compared with the ancient Saints, as followers of the Lamb of God who has taken away our sins by His own blood, we are bound to rejoice and give thanks to Him always. (HC 2:22)

2   We have not desired as much from the hand of the Lord through faith and obedience, as we ought to have done, yet we have enjoyed great blessings, and we are not so sensible of this as we should be. (HC 2:308)

3   The brethren have also been very industrious, and supplied me with my winter's wood, for which I am sincerely grateful to each and every one of them, and shall remember, with warm emotions, this

---

Grace
3   Letter of the Prophet and Hyrum Smith to Mr. Tewkesbury (Abijah R. Tewksbury), Nauvoo, 4 June 1844, seeking to restore him to fellowship.

Gratitude
1   Letter to the brethren scattered from Zion, Kirtland, 22 January 1834.
2   Instructions to the Twelve, Kirtland, 12 November 1835.
3   Kirtland, 10 December 1835.

expression of their goodness to me. And in the name of Jesus Christ I invoke the rich benediction of heaven to rest upon them and their families; and I ask my heavenly Father to preserve their health, and that of their wives and children, that they may have strength of body to perform their labors in their several occupations in life, and the use and activity of their limbs, also powers of intellect and understanding hearts, that they may treasure up wisdom, understanding and intelligence above measure, and be preserved from plagues, pestilence, and famine, and from the power of the adversary, and the hands of evil-designing men, and have power over all their enemies, and the way be prepared for them that they may journey to the land of Zion, and be established on their inheritances, to enjoy undisturbed peace and happiness forever, and ultimately be crowned with everlasting life in the celestial Kingdom of God, which blessing I ask in the name of Jesus of Nazareth. Amen. (HC 2:328–29)

4   This being the beginning of a new year, my heart is filled with gratitude to God that He has preserved my life, and the lives of my family, while another year has passed away. We have been sustained and upheld in the midst of a wicked and perverse generation, although exposed to all the afflictions, temptations, and misery that are incident to human life; for this I feel to humble myself in dust and ashes, as it were, before the Lord. (HC 2:352)

5   This is one of the many instances in which I have suddenly been brought from a state of health, to the borders of the grave, and as suddenly restored, for which my heart swells with gratitude to my heavenly Father, and I feel renewedly to dedicate myself and all my powers to His service. (HC 2:493)

6   We would say unto the Saints abroad, let our hearts abound with grateful acknowledgements unto God our Heavenly Father, who hath called us unto His holy calling by the revelation of Jesus Christ, in these last days, and has so mercifully stood by us, and delivered us out of the seventh trouble [see Job 5:19], which happened unto us in the State of Missouri. (HC 3:350–51)

Gratitude
   4   Kirtland, 1 January 1836.
   5   Kirtland, 14 June 1837.
   6   Letter to Oliver Granger from the First Presidency, Nauvoo, 13 May 1839.

7   First of all, I take the liberty to tender you my sincere thanks for the two interesting and consoling visits that you have made me during my almost exiled situation. Tongue cannot express the gratitude of my heart, for the warm and true-hearted friendship you have manifested in these things towards me. (HC 5:103)

8   The righteousness of God . . . sendeth the rain on the just and the unjust, seed time and harvest, for all of which man is ungrateful. (TPJS, p. 317)

9   Minutes: At twelve o'clock, President Joseph Smith commenced by saying, "We all ought to be thankful for the privilege we enjoy this day of meeting so many of the Saints, and for the warmth and brightness of the heavens over our heads; and it truly makes the countenances of this great multitude to look cheerful and gladdens the hearts of all present." (HC 5:327)

Greatness

1   For a man to be great, he must not dwell on small things, though he may enjoy them. (HC 5:298)

Gratitude
  7   Letter to Emma Smith, Nauvoo, 16 August 1842. The exile spoken of refers to the Prophet's going into hiding to avoid attempts by Missouri officials to have him extradited.
  8   Proverbs of the Prophet Joseph Smith, Nauvoo, 1843. Manuscript history, LDS Church Archives.
  9   General conference address, Nauvoo, 6 April 1843.

Greatness
  1   Observation made to Willard Richards in the Prophet's office, Nauvoo, 4 March 1843.

Greed

1   But these men, like Balaam, being greedy for reward, sold us into the hands of those who loved them, for the world loves his own. (HC 3:228)

Guilt

1   A man is his own tormentor and his own condemner. Hence the saying, They shall go into the lake that burns with fire and brimstone. The torment of disappointment in the mind of man is as exquisite as a lake burning with fire and brimstone. I say, so is the torment of man. (HC 6:314)

2   Those who have done wrong always have that wrong gnawing them. . . . You cannot go anywhere but where God can find you out. (HC 6:366)

Happiness

1   The nearer man approaches perfection, the clearer are his views, and the greater his enjoyments, till he has overcome the evils of his life and lost every desire for sin. (HC 2:8)

2   Happiness is the object and design of our existence; and will be the end thereof, if we pursue the path that leads to it; and this path is

---

Greed
   1   Letter to the Church from Liberty Jail, 16 December 1838, in reference to some Latter-day Saints who made arrangements for the arrest of Joseph Smith on 31 October 1838.

Guilt
   1   King Follett Discourse, Nauvoo, 7 April 1844.
   2   Sabbath address, Nauvoo, 12 May 1844.

Happiness
   1   Letter to the brethren scattered from Zion, Kirtland, 22 January 1834.
   2   Essay on happiness, Nauvoo, 27 August 1842.

virtue, uprightness, faithfulness, holiness, and keeping all the commandments of God. . . .

. . . In obedience there is joy and peace unspotted, unalloyed; and as God has designed our happiness—and the happiness of all His creatures, he never has—He never will institute an ordinance or give a commandment to His people that is not calculated in its nature to promote that happiness which He has designed, and which will not end in the greatest amount of good and glory to those who become the recipients of his law and ordinances. (HC 5:134–35)

3   Would you think it strange if I relate what I have seen in vision in relation to this interesting theme [of the resurrection]? Those who have died in Jesus Christ may expect to enter into all that fruition of joy when they come forth, which they possessed or anticipated here. (HC 5:361)

4   If virtue is justified rather than vanity, the best of everything calculated to happify man and dignify society will—yea, must be in Nauvoo. (HC 6:69)

5   Like other honest citizens, I not only (when manhood came,) sought my own peace, prosperity, and happiness, but also the peace, prosperity, and happiness of my friends. (HC 6:88)

Harvest

1   Now we learn by this parable, not only the setting up of the Kingdom in the days of the Savior, which is represented by the good seed, which produced fruit, but also the corruptions of the Church, which are represented by the tares, which were sown by the enemy, which

---

Happiness
3   Remarks upon the death of Lorenzo D. Barnes, Nauvoo, 16 April 1843.
4   Letter to the Saints encouraging them to patronize the Church newspaper, published in the *Times and Seasons*, 1 November 1843.
5   Letter to the "Green Mountain Boys" in Vermont, appealing for their support, Nauvoo, 29 November 1843.

Harvest
1   Letter to the elders of the Church, Kirtland, 1 September 1835.

His disciples would fain have plucked up, or cleansed the Church of, if their views had been favored by the Savior. But He, knowing all things, says, Not so. As much as to say, your views are not correct, the Church is in its infancy, and if you take this rash step, you will destroy the wheat, or the Church, with the tares; therefore it is better to let them grow together until the harvest, or the end of the world, which means the destruction of the wicked, which is not yet fulfilled. . . .

And again, another parable put He forth unto them, having an allusion to the Kingdom that should be set up, just previous to or at the time of the harvest, which reads as follows—"The Kingdom of Heaven is like a grain of mustard seed, which a man took and sowed in his field: which indeed is the least of all seeds: but, when it is grown, it is the greatest among herbs, and becometh a tree, so that the birds of the air come and lodge in the branches thereof." Now we can discover plainly that this figure is given to represent the Church as it shall come forth in the last days. Behold, the Kingdom of Heaven is likened unto it. . . .

". . . Then Jesus sent the multitude away, and went into the house: and His disciples came unto Him, saying, Declare unto us the parable of the tares of the field. He answered and said unto them, He that soweth the good seed is the Son of Man; the field is the world; the good seed are the children of the Kingdom; but the tares are the children of the wicked one." Now let our readers mark the expression— "the field is the world, the tares are the children of the wicked one, the enemy that sowed them is the devil, the harvest is the end of the world, {let them carefully mark this expression—*the end of the world*,} and the reapers are the angels." (HC 2:267, 268, 271)

Hate

1   The Savior said, "It must needs be that offenses come, but woe unto them by whom they come." And again, "Blessed are ye when men shall revile you, and persecute you, and shall say all manner of evil against you falsely for my sake; rejoice and be exceeding glad, for great is your reward in heaven, for so persecuted they the Prophets which were before you."

Hate
1   Letter to the Church from Liberty Jail, 16 December 1838.

Now, dear brethren, if any men ever had reason to claim this promise, we are the men; for we know that the world not only hate us, but they speak all manner of evil of us falsely, for no other reason than that we have been endeavoring to teach the fullness of the Gospel of Jesus Christ. (HC 3:228–29)

2   Renegade "Mormon" dissenters are running through the world and spreading various foul and libelous reports against us, thinking thereby to gain the friendship of the world, because they know that we are not of the world, and that the world hates us; therefore they {the world} make a tool of these fellows {the dissenters}; and by them try to do all the injury they can, and after that they hate them worse than they do us, because they find them to be base traitors and syco-phants.

Such characters God hates; we cannot love them. The world hates them, and we sometimes think that the devil ought to be ashamed of them. (HC 3:230)

3   The work in which we are unitedly engaged is one of no ordinary kind. The enemies we have to contend against are subtle and well skilled in maneuvering; it behooves us to be on the alert to concentrate our energies, and that the best feelings should exist in our midst; and then, by the help of the Almighty, we shall go on from victory to victory, and from conquest to conquest; our evil passions will be subdued, our prejudices depart; we shall find no room in our bosoms for hatred; vice will hide its deformed head, and we shall stand approved in the sight of heaven, and be acknowledged the sons of God. (HC 4:231)

Haun's Mill

1   At Haun's Mill the brethren went contrary to my counsel; if they had not, their lives would have been spared. (HC 5:137)

Hate
   2   Letter to the Church from Liberty Jail, 16 December 1838.
   3   Letter to the Twelve in England, Nauvoo, 15 December 1840. The place-ment of this letter in *HC* implies that it was written in October 1840, but actually it was written on 15 December 1840 (see *PWJS*, p. 480).

Haun's Mill
   1   Conference address, Nauvoo, 29 August 1842.

Healing
See also ADMINISTERING TO THE SICK

1   Waited on my father again, who was very sick. In secret prayer in the morning, the Lord said, "My servant, thy father shall live." I waited on him all this day with my heart raised to God in the name of Jesus Christ, that He would restore him to health, that I might be blessed with his company and advice, esteeming it one of the greatest earthly blessings to be blessed with the society of parents, whose mature years and experience render them capable of administering the most wholesome advice. At evening Brother David Whitmer came in. We called on the Lord in mighty prayer in the name of Jesus Christ, and laid our hands on him, and rebuked the disease. And God heard and answered our prayers—to the great joy and satisfaction of our souls. Our aged father arose and dressed himself, shouted, and praised the Lord. (HC 2:289)

2   You need an endowment, brethren, in order that you may be prepared and able to overcome all things; and those that reject your testimony will be damned. The sick will be healed, the lame made to walk, the deaf to hear, and the blind to see, through your instrumentality. But let me tell you, that you will not have power, after the endowment to heal those that have not faith, nor to benefit them, for you might as well expect to benefit a devil in hell as such as are possessed of his spirit, and are willing to keep it; for they are habitations for devils, and only fit for his society. (HC 2:309)

3   About this time much sickness began to manifest itself among the brethren, as well as among the inhabitants of the place, so that this week and the following were generally spent in visiting the sick and administering to them; some had faith enough and were healed; others had not. (HC 4:3)

4   What is the sign of the healing of the sick? The laying on of hands is the sign or way marked out by James, and the custom of the ancient

---

Healing
1   Kirtland, 11 October 1835.
2   Instructions to the Twelve, Kirtland, 12 November 1835.
3   Nauvoo, July 1839.
4   Sabbath address, Nauvoo, 20 March 1842.

Saints as ordered by the Lord, and we cannot obtain the blessing by pursuing any other course except the way marked out by the Lord. What if we should attempt to get the gift of the Holy Ghost through any other means except the signs or way which God hath appointed—would we obtain it? Certainly not; all other means would fail. The Lord says do so and so, and I will bless you. (HC 4:555)

Health

1   It is the will of God that man should repent and serve Him in health, and in the strength and power of his mind, in order to secure His blessing, and not wait until he is called to die. (HC 4:554)

2   If we would be sober and watch in fasting and prayer, God would turn away sickness from our midst. (HC 6:52)

Heart

1   Remember God sees the secret springs of human action, and knows the hearts of all living. . . .
    It is in vain to try to hide a bad spirit from the eyes of them who are spiritual, for it will show itself in speaking and in writing, as well as in all our other conduct. It is also needless to make great pretensions when the heart is not right; the Lord will expose it to the view of His faithful Saints. (HC 1:317)

2   God [has] power to soften the hearts of all men. (HC 1:455)

Health
   1   Sabbath address, Nauvoo, 20 March 1842.
   2   Remarks upon the death of James Adams, Nauvoo, 9 October 1843.

Heart
   1   Letter to William W. Phelps in Missouri, written from Kirtland, 14 January 1833. According to Dean Jessee this letter was dated 11 January (see *PWJS*, p. 262).
   2   Letter to the exiled Saints in Missouri, Kirtland, 10 December 1833.

3   We received some letters last evening. . . . And we need not say to you that the floodgates of our hearts were lifted and our eyes were a fountain of tears, but those who have not been enclosed in the walls of prison without cause or provocation, can have but little idea how sweet the voice of a friend is; one token of friendship from any source whatever awakens and calls into action every sympathetic feeling; it brings up in an instant everything that is passed; it seizes the present with the avidity of lightning; it grasps after the future with the fierceness of a tiger; it moves the mind backward and forward, from one thing to another, until finally all enmity, malice and hatred, and past differences, misunderstandings and mismanagements are slain victorious at the feet of hope; and when the heart is sufficiently contrite, then the voice of inspiration steals along and whispers. . . .

How much more dignified and noble are the thoughts of God, than the vain imaginations of the human heart! (HC 3:293, 295)

4   The truth shall break down and dash in pieces all such bigoted Pharisaism; the sects shall be sifted, the honest in heart brought out, and their priests left in the midst of their corruption. (HC 4:426)

5   I love my father and his memory; and the memory of his noble deeds rests with ponderous weight upon my mind, and many of his kind and parental words to me are written on the tablet of my heart. (HC 5:126)

6   Out of the abundance of the heart of man the mouth speaketh. . . .
. . . You don't know me; you never knew my heart. No man knows my history. I cannot tell it: I shall never undertake it. I don't blame any one for not believing my history. If I had not experienced what I have, I would not have believed it myself. I never did harm any man since I was born in the world. My voice is always for peace. (HC 6:315, 317)

7   My heart is large enough for all men. (HC 6:459)

Heart
   3   Letter to the Saints from Liberty Jail, 20–25 March 1839.
   4   Conference address, Nauvoo, 2 October 1841.
   5   Nauvoo, 22 August 1842.
   6   King Follett Discourse, Nauvoo, 7 April 1844.
   7   Letter to Washington Tucker, 12 June 1844.

8 *History Entry:* Several of the officers of the troops in Carthage, and other gentlemen, curious to see the Prophet, visited Joseph in his room. General Smith asked them if there was anything in his appearance that indicated he was the desperate character his enemies represented him to be; and he asked them to give him their honest opinion on the subject. The reply was, "No, sir, your appearance would indicate the very contrary, General Smith; but we cannot see what is in your heart, neither can we tell what are your intentions." To which Joseph replied, "Very true, gentlemen, you cannot see what is in my heart, and you are therefore unable to judge me or my intentions; but I can see what is in your hearts, and will tell you what I see. I can see that you thirst for blood, and nothing but my blood will satisfy you." (HC 6:566)

Heathens

1 To say that the heathens would be damned because they did not believe the Gospel would be preposterous, and to say that the Jews would all be damned that do not believe in Jesus would be equally absurd; for "how can they believe on him of whom they have not heard, and how can they hear without a preacher, and how can he preach except he be sent;" consequently neither Jew nor heathen can be culpable for rejecting the conflicting opinions of sectarianism, nor for rejecting any testimony but that which is sent of God, for as the preacher cannot preach except he be sent, so the hearer cannot believe without he hear a "sent" preacher, and cannot be condemned for what he has not heard, and being without law, will have to be judged without law. (HC 4:598)

Heart
    8   Carthage, Illinois, 25 June 1844.

Heathens
    1   Editorial in the *Times and Seasons*, 15 April 1842.

2 There will be wicked men on the earth during the thousand years. The heathen nations who will not come up to worship will be visited with the judgments of God, and must eventually be destroyed from the earth. (*HC* 5:212)

Heaven

See also CELESTIAL KINGDOM; DEGREES OF GLORY

1 Upon my return from Amherst conference, I resumed the translation of the Scriptures. From sundry revelations which had been received, it was apparent that many important points touching the salvation of man, had been taken from the Bible, or lost before it was compiled. It appeared self-evident from what truths were left, that if God rewarded every one according to the deeds done in the body the term "Heaven," as intended for the Saints' eternal home must include more kingdoms than one. Accordingly, on the 16th of February, 1832, while translating St. John's Gospel, myself and Elder Rigdon saw the following vision: [D&C 76]. (*HC* 1:245)

2 When I consider that soon the heavens are to be shaken, and the earth tremble and reel to and fro; and that the heavens are to be unfolded as a scroll when it is rolled up; and that every mountain and island are to flee away, I cry out in my heart, What manner of persons ought we to be in all holy conversation and godliness! (*HC* 1:442)

3 Men of the present time testify of heaven and hell, and have never seen either; and I will say that no man knows these things without this. (*HC* 3:390)

Heathens
  2 In conversation with Judge James Adams, Springfield, Illinois, 30 December 1842. There is a footnote accompanying this quotation in *TPJS* (pp. 268–69) indicating that the "wicked" referred to as living on earth during the Millennium are those of a terrestrial nature but who have not yet received the gospel (see D&C 84:49–53).

Heaven
  1 The Prophet's view of the vision of the glories (D&C 76), Hiram, Ohio, 16 February 1832.
  2 Letter to Moses C. Nickerson, written from Kirtland, 19 November 1833.
  3 Discourse on the priesthood, given sometime before 8 August 1839, Commerce (Nauvoo). For a discussion on the dating of this discourse, see *WJS*, p. 22.

4   Could you gaze into heaven five minutes, you would know more than you would by reading all that ever was written on the subject. (*HC* 6:50)

Heavenly Father
See GOD

Hell
See also DAMNATION

1   What is the damnation of hell? To go with that society who have not obeyed His commands. (*HC* 4:555)

2   There has been much said about the word hell, and the sectarian world have preached much about it, describing it to be a burning lake of fire and brimstone. But what is hell? It is another modern term, and is taken from hades. I'll hunt after hades as Pat did for the woodchuck.

Hades, the Greek, or Shaole, the Hebrew: these two significations mean a world of spirits. Hades, Shaole, paradise, spirits in prison, are all one; it is a world of spirits.

The righteous and the wicked all go to the same world of spirits until the resurrection. "I do not think so," says one. If you will go to my house any time, I will take my lexicon and prove it to you.

The great misery of departed spirits in the world of spirits, where they go after death, is to know that they come short of the glory that others enjoy and that they might have enjoyed themselves, and they are their own accusers. (*HC* 5:425)

3   I see no faults in the Church, and therefore let me be resurrected with the Saints, whether I ascend to heaven or descend to hell, or go to any other place. And if we go to hell, we will turn the devils out of

---

Heaven
   4   Remarks upon the death of James Adams, Nauvoo, 9 October 1843.

Hell
   1   Sabbath address, Nauvoo, 20 March 1842.
   2   Sabbath address, Nauvoo, 11 June 1843.
   3   Sabbath address, Nauvoo, 23 July 1843.

doors and make a heaven of it. Where this people are, there is good society. What do we care where we are, if the society be good? (HC 5:517)

High-mindedness

1   If there are any among you who aspire after their own aggrandizement, and seek their own opulence, while their brethren are groaning in poverty, and are under sore trials and temptations, they cannot be benefited by the intercession of the Holy Spirit, which maketh intercession for us day and night with groanings that cannot be uttered.

We ought at all times to be very careful that such high-mindedness shall never have place in our hearts; but condescend to men of low estate, and with all long-suffering bear the infirmities of the weak. (HC 3:299)

History

1   You don't know me; you never knew my heart. No man knows my history. I cannot tell it: I shall never undertake it. I don't blame any one for not believing my history. If I had not experienced what I have, I would not have believed it myself. I never did harm any man since I was born in the world. My voice is always for peace.

I cannot lie down until all my work is finished. I never think any evil, nor do anything to the harm of my fellow-man. When I am called by the trump of the archangel and weighed in the balance, you will all know me then. I add no more. God bless you all. Amen. (HC 6:317)

2   *Words of Oliver B. Huntington:* On another occasion, when Joseph was sitting in Dimick's shop waiting for something, he got on a won-

---

High-mindedness
    1   Letter to the Saints from Liberty Jail, 20–25 March 1839.

History
    1   King Follett Discourse, Nauvoo, 7 April 1844.
    2   Recollection of Oliver B. Huntington, published in the *Young Woman's Journal,* July 1891.

derful strain of relating the history of the world in the past, recounting many strange things I never had read or heard of before. When he came to the present times, he did not stop, but went on and related the principal events that will transpire in the history of the world down to the time when the angel will declare that time shall be no longer.

Although I did not see the events with my natural eyes, the vividness of their appearance to my mind was next to reality. He declared the succession of events with as great clearness as one of us can repeat the events of our past lives. (*TK*, p. 66)

Holy Ghost
See also GIFT OF THE HOLY GHOST

1   Meantime we continued to translate, at intervals, when not under the necessity of attending to the numerous inquirers who now began to visit us—some for the sake of finding the truth others for the purpose of putting hard questions, and trying to confound us. Among the latter class were several learned priests, who generally came for the purpose of disputation. However, the Lord continued to pour out upon us His Holy Spirit, and as often as we had need, He gave us in that moment what to say; so that although unlearned and inexperienced in religious controversies, yet we were able to confound those learned priests of the day; whilst at the same time we were enabled to convince the honest in heart that we had obtained, through the mercy of God, the true and everlasting Gospel of Jesus Christ; and occasionally we administered the ordinance of baptism for the remission of sins to such as believed. (HC 1:59)

2   We now proceeded to call out and ordain some others of the brethren to different offices of the Priesthood, according as the Spirit manifested unto us. (HC 1:79)

Holy Ghost
1   Fayette, New York, June 1829.
2   Organization of the Church at the home of Peter Whitmer, Sr., at Fayette, New York, 6 April 1830.

3 We had much of the power of God manifested amongst us; the Holy Ghost came upon us, and filled us with joy unspeakable; and peace, and faith, and hope, and charity abounded in our midst. (*HC* 1:115)

4 *Words of Daniel Tyler:* During his short stay, he [Joseph Smith] preached at my father's residence. He read the third chapter of John and explained much of it, making it so plain that a child could not help understanding it, if he paid attention. I recollect distinctly the substance of his remarks on the third verse—"Except a man be born again he cannot *see* the Kingdom of God."

The birth here spoken of, the Prophet said, was not the gift of the Holy Ghost, which was promised after baptism, but was an illumination of the mind by the Spirit which attended the preaching of the gospel by the elders of the Church. The people wondered why they had not previously understood the plain declarations of scripture as explained by the Elders, as they had read them hundreds of times. When they afterward read the Bible, it was a new book to them. This was being born again to *see* the kingdom of God. They were not in it, but could see it from the outside, which they could not do until the Spirit of the Lord took the veil from before their eyes. It resulted in a change of heart, but not of state; they were converted, but were yet in their sins. For instance, although Cornelius had seen an holy angel, and on the preaching of Peter the Holy Ghost was poured out upon him and his household, they were only born again to *see* the kingdom of God. Had they not been baptized afterwards they would not have been saved. (See Acts, 10th chapter.) (*TK*, p. 50)

5 Speaking of Christ, he [Peter] says that God raised Him from the dead, and we (the apostles) are His witnesses of these things, and so is the Holy Ghost, whom God had given to them that obey Him (see Acts v). So that after the testimony of the Scriptures on this point,

---

Holy Ghost

   3 A conference of the Church wherein the confusion created by Hiram Page's "revelation" through a certain stone was resolved. All present "renounced the stone and all things connected therewith," 26 September 1830.

   4 Daniel Tyler's recollection of the Prophet's visit to the home of his father, Andrew Tyler, probably in the fall of 1833.

   5 Letter to the brethren scattered from Zion, Kirtland, 22 January 1834.

the assurance is given by the Holy Ghost, bearing witness to those who obey Him, that Christ Himself has assuredly risen from the dead. (HC 2:19)

6   We have a fervent desire that in your general conferences everything should be discussed with a great deal of care and propriety, lest you grieve the Holy Spirit, which shall be poured out at all times upon your heads, when you are exercised with those principles of righteousness that are agreeable to the mind of God, and are properly affected one toward another, and are careful by all means to remember, those who are in bondage, and in heaviness, and in deep affliction for your sakes. And if there are any among you who aspire after their own aggrandizement, and seek their own opulence, while their brethren are groaning in poverty, and are under sore trials and temptations, they cannot be benefited by the intercession of the Holy Spirit, which maketh intercession for us day and night with groanings that cannot be uttered. (HC 3:299)

7   The first Comforter or Holy Ghost has no other effect than pure intelligence. It is more powerful in expanding the mind, enlightening the understanding, and storing the intellect with present knowledge, of a man who is of the literal seed of Abraham, than one that is a Gentile, though it may not have half as much visible effect upon the body; for as the Holy Ghost falls upon one of the literal seed of Abraham, it is calm and serene; and his whole soul and body are only exercised by the pure spirit of intelligence; while the effect of the Holy Ghost upon a Gentile, is to purge out the old blood, and make him actually of the seed of Abraham. That man that has none of the blood of Abraham (naturally) must have a new creation by the Holy Ghost. In such a case, there may be more of a powerful effect upon the body, and visible to the eye, than upon an Israelite, while the Israelite at first might be far before the Gentile in pure intelligence. (HC 3:380)

8   We believe that the holy men of old spake as they were moved by the Holy Ghost, and that holy men in these days speak by the same principle; we believe in its being a comforter and a witness bearer,

---

Holy Ghost
   6   Letter to the Saints from Liberty Jail, 20–25 March 1839.
   7   Instructions to the Twelve, Commerce (Nauvoo), 27 June 1839.
   8   Editorial in the *Times and Seasons*, 15 June 1842.

that it brings things past to our remembrance, leads us into all truth, and shows us of things to come; we believe that "no man can know that Jesus is the Christ, but by the Holy Ghost." (HC 5:27)

9 *Words of Franklin D. Richards:* Joseph also said that the Holy Ghost is now in a state of probation which if he should perform in righteousness he may pass through the same or a similar course of things that the Son has. (WJS, p. 245; standardized)

10 The Holy Ghost is God's messenger to administer in all those priesthoods [three grand orders of the priesthood: Melchizedek, Patriarchal, and Levitical]. (HC 5:555)

11 No man can receive the Holy Ghost without receiving revelations. The Holy Ghost is a revelator. (HC 6:58)

12 But the Holy Ghost is yet a spiritual body and waiting to take to himself a body, as the Savior did or as God did or the gods before them took bodies; for the Savior says the work that my Father did do I also. . . . He took himself a body and then laid down his life that he might take it up again. (WJS, p. 382; standardized)

Home Teaching

1 *Words of William Farrington Cahoon:* I was called and ordained to act as a teacher to visit the families of the Saints. I got along very well

---

Holy Ghost
   9 Sabbath address, Nauvoo, 27 August 1843. Reported by Franklin D. Richards.
   10 Sabbath address, Nauvoo, 27 August 1843.
   11 Sabbath address, Nauvoo, 15 October 1843.
   12 Sabbath address, Nauvoo, 16 June 1844. Reported by George Laub.

Home Teaching
   1 Recollection of William Farrington Cahoon, published in the *Juvenile Instructor*, 15 August 1892. *Home teaching* is a modern term for the function of priesthood holders being assigned to visit the homes of the Saints in the capacity as teachers.

till I found that I was obliged to call and pay a visit to the Prophet. Being young, only about seventeen years of age, I felt my weakness in visiting the Prophet and his family in the capacity of a teacher. I almost felt like shrinking from duty. Finally I went to his door and knocked, and in a minute the Prophet came to the door. I stood there trembling, and said to him, "Brother Joseph, I have come to visit you in the capacity of a teacher, if it is convenient for you."

He said, "Brother William, come right in, I am glad to see you; sit down in that chair there and I will go and call my family in."

They soon came in and took seats. He then said, "Brother William, I submit myself and family into your hands."

He then took his seat. "Now Brother William," said he, "ask all the questions you feel like."

By this time all my fears and trembling had ceased, and I said, "Brother Joseph, are you trying to live your religion?"

He answered, "Yes."

I then said, "Do you pray in your family?"

He said, "Yes."

"Do you teach your family the principles of the gospel?"

He replied, "Yes, I am trying to do it."

"Do you ask a blessing on your food?"

He answered, "Yes."

"Are you trying to live in peace and harmony with all your family?"

He said that he was.

I then turned to Sister Emma, his wife, and said, "Sister Emma, are you trying to live your religion? Do you teach your children to obey their parents? Do you try to teach them to pray?"

To all these questions she answered, "Yes, I am trying to do so."

I then turned to Joseph and said, "I am now through with my questions as a teacher; and now if you have any instructions to give, I shall be happy to receive them."

He said, "God bless you, Brother William; and if you are humble and faithful, you shall have power to settle all difficulties that may come before you in the capacity of a teacher."

As a teacher, I then left my parting blessing upon him and his family and took my departure. (*TK*, pp. 132–33)

Honesty

1   My heart is full of desire this day, to be blessed of the God of Abraham, with prosperity, until I shall be able to pay all my debts, for it is the delight of my soul to be honest. (*PJS* 1:98)

2   Be honest one with another, for it seems that some have come short of these things. (*HC* 3:233)

3   Act honestly before God and man. Beware of Gentile sophistry; such as bowing and scraping unto men in whom you have no confidence. Be honest, open, and frank in all your intercourse with mankind. (*HC* 3:384)

4   *Minutes:* Joseph said that an equality [of property or knowledge] would not answer, for he says if we were equal in property at present, in six months we would be worse than ever, for there [are] too many dishonest men amongst us. (*WJS*, p. 68; standardized)

5   There is a straight way to do all things and it is invariably the safest and the best. (*PWJS*, p. 568)

6   More honesty and familiarity in societies would make less hypocrisy and flattery in all branches of the community; and open, frank, candid decorum to all men, in this boasted land of liberty, would beget esteem, confidence, union, and love; and the neighbor from any state or from any country, of whatever color, clime or tongue, could rejoice when he put his foot on the sacred soil of freedom, and exclaim, The very name of "*American*" is fraught with

---

Honesty

1   Kirtland, 23 September 1835.
2   Letter to the Church from Liberty Jail, 16 December 1838.
3   Instructions to the Apostles and Seventies departing for missions to England, Commerce (Nauvoo), 2 July 1839.
4   Instructions at a meeting of the Nauvoo Lyceum, 30 March 1841, as recorded in William P. McIntire's Minute Book, LDS Church Archives.
5   Letter to Reuben McBride, Nauvoo, 18 January 1844.
6   A pamphlet containing the Prophet's political platform, entitled *Views of the Powers and Policy of the Government of the United States*, Nauvoo, 7 February 1844.

"friendship!" Oh, then, create confidence, restore freedom, break down slavery, banish imprisonment for debt, and be in love, fellowship and peace with all the world! Remember that honesty is not subject to law. The law was made for transgressors. Wherefore a . . . good name is better than riches. (*HC* 6:205–6)

7   No one can ever enter the celestial kingdom unless he is strictly honest. (*JSP*, p. 104)

Honor

1   *Words of Sarah M. Pomeroy:* It was quite an exciting time just then [in 1843]. The Prophet had been falsely accused of an attempt to murder Governor Boggs of Missouri. Porter Rockwell, a firm friend of Joseph, had been kidnapped and taken to Missouri as an accomplice, and was about to have his trial. Joseph requested my father to lend him a hundred dollars to pay the lawyer who defended Porter Rockwell, and father freely counted out the money.

"This shall be returned within three days, if I am alive," said the Prophet, and departed.

My aunt, Father's sister, was quite wrathful. "Don't you know, Thomas," said she, "you will never see a cent of that money again. Here are your family without a home, and you throw your money away."

"Don't worry, Katie," Father replied, "if he cannot pay it, he is welcome to it."

This conversation was held before us children, and I thought seriously about it. Would he pay it, or would he not? But I had strong faith that he would.

The day came when it was to be paid—a cold, wet, rainy day. The day passed. Night came—9 o'clock, 10 o'clock, and we all retired for

---

Honesty
7   Statement recalled by Milo Andrus, who heard Joseph speak in Nauvoo. Joseph Smith Papers, LDS Church Archives.

Honor
1   Reminiscence of Sarah M. Pomeroy, published in the *Young Woman's Journal*, December 1906.

the night. Shortly after there was a knock at the door. Father arose and went to it, and there in the driving rain stood the Prophet Joseph.

"Here Brother Thomas, is the money." A light was struck, and he counted out the hundred dollars in gold.

He said, "Brother Thomas, I have been trying all day to raise this sum, for my honor was at stake. God bless you."

My aunt had nothing to say. She afterwards left the Church. (*TK*, pp. 171–72)

2   Make honor the standard with all men. Be sure that good is rendered for evil in all cases; and the whole nation, like a kingdom of kings and priests, will rise up in righteousness, and be respected as wise and worthy on earth, and as just and holy for heaven, by Jehovah, the Author of perfection. (*HC* 6:205)

Hope

1   Reflect for a moment, brethren, and enquire, whether you would consider yourselves worthy a seat at the marriage feast with Paul and others like him, if you had been unfaithful? Had you not fought the good fight, and kept the faith, could you expect to receive? Have you a promise of receiving a crown of righteousness from the hand of the Lord, with the Church of the First Born? Here then, we understand, that Paul rested his hope in Christ, because he had kept the faith, and loved his appearing and from His hand he had a promise of receiving a crown of righteousness. (*HC* 2:20)

2   The only difference between the old and young dying is, one lives longer in heaven and eternal light and glory than the other, and is freed a little sooner from this miserable, wicked world. Notwithstanding all this glory, we for a moment lose sight of it, and mourn the loss, but we do not mourn as those without hope. (*HC* 4:554)

Honor
   2   A pamphlet containing the Prophet's political platform, entitled *Views of the Powers and Policy of the Government of the United States*, Nauvoo, 7 February 1844.

Hope
   1   Letter to the brethren scattered from Zion, Kirtland, 22 January 1834.
   2   Sabbath address, Nauvoo, 20 March 1842.

3 What have we to console us in relation to the dead? We have reason to have the greatest hope and consolation for our dead of any people on the earth; for we have seen them walk worthily in our midst, and seen them sink asleep in the arms of Jesus; and those who have died in the faith are now in the celestial kingdom of God. And hence is the glory of the sun. (HC 6:315)

House of Israel

1 On the second day of August, I assisted the Colesville branch of the Church to lay the first log, for a house, as a foundation of Zion in Kaw township, twelve miles west of Independence. The log was carried and placed by twelve men, in honor of the twelve tribes of Israel. (HC 1:196)

2 By it we learn that our western tribes of Indians are descendants from that Joseph which was sold into Egypt, and that the land of America is a promised land unto them, and unto it all the tribes of Israel will come, with as many of the Gentiles as shall comply with the requisitions of the new covenant. But the tribe of Judah will return to old Jerusalem. . . .

And now I am prepared to say by the authority of Jesus Christ, that not many years shall pass away before the United States shall present such a scene of *bloodshed* as has not a parallel in the history of our nation; pestilence, hail, famine, and earthquake will sweep the wicked of this generation from off the face of the land, to open and prepare the way for the return of the lost tribes of Israel from the north country. (HC 1:315)

3 As watchmen to the house of Israel—as shepherds over the flock which is now scattered over a vast extent of country, and the anxiety

Hope
3 King Follett Discourse, Nauvoo, 7 April 1844.

House of Israel
1 Dedication of Zion, Kaw Township, Missouri, 2 August 1831.
2 Letter to N. E. Seaton (N. C. Saxton), a newspaper editor in Rochester, N.Y., Kirtland, 4 January 1833.
3 Proclamation of the First Presidency, Nauvoo, 15 January 1841.

we feel for their prosperity and everlasting welfare, and for the carrying out the great and glorious purposes of our God, to which we have been called, we feel to urge its necessity, and say—Let the Saints come here; this is the word of the Lord, and in accordance with the great work of the last days. (HC 4:271)

Humility

1   And thus was this error [Oliver Cowdery's claim that he had discovered an error in one of the revelations, viz., D&C 20:37] rooted out, which having its rise in presumption and rash judgment, was the more particularly calculated (when once fairly understood) to teach each and all of us the necessity of humility and meekness before the Lord, that He might teach us of His ways, that we might walk in His paths, and live by every word that proceedeth forth from His mouth. (HC 1:105)

2   Great harmony prevailed; several were ordained; faith was strengthened; and humility, so necessary for the blessing of God to follow prayer, characterized the Saints. (HC 1:176–77)

3   [A general epistle from Zion] was read by the brethren in Kirtland with feelings of the deepest interest, knowing as we did, that the anger of the Lord was kindled against you, and nothing but repentance, of the greatest humility, would turn it away. (HC 1:340)

4   Had you made such confession as you were required to, at Chippeway, all things would have worked together for your good, and as I told you; but you did not manifest that degree of humility to the brethren that was required, but remained obstinate; for that reason God withdrew His Spirit from you, and left you in darkness. (HC 1:370)

Humility
1   The Prophet's visit to Oliver Cowdery and the Whitmer family, Fayette, New York, summer 1830. Joseph and Emma were living in Harmony, Pennsylvania.
2   Conference of the Church held at Kirtland, Ohio, June 1831.
3   Letter to the brethren in Zion, Kirtland, 21 April 1833.
4   Letter to John Smith (not the Prophet's uncle), Kirtland, 2 July 1833.

5 We seek not gold or silver or this world's goods, nor honors nor the applause of men; but we seek to please him [God], and to do the will of him who hath power not only to destroy the body, but to cast the soul into hell! Ah! men should not attempt to steady the ark of God! (*PWJS*, p. 317; standardized)

6 Brother Ezra Thayre and Joseph Hancock are sick with the cholera. Thomas Heyes was taken today. Previous to crossing the Mississippi river I had called the camp together and told them that in consequence of the disobedience of some who had been unwilling to listen to my words, but had rebelled, God had decreed that sickness should come upon the camp, and if they did not repent and humble themselves before God they should die like sheep with the rot; that I was sorry, but could not help it. The scourge must come; repentance and humility may mitigate the chastisement, but cannot altogether avert it. But there were some who would not give heed to my words. (HC 2:106–7)

7 The true principle of honor in the Church of the Saints, that the more a man is exalted, the more humble he will be, if actuated by the Spirit of the Lord, seemed to have been overlooked. (*PJS* 1:23)

8 *Minutes*: President Joseph Smith, Jun., arose, and said, . . . that Brother Jared Carter . . . , not being sufficiently humble to deliver just the message that was required, . . . stumbled and could not get the Spirit. (HC 2:280)

9 Thus came the word of the Lord unto me concerning the Twelve, saying—

Humility

5   Letter to Edward Partridge and others in Missouri, Kirtland, 30 March 1834.
6   Events of Zion's Camp in Missouri, June 1834.
7   The Prophet assembled with Oliver Cowdery, Sidney Rigdon, and Frederick G. Williams to ordain Oliver Cowdery to the office of Assistant President of the Church, 5 December 1834.
8   Minutes of a high council meeting, Kirtland, 19 September 1835.
9   A revelation concerning the Twelve Apostles, Kirtland, 3 November 1835.

Behold they are under condemnation, because they have not been sufficiently humble in my sight, and in consequence of their covetous desires, in that they have not dealt equally with each other in the division of the monies which came into their hands, nevertheless, some of them dealt equally, therefore they shall be rewarded; but verily I say unto you, they must all humble themselves before me, before they will be accounted worthy to receive an endowment, to go forth in my name unto all nations.

. . . The residue [of the Twelve] are not sufficiently humble before me. (HC 2:300, 301)

10 I then addressed them and gave much instruction calculated to guard them against self-sufficiency, self-righteousness, and self-importance; touching upon many subjects of importance and value to all who wish to walk humbly before the Lord, and especially teaching them to observe charity, wisdom and fellow-feeling, with love one towards another in all things, and under all circumstances. (HC 3:383)

11 Long-suffering, patience, and mercy have ever characterized the dealings of our heavenly Father towards the humble and penitent. (HC 4:163)

12 It would be gratifying to my mind to see the Saints in Kirtland flourish, but think the time is not yet come; and I assure you it never will until a different order of things be established and a different spirit manifested. When confidence is restored, when pride shall fall, and every aspiring mind be clothed with humility as with a garment, and selfishness give place to benevolence and charity, and a united determination to live by every word which proceedeth out of the mouth of the Lord is observable, then, and not till then, can peace, order and love prevail.

It is in consequence of aspiring men that Kirtland has been forsaken. How frequently has your humble servant been envied in his office by such characters, who endeavored to raise themselves to power at his expense, and seeing it impossible to do so, resorted to foul slan-

---

Humility

10 Instructions to the Apostles and Seventies departing for missions to England, Commerce (Nauvoo), 2 July 1839.

11 Letter to William W. Phelps, Nauvoo, 22 July 1840.

12 Letter to Oliver Granger in Kirtland, sent from Nauvoo, July 1840.

der and abuse, and other means to effect his overthrow. Such characters have ever been the first to cry out against the Presidency, and publish their faults and foibles to the four winds of heaven. (HC 4:166)

13 God exalts the humble, and debases the haughty. (HC 6:74)

Hypnotism (Mesmerism)

1 In the morning, had an interview with a lecturer on Mesmerism and Phrenology. Objected to his performing in the city. (HC 5:383)

Hypocrisy

1 It is against my principles to act the part of a hypocrite or to dissemble [to conceal one's true feelings] in anywise whatever with any man. (HC 5:312)

2 I love that man better who swears a stream as long as my arm yet deals justice to his neighbors and mercifully deals his substance to the poor, than the long, smooth-faced hypocrite. (HC 5:401)

Humility
13 Letter to James Arlington Bennett, Nauvoo, 13 November 1843.

Hypnotism (Mesmerism)
1 Nauvoo, 6 May 1843. In the handwritten version of Church history, the following words were included but crossed out: "Thought we had been imposed upon enough by such kind of things" (History of Joseph Smith, LDS Church Archives; see Bitton and Bunker, "Phrenology Among the Mormons," p. 60).

Hypocrisy
1 Letter to Sidney Rigdon, Nauvoo, 27 March 1843.
2 Sabbath address, Nauvoo, 21 May 1843.

Idleness

1 We are not willing to idle any time away which can be spent to useful purposes. (HC 1:369)

2 The Priests, too, should not be idle: their duties are plain, and unless they do them diligently, they cannot expect to be approved. (HC 2:229)

Ignorance

1 If the Church knew all the commandments, one half they would condemn through prejudice and ignorance. (HC 2:477)

2 We have been misrepresented and misunderstood, and belied, and the purity and integrity and uprightness of our hearts have not been known—and it is through ignorance—yea, the very depths of ignorance is the cause of it; and not only ignorance, but on the part of some, gross wickedness and hypocrisy also; for some, by a long face and sanctimonious prayers, and very pious sermons, had power to lead the minds of the ignorant and unwary, and thereby obtain such influence that when we approached their iniquities the devil gained great advantage. (HC 3:231–32)

3 But I beg leave to say unto you, brethren, that ignorance, superstition and bigotry placing itself where it ought not, is oftentimes in the way of the prosperity of this Church. (HC 3:296)

4 There are a great many wise men and women too in our midst who are too wise to be taught; therefore they must die in their igno-

---

Idleness
  1 Letter to the brethren in Zion, Kirtland, 2 July 1833.
  2 Letter to the Saints in Missouri published in the *Messenger and Advocate*, June 1835.

Ignorance
  1 Solemn assembly in the Kirtland Temple, 6 April 1837.
  2 Letter to the Church from Liberty Jail, 16 December 1838.
  3 Letter to the Saints from Liberty Jail, 20–25 March 1839.
  4 Sabbath address, Nauvoo, 11 June 1843.

rance, and in the resurrection they will find their mistake. Many seal up the door of heaven by saying, So far God may reveal and I will believe. (HC 5:424)

5   He that believeth in our chartered rights may come here and be saved; and he that does not shall remain in ignorance. (HC 5:467)

6   They are ready to destroy me for the least foible, and publish my imaginary failings from Dan to Beersheba, though they are too ignorant of the things of God, which have been revealed to me, to judge of my actions, motives or conduct, in any correct manner whatever.

The only principle upon which they judge me is by comparing my acts with the foolish traditions of their fathers and nonsensical teachings of hireling priests, whose object and aim were to keep the people in ignorance for the sake of filthy lucre; or as the prophet says, to feed themselves, not the flock. (HC 5:516–17)

Independence

1   Say to Brother Gilbert that we have no means in our power to assist him in a pecuniary way, as we know not the hour when we shall be sued for debts which we have contracted ourselves in New York. Say to him that he must exert himself to the utmost to obtain means himself, to replenish his store, for it must be replenished, and it is his duty to attend to it. (HC 1:365)

2   There are many things of much importance, on which you ask counsel, but which I think you will be perfectly able to decide upon, as you are more conversant with the peculiar circumstances than I am;

Ignorance
   5   Address regarding his arrest at Dixon, Illinois, Nauvoo, 30 June 1843.
   6   Sabbath address, Nauvoo, 23 July 1843.

Independence
   1   Letter to the brethren in Zion, Kirtland, 25 June 1833. The section that appears here is addressed to Edward Partridge.
   2   Letter to the Twelve in England, Nauvoo, 15 December 1840. The placement of this letter in HC implies that it was written in October 1840, but actually it was written on 15 December 1840 (see PWJS, p. 480).

and I feel great confidence in your united wisdom; therefore you will excuse me for not entering into detail. If I should see anything that is wrong, I would take the privilege of making known my mind to you, and pointing out the evil. (*HC* 4:228–29)

3   We can only live by worshiping our God; all must do it for themselves; none can do it for another. . . . Men or women could not be compelled into the kingdom of God. (*HC* 5:24)

Indians
See also LAMANITES

1   By it [the Book of Mormon] we learn that our western tribes of Indians are descendants from that Joseph which was sold into Egypt, and that the land of America is a promised land unto them. (*HC* 1:315)

2   Much has been said and done of late by the general government in relation to the Indians (Lamanites) within the territorial limits of the United States. One of the most important points in the faith of the Church of the Latter-day Saints, through the fullness of the everlasting Gospel, is the gathering of Israel (of whom the Lamanites constitute a part). (*HC* 2:357)

3   The remnant [of Book of Mormon peoples] are the Indians that now inhabit this country. (*HC* 4:538)

Independence
  3   Remarks to the Relief Society, Nauvoo, 9 June 1842.

Indians
  1   Letter to N. E. Seaton (N. C. Saxton), a newspaper editor in Rochester, N.Y., Kirtland, 4 January 1833.
  2   Meeting of the high council at Kirtland, 6 January 1836.
  3   Letter to John Wentworth, editor of the *Chicago Democrat*, Nauvoo, 1 March 1842.

Infant Baptism

1 The doctrine of baptizing children, or sprinkling them, or they must welter in hell, is a doctrine not true, not supported in Holy Writ, and is not consistent with the character of God. All children are redeemed by the blood of Jesus Christ, and the moment that children leave this world, they are taken to the bosom of Abraham. The only difference between the old and young dying is, one lives longer in heaven and eternal light and glory than the other, and is freed a little sooner from this miserable, wicked world. Notwithstanding all this glory, we for a moment lose sight of it, and mourn the loss, but we do not mourn as those without hope. (HC 4:554)

2 "Do you believe in the baptism of infants?" asks the Presbyterian. No. "Why?" Because it is nowhere written in the Bible. Circumcision is not baptism, neither was baptism instituted in the place of circumcision. Baptism is for remission of sins. Children have no sins. Jesus blessed them and said, "Do what you have seen me do." Children are all made alive in Christ, and those of riper years through faith and repentance. (HC 5:499)

Influence

1 It is our duty to concentrate all our influence to make popular that which is sound and good, and unpopular that which is unsound. 'Tis right, politically, for a man who has influence to use it, as well as for a man who has no influence to use his. From henceforth I will maintain all the influence I can get. (HC 5:286)

Infant Baptism
1 Sabbath address, Nauvoo, 20 March 1842.
2 Sabbath address, Nauvoo, 9 July 1843.

Influence
1 Address at the temple site in Nauvoo, 21 February 1843.

Innocence

1 Females, if they are pure and innocent, can come in the presence of God; for what is more pleasing to God than innocence; you must be innocent, or you cannot come up before God; if we would come before God, we must keep ourselves pure, and He is pure. (HC 4:605)

2 Virtue and innocence need no artificial covering. (HC 6:218)

Integrity

1 We would say to the brethren, seek to know God in your closets, call upon him in the fields. Follow the directions of the Book of Mormon, and pray over, and for your families, your cattle, your flocks, your herds, your corn, and all things that you possess; ask the blessing of God upon all your labors, and everything that you engage in. Be virtuous and pure; be men of integrity and truth; keep the commandments of God; and then you will be able more perfectly to understand the difference between right and wrong—between the things of God and the things of men; and your path will be like that of the just, which shineth brighter and brighter unto the perfect day. (HC 5:31)

2 I proclaim, in the name of the Lord God Almighty, that I will fellowship nothing in the Church but virtue, integrity, and uprightness. (HC 6:58)

3 To close, I would admonish you, before you let your "*candor compel*" you again to write upon a subject great as the salvation of man, consequential as the life of the Savior, broad as the principles of eternal truth, and valuable as the jewels of eternity, to read in the 8th section

---

Innocence
  1 Remarks to the Relief Society, Nauvoo, 28 April 1842.
  2 Article entitled "Pacific Innuendo," Nauvoo, 17 February 1844.

Integrity
  1 Editorial in the *Times and Seasons*, 15 June 1842.
  2 Sabbath address, Nauvoo, 15 October 1843.
  3 Letter to John C. Calhoun, Nauvoo, 2 January 1844.

and 1st article of the Constitution of the United States, the *first*, *fourteenth* and *seventeenth* "specific" and not very "limited powers" of the Federal Government, what can be done to protect the lives, property, and rights of a virtuous people, when the administrators of the law and law-makers are unbought by bribes, uncorrupted by patronage, untempted by gold, unawed by fear, and uncontaminated tangling alliances—even like Caesar's wife, not only *unspotted*, *but unsuspected!* And God, who cooled the heat of a Nebuchadnezzar's furnace or shut the mouths of lions for the honor of a Daniel, will raise your mind above the narrow notion that the General Government has no power, to the sublime idea that Congress, with the President as Executor, is as almighty in its sphere as Jehovah is in his. (HC 6:160)

Intelligence (Attribute)

1   There is a superior intelligence bestowed upon such as obeyed the Gospel with full purpose of heart, which, if sinned against, the apostate is left naked and destitute of the Spirit of God. (HC 2:23)

2   I therefore availed myself of this favorable opportunity to drop a few words upon this subject, by way of advice, that they might improve their minds and cultivate their powers of intellect in a proper manner, that they might not incur the displeasure of heaven; that they should handle sacred things very sacredly, and with due deference to the opinions of others, and with an eye single to the glory of God. (HC 2:318)

3   [By coming to Nauvoo the Saints will] be in a situation where they can have the advantages of instruction from the Presidency and other authorities of the Church, and rise higher and higher in the scale of intelligence until they can "comprehend with all Saints what is the breadth and length, and depth and height; and to know the love of Christ which passeth knowledge." (HC 4:186)

Intelligence (Attribute)
1   Letter to the brethren scattered from Zion, Kirtland, 22 January 1834.
2   Counsel given to a few Saints in Father Smith's home, Kirtland, 18 November 1835.
3   Letter to the Saints from the First Presidency, Nauvoo, 31 August 1840.

Intelligence (Self-Existent)

1   The spirit of man is not a created being; it existed from eternity, and will exist to eternity. Anything created cannot be eternal; and earth, water, etc., had their existence in an elementary state, from eternity. (HC 3:387)

2   I have another subject to dwell upon, which is calculated to exalt man; but it is impossible for me to say much on this subject. I shall therefore just touch upon it, for time will not permit me to say all. It is associated with the subject of the resurrection of the dead,—namely, the soul—the mind of man—the immortal spirit. Where did it come from? All learned men and doctors of divinity say that God created it in the beginning; but it is not so: the very idea lessens man in my estimation. I do not believe the doctrine; I know better. Hear it, all ye ends of the world; for God has told me so; and if you don't believe me, it will not make the truth without effect. . . .

We say that God Himself is a self-existing being. Who told you so? It is correct enough; but how did it get into your heads? Who told you that man did not exist in like manner upon the same principles? Man does exist upon the same principles. . . .

The mind or the intelligence which man possesses is co-equal {co-eternal} with God himself. . . .

I am dwelling on the immortality of the spirit of man. Is it logical to say that the intelligence of spirits is immortal, and yet that it has a beginning? The intelligence of spirits had no beginning, neither will it have an end. . . .

Intelligence (Self-Existent)

1   Discourse on the priesthood, given sometime before 8 August 1839, Commerce (Nauvoo). For a discussion on the dating of this discourse, see *WJS*, p. 22. In *TPJS* (p. 158) Elder Joseph Fielding Smith commented on this statement as follows: "In saying the spirit of man is not created the Prophet without any doubt had in mind the intelligence as explained in the *Doctrine and Covenants*, Sec. 93:29: 'Man was also in the beginning with God. Intelligence, or the light of truth, was not created or made, neither indeed can be.' From this we gather that the intelligence in man was not created, but the Prophet taught very clearly that man is in very deed the offspring of God, and that the spirits of men were born in the spirit world the children of God."

2   King Follett Discourse, Nauvoo, 7 April 1844.

Intelligence is eternal and exists upon a self-existent principle. It is a spirit from age to age and there is no creation about it. . . .

The first principles of man are self-existent with God. (*HC* 6:310, 311, 312)

Intemperance

1   I was informed today that a man by the name of Clark, who was under the influence of ardent spirits froze to death last night, near this place. How long, O Lord, will this monster intemperance find its victims on the earth! I fear until the earth is swept with the wrath and indignation of God, and Christ's kingdom becomes universal. O, come, Lord Jesus, and cut short Thy work in righteousness. (*HC* 2:406)

2   In all things be temperate; abstain from drunkenness, and from swearing, and from all profane language, and from everything which is unrighteous or unholy; also from enmity, and hatred, and covetousness, and from every unholy desire. Be honest one with another. (*HC* 3:233)

3   What added greatly to the happiness we experienced on this interesting occasion, is the fact that we heard no obscene or profane language; neither saw we any one intoxicated. Can the same be said of a similar assemblage in any other city in the Union? Thank God that the intoxicating beverage, the bane of humanity in these last days, is becoming a stranger in Nauvoo. (*HC* 4:330–31)

Israel
See CHILDREN OF ISRAEL; HOUSE OF ISRAEL

Intemperance
1   Reflections on intemperance, Kirtland, 12 March 1836.
2   Letter to the Church from Liberty Jail, 16 December 1838.
3   Remarks regarding the cornerstone laying ceremony for the Nauvoo Temple, 6 April 1841.

Jacob

1 The Lord says, that Jacob is the lot of his inheritance. He found him in a desert land, and in the waste, howling wilderness; He led him about, He instructed him, He kept him as the apple of His eye, etc.; which will show . . . that it is necessary for men to receive an understanding concerning the laws of the heavenly kingdom, before they are permitted to enter it: we mean the celestial glory. (HC 2:8)

2 Jacob and Joseph were no doubt, embalmed in the manner of the Egyptians, as they died in that country, Gen. 1:2, 3, 26. (T&S 3:782)

3 Paul ascended into the third heavens, and he could understand the three principal rounds of Jacob's ladder—the telestial, the terrestrial, and the celestial glories or kingdoms, where Paul saw and heard things which were not lawful for him to utter. (HC 5:402)

Jaredites

1 Jared and his brother came on to this continent from the confusion and scattering at the Tower, and lived here more than a thousand years, and covered the whole continent from sea to sea, with towns and cities. (T&S 3:922)

Jehovah

1 The great Jehovah contemplated the whole of the events connected with the earth, pertaining to the plan of salvation, before it

---

Jacob
1 Letter to the brethren scattered from Zion, Kirtland, 22 January 1834.
2 Editorial in the *Times and Seasons*, Nauvoo, 2 May 1842.
3 Sabbath address, Nauvoo, 21 May 1843.

Jaredites
1 Editorial in the *Times and Seasons*, 15 September 1842.

Jehovah
1 Editorial in the *Times and Seasons*, 15 April 1842.

rolled into existence, or ever "the morning stars sang together" for joy; the past, the present, and the future were and are, with Him, one eternal "now;" He knew of the fall of Adam, the iniquities of the antediluvians, of the depth of iniquity that would be connected with the human family, their weakness and strength, their power and glory, apostasies, their crimes, their righteousness and iniquity; He comprehended the fall of man, and his redemption; He knew the plan of salvation and pointed it out; He was acquainted with the situation of all nations and with their destiny; He ordered all things according to the council of His own will; He knows the situation of both the living and the dead, and has made ample provision for their redemption, according to their several circumstances, and the laws of the kingdom of God, whether in this world, or in the world to come. (HC 4:597)

2   It has been the design of Jehovah, from the commencement of the world, and is His purpose now, to regulate the affairs of the world in His own time, to stand as head of the universe, and take the reins of government in His own hand. When that is done, judgment will be administered in righteousness; anarchy and confusion will be destroyed, and "nations will learn war no more." (HC 5:63)

3   O Thou, who seest and knowest the hearts of all men—Thou eternal, omnipotent, omniscient, and omnipresent Jehovah—God—Thou Eloheim, that sittest, as saith the Psalmist, "enthroned in heaven," look down upon Thy servant Joseph at this time; and let faith on the name of Thy Son Jesus Christ, to a greater degree than Thy servant ever yet has enjoyed, be conferred upon him, even the faith of Elijah; and let the lamp of eternal life be lit up in his heart, never to be taken away; and let the words of eternal life be poured upon the soul of Thy servant. (HC 5:127)

Jehovah

2   Editorial in the *Times and Seasons*, 15 July 1842.

3   Reflections and prayer while in hiding in Nauvoo, August 1842. It seems clear that Joseph Smith is using "Jehovah" in this instance to refer to God the Father, although generally Jehovah refers to Jesus Christ (see, for example, D&C 110:1–4). Name-titles such as Elohim and Jehovah are not always used to refer to a single individual. See *Encyclopedia of Mormonism*, s. v. "Jehovah, Jesus Christ."

4   That friendship which intelligent beings would accept as sincere must arise from love, and that love grow out of virtue, which is as much a part of religion as light is a part of Jehovah. (*HC* 6:73)

Jesus Christ
See also ATONEMENT; SECOND COMING

1   Whenever the Lord revealed Himself to men in ancient days, and commanded them to offer sacrifice to Him, that it was done that they might look forward in faith to the time of His coming, and rely upon the power of that atonement for a remission of their sins. (*HC* 2:17)

2   Who, among all the Saints in these last days, can consider himself as good as our Lord? Who is as perfect? Who is as pure? Who is as holy as He was? Are they to be found? He never transgressed or broke a commandment or law of heaven—no deceit was in His mouth, neither was guile found in His heart. And yet one that ate with Him, who had often drunk of the same cup, was the first to lift up his heel against Him. Where is one like Christ? He cannot be found on earth. Then why should His followers complain, if from those whom they once called brethren, and considered as standing in the nearest relation in the everlasting covenant they should receive persecution? (*HC* 2:23)

3   The Son, who was in the bosom of the Father, [is] a personage of tabernacle, made or fashioned like unto man, being in the form and likeness of man, or rather man was formed after his likeness and in his image; he is also the express image and likeness of the personage of

---

Jehovah
   4   Letter to James Arlington Bennett, Nauvoo, 13 November 1843.

Jesus Christ
   1   Letter to the brethren scattered from Zion, Kirtland, 22 January 1834.
   2   Letter to the brethren scattered from Zion, Kirtland, 22 January 1834.
   3   Lectures on Faith, delivered to a school of the elders, Kirtland, December 1834. Although the Lectures on Faith were not written only by Joseph Smith, he reviewed them carefully and prepared them for publication (see Larry E. Dahl and Charles D. Tate, Jr., eds., *The Lectures on Faith in Historical Perspective*, p. 10).

the Father, possessing all the fullness of the Father, or the same fullness with the Father; being begotten of him, and ordained from before the foundation of the world to be a propitiation for the sins of all those who should believe on his name, and is called the Son because of the flesh, and descended in suffering below that which man can suffer; or, in other words, suffered greater sufferings, and was exposed to more powerful contradictions than any man can be. But, notwithstanding all this, he kept the law of God, and remained without sin, showing thereby that it is in the power of man to keep the law and remain also without sin; and also, that by him a righteous judgment might come upon all flesh, that all who walk not in the law of God may justly be condemned by the law, and have no excuse for their sins. And he being the Only Begotten of the Father, full of grace and truth, and having overcome, received a fullness of the glory of the Father, possessing the same mind with the Father, which mind is the Holy Spirit, that bears record of the Father and the Son. (*LF* 5:2)

4 The Lord wants the wheat and tares to grow together; for Zion must be redeemed with judgment, and her converts with righteousness. (*HC* 2:228)

5 How have we come at the Priesthood in the last days? It came down, down, in regular succession. Peter, James, and John had it given to them and they gave it to others. Christ is the Great High Priest; Adam next. Paul speaks of the Church coming to an innumerable company of angels—to God the Judge of all—the spirits of just men made perfect; to Jesus the Mediator of the new covenant. (*HC* 3:387–88)

6 [Adam was he] to whom Christ was first revealed, and through whom Christ has been revealed from heaven, and will continue to be revealed from henceforth. (*HC* 4:207)

Jesus Christ

  4 Letter to the Saints in Missouri published in the *Messenger and Advocate*, June 1835.

  5 Discourse on the priesthood, given sometime before 8 August 1839, Commerce (Nauvoo). For a discussion on the dating of this discourse, see *WJS*, p. 22.

  6 Article on priesthood read at general conference, Nauvoo, 5 October 1840.

7   None ever were perfect but Jesus; and why was He perfect? Because He was the Son of God, and had the fullness of the Spirit, and greater power than any man. But notwithstanding their vanity, men look forward with hope (because they are "subjected in hope") to the time of their deliverance. (*HC* 4:358–59)

8   Jesus Christ became a ministering spirit (while His body was lying in the sepulchre) to the spirits in prison, to fulfill an important part of His mission, without which He could not have perfected His work, or entered into His rest. After His resurrection He appeared as an angel to His disciples. . . .
. . . Jesus Christ went in body after His resurrection, to minister to resurrected bodies. (*HC* 4:425)

9   *Report of Eliza R. Snow:* President Smith arose and called the attention of the meeting to the 12th chapter 1st Corinthians—"Now concerning spiritual gifts, I would not have you ignorant." Said that the passage in the third verse, which reads, "No man can say that Jesus is the Lord, but by the Holy Ghost," should be translated "no man can *know* that Jesus is the Lord, but by the Holy Ghost." (*HC* 4:602–3)

10   When Egypt was under the superintendence of Joseph it prospered, because he was taught of God; when they oppressed the Israelites, destruction came upon them. When the children of Israel were chosen with Moses at their head, they were to be a peculiar people, among them God should place His name; their motto was: "The Lord is our lawgiver; the Lord is our Judge; the Lord is our King, and He shall reign over us." While in this state they might truly say, "Happy is that people, whose God is the Lord." Their government was a theocracy; they had God to make their laws, and men chosen by Him to administer them; He was their God, and they were His people. Moses received the word of the Lord from God Himself; he was the mouth of God to Aaron, and Aaron taught the people, in both civil and eccle-

---

Jesus Christ
7   Sabbath address, Nauvoo, 16 May 1841.
8   General conference address, Nauvoo, 3 October 1841.
9   Remarks to the Relief Society, Nauvoo, 28 April 1842.
10   Editorial in the *Times and Seasons*, 15 July 1842.

siastical affairs; they were both one, there was no distinction; so will it be when the purposes of God shall be accomplished: when "the Lord shall be King over the whole earth," and "Jerusalem His throne." "The law shall go forth from Zion, and the word of the Lord from Jerusalem." (HC 5:64)

11 He, the Lord [is] a priest forever, after the order of Melchisedec, and the anointed son of God, from before the foundation of the world. . . .

. . . If Enoch was righteous enough to come into the presence of God, and walk with him, he must have become so by keeping his commandments, and so of every righteous person, whether it was Noah, . . . Abraham, . . . Jacob, . . . Moses, . . . or whether it was Jesus Christ himself, who had no need of repentance, having . . . no sin; according to his solemn declaration to John:—now let me be baptised: for no man can enter the kingdom without obeying this ordinance: for thus it becometh us to fulfil all righteousness. Surely, then, if it became John and Jesus Christ, the Saviour, to fulfil all righteousness to be baptised—so surely, then, it will become every other person that seeks the kingdom of heaven to go and do likewise; for he is the door, and if any person climbs up any other way, the same is a thief and a robber!

In the former ages of the world, before the Saviour came in the flesh, "the saints" were baptised in the name of Jesus Christ to come, because there never was any other name whereby men could be saved; and after he came in the flesh and was crucified, then the saints were baptised in the name of Jesus Christ, crucified, risen from the dead and ascended into heaven, that they might be buried in baptism like him, and be raised in glory like him, that as there was but one Lord, one faith, one baptism, and one God and father of us all, even so there was but one door to the mansions of bliss. (T&S 3:905)

12 Christ came according to the words of John, and He was greater than John, because He held the keys of the Melchisedek Priesthood and kingdom of God, and had before revealed the priesthood of Moses, yet Christ was baptized by John to fulfill all righteousness. (HC 5:258)

Jesus Christ
11 Editorial in the *Times and Seasons*, 1 September 1842.
12 Sabbath address, Nauvoo, 22 January 1843.

13 How was the least in the kingdom of heaven greater than [John the Baptist]?

In reply I asked—Whom did Jesus have reference to as being the least? Jesus was looked upon as having the least claim in God's kingdom, and {seemingly} was least entitled to their credulity as a prophet; as though He had said—"He that is considered the least among you is greater than John—that is I myself." (*HC* 5:261)

14 The Lord deals with this people as a tender parent with a child, communicating light and intelligence and the knowledge of his ways as they can bear it. (*HC* 5:402)

15 If a man gets a fullness of the priesthood of God, he has to get it in the same way that Jesus Christ obtained it, and that was by keeping all the commandments and obeying all the ordinances of the house of the Lord. (*HC* 5:424)

16 It always has been when a man was sent of God with the priesthood and he began to preach the fullness of the gospel, that he was thrust out by his friends, who are already to butcher him if he teach things which they imagine to be wrong; and Jesus was crucified upon this principle. (*HC* 5:425)

17 As the Father hath power in Himself, so hath the Son power in Himself, to lay down His life and take it again, so He has a body of His own. The Son doeth what He hath seen the Father do: then the Father hath some day laid down His life and taken it again; so He has a body of His own; each one will be in His own body; and yet the sectarian world believe the body of the Son is identical with the Father's. (*HC* 5:426)

18 Salvation could not come to the world without the mediation of Jesus Christ. . . .

Jesus Christ
   13 Sabbath address, Nauvoo, 29 January 1843.
   14 Sabbath address, Nauvoo, 21 May 1843.
   15 Sabbath address, Nauvoo, 11 June 1843.
   16 Sabbath address, Nauvoo, 11 June 1843.
   17 Sabbath address, Nauvoo, 11 June 1843.
   18 Sabbath address, Nauvoo, 27 August 1843.

Jesus Christ is the heir of this Kingdom—the only begotten of the Father according to the flesh, and holds the keys over all this world. (*HC* 5:555, 556)

19 This generation is as corrupt as the generation of the Jews that crucified Christ; and if He were here to-day, and should preach the same doctrine He did then, they would put Him to death. (*HC* 6:58)

20 The scriptures inform us that Jesus said, as the Father hath power in himself, even so hath the Son power—to do what? Why, what the Father did. The answer is obvious—in a manner to lay down his body and take it up again. Jesus, what are you going to do? To lay down my life as my Father did, and take it up again. . . .
. . . What did Jesus do? Why, I do the things I saw my Father do when worlds came rolling into existence. My Father worked out His kingdom with fear and trembling, and I must do the same; and when I get my kingdom, I shall present it to My Father, so that He may obtain kingdom upon kingdom, and it will exalt Him in glory. He will then take a higher exaltation, and I will take His place, and thereby become exalted myself. So that Jesus treads in the tracks of His Father, and inherits what God did before; and God is thus glorified and exalted in the salvation and exaltation of all His children. (*HC* 6:305, 306)

21 My object was to preach the scriptures, and preach the doctrine they contain, there being a God above, the Father of our Lord Jesus Christ. (*HC* 6:474)

22 If Abraham reasoned thus—If Jesus Christ was the Son of God, and John discovered that God the Father of Jesus Christ had a Father, you may suppose that He had a Father also. Where was there ever a son without a father? And where was there ever a father without first being a son? Whenever did a tree or anything spring into existence without a progenitor? And everything comes in this way. Paul says that which is earthly is in the likeness of that which is heavenly. Hence if Jesus had a Father, can we not believe that *He* had a Father

---

Jesus Christ

19 Sabbath address, Nauvoo, 15 October 1843.
20 King Follett Discourse, Nauvoo, 7 April 1844.
21 Sabbath address, Nauvoo, 16 June 1844.
22 Sabbath address, Nauvoo, 16 June 1844.

also? I despise the idea of being scared to death at such a doctrine, for the Bible is full of it.

I want you to pay particular attention to what I am saying. Jesus said that the Father wrought precisely in the same way as His Father had done before Him. As the Father had done before. He laid down His life, and took it up the same as His Father had done before. He did as He was sent, to lay down His life and take it up again; and then was committed unto Him the keys, &c. I know it is good reasoning. (*HC* 6:476–77)

23 Our lives have already become jeopardized by revealing the wicked and bloodthirsty purposes of our enemies; and for the future we must cease to do so. All we have said about them is truth, but it is not always wise to relate all the truth. Even Jesus, the Son of God had to refrain from doing so, and had to restrain His feelings many times for the safety of Himself and His followers, and had to conceal the righteous purposes of His heart in relation to many things pertaining to His Father's kingdom. When still a boy He had all the intelligence necessary to enable Him to rule and govern the kingdom of the Jews, and could reason with the wisest and most profound doctors of law and divinity, and make their theories and practice to appear like folly compared with the wisdom He possessed; but He was a boy only, and lacked physical strength even to defend His own person, and was subject to cold, to hunger and to death. So it is with the Church of Jesus Christ of Latter-day Saints; we have the revelation of Jesus, and the knowledge within us is sufficient to organize a righteous government upon the earth, and to give universal peace to all mankind, if they would receive it, but we lack the physical strength, as did our Savior when a child, to defend our principles, and we have of necessity to be afflicted, persecuted and smitten, and to bear it patiently until Jacob is of age, then he will take care of himself. (*HC* 6:608–9)

Jesus Christ
23 Carthage Jail, 27 June 1844.

Jews

1 They are the Twelve Apostles, who are called to the office of the Traveling High Council . . . ; and they are to travel and preach among the Gentiles, until the Lord shall command them to go to the Jews. (HC 2:200)

2 That the doctrine of eternal judgment was perfectly understood by the Apostles, is evident from several passages of Scripture. Peter preached repentance and baptism for the remission of sins to the Jews who had been led to acts of violence and blood by their leaders; but to the rulers he said, "I would that through ignorance ye did it, as did also those ye ruled." "Repent, therefore, and be converted, that your sins may be blotted out, when the times of refreshing (redemption) shall come from the presence of the Lord, for He shall send Jesus Christ, who before was preached unto you." (HC 4:359)

3 This generation is as corrupt as the generation of the Jews that crucified Christ; and if He were here to-day, and should preach the same doctrine He did then, they would put Him to death. (HC 6:58)

John the Baptist

1 Let us come into new Testament times. . . . We will commence with John the Baptist. When Herod's edict went forth to destroy the young children, John was about six months older than Jesus, and came under this hellish edict, and Zacharias caused his mother to take him into the mountains, where he was raised on locusts and wild honey. When his father refused to discover [disclose] his hiding place, and being the officiating high priest at the Temple that year, was slain by Herod's order, between the porch and the altar, as Jesus said. John's

---

Jews
 1 Instructions to the Twelve, Kirtland, 27 February 1835.
 2 Sabbath address, Nauvoo, 16 May 1841.
 3 Sabbath address, Nauvoo, 15 October 1843.

John the Baptist
 1 Editorial in the *Times and Seasons*, 1 September 1842.

head was taken to Herod, the son of this infant murderer, *in a charger*—notwithstanding there was never a greater prophet born of a woman than him! (*T&S* 3:902)

2   As touching the Gospel and baptism that John preached, I would say that John came preaching the Gospel for the remission of sins; he had his authority from God, and the oracles of God were with him, and the kingdom of God for a season seemed to rest with John alone. The Lord promised Zacharias that he should have a son who was a descendant of Aaron, the Lord having promised that the priesthood should continue with Aaron and his seed throughout their generations. Let no man take this honor upon himself, except he be called of God, as was Aaron; and Aaron received his call by revelation. An angel of God also appeared unto Zacharias while in the Temple, and told him that he should have a son, whose name should be John, and he should be filled with the Holy Ghost. Zacharias was a priest of God, and officiating in the Temple, and John was a priest after his father, and held the keys of the Aaronic Priesthood, and was called of God to preach the Gospel of the kingdom of God. The Jews, as a nation, having departed from the law of God and the Gospel of the Lord, prepared the way for transferring it to the Gentiles.

But, says one, the kingdom of God could not be set up in the days of John, for John said the kingdom was at hand. But I would ask if it could be any nearer to them than to be in the hands of John. The people need not wait for the days of Pentecost to find the kingdom of God, for John had it with him, and he came forth from the wilderness crying out, "Repent ye, for the kingdom of heaven is nigh at hand," as much as to say, "Out here I have got the kingdom of God and I am coming after you; I have got the kingdom of God, and you can get it, and I am coming after you; and if you don't receive it, you will be damned;" and the scriptures represent that all Jerusalem went out unto John's baptism. There was a legal administrator, and those that were baptized were subjects for a king; and also the laws and oracles of God were there; therefore the kingdom of God was there; for no man could have better authority to administer than John; and our Savior submitted to that authority Himself, by being baptized by John; therefore the kingdom of God was set up on the earth, even in the days of John. . . .

John the Baptist
2   Sabbath address, Nauvoo, 22 January 1843.

John was a priest after the order of Aaron, and had the keys of that priesthood, and came forth preaching repentance and baptism for the remission of sins, but at the same time cries out, "There cometh one mightier than I after me, the latchet of whose shoes I am not worthy to stoop down and unloose," and Christ came according to the words of John, and He was greater than John, because He held the keys of the Melchisedek Priesthood and kingdom of God, and had before revealed the priesthood of Moses, yet Christ was baptized by John to fulfill all righteousness; and Jesus in His teachings says, "Upon this rock I will build my Church, and the gates of hell shall not prevail against it." What rock? Revelation.

Again he says, "Except a man be born of water and of the Spirit, he cannot enter into the kingdom of God;" and, "heaven and earth shall pass away, but my words shall not pass away." If a man is born of water and of the Spirit, he can get into the kingdom of God. It is evident the kingdom of God was on the earth, and John prepared subjects for the kingdom, by preaching the Gospel to them and baptizing them, and he prepared the way before the Savior, or came as a forerunner, and prepared subjects for the preaching of Christ; and Christ preached through Jerusalem on the same ground where John had preached; and when the apostles were raised up, they worked in Jerusalem, and Jesus commanded them to tarry there until they were endowed with power from on high. Had they not work to do in Jerusalem? They did work, and prepared a people for the Pentecost. The kingdom of God was with them before the day of Pentecost, as well as afterwards; and it was also with John, and he preached the same Gospel and baptism that Jesus and the apostles preached after him. The endowment was to prepare the disciples for their missions unto the world. (HC 5:257–59)

3   The question arose from the saying of Jesus—"Among those that are born of women there is not a greater prophet than John the Baptist; but he that is least in the kingdom of God is greater than he." How is it that John was considered one of the greatest prophets? His miracles could not have constituted his greatness.

First. He was entrusted with a divine mission of preparing the way before the face of the Lord. Whoever had such a trust committed to him before or since? No man.

John the Baptist
3   Sabbath address, Nauvoo, 29 January 1843.

Secondly. He was entrusted with the important mission, and it was required at his hands, to baptize the Son of Man. Whoever had the honor of doing that? Whoever had so great a privilege and glory? Whoever led the Son of God into the waters of baptism, and had the privilege of beholding the Holy Ghost descend in the form of a dove, or rather in the *sign* of a dove, in witness of that administration? The sign of the dove was instituted before the creation of the world, a witness for the Holy Ghost, and the devil cannot come in the sign of a dove. The Holy Ghost is a personage, and is in the form of a personage. It does not confine itself to the *form* of the dove, but in *sign* of the dove. The Holy Ghost cannot be transformed into a dove; but the sign of a dove was given to John to signify the truth of the deed, as the dove is an emblem or token of truth and innocence.

Thirdly. John, at that time, was the only legal administrator in the affairs of the kingdom there was then on the earth, and holding the keys of power. The Jews had to obey his instructions or be damned, by their own law; and Christ Himself fulfilled all righteousness in becoming obedient to the law which he had given to Moses on the mount, and thereby magnified it and made it honorable, instead of destroying it. The son of Zacharias wrested the keys, the kingdom, the power, the glory from the Jews, by the holy anointing and decree of heaven, and these three reasons constitute him the greatest prophet born of a woman.

Second question:—How was the least in the kingdom of heaven greater than he?

In reply I asked—Whom did Jesus have reference to as being the least? Jesus was looked upon as having the least claim in God's kingdom, and {seemingly} was least entitled to their credulity as a prophet; as though He had said—"He that is considered the least among you is greater than John—that is I myself." (HC 5:260–61)

4   And again, Matth. 11 Chap., 12 and 13 v.—"And from the days of John the Baptist, until now, the Kingdom of Heaven suffereth violence, and the violent take it by force. For all the prophets and the law prophesied until John." John held the Aaronic Priesthood and was a legal administrator, and the forerunner of Christ, and came to prepare the way before him.

John the Baptist
   4   Sabbath address, Nauvoo, 23 July 1843.

. . . John was a priest after the order of Aaron before Christ.

See Exodus 30 Chap. 30 and 31 v.—"And thou shalt anoint Aaron and his sons, and consecrate them, that they may minister unto me in the priest's office. And thou shalt speak unto the children of Israel, saying, This shall be an holy anointing oil unto me throughout your generations." Also Exodus 40 Chap., 15 v.—"And thou shalt anoint them as thou didst anoint their father (Aaron) that they may minister unto me in the priest's office; for their anointing shall surely be an everlasting Priesthood throughout their generations."

Here is a little of law which must be fulfilled. The Levitical Priesthood is forever hereditary—fixed on the head of Aaron and his sons forever, and was in active operation down to Zacharias the father of John. Zacharias would have had no child had not God given him a son. He sent his angel to declare unto Zacharias that his wife Elizabeth should bear him a son, whose name was to be called John.

The keys of the Aaronic Priesthood were committed unto him, and he was as the voice of one crying in the wilderness saying: "Prepare ye the way of the Lord and make his paths straight."

The Kingdom of heaven suffereth violence, etc.

The kingdom of heaven continueth in authority until John.

The authority taketh it by absolute power.

John having the power took the Kingdom by authority.

How have you obtained all this great knowledge? By the gift of the Holy Ghost.

Wrested the Kingdom from the Jews.

Of these stony Gentiles—these dogs—to raise up children unto Abraham.

The Savior said unto John, I must be baptized by you. Why so? To fulfil all righteousness. John refuses at first, but afterwards obeyed by administering the ordinance of baptism unto him, Jesus having no other legal administrator to apply to.

There is no salvation between the two lids of the Bible without a legal administrator. Jesus was then the legal administrator, and ordained His Apostles. (*TPJS*, pp. 318–19)

5   John's mission was limited to preaching and baptizing; but what he did was legal; and when Jesus Christ came to any of John's disciples, He baptized them with fire and the Holy Ghost.

John the Baptist
   5   Sabbath address, Nauvoo, 10 March 1844.

We find the apostles endowed with greater power than John: their office was more under the spirit and power of Elijah than Elias.

In the case of Phillip when he went down to Samaria, when he was under the spirit of Elias, he baptized both men and women. When Peter and John heard of it, they went down and laid hands upon them, and they received the Holy Ghost. This shows the distinction between the two powers.

When Paul came to certain disciples, he asked if they had received the Holy Ghost? They said, No. Who baptized you, then? We were baptized unto John's baptism. No, you were not baptized unto John's baptism, or you would have been baptized by John. And so Paul went and baptized them, for he knew what the true doctrine was, and he knew that John had not baptized them. And these principles are strange to me, that men who have read the Scriptures of the New Testament are so far from it.

What I want to impress upon your minds is the difference of power in the different parts of the Priesthood, so that when any man comes among you, saying, "I have the spirit of Elias," you can know whether he be true or false; for any man that comes, having the spirit and power of Elias, he will not transcend his bounds.

John did not transcend his bounds, but faithfully performed that part belonging to his office; and every portion of the great building should be prepared right and assigned to its proper place; and it is necessary to know who holds the keys of power, and who does not, or we may be likely to be deceived. (HC 6:250–51)

John the Revelator

1   *Report of John Whitmer:* The Spirit of the Lord fell upon Joseph in an unusual manner, and he prophesied that John the Revelator was then among the Ten Tribes of Israel who had been led away by Shalmaneser, king of Assyria, to prepare them for their return from their long dispersion, to again possess the land of their fathers. (HC 1:176)

2   John upon the isle of Patmos, saw the same thing concerning the last days, which Enoch saw. (HC 2:261)

John the Revelator
1   Conference of the Church, Kirtland, 3–6 June 1831.
2   Letter to the elders of the Church, Kirtland, 1 September 1835.

3   John had the curtains of heaven withdrawn, and by vision looked through the dark vista of future ages, and contemplated events that should transpire throughout every subsequent period of time, until the final winding up scene—while he gazed upon the glories of the eternal world, saw an innumerable company of angels and heard the voice of God—it was in the Spirit, on the Lord's day, unnoticed and unobserved by the world. (HC 5:30)

4   There is a grand difference and distinction between the visions and figures spoken of by the ancient prophets, and those spoken of in the revelations of John. The things which John saw had no allusion to the scenes of the days of Adam, Enoch, Abraham or Jesus, only so far as is plainly represented by John, and clearly set forth by him. John saw that only which was lying in futurity and which was shortly to come to pass. See Rev. i: 1–3, which is a key to the whole subject. (HC 5:341–42)

Joseph of Egypt

1   The learning of the Egyptians, and their knowledge of astronomy was no doubt taught them by Abraham and Joseph, as their records testify, who received it from the Lord. . . .
When Egypt was under the superintendence of Joseph it prospered, because he was taught of God. (HC 5:63, 64)

Joseph Smith Translation
See BIBLE, JOSEPH SMITH TRANSLATION OF THE

John the Revelator
   3   Editorial in the *Times and Seasons*, 15 June 1842.
   4   General conference address, Nauvoo, 8 April 1843.

Joseph of Egypt
   1   Editorial in the *Times and Seasons*, 15 July 1842.

Journals

1   Since I have been engaged in laying the foundation of the
Church of Jesus Christ of Latter-day Saints, I have been prevented in
various ways from continuing my journal and history in a manner satisfactory to myself or in justice to the cause. Long imprisonments,
vexatious and long-continued law-suits, the treachery of some of my
clerks, the death of others, and the poverty of myself and brethren
from continued plunder and driving, have prevented my handing
down to posterity a connected memorandum of events desirable to all
lovers of truth; yet I have continued to keep up a journal in the best
manner my circumstances would allow, and dictate for my history
from time to time, as I have had opportunity so that the labors and
suffering of the first Elders and Saints of this last kingdom might not
wholly be lost to the world. (HC 4:470)

2   *Words of Oliver B. Huntington:* He advised the elders all to keep
daily journals. "For," said he, "your journals will be sought after as history and scripture. That is the way the New Testament came, what we
have of it, though much of the matter there was written by the apostles
from their memory of what had been done, because they were not
prompt in keeping daily journals."
    I have kept a journal as he directed. (*TK,* p. 65)

Judas Iscariot

1   From apostates the faithful have received the severest persecutions. Judas was rebuked and immediately betrayed his Lord into the
hands of His enemies, because Satan entered into him. . . . What
nearer friend on earth, or in heaven, had Judas than the Savior? And
his first object was to destroy Him. (HC 2:23)

Journals
   1   Nauvoo, 11 December 1841.
   2   Recollection of Oliver B. Huntington, published in the *Young Woman's
       Journal,* July 1891.

Judas Iscariot
   1   Letter to the brethren scattered from Zion, Kirtland, 22 January 1834.

2   Must the new ones that are chosen to fill the places of those that are fallen, of the quorum of the Twelve, begin to exalt themselves, until they exalt themselves so high that they will soon tumble over and have a great fall, and go wallowing through the mud and mire and darkness, Judas like, to the buffetings of Satan, as several of the quorum have done, or will they learn wisdom and be wise? O God! give them wisdom, and keep them humble, I pray. (HC 3:384)

Judging

1   No man is capable of judging a matter, in council, unless his own heart is pure; and that we are frequently so filled with prejudice, or have a beam in our own eye, that we are not capable of passing right decisions. (HC 2:25)

2   After so long a time, I dictate a few lines to you, to let you know that I am in Kirtland, and that I found all well when I arrived, as pertaining to health; but our common adversary had taken the advantage of our Brother Sylvester Smith, and others, who gave a false coloring to almost every transaction, from the time we left Kirtland, until we returned, and thereby stirred up a great difficulty in the Church against me. Accordingly I was met in the face and eyes, as soon as I had got home, with a catalogue of charges as black as the author of lies himself; and the cry was Tyrant—Pope—King—Usurper—Abuser of men—Angel—False Prophet—Prophesying lies in the name of the Lord—Taking consecrated monies—and every other lie to fill up and complete the catalogue. Such experiences may be necessary to perfect the Church, and render our traducers mete for the devourer, and the shaft of the destroying angel. (HC 2:144)

Judas Iscariot
>   2   Instructions to the Apostles and Seventies departing for missions to England, Commerce (Nauvoo), 2 July 1839.

Judging
>   1   A council of high priests and elders at the Prophet's home in Kirtland, 12 February 1834.
>   2   Letter written from Kirtland to the high council in Zion, 16 August 1834.

3 I preached to the Saints, setting forth the evils that existed, and that would exist, by reason of hasty judgment, or decisions upon any subject given by any people, or in judging before they had heard both sides of a question. (HC 3:27)

4 Explained concerning the coming of the Son of Man; also that it is a false idea that the Saints will escape all the judgments, whilst the wicked suffer; for all flesh is subject to suffer, and "the righteous shall hardly escape;" still many of the Saints will escape, for the just shall live by faith; yet many of the righteous shall fall prey to disease, to pestilence, etc., by reason of the weakness of the flesh, and yet be saved in the Kingdom of God. So that it is an unhallowed principle to say that such and such have transgressed because they have been preyed upon by disease or death, for all flesh is subject to death; and the Savior has said, "Judge not, lest ye be judged." (HC 4:11)

5 *Minutes:* The President rose, made some observations on the business of the Conference, exhorted the brethren who had charges to make against individuals, and made some very appropriate remarks respecting the pulling the beam out of their own eye, that they may see more clearly the mote which was in their brother's eye. (HC 4:105)

6 I advise all of you to be careful what you do, or you may by-and-by find out that you have been deceived. Stay yourselves; do not give way; don't make any hasty moves, you may be saved. If a spirit of bitterness is in you, don't be in haste. You may say, that man is a sinner. Well, if he repents, he shall be forgiven. Be cautious: await. When you find a spirit that wants bloodshed,—murder, the same is not of God, but is of the devil. Out of the abundance of the heart of man the mouth speaketh. (HC 6:315)

7 *Words of Jesse W. Crosby:* I went one day to the Prophet with a sister. She had a charge to make against one of the brethren for scandal.

Judging
  3 Sabbath address, Far West, 6 May 1838.
  4 Sabbath address, Commerce (Nauvoo), 29 September 1839.
  5 Minutes of a general conference of the Church, Nauvoo, 6 April 1840.
  6 King Follett Discourse, Nauvoo, 7 April 1844.
  7 Recollection of Jesse W. Crosby, reported in "Stories from the Notebook of Martha Cox, Grandmother of Fern Cox Anderson," LDS Church Archives.

When her complaint had been heard the Prophet asked her if she was quite sure that what the brother had said of her was utterly untrue.

She was quite sure that it was.

He then told her to think no more about it, for it could not harm her. If untrue it could not live, but the truth will survive. Still she felt that she should have some redress.

Then he offered her his method of dealing with such cases for himself. When an enemy had told a scandalous story about him, which had often been done, before he rendered judgment he paused and let his mind run back to the time and place and setting of the story to see if he had not by some unguarded word or act laid the block on which the story was built. If he found that he had done so, he said that in his heart he then forgave his enemy, and felt thankful that he had received warning of a weakness that he had not known he possessed.

Then he said to the sister that he would have her to do the same: search her memory thoroughly and see if she had not herself unconsciously laid the foundation for the scandal that annoyed her.

The sister thought deeply for a few moments and then confessed that she believed that she had.

Then the Prophet told her that in her heart she could forgive that brother who had risked his own good name and her friendship to give her this clearer view of herself.

The sister thanked her advisor and went away in peace. (*TK*, p. 144)

Judgment

1   We do not present this little volume [the Doctrine and Covenants] with any other expectation than that we are to be called to answer to every principle advanced, in that day when the secrets of all hearts will be revealed, and the reward of every man's labor be given him. (*HC* 2:251)

Judgment
   1   Preface to the first edition of the Doctrine and Covenants, signed by Joseph Smith, Oliver Cowdery, Sidney Rigdon, and Frederick G. Williams, Kirtland, dated 17 February 1835.

2   May God reward our enemies according to their works. (HC 3:351)

3   I want the innocent to go free—rather spare ten iniquitous among you, than condemn one innocent one. "Fret not thyself because of evil doers." God will see to it. (HC 5:20–21)

4   The great misery of departed spirits in the world of spirits, where they go after death, is to know that they come short of the glory that others enjoy and that they might have enjoyed themselves, and they are their own accusers. (HC 5:425)

5   Wherefore let the rich and the learned, the wise and the noble, the poor and the needy, the bond and the free, both black and white, take heed to their ways, and a leave to the knowledge of God, and execute justice and judgment upon the earth in righteousness, and prepare to meet the judge of the quick and the dead, for the hour of His coming is nigh. (HC 6:93)

6   As they concocted scenes of bloodshed in this world, so they shall rise to that resurrection which is as the lake of fire and brimstone. Some shall rise to the everlasting burnings of God; for God dwells in everlasting burnings and some shall rise to the damnation of their own filthiness, which is as exquisite a torment as the lake of fire and brimstone. (HC 6:317)

Keys of the Kingdom of God

1   *Words of Philo Dibble:* On invitation of Father Johnson, of Hiram, Ohio, Joseph removed his family to his home, to translate the New Testament.

Judgment
2   Letter from the First Presidency to Oliver Granger written from Commerce (Nauvoo), 14 May 1839.
3   Remarks to the Relief Society, Nauvoo, 26 May 1842.
4   Sabbath address, Nauvoo, 11 June 1843.
5   Letter to the "Green Mountain Boys" in Vermont, appealing for their support, Nauvoo, 29 November 1843.
6   King Follett Discourse, Nauvoo, 7 April 1844.

Keys of the Kingdom of God
1   Recollection of Philo Dibble, published in "Philo Dibble's Narrative."

At this time Sidney Rigdon was left to preside at Kirtland and frequently preached to us. Upon one occasion he said the keys of the kingdom were taken from us. On hearing this, many of his hearers wept, and when some one undertook to dismiss the meeting by prayer he said praying would do them no good, and the meeting broke up in confusion.

Brother Hyrum came to my house the next morning and told me all about it, and said it was false, and that the keys of the kingdom were still with us. He wanted my carriage and horses to go to the town of Hiram and bring Joseph. The word went abroad among the people immediately that Sidney was going to expose "Mormonism."

Joseph came up to Kirtland a few days afterwards and held a meeting in a large barn. Nearly all the inhabitants of Kirtland turned out to hear him. The barn was filled with people, and others, unable to get inside, stood around the door as far as they could hear.

Joseph arose in our midst and spoke in mighty power, saying: "I can contend with wicked men and devils—yes, with angels. No power can pluck those keys from me, except the power that gave them to me; that was Peter, James and John. But for what Sidney has done, the devil shall handle him as one man handles another."

Thomas B. Marsh's wife went from the meeting and told Sidney what Joseph had said, and he replied: "Is it possible that I have been so deceived? But if Joseph says so, it is so."

About three weeks after this, Sidney was lying on his bed alone. An unseen power lifted him from the bed, threw him across the room, and tossed him from one side of the room to the other. The noise being heard in the adjoining room, his family went in to see what was the matter, and found him going from one side of the room to the other, from the effects of which Sidney was laid up for five or six weeks. Thus was Joseph's prediction in regard to him verified. (*TK*, p. 67)

2   The fundamental principles, government, and doctrine of the Church are vested in the keys of the kingdom. (*HC* 1:338)

3   The keys have to be brought from heaven whenever the Gospel is sent. When they are revealed from heaven, it is by Adam's authority.

Keys of the Kingdom of God
2   Letter to one of Jared Carter's brothers, written at the request of Jared Carter, Kirtland, 13 April 1833.
3   Discourse on the priesthood, given sometime before 8 August 1839, Commerce (Nauvoo). For a discussion on the dating of this discourse, see *WJS*, p. 22.

Daniel in his seventh chapter speaks of the Ancient of Days; he means the oldest man, our Father Adam, Michael, he will call his children together and hold a council with them to prepare them for the coming of the Son of Man. He (Adam) is the father of the human family, and presides over the spirits of all men, and all that have had the keys must stand before him in this grand council. . . .

. . . The Savior, Moses, and Elias, gave the keys to Peter, James, and John, on the mount, when they were transfigured before him. (HC 3:386–87)

4 [The Melchizedek Priesthood] holds the highest authority which pertains to the Priesthood, and the keys of the Kingdom of God in all ages of the world to the latest posterity on the earth. . . .

The next great, grand Patriarch {after Enoch} who held the keys of the Priesthood was Lamech. . . . The Priesthood continued from Lamech to Noah. . . .

Thus we behold the keys of this Priesthood consisted in obtaining the voice of Jehovah that He talked with him {Noah} in a familiar and friendly manner, that He continued to him the keys, the covenants, the power and the glory, with which He blessed Adam at the beginning; and the offering of sacrifice, which also shall be continued at the last time; for all the ordinances and duties that ever have been required by the Priesthood, under the directions and commandments of the Almighty in any of the dispensations, shall all be had in the last dispensation. . . .

Elijah was the last Prophet that held the keys of the Priesthood, and who will, before the last dispensation, restore the authority and deliver the keys of the Priesthood, in order that all the ordinances may be attended to in righteousness. . . . Why send Elijah? Because he holds the keys of the authority to administer in all the ordinances of the Priesthood; and without the authority is given, the ordinances could not be administered in righteousness. (HC 4:207, 210–11)

5 The Apostles in ancient times held the keys of this Priesthood— of the mysteries of the Kingdom of God, and consequently were enabled to unlock and unravel all things pertaining to the government

---

Keys of the Kingdom of God
4 Article on priesthood read at general conference, Nauvoo, 5 October 1840.
5 Editorial in the *Times and Seasons*, 1 April 1842.

of the Church, the welfare of society, the future destiny of men, and the agency, power and influence of spirits. (HC 4:574)

6   John [the Baptist] was a priest after his father, and held the keys of the Aaronic Priesthood. . . .

John was a priest after the order of Aaron, and had the keys of that priesthood, and came forth preaching repentance and baptism for the remission of sins, but at the same time cries out, "There cometh one mightier than I after me, the latchet of whose shoes I am not worthy to stoop down and unloose," and Christ came according to the words of John, and He was greater than John, because He held the keys of the Melchisedek Priesthood and kingdom of God. (HC 5:257, 258)

7   John [the Baptist], at that time, was the only legal administrator in the affairs of the kingdom there was then on the earth, and holding the keys of power. The Jews had to obey his instructions or be damned, by their own law; and Christ Himself fulfilled all righteousness in becoming obedient to the law which he had given to Moses on the mount, and thereby magnified it and made it honorable, instead of destroying it. The son of Zacharias wrested the keys, the kingdom, the power, the glory from the Jews, by the holy anointing and decree of heaven. (HC 5:261)

8   Any person that had seen the heavens opened knows that there are three personages in the heavens who hold the keys of power, and one presides over all. (HC 5:426)

9   The sacrifice required of Abraham in the offering up of Isaac, shows that if a man would attain to the keys of the kingdom of an endless life, he must sacrifice all things. . . .

. . . Those holding the fullness of the Melchizedek Priesthood are kings and priests of the Most High God, holding the keys of power and blessings. (HC 5:555)

Keys of the Kingdom of God

6   Sabbath address, Nauvoo, 22 January 1843.
7   Sabbath address, Nauvoo, 29 January 1843.
8   Sabbath address, Nauvoo, 11 June 1843.
9   Sabbath address, Nauvoo, 27 August 1843.

10 I shall read the 24th chapter of Matthew, and give it a literal rendering and reading; and when it is rightly understood, it will be edifying. {He then read and translated it from the German}.

I thought the very oddity of its rendering would be edifying anyhow—"*And it will preached be, the Gospel of the kingdom, in the whole world, to a witness over all people: and then will the end come.*" . . .

The Savior said when these tribulations should take place, it should be committed to a man who should be a witness over the whole world: the keys of knowledge, power and revelations should be revealed to a witness who should hold the testimony to the world. It has always been my province to dig up hidden mysteries—new things—for my hearers. Just at the time when some men think that I have no right to the keys of the Priesthood—just at that time I have the greatest right. . . .

All the testimony is that the Lord in the last days would commit the keys of the priesthood to a witness over all people. Has the Gospel of the kingdom commenced in the last days? And will God take it from the man until He takes him Himself? (HC 6:363–64)

Keys of Understanding

1 How vain and trifling have been our spirits, our conferences, our councils, our meetings, our private as well as public conversations—too low, too mean, too vulgar, too condescending for the dignified characters of the called and chosen of God, according to the purposes of His will, from before the foundation of the world! We are called to hold the keys of the mysteries of those things that have been kept hid from the foundation of the world until now. Some have tasted a little of these things, many of which are to be poured down from heaven upon the heads of babes; yea, upon the weak, obscure and despised ones of the earth. Therefore we beseech of you, brethren, that you bear with those who do not feel themselves more worthy than yourselves, while we exhort one another to a reformation with one and all, both old and young, teachers and taught, both high and low, rich and

---

Keys of the Kingdom of God
 10 Sabbath address, Nauvoo, 12 May 1844.

Keys of Understanding
  1   Letter to the Saints from Liberty Jail, 20–25 March 1839.

poor, bond and free, male and female; let honesty, and sobriety, and candor, and solemnity, and virtue, and pureness, and meekness, and simplicity crown our heads in every place; and in fine, become as little children, without malice, guile or hypocrisy. (HC 3:295–96)

2   A key: Every principle proceeding from God is eternal, and any principle which is not eternal is of the devil. The sun has no beginning or end; the rays which proceed from himself have no bounds, consequently are eternal. (*WJS*, p. 60; standardized)

3   If any person should ask me if I were a prophet, I should not deny it, as that would give me the lie; for, according to John, the testimony of Jesus is the spirit of prophecy; therefore, if I profess to be a witness or teacher, and have not the spirit of prophecy, which is the testimony of Jesus, I must be a false witness; but if I be a true teacher and witness, I must possess the spirit of prophecy, and that constitutes a prophet; and any man who says he is a teacher or a preacher of righteousness, and denies the spirit of prophecy, is a liar, and the truth is not in him; and by this key false teachers and imposters may be detected. (HC 5:215–16)

4   I have a key by which I understand the scriptures. I enquire, what was the question which drew out the answer, or caused Jesus to utter the parable? It is not national; it does not refer to Abraham, Israel or the Gentiles, in a national capacity, as some suppose. To ascertain its meaning, we must dig up the root and ascertain what it was that drew the saying out of Jesus. (HC 5:261)

5   First chapter, Second Epistle of Peter. The first four verses are the preface to the whole subject. There are three grand keys to unlock the whole subject. First what is the knowledge of God; second what is it to make our calling and election sure; third and last is how to make

---

Keys of Understanding

2   Lecture given at the Nauvoo Lyceum, 5 January 1841, as reported by William Clayton. (The lyceum met weekly at different locations in Nauvoo for several months, beginning 5 January 1841.)

3   Remarks to a group of politicians and lawyers, Springfield, Illinois, 1 January 1843.

4   Sabbath address, Nauvoo, 29 January 1843.

5   Sabbath address, Nauvoo, 21 May 1843, as reported by James Burgess.

our calling and election sure. Ans[wer]: it is to obtain a promise from God for myself that I shall have eternal life. That is the more sure word of prophecy. (*WJS*, p. 209; standardized)

Kindness

1   The kindness of a man should never be forgotten. (*HC* 1:444)

2   It should be the duty of the Elder to stand up boldly for the cause of Christ, and warn that people with one accord to repent and be baptized for the remission of sins, and for the Holy Ghost, always commanding them in the name of the Lord, in the spirit of meekness, to be kindly affectionate one toward another, that the fathers should be kind to their children, husbands to their wives, masters to their slaves or servants, children obedient to their parents, wives to their husbands, and slaves or servants to their masters. (*HC* 2:263–64)

3   To those who have suffered so much abuse, and borne the cruelties and insults of wicked men so long, on account of those principles which we have been instructed to teach to the world, a feeling of sympathy and kindness is something like the refreshing breeze and cooling stream at the present season of the year, and are, I assure you, duly appreciated by us. (*HC* 4:177)

4   When you go home, never give a cross or unkind word to your husbands, but let kindness, charity and love crown your works henceforward. (*HC* 4:607)

5   Nothing is so much calculated to lead people to forsake sin as to take them by the hand, and watch over them with tenderness. When persons manifest the least kindness and love to me, O what power it has over my mind, while the opposite course has a tendency to harrow up all the harsh feelings and depress the human mind. (*HC* 5:23–24)

Kindness
1   Kirtland, 19 November 1833.
2   Letter to the elders of the Church, Kirtland, 1 September 1835.
3   Letter to John C. Bennett, 8 August 1840, bidding him welcome to Nauvoo.
4   Remarks to the Relief Society, Nauvoo, 28 April 1842.
5   Remarks to the Relief Society, Nauvoo, 9 June 1842.

6   If a man fails in kindness, justice, and mercy, he will be damned. (*WJS*, p. 206; standardized)

7   Wise men ought to have understanding enough to conquer men with kindness.

   "A soft answer turneth away wrath," says the wise man; and it will be greatly to the credit of the Latter-day Saints to show the love of God, by now kindly treating those who may have, in an unconscious moment, done wrong; for truly said Jesus, Pray for thine enemies. (*HC* 6:219)

Kingdom of God

1   What constitutes the kingdom of God? Where there is a prophet, a priest, or a righteous man unto whom God gives His oracles, there is the kingdom of God; and where the oracles of God are not, there the kingdom of God is not. . . .

   Whenever men can find out the will of God and find an administrator legally authorized from God, there is the kingdom of God; but where these are not, the kingdom of God is not. All the ordinances, systems, and administrations on the earth are of no use to the children of men, unless they are ordained and authorized of God; for nothing will save a man but a legal administrator; for none others will be acknowledged either by God or angels. (*HC* 5:257, 259)

2   It is one thing to see the kingdom of God, and another thing to enter into it. We must have a change of heart to see the kingdom of God, and subscribe the articles of adoption to enter therein. (*HC* 6:58)

Kindness
   6   Sabbath address, Nauvoo, 21 May 1843, as reported by Martha Jane Knowlton Coray.
   7   Article entitled "Pacific Innuendo," Nauvoo, 17 February 1844.

Kingdom of God
   1   Sabbath address, Nauvoo, 22 January 1843.
   2   Sabbath address, Nauvoo, 15 October 1843.

Kingdom of Heaven

1   In the 22nd chapter of Luke's account of the Messiah, we find the kingdom of heaven likened unto a king who made a marriage for his son. That this son was the Messiah will not be disputed, since it was the kingdom of heaven that was represented in the parable; and that the Saints, or those who are found faithful to the Lord, are the individuals who will be found worthy to inherit a seat at the marriage-supper, is evident from the sayings of John in the Revelation where he represents the sound which he heard in heaven to be like a great multitude, or like the voice of mighty thunderings, saying, the Lord God Omnipotent reigneth. (*HC* 2:19)

2   *Minutes:* We wish you to understand that your duty requires you to seek first the kingdom of heaven and its righteousness; that is, attend to the first things first, and then all things will be added. (*HC* 2:240)

3   And again, another parable put He forth unto them, having an allusion to the Kingdom that should be set up, just previous to or at the time of the harvest, which reads as follows—"The Kingdom of Heaven is like a grain of mustard seed, which a man took and sowed in his field: which indeed is the least of all seeds: but, when it is grown, it is the greatest among herbs, and becometh a tree, so that the birds of the air come and lodge in the branches thereof." Now we can discover plainly that this figure is given to represent the Church as it shall come forth in the last days. Behold, the Kingdom of Heaven is likened unto it. . . .

   The Kingdom of heaven is like unto a mustard seed. Behold, then is not this the Kingdom of heaven that is raising its head in the last days in the majesty of its God, even the Church of the Latter-day Saints, like an impenetrable, immovable rock in the midst of the mighty deep, exposed to the storms and tempests of Satan, but has,

---

Kingdom of Heaven

   1   Letter to the brethren scattered from Zion, Kirtland, 22 January 1834.
   2   Minutes of the high council at Kirtland, 4 August 1835. B. H. Roberts notes that "it appears that the minutes of this High Council at Kirtland were intended to be sent to the Twelve as a communication" (*HC* 2:241).
   3   Letter to the elders of the Church, Kirtland, 1 September 1835.

thus far, remained steadfast, and is still braving the mountain waves of opposition, which are driven by the tempestuous winds of sinking crafts, which have {dashed} and are still dashing with tremendous foam across its triumphant brow. (HC 2:268)

4   Of all the other criterions whereby we may judge of the vanity of these things, one will be always found true, namely, that we will always find such characters glorying in their own wisdom and their own works; whilst the humble Saint gives all the glory to God the Father, and to His Son Jesus Christ, whose yoke is easy and whose burden is light, and who told His disciples that unless they became like little children they could not enter the Kingdom of Heaven. (HC 4:8)

5   *Clerk's Report:* Brother Wilkie now feels anxious to do right in all things, and especially to pay his tithing to the full. President Joseph showed him the principles of consecration and the means whereby he might realize the fullness of the blessings of the celestial kingdom. . . .

    May the Lord grant his Spirit and peace to abide upon Brother Wilkie and his companion through the remainder of their days; may their hearts expand and become enlarged to receive the fullness of the blessings of the kingdom of heaven. (HC 6:265)

Knowledge

1   Many, having a zeal not according to knowledge, and not understanding the pure principles of the doctrine of the Church, have, no doubt, in the heat of enthusiasm, taught and said many things which were derogatory to the genuine character and principles of the Church; and for these things we are heartily sorry, and would apologize, if apology would do any good. (HC 2:255)

Kingdom of Heaven
   4   A letter to Isaac Galland, Commerce (Nauvoo), 11 September 1839.
   5   Instruction and blessing for John Wilkie, Nauvoo, 15 March 1844.

Knowledge
   1   Letter to the elders of the Church, Kirtland, 1 September 1835.

2   Spent this day at home, endeavoring to treasure up knowledge for the benefit of my calling. . . .

At home. Continued my studies. O may God give me learning, even language; and endue me with qualifications to magnify His name while I live. (*HC* 2:344)

3   Many . . . dishonor themselves and the Church, and bring persecution swiftly upon us, in consequence of their zeal without knowledge. (*HC* 2:394)

4   *Words of Howard Coray:* Knowing the meagerness of his [the Prophet's] education, I was truly gratified at seeing his great ease, even in the company of the most scientific minds, and the ready, off-hand manner in which he would answer their questions. I heard him say that God had given him the key of knowledge by which he could trace any subject through all its ramifications. (*TK*, pp. 133–34)

5   [The Melchizedek Priesthood] is the channel through which all knowledge, doctrine, the plan of salvation, and every important matter is revealed from heaven. (*HC* 4:207)

6   The "University of the City of Nauvoo" will enable us to teach our children wisdom, to instruct them in all the knowledge and learning, in the arts, sciences, and learned professions. We hope to make this institution one of the great lights of the world, and by and through it to diffuse that kind of knowledge which will be of practicable utility, and for the public good, and also for private and individual happiness. (*HC* 4:269)

7   As far as we degenerate from God, we descend to the devil and lose knowledge, and without knowledge we cannot be saved. . . .

Knowledge
  2   Kirtland, 22 December 1835.
  3   Remarks at a meeting of several priesthood quorums in the schoolroom of the Kirtland Temple, 12 February 1836.
  4   Recollection of Howard Coray, Nauvoo, about 1840, journal of Howard Coray, BYU Library.
  5   Article on priesthood read at general conference, Nauvoo, 5 October 1840.
  6   Proclamation of the First Presidency, Nauvoo, 15 January 1841.
  7   Sabbath address, Nauvoo, 10 April 1842.

... A man is saved no faster than he gets knowledge, for if he does not get knowledge, he will be brought into captivity by some evil power in the other world, as evil spirits will have more knowledge, and consequently more power than many men who are on the earth. Hence it needs revelation to assist us, and give us knowledge of the things of God. (*HC* 4:588)

8   The exaltation and happiness of any community, goes hand in hand with the knowledge possessed by the people, when applied to laudable ends; whereupon we can exclaim like the wise man; righteousness exalteth a nation; for righteousness embraces knowledge and knowledge is power. (*T&S* 3:889)

9   We cannot keep all the commandments without first knowing them, and we cannot expect to know all, or more than we now know unless we comply with or keep those we have already received. (*HC* 5:135)

10   If we get puffed up by thinking that we have much knowledge, we are apt to get a contentious spirit, and correct knowledge is necessary to cast out that spirit.
   The evil of being puffed up with correct (though useless) knowledge is not so great as the evil of contention. Knowledge does away with darkness, suspense and doubt; for these cannot exist where knowledge is. . . .
   In knowledge there is power. God has more power than all other beings, because he has greater knowledge; and hence he knows how to subject all other beings to Him. He has power over all. (*HC* 5:340)

11   It is not wisdom that we should have all knowledge at once presented before us; but that we should have a little at a time; then we can comprehend it. . . .
   Add to your faith knowledge, &c. The principle of knowledge is the principle of salvation. This principle can be comprehended by the faithful and diligent; and every one that does not obtain knowledge

Knowledge
   8   Editorial in the *Times and Seasons*, 15 August 1842.
   9   Essay on happiness, Nauvoo, 27 August 1842.
   10   General conference address, Nauvoo, 8 April 1843.
   11   Sabbath address at Yelrome (Morley's Settlement), Illinois, 14 May 1843.

sufficient to be saved will be condemned. The principle of salvation is given us through the knowledge of Jesus Christ. (HC 5:387)

12 When a man is reined up continually by excitement, he becomes strong and gains power and knowledge; but when he relaxes for a season, he loses much of his power and knowledge. (HC 5:389)

13 Knowledge is power; and the man who has the most knowledge has the greatest power. (HC 5:392)

14 The Lord deals with this people as a tender parent with a child, communicating light and intelligence and the knowledge of his ways as they can bear it. . . .

. . . There could not anything be given, pertaining to life and godliness, without knowledge. . . .

Salvation is for a man to be saved from all his enemies; for until a man can triumph over death, he is not saved. A knowledge of the priesthood alone will do this. (HC 5:402, 403)

15 There are a great many wise men and women too in our midst who are too wise to be taught; therefore they must die in their ignorance, and in the resurrection they will find their mistake. Many seal up the door of heaven by saying, So far God may reveal and I will believe. (HC 5:424)

16 When God offers a blessing or knowledge to a man, and he refuses to receive it, he will be damned. The Israelites prayed that God would speak to Moses and not to them; in consequence of which he cursed them with a carnal law. (HC 5:555)

17 All men know that they must die. And it is important that we should understand the reasons and causes of our exposure to the vicissitudes of life and of death, and the designs and purposes of God in our

---

Knowledge
12 Sabbath address at Yelrome (Morley's Settlement), Illinois, 14 May 1843.
13 Items of doctrine given at Ramus, Illinois, 17 May 1843.
14 Sabbath address, Nauvoo, 21 May 1843.
15 Sabbath address, Nauvoo, 11 June 1843.
16 Sabbath address, Nauvoo, 27 August 1843.
17 Remarks upon the death of James Adams, Nauvoo, 9 October 1843.

coming into the world, our sufferings here, and our departure hence. What is the object of our coming into existence, then dying and falling away, to be here no more? It is but reasonable to suppose that God would reveal something in reference to the matter, and it is a subject we ought to study more than any other. We ought to study it day and night, for the world is ignorant in reference to their true condition and relation. If we have any claim on our Heavenly Father for anything, it is for knowledge on this important subject. Could we read and comprehend all that has been written from the days of Adam, on the relation of man to God and angels in a future state, we should know very little about it. Reading the experience of others, or the revelation given to them, can never give us a comprehensive view of our condition and true relation to God. Knowledge of these things can only be obtained by experience through the ordinances of God set forth for that purpose. Could you gaze into heaven five minutes, you would know more than you would by reading all that ever was written on the subject. (HC 6:50)

18 Angels have advanced higher in knowledge and power than spirits.
    . . . I anointed him [Judge Adams, now dead] to the patriarchal power—to receive the keys of knowledge and power, by revelation to himself. (HC 6:51–52)

19 We have received a portion of knowledge from God by immediate revelation, and from the same source we can receive all knowledge. . . .
    . . . There has been a great difficulty in getting anything into the heads of this generation. It has been like splitting hemlock knots with a corn-dodger for a wedge, and a pumpkin for a beetle. Even the Saints are slow to understand. (HC 6:183, 184)

20 If we start right, it is easy to go right all the time; but if we start wrong we may go wrong, and it will be a hard matter to get right. (HC 6:303)

21 Knowledge saves a man; and in the world of spirits no man can be exalted but by knowledge. So long as a man will not give heed to the

---

Knowledge
18 Remarks upon the death of James Adams, Nauvoo, 9 October 1843.
19 Sabbath address, Nauvoo, 21 January 1844.
20 King Follett Discourse, Nauvoo, 7 April 1844.
21 King Follett Discourse, Nauvoo, 7 April 1844.

commandments, he must abide without salvation. If a man has knowledge, he can be saved; although, if he has been guilty of great sins, he will be punished for them. But when he consents to obey the gospel, whether here or in the world of spirits, he is saved. (HC 6:314)

22 I say there are Gods many and Lords many, but to us only one, and we are to be in subjection to that one, and no man can limit the bounds or the eternal existence of eternal time. Hath he beheld the eternal world, and is he authorized to say that there is only one God? He makes himself a fool if he thinks or says so, and there is an end of his career or progress in knowledge. He cannot obtain all knowledge, for he has sealed up the gate to it. (HC 6:474–75)

23 Our lives have already become jeopardized by revealing the wicked and bloodthirsty purposes of our enemies; and for the future we must cease to do so. All we have said about them is truth, but it is not always wise to relate all the truth. Even Jesus, the Son of God had to refrain from doing so, and had to restrain His feelings many times for the safety of Himself and His followers, and had to conceal the righteous purposes of His heart in relation to many things pertaining to His Father's kingdom. When still a boy He had all the intelligence necessary to enable Him to rule and govern the kingdom of the Jews, and could reason with the wisest and most profound doctors of law and divinity, and make their theories and practice appear like folly compared with the wisdom He possessed; but He was a boy only, and lacked physical strength even to defend His own person, and was subject to cold, to hunger and to death. So it is with the Church of Jesus Christ of Latter-day Saints; we have the revelations of Jesus, and the knowledge within us is sufficient to organize a righteous government upon the earth, and to give universal peace to all mankind, if they would receive it, but we lack the physical strength, as did our Savior when a child, to defend our principles, and we have of necessity to be afflicted, persecuted and smitten, and to bear it patiently until Jacob is of age, then he will take care of himself. (HC 6:608–9)

Knowledge
22 Sabbath address, Nauvoo, 16 June 1844.
23 Carthage Jail, 27 June 1844.

Lamanites

See also INDIANS

1 *Words of Lucy Mack Smith:* During our evening conversations, Joseph would occasionally give us some of the most amusing recitals that could be imagined. He would describe the ancient inhabitants of this continent, their dress, mode of traveling, and the animals upon which they rode; their cities, their buildings, with every particular; their mode of warfare; and also their religious worship. This he would do with as much ease, seemingly, as if he had spent his whole life among them. (*HJS*, p. 83)

2 We discovered some antiquities about one mile west of the camp, consisting of stone mounds, apparently erected in square piles, though somewhat decayed and obliterated by the weather of many years. These mounds were probably erected by the aborigines of the land, to secrete treasures. (*HC* 3:37)

3 *Report of Wilford Woodruff:* The Spirit of God rested upon the Lamanites, especially the orator. Joseph was much affected and shed tears. He arose and said unto them: "I have heard your words. They are true. The Great Spirit has told you the truth. I am your friend and brother, and I wish to do you good. Your fathers were once a great people. They worshiped the Great Spirit. The Great Spirit did them good. He was their friend; but they left the Great Spirit, and would not hear his words or keep them. The Great Spirit left them, and they began to kill one another, and they have been poor and afflicted until now.

"The Great Spirit has given me a book, and told me that you will soon be blessed again. The Great Spirit will soon begin to talk with you and your children. This is the book which your fathers made. I wrote upon it (showing them the Book of Mormon). This tells what you will have to do. I now want you to begin to pray to the Great

---

Lamanites
1 Lucy Mack Smith's account of the Prophet's familiarity with ancient Book of Mormon peoples.
2 The Prophet and others were involved in selecting lands for the settlement of the Saints in northern Missouri, 22 April 1838.
3 Interview with several Potawatomi chiefs, Nauvoo, 2 July 1843.

Spirit. I want you to make peace with one another, and do not kill any more Indians: it is not good. Do not kill white men; it is not good; but ask the Great Spirit for what you want, and it will not be long before the Great Spirit will bless you, and you will cultivate the earth and build good houses like white men. We will give you something to eat and to take home with you."

When the Prophet's words were interpreted to the chiefs, they all said it was good. The chief asked, "How many moons would it be before the Great Spirit would bless them?" He {Joseph} told them, Not a great many. (HC 5:480–81)

4   At one p.m., had a talk with the Sac and Fox Indians in my back kitchen. They said—"When our fathers first came here, this land was inhabited by the Spanish; when the Spaniards were driven off, the French came, and then the English and Americans; and our fathers talked a great deal with the Big Spirit." They complained that they had been robbed of their lands by the whites, and cruelly treated.

I told them I knew they had been wronged, but that we had bought this land and paid our money for it. I advised them not to sell any more land, but to cultivate peace with the different tribes and with all men, as the Great Spirit wanted them to be united and to live in peace. "The Great Spirit has enabled me to find a book {showing them the Book of Mormon}, which told me about your fathers, and Great Spirit told me, 'You must send to all the tribes that you can, and tell them to live in peace;' and when any of our people come to see you, I want you to treat them as we treat you."

At 3 p.m., the Indians commenced a war dance in front of my old house. Our people commenced with music and firing cannon. After the dance, which lasted about two hours, the firing of cannon closed the exercise, and with our music marched back to the office. Before they commenced dancing, the Saints took up a collection to get the Indians food. (HC 6:402)

5   *Words of Benjamin F. Johnson:* He [Joseph Smith] taught us that the Saints would fill the great West, and through Mexico and Central and South America we would do a great work for the redemption of the remnant of Jacob. (TK, pp. 95–96)

Lamanites
   4   Nauvoo, 23 May 1844.
   5   Letter of Benjamin F. Johnson to George S. Gibbs, 1903.

Lamb's Book of Life

1   Until we have perfect love we are liable to fall, and when we have a testimony that our names are sealed in the Lamb's book of life we have perfect love, and then it is impossible for false Christs to deceive us. (*FWR*, p. 23; standardized)

2   If the saints in the days of the Apostles were privileged to take the saints for example and lay hold of the same promises and attain to the same exalted privileges of knowing that their names were writen in the Lamb's book of life, and that they were sealed there as a perpetual memorial before the face of the Most High, will not the same faithfulness, the same purity of heart, and the same faith bring the same assurance of eternal life, and that in the same manner, to the children of men now in this age of the world? (*PWJS*, p. 300; standardized)

3   Let this prayer ever be recorded before Thy face. Give Thy Holy Spirit unto my brethren, unto whom I write; send Thine angels to guard them, and deliver them from all evil; and when they turn their faces toward Zion, and bow down before Thee and pray, may their sins never come up before Thy face, neither have place in the book of Thy remembrance; and may they depart from all their iniquities. Provide food for them as Thou doest for the ravens; provide clothing to cover their nakedness, and houses that they may dwell therein; give unto them friends in abundance, and let their names be recorded in the Lamb's book of life, eternally before Thy face. Amen. (*HC* 1:456)

Language

1   This day I have been walking through the most splendid part of the City of New York. The buildings are truly great and wonderful to the astonishing of every beholder, and the language of my heart is like

---

Lamb's Book of Life
1   Minutes of a conference held at Orange, Ohio, 25 October 1831.
2   Letter to Silas Smith, the Prophet's uncle, Kirtland, 26 September 1833.
3   A letter to the exiled Saints in Missouri, Kirtland, 10 December 1833.

Language
1   Letter to Emma Smith from New York City, 13 October 1832.

this: Can the great God of all the earth, maker of all things magnificent and splendid, be displeased with man for all these great inventions sought out by them? My answer is no, it cannot be, seeing these works are calculated to make men comfortable, wise, and happy; therefore, not for the works can the Lord be displeased, only against man is the anger of the Lord kindled because they give him not the glory; therefore their iniquities shall be visited upon their heads and their works shall be burned up with unquenchable fire. (*PWJS*, pp. 252–53; standardized)

2   Oh, Lord, deliver us in due time from the little, narrow prison, almost as it were, total darkness of paper, pen and ink;—and a crooked, broken, scattered and imperfect language. (HC 1:299)

3   If this life were all, we should be led to query, whether or not there was really any substance in existence, and we might with propriety say, "Let us eat, drink, and be merry, for to morrow we die!" But if this life is all, then why this constant toiling, why this continual warfare, and why this unceasing trouble? But this life is not all, the voice of *reason*, the language of *inspiration*, and the Spirit of the living God, our Creator, teaches us, as we hold the record of truth in our hands, that this is not the case, that this is not so; for, the heavens declare the glory of a God, and the firmament showeth His handiwork; and a moment's reflection is sufficient to teach every man of common intelligence, that all these are not the mere productions of *chance*, nor could they be supported by any power less than an Almighty hand. . . . Man is unable, without assistance beyond what has been given to those before, of expressing in words the greatness of this important subject [the gospel]. (HC 2:14)

4   But when you are endowed and prepared to preach the Gospel to all nations, kindred, and tongues, in their own languages, you must faithfully warn all, and bind up the testimony, and seal up the law, and the destroying angel will follow close at your heels, and exercise his tremendous mission upon the children of disobedience; and destroy

Language
   2   Letter to William W. Phelps in Missouri, written from Kirtland, 27 November 1832.
   3   Letter to the brethren scattered from Zion, Kirtland, 22 January 1834.
   4   Instructions to the Twelve, Kirtland, 12 November 1835.

the workers of iniquity, while the Saints will be gathered out from among them, and stand in holy places ready to meet the Bridegroom when he comes. (HC 2:309)

5   One of the most important points in the faith of the Church of the Latter-day Saints, through the fullness of the everlasting Gospel, is the gathering of Israel (of whom the Lamanites constitute a part)— that happy time when Jacob shall go up to the house of the Lord, to worship Him in spirit and in truth, to live in holiness; when the Lord will restore His judges as at the first, and His counselors as at the beginning; when every man may sit under his own vine and fig tree, and there will be none to molest or make afraid; when He will turn to them a pure language, and the earth will be filled with sacred knowledge, as the waters cover the great deep; when it shall not longer be said, the Lord lives that brought up the children of Israel out of the land of Egypt, but the Lord lives that brought up the children of Israel from the land of the north, and from all the lands whither He has driven them. (HC 2:357)

6   *19 January 1836.* This day we commenced reading in our Hebrew Bibles with much success. It seems as if the Lord opens our minds in a marvelous manner, to understand His word in the original language. (HC 2:376)

7   *4 February 1836.* We have a great want of books, but are determined to do the best we can. May the Lord help us to obtain this language, that we may read the Scriptures in the language in which they were given. (HC 2:391)

8   *17 February 1836.* Attended the school and read and translated with my class as usual. My soul delights in reading the word of the Lord in the original, and I am determined to pursue the study of the languages, until I shall become master of them, if I am permitted to live long enough. At any rate, so long as I do live, I am determined to make this my object; and with the blessing of God, I shall succeed to my satisfaction. (HC 2:396)

Language
5   Meeting of the high council at Kirtland, 6 January 1836.
6–8 References to the Hebrew school held in Kirtland and the Prophet's interest in learning languages, January–February 1836.

9 With emotions known only to God do I write this letter. The contemplations of the mind under these circumstances defy the pen or tongue or angels to describe or paint to the human being who never experienced what we experience. (*PWJS*, p. 425; standardized)

10 We may come to Jesus to ask Him; He will know all about it; if He comes to a little child, He will adapt himself to the language and capacity of a little child. (*HC* 3:392)

11 In this important and interesting book [the Book of Mormon] the history of ancient America is unfolded, from its first settlement by a colony that came from the Tower of Babel, at the confusion of languages to the beginning of the fifth century of the Christian Era. (*HC* 4:537)

12 O that I had the language of the archangel to express my feelings once to my friends! But I never expect to in this life. (*HC* 5:362)

13 Peter penned the most sublime language of any of the apostles. (*HC* 5:392)

Last Days

1 The day was spent in a very agreeable manner, in giving and receiving knowledge which appertained to this last kingdom—it being just 1800 years since the Savior laid down His life that men might

---

Language
9 Letter to Emma Smith from Liberty Jail, 4 April 1839. Original copy at Yale University library.
10 Discourse on the priesthood, given sometime before 8 August 1839, Commerce (Nauvoo). For a discussion on the dating of this discourse, see *WJS*, p. 22.
11 Letter to John Wentworth, editor of the *Chicago Democrat*, Nauvoo, 1 March 1842.
12 Remarks upon the death of Lorenzo D. Barnes, Nauvoo, 16 April 1843.
13 Items of doctrine given at Ramus, Illinois, 17 May 1843.

Last Days
1 Reference to instructions given at a meeting at the ferry on the Big Blue River, Jackson County, Missouri, 6 April 1833.

have everlasting life, and only three years since the Church had come out of the wilderness, preparatory for the last dispensation. (*HC* 1:337)

2   For God hath so ordained, that His work shall be cut short in righteousness, in the last days. (HC 2:262)

3   Now let our readers mark the expression—"the field is the world, the tares are the children of the wicked one, the enemy that sowed them is the devil, the harvest is the end of the world, {let them carefully mark this expression—*the end of the world*,} and the reapers are the angels."

Now men cannot have any possible grounds to say that this is figurative, or that it does not mean what it says; for he is now explaining what He has previously spoken in parables; and according to this language, the end of the world is the destruction of the wicked, the harvest and the end of the world have an allusion directly to the human family in the last days, instead of the earth, as many have imagined; and that which shall precede the coming of the Son of Man, and the restitution of all things spoken of by the mouth of all the holy prophets since the world began. (HC 2:271)

4   We have to congratulate the Saints on the progress of the great work of the "last days," for not only has it spread through the length and breadth of this vast continent, but on the continent of Europe, and on the islands of the sea, it is spreading in a manner entirely unprecedented in the annals of time. (HC 4:267)

5   Truly this is a day long to be remembered by the Saints of the last days,—a day in which the God of heaven has begun to restore the ancient order of His kingdom unto His servants and His people,—a day in which all things are concurring to bring about the completion of the fullness of the Gospel, a fullness of the dispensation of dispensations,

---

Last Days

2   Letter to the elders of the Church, Kirtland, 1 September 1835.

3   Letter to the elders of the Church, Kirtland, 1 September 1835. Here reference is being made to the parable of the wheat and the tares (see Matthew 13:24–30, 36–43).

4   Proclamation of the First Presidency, Nauvoo, 15 January 1841.

5   Nauvoo, 6 January 1842.

even the fullness of times; a day in which God has begun to make manifest and set in order in His Church those things which have been, and those things which the ancient prophets and wise men desired to see but died without beholding them; a day in which those things begin to be made manifest, which have been hid from before the foundation of the world, and which Jehovah has promised should be made known in His own due time unto His servants, to prepare the earth for the return of His glory, even a celestial glory, and a kingdom of Priests and kings to God and the Lamb, forever, on Mount Zion. (HC 4:492–93)

6   This book [the Book of Mormon] also tells us that . . . the last of their prophets who existed among them was commanded to write an abridgment of their prophecies, history, &c, and to hide it up in the earth, and that it should come forth and be united with the Bible for the accomplishment of the purposes of God in the last days. (HC 4:538)

7   Brother Shearer inquired the meaning of the "little leaven which a woman hid in the three measures of meal." I replied, it alluded expressly to the last days, when there should be little faith on the earth, and it should leaven the whole world; also there shall be safety in Zion and Jerusalem, and in the remnants whom the Lord our God shall call. The three measures refer directly to the Priesthood, truth springing up on a fixed principle, to the three in the Grand Presidency, confining the oracles to a certain head on the principle of three. (HC 5:207)

8   In the former days God sent His servants to fight; but in the last days, He has promised to fight the battle Himself. (HC 5:356)

9   Many things are insoluble to the children of men in the last days: for instance, that God should raise the dead, and forgetting that things have been hid from before the foundation of the world, which are to be revealed to babes in the last days. (HC 5:424)

Last Days

6   Letter to John Wentworth, editor of the *Chicago Democrat*, Nauvoo, 1 March 1842.
7   Nauvoo, 20 December 1842.
8   Remarks to Saints newly arrived from England, Nauvoo, 13 April 1843.
9   Sabbath address, Nauvoo, 11 June 1843.

10 Our worthy Brother, Elder George J. Adams, has been appointed by the First Presidency of the Church of Jesus Christ of Latter-day Saints at Nauvoo to present to them the importance, as well as the things connected with his mission to Russia, to introduce the fullness of the Gospel to the people of that vast empire, and also to which is attached some of the most important things concerning the advancement and building up of the kingdom of God in the last days, which cannot be explained at this time. (*HC* 6:41)

11 In the days of Noah, God destroyed the world by a flood, and He has promised to destroy it by fire in the last days: but before it should take place, Elijah should first come and turn the hearts of the fathers to the children, &c. (*HC* 6:251)

12 Woe, woe be to that man or set of men who lift up their hands against God and His witness in these last days: for they shall deceive almost the very chosen ones! (*HC* 6:364)

Law of the Harvest

1 We can only say, that if an anticipation of the joys of the celestial glory, as witnessed to the hearts of the humble is not sufficient, we will leave to yourselves the result of your own diligence; for God ere long, will call all His servants before Him, and there from His own hand they will receive a just recompense and a righteous reward for all their labors. (*HC* 2:14–15)

2 Do good and work righteousness with an eye single to the glory of God, and you shall reap your reward when the Lord recompenses every one according to his work. (*HC* 2:229–30)

Last Days

 10 Announcement published in the *Times and Seasons*, 1 October 1843.

 11 Sabbath address, Nauvoo, 10 March 1844.

 12 Sabbath address, Nauvoo, 12 May 1844.

Law of the Harvest

 1 Letter to the brethren scattered from Zion, Kirtland, 22 January 1834.

 2 Letter to the Saints in Missouri published in the *Messenger and Advocate*, June 1835.

3   Remember that whatsoever measure you mete out to others, it shall be measured to you again. (HC 3:233)

4   He that sows sparingly, shall also reap sparingly, so that if the brethren want a plentiful harvest, they will do well to be at the place of labor in good season in the morning, bringing all necessary tools. (HC 4:517)

Law of Moses

1   It is said again, in Gal. iii:19, that the law (of Moses, or the Levitical law) was "added" because of transgression. What, we ask, was this law added to, if it was not added to the Gospel? It must be plain that it was added to the Gospel, since we learn that they had the Gospel preached to them. (HC 2:17)

2   Again, if men sin wilfully after they have received the knowledge of the truth, there remaineth no more sacrifice for sin, but a certain fearful looking for of judgment and fiery indignation to come, which shall devour these adversaries. For he who despised Moses' law died without mercy under two or three witnesses. Of how much more severe punishment suppose ye, shall he be thought worthy, who hath sold his brother, and denied the new and everlasting covenant by which he was sanctified, calling it an unholy thing, and doing despite to the Spirit of grace. (HC 3:232)

3   It is not to be understood that the law of Moses will be established again with all its rites and variety of ceremonies; this has never been spoken of by the Prophets; but those things which existed prior to Moses' day, namely, sacrifice, will be continued. (HC 4:212)

Law of the Harvest
  3   Letter to the Church from Liberty Jail, 16 December 1838.
  4   Announcement regarding work on the Nauvoo Temple, 21 February 1842.

Law of Moses
  1   Letter to the brethren scattered from Zion, Kirtland, 22 January 1834.
  2   Letter to the Church from Liberty Jail, 16 December 1838.
  3   Article on priesthood read at general conference, Nauvoo, 5 October 1840.

4 All priesthood is Melchizedek; but there are different portions or degrees of it. That portion which brought Moses to speak with God face to face was taken away; but that which brought the ministry of angels remained. All the prophets had the Melchizedek Priesthood and [were] ordained by God himself. (*WJS*, p. 59; standardized)

5 When the children of Israel were chosen with Moses at their head, they were to be a peculiar people, among whom God should place His name; their motto was: "The Lord is our lawgiver; the Lord is our Judge; the Lord is our King, and He shall reign over us." While in this state they might truly say, "Happy is that people, whose God is the Lord." Their government was a theocracy; they had God to make their laws, and men chosen by Him to administer them; He was their God, and they were His people. Moses received the word of the Lord from God Himself; he was the mouth of God to Aaron, and Aaron taught the people, in both civil and ecclesiastical affairs; they were both one, there was no distinction; so will it be when the purposes of God shall be accomplished: when "the Lord shall be King over the whole earth," and "Jerusalem His throne." "The law shall go forth from Zion, and the word of the Lord from Jerusalem." (*HC* 5:64)

6 Moses [was] the man who wrote of Christ, and brought forth the law by commandment, as a school master to bring men to Christ. (*T&S* 3:905)

7 John [the Baptist], at that time, was the only legal administrator in the affairs of the kingdom there was then on the earth, and holding the keys of power. The Jews had to obey his instructions or be damned, by their own law; and Christ Himself fulfilled all righteousness in becoming obedient to the law which he had given to Moses on the mount, and thereby magnified it and made it honorable, instead of destroying it. (*HC* 5:261)

Law of Moses
   4 Lecture given at the Nauvoo Lyceum, 5 January 1841, as reported by William Clayton. (The lyceum met weekly at different locations in Nauvoo for several months, beginning 5 January 1841.)
   5 Editorial in the *Times and Seasons*, 15 July 1842.
   6 Editorial in the *Times and Seasons*, 1 September 1842.
   7 Sabbath address, Nauvoo, 29 January 1843.

8   The law revealed to Moses in Horeb never was revealed to the children of Israel as a nation. (*HC* 5:555)

Laws of God

1   It is not our intention by these remarks, to attempt to place the law of man on a parallel with the law of heaven; because we do not consider that it is formed in the same wisdom and propriety; neither do we consider that it is sufficient in itself to bestow anything on man in comparison with the law of heaven, even should it promise it. . . . The law of heaven is presented to man, and as such guarantees to all who obey it a reward far beyond any earthly consideration; though it does not promise that the believer in every age should be exempt from the afflictions and troubles arising from different sources in consequence of the acts of wicked men on earth. . . . Then, certainly, if the law of man is binding upon man when acknowledged, how much more must the law of heaven be! And as much as the law of heaven is more perfect than the law of man, so much greater must be the reward if obeyed. The law of man promises safety in temporal life; but the law of God promises that life which is eternal, even an inheritance at God's own right hand, secure from all the powers of the wicked one. . . .

As we previously remarked, all well established and properly organized governments have certain fixed and prominent laws for the regulation and management of the same. If man has grown to wisdom and is capable of discerning the propriety of laws to govern nations, what less can be expected from the Ruler and Upholder of the universe? Can we suppose that He has a kingdom without laws? Or do we believe that it is composed of an innumerable company of beings who are entirely beyond all law? Consequently have need of nothing to govern or regulate them? Would not such ideas to be a reproach to our Great Parent, and at variance with His glorious intelligence? Would it

---

Law of Moses
   8   Sabbath address, Nauvoo, 27 August 1843. The "law" referred to here is undoubtedly the fulness of the gospel, written on the first tables of stone, which Moses broke. The second set contained the law of Moses. (See JST, Exodus 32:15–19; 34:1–2)

Laws of God
   1   Letter to the brethren scattered from Zion, Kirtland, 22 January 1834.

not be asserting that man had found out a secret beyond Deity? That he had learned that it was good to have laws, while God after existing from eternity and having power to create man, had not found out that it was proper to have laws for His government? We admit that God is the great source and fountain from whence proceeds all good; that He is perfect intelligence, and that His wisdom is alone sufficient to govern and regulate the mighty creations and worlds which shine and blaze with such magnificence and splendor over our heads, as though touched with His finger and moved by His Almighty word. And if so, it is done and regulated by law; for without law all must certainly fall into chaos. . . . God is the source of all good; consequently, then, he was the first Author of law, or the principle of it, to mankind. (HC 2:7, 8, 12, 13)

2   My soul delighteth in the law of the Lord, for He forgiveth my sins, and will confound mine enemies. (HC 2:46)

3   God has made certain decrees which are fixed and immovable; for instance,—God set the sun, the moon, and the stars in the heavens, and gave them their laws, conditions and bounds, which they cannot pass, except by His commandments; they all move in perfect harmony in their sphere and order, and are as lights, wonders and signs unto us. The sea also has its bounds which it cannot pass. (HC 4:554)

4   He [God] will judge them, "not according to what they have not, but according to what they have," those who have lived without law, will be judged without law, and those who have a law, will be judged by that law. (HC 4:596)

5   The Almighty God has taught me the principle of law. (HC 5:471)

6   The organization of the spiritual and heavenly worlds, and of spiritual and heavenly beings, was agreeable to the most perfect order and

---

Laws of God
2   Kirtland, 1 April 1834.
3   Sabbath address, Nauvoo, 20 March 1842.
4   Editorial in the *Times and Seasons*, 15 April 1842.
5   Address regarding his arrest at Dixon, Illinois, Nauvoo, 30 June 1843.
6   Remarks upon the death of James Adams, Nauvoo, 9 October 1843.

harmony: their limits and bounds were fixed irrevocably, and voluntarily subscribed to in their heavenly estate by themselves, and were by our first parents subscribed to upon the earth. Hence the importance of embracing and subscribing to principles of eternal truth by all men upon the earth that expect eternal life. (HC 6:51)

Laws of the Land

1   Make yourselves acquainted with the commandments of the Lord, and the laws of the state, and govern yourselves accordingly. (HC 1:341)

2   All regularly organized and well established governments have certain laws by which, more or less, the innocent are protected and the guilty punished. The fact admitted, that certain laws are good, equitable and just, ought to be binding upon the individual who admits this, and lead him to observe in the strictest manner an obedience to those laws. These laws when violated, or broken by the individual, must, in justice, convict his mind with a double force, if possible, of the extent and magnitude of his crime; because he could have no plea of ignorance to produce; and his act of transgression was openly committed against light and knowledge. But the individual who may be ignorant and imperceptibly transgresses or violates laws, though the voice of the country requires that he should suffer, yet he will never feel that remorse of conscience that the other will, and that keen, cutting reflection will never rise in his breast that otherwise would, had he done the deed, or committed the offense in full conviction that he was breaking the law of his country, and having previously acknowledged the same to be just. . . . The laws of men may guarantee to a people protection in the honorable pursuits of this life, and the temporal happiness arising from a protection against unjust insults and injuries; and when this is said, all is said, that can be in truth, of the power, extent, and influence of the laws of men, exclusive of the law of God. . . .

It is reasonable to suppose, that man departed from the first teachings, or instructions which he received from heaven in the first

---

Laws of the Land
1   Letter to the brethren in Zion, Kirtland, 21 April 1833.
2   Letter to the brethren scattered from Zion, Kirtland, 22 January 1834.

age, and refused by his disobedience to be governed by them. Consequently, he formed such laws as best suited his own mind, or as he supposed, were best adapted to his situation. But that God has influenced man more or less since that time in the formation of law for His benefit we have no hesitancy in believing; for, as before remarked, being the source of all good, every just and equitable law was in a greater or less degree influenced by Him. And though man in his own supposed wisdom would not admit the influence of a power superior to his own, yet for wise and great purposes, for the good and happiness of His creatures, God has instructed man to form wise and wholesome laws, since he had departed from Him and refused to be governed by those laws which God had given by His own voice from on high in the beginning. (HC 2:7, 15)

3   *The Political Motto of the Church of Latter-day Saints:* The Constitution of our country formed by the Fathers of liberty. Peace and good order in society. Love to God, and good will to man. All good and wholesome laws, virtue and truth above all things, and aristarchy, live for ever! But woe to tyrants, mobs, aristocracy, anarchy, and toryism, and all those who invent or seek out unrighteous and vexatious law suits, under the pretext and color of law, or office, either religious or political. Exalt the standard of Democracy! Down with that of priestcraft, and let all the people say Amen! that the blood of our fathers may not cry from the ground against us. Sacred is the memory of that blood which bought for us our liberty. (HC 3:9)

4   Should any person be guilty of exciting the people to riot or rebellion, or of participating in a mob, or any other unlawful riotous or tumultuous assemblage of the people, or of refusing to obey any civil officer, executing the ordinances of the city, or the general laws of the state or United States, or of neglecting or refusing to obey promptly, any military order for the due execution of said law or ordinances, he shall, on conviction thereof as aforesaid, be fined or imprisoned, or both, as aforesaid. (HC 4:307)

Laws of the Land

   3 Far West, Missouri, March 1838. The word *aristarchy* in this entry means "the rule of those who actually *are* the best" (see *BYU Studies* 5 [Spring and Summer 1964]: 192).

   4 An ordinance presented by Joseph Smith and passed by the Nauvoo City Council, 1 March 1841.

5 We will keep the laws of the land; we do not speak against them; we never have. (*HC* 5:257)

6 The Constitution is not a law, but it empowers the people to make laws. . . .

. . . Powers not delegated to the states or reserved from the states are constitutional. The Constitution acknowledges that the people have all power not reserved to itself. (*HC* 5:289)

7 If I lose my life in a good cause I am willing to be sacrificed on the altar of virtue, righteousness and truth, in maintaining the laws and Constitution of the United States, if need be, for the general good of mankind. (*HC* 6:211)

8 The constitution expects every man to do his duty; and when he fails the law urges him; or should he do too much, the same master rebukes him. (*HC* 6:220)

9 We have ever held ourselves amenable to the law; and, for myself, sir, I am ever ready to conform to and support the laws and Constitution, even at the expense of my life. I have never in the least offered any resistance to law or lawful process, which is a well-known fact to the general public. (*HC* 6:526)

10 We are desirous to fulfill the law in every particular, and are responsible for our acts. (*HC* 6:585)

Laws of the Land
  5 Sabbath address, Nauvoo, 22 January 1843.
  6 Views on Constitutional powers expounded to Nauvoo City Council, 25 February 1843.
  7 Views of the Prophet on his candidacy for president of the United States, Nauvoo, 8 February 1844.
  8 Article entitled "Pacific Innuendo," Nauvoo, 17 February 1844.
  9 Letter to Governor Thomas Ford, Nauvoo, 22 June 1844.
  10 Interview between the Prophet and Governor Thomas Ford, 26 June 1844, as reported by Elder John Taylor.

Lawyers

1 Many lawyers contend for those things which are against the rights of men, and I can only excuse them because of their ignorance. Go forth and advocate the laws and rights of the people, ye lawyers. If not, don't get into my hands, or under the lash of my tongue. (HC 5:468–69)

2 All ye lawyers who have no business, only as you hatch it up, would to God you would go to work or run away! (HC 6:59)

Laying on of Hands

1 We now became anxious to have that promise realized to us, which the angel that conferred upon us the Aaronic Priesthood had given us, viz., that provided we continued faithful, we should also have the Melchizedek Priesthood, which holds the authority of the laying on of hands for the gift of the Holy Ghost. (HC 1:60)

2 *Report of Don Carlos Smith:* He [Joseph Smith] then briefly stated the principles of faith, repentance, and baptism for the remission of sins, these were believed by some of the righteous societies of the day, but the doctrine of laying on of hands for the gift of the Holy Ghost was discarded by them. (HC 4:359)

3 The scriptural way of attaining the gift of the Holy Ghost is by baptism, and by laying on of hands. (HC 4:579)

4 *Report of Eliza R. Snow:* Respecting females administering for the healing of the sick, he [Joseph Smith] further remarked, there could

---

Lawyers
1 Address regarding his arrest at Dixon, Illinois, Nauvoo, 30 June 1843.
2 Sabbath address, Nauvoo, 15 October 1843.

Laying on of Hands
1 Fayette, New York, June 1829.
2 Sabbath address, Nauvoo, 16 May 1841.
3 Editorial in the *Times and Seasons*, 1 April 1842.
4 Remarks to the Relief Society, Nauvoo, 28 April 1842. For recent commentary concerning women laying on hands, see Dallin H. Oaks, "The Relief Society and the Church," *Ensign* 22 (May 1992): 36.

be no devil in it, if God gave His sanction by healing; that there could be no more sin in any female laying hands on and praying for the sick, than in wetting the face with water; it is no sin for anybody to administer that has faith, or if the sick have faith to be healed by their administration. (HC 4:604)

Learning
See EDUCATION

Lectures on Faith

1   Our school for the Elders was now well attended, and with the lectures on theology, which were regularly delivered, absorbed for the time being everything else of a temporal nature. (HC 2:175–76)

2   During the month of January, I was engaged in the school of the Elders, and in preparing the lectures on theology for publication in the book of Doctrine and Covenants, which the committee appointed last September were now compiling. (HC 2:180)

3   The first part of the book [the Doctrine and Covenants] will be found to contain a series of lectures as delivered before a theological class in this place, and in consequence of their embracing the important doctrine of salvation, we have arranged them in the following work. (HC 2:250)

Legal Administrator
See AUTHORITY

Lectures on Faith
1   Kirtland, 1 December 1834.
2   Kirtland, January 1835.
3   Preface to the first edition of the Doctrine and Covenants, signed by Joseph Smith, Oliver Cowdery, Sidney Rigdon, and Frederick G. Williams, Kirtland, dated 17 February 1835.

Leisure

1 *Words of William M. Allred:* He [Joseph Smith] said it tried some of the pious folks to see him play ball with the boys. He then related a story of a certain prophet who was sitting under the shade of a tree amusing himself in some way, when a hunter came along with his bow and arrow, and reproved him. The prophet asked him if he kept his bow strung up all the time. The hunter answered that he did not. The prophet asked why, and he said it would lose its elasticity if he did. The prophet said it was just so with his mind, he did not want it strung up all the time. (JSMS, p. 16)

Liberty

1 I want the liberty of thinking and believing as I please. It feels so good not to be trammelled. (HC 5:340)

2 It is a love of liberty which inspires my soul—civil and religious liberty to the whole of the human race. Love of liberty was diffused into my soul by my grandfathers while they dandled me on their knees; and shall I want friends? No. (HC 5:498)

3 No honest man can doubt for a moment but the glory of American liberty is on the wane, and that calamity and confusion will sooner or later destroy the peace of the people. (HC 6:204)

Leisure
1 Reminiscence of William M. Allred, published in the *Juvenile Instructor*, 1 August 1892.

Liberty
1 Conference address, Nauvoo, 8 April 1843.
2 Sabbath address, Nauvoo, 9 July 1843.
3 A pamphlet containing the Prophet's political platform, entitled *Views of the Powers and Policy of the Government of the United States*, Nauvoo, 7 February 1844.

Lies

1   I know that something will soon take place to stir up this generation to see what they have been doing, and that their fathers have inherited lies and they have been led captive by the devil, to no profit;
but they know not what they do. Do not have any feelings of enmity
towards any son or daughter of Adam. (HC 3:286)

2   It is best to let Sharp publish what he pleases and go to the devil,
and the more lies he prints the sooner he will get through. (HC
4:487)

3   I then made some pertinent remarks before the council, concerning those who had been guilty of circulating false reports, &c., and
said:
    . . . If they will not repent and stop their lyings and surmisings, let
God curse them, and let their tongues cleave to the roofs of their
mouths. (HC 5:13, 14)

4   Mr. Sollars stated that James Mullone, of Springfield, told him as
follows:—"I have been to Nauvoo, and seen Joe Smith, the Prophet:
he had a gray horse, and I asked him where he got it; and Joe said,
'You see that white cloud.' 'Yes.' 'Well, as it came along, I got the
horse from that cloud.'" This is a fair specimen of the ten thousand
foolish lies circulated by this generation to bring the truth and its advocates into disrepute. (HC 5:218)

5   The men who seek our destruction and cry thief, treason, riot,
&c., are those who themselves violate the laws, steal and plunder
from their neighbors, and seek to destroy the innocent, heralding
forth lies to screen themselves from the just punishment of their
crimes by bringing destruction upon this innocent people. I call God,

---

Lies
  1   Letter from Liberty Jail to Mrs. Norman Bull (Buell), 15 March 1839.
  2   Conversation with Calvin Warren about Thomas Sharp, newspaper editor
      of the *Warsaw Signal*, 30 December 1841.
  3   Meeting of the Nauvoo City Council, 19 May 1842.
  4   Springfield, Illinois, at the home of a Mr. Sollars, 2 January 1843.
  5   Address to the Nauvoo Legion, 18 June 1844.

angels and all men to witness that we are innocent of the charges which are heralded forth through the public prints against us by our enemies; and while they assemble together in unlawful mobs to take away our rights and destroy our lives, they think to shield themselves under the refuge of lies which they have thus wickedly fabricated. (*HC* 6:498)

Life

1   If in this life we receive our all; if when we crumble back to dust we are no more, from what source did we emanate, and what was the purpose of our existence? If this life were all, we should be led to query, whether or not there was really any substance in existence, and we might with propriety say, "Let us eat, drink, and be merry, for to morrow we die!" But if this life is all, then why this constant toiling, why this continual warfare, and why this unceasing trouble? But this life is not all, the voice of *reason*, the language of *inspiration*, and the Spirit of the living God, our Creator, teaches us, as we hold the record of truth in our hands, that this is not the case, that this is not so; for, the heavens declare the glory of a God, and the firmament showeth His handiwork; and a moment's reflection is sufficient to teach every man of common intelligence, that all these are not the mere productions of *chance*, nor could they be supported by any power less than an Almighty hand. (*HC* 2:14)

Light

1   There is a superior intelligence bestowed upon such as obeyed the Gospel with full purpose of heart, which, if sinned against, the apostate is left naked and destitute of the Spirit of God, and he is, in truth, nigh unto cursing, and his end is to be burned. When once that light which was in them is taken from them they become as much darkened as

---

Life
   1   Letter to the brethren scattered from Zion, Kirtland, 22 January 1834.

Light
   1   Letter to the brethren scattered from Zion, Kirtland, 22 January 1834.

they were previously enlightened, and then, no marvel, if all their power should be enlisted against the truth, and they, Judas like, seek the destruction of those who were their greatest benefactors. (HC 2:23)

2   We understand from this saying, that those who had been previously looking for a Messiah to come, according to the testimony of the Prophets, and were then, at that time looking for a Messiah, but had not sufficient light, on account of their unbelief, to discern Him to be their Savior; and He being the true Messiah, consequently they must be disappointed, and lose even all the knowledge, or have taken away from them all the light, understanding, and faith which they had upon this subject; therefore he that will not receive the greater light, must have taken away from him all the light which he hath; and if the light which is in you become darkness, behold, how great is that darkness! (HC 2:265)

3   He loves darkness rather than light, because his deeds are evil. (HC 4:581)

4   We are all responsible to God for the manner we improve the light and wisdom given by our Lord to enable us to save ourselves. (HC 4:606)

5   Concerning Brother James Adams, it should appear strange that so good and so great a man was hated. The deceased ought never to have had an enemy. But so it was. Wherever light shone, it stirred up darkness. Truth and error, good and evil cannot be reconciled. (HC 6:51)

6   May the Lord grant his Spirit and peace to abide upon Brother Wilkie and his companion through the remainder of their days; may their hearts expand and become enlarged to receive the fullness of the blessings of the kingdom of heaven; may they have the light of eternal

---

Light
   2   Letter to the elders of the Church, Kirtland, 1 September 1835.
   3   Editorial in the *Times and Seasons*, 1 April 1842.
   4   Remarks to the Relief Society, Nauvoo, 28 April 1842.
   5   Remarks upon the death of James Adams, Nauvoo, 9 October 1843.
   6   Blessing upon John Wilkie, Nauvoo, 15 March 1844.

truth continually springing up in them like a well of living water; may they be shielded from the powers of Satan and the influence of designing men, and their faith increase from day to day until they shall have power to lay hold on the blessings of God and the gifts of the Spirit until they are satisfied. (HC 6:265)

Light-mindedness

1   As to our light speeches, which may have escaped our lips from time to time, they have nothing to do with the fixed purposes of our hearts. (HC 3:227)

2   How vain and trifling have been our spirits, our conferences, our councils, our meetings, our private as well as public conversations—too low, too mean, too vulgar, too condescending for the dignified characters of the called and chosen of God, according to the purposes of His will, from before the foundation of the world! We are called to hold the keys of the mysteries of those things that have been kept hid from the foundation of the world until now. . . . Let honesty, and sobriety, and candor, and solemnity, and virtue, and pureness, and meekness, and simplicity crown our heads in every place; and in fine, become as little children, without malice, guile or hypocrisy. (HC 3:295–96)

3   Let the Elders and Saints do away with lightmindedness, and be sober. (HC 6:52)

Light of Christ

1   We could not help beholding the exertions of Satan to blind the eyes of the people, so as to hide the true light that lights every man that comes into the world. (HC 1:206)

Light-mindedness
1   Letter to the Church from Liberty Jail, 16 December 1838.
2   Letter to the Saints from Liberty Jail, 20–25 March 1839.
3   Remarks upon the death of James Adams, Nauvoo, 9 October 1843.

Light of Christ
1   Observations about a journey from Kirtland to Missouri and back, June–August, 1831.

Light of the World

1   John was very particular to tell the people, he was not that Light, but was sent to bear witness of that Light.

He told the people that his mission was to preach repentance and baptize with water; but it was He that should come after him that should baptize with fire and the Holy Ghost. (HC 6:250)

Lion

1   It is true that I once suffered an ass to feed in my pasture. He ate at my crib and drank at my waters; but possessing the true nature of an ass, he began to foul the water with his feet, and to trample under foot the green grass and destroy it. I therefore put him out of my pasture, and he began to bray. Many of the lions in the adjoining jungles, mistaking the braying for the roaring of a lion, commenced roaring. When I proclaimed this abroad many of the lions began to enquire into the matter. A few, possessing a more noble nature than many of their fellows, drew near, and viewing the animal found that he was nothing more than a decrepit, broken down, worn out ass, that had scarcely anything left but his ears and voice.

Whereupon many of the lions felt indignant at the lion of Warsaw, the lion of Quincy, the lion of Sangamon, the lion of Alton, and several other lions, for giving a false alarm, for dishonoring their race, and for responding to the voice of so base an animal as an ass. And they felt ashamed of themselves for being decoyed into such base ribaldry and foul-mouthed slander. But there were many that lost sight of their dignity, and continued to roar, although they knew well that they were following the braying of so despicable a creature. (HC 5:275)

2   "The righteous are as bold as a lion." (HC 6:170)

Light of the World
    1   Sabbath address, Nauvoo, 10 March 1844.

Lion
    1   The Prophet's parable of the lions of the press, published in the *Times and Seasons*, 15 February 1843. It has reference to John C. Bennett and the Illinois newspaper editors.
    2   Nauvoo, 5 January 1844. The prophet is apparently quoting Proverbs 28:1.

Long-suffering

1 I started to ride to Painesville with my family and scribe. When we were passing through Mentor Street, we overtook a team, with two men in a sleigh; I politely asked them to let me pass. They granted my request, and as we passed them they bawled out, "Do you get any revelations lately?" with an addition of blackguard language that I did not understand. This is a fair sample of the character of the Mentor Street inhabitants, who are ready to abuse and scandalize men who never laid a straw in their way; and, in fact, those whose faces they never saw, and {whom they} cannot bring an accusation against, either of a temporal or spiritual nature, except their firm belief in the fullness of the Gospel. I was led to marvel at the longsuffering and condescension of our heavenly Father in permitting these ungodly wretches to possess this goodly land. (HC 2:323)

2 He said he had manifested long-suffering, forbearance and patience towards the Church, and also to his enemies; and we must bear with each other's failings, as an indulgent parent bears with the foibles of his children.

. . . As you increase in innocence and virtue, as you increase in goodness, let your hearts expand, let them be enlarged towards others; you must be long-suffering, and bear with the faults and errors of mankind. (HC 4:606)

3 How oft have wise men and women sought to dictate Brother Joseph by saying, "O, if I were Brother Joseph, I would do this and that;" but if they were in Brother Joseph's shoes they would find that men or women could not be compelled into the kingdom of God, but must be dealt with in long-suffering, and at last we shall save them. The way to keep all the Saints together, and keep the work rolling, is to wait with all long-suffering, till God shall bring such characters to justice. There should be no license for sin, but mercy should go hand in hand with reproof. (HC 5:24)

Long-suffering
1 Kirtland, 2 December 1835.
2 Remarks to the Relief Society, Nauvoo, 28 April 1842.
3 Remarks to the Relief Society, Nauvoo, 9 June 1842.

Lord's Prayer

1   *Words of Edward Stevenson:* He taught that the Lord's prayer should state, "Leave us not in temptation"—not, "Lead us not into temptation." (Matthew 6:13.) (*TK,* p. 87)

Lost Tribes of Israel

1   *Report of John Whitmer:* The Spirit of the Lord fell upon Joseph in an unusual manner, and he prophesied that John the Revelator was then among the Ten Tribes of Israel who had been led away by Shalmaneser, king of Assyria, to prepare them for their return from their long dispersion, to again possess the land of their fathers. (*HC* 1:176)

2   And now I am prepared to say by the authority of Jesus Christ, that not many years shall pass away before the United States shall present such a scene of *bloodshed* as has not a parallel in the history of our nation; pestilence, hail, famine, and earthquake will sweep the wicked of this generation from off the face of this land, to open and prepare the way for the return of the lost tribes of Israel from the north country. (*HC* 1:315)

3   It has been said by many of the learned and wise men, or historians, that the Indians or aborigines of this continent, are of the scattered tribes of Israel. It has been conjectured by many others, that the aborigines of this continent are not of the tribes of Israel, but the ten tribes have been led away into some unknown regions of the north. Let this be as it may, the prophecy I have just quoted [Deuteronomy 30:1–4] "will fetch them," in the last days, and place them in the land which their fathers possessed. (*HC* 2:261)

Lord's Prayer
1   Autobiography of Edward Stevenson, LDS Church Archives.

Lost Tribes of Israel
1   Conference of the Church, Kirtland, 3–6 June 1831.
2   Letter to N. E. Seaton (N. C. Saxton), a newspaper editor in Rochester, N.Y., Kirtland, 4 January 1833.
3   Letter to the elders of the Church, Kirtland, 1 September 1835.

Editors' Note: There are several theories about the location of the ten tribes attributed to Joseph Smith by individuals but which were not publicly taught by the Prophet. These theories are not consistent with one another and have no scriptural or official Church documentation. Hence, the editors have chosen not to include them here.

Love
See also CHARITY

1   Until we have perfect love we are liable to fall; and when we have a testimony that our names are sealed in the Lamb's book of life, we have perfect love, and then it is impossible for false Christs to deceive us. (FWR, p. 23; standardized)

2   It was my endeavor to so organize the Church, that the brethren might eventually be independent of every incumbrance beneath the celestial kingdom, by bonds and covenants of mutual friendship, and mutual love.

On the 28th and 29th, I visited the brethren above Big Blue river, in Kaw township, a few miles west of Independence, and received a welcome only known by brethren and sisters united as one in the same faith, and by the same baptism, and supported by the same Lord. The Colesville branch, in particular, rejoiced as the ancient Saints did with Paul. (HC 1:269)

3   That person who never forsaketh his trust, should ever have the highest place of regard in our hearts, and our love should never fail, but increase more and more, and this is my disposition and these my sentiments. (HC 1:444)

4   We call to remembrance the ties with which we are bound to those who embrace the everlasting covenant, and the fellowship and love with which the hearts of the children of our Lord's kingdom should be united. (HC 2:4)

Love
  1   Minutes of a conference held at Orange, Ohio, 25 October 1831.
  2   Kaw township, Missouri, April 1832.
  3   Kirtland, 19 November 1833.
  4   Letter to the brethren scattered from Zion, Kirtland, 22 January 1834.

5 Dear Brethren:—It is a duty which every Saint ought to render to his brethren freely—to always love them, and ever succor them. To be justified before God we must love one another: we must overcome evil; we must visit the fatherless and the widow in their affliction, and we must keep ourselves unspotted from the world. (HC 2:229)

6 I frequently rebuke and admonish my brethren, and that because I love them, not because I wish to incur their displeasure, or mar their happiness. Such a course of conduct is not calculated to gain the good will of all, but rather the ill will of many; therefore, the situation in which I stand is an important one; so, you see, brethren, the higher the authority, the greater the difficulty of the station; but these rebukes and admonitions become necessary, from the perverseness of the brethren, for their temporal as well as spiritual welfare. They actually constitute a part of the duties of my station and calling. Others have other duties to perform, that are important, and far more enviable, and may be just as good, like the feet and hands, in their relation to the human body—neither can claim priority, or say to the other, I have no need of you. (HC 2:478)

7 There is a love from God that should be exercised toward those of our faith, who walk uprightly, which is peculiar to itself, but it is without prejudice; it also gives scope to the mind, which enables us to conduct ourselves with greater liberality towards all that are not of our faith, than what they exercise towards one another. These principles approximate nearer to the mind of God, because it is like God, or Godlike. (HC 3:304)

8 Love is one of the chief characteristics of Deity, and ought to be manifested by those who aspire to be the sons of God. A man filled with the love of God, is not content with blessing his family alone, but ranges through the whole world, anxious to bless the whole

---

Love
5   Letter to the Saints in Missouri published in the *Messenger and Advocate*,
     June 1835.
6   Solemn assembly in the Kirtland Temple, 6 April 1837.
7   Letter to the Saints from Liberty Jail, 20–25 March 1839.
8   Letter to the Twelve in England, Nauvoo, 15 December 1840. The placement of this letter in *HC* implies that it was written in October 1840, but actually it was written on 15 December 1840 (see *PWJS*, p. 480).

human race. This has been your feeling, and caused you to forego the pleasures of home, that you might be a blessing to others, who are candidates for immortality, but strangers to truth; and for so doing, I pray that heaven's choicest blessings may rest upon you. (HC 4:227)

9 It is with unspeakable delight that I contemplate them [certain elders of the Church] as my friends and brethren. I love them with a perfect love; and I hope they love me, and have no reason to doubt that they do. (HC 5:156)

10 *Words of George A. Smith:* Joseph wrapped his arms around me, and squeezed me to his bosom and said, "George A., I love you as I do my own life." I felt so affected, I could hardly speak, but replied, "I hope, Brother Joseph, that my whole life and actions will ever prove my feelings, and the depth of my affection towards you." (HC 5:391)

11 If we would secure and cultivate the love of others, we must love others, even our enemies as well as friends.

Sectarian priests cry out concerning me, and ask, "Why is it this babbler gains so many followers, and retains them?" I answer, It is because I possess the principle of love. All I can offer the world is a good heart and a good hand. (HC 5:498)

12 It is a time-honored adage that love begets love. Let us pour forth love—show forth our kindness unto all mankind, and the Lord will reward us with everlasting increase; cast our bread upon the waters and we shall receive it after many days, increased to a hundredfold. . . .

I do not dwell upon your faults, and you shall not upon mine. Charity, which is love, covereth a multitude of sins, and I have often covered up all the faults among you; but the prettiest thing is to have no faults at all. We should cultivate a meek, quiet and peaceable spirit. (HC 5:517)

Love

9 Letter to James Arlington Bennett, Nauvoo, 8 September 1842.

10 An excerpt from the journal of George A. Smith under date of 15 May 1843.

11 Sabbath address, Nauvoo, 9 July 1843.

12 Sabbath address, Nauvoo, 23 July 1843.

13 And as the new commandment given anciently was *to love one another*, even so the works of the Saints at home and abroad will bear its own testimony whether *they love the brethren*. (HC 6:69)

14 How far you are capable of being "a most undeviating friend, without being governed by the smallest religious influence," will best be decided by your survivors, as all past experience most assuredly proves. Without controversy, that friendship which intelligent beings would accept as sincere must arise from love, and that love grow out of virtue, which is as much a part of religion as light is a part of Jehovah. Hence the saying of Jesus, "Greater love hath no man than this, that a man lay down his life for his friends." (HC 6:73)

15 Filled with a love almost unspeakable, and moved by a desire pleasant as the dew of heaven, I supplicate not only our Father above, but also the civil, the enlightened, the intelligent, the social, and the best inhabitants of Missouri. (HC 6:246)

16 I have intended my remarks to all, both rich and poor, bond and free, great and small. I have no enmity against any man. I love you all; but I hate some of your deeds. I am your best friend, and if persons miss their mark it is their own fault. If I reprove a man, and he hates me, he is a fool; for I love all men, especially these my brethren and sisters. (HC 6:317)

17 Brethren and sisters, love one another; love one another and be merciful to your enemies. (JSP, p. 116)

18 God has tried you. You are a good people; therefore I love you with all my heart. Greater love hath no man than that he should lay

---

Love

13 Letter to the Saints encouraging them to patronize the Church newspaper, published in the *Times and Seasons*, 1 November 1843.

14 Letter to James Arlington Bennett, Nauvoo, 13 November 1843.

15 An appeal for peace and goodwill, addressed to the people of Missouri, Nauvoo, 8 March 1844.

16 King Follett Discourse, Nauvoo, 7 April 1844.

17 Sabbath address, Nauvoo, 16 June 1844. Recalled by Lucy M. Smith, published in the *Juvenile Instructor*, 1 August 1892.

18 Address to the Nauvoo Legion, 18 June 1844.

down his life for his friends. You have stood by me in the hour of trouble, and I am willing to sacrifice my life for your preservation. (HC 6:500)

Magnifying One's Calling

1   We feel to rebuke the Elders of that branch of the Church of Christ, for not magnifying their office, and letting the transgressor go unpunished. (HC 1:371)

2   On the subject of ordination, a few words are necessary. In many instances there has been too much haste in this thing, and the admonition of Paul has been too slightingly passed over, which says, "Lay hands suddenly upon no man." Some have been ordained to the ministry, and have never acted in that capacity, or magnified their calling at all. Such may expect to lose their appointment, except they awake and magnify their office. Let the Elders abroad be exceedingly careful upon this subject, and when they ordain a man to the holy ministry, let him be a faithful man, who is able to teach others also; that the cause of Christ suffer not. It is not the multitude of preachers that is to bring about the glorious millennium! but it is those who are "called, and chosen, and faithful." (HC 1:468)

3   Everyone should aspire only to magnify his own office and calling. (HC 4:606)

Manifestations

1   If God gives you a manifestation, keep it to yourselves; be watchful and prayerful, and you shall have a prelude of those joys that God will pour out on that day [anticipated solemn assembly]. (HC 2:309)

Magnifying One's Calling
  1   Letter to the brethren in Zion, Kirtland, 2 July 1833.
  2   Letter to the elders of the Church, published in *The Evening and the Morning Star*, Kirtland, December 1833.
  3   Remarks to the Relief Society, Nauvoo, 28 April 1842.

Manifestations
  1   Instructions to the Twelve, Kirtland, 12 November 1835.

2   Mr. Irving, falling into the common error of considering all supernatural manifestations to be of God, took them to London with him,
and introduced them into his church. (HC 4:578)

Mankind

1   Mankind will persist in self-justification until all their iniquity is
exposed, and their character past being redeemed, and that which is
treasured up in their hearts be exposed to the gaze of mankind. (HC
1:316)

2   It is in vain to warn and give precepts, for all men are naturally
disposed to walk in their own paths as they are pointed out by their
own fingers and are not willing to consider and walk in the path
which is pointed out by another, saying, This is the way, walk ye in it,
although he should be an unerring director, and the Lord his God sent
him. (HC 1:408)

3   I have learned in my travels that man is treacherous and selfish,
but few excepted. (HC 1:443)

4   It is the will of God that man should repent and serve Him in
health, and in the strength and power of his mind, in order to secure
His blessing, and not wait until he is called to die. (HC 4:554)

5   Now, in this world, mankind are naturally selfish, ambitious and
striving to excel one above another; yet some are willing to build up
others as well as themselves. (HC 5:388)

Manifestations
   2   Editorial in the *Times and Seasons*, 1 April 1842.

Mankind
   1   Letter to William W. Phelps in Missouri, written from Kirtland, 14 Janu-
       ary 1833. According to Dean Jessee this letter was dated 11 January (see
       PWJS, p. 262).
   2   Letter to Vienna Jacques, Kirtland, 4 September 1833.
   3   Kirtland, 19 November 1833.
   4   Sabbath address, Nauvoo, 20 March 1842.
   5   Sabbath address at Yelrome (Morley's Settlement), Illinois, 14 May 1843.

6 I do not think there have been many good men on the earth since the days of Adam; but there was one good man and his name was Jesus. Many persons think a prophet must be a great deal better than anybody else. Suppose I would condescend—yes, I will call it condescend, to be a great deal better than any of you, I would be raised up to the highest heaven; and who should I have to accompany me? (HC 5:401)

7 It is the constitutional disposition of mankind to set up stakes and set bounds to the works and ways of the Almighty. (HC 5:529)

8 Men will set up stakes and say thus far will we go and no farther. (WJS, p. 246)

9 What was the design of the Almighty in making man? It was to exalt him to be as God. The scripture says ye are Gods, and it cannot be broken—heirs of God and joint heirs . . . with Jesus Christ, equal with him, possessing all power, &c. (WJS, p. 247; standardized)

10 I say to all those who are disposed to set up stakes for the Almighty, You will come short of the glory of God. (HC 5:554)

11 The best men bring forth the best works. (HC 6:315)

12 You cannot go anywhere but where God can find you out. (HC 6:366)

13 When men open their lips against these truths they do not injure me, but injure themselves. . . . When things that are of the greatest importance are passed over by weak-minded men without even a thought, I want to see truth in all its bearings and hug it to my bosom.

Mankind
6 Sabbath address, Nauvoo, 21 May 1843.
7 Remarks at the funeral of Judge Elias Higbee, Nauvoo, 13 August 1843.
8 Sabbath address, Nauvoo, 27 August 1843, as reported by James Burgess.
9 Sabbath address, Nauvoo, 27 August 1843, as reported by James Burgess.
10 Sabbath address, Nauvoo, 27 August 1843.
11 King Follett Discourse, Nauvoo, 7 April 1844.
12 Sabbath address, Nauvoo, 12 May 1844.
13 Sabbath address, Nauvoo, 16 June 1844.

I believe all that God ever revealed, and I never hear of a man being damned for believing too much; but they are damned for unbelief. (HC 6:477)

Marriage

1   I had an invitation to attend a wedding at Brother Hyrum Smith's in the evening; also to solemnize the matrimonial ceremony between Newel Knight and Lydia Goldthwaite. My wife accompanied me. On our arrival a considerable company had collected. The bridegroom and bride came in, and took their seats, which gave me to understand that they were ready. After prayers, I requested them to rise, and join hands. I then remarked that marriage was an institution of heaven, instituted in the garden of Eden; that it was necessary it should be solemnized by the authority of the everlasting Priesthood. The ceremony was original with me, and in substance as follows—You covenant to be each other's companions through life, and discharge the duties of husband and wife in every respect; to which they assented. I then pronounced them husband and wife in the name of God, and also pronounced upon them the blessings that the Lord conferred upon Adam and Eve in the garden of Eden, that is, to multiply and replenish the earth, with the addition of long life and prosperity. Dismissed them and returned home. (HC 2:320)

2   It is the duty of a husband to love, cherish, and nourish his wife, and cleave unto her and none else; he ought to honor her as himself, and he ought to regard her feelings with tenderness, for she is his flesh, and his bone, designed to be an help unto him, both in temporal, and spiritual things; one into whose bosom he can pour all his complaints without reserve, who is willing (being designed) to take part of his burden, to soothe and encourage his feelings by her gentle voice. It is the place of the man, to stand at the head of his family, and be lord of his own house, not to rule over his wife as a tyrant, neither as one who is fearful or jealous that his wife will get out of her place, and prevent him from exercising his authority. It is his duty to be a

---

Marriage
1   Kirtland, 24 November 1835.
2   Editorial published in the *Elders' Journal*, August 1838.

man of God (for a man of God is a man of wisdom,) ready at all times to obtain from the scriptures, the revelations, and from on high, such instructions as are necessary for the edification, and salvation of his household.—And on the other hand, it is the duty of the wife, to be in subjection to her husband at all times, not as a servant, neither as one who fears a tyrant, or a master, but as one, who, in meekness, and the love of God, regards the laws and institutions of Heaven, looks up to her husband for instruction, edification and comfort. (*EJ* 1:61–62)

3 You need not be teasing your husbands because of their deeds, but let the weight of your innocence, kindness and affection be felt, which is more mighty than a millstone hung about the neck; not war, not jangle, not contradiction, or dispute, but meekness, love, purity— these are the things that should magnify you in the eyes of all good men. (HC 4:605)

4 Except a man and his wife enter into an everlasting covenant and be married for eternity, while in this probation, by the power and authority of the Holy Priesthood, they will cease to increase when they die; that is, they will not have any children after the resurrection. But those who are married by the power and authority of the priesthood in this life, and continue without committing the sin against the Holy Ghost, will continue to increase and have children in the celestial glory. (HC 5:391)

5 I . . . slightly touched upon the subject of the everlasting covenant, showing that a man and his wife must enter into that covenant in the world, or he will have no claim on her in the next world. But on account of the unbelief of the people, I cannot reveal the fullness of these things at present. (HC 5:510)

6 *Words of Lucy Walker Kimball:* He [Joseph Smith] often referred to the feelings that should exist between husbands and wives. . . . He said men must beware how they treat their wives. They were given

---

Marriage
3 Remarks to the Relief Society, Nauvoo, 28 April 1842.
4 Instruction given to a few Saints at the home of Benjamin F. Johnson, Ramus, Illinois, 16 May 1843.
5 Sabbath address, Nauvoo, 16 July 1843.
6 Recollection of Lucy Walker Kimball.

them for a holy purpose that the myriads of spirits waiting for tabernacles might have pure and healthy bodies. He also said many would
awake in the morning of the resurrection sadly disappointed; for they,
by transgression, would have neither wives nor children, for they
surely would be taken from them, and given to those who should
prove themselves worthy. Again he said, a woman would have her
choice; this was a privilege that could not be denied her. (Walker and
Stevenson, comps., *Ancestry and Descendants of John Walker*, p. 32)

7   *Words of Jesse W. Crosby:* One day when the Prophet carried to my
house a sack of flour he had borrowed, my wife remarked that he had
returned more than he had received. He answered that it should be so;
that anything borrowed should be returned always with interest to the
lender. "Thus," he said, "the borrower, if he be honest, is a slave to the
lender." Some of the home habits of the Prophet—such as building
kitchen fires, carrying out ashes, carrying in wood and water, assisting
in the care of the children, etc.—were not in accord with my idea of a
great man's self-respect. The above incident of the Prophet carrying
the sack of flour gave me the opportunity to give him some corrective
advice which I had desired to do for a long time. I reminded him of
every phase of his greatness and called to his mind the multitude of
tasks he performed that were too menial for such as he; to fetch and
carry flour was too great a humiliation. "Too terrible a humiliation," I
repeated, "for you who are the head, and you should not do it."

The Prophet listened quietly to all I had to say, then made his answer in these words: "If there be humiliation in a man's house, who
but the head of that house should or could bear that humiliation?"

Sister Crosby was a very hardworking woman, taking much more
responsibility in her home than most women take. Thinking to give
the Prophet some light on home management, I said to him, "Brother
Joseph, my wife does much more hard work than does your wife."

Brother Joseph replied by telling me that if a man cannot learn in
this life to appreciate a wife and do his duty to her, in properly taking
care of her, he need not expect to be given one in the hereafter.

His words shut my mouth as tight as a clam. I took them as terrible reproof. After that I tried to do better by the good wife I had and
tried to lighten her labors. (*TK*, p. 145)

Marriage

7   Recollection of Jesse W. Crosby, reported in "Stories from the Notebook of
   Martha Cox, Grandmother of Fern Cox Anderson," LDS Church Archives.

Martyrdom

1   *Words of Edward Stevenson:* During the Prophet's visit [to Michigan, fall 1834], he came to our house. My heart swelled with love as I selected and presented him with some of our choice apples. While looking over our copy of a large English Book of Martyrs, he expressed sympathy for the Christian martyrs and a hope for their salvation. He asked to borrow the book, promising to return it when he should meet us again in Missouri. On returning it he said, "I have, by the aid of the Urim and Thummim {Seer Stone?}, seen those martyrs. They were honest, devoted followers of Christ, according to the light they possessed. They will be saved." (*TK*, p. 85)

2   However, thank God, we have been delivered. And although some of our beloved brethren have had to seal their testimony with their blood, and have died martyrs to the cause of truth—
> Short though bitter was their pain,
> Everlasting is their joy.

Let us not sorrow as "those without hope;" the time is fast approaching when we shall see them again and rejoice together, without being afraid of wicked men. Yes, those who have slept in Christ, shall He bring with Him, when He shall come to be glorified in His Saints, and admired by all those who believe, but to take vengeance upon His enemies and all those who obey not the Gospel. (*HC* 3:330)

3   On my part, I am ready to be offered up a sacrifice in that way that can bring to pass the greatest benefit and good to those who must necessarily be interested in this important matter. (*HC* 5:159)

4   I understand my mission and business. God Almighty is my shield; and what can man do if God is my friend? I shall not be sacrificed until my time comes; then I shall be offered freely. (*HC* 5:259)

5   I defy all the world to destroy the work of God; and I prophesy they never will have power to kill me till my work is accomplished, and I am ready to die. (*HC* 6:58)

Martyrdom
1   Autobiography of Edward Stevenson, LDS Church Archives.
2   Reflections on Missouri persecutions and confinement in Liberty Jail, Quincy, Illinois, 22 April 1839.
3   Letter to James Arlington Bennett, Nauvoo, 8 September 1842.
4   Sabbath address, Nauvoo, 22 January 1843.
5   Sabbath address, Nauvoo, 15 October 1843.

6   God will always protect me until my mission is fulfilled. (*HC* 6:365)

7   *Words of Daniel Tyler:* In a discourse in Far West, Missouri, Joseph Smith said, "Many of the elders of this Church will yet be martyred."

When the massacre took place at Brother Haun's mill, I felt in hopes that that was the fulfillment of the prediction. Subsequently, when he and his brother Hyrum were martyred in Carthage jail, I hoped that that would be the entire amount of those who would seal their testimony with their blood; but alas, several have since had their blood shed for the testimony of Jesus. (*TK*, p. 52)

8   *Words of Lucy Walker Kimball:* He [Joseph Smith] well knew that he must sacrifice his life for the principles God had revealed through him. Death had no terrors for him although life was dear. I have often heard him say he expected to seal his testimony with his blood. (*TK*, p. 139)

Masonry

1   *Words of Heber C. Kimball:* There is a similarity of priesthood in Masonry. Bro[ther] Joseph says Masonry was taken from priesthood but has become degenerated. (Stanley B. Kimball, *Heber C. Kimball: Mormon Patriarch and Pioneer*, p. 85; standardized)

2   *Words of Benjamin F. Johnson:* He [Joseph Smith] told me Freemasonry, as at present, was the apostate endowments, as sectarian religion was the apostate religion. (Johnson, *My Life's Review*, p. 96)

3   The secret of masonry is to keep a secret. (*HC* 6:59)

Martyrdom
   6   Sabbath address, Nauvoo, 12 May 1844.
   7   Recollection of Daniel Tyler, published in the *Juvenile Instructor*, 15 February 1892.
   8   Recollection of Lucy Walker Kimball, published in the *Woman's Exponent*, November 1910.

Masonry
   1   Letter from Heber C. Kimball to Parley P. Pratt, 17 June 1842.
   2   Recollection of Benjamin F. Johnson.
   3   Sabbath address, Nauvoo, 15 October 1843.

Matter

1   In tracing the thing to the foundation, and looking at it philo-
sophically, we shall find a very material difference between the body
and the spirit; the body is supposed to be organized matter, and the
spirit, by many, is thought to be immaterial, without substance. With
this latter statement we should beg leave to differ, and state that spirit
is a substance; that it is material, but that it is more pure, elastic and
refined matter than the body; that it existed before the body, can exist
in the body; and will exist separate from the body, when the body will
be mouldering in the dust; and will in the resurrection, be again
united with it. (HC 4:575)

2   God had materials to organize the world out of chaos—chaotic
matter, which is element, and in which dwells all the glory. Element
had an existence from the time He had. The pure principles of element are principles which never can be destroyed; they may be organized and re-organized, but not destroyed. They had no beginning and
can have no end. (HC 6:308–9)

3   *Words of Benjamin F. Johnson:* He [Joseph Smith] was the first to
teach in this age "substantialism," the eternity of matter, that no part
or particle of the great universe could become annihilated or destroyed; that light and life and spirit were one; that all light and heat
are the "glory of God," which is His power, that fills the "immensity of
space," and is the life of all things, and permeates with latent life, and
heat, every particle of which all worlds are composed; that light or
spirit, and gross matter, are the two first great primary principles of the
universe, or of being; that they are self-existent, co-existent, inde-
structible, and eternal, and from these two elements both our spirits
and our bodies were formulated. (TK, p. 95)

Matter
1   Editorial in the *Times and Seasons*, 1 April 1842.
2   King Follett Discourse, Nauvoo, 7 April 1844.
3   Letter of Benjamin F. Johnson to George S. Gibbs, 1903.

Mediation

1   Salvation could not come to the world without the mediation of Jesus Christ. (*HC* 5:555)

Meditation

1   I returned home, being much fatigued from riding in the rain. Spent the remainder of the day in reading and meditation. (*HC* 2:287)

2   Spent the rest of the day in reading and meditation. (*HC* 2:288)

3   Spent the day at home in reading, meditation and prayer. (*HC* 2:398)

4   I was engaged in reading, meditation, &c., mostly with my family. (*HC* 4:601)

5   It is my meditation all the day, and more than my meat and drink, to know how I shall make the Saints of God comprehend the visions that roll like an overflowing surge before my mind. (*HC* 5:362)

Meekness

1   When we rebuke, do it in all meekness. (*HC* 1:341)

Mediation
   1   Sabbath address, Nauvoo, 27 August 1843.

Meditation
   1   Kirtland, 5 October 1835.
   2   Kirtland, 6 October 1835.
   3   Kirtland, 21 February 1836.
   4   Nauvoo, 25–27 April 1842.
   5   Remarks upon the death of Lorenzo D. Barnes, Nauvoo, 16 April 1843.

Meekness
   1   Letter to the brethren in Zion, Kirtland, 21 April 1833.

2   Go in all meekness, in sobriety, and preach Jesus Christ and Him crucified; not to contend with others on account of their faith, or systems of religion, but pursue a steady course. This I delivered by way of commandment; and all who observe it not, will pull down persecution upon their heads, while those who do, shall always be filled with the Holy Ghost; this I pronounced as a prophecy, and sealed with hosanna and amen. (HC 2:431)

3   Some of the company thought I was not a very meek Prophet; so I told them: "I am meek and lowly in heart," and will personify Jesus for a moment, to illustrate the principle, and cried out with a loud voice, "Woe unto you, ye doctors; woe unto you, ye lawyers; woe unto you, ye scribes, Pharisees, and hypocrites!" &c. But you cannot find the place where I ever went that I found fault with their food, their drink, their house, their lodgings; no, never; and this is what is meant by the meekness and lowliness of Jesus. (HC 5:218)

Meetings

1   *Minutes:* Certain points were discussed by Brother Joseph Smith, Jr., who said that the elders present were to tarry until the morrow and hold a meeting so that the members might understand the ancient manner of conducting meetings as they were led by the Holy Ghost. Also said that this was not perfectly known by many of the elders of this church. (FWR, p. 17; standardized)

2   *Minutes:* President Joseph Smith stated that the business of the conference had closed, and the remainder would be devoted to instruction. It is an insult to a meeting for persons to leave just before its close. If they must go out, let them go half an hour before. No gentlemen will go out of a meeting just at closing. (HC 5:338–39)

Meekness
  2   Solemn assembly in the Kirtland Temple, 30 March 1836.
  3   Springfield, Illinois, at the home of a Mr. Sollars, 2 January 1843.

Meetings
  1   Minutes of a conference held in Hiram, Ohio, 11 October 1831.
  2   Minutes of a general conference, Nauvoo, 7 April 1843.

3   As president of this house [the Nauvoo Temple], I forbid any man leaving just as we are going to close the meeting. He is no gentleman who will do it. I don't care who does it, even if it were the king of England. I forbid it. (HC 5:363)

4   In so large a congregation it is necessary that the greatest order and decorum be observed. I request this at your hands, and believe that you will all keep good order. (HC 6:288)

Melchizedek

1   The King of Shiloam, (Salem) had power and authority over that of Abraham, holding the key and the power of endless life. . . .
    The sacrifice required of Abraham in the offering up of Isaac, shows that if a man would attain to the keys of the kingdom of an endless life; he must sacrifice all things. . . .
    What was the power of Melchizedek? . . . Those holding the fullness of the Melchizedek Priesthood are kings and priests of the Most High God, holding the keys of power and blessings. In fact, that priesthood is a perfect law of theocracy, and stands as God to give laws to the people, administering endless lives to the sons and daughters of Adam.
    Abraham says to Melchizedek, I believe all that thou hast taught me concerning the priesthood and the coming of the Son of Man; so Melchizedek ordained Abraham and sent him away. Abraham rejoiced, saying, Now I have a priesthood. (HC 5:554–55)

Melchizedek Priesthood
   See PRIESTHOOD, MELCHIZEDEK

Members
   See SAINTS

Meetings
   3   Remarks upon the death of Lorenzo D. Barnes, Nauvoo, 16 April 1843.
   4   General conference address, Nauvoo, 5 April 1844.

Melchizedek
   1   Sabbath address, Nauvoo, 27 August 1843.

Mercy

1   Ever keep in exercise the principle of mercy, and be ready to forgive our brother on the first intimations of repentance, and asking
forgiveness; and should we even forgive our brother, or even our
enemy, before he repent or ask forgiveness, our heavenly Father would
be equally as merciful unto us. (HC 3:383)

2   Long-suffering, patience, and mercy have ever characterized the
dealings of our heavenly Father towards the humble and penitent.
(HC 4:163)

3   There is never a time when the spirit is too old to approach God.
All are within the reach of pardoning mercy, who have not committed the unpardonable sin, which hath no forgiveness. (HC 4:425)

4   Don't envy the finery and fleeting show of sinners, for they are in
a miserable situation; but as far as you can, have mercy on them. (HC
4:607)

5   There is another error which opens a door for the adversary to
enter. As females possess refined feelings and sensitiveness, they are
also subject to overmuch zeal, which must ever prove dangerous, and
cause them to be rigid in a religious capacity—{they} should be armed
with mercy, notwithstanding the iniquity among us. (HC 5:19)

6   *Report of Eliza R. Snow:* President Joseph Smith continued his address; said he was going to preach mercy. Suppose that Jesus Christ
and holy angels should object to us on frivolous things, what would
become of us? We must be merciful to one another, and overlook
small things. (HC 5:23)

Mercy
   1   Instructions to the Apostles and Seventies departing for missions to En-
       gland, Commerce (Nauvoo), 2 July 1839.
   2   Letter to William W. Phelps, Nauvoo, 22 July 1840.
   3   General conference address, Nauvoo, 3 October 1841.
   4   Remarks to the Relief Society, Nauvoo, 28 April 1842.
   5   Remarks to the Relief Society, Nauvoo, 26 May 1842.
   6   Remarks to the Relief Society, Nauvoo, 9 June 1842.

7   There should be no license for sin, but mercy should go hand in hand with reproof. (HC 5:24)

Messiah
See JESUS CHRIST

Millennium

1   It is not the multitude of preachers that is to bring about the glorious millennium! but it is those who are "called, and chosen, and faithful." (HC 1:468)

2   *Minutes:* Joseph said that the wicked will not all be destroyed at the coming of Christ, and also there will be wicked during the Millennium. For instance, Isaiah says the days of an infant shall be as the age of a tree; also Zachariah says all who do not come up year by year with their gifts to the priests of the tabernacle that no rain shall fall upon them. And that Jesus will be a resident on the earth a thousand {years} with the Saints is not the case but will reign over the Saints and come down and instruct [them] as he did the five hundred brethren (1st Cor. 15), and those of the first resurrection will also reign with him over the Saints. Then after the little season is expired and the earth undergoes its last change and is glorified, then will all the meek inherit the earth wherein dwelleth [the] righteous. (*WJS*, p. 65; standardized)

3   This [the Millennium] is the only thing that can bring about the "restitution of all things spoken of by all the holy Prophets since the world was"—"the dispensation of the fullness of times, when God

---

Mercy
  7   Remarks to the Relief Society, Nauvoo, 9 June 1842.

Millennium
  1   Letter to the elders of the Church, published in *The Evening and the Morning Star*, Kirtland, December 1833.
  2   Remarks at the Nauvoo Lyceum meeting, 16 March 1841, as recorded in William P. McIntire's Minute Book, LDS Church Archives.
  3   Editorial in the *Times and Seasons*, 15 July 1842.

shall gather together all things in one." Other attempts to promote universal peace and happiness in the human family have proved abortive; every effort has failed; every plan and design has fallen to the ground; it needs the wisdom of God, the intelligence of God, and the power of God to accomplish this. The world has had a fair trial for six thousand years; the Lord will try the seventh thousand Himself; "He whose right it is, will possess the kingdom, and reign until He has put all things under His feet;" iniquity will hide its hoary head, Satan will be bound, and the works of darkness destroyed; righteousness will be put to the line, and judgment to the plummet, and "he that fears the Lord will alone be exalted in that day." To bring about this state of things, there must of necessity be great confusion among the nations of the earth; "distress of nations with perplexity." (HC 5:64–65)

4 Christ and the resurrected Saints will reign over the earth during the thousand years. They will not probably dwell upon the earth, but will visit it when they please, or when it is necessary to govern it. There will be wicked men on the earth during the thousand years. The heathen nations who will not come up to worship will be visited with the judgments of God, and must eventually be destroyed from the earth. (HC 5:212)

5 The battle of Gog and Magog will be after the millennium. The remnant of all the nations that fight against Jerusalem were commanded to go up to Jerusalem to worship in the millennium. (HC 5:298)

6 Christians should cease wrangling and contending with each other, and cultivate the principles of union and friendship in their midst; and they will do it before the millennium can be ushered in and Christ takes possession of His kingdom. (HC 5:499)

Millennium

4 In conversation with Judge James Adams, Springfield, Illinois, 30 December 1842. There is a footnote accompanying this quotation in *TPJS* (pp. 268–69) indicating that the "wicked" referred to as living on earth during the Millennium are those of a terrestrial nature but who have not yet received the gospel (see D&C 84:49–53).

5 Nauvoo, 4 March 1843.

6 Sabbath address, Nauvoo, 9 July 1843.

7   Friendship is one of the grand fundamental principles of "Mormonism"; {it is designed} to revolutionize and civilize the world, and cause wars and contentions to cease and men to become friends and brothers. Even the wolf and the lamb shall dwell together; the leopard shall lie down with the kid, the calf, the young lion and the fatling; and a little child shall lead them; the bear and the cow shall lie down together, and the sucking child shall play on the hole of the asp, and the weaned child shall play on the cockatrice's den; and they shall not hurt or destroy in all my holy mountains, saith the Lord of hosts. (Isaiah.) (*HC* 5:517)

Ministering Angels
See also ANGELS

1   *Minutes:* [President Joseph Smith] explained the difference between an angel and a ministering spirit; the one a resurrected or translated body, with its spirit ministering to embodied spirits—the other a disembodied spirit, visiting and ministering to disembodied spirits. Jesus Christ became a ministering spirit (while His body was lying in the sepulchre) to the spirits in prison, to fulfill an important part of His mission, without which He could not have perfected His work, or entered into His rest. After His resurrection He appeared as an angel to His disciples. (*HC* 4:425)

2   There have also been ministering angels in the Church which were of Satan appearing as an angel of light. A sister in the state of New York had a vision, who said it was told her that if she would go to a certain place in the woods, an angel would appear to her. She went at the appointed time, and saw a glorious personage descending, arrayed in white, with sandy colored hair; he commenced and told her to fear God, and said that her husband was called to do great things, but that he must not go more than one hundred miles from home, or

---

Millennium
   7   Sabbath address, Nauvoo, 23 July 1843.

Ministering Angels
   1   General conference address, Nauvoo, 3 October 1841.
   2   Editorial in the *Times and Seasons*, 1 April 1842.

he would not return; whereas God had called him to go to the ends of the earth, and he has since been more than one thousand miles from home, and is yet alive. Many true things were spoken by this personage, and many things were false. How, it may be asked, was this known to be a bad angel? By the color of his hair; that is one of the signs that he can be known by, and by his contradicting a former revelation. (HC 4:581)

3   The organization of the spiritual and heavenly worlds, and of spiritual and heavenly beings, was agreeable to the most perfect order and harmony: their limits and bounds were fixed irrevocably, and voluntarily subscribed to in their heavenly estate by themselves, and were by our first parents subscribed to upon the earth. Hence the importance of embracing and subscribing to principles of eternal truth by all men upon the earth that expect eternal life. (HC 6:51)

Miracles

1   Amongst those who attended our meetings regularly, was Newel Knight, son of Joseph Knight. He and I had many serious conversations on the important subject of man's eternal salvation. We had got into the habit of praying much at our meetings, and Newel had said that he would try and take up his cross, and pray vocally during meeting; but when we again met together, he rather excused himself. I tried to prevail upon him, making use of the figure, supposing that he should get into a mud-hole, would he not try to help himself out? And I further said that we were willing now to help him out of the mud-hole. He replied, that provided he had got into a mud-hole through carelessness, he would rather wait and get out himself, than to have others help him; and so he would wait until he could get into the woods by himself, and there he would pray. Accordingly, he deferred praying until next morning, when he retired into the woods; where, according to his own account afterwards, he made several attempts to

---

Ministering Angels
    3   Remarks upon the death of James Adams, Nauvoo, 9 October 1843.

Miracles
    1   Colesville, New York, April 1830.

pray, but could scarcely do so, feeling that he had not done his duty, in refusing to pray in the presence of others. He began to feel uneasy, and continued to feel worse both in mind and body, until, upon reaching his own house, his appearance was such as to alarm his wife very much. He requested her to go and bring me to him. I went and found him suffering very much in his mind, and his body acted upon in a very strange manner; his visage and limbs distorted and twisted in every shape and appearance possible to imagine; and finally he was caught up off the floor of the apartment, and tossed about most fearfully.

His situation was soon made known to his neighbors and relatives, and in a short time as many as eight or nine grown persons had got together to witness the scene. After he had thus suffered for a time, I succeeded in getting hold of him by the hand, when almost immediately he spoke to me, and with great earnestness requested me to cast the devil out of him, saying that he knew he was in him, and that he also knew that I could cast him out.

I replied, "If you know that I can, it shall be done;" and then almost unconsciously I rebuked the devil, and commanded him in the name of Jesus Christ to depart from him; when immediately Newel spoke out and said that he saw the devil leave him and vanish from his sight. This was the first miracle which was done in the Church, or by any member of it; and it was done not by man, nor by the power of man, but it was done by God, and by the power of godliness; therefore, let the honor and the praise, the dominion and the glory, be ascribed to the Father, Son, and Holy Spirit, for ever and ever. Amen. (HC 1:82–83)

2   When we arrived, some of the young Elders were about engaging in a debate on the subject of miracles. The question—"Was it, or was it not, the design of Christ to establish His Gospel by miracles?" After an interesting debate of three hours or more, during which time much talent was displayed, it was decided, by the President of the debate, in the negative, which was a righteous decision. (HC 2:317)

3   The Egyptians were not able to discover the difference between the miracles of Moses and those of the magicians until they came to

---

Miracles

2   Gathering of a few Saints in Father Smith's home, Kirtland, 18 November 1835.

3   Editorial in the *Times and Seasons*, 1 April 1842.

be tested together; and if Moses had not appeared in their midst, they would unquestionably have thought that the miracles of the magicians were performed through the mighty power of God, for they were great miracles that were performed by them—a supernatural agency was developed, and great power manifested. (HC 4:571)

4   It is not to be wondered at that men should be ignorant, in a great measure, of the principles of salvation, and more especially of the nature, office, power, influence, gifts, and blessings of the gift of the Holy Ghost; when we consider that the human family have been enveloped in gross darkness and ignorance for many centuries past, without revelation, or any just criterion {by which} to arrive at a knowledge of the things of God, which can only be known by the Spirit of God. Hence it not infrequently occurs, that when the Elders of this Church preach to the inhabitants of the world, that if they obey the Gospel they shall receive the gift of the Holy Ghost, that the people expect to see some wonderful manifestation, some great display of power, or some extraordinary miracle performed; and it is often the case that young members of this Church for want of better information, carry along with them their old notions of things, and sometimes fall into egregious errors. . . .

The human family are very apt to run to extremes, especially in religious matters, and hence people in general, either want some miraculous display, or they will not believe in the gift of the Holy Ghost at all. . . .

The Lord cannot always be known by the thunder of His voice, by the display of His glory or by the manifestation of His power; and those that are the most anxious to see these things, are the least prepared to meet them, and were the Lord to manifest His power as He did to the children of Israel, such characters would be the first to say, "Let not the Lord speak any more, lest we His people die." (HC 5:26–27, 31)

5   Why did not God deliver Micaiah from the hands of his persecutors? Why did not Jeremiah *"work a miracle or two"* to help him out of

---

Miracles

4   Editorial in the *Times and Seasons*, 15 June 1842.

5   Response to a newspaper reporter's challenge that Joseph Smith prove his prophetic powers by performing a miracle, published in the *Times and Seasons*, 15 February 1843.

the dungeon? It would have been *"very convenient."* Why did not Zachariah, by a miracle, prevent the people from slaying him? Why did not our Savior come down from the cross? The people asked Him to do it; and besides, He had "saved others," and could not save Himself, so said the people. Why did He not prove His mission by working a miracle and coming down? Why did not Paul, by a miracle, prevent the people from stoning and whipping him? It would have been "very convenient." Or why did the Saints of God in every age have to wander about in sheep-skins or goat-skins, being tempted, tried, and sawn asunder, of whom the world was not worthy? I would here advise my worthy friend, before he talks of "proving missions," "working miracles," or any "convenience" of that kind, to read his Bible a little more, and the garbled stories of political demagogues less. (HC 5:276)

6   Miracles are the fruits of faith. (HC 5:355)

Missionary Work

1   A desire was manifested by all the Saints to go forward and labor with all their powers to spread the great and glorious principles of truth, which had been revealed by our Heavenly Father. A number were baptized during the conference, and the word of the Lord spread and prevailed. (HC 1:118)

2   I ask God in the name of Jesus, to . . . cause that His word may speedily go forth to the nations of the earth, to the accomplishing of His great work in bringing about the restoration of the house of Israel. (HC 1:451)

3   Let the Elders be exceedingly careful about unnecessarily disturbing and harrowing up the feelings of the people. Remember that your

---

Miracles
   6   Remarks to the Saints newly arrived from England, Nauvoo, 13 April 1843.

Missionary Work
   1   A conference of the Church held at Fayette, New York, 26 September 1830.
   2   Dedication of a printing establishment in Kirtland, 6 December 1833.
   3   Letter to the elders of the Church, published in *The Evening and the Morning Star*, Kirtland, December 1833.

business is to preach the Gospel in all humility and meekness, and warn sinners to repent and come to Christ. Avoid contentions and vain disputes with men of corrupt minds, who do not desire to know the truth. Remember that "it is a day of warning, and not a day of many words." If they receive not your testimony in one place, flee to another, remembering to cast no reflections, nor throw out any bitter sayings. If you do your duty, it will be just as well with you, as though all men embraced the Gospel.

Be careful about sending boys to preach the Gospel to the world; if they go, let them be accompanied by some one who is able to guide them in the proper channel, lest they become puffed up, and fall under condemnation, and into the snare of the devil. Finally, in these critical times, be careful; call on the Lord day and night; beware of pride; beware of false brethren, who will creep in among you to spy out your liberties. Awake to righteousness, and sin not; let your light shine, and show yourselves workmen that need not be ashamed, rightly dividing the word of truth. Apply yourselves diligently to study, that your minds may be stored with all necessary information. (HC 1:468–69)

4   The classes, being mostly Elders gave the most studious attention to the all-important object of qualifying themselves as messengers of Jesus Christ, to be ready to do His will in carrying glad tidings to all that would open their eyes, ears and hearts. (HC 2:176)

5   *Minutes:* Voted, that all the Elders of the Church are bound to travel in the world to preach the Gospel, with all their might, mind, and strength, when their circumstances will admit of it; and that the door is now opened. (HC 2:222)

6   *Words of George A. Smith:* On May 30, 1835, I was appointed on a mission to preach the gospel in the East. . . .

I called to see Cousin Joseph. He gave me a Book of Mormon, shook hands with me and said: "Preach short sermons, make short prayers, and deliver your sermons with a prayerful heart." (*TK*, p. 49)

Missionary Work

4   Description of the School of the Elders, Kirtland, 1 December 1834.

5   Minutes of a general council of the priesthood, Kirtland, 2 May 1835.

6   Recollection of George A. Smith contained in *Family of George A. Smith.*

7 *Now,* the Lord wants the wheat and tares to grow together; for Zion must be redeemed with judgment, and her converts with righteousness. Every Elder that can, after providing for his family (if he has any) and paying his debts, must go forth and clear his skirts from the blood of this generation. . . . Let every one labor to prepare himself for the vineyard, sparing a little time to comfort the mourners, to bind up the broken-hearted, to reclaim the backslider, to bring back the wanderer, to re-invite into the kingdom such as have been cut off, by encouraging them to lay to while the day lasts, and work righteousness, and, with one heart and one mind, prepare to help to redeem Zion, that goodly land of promise, where the willing and obedient shall be blessed. (HC 2:228–29)

8 And first, it becomes an Elder when he is traveling through the world, warning the inhabitants of the earth to gather together, that they may be built up an holy city unto the Lord, instead of commencing with children, or those who look up to parents or guardians to influence their minds, thereby drawing them from their duties, which they rightfully owe these legal guardians, they should commence their labors with parents, or guardians; and their teachings should be such as are calculated to turn the hearts of the fathers to the children, and the hearts of the children to the fathers; and no influence should be used with children, contrary to the consent of their parents or guardians; but all such as can be persuaded in a lawful and righteous manner, and with common consent. . . . But otherwise let the responsibility rest upon the heads of parents or guardians, and all condemnation or consequences be upon their heads, according to the dispensation which he hath committed unto us; for God hath so ordained, that His work shall be cut short in righteousness, in the last days; therefore, first teach the parents, and then, with their consent, persuade the children to embrace the Gospel also. And if children embrace the Gospel, and their parents or guardians are unbelievers, teach them to stay at home and be obedient to their parents or guardians, if they require it; but if they consent to let them gather with the people of God, let them do so, and there shall be no wrong;

Missionary Work

  7 Letter to the Saints in Missouri published in the *Messenger and Advocate,* June 1835.

  8 Letter to the elders of the Church, Kirtland, 1 September 1835.

and let all things be done carefully and righteously and God will extend to all such His guardian care.

And secondly, it is the duty of the Elders, when they enter into any house, to let their labors and warning voice be unto the master of that house; and if he receive the Gospel, then he may extend his influence to his wife also, with consent, that peradventure she may receive the Gospel; but if a man receive not the Gospel, but gives his consent that his wife may receive it, and she believes, then let her receive it. But if a man forbid his wife, or his children, before they are of age, to receive the Gospel, then it should be the duty of the Elder to go his way, and use no influence against him, and let the responsibility be upon his head; shake off the dust of thy feet as a testimony against him, and thy skirts shall then be clear of their souls. Their sins are not to be answered upon such as God hath sent to warn them to flee the wrath to come, and save themselves from this untoward generation. The servants of God will not have gone over the nations of the Gentiles, with a warning voice, until the destroying angel will commence to waste the inhabitants of the earth, and as the prophet hath said, "It shall be a vexation to hear the report." I speak thus because I feel for my fellow men; I do it in the name of the Lord, being moved upon by the Holy Spirit. Oh, that I could snatch them from the vortex of misery, into which I behold them plunging themselves, by their sins; that I might be enabled by the warning voice, to be an instrument of bringing them to unfeigned repentance, that they might have faith to stand in the evil day!

Thirdly, it should be the duty of an Elder, when he enters into a house, to salute the master of that house, and if he gain his consent, then he may preach to all that are in that house; but if he gain not his consent, let him not go unto his slaves, or servants, but let the responsibility be upon the head of the master of that house, and the consequences thereof, and the guilt of that house is no longer upon his skirts, he is free; therefore, let him shake off the dust of his feet, and go his way. But if the master of that house give consent, the Elder may preach to his family, his wife, his children and his servants, his man-servants, or his maid-servants, or his slaves; then it should be the duty of the Elder to stand up boldly for the cause of Christ, and warn that people with one accord to repent and be baptized for the remission of sins, and for the Holy Ghost, always commanding them in the name of the Lord, in the spirit of meekness, to be kindly affectionate one toward another, that the fathers should be kind to

their children, husbands to their wives, masters to their slaves or servants, children obedient to their parents, wives to their husbands, and
slaves or servants to their masters. (HC 2:262–64)

9 When you are endowed and prepared to preach the Gospel to all
nations, kindred, and tongues, in their own languages, you must faithfully warn all, and bind up the testimony, and seal up the law, and the
destroying angel will follow close at your heels, and exercise his
tremendous mission upon the children of disobedience; and destroy
the workers of iniquity, while the Saints will be gathered out from
among them, and stand in holy places ready to meet the Bridegroom
when he comes. (HC 2:309)

10 [The assembly] voted that the Twelve and Seventy see that the
calls for preaching in the region round about Kirtland be attended to,
and filled by judicious Elders of this Church. (HC 2:400)

11 Before closing this communication, I beg leave to drop a word to
the traveling Elders. You know, brethren, that great responsibility
rests upon you; and that you are accountable to God, for all you teach
the world. . . .

I do most sincerely hope that no one who is authorized from this
Church to preach the Gospel, will so far depart from the Scriptures, as
to be found stirring up strife and sedition against our brethren of the
South. (HC 2:440)

12 No man can preach the Gospel without the Holy Ghost.
. . . After all has been said, the greatest and most important duty
is to preach the Gospel. (HC 2:477, 478)

13 When the Twelve or any other witnesses stand before the congregations of the earth, and they preach in the power and demonstration
of the Spirit of God, and the people are astonished and confounded at

---

Missionary Work
9 Instructions to the Twelve, Kirtland, 12 November 1835.
10 Priesthood meeting, Kirtland, 24 February 1836.
11 Letter on abolition published in the *Messenger and Advocate*, April 1836.
12 Solemn assembly in the Kirtland Temple, 6 April 1837.
13 Instructions to the Apostles and Seventies departing for missions to England, Commerce (Nauvoo), 2 July 1839.

the doctrine, and say, "That man has preached a powerful discourse, a great sermon," then let that man or those men take care that they do not ascribe the glory unto themselves, but be careful that they are humble, and ascribe the praise and glory to God and the Lamb; for it is by the power of the Holy Priesthood and the Holy Ghost that they have power thus to speak. What art thou, O man, but dust? And from whom receivest thou thy power and blessings, but from God? (HC 3:384)

14 In England many hundreds have of late been added to our numbers; but so, even so, it must be, for "Ephraim he hath mixed himself among the people." And the Savior He hath said, "My sheep hear my voice;" and also, "He that heareth you, heareth me." (HC 4:8)

15 After others had spoken I spoke and explained concerning the uselessness of preaching to the world about great judgments, but rather to preach the simple Gospel. (HC 4:11)

16 *Minutes:* Having now got through the business matters, the President [Joseph Smith] proceeded to give instruction to the Elders respecting preaching the Gospel, and pressed upon them the necessity of getting the Spirit, so that they might preach with the Holy Ghost sent down from heaven; to be careful in speaking on those subjects which are not clearly pointed out in the word of God, which lead to speculation and strife. (HC 4:13)

17 Those engaged in seeking the outcasts of Israel, and the dispersed of Judah, cannot fail to enjoy the Spirit of the Lord and have the choicest blessings of Heaven rest upon them in copious effusions.

. . . He who scattered Israel has promised to gather them; therefore inasmuch as you are to be instrumental in this great work, He will endow you with power, wisdom, might, and intelligence, and every qualification necessary; while your minds will expand wider and wider, until you can circumscribe the earth and the heavens, reach

---

Missionary Work

14 Letter to Isaac Galland, Commerce (Nauvoo), 11 September 1839.

15 Sabbath address, Commerce (Nauvoo), 29 September 1839.

16 Minutes of a general conference of the Church, Commerce (Nauvoo), 6 October 1839.

17 Letter to Orson Hyde and John E. Page, Nauvoo, 14 May 1840.

forth into eternity, and contemplate the mighty acts of Jehovah in all
their variety and glory. (HC 4:128, 129)

18 Be assured, beloved brethren, that I am no disinterested observer
of the things which are transpiring on the face of the whole earth; and
amidst the general movements which are in progress, none is of more
importance than the glorious work in which you are now engaged.
(HC 4:226)

19 When the apostles were raised up, they worked in Jerusalem, and
Jesus commanded them to tarry there until they were endowed with
power from on high. Had they not work to do in Jerusalem? They did
work, and prepared a people for the Pentecost. . . . The endowment
was to prepare the disciples for their missions unto the world.
. . . We don't ask any people to throw away any good they have
got; we only ask them to come and get more. What if all the world
should embrace this Gospel? They would then see eye to eye, and the
blessings of God would be poured out upon the people, which is the
desire of my whole soul. Amen. (HC 5:259)

20 Oh, ye elders of Israel, hearken to my voice; and when you are
sent into the world to preach, tell those things you are sent to tell;
preach and cry aloud, "Repent ye, for the kingdom of heaven is at
hand; repent and believe the Gospel." Declare the first principles, and
let mysteries alone, lest ye be overthrown. Never meddle with the visions of beasts and subjects you do not understand. . . . Preach those
things the Lord has told you to preach about—repentance and baptism for the remission of sins. (HC 5:344)

21 As Paul said he had to become all things to all men, that he might
thereby save some, so must the elders of the last days do; and, being
sent out to preach the Gospel and warn the world of the judgments to

---

Missionary Work

18 Letter to the Twelve in England, Nauvoo, 15 December 1840. The place-
    ment of this letter in *HC* implies that it was written in October 1840, but
    actually it was written on 15 December 1840 (see *PWJS*, p. 480).
19 Sabbath address, Nauvoo, 22 January 1843.
20 General conference address, Nauvoo, 8 April 1843.
21 To the editor of the *Times and Seasons*, published in the 15 May 1843 issue
    of that paper.

come, we are sure, when they teach as directed by the Spirit, according to the revelations of Jesus Christ, that they will preach the truth and prosper without complaint. (HC 5:404)

22 It always has been when a man was sent of God with the priesthood and he began to preach the fullness of the gospel, that he was thrust out by his friends, who are ready to butcher him if he teach things which they imagine to be wrong; and Jesus was crucified upon this principle. (HC 5:425)

Missouri

1 I received, by a heavenly vision, a commandment in June following, to take my journey to the western boundaries of the State of Missouri, and there designate the very spot which was to be the central place for the commencement of the gathering together of those who embrace the fullness of the everlasting Gospel. . . . After viewing the country, seeking diligently at the hand of God, He manifested Himself unto us, and designated, to me and others, the very spot upon which He designed to commence the work of the gathering, and the upbuilding of an "holy city," which should be called Zion—Zion, because it is a place of righteousness, and all who build thereon are to worship the true and living God, and all believe in one doctrine, even the doctrine of our Lord and Savior Jesus Christ. (HC 2:254)

Moderation

1 But in all matters, temporal or spiritual, preaching the Gospel of Jesus Christ, or in leading an army to battle, victory almost entirely depends upon good order and moderation. (HC 5:389)

Missionary Work
   22 Sabbath address, Nauvoo, 11 June 1843.

Missouri
   1 Letter to the elders of the Church, Kirtland, 1 September 1835.

Moderation
   1 Sabbath address at Yelrome (Morley's Settlement), Illinois, 14 May 1843.

Mormonism, Mormons

1   In the first place, I have stated above that Mormonism is truth. In other words, the doctrine of the Latter-day Saints is truth; for the name Mormon, and Mormonism, was given to us by our enemies, but Latter-day Saints was the real name by which the Church was organized. (*PWJS*, p. 420; standardized)

2   Hell may pour forth its rage like the burning lava of mount Vesuvius, or of Etna, or of the most terrible of the burning mountains; and yet shall "Mormonism" stand. Water, fire, truth and God are all realities. Truth is "Mormonism." God is the author of it. He is our shield. It is by Him we received our birth. It was by His voice that we were called to a dispensation of His Gospel in the beginning of the fullness of times. It was by Him we received the Book of Mormon; and it is by Him that we remain unto this day; and by Him we shall remain, if it shall be for our glory; and in His Almighty name we are determined to endure tribulation as good soldiers unto the end. (*HC* 3:297)

3   Sir:—Through the medium of your paper, I wish to correct an error among men that profess to be learned, liberal and wise; and I do it the more cheerfully, because I hope sober-thinking and sound-reasoning people will sooner listen to the voice of truth, than be led astray by the vain pretensions of the self-wise. The error I speak of, is the definition of the word "Mormon." It has been stated that this word was derived from the Greek word *mormo*. This is not the case. There was no Greek or Latin upon the plates from which I, through the grace of God, translated the Book of Mormon. Let the language of that book speak for itself. On the 523d page, of the fourth edition, it reads: "And now behold we have written this record according to our knowledge in the characters, which are called among us the *Reformed Egyptian*, being handed down and altered by us, according to our manner of speech; and if our plates had been sufficiently large, we

---

Mormonism, Mormons
1   Letter to Isaac Galland, written while the Prophet was imprisoned in Liberty Jail, 22 March 1839.
2   Letter to the Saints from Liberty Jail, 20–25 March 1839.
3   Letter to the editor of the *Times and Seasons*, published in the 15 May 1843 issue of that paper.

should have written in Hebrew: but the Hebrew hath been altered by us, also; and if we could have written in Hebrew, behold ye would have had no imperfection in our record, but the Lord knoweth the things which we have written, and also, that none other people knoweth our language; therefore he hath prepared means for the interpretation thereof."

Here then the subject is put to silence, for *"none other people knoweth our language,"* therefore the Lord, and not man, had to interpret, after the people were all dead. . . . I may safely say that the word Mormon stands independent of the learning and wisdom of this generation.—Before I give a definition, however, to the word, let me say that the Bible in its widest sense, means *good;* for the Savior says according to the gospel of John, "I am the *good* shepherd;" and it will not be beyond the common use of terms, to say that good is among the most important in use, and though known by various names in different languages, still its meaning is the same, and is ever in opposition to *bad.* We say from the Saxon, *good;* the Dane, *god;* the Goth, *goda;* the German, *gut;* the Dutch, *goed;* the Latin, *bonus;* the Greek, *kalos;* the Hebrew, *tob;* and the Egyptian, *mon.* Hence, with the addition of *more,* or the contraction, *mor,* we have the word "Mormon"; which means, literally, *more good. (T&S* 4:194)

4   One of the grand fundamental principles of "Mormonism" is to receive truth, let it come from whence it may. (HC 5:499)

5   Have the Presbyterians any truth? Yes. Have the Baptists, Methodists, &c., any truth? Yes. They all have a little truth mixed with error. We should gather all the good and true principles in the world and treasure them up, or we shall not come out true "Mormons." (HC 5:517)

Moses
See LAW OF MOSES

Mormonism, Mormons
  4   Sabbath address, Nauvoo, 9 July 1843.
  5   Sabbath address, Nauvoo, 23 July 1843.

Mother in Heaven

1 *Words of Susa Young Gates:* An interesting sidelight is given to this time [during which the hymn "O My Father" was written] through a possible glimpse of the thought-kernel which grew into such fragrant bloom in the full-voiced poem of Sister [Eliza R.] Snow. It was told by Aunt Zina D. Young to the writer as to many others during her life. Father Huntington lost his wife under the most trying circumstances. Her children were left desolate. One day, when her daughter Zina was speaking with the Prophet Joseph Smith concerning the loss of her mother and her intense grief, she asked the question:

"Will I know my mother as my mother when I get over on the Other Side?"

"Certainly you will," was the instant reply of the Prophet. "More than that, you will meet and become acquainted with your eternal Mother, the wife of your Father in Heaven."

"And have I then a Mother in Heaven?" exclaimed the astonished girl.

"You assuredly have. How could a Father claim His title unless there were also a Mother to share that parenthood?"

It was about this time that Sister Snow learned the same glorious truth from the same inspired lips, and at once she was moved to express her own great joy and gratitude in the moving words of the hymn, "O My Father," which includes the pregnant couplet:

"Truth is reason; truth eternal
Tells me I've a mother there."

(Gates, *History of the Young Ladies MIA*, p. 16)

Mourning

1 All children are redeemed by the blood of Jesus Christ, and the moment that children leave this world, they are taken to the bosom of

---

Mother in Heaven
    1 Recollection of Zina Diantha Huntington Young reported by Susa Young Gates.

Mourning
    1 Sabbath address, Nauvoo, 20 March 1842.

Abraham. The only difference between the old and young dying is, one lives longer in heaven and eternal light and glory than the other, and is freed a little sooner from this miserable, wicked world. Notwithstanding all this glory, we for a moment lose sight of it, and mourn the loss, but we do not mourn as those without hope. (HC 4:554)

2   All your losses will be made up to you in the resurrection, provided you continue faithful. By the vision of the Almighty I have seen it.

More painful to me are the thoughts of annihilation than death. If I have no expectation of seeing my father, mother, brothers, sisters and friends again, my heart would burst in a moment, and I should go down to my grave.

The expectation of seeing my friends in the morning of the resurrection cheers my soul and makes me bear up against the evils of life. It is like their taking a long journey, and on their return we meet them with increased joy.

God has revealed His Son from the heavens and the doctrine of the resurrection also; and we have a knowledge that those we bury here God will bring up again, clothed upon and quickened by the Spirit of the great God; and what mattereth it whether we lay them down, or we lay down with them, when we can keep them no longer? Let these truths sink down in your hearts, that we may even here begin to enjoy that which shall be in full hereafter.

. . . When others rejoice, I rejoice; when they mourn, I mourn. (HC 5:362)

3   These are the first principles of consolation. How consoling to the mourners when they are called to part with a husband, wife, father, mother, child, or dear relative, to know that, although the earthly tabernacle is laid down and dissolved, they shall rise again to dwell in everlasting burnings in immortal glory, not to sorrow, suffer, or die any more, but they shall be heirs of God and joint heirs with Jesus Christ. (HC 6:306)

4   You mourners have occasion to rejoice, speaking of the death of Elder King Follett; for your husband and father is gone to wait until

---

Mourning

  2   Remarks upon the death of Lorenzo D. Barnes, Nauvoo, 16 April 1843.
  3   King Follett Discourse, Nauvoo, 7 April 1844.
  4   King Follett Discourse, Nauvoo, 7 April 1844.

the resurrection of the dead—until the perfection of the remainder; for at the resurrection your friend will rise in perfect felicity and go to celestial glory. (HC 6:315)

Murder

1   The time of redemption here [Acts 3:19–20] had reference to the time when Christ should come; then, and not till then, would their sins be blotted out. Why? Because they were murderers, and no murderer hath eternal life. Even David must wait for those times of refreshing, before he can come forth and his sins be blotted out. For Peter, speaking of him says, "David hath not yet ascended into heaven, for his sepulchre is with us to this day." His remains were then in the tomb. Now, we read that many bodies of the Saints arose at Christ's resurrection, probably all the Saints, but it seems that David did not. Why? Because he had been a murderer. If the ministers of religion had a proper understanding of the doctrine of eternal judgment, they would not be found attending the man who forfeited his life to the injured laws of his country, by shedding innocent blood; for such characters cannot be forgiven, until they have paid the last farthing. The prayers of all the ministers in the world can never close the gates of hell against a murderer. (HC 4:359)

2   God said, "Thou shalt not kill;" at another time He said, "Thou shalt utterly destroy." This is the principle on which the government of heaven is conducted—by revelation adapted to the circumstances in which the children of the kingdom are placed. Whatever God requires is right, no matter what it is, although we may not see the reason thereof till long after the events transpire. (HC 5:135)

3   A murderer, for instance, one that sheds innocent blood, cannot have forgiveness. David sought repentance at the hand of God carefully with tears, for the murder of Uriah; but he could only get it through hell: he got a promise that his soul should not be left in hell.

Murder
1   Sabbath address, Nauvoo, 16 May 1841.
2   Essay on happiness, Nauvoo, 27 August 1842.
3   Sabbath address, Nauvoo, 10 March 1844.

Although David was a king, he never did obtain the spirit and power of Elijah and the fullness of the Priesthood; and the Priesthood that he received, and the throne and kingdom of David is to be taken from him and given to another by the name of David in the last days, raised up out of his lineage.

Peter referred to the same subject on the day of Pentecost, but the multitude did not get the endowment that Peter had; but several days after, the people asked "What shall we do?" Peter says, "I would ye had done it ignorantly," speaking of crucifying the Lord, &c. He did not say to them, "Repent and be baptized, for the remission of your sins;" but he said, "Repent ye therefore, and be converted, that your sins may be blotted out, when the times of refreshing shall come from the presence of the Lord." (Acts iii. 19.)

This is the case with murderers. They could not be baptized for the remission of sins for they had shed innocent blood. (HC 6:253)

4   Rejoice, O Israel! Your friends who have been murdered for the truth's sake in the persecutions shall triumph gloriously in the celestial world, while their murderers shall welter for ages in torment, even until they shall have paid the uttermost farthing. I say this for the benefit of strangers. (HC 6:315)

Murmuring

1   When I contemplate upon all things that have been manifested, I am aware that I ought not to murmur, and do not murmur, only in this, that those who are innocent are compelled to suffer for the iniquities of the guilty. (HC 1:454)

2   *Words of George A. Smith:* During our noon meal, near the place where the town of Pittsfield stands, Joseph stood on a wagon while he made a speech to the camp. He said: "The Lord is displeased with us.

Murder
4   King Follett Discourse, Nauvoo, 7 April 1844.

Murmuring
1   Letter to the exiled Saints in Missouri, Kirtland, 10 December 1833.
2   Recollection of George A. Smith regarding events of Zion's Camp, mid-1834, contained in *Family of George A. Smith.*

Our murmuring and fault finding and want of humility has kindled the anger of the Lord against us. A severe scourge will come upon the camp, and many will die like sheep with rot, and we cannot help it. It must come. But by repentance and humility and the prayer of faith, the chastisement may be alleviated, but cannot be entirely turned away, for as the Lord lives, this camp must suffer a severe scourge for their wickedness and rebellion. I say it in the name of the Lord."

This prophecy struck me to the heart. I thought we should probably get into battle with the mob and some of us get killed. Little thought I that within four weeks a dozen of my brethren would be laid in the ground without coffins, by the fell hand of the plague. But it was so, and I learned ever after to heed the counsels of the Prophet, and not murmur at the dispensations of Providence. (*TK*, p. 48)

3   Now for persons to do things, merely because they are advised to do them, and yet murmur all the time they are doing them, is of no use at all; they might as well not do them. (*T&S* 1:29)

4   If the Church would cease from these bickerings and murmurings, and be of one mind, the Lord would visit them with health and every needed good. (*WJS*, p. 37; standardized)

5   *Minutes:* President Joseph Smith . . . made some very appropriate remarks concerning . . . the inconsistency, folly, and danger of murmuring against the dispensation of Jehovah. (*HC* 4:583)

6   I showed them that it was generally in consequence of the brethren disregarding or disobeying counsel that they became dissatisfied and murmured; and many when they arrived here, were dissatisfied with the conduct of some of the Saints, because everything was not done perfectly right, and they get angry, and thus the devil gets advantage over them to destroy them. (*HC* 5:181)

Murmuring
3   Letter to the Saints published in the *Times and Seasons*, December 1839.
4   Instruction at a Thursday fast meeting, Nauvoo, 30 July 1840, as reported by John Smith.
5   Minutes of a general conference of the Church, Nauvoo, 7 April 1842.
6   Instructions to a group of Saints who had newly arrived in Nauvoo, 29 October 1842.

7 While Jesus was teaching the people, all the publicans and sinners drew near to hear Him; "and the Pharisees and scribes murmured, saying, This man receiveth sinners, and eateth with them." This is the keyword which unlocks the parable of the prodigal son. It was given to answer the murmurings and questions of the Sadducees and Pharisees. . . . This represents hunting after a few individuals, or one poor publican, which the Pharisees and Sadducees despised.

He also gave them the parable of the woman and her ten pieces of silver, and how she lost one, and searching diligently, found it again, which gave more joy among the friends and neighbors than the nine which were not lost; like I say unto you, there is joy in the presence of the angels of God over one sinner that repenteth, more than over ninety-and-nine just persons that are so righteous; they will be damned anyhow; you cannot save them. (HC 5:261, 262)

8 There is a great deal of murmuring in the Church about me; but I don't care anything about it. I like to hear it thunder, and I like to hear the Saints grumble; for the growling dog gets the sorest head. If any man is poor and afflicted, let him come and tell of it, and not complain or grumble about it. (HC 5:285)

9 Some would complain with what God Himself would do. (HC 6:237)

10 At all events, the people ought not to complain of the officers; but if they are not satisfied, they should complain to the lawmakers by petition. (HC 6:237)

Music

1 *Minutes:* President Joseph Smith called upon the choir to sing a hymn, and remarked that "tenor charms the ear, bass, the heart." (HC 5:339)

Murmuring
7 Sabbath address, Nauvoo, 29 January 1843.
8 Address at the temple site in Nauvoo, 21 February 1843.
9 Remarks at meeting at temple in Nauvoo, 7 March 1844.
10 Remarks at meeting at temple in Nauvoo, 7 March 1844.

Music
1 General conference address, Nauvoo, 8 April 1843.

2   In the evening, several of the Twelve and others called to visit me. My family sang hymns. (HC 6:79)

3   This morning, about one o'clock, I was aroused by an English sister, Lettice Rushton, widow of Richard Rushton, Senior, (who, ten years ago, lost her sight,) accompanied by three of her sons, with their wives, and her two daughters, with their husbands, and several of her neighbors, singing, "Mortals, awake! with angels join," &c., which caused a thrill of pleasure to run through my soul. All of my family and boarders arose to hear the serenade, and I felt to thank my Heavenly Father for their visit, and blessed them in the name of the Lord. They also visited my brother Hyrum, who was awakened from his sleep. He arose and went out of doors. He shook hands with and blessed each one of them in the name of the Lord, and said that he thought at first that a cohort of angels had come to visit him, it was such heavenly music to him. . . .

A large party supped at my house, and spent the evening in music, dancing, &c., in a most cheerful and friendly manner. (HC 6:134)

4   *History Entry:* 3:15 p.m.—The guard began to be more severe in their operations, threatening among themselves, and telling what they would do when the excitement was over.

Elder Taylor sang the following:—*The Poor Wayfaring Man of Grief.* . . .

When he got through, Joseph requested him to sing it again, which he did. (HC 6:614, 615)

Mysteries

1   Strive not about the mysteries of the kingdom; cast not your pearls before swine, give not the bread of the children to dogs, lest you

---

Music
2   Nauvoo, 20 November 1843.
3   Christmas Day, Nauvoo, 25 December 1843.
4   Carthage Jail, 27 June 1844.

Mysteries
1   Letter to the Saints in Missouri published in the *Messenger and Advocate*, June 1835.

and the children should suffer, and you thereby offend your righteous Judge. (*HC* 2:230)

2 We are called to hold the keys of the mysteries of those things that have been kept hid from the foundation of the world until now. Some have tasted a little of these things, many of which are to be poured down from heaven upon the heads of babes; yea, upon the weak, obscure and despised ones of the earth. (*HC* 3:296)

3 Many men will say, "I will never forsake you, but will stand by you at all times." But the moment you teach them some of the mysteries of the kingdom of God that are retained in the heavens and are to be revealed to the children of men when they are prepared for them, they will be the first to stone you and put you to death. It was this same principle that crucified the Lord Jesus Christ, and will cause the people to kill the prophets in this generation. (*HC* 5:424)

4 I advise all to go on to perfection, and search deeper and deeper into the mysteries of Godliness. (*HC* 6:363)

Nauvoo

1 The City Charter of Nauvoo is of my own plan and device. I concocted it for the salvation of the Church, and on principles so broad, that every honest man might dwell secure under its protective influence without distinction of sect or party. (*HC* 4:249)

2 The name of our city (Nauvoo) is of Hebrew origin, and signifies a beautiful situation, or place, carrying with it, also, the idea of rest; and is truly descriptive of the most delightful location. It is situated on the east bank of the Mississippi river, at the head of the Des Moines

---

Mysteries
2   Letter to the Saints from Liberty Jail, 20–25 March 1839.
3   Sabbath address, Nauvoo, 11 June 1843.
4   Sabbath address, Nauvoo, 12 May 1844.

Nauvoo
1   Nauvoo, December 1840.
2   Proclamation of the First Presidency, Nauvoo, 15 January 1841.

Rapids, in Hancock county, bounded on the east by an extensive prairie of surpassing beauty, and on the north, west, and south, by the Mississippi. . . .

The "University of the City of Nauvoo" will enable us to teach our children wisdom, to instruct them in all the knowledge and learning, in the arts, sciences, and learned professions. We hope to make this institution one of the great lights of the world, and by and through it to diffuse that kind of knowledge which will be of practicable utility, and for the public good, and also for private and individual happiness. (HC 4:268, 269)

3   Here the Temple must be raised, the University built, and other edifices erected which are necessary for the great work of the last days, and which can only be done by a concentration of energy and enterprise. (HC 4:362)

4   In regard to moral principles there is no city either in this State, or in the United States, that can compare with the city of Nauvoo; you may live in our city for a month and not hear an oath sworn, you may be here as long and not see one person intoxicated so notorious are we for sobriety, that at the time the Washingtonian convention passed through our city a meeting was called for them; but they expressed themselves at a loss what to say, as there were no drunkards to speak to; so that whether as a civil, moral or religious community we think that we can say without vanity that we are as orderly as any other community, in any town or city in this State, or in the United States; and we are laying a foundation for agricultural and manufactoring purposes, that bids fair to rival if not to exceed, any city in the western country. (T&S 3:832)

5   The building of the Nauvoo House is just as sacred in my view as the Temple. I want the Nauvoo House built. It *must* be built. Our salvation {as a city} depends upon it.

When men have done what they can or will do for the Temple, let them do what they can for the Nauvoo House. We never can accomplish one work at the expense of another. . . .

Nauvoo
3   Letter to the Saints, Nauvoo, 24 May 1841.
4   Response to a letter by William Law, published in the *Times and Seasons*, 1 July 1842.
5   Address at the temple site in Nauvoo, 21 February 1843.

The finishing of the Nauvoo House is like a man finishing a fight; if he gives up, he is killed; if he holds out a little longer, he may live. (HC 5:285)

6   It is necessary that this conference give importance to the Nauvoo House. A prejudice exists against building it, in favor of the Temple; and the conference is required to give stress to the building of the Nauvoo House. This is the most important matter for the time being; for there is no place in this city where men of wealth, character and influence from abroad can go to repose themselves, and it is necessary we should have such a place. The Church must build it or abide the result of not fulfilling the commandment. (HC 5:328)

7   *History Entry:* Joseph paused when they got to the Temple, and looked with admiration first on that, and then on the city, and remarked, "This is the loveliest place and the best people under the heavens; little do they know the trials that await them." (HC 6:554)

New Jerusalem

1   On the 19th of June, in company with Sidney Rigdon, Martin Harris, Edward Partridge, William W. Phelps, Joseph Coe, Algernon S. Gilbert and his wife, I started from Kirtland, Ohio, for the land of Missouri, agreeable to the commandment before received [D&C 56], wherein it was promised that if we were faithful, the land of our inheritance, even the place for the city of the New Jerusalem, should be revealed. (HC 1:188)

2   "Behold this people will I establish in this land, unto the fulfilling of the covenant which I made with your father Jacob, and it shall be a New Jerusalem." [3 Nephi 20:22.] Now we learn from the Book of Mormon the very identical continent and spot of land upon which the New Jerusalem is to stand, and it must be caught up according to the vision of John upon the isle of Patmos.

Nauvoo
  6   General conference address, Nauvoo, 6 April 1843.
  7   En route to Carthage, leaving Nauvoo for the last time, 24 June 1844.

New Jerusalem
  1   Kirtland, 19 June 1831.
  2   Letter to the elders of the Church, Kirtland, 1 September 1835.

Now many will feel disposed to say, that this New Jerusalem spoken of, is the Jerusalem that was built by the Jews on the eastern continent. But you will see, from Revelation xxi:2, there was a New Jerusalem coming down from God out of heaven, adorned as a bride for her husband; that after this, the Revelator was caught away in the Spirit, to a great and high mountain, and saw the great and holy city descending out of heaven from God. Now there are two cities spoken of here. As everything cannot be had in so narrow a compass as a letter, I shall say with brevity, that there is a New Jerusalem to be established on this continent, and also Jerusalem shall be rebuilt on the eastern continent (See Book of Mormon, Ether xiii:1–12). "Behold, Ether saw the days of Christ, and he spake also concerning the house of Israel, and the Jerusalem from whence Lehi should come; after it should be destroyed, it should be built up again, a holy city unto the Lord, wherefore it could not be a New Jerusalem, for it had been in a time of old." This may suffice, upon the subject of gathering, until my next. (HC 2:261–62)

Noah

1   The Priesthood was first given to Adam; he obtained the First Presidency, and held the keys of it from generation to generation. He obtained it in the Creation, before the world was formed, as in Gen. i:26, 27, 28. He had dominion given him over every living creature. He is Michael the Archangel, spoken of in the Scriptures. Then to Noah, who is Gabriel; he stands next in authority to Adam in the Priesthood; he was called of God to this office, and was the father of all living in his day, and to him was given the dominion. These men held keys first on earth, and then in heaven. (HC 3:385–86)

2   Thus we behold the keys of this Priesthood consisted in obtaining the voice of Jehovah that He talked with him {Noah} in a familiar and friendly manner, that He continued to him the keys, the covenants, the power and the glory, with which He blessed Adam at the begin-

---

Noah

1   Discourse on the priesthood, given sometime before 8 August 1839, Commerce (Nauvoo). For a discussion on the dating of this discourse, see *WJS*, p. 22.

2   Article on priesthood read at general conference, Nauvoo, 5 October 1840.

ning; and the offering of sacrifice, which also shall be continued at the last time. (HC 4:210)

3   The construction of the first vessel was given to Noah, by revela-tion. The design of the ark was given by God, "a pattern of heavenly things." (HC 5:63)

4   As Noah was a preacher of righteousness he must have been bap-tised and ordained to the priesthood by the laying on of the hands, &c. (T&S 3:904)

Obedience

1   The . . . glorious manifestations of the powers of the Priesthood, the gifts and blessings of the Holy Ghost, and the goodness and con-descension of a merciful God [are] unto such as obey the everlasting Gospel of our Lord Jesus Christ. (HC 1:85–86)

2   *Words of Philo Dibble:* I was with Joseph the morning after he was tarred and feathered by a mob in the town of Hiram, Ohio. After he had washed and dressed in clean clothes, I heard him say to Sidney Rigdon, who was also tarred and feathered, "Now, Sidney, we are ready to go on that mission."
    He had reference to a command of God to go to Jackson County, Missouri, and which they had deferred to comply with until they should have accomplished some work which they had planned, but never did accomplish. (TK, p. 68)

3   Now, Brother William [W. Phelps], if what I have said is true, how careful men ought to be what they do in the last days, lest they are cut

Noah
   3   Editorial in the *Times and Seasons*, 15 July 1842.
   4   Editorial in the *Times and Seasons*, 1 September 1842.

Obedience
   1   First conference of the Church, Fayette, New York, 9 June 1830.
   2   Recollection of Philo Dibble, published in the *Juvenile Instructor*, 15 May 1892.
   3   Letter to William W. Phelps in Missouri, written from Kirtland, 27 No-vember 1832.

short of their expectations, and they that think they stand should fall, because they keep not the Lord's commandments; whilst you, who do the will of the Lord and keep His commandments, have need to rejoice with unspeakable joy, for such shall be exalted very high, and shall be lifted up in triumph above all the kingdoms of this world. (HC 1:299)

4   You will see that the Lord commanded us, in Kirtland, to build a house of God, and establish a school for the Prophets, this is the word of the Lord to us, and we must, yea, the Lord helping us, we will obey: as on conditions of our obedience He has promised us great things; yea, even a visit from the heavens to honor us with His own presence. We greatly fear before the Lord lest we should fail of this great honor, which our Master proposes to confer on us; we are seeking for humility and great faith lest we be ashamed in His presence. (HC 1:316–17)

5   Great preparations were making to commence a house of the Lord; and notwithstanding the Church was poor, yet our unity, harmony and charity abounded to strengthen us to do the commandments of God. (HC 1:349)

6   Live in strict obedience to the commandments of God, and walk humbly before Him, and He will exalt thee in His own due time. (HC 1:408)

7   I have no doubt but that you will agree with me that men will be held accountable for the things which they have done and not for the things they have not, or that all the light and intelligence communicated to them from their beneficent creator, whether it is much or little, by the same they in justice will be judged, and that they are required to yield obedience and improve upon that and that only which is given, for man is not to live by bread alone but by every word that proceeds out of the mouth of God. (PWJS, p. 298; standardized)

Obedience

4   Letter to William W. Phelps in Missouri, written from Kirtland, 14 January 1833. According to Dean Jessee this letter was dated 11 January (see PWJS, p. 262).

5   Kirtland, 1 June 1833.

6   Letter to Vienna Jacques, Kirtland, 4 September 1833.

7   Letter to Silas Smith, the Prophet's uncle, Kirtland, 26 September 1833.

8 We take the sacred writings into our hands, and admit that they were given by direct inspiration for the good of man. We believe that God condescended to speak from the heavens and declare His will concerning the human family, to give them just and holy laws, to regulate their conduct, and guide them in a direct way, that in due time He might take them to Himself, and make them joint heirs with His Son. But when this fact is admitted, that the immediate will of heaven is contained in the Scriptures, are we not bound as rational creatures to live in accordance to all its precepts? Will the mere admission, that this is the will of heaven ever benefit us if we do not comply with all its teachings? Do we not offer violence to the Supreme Intelligence of heaven, when we admit the truth of its teachings, and do not obey them? Do we not descend below our own knowledge, and the better wisdom which heaven has endowed us with, by such a course of conduct? For these reasons, if we have direct revelations given us from heaven, surely those revelations were never given to be trifled with, without the trifler's incurring displeasure and vengeance upon his own head, if there is any justice in heaven; and that there is must be admitted by every individual who admits the truth and force of God's teachings, His blessings and cursings, as contained in the sacred volume. (HC 2:11)

9 Unless they [the brethren of the Church] do the will of God, God will not help them; and if God does not help them, all is vain. (HC 2:48)

10 No month ever found me more busily engaged than November; but as my life consisted of activity and unyielding exertions, I made this my rule: *When the Lord commands, do it.* (HC 2:170)

11 The feelings of the brethren on leaving Kirtland and parting with those who were left behind were somewhat peculiar, notwithstanding the scenes they had passed through in Kirtland; but the consciousness of doing the will of their heavenly Father, and obeying His commandments in journeying to Zion, over balanced every other consideration

---

Obedience
8 Letter to the brethren scattered from Zion, Kirtland, 22 January 1834.
9 Letter to Orson Hyde in New York State from the First Presidency, Kirtland, 7 April 1834.
10 Kirtland, November 1834.
11 Kirtland, 6 July 1838.

that could possibly be presented to their minds, and buoyed up their spirits, and helped them to overcome the weaknesses and infirmities of human nature which men are subject to here on the earth. (HC 3:100–101)

12 It is likewise very satisfactory to my mind, that there has been such a good understanding between you, and that the Saints have so cheerfully hearkened to council, and vied with each other in this labor of love, and in the promotion of truth and righteousness. This is as it should be in the Church of Jesus Christ; unity is strength. "How pleasing it is for brethren to dwell together in unity!" Let the Saints of the Most High ever cultivate this principle, and the most glorious blessings must result, not only to them individually, but to the whole Church—the order of the kingdom will be maintained, its officers respected, and its requirements readily and cheerfully obeyed. (HC 4:227)

13 Let us realize that we are not to live to ourselves, but to God; by so doing the greatest blessings will rest upon us both in time and in eternity. (HC 4:231)

14 Let those who come up to this place be determined to keep the commandments of God, and not be discouraged by those things we have enumerated, and then they will be prospered—the intelligence of heaven will be communicated to them, and they will, eventually, see eye to eye, and rejoice in the full fruition of that glory which is reserved for the righteous. (HC 4:273)

15 God did elect or predestinate, that all those who would be saved, should be saved in Christ Jesus, and through obedience to the Gospel; but He passes over no man's sins, but visits them with correction, and

---

Obedience

12 Letter to the Twelve in England, Nauvoo, 15 December 1840. The placement of this letter in *HC* implies that it was written in October 1840, but actually it was written on 15 December 1840 (see *PWJS*, p. 480).

13 Letter to the Twelve in England, Nauvoo, 15 December 1840. The placement of this letter in *HC* implies that it was written in October 1840, but actually it was written on 15 December 1840 (see *PWJS*, p. 480).

14 Proclamation of the First Presidency, Nauvoo, 15 January 1841.

15 Sabbath address, Nauvoo, 16 May 1841.

if His children will not repent of their sins He will discard them. (*HC* 4:360)

16 When instructed, we must obey that voice, observe the laws of the kingdom of God, that the blessing of heaven may rest down upon us. (*HC* 4:570)

17 Be virtuous and pure; be men of integrity and truth; keep the commandments of God; and then you will be able more perfectly to understand the difference between right and wrong—between the things of God and the things of men; and your path will be like that of the just, which shineth brighter and brighter unto the perfect day. (*HC* 5:31)

18 [Abraham] prospered exceedingly in all that he put his hand unto; it was because he and his family obeyed the counsel of the Lord. (*HC* 5:64)

19 As a Church and a people it behooves us to be wise, and to seek to know the will of God, and then be willing to do it; for "blessed is he that heareth the word of the Lord, and keepeth it," say the Scriptures. "Watch and pray always," says our Savior, "that ye may be accounted worthy to escape the things that are to come on the earth, and to stand before the Son of Man." If Enoch, Abraham, Moses, and the children of Israel, and all God's people were saved by keeping the commandments of God, we, if saved at all, shall be saved upon the same principle. . . .

We have been chastened by the hand of God heretofore for not obeying His commands, although we never violated any human law, or transgressed any human precept; yet we have treated lightly His commands, and departed from His ordinances, and the Lord has chastened us sore, and we have felt His arm and kissed the rod; let us be wise in time to come and ever remember that "to obey is better than sacrifice, and to hearken than the fat of rams." The Lord has told us to build the Temple and the Nauvoo House; and that command is as

---

Obedience

16 Remarks to the Relief Society, Nauvoo, 30 March 1842.
17 Editorial in the *Times and Seasons*, 15 June 1842.
18 Editorial in the *Times and Seasons*, 15 July 1842.
19 Editorial in the *Times and Seasons*, 15 July 1842.

binding upon us as any other; and that man who engages not in these things is as much a transgressor as though he broke any other commandment; he is not a doer of God's will, not a fulfiller of His laws. (HC 5:65)

20 Happiness is the object and design of our existence; and will be the end thereof, if we pursue the path that leads to it; and this path is virtue, uprightness, faithfulness, holiness, and keeping all the commandments of God. But we cannot keep all the commandments without first knowing them, and we cannot expect to know all, or more than we now know unless we comply with or keep those we have already received. (HC 5:134–35)

21 In obedience there is joy and peace unspotted, unalloyed. (HC 5:135)

22 We have no claim in our eternal compact, in relation to eternal things, unless our actions and contracts and all things tend to this. (HC 5:403)

23 If a man gets a fullness of the priesthood of God, he has to get it in the same way that Jesus Christ obtained it, and that was by keeping all the commandments and obeying all the ordinances of the house of the Lord. . . .

Any man may believe that Jesus Christ is the Son of God, and be happy in that belief, and yet not obey his commandments, and at last be cut down for disobedience to the Lord's righteous requirements. (HC 5:424, 426)

24 All blessings that were ordained for man by the Council of Heaven were on conditions of obedience to the law thereof. (WJS, p. 232; standardized)

Obedience

20 Essay on happiness, Nauvoo, 27 August 1842.

21 Essay on happiness, Nauvoo, 27 August 1842.

22 Sabbath address, Nauvoo, 21 May 1843.

23 Sabbath address, Nauvoo, 11 June 1843.

24 Sabbath address, Nauvoo, 16 July 1843, as reported by Franklin D. Richards.

25 If men would acquire salvation, they have got to be subject, before they leave this world, to certain rules and principles, which were fixed by an unalterable decree before the world was. (HC 6:50–51)

26 Any person who is exalted to the highest mansion has to abide a celestial law, and the whole law too. (HC 6:184)

27 To get salvation we must not only do some things, but everything which God has commanded. Men may preach and practice everything except those things which God commands us to do, and will be damned at last. We may tithe mint and rue, and all manner of herbs, and still not obey the commandments of God. The object with me is to obey and teach others to obey God in just what He tells us to do. It mattereth not whether the principle is popular or unpopular, I will always maintain a true principle, even if I stand alone in it. (HC 6:223)

28 All things whatsoever God in his infinite wisdom has seen fit and proper to reveal to us, while we are dwelling in mortality, in regard to our mortal bodies, are revealed to us in the abstract, and independent of affinity of this mortal tabernacle, but are revealed to our spirits precisely as though we had no bodies at all; and those revelations which will save our spirits will save our bodies. God reveals them to us in view of no eternal dissolution of the body, or tabernacle. Hence the responsibility, the awful responsibility, that rests upon us in relation to our dead; for all the spirits who have not obeyed the Gospel in the flesh must either obey it in the spirit or be damned. . . .

. . . So long as a man will not give heed to the commandments, he must abide without salvation. If a man has knowledge, he can be saved; although, if he has been guilty of great sins, he will be punished for them. But when he consents to obey the gospel, whether here or in the world of spirits, he is saved. . . .

. . . All will suffer until they obey Christ himself. (HC 6:312–13, 314)

Obedience

25 Remarks upon the death of James Adams, Nauvoo, 9 October 1843.
26 Sabbath address, Nauvoo, 21 January 1844.
27 Remarks after a sermon given by an Episcopalian minister, Nauvoo, 21 February 1844.
28 King Follett Discourse, Nauvoo, 7 April 1844.

Offense

1   Perhaps our brethren will say, because we thus write, that we are offended at these characters. If we are, it is not for a word, neither because they reproved in the gate—but because they have been the means of shedding innocent blood. Are they not murderers then at heart? Are not their consciences seared as with a hot iron? We confess that we are offended; but the Savior said, "It must needs be that offenses come, but woe unto them by whom they come." (HC 3:228)

2   I hope that even in Kirtland there are some who do not make a man an offender for a word, but are disposed to stand forth in defense of righteousness and truth. (HC 4:165)

Opposition
See PERSECUTION

Optimism

1   I write these few lines to inform you that we feel determined in this place not to be dismayed if hell boils over all at once. We feel to hope for the best, and determined to prepare for the worst. (HC 6:485–86)

Order

1   Such scenes as these were calculated to inspire our hearts with joy unspeakable, and fill us with awe and reverence for that Almighty

---

Offense
1   Letter to the Church from Liberty Jail, 16 December 1838.
2   Letter to Oliver Granger in Kirtland, sent from Nauvoo, July 1840.

Optimism
1   Letter to John Smith, the Prophet's uncle, Nauvoo, 17 June 1844.

Order
1   Reflections on the early events of the Restoration, New York, Summer 1830.

Being, by whose grace we had been called to be instrumental in bringing about, for the children of men, the enjoyment of such glorious blessings as were now at this time poured out upon us. To find ourselves engaged in the very same order of things as observed by the holy Apostles of old . . . create[d] within us sensations of rapturous gratitude (HC 1:85, 86)

2   On the top of the mound were stones which presented the appearance of three altars having been erected one above the other, according to the ancient order. (HC 2:79)

3   The endowment you are so anxious about, you cannot comprehend now, nor could Gabriel explain it to the understanding of your dark minds; but strive to be prepared in your hearts, be faithful in all things, that when we meet in the solemn assembly, that is, when such as God shall name out of all the official members shall meet, we must be clean every whit. Let us be faithful and silent, brethren, and if God gives you a manifestation, keep it to yourselves; be watchful and prayerful, and you shall have a prelude of those joys that God will pour out on that day. Do not watch for iniquity in each other, if you do you will not get an endowment, for God will not bestow it on such. But if we are faithful, and live by every word that proceeds forth from the mouth of God, I will venture to prophesy that we shall get a blessing that will be worth remembering, if we should live as long as John the Revelator; our blessings will be such as we have not realized before, nor received in this generation. The order of the house of God has been, and ever will be, the same, even after Christ comes; and after the termination of the thousand years it will be the same; and we shall finally enter into the celestial Kingdom of God, and enjoy it forever. (HC 2:309)

4   Attended a sumptuous feast at Bishop Newel K. Whitney's. This feast was after the order of the Son of God—the lame, the halt, and the blind were invited, according to the instructions of the Savior. (HC 2:362)

Order
  2   Events of Zion's Camp, along the Illinois River near present-day Griggsville, 3 June 1834.
  3   Instructions to the Twelve, Kirtland, 12 November 1835.
  4   Kirtland, 7 January 1836.

5   Each should speak in his turn and in his place, and in his time and season, that there may be perfect order in all things; and that every man, before he makes an objection to any item that is brought before a council for consideration, should be sure that he can throw light upon the subject rather than spread darkness, and that his objection be founded in righteousness. (HC 2:370)

6   I doubt whether the pages of history can boast of a more splendid and innocent wedding and feast than this, for it was conducted after the order of heaven, which has a time for all things; and this being a time of rejoicing, we heartily embraced it and conducted ourselves accordingly. (HC 2:378)

7   I labored with each of these quorums for some time to bring them to the order which God had shown to me, which is as follows: The first part to be spent in solemn prayer before God, without any talking or confusion; and the conclusion with a sealing prayer by President Rigdon, when all the quorums were to shout with one accord a solemn hosanna to God and the Lamb, with an Amen, Amen and Amen. (HC 2:391)

8   Paul perfectly understood the purposes of God in relation to His connection with man, and that glorious and perfect order which He established in Himself, whereby he sent forth power, revelations, and glory.
   God will not acknowledge that which He has not called, ordained, and chosen. (HC 4:208)

9   The Almighty is a lover of order and good government. (HC 4:339)

10   Truly this is a day long to be remembered by the Saints of the last days,—a day in which the God of heaven has begun to restore the an-

---

Order
   5   Minutes of a priesthood meeting, Kirtland, 15 January 1836.
   6   Kirtland, 20 January 1836. Wedding celebration for John F. Boynton and Susan Lowell.
   7   Kirtland, 6 February 1836.
   8   Article on priesthood read at general conference, Nauvoo, 5 October 1840.
   9   Report of the First Presidency at general conference, Nauvoo, 7 April 1841.
   10 Nauvoo, 6 January 1842.

cient order of His kingdom unto His servants and His people,—a day in which all things are concurring to bring about the completion of the fullness of the Gospel, a fullness of the dispensation of dispensations, even the fullness of times; a day in which God has begun to make manifest and set in order in His Church those things which have been, and those things which the ancient prophets and wise men desired to see but died without beholding them. (HC 4:492)

11 This book [the Book of Mormon] also tells us that our Savior made His appearance upon this continent after His resurrection; that He planted the Gospel here in all its fulness, and richness, and power, and blessing; that they had Apostles, Prophets, Pastors, Teachers, and Evangelists; the same order, the same priesthood, the same ordinances, gifts, powers, and blessings, as were enjoyed on the eastern continent. (HC 4:538)

12 And now as the great purposes of God are hastening to their accomplishment, and the things spoken of in the Prophets are fulfilling, as the kingdom of God is established on the earth, and the ancient order of things restored, the Lord has manifested to us this day and privilege, and we are commanded to be baptized for our dead. (HC 4:599)

13 The organization of the spiritual and heavenly worlds, and of spiritual and heavenly beings, was agreeable to the most perfect order and harmony; their limits and bounds were fixed irrevocably, and voluntarily subscribed to in their heavenly estate by themselves, and were by our first parents subscribed to upon the earth. Hence the importance of embracing and subscribing to principles of eternal truth by all men upon the earth that expect eternal life. (HC 6:51)

Order

11 Letter to John Wentworth, editor of the *Chicago Democrat*, Nauvoo, 1 March 1842.

12 Editorial in the *Times and Seasons*, 15 April 1842.

13 Remarks upon the death of James Adams, Nauvoo, 9 October 1843.

Ordinances

1   If Abel was taught of the coming of the Son of God, was he not taught also of His ordinances? We all admit that the Gospel has ordinances, and if so, had it not always ordinances, and were not its ordinances always the same? (HC 2:16)

2   [God] set the ordinances to be the same forever and ever, and set Adam to watch over them, to reveal them from heaven to man, or to send angels to reveal them. . . .
  . . . Cain also being authorized to offer sacrifice, but not offering it in righteousness, was cursed. It signifies, then, that the ordinances must be kept in the very way God has appointed; otherwise their Priesthood will prove a cursing instead of a blessing. . . .
  . . . All the ordinances and duties that ever have been required by the Priesthood, under the directions and commandments of the Almighty in any of the dispensations, shall all be had in the last dispensation, therefore all things had under the authority of the Priesthood at any former period, shall be had again, bringing to pass the restoration spoken of by the mouth of all the Holy Prophets. . . .
  Elijah was the last Prophet that held the keys of the Priesthood, and who will, before the last dispensation, restore the authority and deliver the keys of the Priesthood, in order that all the ordinances may be attended to in righteousness. . . . Why send Elijah? Because he holds the keys of the authority to administer in all the ordinances of the Priesthood; and without the authority is given, the ordinances could not be administered in righteousness. (HC 4:208, 209, 210–11)

3   It may be asked, where is there anything in all this that is wrong? [In the Irvingites' church]. . . .
  Mr. Baxter received the spirit on asking for it, without attending to the ordinances, and began to prophesy, whereas the scriptural way of attaining the gift of the Holy Ghost is by baptism, and by laying on of hands. (HC 4:579)

Ordinances
  1   Letter to the brethren scattered from Zion, Kirtland, 22 January 1834.
  2   Article on priesthood read at general conference, Nauvoo, 5 October 1840.
  3   Editorial in the *Times and Seasons*, 1 April 1842.

4   The order and ordinances of the kingdom were instituted by the priesthood in the Council of Heaven before the world was. (*WJS*, p. 215; standardized)

5   The main object [of gathering the people of God in any age] was to build unto the Lord a house whereby He could reveal unto His people the ordinances of His house and the glories of His kingdom, and teach the people the way of salvation; for there are certain ordinances and principles that, when they are taught and practiced, must be done in a place or house built for that purpose. . . .

All men who become heirs of God and joint-heirs with Jesus Christ will have to receive the fulness of the ordinances of his kingdom; and those who will not receive all the ordinances will come short of the fullness of that glory, if they do not lose the whole. . . .

. . . Jesus said unto the Jews, "How oft would I have gathered thy children together, even as a hen gathereth her chickens under her wings, and ye would not!"—that they might attend to the ordinances of baptism for the dead as well as other ordinances of the priesthood, and receive revelations from heaven, and be perfected in the things of the kingdom of God—but they would not. This was the case on the day of Pentecost: those blessings were poured out on the disciples on that occasion. . . .

. . . Why gather the people together in this place? For the same purpose that Jesus wanted to gather the Jews—to receive the ordinances, the blessings, and glories that God has in store for His Saints.

I will now ask this assembly and all the Saints if you will now build this house and receive the ordinances and blessings which God has in store for you; or will you not build unto the Lord this house, and let Him pass by and bestow these blessings upon another people? I pause for a reply. (*HC* 5:423, 424, 425, 427)

6   Reading the experience of others, or the revelation given to *them*, can never give *us* a comprehensive view of our condition and true relation to God. Knowledge of these things can only be obtained by experience through the ordinances of God set forth for that purpose. (*HC* 6:50)

Ordinances

4   Sabbath address, Nauvoo, 11 June 1843, as reported by Franklin D. Richards.

5   Sabbath address, Nauvoo, 11 June 1843.

6   Remarks upon the death of James Adams, Nauvoo, 9 October 1843.

7   The question is frequently asked "Can we not be saved without going through with all those ordinances, &c.?" I would answer, No, not the fullness of salvation. Jesus said, "There are many mansions in my Father's house, and I will go and prepare a place for you." *House* here named should have been translated kingdom; and any person who is exalted to the highest mansion has to abide a celestial law, and the whole law too. (HC 6:184)

Ordinations

1   I met in company with the several quorums in the school room in the temple, at evening, to take into consideration the subject of ordination. I made some remarks upon the subject of our meeting, which were as follows: Many are desiring to be ordained to the ministry, who are not called, consequently the Lord is displeased. Secondly, many already have been ordained, who ought not to hold official stations in the Church, because they dishonor themselves and the Church, and bring persecution swiftly upon us, in consequence of their zeal without knowledge. (HC 2:394)

Palestine Mission

1   To all people unto whom these presents shall come, Greeting—
   Be it known that we, the constituted authorities of the Church of Jesus Christ of Latter-day Saints, assembled in Conference at Nauvoo, Hancock county, and state of Illinois, on the sixth day of April, in the year of our Lord, one thousand eight hundred and forty, considering an important event at hand, an event involving the interest and fate

---

Ordinances
   7   Sabbath address, Nauvoo, 21 January 1844.

Ordinations
   1   Remarks at a meeting of several priesthood quorums in the schoolroom of the Kirtland Temple, 12 February 1836.

Palestine Mission
   1   Credentials given to Orson Hyde as a missionary to Palestine, Nauvoo, April 1840.

of the Gentile nations throughout the world—from the signs of the times and from declarations contained in the oracles of God, we are forced to come to this conclusion. The Jewish nations have been scattered abroad among the Gentiles for a long period; and in our estimation, the time of the commencement of their return to the Holy Land has already arrived. As this scattered and persecuted people are set among the Gentiles as a sign unto them of the second coming of the Messiah, and also of the overthrow of the present kingdoms and governments of the earth, by the potency of His Almighty arm in scattering famine and pestilence like the frosts and snows of winter, and sending the sword with nation against nation to bathe it in each other's blood; it is highly important, in our opinion, that the present views and movements of the Jewish people be sought after and laid before the American people, for their consideration, their profit and their learning. (HC 4:112–13)

Parables

1   [Quoting Matthew 13:10–12] "And the disciples came and said unto Him, Why speakest thou unto them in parables? {I would here remark, that the 'them' made use of in this interrogation, is a personal pronoun, and refers to the multitude.} He answered and said unto them, {that is unto the disciples,} because it is given unto *you* to know the mysteries of the Kingdom of Heaven, but to *them*, {that is, unbelievers,} it is not given; for whosoever hath, to him shall be given, and he shall have more abundance; but whosoever hath not, from him shall be taken away, even that he hath." (HC 2:265)

2   The very reason why the multitude, or the world, as they were designated by the Savior, did not receive an explanation upon His parables, was because of unbelief. (HC 2:267)

3   In reference to the prodigal son, I said it was a subject I had never dwelt upon; that it was understood by many to be one of the intricate

---

Parables

1   Letter to the elders of the Church, Kirtland, 1 September 1835.
2   Letter to the elders of the Church, Kirtland, 1 September 1835.
3   Sabbath address, Nauvoo, 29 January 1843.

subjects of the scriptures; and even the Elders of this Church have preached largely upon it, without having any rule of interpretation. What is the rule of interpretation? Just no interpretation at all. Understand it precisely as it reads. I have a key by which I understand the scriptures. I enquire, what was the question which drew out the answer, or caused Jesus to utter the parable? It is not national; it does not refer to Abraham, Israel or the Gentiles, in a national capacity, as some suppose. To ascertain its meaning, we must dig up the root and ascertain what it was that drew the saying out of Jesus.

While Jesus was teaching the people, all the publicans and sinners drew near to hear Him; "and the Pharisees and scribes murmured, saying, This man receiveth sinners, and eateth with them." This is the keyword which unlocks the parable of the prodigal son. It was given to answer the murmurings and questions of the Sadducees and Pharisees, who were querying, finding fault, and saying, "How is it that this man, as great as He pretends to be, eats with publicans and sinners?" Jesus was not put to it so, but He could have found something to illustrate His subject, if He had designed it for a nation or nations; but He did not. It was for men in an individual capacity; and all straining on this point is a bubble. "This man receiveth sinners and eateth with them." (HC 5:261–62)

Parents

1   It [is] one of the greatest earthly blessings to be blessed with the society of parents, whose mature years and experience render them capable of administering the most wholesome advice. (HC 2:289)

2   *Minutes:* "[Brother Elliot] ought to have trained his child in a way that she would not have required the rod at the age of fifteen years." (HC 2:295)

3   And when [I] reflect with what care, and with what unremitting diligence our parents have striven to watch over us, and how many

---

Parents
 1   Kirtland, 11 October 1835.
 2   High council's quoted decision, Kirtland, 29 October 1835.
 3   Letter to William Smith, the Prophet's brother, Kirtland, 18 December 1835.

hours of sorrow and anxiety they have spent, over our cradles and bed-sides, in times of sickness, how careful we ought to be of their feelings in their old age! It cannot be a source of sweet reflection to us, to say or do anything that will bring their gray hairs down with sorrow to the grave. (HC 2:342)

4 Words and language are inadequate to express the gratitude that I owe to God for having given me so honorable a parentage. (HC 5:126)

Patience

1 We have been making every exertion, and used all the means at our command to lay a foundation that will now begin to enable us to meet our pecuniary engagements, and no doubt in our minds to the entire satisfaction of all those concerned, if they will but exercise a small degree of patience, and stay a resort to coercive measures which would kill us in the germ, even before we can (by reason of the sea-son) begin to bud and blossom in order to bring forth a plentiful yield of fruit. (HC 4:407)

2 Patience is heavenly, obedience is noble, forgiveness is merciful, and exaltation is godly; and he that holds out faithful to the end shall in no wise lose his reward. (HC 6:427)

Patriarch

1 An Evangelist is a Patriarch, even the oldest man of the blood of Joseph or of the seed of Abraham. Wherever the Church of Christ is

---

Parents
    4 Nauvoo, 22 August 1842.

Patience
    1 Letter to Horace R. Hotchkiss, Nauvoo, 25 August 1841.
    2 Letter of the Prophet and Hyrum Smith to Mr. Tewkesbury (Abijah R. Tewksbury), Nauvoo, 4 June 1844, seeking to restore him to fellowship.

Patriarch
    1 Instructions to the Twelve, Commerce (Nauvoo), 27 June 1839.

established in the earth, there should be a Patriarch for the benefit of the posterity of the Saints, as it was with Jacob in giving his patriarchal blessing unto his sons, etc. (HC 3:381)

Patriotism

1 *Minutes:* The Legion was called out to celebrate our National Independence (the 4th being Sunday), and was reviewed by Lieutenant-General Joseph Smith, who made an eloquent and patriotic speech to the troops, and strongly testified of his regard for our national welfare, and his willingness to lay down his life in defense of his country, and closed with these remarkable words, "I would ask no greater boon, than to lay down my life for my country." (HC 4:382)

2 I now subscribe myself your friend, and a patriot and lover of my country, pleading at their feet for protection and deliverance, by the justice of their Constitution. (HC 5:159)

3 By this I discover a spark of liberty burning in the bosom of the writer. May it continue to burn and burn, till it once more fires the whole land with its heavenly influence. (HC 5:172)

4 I was born in Sharon, Vermont, in 1805, where the first quarter of my life grew with the growth and strengthened with the strength of that "first-born" State of the "United Thirteen." From the old "French War" to the final consummation of American Independence, my fathers, heart to heart, and shoulder to shoulder, with the noble fathers of our liberty, fought and bled; and with the most of that venerable band of patriots, they have gone to rest, bequeathing a glorious country, with all her inherent rights, to millions of posterity. (HC 6:88)

5 Where is the strength of Government? Where is the patriotism of a Washington, a Warren, and Adams? And where is a spark from the

---

Patriotism
1 Nauvoo Legion minutes, Nauvoo, 3 July 1841.
2 Letter to James Arlington Bennett, Nauvoo, 8 September 1842.
3 Response to James Arlington Bennett's letter, Nauvoo, 16 October 1842.
4 Letter to the "Green Mountain Boys" in Vermont, appealing for their support, Nauvoo, 29 November 1843.
5 Letter to John C. Calhoun, Nauvoo, 2 January 1844.

watch-fire of '76, by which one candle might be lit that would glimmer upon the confines of Democracy? . . .

. . . While I have powers of body and mind—while water runs and grass grows—while virtue is lovely and vice hateful; and while a stone points out a sacred spot where a fragment of American liberty once was, I or my posterity will plead the cause of injured innocence, until Missouri makes atonement for all her sins, or sinks disgraced, degraded, and damned to hell, "where the worm dieth not, and the fire is not quenched." (HC 6:158–59)

6   The elder Adams, in his inaugural address, gives national pride such a grand turn of justification, that every honest citizen must look back upon the infancy of the United States with an approving smile, and rejoice that patriotism in their rulers, virtue in the people, and prosperity in the Union once crowded the expectations of hope, unveiled the sophistry of the hypocrite, and silenced the folly of foes. Mr. Adams said, "If national pride is ever justifiable or excusable, it is when it springs not from *power* or riches, grandeur or glory, but from conviction of national innocence, information, and benevolence." (HC 6:200)

7   To the Honorable the Senate and House of Representatives of the United States of America, in Congress Assembled:

Your memorialist, a free-born citizen of these United States, respectfully showeth that from his infancy his soul has been filled with the most intense and philanthropic interest for the welfare of his native country; and being fired with an ardor which floods cannot quench, crowns cannot conquer, nor diplomatic intrigue corrupt, to see those principles which emanated from the bosoms of the fathers of seventy-six, and which cost the noblest talents and richest blood of the nation, maintained inviolate and perpetuated to future generations; and the proud eagle of American freedom soar triumphant over every party prejudice and local sinistry, and spread her golden pinions over every member of the human family, who shall stretch forth their hands for succor from the lion's paw or the oppressor's grasp; and

---

Patriotism

6   A pamphlet containing the Prophet's political platform, entitled *Views of the Powers and Policy of the Government of the United States*, Nauvoo, 7 February 1844.

7   Memorial to Congress, Nauvoo, 26 March 1844.

firmly trusting in the God of liberty, that He has designed universal peace and goodwill, union, and brotherly love to all the great family of man, your memorialist asks your honorable body to pass the following:—[An ordinance for the protection of United States citizens emigrating to the territories.] (*HC* 6:275)

8   Keep the peace by being cool, considerate, virtuous, unoffending, manly, and patriotic, as the true sons of liberty ever have been, and honorably maintain the precious boon our illustrious fathers won. (*HC* 6:449)

Paul

1   That those only are the individuals who keep the commandments of the Lord and walk in his statutes to the end, that are permitted to set at this glorious feast, is evident from the following items: In Paul's last letter to Timothy, which was written just previous to his death, he says, I have fought a good fight, I have finished my course, I have kept the faith: henceforth there is laid up for me a crown of righteousness which the Lord, the righteous Judge shall give me at that day: and not to me only, but unto all them also that love his appearing. No one who believes the account, will doubt for a moment this assertion of Paul which was made, as he knew, just before he was to take his leave of this world. Though he once, according to his own word, persecuted the church of God and wasted it, yet after embracing the faith, his labors were unceasing to spread the glorious news; and like a faithful soldier, when called to give his life in the cause which he had espoused, he laid it down, as he says, with an assurance of an eternal crown. Follow the labors of this apostle from the time of his conversion to the time of his death, and you will have a fair sample of industry and patience in promulgating the gospel of Christ: Whipped, stoned, and derided, the moment he escaped the hands of his persecutors, he, as zealously as ever, proclaimed the doctrine of the Savior.

Patriotism
   8   Proclamation to the citizens of Nauvoo, 11 June 1844.

Paul
   1   Letter from the elders in Kirtland to the brethren abroad, March 1834.

And all may know, that he did not embrace the faith for the honor of this life, nor for the gain of earthly goods. What then could have induced him to undergo all this toil? It was, as he said, that he might obtain that crown of righteousness from the hand of God. No one, we presume, will doubt the faithfulness of Paul to the end: None will say, that he did not keep the faith, that he did not fight the good fight, that he did not preach and persuade to the last: And what was he to receive? A crown of righteousness. And what shall others receive who do not labor faithfully, and continue to the end? We leave such to search out their own promises if any they have; and if they have any they are welcome to them, on our part, for the Lord says, that every man is to receive according to his works. Reflect for a moment, brethren, and enquire, whether you would consider yourselves worthy a seat at the marriage feast with Paul and others like him, if you had been unfaithful? Had you not fought the good fight, and kept the faith, could you expect to receive; have you a promise of receiving a crown of righteousness from the hand of the Lord, with the church of the first born? Here then, we understand, that Paul rested his hope in Christ because he had kept the faith, and loved his appearing; and from his hand he had a promise of receiving a crown of righteousness. (*E&MS* 2:144)

2   [Paul] is about 5 foot high; very dark hair; dark complexion; dark skin; large Roman nose; sharp face; small black eyes, penetrating as eternity; round shoulders; a whining voice, except when elevated, and then it almost resembles the roaring of a lion. He was a good orator, . . . active and diligent, always employing himself in doing good to his fellowmen. (*WJS*, p. 59; standardized)

3   Paul ascended into the third heavens, and he could understand the three principal rounds of Jacob's ladder—the telestial, the terrestrial, and the celestial glories or kingdoms, where Paul saw and heard things which were not lawful for him to utter. (*HC* 5:402)

Paul
2   Lecture given at the Nauvoo Lyceum, 5 January 1841, as reported by William Clayton. (The lyceum met weekly at different locations in Nauvoo for several months, beginning 5 January 1841.)
3   Sabbath address, Nauvoo, 21 May 1843.

Peace

1   We want to live in peace with all men; and equal rights is all we ask. (*HC* 2:122)

2   Some may have cried peace, but the Saints and the world will have little peace from henceforth. . . .
  . . . The time is soon coming, when no man will have any peace but in Zion and her stakes. (*HC* 3:390, 391)

3   We should cultivate a meek, quiet and peaceable spirit. (*HC* 5:517)

4   Our motto, then, is Peace with all! If we have joy in the love of God, let us try to give a reason of that joy, which all the world cannot gainsay or resist. And may be, like as when Paul started with recommendations to Damascus to persecute the Saints, some one who has raised his hand against us with letters to men in high places may see a light at noonday, above the brightness of the sun, and hear the voice of Jesus saying, "It is hard for thee to kick against the pricks." (*HC* 6:220)

5   Jesus said: "Blessed are the peacemakers, for they shall be called the children of God." Wherefore if the nation, a single State, community, or family ought to be grateful for anything, it is peace.
  Peace, lovely child of heaven!—peace like light from the same great parent, gratifies, animates, and happifies the just and the unjust, and is the very essence of happiness below, and bliss above.
  He that does not strive with all his powers of body and mind, with all his influence at home and abroad, and to cause others to do so

---

Peace
1   Statement of the intent of Zion's Camp, Clay County, Missouri, 22 June 1834.
2   Discourse on the priesthood, given sometime before 8 August 1839, Commerce (Nauvoo). For a discussion on the dating of this discourse, see *WJS*, p. 22.
3   Sabbath address, Nauvoo, 23 July 1843.
4   Article entitled "Pacific Innuendo," Nauvoo, 17 February 1844.
5   An appeal for peace and goodwill, addressed to the people of Missouri, Nauvoo, 8 March 1844.

too—to seek peace and maintain it for his own benefit and convenience, and for the honor of his State, nation, and country, has no claim on the clemency of man; nor should he be entitled to the friendship of woman or the protection of government.

He is the canker-worm to gnaw his own vitals; and the vulture to prey upon his own body; and he is, as to his own prospects and prosperity in life, a *felo-de-se* of his own pleasure.

A community of such beings are not far from hell on earth, and should be let alone as unfit for the smiles of the free or praise of the brave.

But the peacemaker, O give ear to him! for the words of his mouth and his doctrine drop like the rain, and distil as the dew. They are like the gentle mist upon the herbs, and as the moderate shower upon the grass. (HC 6:245)

Perfection

1   The nearer man approaches perfection, the clearer are his views, and the greater his enjoyments, till he has overcome the evils of his life and lost every desire for sin; and like the ancients, arrives at that point of faith where he is wrapped in the power and glory of his Maker, and is caught up to dwell with Him. But we consider that this is a station to which no man ever arrived in a moment: he must have been instructed in the government and laws of that kingdom by proper degrees, until his mind is capable in some measure of comprehending the propriety, justice, equality, and consistency of the same. (HC 2:8)

2   We admit that God is the great source and fountain from whence proceeds all good; that He is perfect intelligence. (HC 2:12)

3   Remember, brethren, that He has called you unto holiness; and need we say, to be like Him in purity? How wise, how holy; how chaste, and how perfect, then, you ought to conduct yourselves in His

---

Perfection
1   Letter to the brethren scattered from Zion, Kirtland, 22 January 1834.
2   Letter to the brethren scattered from Zion, Kirtland, 22 January 1834.
3   Letter to the brethren scattered from Zion, Kirtland, 22 January 1834.

sight; and remember, too, that His eyes are continually upon you. (HC 2:13)

4   If we can credit the account, God conversed with him [Abraham] from time to time, and directed him in the way he should walk, saying, "I am the Almighty; walk before me, and be thou perfect." (HC 2:439)

5   By learning the Spirit of God and understanding it, you may grow into the principle of revelation, until you become perfect in Christ Jesus. (HC 3:381)

6   We would wish the Saints to understand that, when they come here, they must not expect perfection, or that all will be harmony, peace, and love; if they indulge these ideas, they will undoubtedly be deceived, for here there are persons, not only from different states, but from different nations, who, although they feel a great attachment to the cause of truth, have their prejudices of education, and, consequently, it requires some time before these things can be overcome. Again, there are many that creep in unawares, and endeavor to sow discord, strife, and animosity in our midst, and by so doing, bring evil upon the Saints. These things we have to bear with, and these things will prevail either to a greater or less extent until "the floor be thoroughly purged," and "the chaff be burnt up." Therefore, let those who come up to this place be determined to keep the commandments of God, and not be discouraged by those things we have enumerated, and then they will be prospered—the intelligence of heaven will be communicated to them, and they will, eventually, see eye to eye, and rejoice in the full fruition of that glory which is reserved for the righteous. (HC 4:272–73)

7   None ever were perfect but Jesus; and why was He perfect? Because He was the Son of God, and had the fullness of the Spirit, and greater power than any man. (HC 4:358)

Perfection

   4   Letter on abolition published in the *Messenger and Advocate*, Kirtland, April 1836.
   5   Instructions to the Twelve, Commerce (Nauvoo), 27 June 1839.
   6   Proclamation of the First Presidency, Nauvoo, 15 January 1841.
   7   Sabbath address, Nauvoo, 16 May 1841.

8 Be virtuous and pure; be men of integrity and truth; keep the commandments of God; and then you will be able more perfectly to understand the difference between right and wrong—between the things of God and the things of men; and your path will be like that of the just, which shineth brighter and brighter unto the perfect day. (HC 5:31)

9 I showed them that it was generally in consequence of the brethren disregarding or disobeying counsel that they became dissatisfied and murmured; and many when they arrived here, were dissatisfied with the conduct of some of the Saints, because everything was not done perfectly right, and they get angry, and thus the devil gets advantage over them to destroy them. I told them I was but a man, and they must not expect me to be perfect; if they expected perfection from me, I should expect it from them; but if they would bear with my infirmities and the infirmities of the brethren, I would likewise bear with their infirmities. (HC 5:181)

10 Says one, "I cannot believe in the salvation of beasts." Any man who would tell you that this could not be, would tell you that the revelations are not true. John heard the words of the beasts giving glory to God, and understood them. . . . The four beasts were four of the most noble animals that had filled the measure of their creation, and had been saved from other worlds, because they were perfect: they were like angels in their sphere. (HC 5:343)

11 Look at Heb. vi. 1 for contradictions—"Therefore leaving the principles of the doctrine of Christ, let us go on unto perfection." If a man leaves the principles of the doctrine of Christ, how can he be saved in the principles? This is a contradiction. I don't believe it. I will render it as it should be—"Therefore *not* leaving the principles of the doctrine of Christ, let us go on unto perfection, not laying again the foundation of repentance from dead works, and of faith toward God, of the doctrine of baptisms, and of laying on of hands, and of resurrection of the dead, and of eternal judgment." (HC 6:58)

Perfection

  8 Editorial in the *Times and Seasons*, 15 June 1842.

  9 The Prophet counsels a group of Saints newly arrived in Nauvoo, 29 October 1842.

 10 General conference address, Nauvoo, 8 April 1843.

 11 Sabbath address, Nauvoo, 15 October 1843.

Persecution

1 The Book of Mormon (the stick of Joseph in the hands of Ephraim,) had now been published for some time, and as the ancient prophet had predicted it, "It was accounted as a strange thing." No small stir was created by its appearance. Great opposition and much persecution followed the believers of its authenticity. But it had now come to pass that truth had sprung out of the earth, and righteousness had looked down from heaven, so we feared not our opponents, knowing that we had both truth and righteousness on our side, that we had both the Father and the Son, because we had the doctrines of Christ, and abided in them; and therefore we continued to preach and to give information to all who were willing to hear. (HC 1:84)

2 Myself and Elder Rigdon continued to preach in Shalersville, Ravenna, and other places, setting forth the truth, vindicating the cause of our Redeemer; showing that the day of vengeance was coming upon this generation like a thief in the night; that prejudice, blindness and darkness filled the minds of many, and caused them to persecute the true Church, and reject the true light; by which means we did much towards allaying the excited feelings which were growing out of the scandalous letters then being published in the *Ohio Star*, at Ravenna, by the before-mentioned apostate, Ezra Booth. (HC 1:241)

3 This one thing is sure, that they who will live godly in Christ Jesus, shall suffer persecution; and before their robes are made white in the blood of the Lamb, it is to be expected, according to John the Revelator, they will pass through great tribulation. (HC 1:449)

4 Those who cannot endure persecution, and stand in the day of affliction, cannot stand in the day when the Son of God shall burst the veil, and appear in all the glory of His Father, with all the holy angels. (HC 1:468)

Persecution
1 Fayette, New York, April 1830.
2 Hiram, Ohio, December 1831.
3 Letter to the brethren in Missouri, Kirtland, 5 December 1833.
4 Letter to the elders of the Church, published in *The Evening and the Morning Star*, December 1833.

5 I am suffering under the tongue of slander for Christ's sake, unceasingly. God have mercy on such, if they will quit their lying. (HC 2:169)

6 Mountain waves of opposition . . . [are] urged onward with redoubled fury by the enemy of righteousness, with his pitchfork of lies, as you will see fairly represented in a cut contained in Mr. Howe's *Mormonism Unveiled*[.] And we hope that this adversary of truth will continue to stir up the sink of iniquity, that the people may the more readily discern between the righteous and the wicked. (HC 2:268)

7 The chariot wheels of the Kingdom are still rolling on, impelled by the mighty arm of Jehovah; and in spite of all opposition, will still roll on, until His words are all fulfilled. (HC 2:270)

8 Our religious principles are before the world ready for the investigation of all men, yet we are aware that all the persecution against our friends has arisen in consequence of calumnies and misconstructions without foundation in truth and righteousness. This we have endured in common with all other religious societies at their first commencement. (HC 2:460)

9 We have not complained at the Great God, we murmured not, but peaceably left all; and retired into the back country, in the broad and wild prairies, in the barren and desolate plains, and there commenced anew; we made the desolate places to bud and blossom as the rose; and now the fiend-like race is disposed to give us no rest. Their father the devil, is hourly calling upon them to be up and doing, and they, like willing and obedient children, need not the second admonition; but in the name of Jesus Christ the Son of the living God, we will endure it no longer, if the great God will arm us with courage, with strength and with power, to resist them in their persecutions. We will not act on the offensive, but always on the defensive; our rights

---

Persecution
    5   Kirtland, 16 October 1834.
    6   Letter to the elders of the Church, Kirtland, 1 September 1835.
    7   Letter to the elders of the Church, Kirtland, 1 September 1835.
    8   Letter to John Thornton and others, Kirtland, 25 July 1836.
    9   Far West, Missouri, 1 September 1838.

and our liberties shall not be taken from us, and we peaceably submit
to it, as we have done heretofore, but we will avenge ourselves of our
enemies, inasmuch as they will not let us alone. (*HC* 3:68)

10 Know assuredly, dear brethren, that it is for the testimony of Jesus
that we are in bonds and in prison. But we say unto you, that we consider that our condition is better (notwithstanding our sufferings)
than that of those who have persecuted us, and smitten us, and borne
false witness against us; and we most assuredly believe that those who
do bear false witness against us, do seem to have a great triumph over
us for the present. . . .

Dear brethren, do not think that our hearts faint, as though some
strange thing had happened unto us, for we have seen and been assured of all these things beforehand, and have an assurance of a better
hope than that of our persecutors. Therefore God hath made broad
our shoulders for the burden. We glory in our tribulation, because we
know that God is with us, that He is our friend, and that He will save
our souls. We do not care for them that can kill the body; they cannot
harm our souls. We ask no favors at the hands of mobs, nor of the
world, nor of the devil, nor of his emissaries the dissenters, and those
who love, and make, and swear falsehoods, to take away our lives. We
have never dissembled, nor will we for the sake of our lives. . . .

. . . "Blessed are ye when men shall revile you, and persecute you,
and shall say all manner of evil against you falsely for my sake; rejoice
and be exceeding glad, for great is your reward in heaven, for so persecuted they the Prophets which were before you."

Now, dear brethren, if any men ever had reason to claim this
promise, we are the men; for we know that the world not only hate us,
but they speak all manner of evil of us falsely, for no other reason than
that we have been endeavoring to teach the fullness of the Gospel of
Jesus Christ. . . .

Was it for committing adultery that we were assailed? We are
aware that that false slander has gone abroad, for it has been reiterated
in our ears. These are falsehoods also. Renegade "Mormon" dissenters
are running through the world and spreading various foul and libelous
reports against us, thinking thereby to gain the friendship of the
world, because they know that we are not of the world, and that the

---

Persecution
10 Letter to the Church from Liberty Jail, 16 December 1838.

world hates us; therefore they {the world} make a tool of these fellows {the dissenters}; and by them try to do all the injury they can, and after that they hate them worse than they do us, because they find them to be base traitors and sycophants. (HC 3:226–27, 228–29, 230)

11 Nothing therefore can separate us from the love of God and fellowship one with another; and . . . every species of wickedness and cruelty practiced upon us will only tend to bind our hearts together and seal them together in love. (HC 3:290)

12 Hell may pour forth its rage like the burning lava of mount Vesuvius, or of Etna, or of the most terrible of the burning mountains; and yet shall "Mormonism" stand. (HC 3:297)

13 The persecutions we suffered in Missouri were but the prelude to a far more glorious display of the power of truth, and of the religion we have espoused. (HC 4:271)

14 Persecution has not stopped the progress of truth, but has only added fuel to the flame, it has spread with increasing rapidity. . . .
. . . No unhallowed hand can stop the work from progressing; persecutions may rage, mobs may combine, armies may assemble, calumny may defame, but the truth of God will go forth boldly, nobly, and independent, till it has penetrated every continent, visited every clime, swept every country, and sounded in every ear, till the purposes of God shall be accomplished, and the Great Jehovah shall say the work is done. (HC 4:540)

15 All those that rise up against me will surely feel the weight of their iniquity upon their own heads. . . .
When I do the best I can—when I am accomplishing the greatest good, then the most evils and wicked surmisings are got up against me. . . .

Persecution
11 Letter to the Saints from Liberty Jail, 20–25 March 1839.
12 Letter to the Saints from Liberty Jail, 20–25 March 1839.
13 Proclamation of the First Presidency, Nauvoo, 15 January 1841.
14 Letter to John Wentworth, editor of the *Chicago Democrat*, Nauvoo, 1 March 1842.
15 Remarks to the Relief Society, Nauvoo, 31 August 1842.

. . . The enemies of this people will never get weary of their persecution against the Church, until they are overcome. I expect they will array everything against me that is in their power to control, and that we shall have a long and tremendous warfare. He that will war the true Christian warfare against the corruptions of these last days will have wicked men and angels of devils, and all the infernal powers of darkness continually arrayed against him. When wicked and corrupt men oppose, it is a criterion to judge if a man is warring the Christian warfare. When all men speak evil of you falsely, blessed are ye, &c. Shall a man be considered bad, when men speak evil of him? No. If a man stands and opposes the world of sin, he may expect to have all wicked and corrupt spirits arrayed against him. But it will be but a little season, and all these afflictions will be turned away from us, inasmuch as we are faithful, and are not overcome by these evils. By seeing the blessings of the endowment rolling on, and the kingdom increasing and spreading from sea to sea, we shall rejoice that we were not overcome by these foolish things. (HC 5:140, 141)

16 Abel was slain for his righteousness, and how many more up to the flood is not of much consequence to us now. But if we believe in present revelation, as published in the Times and Seasons last spring, Abraham, the prophet of the Lord, was laid upon the iron bedstead for slaughter; and the book of Jasher, which has not been disproved as a bad author, says he was cast into the fire of the Chaldees. Moses, the man of God, who killed an Egyptian persecutor of the children of Israel, was driven from his country and kindred. Elijah had to flee his country, for they sought his life,—and he was fed by ravens. Daniel was cast into a den of lions: Micah was fed on the bread of affliction; and Jeremiah was cast into the filthy hole under the Temple; and did these afflictions come upon these prophets of the Lord on account of transgression? No! It was the iron hand of persecution—like the chains of Missouri! And mark—when these old prophets suffered, the vengeance of God, in due time, followed and left the wicked opposers of the Lord's anointed like Sodom and Gomorrah; like the Egyptians; like Jezebel, who was eaten by dogs; and like all Israel, which were led away captive, till the Lord had spent his fury upon them—even to this day. (*T&S* 3:902)

Persecution
  16 Editorial in the *Times and Seasons*, 1 September 1842.

17 And where, sir, will be your safety or the safety of your children, if my children can be led to the slaughter with impunity by the hand of murderous rebels? Will they not lead yours to the slaughter with the same impunity? Ought not, then, this oppression, sir, to be checked in the bud, and to be looked down {upon} with just indignation by an enlightened world, before the flame become unextinguishable, and the fire devours the stubble? (HC 5:158)

18 It always has been when a man was sent of God with the priesthood and he began to preach the fullness of the gospel, that he was thrust out by his friends, who are ready to butcher him if he teach things which they imagine to be wrong; and Jesus was crucified upon this principle. (HC 5:425)

19 I defy all the world to destroy the work of God; and I prophesy they never will have power to kill me till my work is accomplished, and I am ready to die. (HC 6:58)

20 Persecution has rolled upon our heads from time to time, from portions of the United States, like peals of thunder, because of our religion; and no portion of the Government as yet has stepped forward for our relief. And in view of these things, I feel it to be my right and privilege to obtain what influence and power I can, lawfully, in the United States, for the protection of injured innocence. (HC 6:210–11)

21 Your friends who have been murdered for the truth's sake in the persecutions shall triumph gloriously in the celestial world, while their murderers shall welter for ages in torment, even until they shall have paid the uttermost farthing. (HC 6:315)

22 It is thought by some that our enemies would be satisfied with my destruction; but I tell you that as soon as they have shed my blood

---

Persecution

17 Letter to James Arlington Bennett, Nauvoo, 8 September 1842.
18 Sabbath address, Nauvoo, 11 June 1843.
19 Sabbath address, Nauvoo, 15 October 1843.
20 Views of the Prophet on his candidacy for president of the United States, Nauvoo, 8 February 1844.
21 King Follett Discourse, Nauvoo, 7 April 1844.
22 Address to the Nauvoo Legion, Nauvoo, 18 June 1844.

they will thirst for the blood of every man in whose heart dwells a single spark of the spirit of the fullness of the Gospel. The opposition of these men is moved by the spirit of the adversary of all righteousness. It is not only to destroy me, but every man and woman who dares believe the doctrines that God hath inspired me to teach to this generation. (HC 6:498)

Perseverance

1   There has quite a number of families gathered up here already; and we anticipate a continuance, especially as upon inquiry we have found that we have not had more than {the usual} ratio of sickness here, notwithstanding the trials we have had, and the hardships to which we have been exposed. Calculating as we do, upon the mercy and power of God in our behalf, we hope to persevere on in every good and useful work, even unto the end, that when we come to be tried in the balance we may not be found wanting. (HC 4:9)

2   It is like the Irishman's digging down the mountain. He does not put his shoulder to it to push it over, but puts it in his wheelbarrow, and carries it away day after day, and perseveres in it until the whole mountain is removed. (HC 5:366)

Peter

1   Now I want you to consider the high standing of Peter; he was now being endowed with power from on high and held the keys of the kingdom of heaven. (PWJS, p. 422)

Perseverance
1   Letter to Isaac Galland, Commerce (Nauvoo), 11 September 1839.
2   Nauvoo, 19 April 1843. The context is a conversation about treating illnesses.

Peter
1   Letter to Isaac Galland, written while the Prophet was imprisoned in Liberty Jail, 22 March 1839.

2   We will now examine the witnesses. As it will be recollected, they were to wait at Jerusalem till they were endowed with power from on high and then go and teach all nations whatsoever the Lord had commanded them. As Peter held the keys of the kingdom, we will examine him first.

Now on the day of Pentecost, when there was a marvelous display of the gifts, according to the promise in Mark, many were pricked in the heart, and said unto Peter, and to the rest of the Apostles, men and brethren what shall we do? Peter said unto them: Repent, and be baptised every one of you in the name of Jesus Christ, for the remission of sins, and ye shall receive the gift of the Holy Ghost, &c.— Here one of the witnesses says in so many words, repent and be baptised. And we are of the opinion that Peter having been taught by the Lord, and commissioned by the Lord, and endowed by the Lord, would be about as correct a counsellor, or ambassador as we or they could enquire of to know the right way to enter into the kingdom. (*T&S* 3:904)

3   Peter penned the most sublime language of any of the apostles. (HC 5:392)

Phrenology

1   *Minutes:* One night Joseph Smith said to D Ells [Dr. Josiah Ells] and to the congregation that he for a length of time thought on phrenology, and that he had a revelation, the Lord rebuking him sharply in crediting such a thing; and further said there was no reality in such a science, but [it] was the works of the devil. (*WJS*, p. 61; standardized)

Peter
2   Editorial in the *Times and Seasons*, 1 September 1842.
3   Items of doctrine given at Ramus, Illinois, 17 May 1843.

Phrenology
1   Lecture given at the Nauvoo Lyceum, 5 January 1841. (The lyceum met weekly at different locations in Nauvoo for several months, beginning 5 January 1841.) Recorded in William P. McIntire's Minute Book, LDS Church Archives.

2   In this day's *Wasp*, I find the following:—

Mr. Editor:

Sir:—I take the liberty to inform you that a large number of persons in different places have manifested a desire to know the phrenological development of Joseph Smith's head. I have examined the Prophet's head, and he is perfectly willing to have the chart published. . . .

A. Crane. . . .

I give the foregoing a place in my history for the gratification of the curious, and not for {any} respect {I entertain for} phrenology. (*HC* 5:52, 55)

3   In the morning, had an interview with a lecturer on Mesmerism and Phrenology. Objected to his performing in the city. (*HC* 5:383)

4   Dr. Turner, a phrenologist, came in. I gratified his curiosity for about an hour by allowing him to examine my head. . . .

In the morning, at home, having a long conversation with a physiologist and mesmeriser. I asked them to prove that the mind of man was seated in one part of the brain more than another. (*HC* 6:56)

Plainness

1   As every letter that comes from Zion must go the rounds of the brethren for inspection, it is necessary that there should be no disguise in them, but that every subject written upon by the brethren should

---

Phrenology
   2   Nauvoo, 2 July 1842.
   3   Nauvoo, 6 May 1843. In the handwritten version of Church history, the following words were included but crossed out: "Thought we had been imposed upon enough by such kind of things" (History of Joseph Smith, LDS Church Archives; see Bitton and Bunker, "Phrenology Among the Mormons," p. 60).
   4   Nauvoo, 13 and 14 October 1843.

Plainness
   1   Letter to the brethren in Zion, Kirtland, 21 April 1833.

be plain to the understanding of all, that no jealousy may be raised, and when we rebuke, do it in all meekness. . . .

Now I would say to Brother Gilbert, that I do not write this by way of chastisement, but to show him the absolute necessity of having all his communications written in a manner to be clearly understood. (HC 1:340–41)

2   The plain simple order of the Gospel of Jesus Christ never has been discerned or acknowledged as the truth, except by a few—among whom were "not many wise men after the flesh, not many mighty, not many noble;" whilst the majority have contented themselves with their own private opinions, or have adopted those of others, according to their address, their philosophy, their formula, their policy, or their fineness may have attracted their attention, or pleased their taste. (HC 4:8)

3   It will be well to study plainness and simplicity in whatever you publish, "for my soul delighteth in plainness." (HC 4:129)

4   If any man attempts to refute what I am about to say, after I have made it plain, let him beware. (HC 5:426)

5   I never design to communicate any ideas but what are simple; for to this end I am sent. (HC 5:529)

Plan of Salvation

1   Who but those who have duly considered the condescension of the Father of our spirits, in providing a sacrifice for His creatures, a plan of redemption, a power of atonement, a scheme of salvation, having as its great objects, the bringing of men back into the presence

---

Plainness
2   Letter to Isaac Galland, Commerce (Nauvoo), 11 September 1839.
3   Letter to Orson Hyde and John E. Page, Nauvoo, 14 May 1840.
4   Sabbath address, Nauvoo, 11 June 1843.
5   Remarks at the funeral of Judge Elias Higbee, Nauvoo, 13 August 1843.

Plan of Salvation
1   Letter to the brethren scattered from Zion, Kirtland, 22 January 1834.

of the King of heaven, crowning them in the celestial glory, and making them heirs with the Son to that inheritance which is incorruptible, undefiled, and which fadeth not away—who but such can realize the importance of a perfect walk before all men, and a diligence in calling upon all men to partake of these blessings? How indescribably glorious are these things to mankind! Of a truth they may be considered tidings of great joy to all people; and tidings, too, that ought to fill the earth and cheer the hearts of every one when sounded in his ears. . . .

The great plan of salvation is a theme which ought to occupy our strict attention, and be regarded as one of heaven's best gifts to mankind. No consideration whatever ought to deter us from showing ourselves approved in the sight of God, according to His divine requirement. (HC 2:5–6, 23)

2   But that man was not able himself to erect a system, or plan with power sufficient to free him from a destruction which awaited him, is evident from the fact that God, as before remarked, prepared a sacrifice in the gift of His own Son who should be sent in due time, to prepare a way, or open a door through which man might enter into the Lord's presence, whence he had been cast out for disobedience. From time to time these glad tidings were sounded in the ears of men in different ages of the world down to the time of Messiah's coming. . . .

. . . For our own part we cannot believe that the ancients in all ages were so ignorant of the system of heaven as many suppose, since all that were ever saved, were saved through the power of this great plan of redemption, as much before the coming of Christ as since; if not, God has had different plans in operation (if we may so express it), to bring men back to dwell with Himself; and this we cannot believe. (HC 2:15, 16)

3   At the first organization in heaven we were all present, and saw the Savior chosen and appointed and the plan of salvation made, and we sanctioned it. (WJS, p. 60; standardized)

Plan of Salvation

2   Letter to the brethren scattered from Zion, Kirtland, 22 January 1834.

3   Lecture given at the Nauvoo Lyceum, 5 January 1841, as reported by William Clayton. (The lyceum met weekly at different locations in Nauvoo for several months, beginning 5 January 1841.)

4 There is a way to release the spirits of the dead; that is by the power and authority of the Priesthood—by binding and loosing on earth. This doctrine appears glorious, inasmuch as it exhibits the greatness of divine compassion and benevolence in the extent of the plan of human salvation.

This glorious truth is well calculated to enlarge the understanding, and to sustain the soul under troubles, difficulties and distresses. (HC 4:425)

5 The great designs of God in relation to the salvation of the human family, are very little understood by the professedly wise and intelligent generation in which we live. Various and conflicting are the opinions of men concerning the plan of salvation, the requisitions of the Almighty, the necessary preparations for heaven, the state and condition of departed spirits, and the happiness or misery that is consequent upon the practice of righteousness and iniquity according to their several notions of virtue and vice. . . .

The great Jehovah contemplated the whole of the events connected with the earth, pertaining to the plan of salvation, before it rolled into existence, or ever "the morning stars sang together" for joy; the past, the present, and the future were and are, with Him, one eternal "now;" He knew of the fall of Adam, the iniquities of the antediluvians, of the depth of iniquity that would be connected with the human family, their weakness and strength, their power and glory, apostasies, their crimes, their righteousness and iniquity; He comprehended the fall of man, and his redemption; He knew the plan of salvation and pointed it out; He was acquainted with the situation of all nations and with their destiny; He ordered all things according to the council of His own will; He knows the situation of both the living and the dead, and has made ample provision for their redemption, according to their several circumstances, and the laws of the kingdom of God, whether in this world, or in the world to come. (HC 4:595, 597)

6 And now as the great purposes of God are hastening to their accomplishment, and the things spoken of in the Prophets are fulfilling,

---

Plan of Salvation

    4 General conference address, Nauvoo, 3 October 1841.

    5 Editorial in the *Times and Seasons*, 15 April 1842.

    6 Editorial in the *Times and Seasons*, 15 April 1842.

as the kingdom of God is established on the earth, and the ancient order of things restored, the Lord has manifested to us this day and privilege, and we are commanded to be baptized for our dead, thus fulfilling the words of Obadiah, when speaking of the glory of the latter-day: "And saviors shall come upon Mount Zion to judge the remnant of Esau, and the kingdom shall be the Lord's." A view of these things reconciles the Scriptures of truth, justifies the ways of God to man, places the human family upon an equal footing, and harmonizes with every principle of righteousness, justice and truth. (*HC* 4:599)

7   All men know that they must die. And it is important that we should understand the reasons and causes of our exposure to the vicissitudes of life and of death, and the designs and purposes of God in our coming into the world, our sufferings here, and our departure hence. What is the object of our coming into existence, then dying and falling away, to be here no more? It is but reasonable to suppose that God would reveal something in reference to the matter, and it is a subject we ought to study more than any other. We ought to study it day and night, for the world is ignorant in reference to their true condition and relation. If we have any claim on our Heavenly Father for anything, it is for knowledge on this important subject. Could we read and comprehend all that has been written from the days of Adam, on the relation of man to God and angels in a future state, we should know very little about it. Reading the experience of others, or the revelation given to *them*, can never give *us* a comprehensive view of our condition and true relation to God. Knowledge of these things can only be obtained by experience through the ordinances of God set forth for that purpose. (*HC* 6:50)

8   I will go back to the beginning before the world was, to show what kind of being God is. What sort of a being was God in the beginning? Open your ears and hear, all ye ends of the earth, for I am going to prove it to you by the Bible, and to tell you the designs of God in relation to the human race, and why He interferes with the affairs of man. . . .
     In the beginning, the head of the Gods called a council of the Gods; and they came together and concocted {prepared} a plan to cre-

<hr>

Plan of Salvation

7   Remarks upon the death of James Adams, Nauvoo, 9 October 1843.
8   King Follett Discourse, Nauvoo, 7 April 1844.

ate the world and people it. When we begin to learn this way, we begin to learn the only true God, and what kind of a being we have got to worship. Having a knowledge of God, we begin to know how to approach Him, and how to ask so as to receive an answer. . . .

Intelligence is eternal and exists upon a self-existent principle. It is a spirit from age to age and there is no creation about it. All the minds and spirits that God ever sent into the world are susceptible of enlargement.

The first principles of man are self-existent with God. God himself, finding he was in the midst of spirits and glory, because he was more intelligent, saw proper to institute laws whereby the rest could have a privilege to advance like himself. The relationship we have with God places us in a situation to advance in knowledge. He has power to institute laws to instruct the weaker intelligences, that they may be exalted with Himself, so that they might have one glory upon another, and all that knowledge, power, glory, and intelligence, which is requisite in order to save them in the world of spirits. (HC 6:305, 308, 311–12)

Planetary Systems

1   I also gave some instructions in the mysteries of the kingdom of God; such as the history of the planets, Abraham's writings upon the planetary systems, etc. (HC 3:27)

2   The learning of the Egyptians, and their knowledge of astronomy was no doubt taught them by Abraham and Joseph, as their records testify, who received it from the Lord. (HC 5:63)

Pledge

1   My life is pledged to carry out this great work. (WJS, p. 218)

Planetary Systems
  1   Sabbath address, Far West, Missouri, 6 May 1838.
  2   Editorial in the *Times and Seasons*, 15 July 1842.

Pledge
  1   Address regarding his arrest at Dixon, Illinois, Nauvoo, 30 June 1843.

2   Another man (I will not call his name,) has been writing to the *New York Tribune*, some of the most disgraceful things possible to name. He says, in that article, that there are a great many donations to the Temple which have been appropriated to other purposes.

His object evidently was to stigmatize the trustee and excite prejudice against us abroad. But I pledge myself that whoever has contributed any old shoes, harness, horses, wagons, or anything else, if he will come forward, I will show that every farthing is on the book and has been appropriated for the building of the Temple.

I pledge myself that if he finds the first farthing that we cannot show where it has been appropriated, I will give him my head for a football. (HC 6:239)

Politeness

1   *Report of Willard Richards:* President Joseph Smith complained of the citizens of Nauvoo. He reproved some young men for crowding on to the ladies' seats on the meeting ground, and laughing and mocking during meeting. (HC 5:531)

Politics

1   *Minutes:* The President commenced making observations . . . that he did not wish to have any political influence, but wished the Saints to use their political franchise to the best of their knowledge. (HC 4:109)

2   The partizans in this county [Hancock County], who expect to divide the friends of humanity and equal rights, will find themselves

---

Pledge
   2   Remarks at meeting at temple in Nauvoo, 7 March 1844.

Politeness
   1   Sabbath address, Nauvoo, 13 August 1843.

Politics
   1   General conference address, Nauvoo, 8 April 1840.
   2   Letter to people of Illinois, dated 20 December 1841, published in the *Times and Seasons*, 1 January 1842.

mistaken—we care not a fig for Whig or Democrat; they are both alike to us, but we shall go for our friends, our tried friends, and the cause of human liberty, which is the cause of God. (HC 4:480)

3 At one p.m. I attended a large and respectable meeting of the citizens of Nauvoo, near the Temple, and addressed them on the principles of government, at considerable length, showing that I did not intend to vote the Whig or Democratic ticket as such, but would go for those who would support good order, &c. (HC 5:19)

4 Dear Sir:—I have of late had repeated solicitations to have something to do in relation to the political farce about dividing the county; but as my feelings revolt at the idea of having anything to do with politics, I have declined, in every instance, having anything to do on the subject. I think it would be well for politicians to regulate their own affairs. I wish to be let alone, that I may attend strictly to the spiritual welfare of the Church.

Please insert the above, and oblige. (HC 5:259)

5 There is one thing more I wish to speak about, and that is political economy. It is our duty to concentrate all our influence to make popular that which is sound and good, and unpopular that which is unsound. 'Tis right, politically, for a man who has influence to use it, as well as for a man who has no influence to use his. From henceforth I will maintain all the influence I can get. In relation to politics, I will speak as a man; but in relation to religion I will speak in authority. (HC 5:286)

6 In relation to national matters, I want it to go abroad unto the whole world that every man should stand on his own merits. The Lord has not given me a revelation concerning politics. I have not asked Him for one. I am a third party, and stand independent and alone. I desire to see all parties protected in their rights. (HC 5:526)

Politics

3 Nauvoo, 26 May 1842.

4 Letter to the editor of the *Wasp*, Nauvoo, 23 January 1843.

5 Address at the temple site in Nauvoo, 21 February 1843.

6 Sabbath address, Nauvoo, 6 August 1843.

7   But, sir, when I leave the dignity and honor I received from heaven, to boost a man into power, through the aid of my friends, where the evil and designing, after the object has been accomplished, can lock up the clemency intended as a reciprocation for such favors, and where the wicked and unprincipled, as a matter of course, would seize the opportunity to flintify the hearts of the nation against me for dabbling at a sly game in politics,—verily I say, when I leave the dignity and honor of heaven, to gratify the ambition and vanity of man or men, may my power cease, like the strength of Samson, when he was shorn of his locks, while asleep in the lap of Delilah. Truly said the Savior, "Cast not your pearls before swine, lest they trample them under their feet, and turn again and rend you."

Shall I, who have witnessed the visions of eternity, and beheld the glorious mansions of bliss, and the regions and the misery of the damned,—shall I turn to be a Judas? Shall I, who have heard the voice of God, and communed with angels, and spake as moved by the Holy Ghost for the renewal of the everlasting covenant, and for the gathering of Israel in the last days,—shall I worm myself into a political hypocrite? Shall I, who hold the keys of the last kingdom, in which is the dispensation of the fullness of all things spoken by the mouths of all the holy Prophets since the world began, under the sealing power of the Melchisedec Priesthood,—shall I stoop from the sublime authority of Almighty God, to be handled as a monkey's cat-paw, and pettify myself into a clown to act the farce of political demagoguery? No—verily no! The whole earth shall bear me witness that I, like the towering rock in the midst of the ocean, which has withstood the mighty surges of the warring waves for centuries, *am impregnable,* and am a faithful friend to virtue, and a fearless foe to vice,—no odds whether the former was sold as a pearl in Asia or hid as a gem in America, and the latter dazzles in palaces or glimmers among the tombs. (HC 6:77–78)

8   Unity is power; and when I reflect on the importance of it to the stability of all governments, I am astounded at the silly moves of per-

---

Politics

7   Letter to James Arlington Bennett, Nauvoo, 13 November 1843; response to Bennett's request that the Prophet use his influence to help Bennett become the governor of Illinois.

8   A pamphlet containing the Prophet's political platform, entitled *Views of the Powers and Policy of the Government of the United States,* Nauvoo, 7 February 1844.

sons and parties to foment discord in order to ride into power on the current of popular excitement; nor am I less surprised at the stretches of power or restrictions of right which too often appear as acts of legislators to pave the way to some favorite political scheme as destitute of intrinsic merit as a wolf's heart is of the milk of human kindness. A Frenchman would say, *"Presque tout aimer richesses et pouvoir."* (Almost all men like wealth and power.)

. . . But the sentiment remains . . . as a pattern for wise men *to study the convenience of the people more than the comfort of the cabinet.* (HC 6:198, 199)

9 I would not have suffered my name to have been used by my friends on anywise as President of the United States, or candidate for that office, if I and my friends could have had the privilege of enjoying our religious and civil rights as American citizens, even those rights which the Constitution guarantees unto all her citizens alike. (*HC* 6:210)

10 Political views and party distinctions never should disturb the harmony of society. (*HC* 6:218)

11 As to politics, I care but little about the presidential chair. I would not give half as much for the office of President of the United States as I would for the one I now hold as Lieutenant-General of the Nauvoo Legion.

We have as good a right to make a political party to gain power to defend ourselves, as for demagogues to make use of our religion to get power to destroy us. In other words, as the world has used the power of government to oppress and persecute us, it is right for us to use it for the protection of our rights. We will whip the mob by getting up a candidate for President. (*HC* 6:243)

Politics

    9   Political meeting, Nauvoo, 8 February 1844.

    10 Article entitled "Pacific Innuendo," Nauvoo, 17 February 1844.

    11 Remarks at meeting at temple in Nauvoo, 7 March 1844.

Pondering

1   A fanciful and flowery and heated imagination beware of; because the things of God are of deep import; and time, and experience, and careful and ponderous and solemn thoughts can only find them out. Thy mind, O man! if thou wilt lead a soul unto salvation, must stretch as high as the utmost heavens, and search into and contemplate the darkest abyss, and the broad expanse of eternity—thou must commune with God. How much more dignified and noble are the thoughts of God, than the vain imaginations of the human heart! None but fools will trifle with the souls of men. (HC 3:295)

Poor

1   The rich are in no wise to cast out the poor, or leave them behind, for it is said that the poor shall inherit the earth. (HC 1:339)

2   First, in relation to the poor: When the Bishops are appointed according to our recommendation, it will devolve upon them to see to the poor, according to the laws of the Church. (HC 1:365)

3   He [Bishop Newel K. Whitney] shall deal with a liberal hand to the poor and the needy, the sick and afflicted, the widow and the fatherless. . . . And it shall come to pass, that according to the measure that he meteth out with a liberal hand to the poor, so shall it be measured to him again by the hand of his God, even an hundred fold. (HC 2:288)

4   When we consecrate our property to the Lord it is to administer to the wants of the poor and needy, for this is the law of God. (HC 3:230)

Pondering
1   Letter to the Saints from Liberty Jail, 20–25 March 1839.

Poor
1   Letter to one of Jared Carter's brothers, written at the request of Jared Carter, Kirtland, 13 April 1833.
2   Letter to the brethren in Zion, Kirtland, 25 June 1833.
3   Blessing upon Bishop Newel K. Whitney, Kirtland, 7 October 1835.
4   Letter to the Church from Liberty Jail, 16 December 1838.

5 Whosoever will, let him come and partake of the poverty of Nauvoo freely, for those who partake of her poverty shall also partake of her prosperity. (*WJS*, p. 416; standardized)

6 The rich cannot be saved without charity, giving to feed the poor when and how God requires. (HC 4:608)

7 The best measure or principle to bring the poor to repentance is to administer to their wants. (HC 5:24–25)

8 *Minutes:* He [Joseph Smith] also prophesied in the name of the Lord, concerning the merchants in the city, that if they and the rich did not open their hearts and contribute to the poor, they would be cursed by the hand of God, and be cut off from the land of the living. (HC 5:35)

9 If any man is poor and afflicted, let him come and tell of it, and not complain or grumble about it. (HC 5:285)

10 Woe to ye rich men, who refuse to give to the poor, and then come and ask me for bread. Away with all your meanness, and be liberal. We need purging, purifying and cleansing. (HC 6:59)

Popularity

1 It is our duty to concentrate all our influence to make popular that which is sound and good, and unpopular that which is unsound. (HC 5:286)

Poor
   5 Discourse, Nauvoo, 19 July 1840, recorded in Howard and Martha Coray Notebook. For a discussion about the recording of this discourse, see *WJS*, pp. 418–19.
   6 Sabbath address, Nauvoo, 1 May 1842.
   7 Remarks to the Relief Society, Nauvoo, 9 June 1842.
   8 Minutes of a public meeting, Nauvoo, 18 June 1842.
   9 Address at the temple site in Nauvoo, 21 February 1843.
   10 Sabbath address, Nauvoo, 15 October 1843.

Popularity
   1 Address at the temple site in Nauvoo, 21 February 1843.

2   And what shall be said of him that, like the "Levite," passes on the other side of the way, when we behold men who "have borne the heat and the burden of the day" struggling against the popular opinions of a vain world, the burlesque of a giddy throng, the vulgarity of a self-wise multitude, and the falsehoods of what may justly be termed the "civilized meanness of the age," and not lending a helping hand? The 25th chapter of Matthew contains the simple answer. (HC 6:69–70)

3   The object with me is to obey and teach others to obey God in just what He tells us to do. It mattereth not whether the principle is popular or unpopular, I will always maintain a true principle, even if I stand alone in it. (HC 6:223)

Posterity

1   Marvelously and miraculously shall the Lord his God provide for him [Bishop Newel K. Whitney], even that he shall be blessed with a fullness of the good things of this earth, and his seed after him from generation to generation. . . . Angels shall guard his house, and shall guard the lives of his posterity, and they shall become very great and very numerous on the earth. (HC 2:288)

2   Stand fast, ye Saints of God, hold on a little while longer, and the storm of life will be past, and you will be rewarded by that God whose servants you are, and who will duly appreciate all your toils and afflictions for Christ's sake and the Gospel's. Your names will be handed down to posterity as Saints of God and virtuous men. (HC 4:337)

3   Let his [Erastus H. Derby's] name be had in everlasting remembrance; let the blessings of Jehovah be crowned upon his posterity

---

Popularity
  2   Letter to the Saints encouraging them to patronize the Church newspaper, published in the *Times and Seasons*, 1 November 1843.
  3   Remarks following the sermon of an Episcopalian minister, Nauvoo, 21 February 1844.

Posterity
  1   Blessing upon Bishop Newel K. Whitney, Kirtland, 7 October 1835.
  2   Minutes of a general conference, Nauvoo, 7 April 1841.
  3   Blessing upon Erastus H. Derby, Nauvoo, 15 August 1842.

after him, for he rendered me consolation in the lonely places of my retreat. (HC 5:107)

4 *Report of Willard Richards:* Four destroying angels holding power over the four quarters of the earth until the servants of God are sealed in their foreheads, which signifies sealing the blessing upon their heads, meaning the everlasting covenant, thereby making their calling and election sure. When a seal is put upon the father and mother, it secures their posterity, so that they cannot be lost, but will be saved by virtue of the covenant of their father and mother. . . .

The speaker continued to teach the doctrine of election and the sealing powers and principles, and spoke of the doctrine of election with the seed of Abraham, and the sealing of blessings upon his posterity, and the sealing of the fathers and children, according to the declarations of the prophets. (HC 5:530–31)

Power
See also KNOWLEDGE

1 Every family should get power by fasting and prayer. (WJS, p. 37; standardized)

2 A man is saved no faster than he gets knowledge, for if he does not get knowledge, he will be brought into captivity by some evil power in the other world, as evil spirits will have more knowledge, and consequently more power than many men who are on the earth. Hence it needs revelation to assist us, and give us knowledge of the things of God. (HC 4:588)

3 In knowledge there is power. God has more power than all other beings, because he has greater knowledge; and hence he knows how to subject all other beings to Him. He has power over all. (HC 5:340)

Posterity
  4 Remarks at the funeral of Judge Elias Higbee, Nauvoo, 13 August 1843.

Power
  1 Instruction at a Thursday fast meeting, Nauvoo, 30 July 1840. The Prophet's words have specific reference to sickness in families.
  2 Sabbath address, Nauvoo, 10 April 1842.
  3 General conference address, Nauvoo, 8 April 1843.

4   *Report of Wilford Woodruff:* President Joseph Smith again arose and said—In relation to the power over the minds of mankind which I hold, I would say, It is in consequence of the power of truth in the doctrines which I have been an instrument in the hands of God of presenting unto them, and not because of any compulsion on my part. (HC 6:273)

5   A brother who works in the *St. Louis Gazette* office came up at the same time, and wanted to know by what principle I got so much power, how many inhabitants and armed men we had, &c. I told him I obtained power on the principles of truth and virtue, which would last when I was dead and gone, &c. (HC 6:343)

Prayer

1   Great harmony prevailed; several were ordained; faith was strengthened; and humility, so necessary for the blessing of God to follow prayer, characterized the Saints. (HC 1:176–77)

2   I have visited a grove which is just back of the town almost every day where I can be secluded from the eyes of any mortal and there give vent to all the feelings of my heart in meditation and prayer. I have called to mind all the past moments of my life, and am left to mourn and shed tears of sorrow for my folly in suffering the adversary of my soul to have so much power over me as he has had in times past. But God is merciful and has forgiven my sins, and I rejoice that he sendeth forth the Comforter unto as many as believe and humbleth themselves before him. (*PWJS*, p. 238; standardized)

3   I urged the necessity of prayer, that the Spirit might be given, that the things of the Spirit might be judged thereby, because the carnal mind cannot discern the things of God. (HC 2:31)

Power
4   Sabbath address, Nauvoo, 24 March 1844.
5   Answer to a brother who worked for the *St. Louis Gazette* and asked about the Prophet's source of power, Nauvoo, 25 April 1844.

Prayer
1   Conference of the Church, Kirtland, Ohio, June 1831.
2   Letter to Emma Smith from Greenville, Indiana, 6 June 1832.
3   Meeting of the high council, Kirtland, 19 February 1834.

4 Every night before retiring to rest, at the sound of the trumpet, we bowed before the Lord in the several tents, and presented our thank-offerings with prayer and supplication; and at the sound of the morning trumpet, about four o'clock, every man was again on his knees before the Lord, imploring His blessing for the day. (HC 2:64–65)

5 Some, by a long face and sanctimonious prayers, and very pious sermons, had power to lead the minds of the ignorant and unwary. (HC 3:232)

6 And now, brethren, after your tribulations, if you do these things, and exercise fervent prayer and faith in the sight of God always, He shall give unto you knowledge by His Holy Spirit, yea by the unspeakable gift of the Holy Ghost, that has not been revealed since the world was until now. (HC 3:296)

7 The best way to obtain truth and wisdom is not to ask it from books, but to go to God in prayer, and obtain divine teaching. (HC 4:425)

8 We would say to the brethren, seek to know God in your closets, call upon him in the fields. Follow the directions of the Book of Mormon, and pray over, and for your families, your cattle, your flocks, your herds, your corn, and all things that you possess; ask the blessing of God upon all your labors, and everything that you engage in. (HC 5:31)

9 The Society [Relief Society] have done well: their principles are to practice holiness. God loves you, and your prayers in my behalf shall avail much: let them not cease to ascend to God continually in my behalf. (HC 5:141)

10 Slack not your duties in your families, but call upon God for his blessings upon you, and your families—upon your flocks and herds, and all that pertains to you—that you may have peace and prosperity—and

Prayer
 4 Events of Zion's Camp, near New Portage, Ohio, 7 May 1834.
 5 Letter to the Church from Liberty Jail, 16 December 1838.
 6 Letter to the Saints from Liberty Jail, 20–25 March 1839.
 7 General conference address, Nauvoo, 3 October 1841.
 8 Editorial in the *Times and Seasons*, 15 June 1842.
 9 Remarks to the Relief Society, Nauvoo, 31 August 1842.
 10 Editorial in the *Times and Seasons*, 15 October 1842.

while you are doing this, "pray for the peace of Zion, for they shall prosper that love her." (*T&S* 3:952)

11 While there, Brother Richards asked if I wanted a wicked man to pray for me? I replied, Yes; if the fervent, affectionate prayer of the righteous man availeth much, a wicked man may avail a little when praying for a righteous man. There is none good but One. The better a man is, the more his prayer will avail. Like the publican and the Pharisee, one was justified rather than the other, showing that both were justified in a degree. The prayer of a wicked man may do a righteous man good, when it does the one who prays no good. (HC 5:208)

12 I have no desire but to do all men good. I feel to pray for all men. (HC 5:259)

13 The effectual prayers of the righteous avail much. (HC 6:303)

14 *Words of Henry William Bigler:* Speaking about praying to our Father in heaven, I once heard Joseph Smith remark, "Be plain and simple, and ask for what you want, just like you would go to a neighbor and say, I want to borrow your horse to go to the mill." (*TK*, p. 100)

15 *Words of John Lyman Smith:* In my early years I used to eat often at the table with Joseph the Prophet. At one time he was called to dinner. I was at play in the room with his son Joseph when he called us to him, and we stood one on each side of him. After he had looked over the table he said, "Lord, we thank Thee for this johnny cake, and ask Thee to send us something better. Amen."

The cornbread was cut and I received a piece from his hand. Before the bread was all eaten, a man came to the door and asked if the Prophet Joseph was at home.

Joseph replied he was, whereupon the visitor said, "I have brought you some flour and a ham."

Prayer
11 Nauvoo, 24 December 1842.
12 Sabbath address, Nauvoo, 22 January 1843.
13 King Follett Discourse, Nauvoo, 7 April 1844.
14 Recollection of Henry William Bigler, published in the *Juvenile Instructor*, 1 March 1892.
15 Recollection of John Lyman Smith, published in the *Juvenile Instructor*, 15 March 1892.

Joseph arose and took the gift, and blessed the man in the name of the Lord. Turning to his wife, Emma, he said, "I knew the Lord would answer my prayer." (*TK*, p. 146)

Prejudice

1   If the Church knew all the commandments, one half they would condemn through prejudice and ignorance. (HC 2:477)

2   We ought always to be aware of those prejudices which sometimes so strangely present themselves, and are so congenial to human nature, against our friends, neighbors, and brethren of the world, who choose to differ from us in opinion and in matters of faith. Our religion is between us and our God. Their religion is between them and their God.

There is a love from God that should be exercised toward those of our faith, who walk uprightly, which is peculiar to itself, but it is without prejudice; it also gives scope to the mind, which enables us to conduct ourselves with greater liberality towards all that are not of our faith, than what they exercise towards one another. These principles approximate nearer to the mind of God, because it is like God, or Godlike. (HC 3:303–4)

Premortality
See also INTELLIGENCE (SELF-EXISTENT)

1   The first step in the salvation of men is the laws of eternal and self-existent principles. Spirits are eternal. At the first organization in heaven we were all present, and saw the Savior chosen and appointed and the plan of salvation made, and we sanctioned it. (*WJS*, p. 60; standardized)

Prejudice
  1   Solemn assembly in the Kirtland Temple, 6 April 1837.
  2   Letter to the Saints from Liberty Jail, 20–25 March 1839.

Premortality
  1   Lecture given at the Nauvoo Lyceum, 5 January 1841, as reported by William Clayton. (The lyceum met weekly at different locations in Nauvoo for several months, beginning 5 January 1841.)

2   It was the design of the councils of heaven before the world was, that the principles and laws of the priesthood should be predicated upon the gathering of the people in every age of the world. . . .

. . . God decreed before the foundation of the world that that ordinance [baptism for the dead] should be administered in a font prepared for that purpose in the house of the Lord. (HC 5:423, 424)

3   The organization of the spiritual and heavenly worlds, and of spiritual and heavenly beings, was agreeable to the most perfect order and harmony: their limits and bounds were fixed irrevocably, and voluntarily subscribed to in their heavenly estate by themselves, and were by our first parents subscribed to upon the earth. Hence the importance of embracing and subscribing to principles of eternal truth by all men upon the earth that expect eternal life. (HC 6:51)

4   In the beginning, the head of the Gods called a council of the Gods; and they came together and concocted {prepared} a plan to create the world and people it. . . .

The first principles of man are self-existent with God. God himself, finding he was in the midst of spirits and glory, because he was more intelligent, saw proper to institute laws whereby the rest could have a privilege to advance like himself. . . .

The contention in heaven was—Jesus said there would be certain souls that would not be saved; and the devil said he would save them all, and laid his plans before the grand council, who gave their vote in favor of Jesus Christ. So the devil rose up in rebellion against God, and was cast down, with all who put up their heads for him. (HC 6:308, 312, 314)

5   *Words of Charles Lambert:* The Prophet used to hold meetings in a log house of his, sometimes twice a week. At one of these, he said he wished he had a people to whom he could reveal what the Lord had shown him. Said he, "But one thing I will say, there are thousands of spirits that have been waiting to come forth in this day and genera-

---

Premortality
  2   Sabbath address, Nauvoo, 11 June 1843.
  3   Remarks upon the death of James Adams, Nauvoo, 9 October 1843.
  4   King Follett Discourse, Nauvoo, 7 April 1844.
  5   Autobiography of Charles Lambert, LDS Church Archives.

tion. Their proper channel is through the priesthood. A way has to be provided. The time has come, and they have got to come anyway." (*TK*, p. 172)

Preparation

1   God has in reserve a time, or period appointed in His own bosom, when He will bring all His subjects, who have obeyed His voice and kept His commandments, into His celestial rest. This rest is of such perfection and glory, that man has need of a preparation before he can, according to the laws of that kingdom, enter it and enjoy its blessings. This being the fact, God has given certain laws to the human family, which, if observed, are sufficient to prepare them to inherit this rest. (HC 2:12)

2   If—verily I say unto you—if the Church with one united effort perform their duties; if they do this, the work shall be complete—if they do not this in all humility, making preparation from this time forth, like Joseph in Egypt, laying up store against the time of famine, every man having his tent, his horses, his chariots, his armory, his cattle, his family, and his whole substance in readiness against the time when it shall be said: To your tents, O Israel! Let not this be noised abroad; let every heart beat in silence, and every mouth be shut. (HC 2:145)

3   Let every one labor to prepare himself for the vineyard, sparing a little time to comfort the mourners; to bind up the broken-hearted; to reclaim the backslider; to bring back the wanderer; to re-invite into the kingdom such as have been cut off, by encouraging them to lay to while the day lasts, and work righteousness, and, with one heart and one mind, prepare to help redeem Zion, that goodly land of promise, where the willing and the obedient shall be blessed. (HC 2:229)

Preparation
1   Letter to the brethren scattered from Zion, Kirtland, 22 January 1834.
2   Letter written from Kirtland to the high council in Zion, 16 August 1834.
3   Letter to the Saints in Missouri published in the *Messenger and Advocate*, June 1835.

4   It seems to be deeply impressed upon our minds that the Saints ought to lay hold of every door that shall seem to be opened unto them, to obtain foothold on the earth, and be making all the preparation that is within their power for the terrible storms that are now gathering in the heavens, "a day of clouds, with darkness and gloominess, and of thick darkness," as spoken of by the Prophets, which cannot be now of a long time lingering. (HC 3:298)

5   The Lord cannot always be known by the thunder of His voice, by the display of His glory or by the manifestation of His power; and those that are the most anxious to see these things, are the least prepared to meet them, and were the Lord to manifest His power as He did to the children of Israel, such characters would be the first to say, "Let not the Lord speak any more, lest we His people die." (HC 5:31)

6   I could explain a hundred fold more than I ever have of the glories of the kingdoms manifested to me in the vision, were I permitted, and were the people prepared to receive them. (HC 5:402)

7   Wherefore let the rich and the learned, the wise and the noble, the poor and the needy, the bond and the free, both black and white, take heed to their ways, and a leave to the knowledge of God, and execute justice and judgment upon the earth in righteousness, and prepare to meet the judge of the quick and the dead, for the hour of His coming is nigh. (HC 6:93)

Presiding

1   Such as have the highest authority should preside. (HC 1:339)

Preparation
   4   Letter to the Saints from Liberty Jail, 20–25 March 1839.
   5   Editorial in the *Times and Seasons*, 15 June 1842.
   6   Sabbath address, Nauvoo, 21 May 1843.
   7   Letter to the "Green Mountains Boys" in Vermont, appealing for their support, Nauvoo, 29 November 1843.

Presiding
   1   Letter to one of Jared Carter's brothers, written at the request of Jared Carter, Kirtland, 13 April 1833.

2   I laid my hands on Brother Oliver Cowdery, and ordained him an assistant-president, saying these words: "In the name of Jesus Christ, who was crucified for the sins of the world, I lay my hands upon thee and ordain thee an assistant-president to the High and Holy Priesthood, in the Church of the Latter-day Saints." (HC 2:176)

3   *Minutes:* The Twelve are not subject to any other than the first Presidency, viz., "myself," said the Prophet, "Sidney Rigdon, and Frederick G. Williams, who are now my Counselors; and where I am not, there is no First Presidency over the Twelve." (HC 2:374)

4   The Presidents or Presidency are over the Church; and revelations of the mind and will of God to the Church, are to come through the Presidency. This is the order of heaven, and the power and privilege of this Priesthood. (HC 2:477)

5   The gift of discerning spirits will be given to the Presiding Elder. (HC 3:392)

6   Any person that had seen the heavens opened knows that there are three personages in the heavens who hold the keys of power, and one presides over all. (HC 5:426)

Pride

1   All men are naturally disposed to walk in their own paths as they are pointed out by their own fingers and are not willing to consider

---

Presiding
2   The Prophet assembled with Oliver Cowdery, Sidney Rigdon, and Frederick G. Williams to ordain Oliver Cowdery to the office of Assistant President of the Church, 5 December 1834.
3   Instructions to the Twelve, Kirtland, 16 January 1836.
4   Solemn assembly in the Kirtland Temple, 6 April 1837.
5   Discourse on the priesthood, given sometime before 8 August 1839, Commerce (Nauvoo). For a discussion on the dating of this discourse, see *WJS*, p. 22.
6   Sabbath address, Nauvoo, 11 June 1843.

Pride
1   Letter to Vienna Jacques, Kirtland, 4 September 1833.

and walk in the path which is pointed out by another, saying, This is the way, walk ye in it, although he should be an unerring director, and the Lord his God sent him. (HC 1:408)

2   Consider for a moment, brethren, the fulfillment of the words of the prophet; for we behold that darkness covers the earth, and gross darkness the minds of the inhabitants thereof—that crimes of every description are increasing among men—vices of great enormity are practiced—the rising generation growing up in the fullness of pride and arrogance—the aged losing every sense of conviction, and seemingly banishing every thought of a day of retribution—intemperance, immorality, extravagance, pride, blindness of heart, idolatry, the loss of natural affection; the love of this world, and indifference toward the things of eternity increasing among those who profess a belief in the religion of heaven, and infidelity spreading itself in consequence of the same—men giving themselves up to commit acts of the foulest kind, and deeds of the blackest dye, blaspheming, defrauding, blasting the reputation of neighbors, stealing, robbing, murdering; advocating error and opposing the truth, forsaking the covenant of heaven, and denying the faith of Jesus—and in the midst of all this, the day of the Lord fast approaching when none except those who have won the wedding garment will be permitted to eat and drink in the presence of the Bridegroom, the Prince of Peace! (HC 2:5)

3   We would say, beware of pride also; for well and truly hath the wise man said, that pride goeth before destruction, and a haughty spirit before a fall. (HC 3:295)

4   If there are any among you who aspire after their own aggrandizement, and seek their own opulence, while their brethren are groaning in poverty, and are under sore trials and temptations, they cannot be benefited by the intercession of the Holy Spirit, which maketh intercession for us day and night with groanings that cannot be uttered. (HC 3:299)

Pride

2   Letter to the brethren scattered from Zion, Kirtland, 22 January 1834.
3   Letter to the Saints from Liberty Jail, 20–25 March 1839.
4   Letter to the Saints from Liberty Jail, 20–25 March 1839.

5 Let the Twelve be humble, and not be exalted, and beware of pride, and not seek to excel one above another, but act for each other's good, and pray for one another, and honor our brother or make honorable mention of his name, and not backbite and devour our brother. (HC 3:383–84)

6 It would be gratifying to my mind to see the Saints in Kirtland flourish, but think the time is not yet come; and I assure you it never will until a different order of things be established and a different spirit manifested. When confidence is restored, when pride shall fall, and every aspiring mind be clothed with humility as with a garment, and selfishness give place to benevolence and charity, and a united determination to live by every word which proceedeth out of the mouth of the Lord is observable, then, and not till then, can peace, order and love prevail.

It is in consequence of aspiring men that Kirtland has been forsaken. How frequently has your humble servant been envied in his office by such characters, who endeavored to raise themselves to power at his expense, and seeing it impossible to do so, resorted to foul slander and abuse, and other means to effect his overthrow. Such characters have ever been the first to cry out against the Presidency, and publish their faults and foibles to the four winds of heaven. (HC 4:166)

7 Let not any man publish his own righteousness, for others can see that for him; sooner let him confess his sins, and then he will be forgiven, and he will bring forth more fruit. When a corrupt man is chastised he gets angry and will not endure it. (HC 4:479)

8 The first principle brought into consideration is aggrandizement. Some think it unlawful; but it is lawful with any man, while he has a disposition to aggrandize all around him. It is a false principle for a man to aggrandize himself at the expense of another. Everything that God does is to aggrandize His kingdom. (HC 5:285)

Pride
5   Instructions to the Apostles and Seventies departing for missions to England, Commerce (Nauvoo), 2 July 1839.
6   Letter to Oliver Granger in Kirtland, sent from Nauvoo, July 1840.
7   Meeting of the Twelve at the Prophet's home, Nauvoo, 19 December 1841.
8   Address at the temple site in Nauvoo, 21 February 1843.

9 Pride goes before destruction, and a haughty spirit before a downfall. (*HC* 6:411)

Priesthood

1 On the subject of ordination, a few words are necessary. In many instances there has been too much haste in this thing, and the admonition of Paul has been too slightingly passed over, which says, "Lay hands suddenly upon no man." Some have been ordained to the ministry, and have never acted in that capacity, or magnified their calling at all. Such may expect to lose their appointment, except they awake and magnify their office. Let the Elders abroad be exceedingly careful upon this subject, and when they ordain a man to the holy ministry, let him be a faithful man, who is able to teach others also; that the cause of Christ suffer not. It is not the multitude of preachers that is to bring about the glorious millennium! but it is those who are "called, and chosen, and faithful." (*HC* 1:468)

2 The Priesthood was first given to Adam; he obtained the First Presidency, and held the keys of it from generation to generation. He obtained it in the Creation, before the world was formed. . . .

The Priesthood is an everlasting principle, and existed with God from eternity, and will to eternity, without beginning of days or end of years. The keys have to be brought from heaven whenever the Gospel is sent. . . .

The Priesthood is everlasting. The Savior, Moses, and Elias, gave the keys to Peter, James, and John, on the mount, when they were transfigured before him. The Priesthood is everlasting—without beginning of days or end of years; without father, mother, etc. If there is no change of ordinances, there is no change of Priesthood. Wherever the ordinances of the Gospel are administered, there is the Priesthood.

Pride
   9 Sabbath address, Nauvoo, 26 May 1844.

Priesthood
   1 Letter to the elders of the Church, published in *The Evening and the Morning Star*, December 1833.
   2 Discourse on the priesthood, given sometime before 8 August 1839, Commerce (Nauvoo). For a discussion on the dating of this discourse, see *WJS*, p. 22.

How have we come at the Priesthood in the last days? It came down, down, in regular succession. Peter, James, and John had it given to them and they gave it to others. Christ is the Great High Priest; Adam next. . . .

. . . Moses sought to bring the children of Israel into the presence of God, through the power of the Priesthood, but he could not. In the first ages of the world they tried to establish the same thing; and there were Eliases raised up who tried to restore these very glories, but did not obtain them; but they prophesied of a day when this glory would be revealed. Paul spoke of the dispensation of the fullness of times, when God would gather together all things in one, etc.; and those men to whom these keys have been given, will have to be there; and they without us cannot be made perfect.

These men are in heaven, but their children are on the earth. Their bowels yearn over us. God sends down men for this reason. "And the Son of Man shall send forth His angels, and they shall gather out of His kingdom all things that give offense and them that do iniquity."—(Matt. xii:41). All these authoritative characters will come down and join hand in hand in bringing about this work. (*HC* 3:385–86, 387–89)

3 There are two Priesthoods spoken of in the Scriptures, viz., the Melchisedek and the Aaronic or Levitical. Although there are two Priesthoods, yet the Melchisedek Priesthood comprehends the Aaronic or Levitical Priesthood, and is the grand head, and holds the highest authority which pertains to the Priesthood, and the keys of the Kingdom of God in all ages of the world to the latest posterity on the earth, and is the channel through which all knowledge, doctrine, the plan of salvation, and every important matter is revealed from heaven.

Its institution was prior to "the foundation of this earth, or the morning stars sang together, or the Sons of God shouted for joy," and is the highest and holiest Priesthood, and is after the order of the Son of God, and all other Priesthoods are only parts, ramifications, powers and blessings belonging to the same, and are held, controlled, and directed by it. It is the channel through which the Almighty commenced revealing His glory at the beginning of the creation of this earth, and through which He has continued to reveal Himself to the

---

Priesthood

3   Article on priesthood read at general conference, Nauvoo, 5 October 1840.

children of men to the present time, and through which He will make known His purposes to the end of time. . . .

This, then, is the nature of the Priesthood; every man holding the Presidency of his dispensation, and one man holding the Presidency of them all, even Adam; and Adam receiving his Presidency and authority from the Lord, but cannot receive a fullness until Christ shall present the Kingdom to the Father, which shall be at the end of the last dispensation.

The power, glory and blessings of the Priesthood could not continue with those who received ordination only as their righteousness continued; for Cain also being authorized to offer sacrifice, but not offering it in righteousness, was cursed. It signifies, then, that the ordinances must be kept in the very way God has appointed; otherwise their Priesthood will prove a cursing instead of a blessing. (HC 4:207, 209)

4   There has been a chain of authority and power from Adam down to the present time. (HC 4:425)

5   The angel told good old Cornelius that he must send for Peter to learn how to be saved: Peter could baptise, and angels could not, so long as there were legal officers in the flesh holding the keys of the kingdom, or the authority of the priesthood. (T&S 3:905)

6   If a man gets a fullness of the priesthood of God, he has to get it in the same way that Jesus Christ obtained it, and that was by keeping all the commandments and obeying all the ordinances of the house of the Lord. (HC 5:424)

7   *Report of Willard Richards:* He [Joseph Smith] then read the 7th chap. Hebrews. . . .

There are three grand orders of priesthood referred to here.

1st. The King of Shiloam, (Salem) had power and authority over that of Abraham, holding the key and the power of endless life. Angels desire to look into it, but they have set up too many stakes. God cursed the children of Israel because they would not receive the last law from Moses.

Priesthood
4   General conference address, Nauvoo, 3 October 1841.
5   Editorial in the *Times and Seasons*, 1 September 1842.
6   Sabbath address, Nauvoo, 11 June 1843.
7   Sabbath address, Nauvoo, 27 August 1843.

The sacrifice required of Abraham in the offering up of Isaac, shows that if a man would attain to the keys of the kingdom of an endless life, he must sacrifice all things. When God offers a blessing or knowledge to a man, and he refuses to receive it, he will be damned. The Israelites prayed that God would speak to Moses and not to them; in consequence of which he cursed them with a carnal law.

What was the power of Melchizedek? 'Twas not the Priesthood of Aaron which administers in outward ordinances, and the offering of sacrifices. Those holding the fullness of the Melchizedek Priesthood are kings and priests of the Most High God, holding the keys of power and blessings. In fact, that priesthood is a perfect law of theocracy, and stands as God to give laws to the people, administering endless lives to the sons and daughters of Adam.

Abraham says to Melchizedek, I believe all that thou hast taught me concerning the priesthood and the coming of the Son of Man; so Melchizedek ordained Abraham and sent him away. Abraham rejoiced, saying, Now I have a priesthood.

Salvation could not come to the world without the mediation of Jesus Christ.

How shall God come to the rescue of this generation? He will send Elijah the prophet. The law revealed to Moses in Horeb never was revealed to the children of Israel as a nation.

Elijah shall reveal the covenants to seal the hearts of the fathers to the children, and the children to the fathers.

The anointing and sealing is to be called, elected and made sure.

"Without father, without mother, without descent, having neither beginning of days nor end of life, but made like unto the Son of God, abideth a priest continually." The Melchizedek Priesthood holds the right from the eternal God, and not by descent from father and mother; and that priesthood is as eternal as God Himself, having neither beginning of days nor end of life.

The 2nd Priesthood is Patriarchal authority. Go to and finish the temple, and God will fill it with power, and you will then receive more knowledge concerning this priesthood.

The 3rd is what is called the Levitical Priesthood, consisting of priests to administer in outward ordinance, made without an oath; but the Priesthood of Melchizedek is by an oath and covenant.

The Holy Ghost is God's messenger to administer in all those priesthoods. (*HC* 5:554–55)

8   A man can do nothing for himself unless God direct him in the right way; and the priesthood is for that purpose. (HC 6:363)

9   All men are liars who say they are of the true Church without the revelations of Jesus Christ and the Priesthood of Melchisedek, which is after the order of the Son of God.

It is in the order of heavenly things that God should always send a new dispensation into the world when men have apostatized from the truth and lost the priesthood; but when men come out and build upon other men's foundations, they do it on their own responsibility, without authority from God; and when the floods come and the winds blow, their foundations will be found to be sand, and their whole fabric will crumble to dust. (HC 6:478–79)

Priesthood, Aaronic

1   The Bishop is a High Priest, and necessarily so, because he is to preside over that particular branch of Church affairs, that is denominated the Lesser Priesthood, and because we have no direct lineal descendant of Aaron, to whom it would of right belong. This is the same, or a branch of the same, Priesthood, which may be illustrated by the figure of the human body, which has different members, which have different offices to perform; all are necessary in their place, and the body is not complete without all the members. (HC 2:477–78)

2   There are two Priesthoods spoken of in the Scriptures, viz., the Melchisedek and the Aaronic or Levitical. Although there are two Priesthoods, yet the Melchisedek Priesthood comprehends the Aaronic or Levitical Priesthood, and is the grand head. . . .

. . . [It] is the highest and holiest Priesthood, and is after the order of the Son of God, and all other Priesthoods are only parts, ramifications, powers and blessings belonging to the same, and are held, controlled, and directed by it. (HC 4:207)

Priesthood
8   Sabbath address, Nauvoo, 12 May 1844.
9   Sabbath address, Nauvoo, 16 June 1844.

Priesthood, Aaronic
1   Solemn assembly in the Kirtland Temple, 6 April 1837.
2   Article on priesthood read at general conference, Nauvoo, 5 October 1840.

3   Answer to the question, Was the priesthood of Melchizedek taken away when Moses died? All priesthood is Melchizedek, but there are different portions or degrees of it. That portion which brought Moses to speak with God face to face was taken away; but that which brought the ministry of angels remained. (*WJS*, p. 59; standardized)

4   As touching the Gospel and baptism that John preached, I would say that John came preaching the Gospel for the remission of sins; he had his authority from God, and the oracles of God were with him, and the kingdom of God for a season seemed to rest with John alone. The Lord promised Zacharias that he should have a son who was a descendant of Aaron, the Lord having promised that the priesthood should continue with Aaron and his seed throughout their generations. Let no man take this honor upon himself, except he be called of God, as was Aaron; and Aaron received his call by revelation. An angel of God also appeared unto Zacharias while in the Temple, and told him that he should have a son, whose name should be John, and he should be filled with the Holy Ghost. Zacharias was a priest of God, and officiating in the Temple, and John was a priest after his father, and held the keys of the Aaronic Priesthood, and was called of God to preach the Gospel of the kingdom of God. . . .

John was a priest after the order of Aaron, and had the keys of that priesthood, and came forth preaching repentance and baptism for the remission of sins, but at the same time cries out, "There cometh one mightier than I after me, the latchet of whose shoes I am not worthy to stoop down and unloose," and Christ came according to the words of John, and He was greater than John, because He held the keys of the Melchisedek Priesthood and kingdom of God. (HC 5:257, 258)

5   See Exodus 30 Chap. 30 and 31 v.—"And thou shalt anoint Aaron and his sons, and consecrate them, that they may minister unto me in the priest's office. And thou shalt speak unto the children of Israel, saying, This shall be an holy anointing oil unto me throughout your generations." Also Exodus 40 Chap., 15 v.—"And thou shalt

---

Priesthood, Aaronic

> **3**   Lecture given at the Nauvoo Lyceum, 5 January 1841, as reported by William Clayton. (The lyceum met weekly at different locations in Nauvoo for several months, beginning 5 January 1841.)
> **4**   Sabbath address, Nauvoo, 22 January 1843.
> **5**   Sabbath address, Nauvoo, 23 July 1843.

anoint them as thou didst anoint their father (Aaron) that they may minister unto me in the priest's office; for their anointing shall surely be an everlasting Priesthood throughout their generations."

Here is a little of law which must be fulfilled. The Levitical Priesthood is forever hereditary—fixed on the head of Aaron and his sons forever, and was in active operation down to Zacharias the father of John. Zacharias would have had no child had not God given him a son. He sent his angel to declare unto Zacharias that his wife Elizabeth should bear him a son, whose name was to be called John.

The keys of the Aaronic Priesthood were committed unto him, and he was as the voice of one crying in the wilderness saying: "Prepare ye the way of the Lord and make his paths straight."

The Kingdom of heaven suffereth violence, etc.

The kingdom of heaven continueth in authority until John.

The authority taketh it by absolute power.

John having the power took the Kingdom by authority.

How have you obtained all this great knowledge? By the gift of the Holy Ghost.

Wrested the Kingdom from the Jews.

Of these stony Gentiles—these dogs—to raise up children unto Abraham.

The Savior said unto John, I must be baptized by you. Why so? To fulfil all righteousness. John refuses at first, but afterwards obeyed by administering the ordinance of baptism unto him, Jesus having no other legal administrator to apply to. (*TPJS*, pp. 318–19)

6   There are three grand principles or orders of priesthood portrayed in this chapter [Hebrews 7].

First, Levitical, which was never able to administer a blessing but only to bind heavy burdens which neither they nor their father [were] able to bear. (*WJS*, p. 245; standardized)

7   In the first place, suffice it to say, I went into the woods to inquire of the Lord, by prayer, His will concerning me, and I saw an angel, and he laid his hands upon my head, and ordained me to a Priest after the order of Aaron, and to hold the keys of this Priesthood, which office

---

Priesthood, Aaronic
   6   Sabbath address, Nauvoo, 27 August 1843.
   7   Sabbath address, Nauvoo, 10 March 1844.

was to preach repentance and baptism for the remission of sins, and also to baptize. But I was informed that this office did not extend to the laying on of hands for the giving of the Holy Ghost; that that office was a greater work, and was to be given afterward; but that my ordination was a preparatory work, or a going before, which was the spirit of Elias; for the spirit of Elias was a going before to prepare the way for the greater, which was the case with John the Baptist. He came crying through the wilderness, "Prepare ye the way of the Lord, make his paths straight." And they were informed, if they could receive it, it was the spirit of Elias; and John was very particular to tell the people, he was not that Light, but was sent to bear witness of that Light.

He told the people that his mission was to preach repentance and baptize with water; but it was He that should come after him that should baptize with fire and the Holy Ghost.

If he had been an imposter, he might have gone to work beyond his bounds, and undertook to have performed ordinances which did not belong to that office and calling, under the spirit of Elias.

The spirit of Elias is to prepare the way for a greater revelation of God, which is the Priesthood of Elias, or the Priesthood that Aaron was ordained unto. And when God sends a man into the world to prepare for a greater work, holding the keys of the power of Elias, it was called the doctrine of Elias, even from the early ages of the world.

John's mission was limited to preaching and baptizing; but what he did was legal; and when Jesus Christ came to any of John's disciples, He baptized them with fire and the Holy Ghost.

We find the apostles endowed with greater power than John: their office was more under the spirit and power of Elijah than Elias. (HC 6:249–50)

8   God made Aaron to be the mouthpiece for the children of Israel, and He will make me be god to you in His stead, and the Elders to be mouth for me. (HC 6:319–20)

Priesthood, Aaronic
   8   General conference address, Nauvoo, 8 April 1844.

Priesthood, Melchizedek

1 *Report:* President Joseph Smith, Jun., addressed the assembly and said, the Melchizedek High Priesthood was no other than the Priesthood of the Son of God; that there are certain ordinances which belong to the Priesthood, from which flow certain results; and the Presidents or Presidency are over the Church; and revelations of the mind and will of God to the Church, are to come through the Presidency. This is the order of heaven, and the power and privilege of this Priesthood. . . . It is also the privilege of the Melchizedek Priesthood, to reprove, rebuke, and admonish, as well as to receive revelation. (*HC* 2:477)

2 [The Melchizedek Priesthood] is the channel through which all knowledge, doctrine, the plan of salvation, and every important matter is revealed from heaven. (*HC* 4:207)

3 Answer to the question, Was the priesthood of Melchizedek taken away when Moses died? All priesthood is Melchizedek, but there are different portions or degrees of it. That portion which brought Moses to speak with God face to face was taken away; but that which brought the ministry of angels remained. All the prophets had the Melchizedek Priesthood and [were] ordained by God himself. (*WJS*, p. 59; standardized)

4 Christ was the head of the Church, the chief corner stone, the spiritual rock upon which the earth was built, and the gates of hell shall not prevail against it. He built up the Kingdom, chose Apostles, and ordained them to the Melchizedek Priesthood, giving them power to administer in the ordinances of the Gospel. (*TPJS*, p. 318)

Priesthood, Melchizedek
1 Solemn assembly in the Kirtland Temple, 6 April 1837.
2 Article on priesthood read at general conference, Nauvoo, 5 October 1840.
3 Lecture given at the Nauvoo Lyceum, 5 January 1841, as reported by William Clayton. (The lyceum met weekly at different locations in Nauvoo for several months, beginning 5 January 1841.)
4 Sabbath address, Nauvoo, 23 July 1843.

5   Respecting the Melchizedek Priesthood, the sectarians never professed to have it; consequently they never could save any one, and would all be damned together. There was an Episcopal priest who said he had the priesthood of Aaron, but had not the priesthood of Melchizedek: and I bear testimony that I never have found the man who claimed the Priesthood of Melchizedek. The power of the Melchizedek priesthood is to have the power of "endless lives;" for the everlasting covenant cannot be broken. . . .

What was the power of Melchizedek? . . . Those holding the fullness of the Melchizedek Priesthood are kings and priests of the Most High God, holding the keys of power and blessings. In fact, that priesthood is a perfect law of theocracy, and stands as God to give laws to the people, administering endless lives to the sons and daughters of Adam. . . .

. . . The Melchizedek Priesthood holds the right from the eternal God, and not by descent from father and mother; and that priesthood is as eternal as God Himself, having neither beginning of days nor end of life. (HC 5:554, 555)

6   *Words of Angus M. Cannon:* I remember Brother Joseph as he addressed an assembly of the Saints in the spring of 1844, under some large oak trees in a hollow south of the Temple. He was discoursing upon the fact that God, in establishing His Church, had provided that only one man was authorized to receive revelations for the Church. It was on this occasion that I heard the Prophet declare he had received the Melchizedek Priesthood under the administration of Peter, James and John. (TK, p. 163)

Principles

1   *Report of Wilford Woodruff:* Then Joseph arose and presented some precious things of the kingdom unto us in the power of the Holy

---

Priesthood, Melchizedek
5   Sabbath address, Nauvoo, 27 August 1843.
6   Remembrance of Angus M. Cannon, published in the *Young Woman's Journal,* December 1906.

Principles
1   Instructions to the Apostles and Seventies departing for missions to England, Commerce (Nauvoo), 2 July 1839, as reported by Wilford Woodruff.

Ghost, yea, precious principles that ought to be engraven upon our hearts and practiced in our lives, some of which are as follows: Ever keep in exercise the principles of mercy, and be ready to forgive our brother on the first intimations of repentance and asking forgiveness. . . . We ought to be willing to repent of and confess all of our own sins, and keep nothing back. . . . Let the Twelve be humble and not be exalted, and beware of pride and not seek to excel one above another, but act for each other's good and honorably make mention of each other's name in our prayers before the Lord and before our fellowmen, and not backbite and devour our brother. . . . When the Twelve or any other witness of Jesus Christ stands before the congregations of the earth and they preach in the power and demonstration of the Holy Ghost, and the people are astonished and confounded at the doctrine, and say that that man has preached a powerful discourse, a great sermon, then let that man or those men take care that they do not ascribe the glory unto themselves but be careful that they are humble and ascribe the praise and glory to God and the Lamb, for it is by the power of the holy priesthood and the Holy Ghost that they have power thus to speak. . . . Let every man be sober, be vigilant, and let all his words be seasoned with grace, and keep in mind that it is a day of warning and not of many words. Act honest before God and man; beware of gentile sophistry, such as bowing and scraping unto men in whom you have no confidence. Be honest, open, and frank in all your intercourse with mankind. (*WJS*, pp. 6–7; standardized)

2   Every principle proceeding from God is eternal, and any principle which is not eternal is of the devil. The sun has no beginning or end; the rays which proceed from himself have no bounds, consequently are eternal. . . .

. . . The first step in the salvation of men is the laws of eternal and self-existent principles. (*WJS*, p. 60; standardized)

3   God has made certain decrees which are fixed and immovable; for instance,—God set the sun, the moon, and the stars in the heavens, and gave them their laws, conditions and bounds, which they cannot

---

Principles

2   Lecture given at the Nauvoo Lyceum, 5 January 1841, as reported by William Clayton. (The lyceum met weekly at different locations in Nauvoo for several months, beginning 5 January 1841.)

3   Sabbath address, Nauvoo, 20 March 1842.

pass, except by His commandments; they all move in perfect harmony in their sphere and order, and are as lights, wonders and signs unto us. The sea also has its bounds which it cannot pass. God has set many signs on the earth, as well as in the heavens; for instance, the oak of the forest, the fruit of the tree, the herb of the field—all bear a sign that seed hath been planted there; for it is a decree of the Lord that every tree, plant, and herb bearing seed should bring forth of its kind, and cannot come forth after any other law or principle. (HC 4:554)

4 If you wish to go where God is, you must be like God, or possess the principles which God possesses, for if we are not drawing towards God in principle, we are going from Him and drawing towards the devil. (HC 4:588)

5 We are only capable of comprehending that certain things exist, which we may acquire by certain fixed principles. If men would acquire salvation, they have got to be subject, before they leave this world, to certain rules and principles, which were fixed by an unalterable decree before the world was. (HC 6:50–51)

6 The object with me is to obey and teach others to obey God in just what He tells us to do. It mattereth not whether the principle is popular or unpopular, I will always maintain a true principle, even if I stand alone in it. (HC 6:223)

7 This is good doctrine. It tastes good. I can taste the principles of eternal life, and so can you. They are given to me by the revelations of Jesus Christ; and I know that when I tell you these words of eternal life as they are given to me, you taste them, and I know that you believe them. You say honey is sweet, and so do I. I can also taste the spirit of eternal life. I know that it is good; and when I tell you of these things which were given me by inspiration of the Holy Spirit, you are bound to receive them as sweet, and rejoice more and more. (HC 6:312)

Principles
  4 Sabbath address, Nauvoo, 10 April 1842.
  5 Remarks upon the death of James Adams, Nauvoo, 9 October 1843.
  6 Remarks following the sermon of an Episcopalian minister, Nauvoo, 21 February 1844.
  7 King Follett Discourse, Nauvoo, 7 April 1844.

Procrastination

1   What chance is there for infidelity when we are parting with our friends almost daily? None at all. The infidel will grasp at every straw for help until death stares him in the face, and then his infidelity takes its flight, for the realities of the eternal world are resting upon him in mighty power; and when every earthly support and prop fails him, he then sensibly feels the eternal truths of the immortality of the soul. We should take warning and not wait for the death-bed to repent, as we see the infant taken away by death, so may the youth and middle aged, as well as the infant be suddenly called into eternity. Let this, then, prove as a warning to all not to procrastinate repentance, or wait till a death-bed, for it is the will of God that man should repent and serve Him in health, and in the strength and power of his mind, in order to secure His blessing, and not wait until he is called to die. (HC 4:553–54)

Profanity

1   *Words of Parley P. Pratt:* In one of those tedious nights [while prisoners in Richmond, Missouri,] we had lain as if in sleep till the hour of midnight had passed, and our ears and hearts had been pained, while we had listened for hours to the obscene jests, the horrid oaths, the dreadful blasphemies and filthy language of our guards, Colonel Price at their head, as they recounted to each other their deeds of rapine, murder, robbery, etc., which they had committed among the "Mormons" while at Far West and vicinity. They even boasted of defiling by force wives, daughters and virgins, and of shooting or dashing out the brains of men, women and children. I had listened till I became so disgusted, shocked, horrified, and so filled with the spirit of indignant justice that I could scarcely refrain from rising upon my feet and rebuking the guards; but had said nothing to Joseph, or anyone else, al-

---

Procrastination
  1   Sabbath address, Nauvoo, 20 March 1842.

Profanity
  1   Recollection of Parley P. Pratt as recorded in his autobiography, Richmond, Missouri, November 1838.

though I lay next to him and knew he was awake. On a sudden he arose to his feet, and spoke in a voice of thunder, or as the roaring lion, uttering, as nearly as I can recollect, the following words:

"*Silence*, ye fiends of the infernal pit! In the name of Jesus Christ I rebuke you, and command you to be still; I will not live another minute and hear such language. Cease such talk, or you or I die *this instant!*"

He ceased to speak. He stood erect in terrible majesty. Chained, and without a weapon; calm, unruffled and dignified as an angel, he looked upon the quailing guards, whose weapons were lowered or dropped to the ground; whose knees smote together, and who, shrinking into a corner, or crouching at his feet, begged his pardon, and remained quiet till a change of guards.

I have seen the ministers of justice, clothed in magisterial robes, and criminals arraigned before them, while life was suspended on a breath, in the courts of England; I have witnessed a Congress in solemn session to give laws to nations; I have tried to conceive of kings, of royal courts, of thrones and crowns; and of emperors assembled to decide the fate of kingdoms; but dignity and majesty have I seen but once, as it stood in chains, at midnight in a dungeon, in an obscure village of Missouri. (HC 3:208)

2   Brethren, from henceforth, let truth and righteousness prevail and abound in you; and in all things be temperate; abstain from drunkenness, and from swearing, and from all profane language, and from everything which is unrighteous or unholy; also from enmity, and hatred, and covetousness, and from every unholy desire. (HC 3:233)

Progression

1   In the evening [I was] with the Twelve and their wives at Elder Woodruff's, at which time I explained many important principles in relation to progressive improvement in the scale of intelligent existence. (HC 4:519)

Profanity
   2   Letter to the Church from Liberty Jail, 16 December 1838.

Progression
   1   A meeting with the Twelve at Wilford Woodruff's home, Nauvoo, 1 March 1842.

2 *Words of a Visitor to Nauvoo:* He [Joseph Smith] said he did not profess to be a very good man, but acknowledged himself a sinner like other men, or, as all men are, imperfect; and it is necessary for all men to grow into the stature of manhood in the Gospel. (*HC* 5:408)

3 Here, then, is eternal life—to know the only wise and true God; and you have got to learn how to be gods yourselves, and to be kings and priests to God, the same as all gods have done before you, namely, by going from one small degree to another, and from a small capacity to a great one; from grace to grace, from exaltation to exaltation, until you attain to the resurrection of the dead, and are able to dwell in everlasting burnings, and to sit in glory, as do those who sit enthroned in everlasting power. And I want you to know that God, in the last days, while certain individuals are proclaiming His name, is not trifling with you or me.

These are the first principles of consolation. How consoling to the mourners when they are called to part with a husband, wife, father, mother, child, or dear relative, to know that, although the earthly tabernacle is laid down and dissolved, they shall rise again to dwell in everlasting burnings in immortal glory, not to sorrow, suffer, or die any more, but they shall be heirs of God and joint heirs with Jesus Christ. What is it? To inherit the same power, the same glory and the same exaltation, until you arrive at the station of a god, and ascend the throne of eternal power, the same as those who have gone before. What did Jesus do? Why, I do the things I saw my Father do when worlds came rolling into existence. My Father worked out His kingdom with fear and trembling, and I must do the same; and when I get my kingdom, I shall present it to My Father, so that He may obtain kingdom upon kingdom, and it will exalt Him in glory. He will then take a higher exaltation, and I will take His place, and thereby become exalted myself. So that Jesus treads in the tracks of His Father, and inherits what God did before; and God is thus glorified and exalted in the salvation and exaltation of all His children. It is plain beyond disputation, and you thus learn some of the first principles of the gospel, about which so much hath been said.

Progression

2   A character sketch on the Prophet from a Boston paper, the *Boston Bee,* 24 May 1843.

3   King Follett Discourse, Nauvoo, 7 April 1844.

When you climb up a ladder, you must begin at the bottom, and ascend step by step, until you arrive at the top; and so it is with the principles of the gospel—you must begin with the first, and go on until you learn all the principles of exaltation. But it will be a great while after you have passed through the veil before you will have learned them. It is not all to be comprehended in this world; it will be a great work to learn our salvation and exaltation even beyond the grave. . . .

. . . All the minds and spirits that God ever sent into the world are susceptible of enlargement.

The first principles of man are self-existent with God. God himself, finding he was in the midst of spirits and glory, because he was more intelligent, saw proper to institute laws whereby the rest could have a privilege to advance like himself. The relationship we have with God places us in a situation to advance in knowledge. He has power to institute laws to instruct the weaker intelligences, that they may be exalted with Himself, so that they might have one glory upon another, and all that knowledge, power, glory, and intelligence, which is requisite in order to save them in the world of spirits. (HC 6:306–7, 311–12)

Promises

1 It would be nonsense to suppose that He [God] would condescend to talk in vain: for it would be in vain, and to no purpose whatever {if the law of God were of no benefit to man}: because, all the commandments contained in the law of the Lord, have the sure promise annexed of a reward to all who obey, predicated upon the fact that they are really the promises of a Being who cannot lie, One who is abundantly able to fulfill every tittle of His word. . . .

. . . And though we cannot claim these promises which were made to the ancients for they are not our property, merely because they were made to the ancient Saints, yet if we are the children of the Most High, and are called with the same calling with which they were called, and embrace the same covenant that they embraced, and are faithful to the testimony of our Lord as they were, we can approach

---

Promises
1 Letter to the brethren scattered from Zion, Kirtland, 22 January 1834.

the Father in the name of Christ as they approached Him, and for ourselves obtain the same promises. These promises, when obtained, if ever by us, will not be because Peter, John, and the other Apostles, with the churches at Sardis, Pergamos, Philadelphia, and elsewhere, walked in the fear of God, and had power and faith to prevail and obtain them; but it will be because we, ourselves, have faith and approach God in the name of His Son Jesus Christ, even as they did; and when these promises are obtained, they will be promises directly to us, or they will do us no good. They will be communicated for our benefit, being our own property (through the gift of God), earned by our own diligence in keeping His commandments, and walking uprightly before Him. If not, to what end serves the Gospel of our Lord Jesus Christ, and why was it ever communicated to us? (HC 2:12, 21–22)

2   Martin Harris having boasted to the brethren that he could handle snakes with perfect safety, while fooling with a black snake with his bare feet, he received a bite on his left foot. The fact was communicated to me, and I took occasion to reprove him, and exhort the brethren never to trifle with the promises of God. I told them it was presumption for any one to provoke a serpent to bite him, but if a man of God was accidentally bitten by a poisonous serpent, he might have faith, or his brethren might have faith for him, so that the Lord would hear his prayer and he might be healed; but when a man designedly provokes a serpent to bite him, the principle is the same as when a man drinks deadly poison knowing it to be such. In that case no man has any claim on the promises of God to be healed. (HC 2:95–96)

3   If there is anything calculated to interest the mind of the Saints, to awaken in them the finest sensibilities, and arouse them to enterprise and exertion, surely it is the great and precious promises made by our heavenly Father to the children of Abraham. (HC 4:128)

4   I now offer to come to you at Carthage on the morrow, as early as shall be convenient for your *posse* to escort us into headquarters, pro-

---

Promises
2   Events of Zion's Camp, Missouri, 16 June 1834.
3   Letter to Orson Hyde and John E. Page, Nauvoo, 14 May 1840.
4   Letter of Joseph and Hyrum Smith to Governor Thomas Ford, Nauvoo, 23 June 1844.

vided we can have a fair trial, not be abused nor have my witnesses abused, and have all things done in due form of law, without partiality, and you may depend on my honor without the show of a great armed force to produce excitement in the minds of the timid. (HC 6:550)

Prophecy

1   The Lord once told me that if at any time I got into deep trouble and could see no way out of it, if I would prophesy in His name, he would fulfill my words. (*TK*, p. 52)

2   I met the quorums in the evening . . . and gave them instructions in relation to the spirit of prophecy, and called upon the congregation to speak, and not to fear to prophesy good concerning the Saints, for if you prophesy the falling of these hills and the rising of the valleys, the downfall of the enemies of Zion and the rising of the kingdom of God, it shall come to pass. Do not quench the Spirit, for the first one that opens his mouth shall receive the Spirit of prophecy.

Brother George A. Smith arose and began to prophesy, when a noise was heard like the sound of a rushing mighty wind, which filled the Temple, and all the congregation simultaneously arose, being moved upon by an invisible power; many began to speak in tongues and prophesy. (HC 2:428)

3   "Do you believe Joseph Smith, Jun., to be a Prophet?"

Yes, and every other man who has the testimony of Jesus. For the testimony of Jesus is the spirit of prophecy. (HC 3:28)

4   *Words of Parley P. Pratt:* As we arose and commenced our march on the morning of the 3d of November, Joseph Smith spoke to me and the other prisoners, in a low, but cheerful and confidential tone; said

---

Prophecy
1   Statement made by the Prophet at a meeting in Kirtland, recalled by Daniel Tyler, published in the *Juvenile Instructor*, 15 February 1892.
2   Events during the dedication of the Kirtland Temple, 27 March 1836.
3   Answers to questions frequently asked the Prophet, Far West, 8 May 1838.
4   Recollection of Parley P. Pratt as recorded in his autobiography. The Prophet's statement was made en route to Jackson County, Missouri, 3 November 1838.

he: "*Be of good cheer, brethren; the word of the Lord came to me last night that our lives should be given us, and that whatever we may suffer during this captivity, not one of our lives should be taken.*" Of this prophecy I testify in the name of the Lord, and, though spoken in secret, its public fulfilment and the miraculous escape of each one of us is too notorious to need my testimony. (*APPP*, p. 164)

5   *Words of Bathsheba W. Smith:* I have heard the Prophet Joseph preach many times. I have heard him prophesy, and I never knew but that everything came to pass that he said. . . .

Joseph Smith attended one of our Relief Society meetings in the lodge room. He opened the meeting by prayer. His voice trembled very much, after which he addressed us and said, "According to my prayer, I will not be with you long to teach and instruct you, and the world will not be troubled with me much longer." (*TK*, p. 123)

6   If any person should ask me if I were a prophet, I should not deny it, as that would give me the lie; for, according to John, the testimony of Jesus is the spirit of prophecy; therefore, if I profess to be a witness or teacher, and have not the spirit of prophecy, which is the testimony of Jesus, I must be a false witness; but if I be a true teacher and witness, I must possess the spirit of prophecy, and that constitutes a prophet; and any man who says he is a teacher or preacher of righteousness, and denies the spirit of prophecy, is a liar, and the truth is not in him; and by this key false teachers and impostors may be detected. (*HC* 5:215–16)

7   Esquire Butterfield asked me "to prophesy how many inhabitants would come to Nauvoo." I said, I will not tell how many inhabitants will come to Nauvoo; but when I went to Commerce, I told the people I would build up a city, and the old inhabitants replied "We will be damned if you can." So I prophesied that I would build up a city, and

---

Prophecy

5   Recollection of Bathsheba W. Smith, published in the *Young Woman's Journal*, December 1905, and in the *Juvenile Instructor*, 1 June 1892. The particular Relief Society meeting recalled here by Bathsheba W. Smith was probably that of 28 April 1842 (see HC 4:604).

6   Remarks to a group of politicians and lawyers, Springfield, Illinois, 1 January 1843.

7   Conversation with Esquire Butterfield, Springfield, Illinois, 5 January 1843.

the inhabitants prophesied that I could not; and we have now about 12,000 inhabitants. I will prophesy that we will build up a great city; for we have the stakes and have only to fill up the interstices. (HC 5:232)

8 Judge, you will aspire to the presidency of the United States; and if ever you turn your hand against me or the Latter-day Saints, you will feel the weight of the hand of Almighty upon you; and you will live to see and know that I have testified the truth to you; for the conversation of this day will stick to you through life. (HC 5:394)

9 I gave some important instructions, and prophesied that within five years we should be out of the power of our old enemies, whether they were apostates or of the world; and told the brethren to record it, that when it comes to pass they need not say they had forgotten the saying. (HC 6:225)

10 I told Stephen Markham that if I and Hyrum were ever taken again we should be massacred, or I was not a prophet of God. (HC 6:546)

11 *History Entry:* Several of the officers of the troops in Carthage, and other gentlemen, curious to see the Prophet, visited Joseph in his room. General Smith asked them if there was anything in his appearance that indicated he was the desperate character his enemies represented him to be; and he asked them to give him their honest opinion on the subject. The reply was, "No, sir, your appearance would indicate the very contrary, General Smith; but we cannot see what is in your heart, neither can we tell what are your intentions." To which Joseph replied, "Very true, gentlemen, you cannot see what is in my heart, and you are therefore unable to judge me or my intentions; but

---

Prophecy
8   Prophecy on the head of Stephen A. Douglas, Carthage, Illinois, 18 May 1843. The prophecy was fulfilled in 1860 when Douglas was soundly defeated by Abraham Lincoln. Douglas indeed turned his hand against the Saints in his political campaigning. Stephen A. Douglas died a heartbroken man in 1861, at forty-eight years of age.
9   Nauvoo, 25 February 1844.
10   Nauvoo, 22 June 1844.
11   Carthage, Illinois, 25 June 1844.

I can see what is in your hearts, and will tell you what I see. I can see that you thirst for blood, and nothing but my blood will satisfy you. It is not for crime of any description that I and my brethren are thus continually persecuted and harassed by our enemies, but there are other motives, and some of them I have expressed, so far as relates to myself; and inasmuch as you and the people thirst for blood, I prophesy, in the name of the Lord, that you shall witness scenes of blood and sorrow to your entire satisfaction. Your souls shall be perfectly satiated with blood, and many of you who are now present shall have an opportunity to face the cannon's mouth from sources you think not of; and those people that desire this great evil upon me and my brethren, shall be filled with regret and sorrow because of the scenes of desolation and distress that await them. They shall seek for peace, and shall not be able to find it. Gentlemen, you will find what I have told you to be true." (HC 6:566)

12 *History Entry:* Soon after Dr. Richards retired to the bed which Joseph had left, and when all were apparently fast asleep, Joseph whispered to Dan Jones, "are you afraid to die?" Dan said, "Has that time come, think you? Engaged in such a cause I do not think that death would have many terrors." Joseph replied, "You will yet see Wales, and fulfill the mission appointed you before you die." (HC 6:601)

13 *History Entry:* Dr. Richards' escape was miraculous; he being a very large man, and in the midst of a shower of balls, yet he stood unscathed, with the exception of a ball which grazed the tip end of the lower part of his left ear. His escape fulfilled literally a prophecy which Joseph made over a year previously, that the time would come that the balls would fly around him like hail, and he should see his friends fall on the right and on the left, but that there should not be a hole in his garment. (HC 6:619)

Prophecy
  12 Prophecy on the head of Dan Jones, Carthage Jail, 26 June 1844.
  13 Carthage Jail, 27 June 1844.

Prophets

1 After this revelation [D&C 1] was received, some conversation was had concerning revelations and language. I received the following: [D&C 67].

After the foregoing [D&C 67] was received, William E. M'Lellin, as the wisest man, in his own estimation, having more learning than sense, endeavored to write a commandment like unto one of the least of the Lord's, but failed; it was an awful responsibility to write in the name of the Lord. The Elders and all present that witnessed this vain attempt of a man to imitate the language of Jesus Christ, renewed their faith in the fulness of the Gospel, and in the truth of the commandments and revelations which the Lord had given to the Church through my instrumentality; and the Elders signified a willingness to bear testimony of their truth to all the world. Accordingly I received the following: [Testimony published in current editions of the Doctrine and Covenants, signed in 1831 by the Twelve]. (HC 1:224, 226)

2 I was this morning introduced to a man from the east. After hearing my name, he remarked that I was nothing but a man, indicating by this expression, that he had supposed that a person to whom the Lord should see fit to reveal His will, must be something more than a man. He seemed to have forgotten the saying that fell from the lips of St. James, that Elias was a man subject to like passions as we are, yet he had such power with God, that He, in answer to his prayers, shut the heavens that they gave no rain for the space of three years and six months; and again, in answer to his prayer, the heavens gave forth rain, and the earth gave forth fruit. Indeed, such is the darkness and ignorance of this generation, that they look upon it as incredible that a man should have any intercourse with his Maker. (HC 2:302)

3 If the Saints in Kirtland deem me unworthy of their prayers when they assemble together, and neglect to bear me up at the throne of heavenly grace, it is a strong and convincing proof to me that they have not the Spirit of God. (HC 4:165)

Prophets
1 Hiram, Ohio, November 1831.
2 Kirtland, 6 November 1835.
3 Letter to Oliver Granger in Kirtland, sent from Nauvoo, July 1840.

4 *Words of Henrietta Cox:* Brother Joseph was sitting with his head bent low, as if in deep thought, and had not spoken for a few minutes, when one of the elders present began to chide him for being bowed in spirit, saying, "Brother Joseph, why don't you hold your head up and talk to us like a man?"

Brother Joseph presently answered the elder by calling his attention to a field of ripening grain, saying that many heads of grain in that field bent low with their weight of valuable store, while others containing no grain to be garnered stood very straight.

Proof of the correctness of his words was given shortly after, for the elder to whom they were addressed soon after apostatized and went back East. (*TK*, p. 147)

5 A man would command his son to dig potatoes and saddle his horse, but before he had done either he would tell him to do something else. This is all considered right; but as soon as the Lord gives a commandment and revokes that decree and commands something else, then the Prophet is considered fallen. (*HC* 4:478)

6 The world always mistook false prophets for true ones, and those that were sent of God, they considered to be false prophets, and hence they killed, stoned, punished and imprisoned the true prophets, and these had to hide themselves "in deserts and dens, and caves of the earth," and though the most honorable men of the earth, they banished them from their society as vagabonds, whilst they cherished, honored and supported knaves, vagabonds, hypocrites, impostors, and the basest of men. (*HC* 4:574)

7 Let the Twelve send all who will support the character of the Prophet, the Lord's anointed; and if all who go will support my character, I prophesy in the name of the Lord Jesus, whose servant I am, that you will prosper in your missions. I have the whole plan of the kingdom before me, and no other person has. (*HC* 5:139)

Prophets
  4 Recollection of Henrietta Cox about events around the spring of 1841, published in the *Juvenile Instructor*, 1 April 1892.
  5 Meeting of the Twelve at the Prophet's home, Nauvoo, 19 December 1841.
  6 Editorial in the *Times and Seasons*, 1 April 1842.
  7 Conference address, Nauvoo, 29 August 1842.

8   Surely "facts are stubborn things." It will be as it ever has been, the world will prove Joseph Smith a true prophet by circumstantial evidence, in experiments, as they did Moses and Elijah. (*T&S* 3:922)

9   Concerning the present state of the Prophet, some of our enemies are ready to say, if he be the prophet of the Lord, why is it that he has to flee from the hand of oppression? Why does not his God deliver him? To this we would answer, that he has delivered him hitherto— but if being delivered out of every difficulty, be a sign of a true prophet, then indeed shall we find them very scarce in the scriptures of eternal truth. Moses had to flee from the land of Egypt, and be a stranger in the land of Midian. Job had to suffer the loss of his camels, his oxen, his asses, his flocks and herds, his children, his property and friends. Abraham, at the command of God had to flee from the hand of persecution and go to a land that the Lord would shew him of. Jacob had to flee, fearing the wrath of his brother, and absent himself fourteen years. Elijah had to hide himself three years and a half from the presence of the king, who sought diligently for him in all the na- tions around to take away his life. Obadiah had to hide the prophets by fifties in a cave, to save them from the hand of persecution. Elisha, David, Jeremiah, Zachariah, and all the prophets more or less had to share the same fate. Paul tells us "that they were tempted, they were tried, they were sawn asunder; that they had to wander about in sheep skins and goat skins, and to HIDE THEMSELVES *in deserts, and dens, and caves of the earth.*" Such is the universal testimony of scripture in regard to the prophets of the Lord, and instead of this being an argu- ment against it, it is one, that goes to establish the truth of the prophet's calling and profession. Our Savior in speaking of these things says—"if they have persecuted you, they will persecute me, if they have called the master of the house Beelzebub, how much more shall they call him of his household"—and he has given it as his coun- sel to flee in time of danger, saying, "but when they persecute you in one city, flee ye to another." We find then, that not only the conduct of your prophet, but that of his persecutors also, has been strictly in accordance with the treatment and proceeding of prophets, and that of their enemies also, in every age of the world. (*T&S* 3:952)

Prophets
  8   Editorial in the *Times and Seasons*, 15 September 1842.
  9   Editorial in the *Times and Seasons*, 15 October 1842.

10 In consequence of rejecting the Gospel of Jesus Christ and the Prophets whom God hath sent, the judgments of God have rested upon people, cities, and nations, in various ages of the world, which was the case with the cities of Sodom and Gomorrah, that were destroyed for rejecting the Prophets. (HC 5:256–57)

11 This morning, I read German, and visited with a brother and sister from Michigan, who thought that "a prophet is always a prophet;" but I told them that a prophet was a prophet only when he was acting as such. (HC 5:265)

12 The popular religionists of the day tell us, forsooth, that the beasts spoken of in the Revelation represent kingdoms. Very well, on the same principle we can say that the twenty-four elders spoken of represent beasts; for they are all spoken of at the same time, and are represented as all uniting in the same acts of praise and devotion.

This learned interpretation is all as flat as a pancake! "What do you use such vulgar expressions for, being a prophet?" Because the old women understand it—they make pancakes. Deacon Homespun said the earth was flat as a pancake, and ridiculed the science which proved to the contrary. The whole argument is flat, and I don't know of anything better to represent it. The world is full of technicalities and misrepresentation, which I calculate to overthrow, and speak of things as they actually exist. (HC 5:344)

13 I am your servant, and it is only through the Holy Ghost that I can do you good. God is able to do His own work.

We do not present ourselves before you as anything but your humble servants, willing to spend and be spent in your service. (HC 5:355)

14 *Words of a Visitor to Nauvoo:* "The Prophet Joseph" (as he is called among his people) said in a conversation with a gentleman present,

---

Prophets

10 Sabbath address, Nauvoo, 22 January 1843.

11 Nauvoo, 8 February 1843.

12 General conference address, Nauvoo, 8 April 1843.

13 Remarks to Saints newly arrived from England, Nauvoo, 13 April 1843.

14 A character sketch on the Prophet from a Boston paper, the *Boston Bee*, 24 May 1843.

that he no more professed to be a prophet than every man must who professes to be a preacher of righteousness or a minister of the new testament.

To be minister of Jesus, a man must testify of Jesus; and to testify of Jesus, a man must have the spirit of prophecy; for, according to John, the testimony of Jesus is the spirit of prophecy.

If a man professes to be a minister of Jesus and has not the spirit of prophecy, he must be a false witness, for he is not in possession of that gift which qualifies him for that office; and the difference between him and the clergy of this generation is, he claims to be in possession of that spirit of prophecy which qualifies him to testify of Jesus and the Gospel of salvation; and the clergy deny that spirit, even the spirit of prophecy, which alone could constitute them true witnesses or testators of the Lord Jesus, and yet claim to be true ministers of salvation. (HC 5:407–8)

15 *Reports of Willard Richards and Wilford Woodruff:* President Joseph Smith remarked—"I am a rough stone. The sound of the hammer and chisel was never heard on me until the Lord took me in hand. I desire the learning and wisdom of heaven alone. I have not the least idea, if Christ should come to the earth and preach such rough things as He preached to the Jews, but that this generation would reject Him for being so rough."

He then took for his text the 37th verse of 23rd chapter of Matthew—"O Jerusalem, Jerusalem, thou that killest the prophets and stonest them which are sent unto thee; how often would I have gathered thy children together, even as a hen gathereth her chickens under her wings, and ye would not." (HC 5:423)

16 It has gone abroad that I proclaimed myself no longer a prophet. I said it last Sabbath ironically: I supposed you would all understand. It was not that I would renounce the idea of being a prophet, but that I had no disposition to proclaim myself such. But I do say that I bear the testimony of Jesus, which is the spirit of prophecy. (HC 5:516)

Prophets
  15 Sabbath address, Nauvoo, 11 June 1843.
  16 Sabbath address, Nauvoo, 23 July 1843.

17 *Words of John Lyman Smith:* When I was playing in the yard of the Mansion, in Nauvoo, with Joseph and Frederick, two of the Prophet's sons, a gentleman drove to the gate and asked if Joseph Smith was at home. The Prophet came forward, and the gentleman drove his horse up to a tie post and left the lines lying loose.

When he was about half way to the house, Joseph said, "Mr., I think you would do well to tie your horse; he might get a scare and run away and break your carriage."

The gentleman replied, "I have driven that horse for some years and never tie him. I am a doctor and cannot afford to tie up at every place I call."

Joseph repeated, "You had better tie, all the same. Your horse might get a scare and run away."

The doctor replied, "No fear."

Joseph seemed quite uneasy, and got up several times from his chair on the porch. Suddenly the horse started up the street and struck a wheel against a post and scattered the pieces for a block or more. The doctor sprang to his feet, and looking after the horse, cried out to Joseph, "I'll be d——d if you ain't a prophet!" (*TK*, p. 146)

18 No man knows my history. I cannot tell it: I shall never undertake it. I don't blame any one for not believing my history. If I had not experienced what I have, I would not have believed it myself. I never did harm any man since I was born in the world. My voice is always for peace.

I cannot lie down until all my work is finished. I never think any evil, nor do anything to the harm of my fellow-man. When I am called by the trump of the archangel and weighed in the balance, you will all know me then. I add no more. God bless you all. Amen. (*HC* 6:317)

19 My enemies say that I *have* been a true prophet. Why, I had rather be a fallen true prophet than a false prophet. When a man goes about prophesying, and commands men to obey his teachings, he must either

---

Prophets

    17 Recollection of John Lyman Smith, published in the *Juvenile Instructor*, 15 March 1892.

    18 King Follett Discourse, Nauvoo, 7 April 1844.

    19 Sabbath address, Nauvoo, 12 May 1844.

be a true or false prophet. False prophets always arise to oppose the true prophets and they will prophesy so very near the truth that they will deceive almost the very chosen ones. (HC 6:364)

20 *Words of Jesse W. Crosby:* With some other brethren, I once went to the Prophet and asked him to give us his opinion on a certain public question. The request was refused. He told us he did not enjoy the right vouchsafed to every American citizen—that of free speech. He said that when he ventured to give his private opinion on any subject of importance, his words were often garbled and their meaning twisted, and then given out as the word of the Lord because they came from him. (*TK,* pp. 144–45)

Punishment

1 *Report of Mathew L. Davis:* He [Joseph Smith] said very little of rewards and punishments; but one conclusion, from what he did say, was irresistible—he contended throughout, that everything which had a *beginning* must have an *ending;* and consequently if the punishment of man *commenced* in the next world, it must, according to his logic and belief have an *end.* (HC 4:79)

2 There is no pain so awful as that of suspense. This is the punishment of the wicked; their doubt, anxiety and suspense cause weeping, wailing and gnashing of teeth. (HC 5:340)

3 If a man has knowledge, he can be saved; although, if he has been guilty of great sins, he will be punished for them. But when he consents to obey the gospel, whether here or in the world of spirits, he is saved.

Prophets
20 Recollection of Jesse W. Crosby, reported in "Stories from the Notebook of Martha Cox, Grandmother of Fern Cox Anderson," LDS Church Archives.

Punishment
1 Letter of Mathew L. Davis to his wife describing the Prophet's discourse in Washington, D.C., 6 February 1840.
2 General conference address, Nauvoo, 8 April 1843.
3 King Follett Discourse, Nauvoo, 7 April 1844.

A man is his own tormentor and his own condemner. Hence the saying, They shall go into the lake that burns with fire and brimstone. The torment of disappointment in the mind of man is as exquisite as a lake burning with fire and brimstone. I say, so is the torment of man. . . .

. . . As they concocted scenes of bloodshed in this world, so they shall rise to that resurrection which is as the lake of fire and brimstone. Some shall rise to the everlasting burnings of God; for God dwells in everlasting burnings and some shall rise to the damnation of their own filthiness, which is as exquisite a torment as the lake of fire and brimstone. (HC 6:314, 317)

Purity

1   And again, it is written, "Behold, now are we the sons of God, and it doth not yet appear what we shall be: but we know that, when He shall appear, we shall be like Him; for we shall see Him as He is. And every man that hath this hope in him, purifieth himself, even as He is pure" (1 John iii:2, 3). (HC 2:20)

2   If we would come before God, we must keep ourselves pure, as He is pure. (HC 4:605)

3   My hands are clean, and my heart pure, from the blood of all men. (HC 5:15)

Rainbow

1   The Lord hath set the bow in the cloud for a sign that while it shall be seen, seed time and harvest, summer and winter shall not fail;

Purity
  1   Letter to the brethren scattered from Zion, Kirtland, 22 January 1834.
  2   Remarks to the Relief Society, Nauvoo, 28 April 1842.
  3   Letter to Mr. Bartlett, editor of the *Quincy Whig*, concerning the assassination attempt on the life of ex-governor Lilburn W. Boggs, Nauvoo, 22 May 1842.

Rainbow
  1   Sabbath address, Nauvoo, 21 May 1843.

but when it shall disappear, woe to that generation, for behold the end cometh quickly. (HC 5:402)

2   I have asked of the Lord concerning His coming; and while asking the Lord, He gave a sign and said, "In the days of Noah I set a bow in the heavens as a sign and token that in any year that the bow should be seen the Lord would not come; but there should be seed time and harvest during that year: but whenever you see the bow withdrawn, it shall be a token that there shall be famine, pestilence, and great distress among the nations, and that the coming of the Messiah is not far distant." (HC 6:254)

Rebellion

1   As we previously remarked, we do not attempt to place the law of man on a parallel with the law of heaven; but we will bring forward another item, to further urge the propriety of yielding obedience to the law of heaven, after the fact is admitted, that the laws of man are binding upon man. Were a king to extend his dominion over the habitable earth, and send forth his laws which were of the most perfect kind, and command his subjects one and all to yield obedience to the same, and add as a reward to those who obeyed them, that at a certain period they should be called to attend the marriage of his son, who in due time was to receive the kingdom, and they should be made equal with him in the same; and fix as a penalty for disobedience that every individual guilty of it should be cast out at the marriage feast, and have no part nor portion with his government, what rational mind could for a moment accuse the king with injustice for punishing such rebellious subjects? In the first place his laws were just, easy to be complied with, and perfect: nothing of a tyrannical nature was required of them; but the very construction of the laws was equity and beauty; and when obeyed would produce the happiest condition possible to all who adhered to them, beside the last great benefit of sitting down

---

Rainbow
  2   Sabbath address, Nauvoo, 10 March 1844.

Rebellion
  1   Letter to the brethren scattered from Zion, Kirtland, 22 January 1834.

with a royal robe in the presence of the king at the great, grand marriage supper of his son, and be made equal with him in all the affairs of the kingdom. (*HC* 2:8–9)

Rebuking

1   After he [Newel Knight] had thus suffered for a time, I succeeded in getting hold of him by the hand, when almost immediately he spoke to me, and with great earnestness requested me to cast the devil out of him, saying that he knew he was in him, and that he also knew that I could cast him out.

I replied, "If you know that I can, it shall be done;" and then almost unconsciously I rebuked the devil, and commanded him in the name of Jesus Christ to depart from him; when immediately Newel spoke out and said that he saw the devil leave him and vanish from his sight. This was the first miracle which was done in the Church, or by any member of it; it was done not by man, nor by the power of man, but it was done by God, and by the power of godliness; therefore, let the honor and the praise, the dominion and the glory, be ascribed to the Father, Son, and Holy Spirit, for ever and ever. Amen. (*HC* 1:82–83)

2   When we rebuke, do it in all meekness. (*HC* 1:341)

3   You know that it is my duty to admonish you, when you do wrong. This liberty I shall always take, and you shall have the same privilege. I take the liberty to admonish you, because of my birthright; and I grant you the privilege, because it is my duty to be humble, and receive rebuke and instruction from a brother, or a friend. (*HC* 2:343)

4   A frank and open rebuke provoketh a good man to emulation; and in the hour of trouble he will be your best friend; but on the other hand, it will draw out all the corruptions of corrupt hearts, and lying

---

Rebuking
1   Colesville, New York, April 1830.
2   Letter to the brethren in Zion, Kirtland, 21 April 1833.
3   Letter to William Smith, the Prophet's brother, Kirtland, 18 December 1835.
4   Letter to the Saints from Liberty Jail, 20–25 March 1839.

and the poison of asps is under their tongues; and they do cause the pure in heart to be cast into prison, because they want them out of their way. (*HC* 3:295)

5   "As finest steel doth show a brighter polish
     The more you rub the same,
E'en so in love rebuke will ne'er demolish
     A wise man's goodly name." (*HC* 5:300)

6   A good man will speak good things and holy principles, and an evil man evil things. I feel, in the name of the Lord, to rebuke all such bad principles, liars, &c., and I warn all of you to look out whom you are going after. (*HC* 6:366)

Records

1   Our acts are recorded, and at a future day they will be laid before us, and if we should fail to judge right and injure our fellow-beings, they may there, perhaps, condemn us; there they are of great consequence, and to me the consequence appears to be of force, beyond anything which I am able to express. (*HC* 2:26)

2   *Minutes:* After prayer by President Joseph Smith, Jun., he said, if we heard patiently, he could lay before the council an item which would be of importance. He had for himself, learned a fact by experience, which, on recollection, always gave him deep sorrow. It is a fact, if I now had in my possession, every decision which had been had upon important items of doctrine and duties since the commencement of this work, I would not part with them for any sum of money; but we have neglected to take minutes of such things, thinking, perhaps, that

---

Rebuking
  5   A proverb quoted by the Prophet and included in *HC*, Nauvoo, 10 March 1843.
  6   Sabbath address, Nauvoo, 12 May 1844.

Records
  1   A council of high priests and elders at the Prophet's home in Kirtland, 12 February 1834.
  2   Instructions to the Twelve, Kirtland, 27 February 1835.

they would never benefit us afterwards; which, if we had them now, would decide almost every point of doctrine which might be agitated. But this has been neglected, and now we cannot bear record to the Church and to the world, of the great and glorious manifestations which have been made to us with that degree of power and authority we otherwise could, if we now had these things to publish abroad.

Since the Twelve are now chosen, I wish to tell them a course which they may pursue, and be benefited thereafter, in a point of light of which they are not now aware. If they will, every time they assemble, appoint a person to preside over them during the meeting, and one or more to keep a record of their proceedings, and on the decision of every question or item, be it what it may, let such decision be written, and such decision will forever remain upon record, and appear an item of covenant or doctrine. An item thus decided may appear, at the time, of little or no worth, but should it be published, and one of you lay hands on it after, you will find it of infinite worth, not only to your brethren, but it will be a feast to your own souls.

Here is another important item. If you assemble from time to time, and proceed to discuss important questions, and pass decisions upon the same, and fail to note them down, by and by you will be driven to straits from which you will not be able to extricate yourselves, because you may be in a situation not to bring your faith to bear with sufficient perfection or power to obtain the desired information; or, perhaps, for neglecting to write these things when God had revealed them, not esteeming them of sufficient worth, the Spirit may withdraw and God may be angry; and there is, or was, a vast knowledge, of infinite importance, which is now lost. What was the cause of this? It came in consequence of slothfulness, or a neglect to appoint a man to occupy a few moments in writing all these decisions.

Here let me prophesy. The time will come, when, if you neglect to do this thing, you will fall by the hands of unrighteous men. Were you to be brought before the authorities, and be accused of any crime or misdemeanor, and be as innocent as the angels of God, unless you can prove yourselves to have been somewhere else, your enemies will prevail against you; but if you can bring twelve men to testify that you were in a certain place, at that time, you will escape their hand. Now, if you will be careful to keep minutes of these things, as I have said, it will be one of the most important records ever seen; for all such decisions will ever after remain as items of doctrine and covenants. (HC 2:198–99)

Reincarnation

1   He [Robert Matthews, alias Robert Matthias, alias Joshua the Jewish minister] said that he possessed the spirit of his fathers, that he was a literal descendant of Matthias, the Apostle, who was chosen in the place of Judas that fell; that his spirit was resurrected in him; and that this was the way or scheme of eternal life—this transmigration of soul or spirit from father to son.

I told him that his doctrine was of the devil, that he was in reality in possession of a wicked and depraved spirit, although he professed to be the Spirit of truth itself; and he said also that he possessed the soul of Christ. (HC 2:307)

2   *Minutes:* To a remark of Elder Orson Pratt's, that a man's body changes every seven years, President Joseph Smith replied: There is no fundamental principle belonging to a human system that ever goes into another in this world or in the world to come; I care not what the theories of men are. We have the testimony that God will raise us up, and he has the power to do it. If any one supposes that any part of our bodies, that is, the fundamental parts thereof, ever goes into another body he is mistaken. (HC 5:339)

Relief Society

1   *Words of Sarah M. Kimball:* In the [spring of 1842], a Miss Cooke was seamstress for me. The subject of combining our efforts for assisting the Temple hands came up in conversation. She desired to help, but had no means to furnish. I told her I would furnish material if she would make some shirts for the workmen. It was then suggested that some of our neighbors might wish to combine means and efforts with ours, and we decided to invite a few to come and consult with us on

---

Reincarnation
1   Conversation with Robert Matthews, Kirtland, 10 November 1835.
2   Minutes of a general conference, Nauvoo, 7 April 1843.

Relief Society
1   Reminiscence of Sarah M. Kimball, published in the *Woman's Exponent,* 1 September 1883.

the subject of forming a Ladies' Society. The neighboring sisters met in my parlor and decided to organize. I was delegated to call on Sister Eliza R. Snow and ask her to write a constitution and by-laws, and submit them to President Smith prior to our next meeting. When she read them to him, he replied that the constitution and by-laws were the best he had ever seen.

"But," he said, "this is not what you want. Tell the sisters their offering is accepted of the Lord, and he has something better for them than a written constitution. I invite them all to meet with me and a few of the brethren next Thursday afternoon, and I will organize the women under the priesthood after the pattern of the priesthood."

He further said, "The Church was never perfectly organized until the women were thus organized."

He wished to have Sister Emma Smith elected to preside in fulfillment of the revelation which called her an elect lady. (*TK*, p. 131)

2   *Minutes:* The meeting was addressed by President Smith, to illustrate the object of the Society [Relief Society]—that the Society of Sisters might provoke the brethren to good works in looking to the wants of the poor, searching after objects of charity, and in administering to their wants; to assist by correcting the morals and strengthening the virtues of the community. . . .

President Smith further remarked that an organization to show them how to go to work would be sufficient. He proposed that the sisters elect a presiding officer to preside over them, and let that presiding officer choose two counselors to assist in the duties of her office; that he would ordain them to preside over the Society, and let them preside just as [the] Presidency preside over the Church: and if they need his instruction ask him, [and he] will give it from time to time.

Let this presidency serve as a constitution, all their decisions be considered law, and acted upon as such.

If any officers are wanted to carry out the designs of the institution, let them be appointed and set apart, as deacons, teachers, etc., are among us.

The minutes of your meetings will be precedent for you to act upon, your constitution and law.

He then suggested the propriety of electing a presidency to continue in the office during good behavior, or so long as they shall continue to fill the office with dignity, etc.,—like the First Presidency of the Church.

Motioned by Sister Whitney and seconded by Sister Packard that Mrs. Emma Smith be chosen president. Passed unanimously.

Moved by President Smith that Mrs. Smith proceed to choose her counselors, that they may be ordained to preside over this Society in taking care of the poor, administering to their wants, and attending to the various affairs of this institution.

The presidentess elect then made choice of Mrs. Sarah M. Cleveland and Mrs. Elizabeth Ann Whitney for counselors.

President Smith read the revelation to Emma Smith, from the book of Doctrine and Covenants, and stated that she was ordained at the time the revelation was given to expound the scriptures to all and to teach the female part of [the] community, and that not she alone, but others, may attain to the same blessings. (*WJS*, pp. 104–5; standardized)

3   *Report of Eliza R. Snow:* President Joseph Smith arose. Spoke of the organization of the Female Relief Society; said he was deeply interested, that it might be built up to the Most High in an acceptable manner; that its rules must be observed; that none should be received into it but those who were worthy; proposed a close examination of every candidate; that the society was growing too fast. It should grow up by degrees, should commence with a few individuals, thus have a select society of the virtuous, and those who would walk circumspectly; commended them for their zeal, but said sometimes their zeal was not according to knowledge. One principal object of the institution was to purge out iniquity; said they must be extremely careful in all their examinations, or the consequences would be serious. (*HC* 4:570)

4   You will receive instructions through the order of the Priesthood which God has established, through the medium of those appointed

Relief Society

3   Remarks to the Relief Society, Nauvoo, 30 March 1842.

4   Remarks to the Relief Society, Nauvoo, 28 April 1842. The original handwritten minutes of this meeting of the Relief Society read as follows: "This Society is to get instruction through the order which God has established—thro' the medium of those appointed to lead—and I now turn the key to you in the name of God and this Society shall rejoice and knowledge and intelligence shall flow down from this time." (*WJS*, p. 118)

to lead, guide and direct the affairs of the Church in this last dispensation; and I now turn the key in your behalf in the name of the Lord, and this Society shall rejoice, and knowledge and intelligence shall flow down from this time henceforth; this is the beginning of better days to the poor and needy, who shall be made to rejoice and pour forth blessings on your heads. (HC 4:607)

5 *Words of Elizabeth Ann Whitney:* The Relief Society then was small in numbers, but the Prophet foretold great things concerning the future of this organization, many of which I have lived to see fulfilled; but there are many things which yet remain to be fulfilled in the future.

President Joseph Smith had great faith in the sisters' labors, and ever sought to encourage them in the performance of the duties which pertained to these societies, which he said were not only for benevolent purposes and spiritual improvement, but were actually to save souls. And my testimony to my sisters is that I have seen many demonstrations of the power and blessing of God through the administration of the sisters. (*TK*, p. 41)

Religious Freedom and Tolerance

1 Thus were we persecuted on account of our religious faith—in a country the Constitution of which guarantees to every man the indefeasible right to worship God according to the dictates of his own conscience—and by men, too, who were professors of religion, and who were not backward to maintain the right of religious liberty for themselves, though they could thus wantonly deny it to us. (HC 1:97)

2 The early settlers of Boston (the Emporium of New England), who had fled from their mother country to avoid persecution and death, soon became so lost to principles of justice and religious liberty

---

Relief Society
   5 Reminiscence of Elizabeth Ann Whitney, published in the *Woman's Exponent*, 15 November 1878.

Religious Freedom and Tolerance
   1 Colesville, New York, June 1830.
   2 Salem, Massachusetts, August 1836.

as to whip and hang the Baptist and the Quaker, who like themselves, had fled from tyranny to a land of freedom; and the fathers of Salem from 1692 to 1693, whipped, imprisoned, tortured, and hung many of their citizens for supposed witchcraft; and quite recently,—while boasting of her light and knowledge, of her laws and religion, as surpassed by none on earth,—has New England been guilty of burning a Catholic convent in the vicinity of Charleston, and of scattering the inmates to the four winds; yes, in sight of the very spot where the fire of American Independence was first kindled, where a monument is now erecting in memory of the battle of Bunker Hill, and the fate of the immortal Warren, who bled, who died, on those sacred heights, to purchase religious liberty for his country—in sight of this very spot, have the religionists of the nineteenth century, demolished a noble brick edifice, hurling its inhabitants forth upon a cold, unfeeling world for protection and subsistence. (HC 2:464–65)

3 We believe that the experience of the Saints in times past has been sufficient, that they will from henceforth be always ready to obey the truth without having men's persons in admiration because of advantage. It is expedient that we should be aware of such things; and we ought always to be aware of those prejudices which sometimes so strangely present themselves, and are so congenial to human nature, against our friends, neighbors, and brethren of the world, who choose to differ from us in opinion and in matters of faith. Our religion is between us and our God. Their religion is between them and their God. . . .

Here is a principle also, which we are bound to be exercised with, that is, in common with all men, such as governments, and laws, and regulations in the civil concerns of life. This principle guarantees to all parties, sects, and denominations, and classes of religion, equal, coherent, and indefeasible rights; they are things that pertain to this life; therefore all are alike interested; they make our responsibilities one towards another in matters of corruptible things, while the former principles do not destroy the latter, but bind us stronger, and make our responsibilities not only one to another, but unto God also. (HC 3:303–4)

Religious Freedom and Tolerance
3   Letter to the Saints from Liberty Jail, 20–25 March 1839.

4   And now, sir, this is the sole cause of the persecution against the Mormon people. And now, if they had been Mohammedans, Hottentots, or pagans, or in fine, sir, if their religion was as false as hell, what right would men have to drive them from their homes, and their country, or to exterminate them, so long as their religion did not interfere with the civil rights of men, according to the laws of our country? None at all. . . .

. . . I have the most liberal sentiments and feelings of charity towards all sects, parties, and denominations; and the rights and liberties of conscience I hold most sacred and dear, and despise no man for differing with me in matters of opinion. (*PWJS*, pp. 419, 423–24; standardized)

5   We wish it likewise to be distinctly understood, that we claim no privilege but what we feel cheerfully disposed to share with our fellow citizens of every denomination, and every sentiment of religion; and therefore say, that so far from being restricted to our own faith, let all those who desire to locate themselves in this place, or the vicinity, come, and we will hail them as citizens and friends, and shall feel it not only a duty, but a privilege, to reciprocate the kindness we have received from the benevolent and kind-hearted citizens of the state of Illinois. (HC 4:273)

6   We contemplate a people who have embraced a system of religion, unpopular, and the adherence to which has brought upon them repeated persecutions. A people who, for their love to God, and attachment to His cause, have suffered hunger, nakedness, perils, and almost every privation. A people who, for the sake of their religion, have had to mourn the premature death of parents, husbands, wives, and children. A people, who have preferred death to slavery and hypocrisy, and have honorably maintained their characters, and stood firm and immovable, in times that have tried men's souls. Stand fast, ye Saints of God, hold on a little while longer, and the storm of life will be past, and you will be rewarded by that God whose servants you are, and who will duly appreciate all your toils and afflictions for

---

Religious Freedom and Tolerance
   4   Letter to Isaac Galland, written while the Prophet was imprisoned in Liberty Jail, 22 March 1839.
   5   Proclamation of the First Presidency, Nauvoo, 15 January 1841.
   6   Report of the First Presidency at general conference, Nauvoo, 7 April 1841.

Christ's sake and the Gospel's. Your names will be handed down to posterity as Saints of God and virtuous men. (*HC* 4:337)

7 When we see virtuous qualities in men, we should always acknowledge them, let their understanding be what it may in relation to creeds and doctrine; for all men are, or ought to be free, possessing inalienable rights, and the high and noble qualifications of the laws of nature and of self-preservation, to think, and act, and say as they please, while they maintain a due respect to the rights and privileges of all other creatures, infringing upon none. (*HC* 5:156)

8 The Saints can testify whether I am willing to lay down my life for my brethren. If it has been demonstrated that I have been willing to die for a "Mormon," I am bold to declare before Heaven that I am just as ready to die in defending the rights of a Presbyterian, a Baptist, or a good man of any other denomination; for the same principle which would trample upon the rights of the Latter-day Saints would trample upon the rights of the Roman Catholics, or of any other denomination who may be unpopular and too weak to defend themselves.

It is a love of liberty which inspires my soul—civil and religious liberty to the whole of the human race. Love of liberty was diffused into my soul by my grandfathers while they dandled me on their knees; and shall I want friends? No. (*HC* 5:498)

9 I would not have suffered my name to have been used by my friends on anywise as President of the United States, or candidate for that office, if I and my friends could have had the privilege of enjoying our religious and civil rights as American citizens, even those rights which the Constitution guarantees unto all her citizens alike. But this as a people we have been denied from the beginning. Persecution has rolled upon our heads from time to time, from portions of the United States, like peals of thunder, because of our religion; and no portion of the Government as yet has stepped forward for our relief. And in view of these things, I feel it to be my right and privilege to obtain what influence and power I can, lawfully, in the United States, for the protection of injured innocence. (*HC* 6:210–11)

Religious Freedom and Tolerance
7 Letter to James Arlington Bennett, Nauvoo, 8 September 1842.
8 Sabbath address, Nauvoo, 9 July 1843.
9 Views of the Prophet on his candidacy for president of the United States, Nauvoo, 8 February 1844.

10 As to politics, I care but little about the presidential chair. I would not give half as much for the office of President of the United States as I would for the one I now hold as Lieutenant-General of the Nauvoo Legion.

We have as good a right to make a political party to gain power to defend ourselves, as for demagogues to make use of our religion to get power to destroy us. In other words, as the world has used the power of government to oppress and persecute us, it is right for us to use it for the protection of our rights. We will whip the mob by getting up a candidate for President. (*HC* 6:243)

11 Meddle not with any man for his religion: all governments ought to permit every man to enjoy his religion unmolested. No man is authorized to take away life in consequence of difference of religion, which all laws and governments ought to tolerate and protect, right or wrong. Every man has a natural, and, in our country, a constitutional right to be a false prophet, as well as a true prophet. (*HC* 6:304)

Repentance

1 *Words of Levi W. Hancock:* Joseph said, "Now if you elders have sinned, it will do you no good to preach, if you have not repented." (*TK*, p. 18)

2 I rebuked them sharply, and told them that the Church must feel the wrath of God except they repent of their sins and cast away their murmurings and complainings one of another. (*HC* 1:470)

3 I had called the camp together [on 3 June 1834] and told them that in consequence of the disobedience of some who had been un-

---

Religious Freedom and Tolerance
    10 Remarks at meeting at temple in Nauvoo, 7 March 1844.
    11 King Follett Discourse, Nauvoo, 7 April 1844.

Repentance
    1   Reminiscence of Levi W. Hancock, Kirtland, 4 June 1831.
    2   Kirtland, 26 December 1833. The two brethren rebuked by the Prophet had spoken harshly against a Church leader. At this rebuke, the brethren "confessed their wrongs, and all forgave one another" (*HC* 1:470).
    3   Events of Zion's Camp, Missouri, 20 June 1834.

willing to listen to my words, but had rebelled, God had decreed that sickness should come upon the camp, and if they did not repent and humble themselves before God they should die like sheep with the rot; that I was sorry, but could not help it. The scourge must come; repentance and humility may mitigate the chastisement, but cannot altogether avert it. But there were some who would not give heed to my words. (HC 2:106–7)

4   The hand of the Lord shall be upon them [certain elders who had transgressed], until they repent in sackcloth and ashes, and shall effect their temporal and spiritual interests unless they repent. (HC 2:237)

5   This we believe to be our duty—to teach to all mankind the doctrine of repentance. (HC 2:255)

6   When I was about seventeen years I had another vision of angels, in the night season, after I had retired to bed. I had not been asleep, but was meditating upon my past life and experience. I was well aware I had not kept the commandments, and I repented heartily for all my sins and transgressions, and humbled myself before him whose eye surveys all things at a glance. (PJS 1:127; standardized)

7   You desire to remain in the Church, but forsake your Apostleship. This is the stratagem of the evil one; when he has gained one advantage, he lays a plan for another. . . . When a man falls one step, he must regain that step again, or fall another; he has still more to gain, or eventually all is lost. (HC 2:342, 343)

8   Repentance is a thing that cannot be trifled with every day. Daily transgression and daily repentance is not that which is pleasing in the sight of God. (HC 3:379)

Repentance
  4   Kirtland, 9 July 1835.
  5   Letter to the elders of the Church, Kirtland, 1 September 1835.
  6   Conversation with Robert Matthews (alias Robert Matthias, alias Joshua the Jewish minister), Kirtland, 9 November 1835.
  7   Letter to William Smith, the Prophet's brother, Kirtland, 18 December 1835.
  8   Instructions to the Twelve, Commerce (Nauvoo), 27 June 1839.

9   Again, let the Twelve and all Saints be willing to confess all their sins, and not keep back a part. (*HC* 3:383)

10 God did elect or predestinate, that all those who would be saved, should be saved in Christ Jesus, and through obedience to the Gospel; but He passes over no man's sins, but visits them with correction, and if His children will not repent of their sins He will discard them. (*HC* 4:360)

11 There is never a time when the spirit is too old to approach God. All are within the reach of pardoning mercy, who have not committed the unpardonable sin, which hath no forgiveness, neither in this world, nor in the world to come. (*HC* 4:425)

12 What chance is there for infidelity when we are parting with our friends almost daily? None at all. The infidel will grasp at every straw for help until death stares him in the face, and then his infidelity takes its flight, for the realities of the eternal world are resting upon him in mighty power; and when every earthly support and prop fails him, he then sensibly feels the eternal truths of the immortality of the soul. We should take warning and not wait for the death-bed to repent, as we see the infant taken away by death, so may the youth and middle-aged, as well as the infant be suddenly called into eternity. Let this, then, prove as a warning to all not to procrastinate repentance, or wait till a death-bed, for it is the will of God that man should repent and serve Him in health, and in the strength and power of his mind, in order to secure His blessing, and not wait until he is called to die. (*HC* 4:553–54)

13 Don't envy the finery and fleeting show of sinners, for they are in a miserable situation; but as far as you can, have mercy on them, for in a short time God will destroy them, if they will not repent and turn unto him. (*HC* 4:607)

Repentance
  9 Instructions to the Apostles and Seventies departing for missions to England, Commerce (Nauvoo), 2 July 1839.
  10 Sabbath address, Nauvoo, 16 May 1841.
  11 General conference address, Nauvoo, 3 October 1841.
  12 Sabbath address, Nauvoo, 20 March 1842.
  13 Remarks to the Relief Society, Nauvoo, 28 April 1842.

14 There is now a day of salvation to such as repent and reform;—and they who repent not should be cast out from this society [the Relief Society]; yet we should woo them to return to God, lest they escape not the damnation of hell! . . .

I am advised by some of the heads of the Church to tell the Relief Society to be virtuous, but to save the Church from desolation and the sword; beware, be still, be prudent, repent, reform, but do it in a way not to destroy all around you. I do not want to cloak iniquity—all things contrary to the will of God, should be cast from us, but don't do more hurt than good, with your tongues—be pure in heart. Jesus designs to save the people out of their sins. Said Jesus, "Ye shall do the work, which ye see me do." These are the grand key-words for the society to act upon. (HC 5:20)

15 Christ said He came to call sinners to repentance, to save them. Christ was condemned by the self-righteous Jews because He took sinners into His society; He took them upon the principle that they repented of their sins. It is the object of this society to reform persons, not to take those that are corrupt and foster them in their wickedness; but if they repent, we are bound to take them, and by kindness sanctify and cleanse them from all unrighteousness by our influence in watching over them. (HC 5:23)

16 Sisters of the [Relief] society, shall there be strife among you? I will not have it. You must repent, and get the love of God. Away with self-righteousness. (HC 5:24)

17 The Lord once told me that what I asked for I should have. I have been afraid to ask God to kill my enemies, lest some of them should, peradventure, repent. (HC 6:253)

18 All sins shall be forgiven, except the sin against the Holy Ghost; for Jesus will save all except the sons of perdition. . . . After a man has sinned against the Holy Ghost, there is no repentance for him. . . .

Repentance
14 Remarks to the Relief Society, Nauvoo, 26 May 1842.
15 Remarks to the Relief Society, Nauvoo, 9 June 1842.
16 Remarks to the Relief Society, Nauvoo, 9 June 1842.
17 Sabbath address, Nauvoo, 10 March 1844.
18 King Follett Discourse, Nauvoo, 7 April 1844.

When a man begins to be an enemy to this work, he hunts me, he seeks to kill me, and never ceases to thirst for my blood. He gets the spirit of the devil—the same spirit that they had who crucified the Lord of Life—the same spirit that sins against the Holy Ghost. You cannot save such persons; you cannot bring them to repentance; they make open war, like the devil, and awful is the consequence. (HC 6:314–15)

19 You may say, that man is a sinner. Well, if he repents, he shall be forgiven. Be cautious: await. (HC 6:315)

20 Let us this very day begin anew, and now say, with all our hearts, we will forsake our sins and be righteous. (HC 6:363)

Reproving

1 We admire the confidence and love which our brethren have manifested in them [i.e., in letters], in giving us *sharp, piercing, and cutting* reproofs, which are calculated to wake us up and make us search about ourselves, and put a double watch over ourselves in all things that we do. And we acknowledge that it is our duty to receive all reproofs and chastisements given of the Spirit of the most Holy One. And if being chastised and reproved of what we are guilty seems not to be joyous for the present but grievous, O, how wounding and how poignant must it be to receive chastisements and reproofs for things that we are not guilty of from a source we least expect them, arising from a distrustful, a fearful, and jealous spirit. (*PWJS*, p. 315; standardized)

2 In the spirit of my calling, and in view of the authority of the Priesthood that has been conferred upon me, it would be my duty to

---

Repentance
   19 King Follett Discourse, Nauvoo, 7 April 1844.
   20 Sabbath address, Nauvoo, 2 May 1844.

Reproving
   1   Letter to Edward Partridge and others in Missouri, Kirtland, 30 March 1834.
   2   Letter to William Smith, the Prophet's brother, Kirtland, 18 December 1835.

reprove whatever I esteemed to be wrong, fondly hoping in my heart, that all parties would consider it right, and therefore humble themselves, that Satan might not take the advantage of us. (HC 2:340)

3   *Report of Eliza R. Snow:* He [Joseph Smith] reproved those that were disposed to find fault with the management of the concerns of the Church, saying God had called him to lead the Church, and he would lead it right; those that undertake to interfere will be ashamed when their own folly is made manifest. (HC 4:604)

4   There should be no license for sin, but mercy should go hand in hand with reproof. (HC 5:24)

5   If I did not love men, I would not reprove them. (HC 6:240)

6   I have no enmity against any man. I love you all; but I hate some of your deeds. I am your best friend, and if persons miss their mark it is their own fault. If I reprove a man, and he hates me, he is a fool; for I love all men, especially these my brethren and sisters. (HC 6:317)

Reputation

1   I always take pleasure in extending the reputations of honorable men among honorable men. (HC 6:423)

Reproving
   3   Remarks to the Relief Society, Nauvoo, 28 April 1842.
   4   Remarks to the Relief Society, Nauvoo, 9 June 1842.
   5   Remarks at meeting at temple in Nauvoo, 7 March 1844.
   6   King Follett Discourse, Nauvoo, 7 April 1844.

Reputation
   1   Letter to Judge Pope, Nauvoo, 30 May 1844.

Respect

1　God has respect to the feelings of His Saints, and He will not suffer them to be tantalized with impunity. (HC 1:317)

2　In respecting others, we respect ourselves. (HC 6:221)

Responsibility

1　After all that has been said, the greatest and most important duty is to preach the Gospel. (HC 2:478)

2　The greatest responsibility in this world that God has laid upon us is to seek after our dead. (HC 6:313)

Restoration

1　All of a sudden a vision of the future burst upon [Newel Knight]. He saw there represented the great work which through my instrumentality was yet to be accomplished. (HC 1:85)

2　*Words of Lorenzo Snow:* [Joseph's] remarks were confined principally to his own experiences, especially the visitation of the angel, giving a

---

Respect
1　Letter to William W. Phelps in Missouri, written from Kirtland, 14 January 1833. According to Dean Jessee this letter was dated 11 January (see *PWJS*, p. 262).
2　Letter to the editor of the *Nauvoo Neighbor*, an LDS newspaper, 19 February 1844.

Responsibility
1　Solemn assembly in the Kirtland Temple, 6 April 1837.
2　King Follett Discourse, Nauvoo, 7 April 1844.

Restoration
1　First conference of the Church, Fayette, New York, 9 June 1830.
2　Report on 1831 meeting by Lorenzo Snow, published in the *Improvement Era*, February 1937.

strong and powerful testimony in regard to these marvelous manifestations. He simply bore his testimony to what the Lord had manifested to him, to the dispensation of the gospel which had been committed to him, and to the authority that he possessed. (*TK*, pp. 32–33)

3   The plain fact is this, the power of God begins to fall upon the nations, and the light of the latter-day glory begins to break forth through the dark atmosphere of sectarian wickedness, and their iniquity rolls up into view, and the nations of the Gentiles are like the waves of the sea, casting up mire and dirt, or all in commotion, and they are hastily preparing to act the part allotted them, when the Lord rebukes the nations, when He shall rule them with a rod of iron, and break them in pieces like a potter's vessel. The Lord declared to His servants, some eighteen months since, that He was then withdrawing His Spirit from the earth; and we can see that such is the fact, for not only the churches are dwindling away, but there are no conversions, or but very few: and this is not all, the governments of the earth are thrown into confusion and division; and *Destruction*, to the eye of the spiritual beholder, seems to be written by the finger of an invisible hand, in large capitals, upon almost every thing we behold.

And now what remains to be done, under circumstances like these? I will proceed to tell you what the Lord requires of all people, high and low, rich and poor, male and female, ministers and people, professors of religion and non-professors, in order that they may enjoy the Holy Spirit of God to a fulness and escape the judgments of God, which are almost ready to burst upon the nations of the earth. Repent of all your sins, and be baptized in water for the remission of them, in the name of the Father, and of the Son, and of the Holy Ghost, and receive the ordinance of the laying on of the hands of him who is ordained and sealed unto this power, that ye may receive the Holy Spirit of God; and this is according to the Holy Scriptures, and the Book of Mormon; and the only way that man can enter into the celestial kingdom. These are the requirements of the new covenant, or first principles of the Gospel of Christ; then "Add to your faith, virtue; and to virtue, knowledge; and to knowledge, temperance; and to temperance, patience; and to patience, godliness; and to godliness, brotherly

---

Restoration
3   Letter to N. E. Seaton (N. C. Saxton), a newspaper editor in Rochester, N.Y., Kirtland, 4 January 1833.

kindness; and to brotherly kindness, charity {or love}; for if these things be in you, and abound, they make you that ye shall neither be barren nor unfruitful, in the knowledge of our Lord Jesus Christ." (HC 1:314–15)

4 *Words of Lydia Bailey Knight:* The Prophet bore a faithful testimony that the priesthood was again restored to the earth, and that God and His Son had conferred upon him the keys of the Aaronic and Melchizedek Priesthoods. He stated that the last dispensation had come, and the words of Jesus were now in force: "Go ye into all the world and preach the gospel to every creature. He that believeth and is baptized shall be saved; but he that believeth not shall be damned." . . .

The Prophet then arose and poured forth a golden stream of words, many of which were verily pearls without price, setting forth the restoration of the gospel and the great work that had commenced on the earth. With power he exhorted everyone who was present to seek for the truth of his and his companion's words from the source of all light, all truth, and all religion, and a knowledge of the truth of the same should surely follow. (*TK*, pp. 43, 44)

5 *Words of Wilford Woodruff:* On Sunday [27 April 1834], he [Joseph Smith] called a priesthood meeting. The elders all gathered in a little cabin. There I first heard Joseph Smith speak publicly. He called upon the elders to bear testimony of the gospel of Christ. He then arose and said, "Brethren, I am very much edified and interested in listening to your testimony. But I want to tell you that you know no more concerning the result of this work and what lies before you as the elders of Israel, and before this people, than a parcel of little children."

He told them this work would fill the whole earth, and that all nations would have to hear the proclamation of the gospel. He further said: "This work will fill the Rocky Mountains with tens of thousands of Latter-day Saints, and there will be joined with them the Lamanites who dwell in those mountains who will receive the gospel of Christ at the mouth of the elders of Israel, and they will be united with the Church and the kingdom of God, and bring forth much good." (*TK*, p. 81)

Restoration
  4 Recollection of Lydia Bailey Knight of meetings at Freeman Nickerson's home in Mount Pleasant, Ontario, Canada, October 1833.
  5 Recollection of Wilford Woodruff, published in the *Millennial Star*, 5 October 1891.

6 The above clouds of darkness [anti-Mormon writings] have long been beating like mountain waves upon the immovable rock of the Church of the Latter-day Saints; and notwithstanding all this, the mustard seed is still towering its lofty branches, higher and higher, and extending itself wider and wider; and the chariot wheels of the Kingdom are still rolling on, impelled by the mighty arm of Jehovah; and in spite of all opposition, will still roll on, until His words are all fulfilled. (*HC* 2:270)

7 My grandfather, Asael Smith, long ago predicted that there would be a prophet raised up in his family, and my grandmother was fully satisfied that it was fulfilled in me. My grandfather Asael died in East Stockholm, St. Lawrence county, New York, after having received the Book of Mormon, and read it nearly through; and he declared that I was the very Prophet that he had long known would come in his family. (*HC* 2:443)

8 We are called to hold the keys of the mysteries of those things that have been kept hid from the foundation of the world until now. Some have tasted a little of these things, many of which are to be poured down from heaven upon the heads of babes; yea, upon the weak, obscure and despised ones of the earth. . . .

And now, brethren, after your tribulations, if you do these things, and exercise fervent prayer and faith in the sight of God always, He shall give unto you knowledge by His Holy Spirit, yea by the unspeakable gift of the Holy Ghost, that has not been revealed since the world was until now. (*HC* 3:296)

9 In the first ages of the world they tried to establish the same thing [bringing people into the presence of God]; and there were Eliases raised up who tried to restore these very glories, but did not obtain them; but they prophesied of a day when this glory would be revealed. Paul spoke of the dispensation of the fullness of times, when God would gather together all things in one, etc.; and those men to whom

---

Restoration

6   Letter to the elders of the Church, Kirtland, 1 September 1835.

7   Kirtland, 17 May 1836.

8   Letter to the Saints from Liberty Jail, 20–25 March 1839.

9   Discourse on the priesthood, given sometime before 8 August 1839, Commerce (Nauvoo). For a discussion on the dating of this discourse, see *WJS*, p. 22.

these keys have been given, will have to be there; and they without us cannot be made perfect.

These men are in heaven, but their children are on the earth. Their bowels yearn over us. God sends down men for this reason. "And the Son of Man shall send forth His angels, and they shall gather out of His kingdom all things that give offense and them that do iniquity."—(Matt. xiii:41). All these authoritative characters will come down and join hand in hand in bringing about this work. (HC 3:388–89)

10 The work of the Lord in these last days, is one of vast magnitude and almost beyond the comprehension of mortals. Its glories are past description, and its grandeur unsurpassable. It is the theme which has animated the bosom of prophets and righteous men from the creation of the world down through every succeeding generation to the present time; and it is truly the dispensation of the fullness of times, when all things which are in Christ Jesus, whether in heaven or on the earth, shall be gathered together in Him, and when all things shall be restored, as spoken of by all the holy prophets since the world began; for in it will take place the glorious fulfilment of the promises made to the fathers, while the manifestations of the power of the Most High will be great, glorious, and sublime. . . .

. . . The work which has to be accomplished in the last days is one of vast importance, and will call into action the energy, skill, talent, and ability of the Saints, so that it may roll forth with that glory and majesty described by the prophet; and will consequently require the concentration of the Saints, to accomplish works of such magnitude and grandeur.

The work of the gathering spoken of in the Scriptures will be necessary to bring about the glories of the last dispensation. . . .

Here, then, beloved brethren, is a work to engage in worthy of archangels—a work which will cast into the shade the things which have been heretofore accomplished; a work which kings and prophets and righteous men in former ages have sought, expected, and earnestly desired to see, but died without the sight; and well will it be for those who shall aid in carrying into effect the mighty operations of Jehovah. (HC 4:185–86, 187)

Restoration
10 Letter to the Saints from the First Presidency, Nauvoo, 31 August 1840.

11 Now the purpose in Himself in the winding up scene of the last dispensation is that all things pertaining to that dispensation should be conducted precisely in accordance with the preceding dispensations.

And again, God purposed in Himself that there should not be an eternal fullness until every dispensation should be fulfilled and gathered together in one, and that all things whatsoever, that should be gathered together in one in those dispensations unto the same fullness and eternal glory, should be in Christ Jesus. . . .

. . . All the ordinances and duties that ever have been required by the Priesthood, under the directions and commandments of the Almighty in any of the dispensations, shall all be had in the last dispensation, therefore all things had under the authority of the Priesthood at any former period, shall be had again, bringing to pass the restoration spoken of by the mouth of all the Holy Prophets. (*HC* 4:208, 210–11)

12 The dispensation of the fullness of times will bring to light the things that have been revealed in all former dispensations; also other things that have not been before revealed. He shall send Elijah, the Prophet, &c., and restore all things in Christ. (*HC* 4:426)

13 The new year has been ushered in and continued thus far under the most favorable auspices, and the Saints seem to be influenced by a kind and indulgent Providence in their dispositions and {blessed with} means to rear the Temple of the Most High God, anxiously looking forth to the completion thereof as an event of the greatest importance to the Church and the world, making the Saints in Zion to rejoice, and the hypocrite and sinner to tremble. Truly this is a day long to be remembered by the Saints of the last days,—a day in which the God of heaven has begun to restore the ancient order of His kingdom unto His servants and His people,—a day in which all things are concurring to bring about the completion of the fullness of the Gospel, a fullness of the dispensation of dispensations, even the fullness of times; a day in which God has begun to make manifest and set in order in His

---

Restoration

11 Article on priesthood read at general conference, Nauvoo, 5 October 1840.

12 General conference address, Nauvoo, 3 October 1841.

13 Nauvoo, 6 January 1842.

Church those things which have been, and those things which the ancient prophets and wise men desired to see but died without beholding them; a day in which those things begin to be made manifest, which have been hid from before the foundation of the world, and which Jehovah has promised should be made known in His own due time unto His servants, to prepare the earth for the return of His glory, even a celestial glory, and a kingdom of Priests and kings to God and the Lamb, forever, on Mount Zion, and with him the hundred and forty and four thousand whom John the Revelator saw, all of which is to come to pass in the restitution of all things. (HC 4:492–93)

14 The Savior said when these tribulations should take place, it should be committed to a man who should be a witness over the whole world: the keys of knowledge, power and revelations should be revealed to a witness who should hold the testimony to the world. It has always been my province to dig up hidden mysteries—new things—for my hearers. . . .

All the testimony is that the Lord in the last days would commit the keys of the priesthood to a witness over all people. Has the Gospel of the kingdom commenced in the last days? And will God take it from the man until He takes him Himself? I have read it precisely as the words flowed from the lips of Jesus Christ. John the Revelator saw an angel flying through the midst of heaven, having the everlasting Gospel to preach unto them that dwell on the earth.

The scripture is ready to be fulfilled when great wars, famines, pestilence, great distress, judgments, &c., are ready to be poured out on the inhabitants of the earth. John saw the angel having the holy priesthood, who should preach the everlasting Gospel to all nations. God had an angel—a special messenger—ordained and prepared for that purpose in the last days. Woe, woe be to that man or set of men who lift up their hands against God and His witness in these last days: for they shall deceive almost the very chosen ones! . . .

. . . It is the testimony that I want that I am God's servant, and this people His people. The ancient prophets declared that in the last days the God of heaven should set up a kingdom which should never be destroyed, nor left to other people; and the very time that was calculated on, this people were struggling to bring it out. . . .

Restoration
14 Sabbath address, Nauvoo, 12 May 1844.

I calculate to be one of the instruments of setting up the kingdom of Daniel by the word of the Lord, and I intend to lay a foundation that will revolutionize the whole world. I once offered my life to the Missouri mob as a sacrifice for my people, and here I am. It will not be by sword or gun that this kingdom will roll on: the power of truth is such that all nations will be under the necessity of obeying the Gospel. The prediction is that army will be against army: it may be that the Saints will have to beat their ploughs into swords, for it will not do for men to sit down patiently and see their children destroyed. (HC 6:363–64, 365)

15 *Words of Dan Jones:* Joseph bore a powerful testimony to the guards of the divine authenticity of the Book of Mormon, the restoration of the gospel, the ministration of angels, and the establishment of the kingdom of God again upon the earth, for the sake of which he was at that time incarcerated in the prison, and not because he had violated any law of God or man. (*TK*, p. 186)

16 *Report of John M. Bernhisel's Recollection:* [Joseph Smith said:] "In every previous dispensation, Lucifer had prevailed and driven the priesthood from the earth. But in this last dispensation the reign of the Son of God and His priesthood was firmly established, nevermore to depart; thus all the inhabitants of the world might partake of the gifts and blessings of God. Our integrity to our Father and His righteousness is the only plan whereby we can save ourselves and acquire 'eternal lives and progression,' which is the great blessing God can confer on his faithful sons." (*TK*, p. 177)

Restoration

15 Recollection of Dan Jones concerning experience at Carthage Jail, contained in "The Martyrdom of Joseph and Hyrum Smith," LDS Church Archives.
16 Recollection of John M. Bernhisel, reported in Washington Franklin Anderson, "Reminiscences of John M. Bernhisel," LDS Church Archives.

Resurrection

1 It may be proper for us to notice in this place a few of the many blessings held out in this law of heaven as a reward to those who obey its teachings. God has appointed a day in which He will judge the world, and this He has given an assurance of in that He raised up His Son Jesus Christ from the dead—the point on which the hope of all who believe the inspired record is founded for their future happiness and enjoyment; because, "If Christ be not raised," said Paul to the Corinthians, "your faith is vain; ye are yet in your sins. Then they also which are fallen asleep in Christ are perished" (see I Cor. xv). If the resurrection from the dead be not an important point, or item in our faith, we must confess that we know nothing about it; for if there be no resurrection from the dead, then Christ has not risen; and if Christ has not risen He was not the Son of God; and if He was not the Son of God, there is not nor cannot be a Son of God, if the present book called the Scriptures is true; because the time has gone by when, according to that book, He was to make His appearance. On this subject, however, we are reminded of the words of Peter to the Jewish Sanhedrin, when speaking of Christ, he says that God raised Him from the dead, and we (the apostles) are His witnesses of these things, and so is the Holy Ghost, whom God had given to them that obey Him (see Acts v). So that after the testimony of the Scriptures on this point, the assurance is given by the Holy Ghost, bearing witness to those who obey Him, that Christ Himself has assuredly risen from the dead; and if He has risen from the dead, He will by His power, bring all men to stand before Him: for if He has risen from the dead the bands of the temporal death are broken that the grave has no victory. If then, the grave has no victory, those who keep the sayings of Jesus and obey His teachings have not only a promise of a resurrection from the dead, but an assurance of being admitted into His glorious kingdom; for, He Himself says, "Where I am there also shall my servant be" (see John xii). (HC 2:18–19)

2 Now I understand by this quotation [Moses 7:62], that God clearly manifested to Enoch the redemption which He prepared, by

Resurrection
1 Letter to the brethren scattered from Zion, Kirtland, 22 January 1834.
2 Letter to the elders of the Church, Kirtland, 1 September 1835.

offering the Messiah as a Lamb slain from before the foundation of the world; and by virtue of the same, the glorious resurrection of the Savior, and the resurrection of all the human family, even a resurrection of their corporeal bodies, is brought to pass. (HC 2:260)

3 The doctrines of the resurrection of the dead and the eternal judgment are necessary to preach among the first principles of the Gospel of Jesus Christ. (HC 3:379)

4 Jesus Christ went in body after His resurrection, to minister to resurrected bodies. (HC 4:425)

5 As concerning the resurrection, I will merely say that all men will come from the grave as they lie down, whether old or young; there will not be "added unto their stature one cubit," neither taken from it; all will be raised by the power of God, having spirit in their bodies, and not blood. (HC 4:555)

6 I would esteem it one of the greatest blessings, if I am to be afflicted in this world to have my lot cast where I can find brothers and friends all around me . . . to have the privilege of having our dead buried on the land where God has appointed to gather His Saints together, and where there will be none but Saints, where they may have the privilege of laying their bodies where the Son of Man will make His appearance, and where they may hear the sound of the trump that shall call them forth to behold Him, that in the morn of the resurrection they may come forth in a body, and come up out of their graves and strike hands immediately in eternal glory and felicity, rather than be scattered thousands of miles apart. There is something good and sacred to me in this thing. . . .

I will tell you what I want. If tomorrow I shall be called to lie in yonder tomb, in the morning of the first resurrection let me strike hands with my father, and cry, "My father," and he will say, "My son, my son," as soon as the rock rends and before we come out of our graves. . . .

Resurrection
3 Instructions to the Twelve, Commerce (Nauvoo), 27 June 1839.
4 General conference address, Nauvoo, 3 October 1841.
5 Sabbath address, Nauvoo, 20 March 1842.
6 Remarks upon the death of Lorenzo D. Barnes, Nauvoo, 16 April 1843.

Would you think it strange if I relate what I have seen in vision in relation to this interesting theme? Those who have died in Jesus Christ may expect to enter into all that fruition of joy when they come forth, which they possessed or anticipated here.

So plain was the vision, that I actually saw men, before they had ascended from the tomb, as though they were getting up slowly. They took each other by the hand and said to each other, "My father, my son, my mother, my daughter, my brother, my sister." And when the voice calls for the dead to arise, suppose I am laid by the side of my father, what would be the first joy of my heart? To meet my father, my mother, my brother, my sister; and when they are by my side, I embrace them and they me. . . .

. . . All your losses will be made up to you in the resurrection, provided you continue faithful. By the vision of the Almighty I have seen it. . . .

The expectation of seeing my friends in the morning of the resurrection cheers my soul and makes me bear up against the evils of life. It is like their taking a long journey, and on their return we meet them with increased joy.

God has revealed His Son from the heavens and the doctrine of the resurrection also; and we have a knowledge that those we bury here God will bring up again, clothed upon and quickened by the Spirit of the great God; and what mattereth it whether we lay them down, or we lay down with them, when we can keep them no longer? Let these truths sink down in our hearts, that we may even here begin to enjoy that which shall be in full hereafter. (HC 5:361–62)

7   The spirits in the eternal world are like the spirits in this world. When those have come into this world and received tabernacles, then died and again have risen and received glorified bodies, they will have an ascendency over the spirits who have received no bodies, or kept not their first estate, like the devil. (HC 5:403)

8   Flesh and blood cannot go there; but flesh and bones, quickened by the Spirit of God, can. (HC 6:52)

Resurrection

7   Sabbath address, Nauvoo, 21 May 1843.

8   Remarks upon the death of James Adams, Nauvoo, 9 October 1843. By "there" the Prophet had reference to a resurrected state (see HC 4:555 and 6:366).

9 How consoling to the mourners when they are called to part with a husband, wife, father, mother, child, or dear relative, to know that, although the earthly tabernacle is laid down and dissolved, they shall rise again to dwell in everlasting burnings in immortal glory, not to sorrow, suffer, or die any more, but they shall be heirs of God and joint heirs with Jesus Christ. . . .

You mourners have occasion to rejoice, speaking of the death of Elder King Follett; for your husband and father is gone to wait until the resurrection of the dead—until the perfection of the remainder; for at the resurrection your friend will rise in perfect felicity and go to celestial glory, while many must wait myriads of years before they can receive the like blessings; and your expectations and hopes are far above what man can conceive; for why has God revealed it to us? (HC 6:306, 315)

10 There have been remarks made concerning all men being redeemed from hell; but I say that those who sin against the Holy Ghost cannot be forgiven in this world or in the world to come; they shall die the second death. Those who commit the unpardonable sin are doomed to *Gnolom*—to dwell in hell, worlds without end. As they concocted scenes of bloodshed in this world, so they shall rise to that resurrection which is as the lake of fire and brimstone. Some shall rise to the everlasting burnings of God; for God dwells in everlasting burnings and some shall rise to the damnation of their own filthiness, which is as exquisite a torment as the lake of fire and brimstone. (HC 6:317)

11 "As in Adam all die, even so in Christ shall all be made alive;" all shall be raised from the dead. The Lamb of God hath brought to pass the resurrection, so that all shall rise from the dead.

God Almighty Himself dwells in eternal fire; flesh and blood cannot go there, for all corruption is devoured by the fire. "Our God is a consuming fire." When our flesh is quickened by the Spirit, there will be no blood in this tabernacle. Some dwell in higher glory than others.

. . . All men who are immortal dwell in everlasting burnings. You cannot go anywhere but where God can find you out. All men are born to die, and all men must rise; all must enter eternity. (HC 6:366)

Resurrection
  9 King Follett Discourse, Nauvoo, 7 April 1844.
 10 King Follett Discourse, Nauvoo, 7 April 1844.
 11 Sabbath address, Nauvoo, 12 May 1844.

12 Paul says, "There is one glory of the sun, and another glory of the moon, and another glory of the stars; for one star differeth from another star in glory. So is also the resurrection of the dead." They who obtain a glorious resurrection from the dead, are exalted far above principalities, powers, thrones, dominions and angels, and are expressly declared to be heirs of God and joint heirs with Jesus Christ, all having eternal power. (HC 6:478)

Revelation

1 Whilst thus employed in the work appointed me by my Heavenly Father [arranging and copying the revelations], I received a letter from Oliver Cowdery, the contents of which gave me both sorrow and uneasiness. Not having that letter now in my possession, I cannot of course give it here in full, but merely an extract of the most prominent parts, which I can yet, and expect long to, remember. He wrote to inform me that he had discovered an error in one of the commandments—Book of Doctrine and Covenants: "And truly manifest by their works that they have received of the Spirit of Christ unto a remission of their sins." [See D&C 20:37.]

The above quotation, he said, was erroneous, and added: "I command you in the name of God to erase those words, that no priestcraft be amongst us!"

I immediately wrote to him in reply, in which I asked him by what authority he took upon him to command me to alter or erase, to add to or diminish from, a revelation or commandment from Almighty God.

A few days afterwards I visited him and Mr. Whitmer's family, when I found the family in general of his opinion concerning the words above quoted, and it was not without both labor and perseverance that I could prevail with any of them to reason calmly on the subject. However, Christian Whitmer at length became convinced

---

Resurrection
  12 Sabbath address, Nauvoo, 16 June 1844.

Revelation
  1 Harmony, Pennsylvania, July 1830.

that the sentence was reasonable, and according to Scripture; and finally, with his assistance, I succeeded in bringing, not only the Whitmer family, but also Oliver Cowdery to acknowledge that they had been in error, and that the sentence in dispute was in accordance with the rest of the commandment. And thus was this error rooted out, which having its rise in presumption and rash judgment, was the more particularly calculated (when once fairly understood) to teach each and all of us the necessity of humility and meekness before the Lord, that He might teach us of His ways, that we might walk in His paths, and live by every word that proceedeth forth from His mouth. (HC 1:104–5)

2   To our great grief, however, we soon found that Satan had been lying in wait to deceive, and seeking whom he might devour. Brother Hiram Page had in his possession a certain stone, by which he had obtained certain "revelations" concerning the upbuilding of Zion, the order of the Church, etc., all of which were entirely at variance with the order of God's house, as laid down in the New Testament, as well as in our late revelations. As a conference meeting had been appointed for the 26th day of September, I thought it wisdom not to do much more than to converse with the brethren on the subject, until the conference should meet. Finding, however, that many, especially the Whitmer family and Oliver Cowdery, were believing much in the things set forth by this stone, we thought best to inquire of the Lord concerning so important a matter; and before conference convened, we received the following: [D&C 28] . . .

At length our conference assembled. The subject of the stone previously mentioned was discussed, and after considerable investigation, Brother Page, as well as the whole Church who were present, renounced the said stone, and all things connected therewith, much to our mutual satisfaction and happiness. (HC 1:109–10, 115)

Revelation
2   Fayette, New York, September 1830.

3 Soon after the foregoing revelation was received [D&C 42], a woman came making great pretensions of revealing commandments, laws and other curious matters; and as almost every person has advocates for both theory and practice, in the various notions and projects of the age, it became necessary to inquire of the Lord, when I received the following: [D&C 43]. (*HC* 1:154)

4 *Minutes:* [Joseph Smith] further said that God had often sealed up the heavens because of covetousness in the Church. (*FWR*, p. 23)

5 Respecting the vision you speak of we do not consider ourselves bound to receive any revelation from any one man or woman without his being legally constituted and ordained to that authority, and giving sufficient proof of it.

I will inform you that it is contrary to the economy of God for any member of the Church, or any one, to receive instructions for those in authority, higher than themselves; therefore you will see the impropriety of giving heed to them; but if any person have a vision or a visitation from a heavenly messenger, it must be for his own benefit and instruction; for the fundamental principles, government, and doctrine of the Church are vested in the keys of the kingdom. . . .

. . . And again we never inquire at the hand of God for special revelation only in case of there being no previous revelation to suit the case; and that in a council of High Priests. . . .

It is a great thing to inquire at the hands of God, or to come into His presence; and we feel fearful to approach Him on subjects that are of little or no consequence, to satisfy the queries of individuals, espe-

---

Revelation
3 Kirtland, February 1831. *HC* 1:154 contains the following note: "This woman's name, according to the history of the church kept by John Whitmer, was Hubble. 'She professed to be a prophetess of the Lord, and professed to have many revelations, and knew the Book of Mormon was true, and that she should become a teacher in the church of Christ. She appeared to be very sanctimonious and deceived some who were not able to detect her in her hypocrisy; others, however, had the spirit of discernment and her follies and abominations were manifest.' John Whitmer's *History of the Church*, ch. iii."
4 Minutes of a conference held at Orange, Ohio, 25 October 1831.
5 Letter to one of Jared Carter's brothers, written at the request of Jared Carter, Kirtland, 13 April 1833.

cially about things the knowledge of which men ought to obtain in all sincerity, before God, for themselves, in humility by the prayer of faith; and more especially a Teacher or a High Priest in the Church. (*HC* 1:338, 339)

6   Seeing that the Lord has never given the world to understand, by anything heretofore revealed, that he had ceased forever to speak to his creatures, when sought unto in a proper manner, why should it be thought a thing incredible that he should be pleased to speak again in these last days for their salvation? Perhaps you may be surprised at this assertion, that I should say for the salvation of his creatures in these last days, since we have already in our possession a vast volume of his word, which he has previously given. But you will admit that the word spoken to Noah was not sufficient for Abraham, or it was not required of Abraham to leave the land of his nativity, and seek an inheritance in a strange country upon the word spoken to Noah, but for himself he obtained promises at the hand of the Lord, and walked in that perfection, that he was called the friend of God. Isaac, the promised seed, was not required to rest his hope alone upon the promises made to his father Abraham, but was privileged with the assurance of his approbation, in the sight of Heaven, by the direct voice of the Lord to him. If one man can live upon the revelations given to another, might I not with propriety ask, why the necessity, then, of the Lord's speaking to Isaac as he did, as is recorded in the twenty-sixth chapter of Genesis? For the Lord there repeats, or rather, promises again to perform the oath which he had previously sworn to Abraham; and why this repetition to Isaac? Why was not the first promise as sure for Isaac as it was for Abraham? Was not Isaac Abraham's son? and could he not place implicit confidence in the veracity of his father as being a man of God? Perhaps you may say that he was a very peculiar man, and different from men in these last days, consequently, the Lord favored him with blessings, peculiar and different, as he was different from men of this age. I admit that he was a peculiar man, and not only peculiarly blessed, but greatly blessed. But all the peculiarity that I can discover in the man, or all the difference between him and men in this age, is, that he was more holy and more perfect before God, and came to him with a purer heart, and more faith than men in this day.

Revelation
6   Letter to Silas Smith, the Prophet's uncle, Kirtland, 26 September 1833.

The same might be said on the subject of Jacob's history. Why was it that the Lord spake to him concerning the same promise, after he had made it once to Abraham, and renewed it to Isaac? Why could not Jacob rest contented upon the word spoken to his fathers? When the time of the promise drew nigh for the deliverance of the children of Israel from the land of Egypt, why was it necessary that the Lord should begin to speak to them? The promise or word to Abraham, was, that his seed should serve in bondage, and be afflicted, four hundred years, and after that they should come out with great substance. Why did they not rely upon this promise, and when they had remained in Egypt, in bondage, four hundred years, come out, without waiting for further revelations, but act entirely upon the promise given to Abraham, that they should come out?

Paul said to his Hebrew brethren, that God being more abundantly willing to show unto the heirs of promise the immutability of his counsel, he confirmed it by an oath. He also exhorts them, who, through faith and patience inherit the promises.

Notwithstanding, we (said Paul) have fled for refuge to lay hold upon the hope set before us, which hope we have as an anchor of the soul, both sure and steadfast and which entereth into that within the vail, yet he was careful to press upon them the necessity of continuing on until they, as well as those who then inherited the promises, might have the assurance of their salvation confirmed to them by an oath from the mouth of him who could not lie; for that seemed to be the example anciently, and Paul holds it out to his Hebrew brethren as an object attainable in his day. And why not? I admit that by reading the Scriptures of truth, the saints, in the days of Paul, could learn, beyond the power of contradiction, that Abraham, Isaac, and Jacob had the promise of eternal life confirmed to them by an oath of the Lord, but that promise or oath was no assurance to them of their salvation; but they could, by walking in the footsteps, continuing in the faith of their fathers, obtain, for themselves, an oath for confirmation that they were meet to be partakers of the inheritance with the saints in light.

If the saints, in the days of the apostles, were privileged to take the saints for example, and lay hold of the same promises, and attain to the same exalted privileges of knowing that their names were written in the Lamb's Book of Life, and that they were sealed there as a perpetual memorial before the face of the Most High, will not the same faithfulness, the same purity of heart, and the faith, bring the same assurance of eternal life, and that in the same manner to the

children of men now, in this age of the world? I have no doubt, but
that the holy prophets, and apostles, and saints in ancient days were
saved in the kingdom of God; neither do I doubt but that they held
converse and communion with him while they were in the flesh, as
Paul said to his Corinthian brethren, that the Lord Jesus showed himself to above five hundred saints at one time after his resurrection. Job
said that he knew that his Redeemer lived, and that he should see him
in the flesh in the latter days. I may believe that Enoch walked with
God, and by faith was translated. I may believe that Noah was a perfect man in his generation, and also walked with God. I may believe
that Abraham communed with God, and conversed with angels. I
may believe that Isaac obtained a renewal of the covenant made to
Abraham by the direct voice of the Lord. I may believe that Jacob
conversed with holy angels, and heard the word of his Maker, that he
wrestled with the angel until he prevailed, and obtained a blessing. I
may believe that Elijah was taken to heaven in a chariot of fire with
fiery horses. I may believe that the saints saw the Lord, and conversed
with him face to face after his resurrection. I may believe that the Hebrew church came to Mount Zion, and unto the city of the living
God, the heavenly Jerusalem, and to an innumerable company of angels. I may believe that they looked into eternity, and saw the Judge of
all, and Jesus the Mediator of the New Covenant. But will all this purchase an assurance for me, and waft me to the regions of eternal day,
with my garments spotless, pure and white? Or, must I not rather obtain for myself, by my own faith and diligence in keeping the commandments of the Lord, an assurance of salvation for myself? And
have I not an equal privilege with the ancient saints? And will not the
Lord hear my prayers, and listen to my cries as soon as he ever did
theirs, if I come to him in the manner they did? Or, is he a respecter of
persons? (*HJS*, pp. 233–37)

7 We take the sacred writings into our hands, and admit that they
were given by direct inspiration for the good of man. We believe that
God condescended to speak from the heavens and declare His will
concerning the human family, to give them just and holy laws, to regulate their conduct, and guide them in a direct way, that in due time
He might take them to Himself, and make them joint heirs with His

---

Revelation

7 Letter to the brethren scattered from Zion, Kirtland, 22 January 1834.

Son. But when this fact is admitted, that the immediate will of heaven is contained in the Scriptures, are we not bound as rational creatures to live in accordance to all its precepts? Will the mere admission, that this is the will of heaven ever benefit us if we do not comply with all its teachings? Do we not offer violence to the Supreme Intelligence of heaven, when we admit the truth of its teachings, and do not obey them? Do we not descend below our own knowledge, and the better wisdom which heaven has endowed us with, by such a course of conduct? For these reasons, if we have direct revelations given us from heaven, surely those revelations were never given to be trifled with, without the trifler's incurring displeasure and vengeance upon his own head, if there is any justice in heaven; and that there is must be admitted by every individual who admits the truth and force of God's teachings, His blessings and cursings, as contained in the sacred volume. (HC 2:11)

8 You have given us to understand that there are glaring errors in the revelation, or rather, have shown us the most glaring ones which are not calculated to suit the refinement of the age in which we live, of the great men, &c. We would say, by way of excuse, that we did not think so much of the orthography, or the manner, as we did of the subject matter; as the word of God means what it says, and it is the word of God, as much as Christ was God, although *he* was born in a stable and was rejected by the manner of his birth, notwithstanding he was God. *What a mistake!* (PWJS, p. 315; standardized)

9 It is very difficult for us to communicate to the churches all that God has revealed to us, in consequence of tradition; for we are differently situated from any other people that ever existed upon this earth; consequently those former revelations cannot be suited to our conditions; they were given to other people, who were before us; but in the last days, God was to call a remnant, in which was to be deliverance, as well as in Jerusalem and Zion. Now if God should give no more revelations, where will we find Zion and this remnant? The time is near when desolation is to cover the earth, and then God will have a place of deliverance in His remnant, and in Zion. . . .

Revelation

  8 Letter to Edward Partridge and others in Missouri, Kirtland, 30 March 1834.
  9 Conference of the elders of the Church, Norton, Ohio, 21 April 1834.

Take away the Book of Mormon, and the revelations, and where is our religion? We have none. (HC 2:52)

10 I was this morning introduced to a man from the east. After hearing my name, he remarked that I was nothing but a man, indicating by this expression, that he had supposed that a person to whom the Lord should see fit to reveal His will, must be something more than a man. He seemed to have forgotten the saying that fell from the lips of St. James, that Elias was a man subject to like passions as we are, yet he had such power with God, that He, in answer to his prayers, shut the heavens that they gave no rain for the space of three years and six months; and again, in answer to his prayer, the heavens gave forth rain, and the earth gave forth fruit. Indeed, such is the darkness and ignorance of this generation, that they look upon it as incredible that a man should have any intercourse with his Maker. (HC 2:302)

11 Let us be faithful and silent, brethren, and if God gives you a manifestation, keep it to yourselves; be watchful and prayerful, and you shall have a prelude of those joys that God will pour out on that day. (HC 2:309)

12 It is also the privilege of any officer in this Church to obtain revelations, so far as relates to his particular calling and duty in the Church. All are bound by the principles of virtue and happiness, but one great privilege of the Priesthood is to obtain revelations of the mind and will of God. It is also the privilege of the Melchizedek Priesthood, to reprove, rebuke, and admonish, as well as to receive revelation. (HC 2:477)

13 "Is there anything in the Bible which licenses you to believe in revelation now-a-days?"

Is there anything that does not authorize us to believe so? If there is, we have, as yet, not been able to find it. (HC 3:30)

Revelation

10 Kirtland, 6 November 1835.

11 Instructions to the Twelve, Kirtland, 12 November 1835.

12 Solemn assembly in the Kirtland Temple, 6 April 1837.

13 Answers to questions frequently asked the Prophet, Far West, 8 May 1838.

14 When the heart is sufficiently contrite, then the voice of inspiration steals along and whispers, My son, peace be unto thy soul. (HC 3:293)

15 We are called to hold the keys of the mysteries of those things that have been kept hid from the foundation of the world until now. Some have tasted a little of these things, many of which are to be poured down from heaven upon the heads of babes; yea, upon the weak, obscure and despised ones of the earth. (HC 3:296)

16 There are times coming when God will signify many things which are expedient for the well-being of the Saints; but the times have not yet come, but will come, as fast as there can be found place and reception for them. (HC 3:301–2)

17 The spirit of revelation is in connection with these blessings. A person may profit by noticing the first intimation of the spirit of revelation; for instance, when you feel pure intelligence flowing into you, it may give you sudden strokes of ideas, so that by noticing it, you may find it fulfilled the same day or soon; (i.e.) those things that were presented unto your minds by the Spirit of God, will come to pass; and thus by learning the Spirit of God and understanding it, you may grow into the principle of revelation, until you become perfect in Christ Jesus. (HC 3:381)

18 Do not betray the revelations of God, whether in the Bible, Book of Mormon, or Doctrine and Covenants, or any other that ever was or ever will be given and revealed unto man in this world or that which is to come. Yea, in all your kicking and flounderings, see to it that you do not this thing. (HC 3:385)

Revelation
   14 Letter to the Saints from Liberty Jail, 20–25 March 1839.
   15 Letter to the Saints from Liberty Jail, 20–25 March 1839.
   16 Letter to the Saints from Liberty Jail, 20–25 March 1839.
   17 Instructions to the Twelve, Commerce (Nauvoo), 27 June 1839.
   18 Instructions to the Apostles and Seventies departing for missions to England, Commerce (Nauvoo), 2 July 1839.

19 God has so ordained that when He has communicated, no vision is to be taken but what you see by the seeing of the eye, or what you hear by the hearing of the ear. When you see a vision, pray for the interpretation; if you get not this, shut it up; there must be certainty in this matter. An open vision will manifest that which is more important. Lying spirits are going forth in the earth. There will be great manifestations of spirits, both false and true. (HC 3:391–92)

20 If [Jesus] comes to a little child, He will adapt himself to the language and capacity of a little child. (HC 3:392)

21 It is the privilege of the children of God to come to God and get revelation. . . . When any person receives a vision of heaven, he sees things that he never thought of before. (WJS, pp. 13, 14; standardized)

22 [The Melchizedek Priesthood] is the channel through which all knowledge, doctrine, the plan of salvation, and every important matter is revealed from heaven.

. . . It is the channel through which the Almighty commenced revealing His glory at the beginning of the creation of this earth, and through which He has continued to reveal Himself to the children of men to the present time, and through which He will make known His purposes to the end of time. (HC 4:207)

23 The best way to obtain truth and wisdom is not to ask it from books, but to go to God in prayer, and obtain divine teaching. . . .

Many objections are urged against the Latter-day Saints for not admitting the validity of sectarian baptism, and for withholding fellowship from sectarian churches. Yet to do otherwise would be like putting new wine into old bottles, and putting old wine into new bottles.

Revelation

19 Discourse on the priesthood, given sometime before 8 August 1839, Commerce (Nauvoo). For a discussion on the dating of this discourse, see WJS, p. 22.

20 Discourse on the priesthood, given sometime before 8 August 1839, Commerce (Nauvoo). For a discussion on the dating of this discourse, see WJS, p. 22.

21 Discourse given sometime before 8 August 1839, Commerce (Nauvoo).

22 Article on priesthood read at general conference, Nauvoo, 5 October 1840.

23 General conference address, Nauvoo, 3 October 1841.

What! new revelations in the old churches? New revelations would knock out the bottom of their bottomless pit. New wine into old bottles! The bottles burst and the wine runs out! (HC 4:425, 426)

24 *Report of Wilford Woodruff:* On the subject of revelation, he [Joseph Smith] said, a man would command his son to dig potatoes and saddle his horse, but before he had done either he would tell him to do something else. This is all considered right; but as soon as the Lord gives a commandment and revokes that decree and commands something else, then the Prophet is considered fallen. (HC 4:478)

25 The reason we do not have the secrets of the Lord revealed unto us, is because we do not keep them but reveal them; we do not keep our own secrets, but reveal our difficulties to the world, even to our enemies, then how would we keep the secrets of the Lord? I can keep a secret till Doomsday. (HC 4:479)

26 Unless some person or persons have a communication, or revelation from God, unfolding to them the operation of the spirit, they must eternally remain ignorant of these principles [about the discerning of spirits]; for I contend that if one man cannot understand these things but by the Spirit of God, ten thousand men cannot; it is alike out of the reach of the wisdom of the learned, the tongue of the eloquent, the power of the mighty. And we shall at last have to come to this conclusion, whatever we may think of revelation, that without it we can neither know nor understand anything of God, or the devil; and however unwilling the world may be to acknowledge this principle, it is evident from the multifarious creeds and notions concerning this matter that they understand nothing of this principle, and it is equally as plain that without a divine communication they must remain in ignorance. (HC 4:574)

27 "Christ ascended into heaven, and gave gifts to men; and He gave some Apostles, and some Prophets, and some Evangelists, and some

---

Revelation

24 Meeting of the Twelve at the Prophet's home, Nauvoo, 19 December 1841.
25 Meeting of the Twelve at the Prophet's home, Nauvoo, 19 December 1841.
26 Editorial in the *Times and Seasons*, 1 April 1842.
27 Editorial in the *Times and Seasons*, 1 April 1842.

Pastors and Teachers." And how were Apostles, Prophets, Pastors, Teachers and Evangelists chosen? By prophecy (revelation) and by laying on of hands:—by a divine communication, and a divinely appointed ordinance—through the medium of the Priesthood, organized according to the order of God, by divine appointment. The Apostles in ancient times held the keys of this Priesthood—of the mysteries of the kingdom of God, and consequently were enabled to unlock and unravel all things pertaining to the government of the Church, the welfare of society, the future destiny of men, and the agency, power and influence of spirits; for they could control them at pleasure, bid them depart in the name of Jesus, and detect their mischievous and mysterious operations when trying to palm themselves upon the Church in a religious garb, and militate against the interest of the Church and spread of truth. (HC 4:574)

28 We have also had brethren and sisters who have written revelations, and who have started forward to lead this Church. Such was a young boy in Kirtland, Isaac Russell, of Missouri, and Gladden Bishop, and Oliver Olney of Nauvoo. The boy is now living with his parents who have submitted to the laws of the Church. Mr. Russell stayed in Far West, from whence he was to go to the Rocky Mountains, led by three Nephites; but the Nephites never came, and his friends forsook him, all but some of the blood relations, who have since been nearly destroyed by the mob. Mr. Bishop was tried by the High Council, his papers examined, condemned and burned, and he cut off from the Church. He acknowledged the justice of the decision, and said "that he now saw his error, for if he had been governed by the revelations given before, he might have known that no man was to write revelations for the Church, but Joseph Smith," and begged to be prayed for, and forgiven by the brethren. Mr. Olney has also been tried by the High Council and disfellowshiped, because he would not have his writings tested by the word of God; evidently proving that he loves darkness rather than light, because his deeds are evil. (HC 4:581)

29 A man is saved no faster than he gets knowledge, for if he does not get knowledge, he will be brought into captivity by some evil

---

Revelation

28 Editorial in the *Times and Seasons*, 1 April 1842.

29 Sabbath address, Nauvoo, 10 April 1842.

power in the other world, as evil spirits will have more knowledge, and consequently more power than many men who are on the earth. Hence it needs revelation to assist us, and give us knowledge of the things of God.

What is the reason that the Priests of the day do not get revelation? They ask only to consume it upon their lusts. Their hearts are corrupt, and they cloak their iniquity by saying there are no more revelations. But if any revelations are given of God, they are universally opposed by the priests and Christendom at large; for they reveal their wickedness and abominations. (HC 4:588)

30 The manifestations of the gift of the Holy Ghost, the ministering of angels, or the development of the power, majesty or glory of God were very seldom manifested publicly, and that generally to the people of God, as to the Israelites; but most generally when angels have come, or God has revealed Himself, it has been to individuals in private, in their chamber; in the wilderness or fields, and that generally without noise or tumult. The angel delivered Peter out of prison in the dead of night; came to Paul unobserved by the rest of the crew; appeared to Mary and Elizabeth without the knowledge of others; spoke to John the Baptist whilst the people around were ignorant of it.

When Elisha saw the chariots of Israel and the horsemen thereof, it was unknown to others. When the Lord appeared to Abraham it was at his tent door; when the angels went to Lot, no person knew them but himself, which was the case probably with Abraham and his wife; when the Lord appeared to Moses, it was in the burning bush, in the tabernacle, or in the mountain top; when Elijah was taken in a chariot of fire, it was unobserved by the world; and when he was in a cleft of a rock, there was loud thunder, but the Lord was not in the thunder; there was an earthquake, but the Lord was not in the earthquake; and then there was a still small voice, which was the voice of the Lord, saying, "What doest thou hear, Elijah?" (HC 5:30–31)

31 Spring water tastes best right from the fountain. (WJS, p. 122)

Revelation
30 Editorial in the *Times and Seasons*, 15 June 1842.
31 Sabbath address, Nauvoo, 5 June 1842.

32 We cannot keep all the commandments without first knowing them, and we cannot expect to know all, or more than we now know unless we comply with or keep those we have already received. That which is wrong under one circumstance, may be, and often is, right under another.

God said, "Thou shalt not kill;" at another time He said "Thou shalt utterly destroy." This is the principle on which the government of heaven is conducted—by revelation adapted to the circumstances in which the children of the kingdom are placed. Whatever God requires is right, no matter what it is, although we may not see the reason thereof till long after the events transpire. . . .

. . . Everything that God gives us is lawful and right. (HC 5:135)

33 John Darby came in and said he was going to California with Brewster. I told him I would say, as the Prophet said to Hezekiah, "Go, and prosper; but ye shall not return in peace." Brewster may set out for California, but he will not get there unless somebody shall pick him up by the way, feed him and help him along. Brewster showed me the manuscript he had been writing. I inquired of the Lord, and the Lord told me the book was not true—it was not of Him. If God ever called me, or spake by my mouth, or gave me a revelation, he never gave revelations to that Brewster boy or any of the Brewster race. (HC 5:214)

34 The plea of many in this day is, that we have no right to receive revelations; but if we do not get revelations, we do not have the oracles of God; and if they have not the oracles of God, they are not the people of God. But say you, What will become of the world, or the various professors of religion who do not believe in revelation and the oracles of God as continued to His Church in all ages of the world, when He has a people on earth? I tell you, in the name of Jesus Christ, they will be damned; and when you get into the eternal world, you will find it will be so, they cannot escape the damnation of hell. . . .

. . . Jesus in His teachings says, "Upon this rock I will build my Church, and the gates of hell shall not prevail against it." What rock? Revelation. (HC 5:257, 258)

Revelation
  32 Essay on happiness, Nauvoo, 27 August 1842.
  33 Nauvoo, 31 December 1842.
  34 Sabbath address, Nauvoo, 22 January 1843.

35 I make this broad declaration, that whenever God gives a vision of an image, or beast, or figure of any kind, He always holds Himself responsible to give a revelation or interpretation of the meaning thereof, otherwise we are not responsible or accountable for our belief in it. Don't be afraid of being damned for not knowing the meaning of a vision or figure, if God has not given a revelation or interpretation of the subject. . . .

. . . We never can comprehend the things of God and of heaven, but by revelation. We may spiritualize and express opinions to all eternity; but that is no authority. (HC 5:343, 344)

36 It is my meditation all the day, and more than my meat and drink, to know how I shall make the Saints of God comprehend the visions that roll like an overflowing surge before my mind. (HC 5:362)

37 As Paul said, "the world by wisdom know not God," so the world by speculation are destitute of revelation; and as God in his superior wisdom, has always given his saints, wherever he had any on the earth, the same spirit, and that spirit, as John says, is the true spirit of prophecy, which is the testimony of Jesus, I may safely say that the word Mormon stands independent of the learning and wisdom of this generation. (T&S 4:194)

38 I could explain a hundred fold more than I ever have of the glories of the kingdoms manifested to me in the vision, were I permitted, and were the people prepared to receive them.

The Lord deals with this people as a tender parent with a child, communicating light and intelligence and the knowledge of his ways as they can bear it. (HC 5:402)

39 Where there is no change of priesthood, there is no change of ordinances, says Paul, if God has not changed the ordinances and the priesthood. Howl, ye sectarians! If he has, when and where has He revealed it? Have ye turned revelators? Then why deny revelation?

Revelation
35 General conference address, Nauvoo, 8 April 1843.
36 Remarks upon the death of Lorenzo D. Barnes, Nauvoo, 16 April 1843.
37 Letter to the editor of the *Times and Seasons*, 15 May 1843.
38 Sabbath address, Nauvoo, 21 May 1843.
39 Sabbath address, Nauvoo, 11 June 1843.

Many men will say, "I will never forsake you, but will stand by you at all times." But the moment you teach them some of the mysteries of the kingdom of God that are retained in the heavens and are to be revealed to the children of men when they are prepared for them, they will be the first to stone you and put you to death. It was this same principle that crucified the Lord Jesus Christ, and will cause the people to kill the prophets in this generation. . . .

A man of God should be endowed with wisdom, knowledge, and understanding, in order to teach and lead the people of God. The sectarian priests are blind, and they lead the blind, and they will all fall into the ditch together. They build with hay, wood, and stubble, on the old revelations, without the true priesthood or spirit of revelation. (HC 5:424, 426)

40 I know a man that has been caught up to the third heavens, and can say, with Paul, that we have seen and heard things that are not lawful to utter. (HC 5:556)

41 Believing the Bible to say what it means and mean what it says, and guided by revelation, according to the ancient order of the fathers, to whom came what little light we enjoy, and circumscribed only by the eternal limits of truth, this Church must continue the even tenor of its way. (HC 6:10)

42 Reading the experience of others, or the revelation given to *them*, can never give *us* a comprehensive view of our condition and true relation to God. Knowledge of these things can only be obtained by experience through the ordinances of God set forth for that purpose. Could you gaze into heaven five minutes, you would know more than you would by reading all that ever was written on the subject. . . .

I assure the Saints that truth, in reference to these matters [plan of salvation], can and may be known through the revelations of God in the way of His ordinances, and in answer to prayer. . . .

. . . I anointed [Judge Adams] to the patriarchal power—to receive the keys of knowledge and power, by revelation to himself. He has had

Revelation

40 Sabbath address, Nauvoo, 27 August 1843.

41 Letter to Daniel Rupp, Nauvoo, 7 September 1843.

42 Remarks upon the death of James Adams, Nauvoo, 9 October 1843.

revelations concerning his departure, and has gone to a more important work. (HC 6:50, 51–52)

43 No man can receive the Holy Ghost without receiving revelations. The Holy Ghost is a revelator. (HC 6:58)

44 There are many people assembled here to-day, and throughout the city, and from various parts of the world, who say that they have received to a certainty a portion of the knowledge from God, by revelation, in the way that He has ordained and pointed out.

I shall take the broad ground, then, that we have received a portion of knowledge from God by immediate revelation, and from the same source we can receive all knowledge. (HC 6:183)

45 There are but a very few beings in the world who understand rightly the character of God. The great majority of mankind do not comprehend anything, either that which is past, or that which is to come, as it respects their relationship to God. They do not know, neither do they understand the nature of that relationship; and consequently they know but little above the brute beast, or more than to eat, drink and sleep. This is all man knows about God or His existence, unless it is given by the inspiration of the Almighty.

If a man learns nothing more than to eat, drink and sleep, and does not comprehend any of the designs of God, the beast comprehends the same things. It eats, drinks, sleeps, and knows nothing more about God; yet it knows as much as we, unless we are able to comprehend by the inspiration of Almighty God. . . .

. . . Having a knowledge of God, we begin to know how to approach Him, and how to ask so as to receive an answer.

When we understand the character of God, and know how to come to Him, he begins to unfold the heavens to us, and to tell us all about it. . . .

. . . I can taste the principles of eternal life, and so can you. They are given to me by the revelations of Jesus Christ; and I know that when I tell you these words of eternal life as they are given to me, you

---

Revelation

   43 Sabbath address, Nauvoo, 15 October 1843.
   44 Sabbath address, Nauvoo, 21 January 1844.
   45 King Follett Discourse, Nauvoo, 7 April 1844.

taste them, and I know that you believe them. You say honey is sweet, and so do I. I can also taste the spirit of eternal life. I know that it is good; and when I tell you of these things which were given me by inspiration of the Holy Spirit, you are bound to receive them as sweet, and rejoice more and more.

. . . All things whatsoever God in his infinite wisdom has seen fit and proper to reveal to us, while we are dwelling in mortality, in regard to our mortal bodies, are revealed to us in the abstract, and independent of affinity of this mortal tabernacle, but are revealed to our spirits precisely as though we had no bodies at all; and those revelations which will save our spirits will save our bodies. God reveals them to us in view of no eternal dissolution of the body, or tabernacle. (HC 6:303, 308, 312)

46 When did I ever teach anything wrong from this stand? . . . I never told you I was perfect; but there is no error in the revelations which I have taught. (HC 6:366)

47 All men are liars who say they are of the true Church without the revelations of Jesus Christ and the Priesthood of Melchisedek, which is after the order of the Son of God. (HC 6:478)

48 *Words of Brigham Young:* Joseph said to me in Kirtland, "Brother Brigham, if I was to reveal to this people what the Lord has revealed to me, there is not a man or a woman would stay with me." (JD 9:294)

49 *Words of Howard Coray:* One morning I went as usual into the office to go to work. I found Joseph sitting on one side of a table and Robert B. Thompson on the opposite side, and the understanding I got was that they were hunting in the manuscript of the new translation of the Bible for something on priesthood which Joseph wished to present or have read to the people the next conference. Well, they could not find what they wanted, and Joseph said to Thompson, "Put the manuscript to one side and take some paper, and I will tell you what to write."

Revelation
46 Sabbath address, Nauvoo, 12 May 1844.
47 Sabbath address, Nauvoo, 16 June 1844.
48 Address by Brigham Young, Salt Lake City, 25 May 1862.
49 Sketch of life of Howard Coray, LDS Church Archives.

Brother Thompson took some foolscap paper that was at his elbow and made himself ready for the business. I was seated probably six or eight feet on Joseph's left side, so that I could look almost squarely into the side of his eye. The Spirit of God descended upon him, and a measure of it upon me, insomuch that I could fully realize that God, or the Holy Ghost, was talking through him. I never, neither before or since, have felt as I did on that occasion. (*TK*, p. 135)

Rewards

1   The law of heaven is presented to man, and as such guarantees to all who obey it a reward far beyond any earthly consideration; though it does not promise that the believer in every age should be exempt from the afflictions and troubles arising from different sources in consequence of the acts of wicked men on earth. Still in the midst of all this there is a promise predicated upon the fact that it is the law of heaven, which transcends the law of man, as far as eternal life the temporal; and as the blessings which God is able to give, are greater than those which can be given by man. Then, certainly, if the law of man is binding upon man when acknowledged, how much more must the law of heaven be! And as much as the law of heaven is more perfect than the law of man, so much greater must be the reward if obeyed. The law of man promises safety in temporal life; but the law of God promises that life which is eternal, even an inheritance at God's own right hand, secure from all the powers of the wicked one. (HC 2:7–8)

2   It is a duty which every Saint ought to render to his brethren freely—to always love them, and ever succor them. To be justified before God we must love one another: we must overcome evil; we must visit the fatherless and the widow in their affliction, and we must keep ourselves unspotted from the world; for such virtues flow from the great fountain of pure religion. Strengthening our faith by adding every good quality that adorns the children of the blessed Jesus, we can pray

---

Rewards
1   Letter to the brethren scattered from Zion, Kirtland, 22 January 1834.
2   Letter to the Saints in Missouri published in the *Messenger and Advocate*, June 1835.

in the season of prayer; we can love our neighbor as ourselves, and be faithful in tribulation, knowing that the reward of such is greater in the kingdom of heaven. What a consolation! What a joy! Let me live the life of the righteous, and let my reward be like this! . . .

. . . Do good and work righteousness with an eye single to the glory of God, and you shall reap your reward when the Lord recompenses every one according to his work. (HC 2:229–30)

3   You shall be rewarded according to your deeds. (HC 5:136)

Riches
See also POOR

1   In the last [conference session] which was held at Brother Johnson's, in Hiram, after deliberate consideration, in consequence of the book of revelations, now to be printed, being the foundation of the Church in these last days, and a benefit to the world, showing that the keys of the mysteries of the kingdom of our Savior are again entrusted to man; and the riches of eternity within the compass of those who are willing to live by every word that proceedeth out of the mouth of God—therefore the conference voted that they prize the revelations to be worth to the Church the riches of the whole earth, speaking temporally. The great benefits to the world which result from the Book of Mormon and the revelations which the Lord has seen fit in His infinite wisdom to grant unto us for our salvation, and for the salvation of all that will believe, were duly appreciated. (HC 1:235–36)

2   To devote your time and abilities in the cause of truth and a suffering people may not be the means of exalting you in the eyes of this generation, or securing you the riches of the world, yet by so doing you may rely on the approval of Jehovah, "that blessing which maketh rich and addeth no sorrow." (HC 4:177)

Rewards
    3   Essay on happiness, Nauvoo, 27 August 1842.

Riches
    1   Hiram, Ohio, 12 November 1831.
    2   Letter to John C. Bennett, 8 August 1840, bidding him welcome to Nauvoo.

Righteousness

1   Finally, in these critical times, be careful; call on the Lord day and night; beware of pride; beware of false brethren, who will creep in among you to spy out your liberties. Awake to righteousness, and sin not; let your light shine, and show yourselves workmen that need not be ashamed, rightly dividing the word of truth. Apply yourselves diligently to study, that your minds may be stored with all necessary information. (*HC* 1:468–69)

2   The other class [as contrasted to the obedient] were a set of individuals who disregarded every principle of justice and equity; and this is demonstrated from the fact, that when just laws were issued by the king, which were perfectly equitable, they were so lost to a sense of righteousness that they disregarded those laws, notwithstanding an obedience to them would have produced at the time, as regards their own personal comfort and advantage, the happiest result possible. They were entirely destitute of harmony and virtue, so much so that virtuous laws they despised. They had proven themselves unworthy a place in the joys of the prince, because they had for a series of years lived in open violation of his government. (*HC* 2:10)

3   The praise of men, or the honor of this world, is of no benefit; but if a man is respected in his calling, and considered to be a man of righteousness, the truth may have an influence, many times, by which means they may teach the gospel with success, and lead men unto the kingdom of heaven. (*PJS* 1:25)

4   Righteousness must be the aim of the Saints in all things, and when the covenants are published, they will learn that great things

---

Righteousness
1   Letter to the elders of the Church, published in *The Evening and the Morning Star*, Kirtland, December 1833.
2   Letter to the brethren scattered from Zion, Kirtland, 22 January 1834.
3   The Prophet assembled with Oliver Cowdery, Sidney Rigdon, and Frederick G. Williams to ordain Oliver Cowdery to the office of Assistant President of the Church, 5 December 1834.
4   Letter to the Saints in Missouri published in the *Messenger and Advocate*, June 1835.

must be expected from them. Do good and work righteousness with an eye single to the glory of God. (HC 2:229)

5   Darkness prevails at this time as it did at the time Jesus Christ was about to be crucified. The powers of darkness strove to obscure the glorious Sun of righteousness, that began to dawn upon the world, and was soon to burst in great blessings upon the heads of the faithful; and let me tell you, brethren, that great blessings await us at this time, and will soon be poured out upon us, if we are faithful in all things, for we are even entitled to greater spiritual blessings than they were, because they had Christ in person with them, to instruct them in the great plan of salvation. His personal presence we have not, therefore we have need of greater faith, on account of our peculiar circumstances; and I am determined to do all that I can to uphold you, although I may do many things inadvertently that are not right in the sight of God. (HC 2:308)

6   Brethren, from henceforth, let truth and righteousness prevail and abound in you; and in all things be temperate; abstain from drunkenness, and from swearing, and from all profane language, and from everything which is unrighteous or unholy; also from enmity, and hatred, and covetousness, and from every unholy desire. Be honest one with another, for it seems that some have come short of these things, and some have been uncharitable, and have manifested greediness because of their debts towards those who have been persecuted and dragged about with chains without cause, and imprisoned. . . .

Remember that whatsoever measure you mete out to others, it shall be measured to you again. (HC 3:233)

7   Iniquity will hide its hoary head, Satan will be bound, and the works of darkness destroyed; righteousness will be put to the line, and judgment to the plummet, and "he that fears the Lord will alone be exalted in that day." . . .

. . . As God's people, under His direction, and obedient to His law, we may grow up in righteousness and truth; that when His purposes

---

Righteousness
5   Instructions to the Twelve, Kirtland, 12 November 1835.
6   Letter to the Saints from Liberty Jail, 16 December 1838.
7   Editorial in the *Times and Seasons*, 15 July 1842.

shall be accomplished, we may receive an inheritance among those that are sanctified. (*HC* 5:64, 66)

8   There is one thing under the sun which I have learned and that is that the righteousness of man is sin because it exacteth over much; nevertheless, the righteousness of God is just, because it exacteth nothing at all, but sendeth the rain on the just and the unjust, seed time and harvest, for all of which man is ungrateful. (*TPJS*, p. 317)

9   Righteousness is not that which men esteem holiness. That which the world call righteousness I have not any regard for. To be righteous is to be just and merciful. (*WJS*, p. 206)

10   Those who feel desirous of sowing the seeds of discord will be disappointed on this occasion. It is our purpose to build up and establish the principles of righteousness, and not to break down and destroy. (*HC* 6:288)

Rocky Mountains

1   Passed over the river to Montrose, Iowa, in company with General Adams, Colonel Brewer, and others, and witnessed the installation of the officers of the Rising Sun Lodge Ancient York Masons, at Montrose, by General James Adams, Deputy Grand-Master of Illinois. While the Deputy Grand-Master was engaged in giving the requisite instructions to the Master-elect, I had a conversation with a number of brethren in the shade of the building on the subject of our persecutions in Missouri and the constant annoyance which has followed us since we were driven from that state. I prophesied that the Saints would continue to suffer much affliction and would be driven to the

Righteousness
  8   Proverbs of the Prophet Joseph Smith, Nauvoo, 1843. Manuscript history, LDS Church Archives.
  9   Sabbath address, Nauvoo, 21 May 1843, as reported by Martha Jane Knowlton Coray.
10   General conference address, Nauvoo, 5 April 1844.

Rocky Mountains
  1   Montrose, Iowa, 6 August 1842.

Rocky Mountains, many would apostatize, others would be put to death by our persecutors or lose their lives in consequence of exposure or disease, and some of you will live to go and assist in making settlements and build cities and see the Saints become a mighty people in the midst of the Rocky Mountains. (HC 5:85)

2 *Words of Anson Call:* On the 14th of July, 1843 [6 August 1842?], with quite a number of his brethren, the Prophet crossed the Mississippi River to the town of Montrose, to be present at the installment of the Masonic Lodge of the "Rising Sun." A block schoolhouse had been prepared with shade in front, under which was a barrel of ice water.

Joseph, as he was tasting the cold water, warned the brethren not to be too free with it. With the tumbler still in his hand, he prophesied that the Saints would yet go to the Rocky Mountains. Said he, "This water tastes much like that of the crystal streams that are running from the snow-capped mountains."

I had before seen him in a vision, and now saw his countenance change to white; not the deadly white of a bloodless face, but a living, brilliant white. He seemed absorbed in gazing at something at a great distance, and said, "I am gazing upon the valleys of those mountains."

This was followed by a vivid description of the scenery of these mountains, as I have since become acquainted with it. Pointing to Shadrach Roundy and others, he said, "There are some men here who shall do a great work in that land."

Pointing to me, he said, "There is Anson. He shall go and shall assist in building up cities from one end of the country to the other, and you (rather extending the idea to all those he had spoken of) shall perform as great a work as has been done by man, so that the nations of the earth shall be astonished, and many of them will be gathered in that land and assist in building cities and temples, and Israel shall be made to rejoice."

It is impossible to represent in words the grandeur of Joseph's appearance, his beautiful descriptions of this land, and his wonderful prophetic utterances as they emanated from the glorious inspirations

---

Rocky Mountains

2 Journal of Anson Call, apparently describing the Prophet's visit to Montrose, Iowa, on 6 August 1842, LDS Church Archives. See also *HC* 5:85–86 footnote.

that overshadowed him. There was a force and power in his exclamations of which the following is but a faint echo: "Oh the beauty of those snow-capped mountains! The cool refreshing streams that are running down through those mountain gorges!"

Then looking in another direction, as if there was a change of locality: "Oh the scenes that this people will pass through! The dead that will lie between here and there."

Then turning in another direction as if the scene had again changed: "Oh the apostasy that will take place before my brethren reach that land! But the priesthood shall prevail over its enemies, triumph over the devil and be established upon the earth, never more to be thrown down!" (*TK*, pp. 106–7)

3   I instructed the Twelve Apostles to send out a delegation and investigate the locations of California and Oregon, and hunt out a good location, where we can remove to after the temple is completed, and where we can build a city in a day, and have a government of our own, get up into the mountains, where the devil cannot dig us out, and live in a healthful climate, where we can live as old as we have a mind to. (HC 6:222)

4   Met with the Twelve in the assembly room concerning the Oregon and California Expedition; Hyrum and Sidney present. I told them I wanted an exploration of all that mountain country. Perhaps it would be best to go direct to Santa Fe. "Send twenty-five men: let them preach the Gospel wherever they go. Let that man go that can raise $500, a good horse and mule, a double barrel gun, one-barrel rifle, and the other smooth bore, a saddle and bridle, a pair of revolving pistols, bowie-knife, and a good sabre. Appoint a leader, and let them beat up for volunteers. I want every man that goes to be a king and a priest. When he gets on the mountains he may want to talk with his God; when with the savage nations have power to govern, &c. If we don't get volunteers, wait till after the election." (HC 6:224)

5   *Words of Joseph Lee Robinson*: A pioneer company was organized to search out a land of promise for the Latter-day Saints in the West. The Prophet Joseph had been very anxious to get this people into the

---

Rocky Mountains
3   Nauvoo, 20 February 1844.
4   Nauvoo, 23 February 1844.
5   Journal of Joseph Lee Robinson, LDS Church Archives.

Rocky Mountains. He said at one time he wanted temples built all over the Rocky Mountains. (*TK*, p. 165)

6 *Words of Bathsheba W. Smith:* The Prophet said we would come to the Rocky Mountains, and he had a company of young men selected to hunt a location for a home for the Saints. I heard of it when we were in Illinois, and I remember an old lady coming in and talking to Mother about what Joseph, the Prophet, had said, that we would be in the Rocky Mountains sometime. I said I would like the time to come soon. I would like to get away from our enemies. She gave me a right good scolding, saying it was terrible to think of going to the Rocky Mountains. (*TK*, p. 124)

7 I gave some important instructions, and prophesied that within five years we should be out of the power of our old enemies, whether they were apostates or of the world; and told the brethren to record it, that when it comes to pass they need not say they had forgotten the saying. (HC 6:225)

8 Present—Joseph Smith, Hyrum Smith, Brigham Young, Heber C. Kimball, Willard Richards, Parley P. Pratt, Orson Pratt, John Taylor, George A. Smith, William W. Phelps, John M. Bernhisel, Lucien Woodworth, George Miller, Alexander Badlam, Peter Haws, Erastus Snow, Reynolds Cahoon, Amos Fielding, Alpheus Cutler, Levi Richards, Newel K. Whitney, Lorenzo D. Wasson, and William Clayton, whom I organized into a special council, to take into consideration the subject matter contained in the above letters [from Lyman Wight and George Miller, suggesting that the Church move to the southwest], and also the best policy for this people to adopt to obtain their rights from the nation and insure protection for themselves and children; and to secure a resting place in the mountains, or some uninhabited region, where we can enjoy the liberty of conscience guaranteed to us by the Constitution of our country, rendered doubly sacred by the precious blood of our fathers, and denied to us by the present authorities, who have smuggled themselves into power in the States and Nation. (HC 6:260–61)

Rocky Mountains

6 Recollection of Bathsheba W. Smith, published in the *Young Woman's Journal*, December 1905.
7 Nauvoo, 25 February 1844.
8 Special council meeting, Nauvoo, 11 March 1844.

9   If God ever spake by any man, it will not be five years before this city is in ashes and we in our graves, unless we go to Oregon, California or some other place, if the city does not put down everything which tends to mobocracy, and put down murderers, bogus-makers, and scoundrels. (HC 6:438)

10 *History Entry:* About 9 p.m. Hyrum came out of the Mansion and gave his hand to Reynolds Cahoon, at the same time saying, "A company of men are seeking to kill my brother Joseph, and the Lord has warned him to flee to the Rocky Mountains to save his life. Good-by, Brother Cahoon, we shall see you again." In a few minutes afterwards Joseph came from his family. His tears were flowing fast. He held a handkerchief to his face, and followed after Brother Hyrum without uttering a word. (HC 6:547)

11 *Words of Andrew J. Stewart:* I returned to Nauvoo, June 10, [1844,] to find all the people excited over the destroying of the *Nauvoo Expositor*. I went immediately to the Prophet to learn how and where I was to join Brigham Young. The Prophet said he was glad I had come, but he wanted to change my mission, and take me with him to find a place for the Saints. "For," he said, "the Saints could not build up the Church in the States." They would have to go and find a place in the mountains, where they could find a place to live in peace, and in five years they would not be disturbed or driven away again. He said he had a company made up, but he wanted me, especially, as I had been west on the Indian Land to the Missouri River. . . .

During the time I stayed in the city, I called on the Prophet every day, and was introduced to some of the company who had agreed to go with him. I was surprised that he would have to go into the mountains, or wilderness, and leave that great city and the Temple that was being built. He was eager to get the Temple built and give endowments before we left.

The plan the Prophet proposed was this: I was to go home to Fox River, fifty-five miles west, on the road from Nauvoo to the mountains, take the horse I had given him, and get ready. He would cross

---

Rocky Mountains

   9   Proceedings of the city council against the *Nauvoo Expositor*, 8 June 1844.
   10 Nauvoo, 22 June 1844.
   11 Journal of Andrew J. Stewart, LDS Church Archives.

over the Mississippi River with a few men, come to my place the first night, and the next night go on, for at that time it was only fifteen miles to the Indian Land boundary which was outside of the United States. He said he would start in about a week, and the company could come on later. This was on June 12, 1844.

I went home, taking the horse with me, and got ready for the trip to the mountains. Later, in the evening of June 22, Joseph and Hyrum Smith, and Willard Richards left Nauvoo and crossed the Mississippi River to find the place for the Saints. I heard that the Prophet had crossed the river for the mountains, and expected him every night until I heard that he was martyred. (TK, p. 179)

Sacrament

1   We sanction the decision of the Bishop and his council, in relation to [the teaching of] this doctrine [that the devil, his angels, or the sons of perdition could be restored] being a bar to communion. (HC 1:366)

2   The council adjourned to the day following, March 1st, when, after attending the funeral of Seth Johnson, several who had recently been baptized, were confirmed, and the sacrament was administered to the Church. Previous to the administration, I spoke of the propriety of this institution in the Church, and urged the importance of doing it with acceptance before the Lord, and asked, How long do you suppose a man may partake of this ordinance unworthily, and the Lord not withdraw His Spirit from him? How long will he thus trifle with sacred things, and the Lord not give him over to the buffetings of Satan until the day of redemption! The Church should know if they are unworthy from time to time to partake, lest the servants of God be forbidden to administer it. Therefore our hearts ought to be humble, and we to repent of our sins, and put away evil from among us. (HC 2:204)

Sacrament
  1   Letter to the brethren in Zion, Kirtland, 25 June 1833.
  2   A special meeting held to ordain members of the First Quorum of Seventy, 1 March 1835.

3   In the afternoon administered the Lord's Supper, as we are wont to do on every Sabbath, and the Lord blessed our souls with the out-pouring of His Spirit, and we were made to rejoice in His goodness. (HC 2:408)

4   In the afternoon, I assisted the other Presidents in distributing the Lord's Supper to the Church, receiving it from the Twelve, whose privilege it was to officiate at the sacred desk this day. (HC 2:435)

5   I spoke, and admonished the members of the Church individually to set their houses in order, to make clean the inside of the platter, and to meet on the next Sabbath to partake of the Sacrament, in order that by our obedience to the ordinances, we might be enabled to prevail with God against the destroyer, and that the sick might be healed. (HC 4:4–5)

Sacrifice

1   Let us here observe, that a religion that does not require the sacri-fice of all things never has power sufficient to produce the faith neces-sary unto life and salvation; for, from the first existence of man, the faith necessary unto the enjoyment of life and salvation never could be obtained without the sacrifice of all earthly things. It was through this sacrifice, and this only, that God has ordained that men should enjoy eternal life; and it is through the medium of the sacrifice of all earthly things that men do actually know that they are doing the things that are well pleasing in the sight of God. When a man has of-fered in sacrifice all that he has for the truth's sake, not even with-

---

Sacrament
    3   Kirtland, 20 March 1836.
    4   Solemn assembly in the Kirtland Temple, 30 March 1836.
    5   Sabbath address, Commerce (Nauvoo), 28 July 1839.

Sacrifice
    1   Lectures on Faith, delivered to a school of the elders, Kirtland, December 1834. Although the Lectures on Faith were not written only by Joseph Smith, he reviewed them carefully and prepared them for publication (see Larry E. Dahl and Charles D. Tate, Jr., eds., *The Lectures on Faith in Histor-ical Perspective*, p. 10).

holding his life, and believing before God that he has been called to make this sacrifice because he seeks to do his will, he does know, most assuredly, that God does and will accept his sacrifice and offering, and that he has not, nor will not seek his face in vain. Under these circumstances, then, he can obtain the faith necessary for him to lay hold on eternal life. (*LF* 6:7)

2   Brethren, some of you are angry with me, because you did not fight in Missouri; but let me tell you, God did not want you to fight. He could not organize His kingdom with twelve men to open the Gospel door to the nations of the earth, and with seventy men under their direction to follow in their tracks, unless He took them from a body of men who had offered their lives, and who had made as great a sacrifice as did Abraham. Now the Lord has got His Twelve and His Seventy, and there will be other quorums of Seventies called, who will make the sacrifice, and those who have not made their sacrifices and their offerings now, will make them hereafter. (*HC* 2:182)

3   *Words of Alexander McRae:* During this time, some of our brethren spoke of our being in great danger; and I confess I felt that we were. But Brother Joseph told them "not to fear, that not a hair of their heads should be hurt, and that they should not lose any of their things, even to a bridle, saddle, or blanket; that everything should be restored to them; they had offered their lives for us and the Gospel; that it was necessary the Church should offer a sacrifice, and the Lord accepted the offering." (*HC* 3:258)

4   Therefore let those who can freely make a sacrifice of their time, their talents, and their property, for the prosperity of the kingdom, and for the love they have to the cause of truth, bid adieu to their homes and pleasant places of abode, and unite with us in the great

---

Sacrifice
2   Address to the elders given soon after the calling of the First Quorum of Seventy (the first such quorum in this dispensation), as reported by Joseph Young in his "History of the Organization of the Seventies," Kirtland, February 1835.
3   Excerpt from a letter to the *Deseret News* (2 November 1854) from Alexander McRae in which he quotes Joseph Smith in Liberty Jail, February 1839.
4   Proclamation of the First Presidency, Nauvoo, 15 January 1841.

work of the last days, and share in the tribulation, that they may ultimately share in the glory and triumph. (HC 4:273)

5   Never since the foundation of this Church was laid, have we seen
manifested a greater willingness to comply with the requisitions of Jehovah, a more ardent desire to do the will of God, more strenuous exertions used, or greater sacrifices made than there have been since the
Lord said, "Let the Temple be built by the tithing of my people." (HC
4:609)

6   The sacrifice required of Abraham in the offering up of Isaac,
shows that if a man would attain to the keys of the kingdom of an
endless life, he must sacrifice all things. (HC 5:555)

Sacrifice of Animals

1   But that man was not able himself to erect a system, or plan with
power sufficient to free him from a destruction which awaited him, is
evident from the fact that God, as before remarked, prepared a sacrifice in the gift of His own Son who should be sent in due time, to prepare a way, or open a door through which man might enter into the
Lord's presence, whence he had been cast out for disobedience. From
time to time these glad tidings were sounded in the ears of men in different ages of the world down to the time of Messiah's coming. By
faith in this atonement or plan of redemption, Abel offered to God a
sacrifice that was accepted, which was the firstlings of the flock. Cain
offered of the fruit of the ground, and was not accepted, because he
could not do it in faith, he could have no faith, or could not exercise
faith contrary to the plan of heaven. It must be shedding the blood of
the Only Begotten to atone for man; for this was the plan of redemption, and without the shedding of blood was no remission; and as the
sacrifice was instituted for a type, by which man was to discern the

---

Sacrifice
5   Editorial in the *Times and Seasons*, 2 May 1842.
6   Sabbath address, Nauvoo, 27 August 1843.

Sacrifice of Animals
1   Letter to the brethren scattered from Zion, Kirtland, 22 January 1834.

great Sacrifice which God had prepared; to offer a sacrifice contrary to that, no faith could be exercised, because redemption was not purchased in that way, nor the power of atonement instituted after that order; consequently Cain could have no faith; and whatsoever is not of faith, is sin. But Abel offered an acceptable sacrifice, by which he obtained witness that he was righteous, God Himself testifying of his gifts. Certainly, the shedding of the blood of a beast could be beneficial to no man, except it was done in imitation, or as a type, or explanation of what was to be offered through the gift of God Himself; and this performance done with an eye looking forward in faith on the power of that great Sacrifice for a remission of sins. But however various may have been, and may be at the present time, the opinions of men respecting the conduct of Abel, and the knowledge which he had on the subject of atonement, it is evident in our minds, that he was instructed more fully in the plan than what the Bible speaks of, for how could he offer a sacrifice in faith, looking to God for a remission of his sins in the power of the great atonement, without having been previously instructed in that plan? And further, if he was accepted of God, what were the ordinances performed further than the offering of the firstlings of the flock?

It is said by Paul in his letter to the Hebrew brethren, that Abel obtained witness that he was righteous, God testifying of his gifts. To whom did God testify of the gifts of Abel, was it to Paul? We have very little on this important subject in the forepart of the Bible. But it is said that Abel himself obtained witness that he was righteous. Then certainly God spoke to him: indeed, it is said that God talked with him; and if He did, would He not, seeing that Abel was righteous, deliver to him the whole plan of the Gospel? And is not the Gospel the news of the redemption? How could Abel offer a sacrifice and look forward with faith on the Son of God for a remission of his sins, and not understand the Gospel? The mere shedding of the blood of beasts or offering anything else in sacrifice, could not procure a remission of sins, except it were performed in faith of something to come; if it could, Cain's offering must have been as good as Abel's. . . . The ordinance or institution of offering blood in sacrifice, was only designed to be performed till Christ was offered up and shed His blood—as said before—that man might look forward in faith to that time. . . . Our friends may say, perhaps, that there were never any ordinances except those of offering sacrifices before the coming of Christ, and that it could not be possible before the Gospel to have been administered while the law of sacrifices of blood was in force. But we will recollect that Abraham offered sacrifice, and notwithstanding this, had the Gospel preached to him. That the offering of sacrifice was only to point the mind forward to Christ, we infer from these remarkable words of Jesus to the Jews: "Your Father Abraham rejoiced to see my day: and he saw it, and was glad" (John viii:56). So, then, because the ancients offered sacrifice it did not hinder their hearing the Gospel; but served, as we said before, to open their eyes, and enable them to look forward to the time of the coming of the Savior, and rejoice in His redemption. (HC 2:15–16, 17)

2   It will be necessary here to make a few observations on the doctrine set forth in the above quotation [Malachi 3:3], and it is generally supposed that sacrifice was entirely done away when the Great Sacrifice {i.e., the sacrifice of the Lord Jesus} was offered up, and that there will be no necessity for the ordinance of sacrifice in future: but those who assert this are certainly not acquainted with the duties, privileges and authority of the priesthood, or with the Prophets.

The offering of sacrifice has ever been connected and forms a part of the duties of the Priesthood. It began with the Priesthood, and will be continued until after the coming of Christ, from generation to generation. We frequently have mention made of the offering of sacrifice by the servants of the Most High in ancient days, prior to the law of Moses; which ordinances will be continued when the Priesthood is restored with all its authority, power and blessings. . . .

These sacrifices, as well as every ordinance belonging to the Priesthood, will, when the Temple of the Lord shall be built, and the sons of Levi be purified, be fully restored and attended to in all their powers, ramifications, and blessings. This ever did and ever will exist when the powers of the Melchisedic Priesthood are sufficiently manifest; else how can the restitution of all things spoken of by the holy Prophets be brought to pass? It is not to be understood that the law of Moses will be established again with all its rites and variety of ceremonies; this has never been spoken of by the Prophets; but those things which existed prior to Moses' day, namely, sacrifice, will be continued.

It may be asked by some, what necessity for sacrifice, since the

---

Sacrifice of Animals
 2   Article on priesthood read at general conference, Nauvoo, 5 October 1840.

Great Sacrifice was offered? In answer to which, if repentance, baptism, and faith existed prior to the days of Christ, what necessity for them since that time? The Priesthood has descended in a regular line from father to son, through their succeeding generations. (HC 4:211–12)

3   *Words of Oliver B. Huntington:* I heard the Prophet reply to the question: "Will there ever be any more offering of sheep and heifers and bullocks upon altars, as used to be required of Israel?"

He said: "Yes, there will; for there were never any rites, ordinances of laws in the priesthood of any gospel dispensation upon this earth but what will have to be finished and perfected in this last dispensation of time—the dispensation of all dispensations." (*TK,* p. 62)

Saints

1   And again, the process of laboring with members: We are to deal with them precisely as the Scriptures direct. If thy brother trespass against thee, take him between him and thee alone; and, if he make thee satisfaction, thou hast saved thy brother; and if not, proceed to take another with thee, etc., and when there is no Bishop, they are to be tried by the voice of the Church; and if an Elder, or a High Priest be present, he is to take the lead in managing the business; but if not, such as have the highest authority should preside. (HC 1:338–39)

2   When I contemplate the rapidity with which the great and glorious day of the coming of the Son of Man advances, when He shall come to receive His Saints unto Himself, where they shall dwell in His presence, and be crowned with glory and immortality. . . . I cry out in my heart, What manner of persons ought we to be in all holy conversation and godliness! (HC 1:442)

Sacrifice of Animals
   3   Recollection of Oliver B. Huntington, published in the *Young Woman's Journal,* March 1893.

Saints
   1   Letter to one of Jared Carter's brothers, written at the request of Jared Carter, Kirtland, 13 April 1833.
   2   Letter to Moses C. Nickerson, written from Kirtland, 19 November 1833.

3   It is a duty which every Saint ought to render to his brethren freely—to always love them, and ever succor them. To be justified before God we must love one another: we must overcome evil; we must visit the fatherless and the widow in their affliction, and we must keep ourselves unspotted from the world: for such virtues flow from the great fountain of pure religion. Strengthening our faith by adding every good quality that adorns the children of the blessed Jesus, we can pray in the season of prayer; we can love our neighbor as ourselves, and be faithful in tribulation, knowing that the reward of such is greater in the kingdom of heaven. What a consolation! What a joy! Let me live the life of the righteous, and let my reward be like this! (HC 2:229)

4   Explained concerning the coming of the Son of Man; also that it is a false idea that the Saints will escape all the judgments, whilst the wicked suffer; for all flesh is subject to suffer, and "the righteous shall hardly escape;" still many of the Saints will escape, for the just shall live by faith; yet many of the righteous shall fall prey to disease, to pestilence, etc., by reason of the weakness of the flesh, and yet be saved in the Kingdom of God. (HC 4:11)

5   If you will put away from your midst all evil speaking, backbiting, and ungenerous thoughts and feelings: humble yourselves, and cultivate every principle of virtue and love, then will the blessings of Jehovah rest upon you, and you will yet see good and glorious days; peace will be within your gates, and prosperity in your borders; which may our heavenly Father grant in the name of Jesus Christ, is the prayer of yours in the bonds of the covenant. (HC 4:226)

6   Let the Saints remember that great things depend on their individual exertion, and that they are called to be co-workers with us and the Holy Spirit in accomplishing the great work of the last days; and

---

Saints

   3   Letter to the Saints in Missouri published in the *Messenger and Advocate*, June 1835.
   4   Sabbath address, Commerce (Nauvoo), 29 September 1839.
   5   Letter to the Saints in Kirtland, written from Nauvoo, 19 October 1840.
   6   Letter to the Twelve in England, Nauvoo, 15 December 1840. The placement of this letter in *HC* implies that it was written in October 1840, but actually it was written on 15 December 1840 (see *PWJS*, p. 480).

in consideration of the extent, the blessings and glories of the same, let every selfish feeling be not only buried, but annihilated; and let love to God and man predominate, and reign triumphant in every mind, that their hearts may become like unto Enoch's of old, and comprehend all things, present, past and future, and come behind in no gift, waiting for the coming of the Lord Jesus Christ. (HC 4:230–31)

7 The Saints should be a select people, separate from all the evils of the world—choice, virtuous, and holy. The Lord was going to make of the Church of Jesus Christ a kingdom of Priests, a holy people, a chosen generation, as in Enoch's day, having all the gifts as illustrated to the Church in Paul's epistles and teachings to the churches in his day—that it is the privilege of each member to live long and enjoy health. (HC 4:570)

8 We have thieves among us, adulterers, liars, hypocrites. If God should speak from heaven, he would command you not to steal, not to commit adultery, not to covet, nor deceive, but be faithful over a few things. As far as we degenerate from God, we descend to the devil and lose knowledge, and without knowledge we cannot be saved, and while our hearts are filled with evil, and we are studying evil, there is no room in our hearts for good, or studying good. Is not God good? Then you be good; if He is faithful, then you be faithful. Add to your faith virtue, to virtue knowledge, and seek for every good thing. (HC 4:588)

9 The cause of God is one common cause, in which the Saints are alike all interested; we are all members of the one common body, and all partake of the same spirit, and are baptized into one baptism and possess alike the same glorious hope. The advancement of the cause of God and the building up of Zion is as much one man's business as another's. The only difference is, that one is called to fulfill one duty, and another another duty; "but if one member suffers, all the members suffer with it, and if one member is honored all the rest rejoice with it, and the eye cannot say to the ear, I have no need of thee, nor the

Saints

7   Remarks to the Relief Society, Nauvoo, 30 March 1842.

8   Sabbath address, Nauvoo, 10 April 1842.

9   Editorial in the *Times and Seasons*, 2 May 1842.

head to the foot, I have no need of thee;" party feelings, separate interests, exclusive designs should be lost sight of in the one common
cause, in the interest of the whole. (*HC* 4:609)

10 There has always been, in every age of the church those who have
been opposed to the principles of virtue, who have loved the gain of
this present world, followed the principles of unrighteousness, and
have been the enemies of truth; hence Paul speaks of certain brethren
who "coveted the wages of this present world.". . .

. . . We know that the "net will gather together of every kind,
good and bad," that "the wheat and tares must grow together until the
harvest," and that even at the last there will be five foolish as well as
five wise virgins. (*T&S* 3:868)

11 I see no faults in the Church, and therefore let me be resurrected
with the Saints, whether I ascend to heaven or descend to hell, or go
to any other place. And if we go to hell, we will turn the devils out of
doors and make a heaven of it. Where this people are, there is good
society. What do we care where we are, if the society be good? (*HC*
5:517)

12 I have tried for a number of years to get the minds of the Saints
prepared to receive the things of God; but we frequently see some of
them, after suffering all they have for the work of God, will fly to
pieces like glass as soon as anything comes that is contrary to their
traditions: they cannot stand the fire at all. How many will be able to
abide a celestial law, and go through and receive their exaltation, I am
unable to say, as many are called, but few are chosen. (*HC* 6:185)

Salvation

1 For our own part we cannot believe that the ancients in all ages
were so ignorant of the system of heaven as many suppose, since all

---

Saints
   10 Editorial in the *Times and Seasons*, 1 August 1842.
   11 Sabbath address, Nauvoo, 23 July 1843.
   12 Sabbath address, Nauvoo, 21 January 1844.

Salvation
   1 Letter to the brethren scattered from Zion, Kirtland, 22 January 1834.

that were ever saved, were saved through the power of this great plan of redemption, as much before the coming of Christ as since; if not, God has had different plans in operation (if we may so express it), to bring men back to dwell with Himself; and this we cannot believe. (HC 2:16)

2 The great plan of salvation is a theme which ought to occupy our strict attention, and be regarded as one of heaven's best gifts to mankind. No consideration whatever ought to deter us from showing ourselves approved in the sight of God, according to His divine requirement. Men not unfrequently forget that they are dependent upon heaven for every blessing which they are permitted to enjoy, and that for every opportunity granted them they are to give an account. (HC 2:23–24)

3 Salvation cannot come without revelation; it is in vain for anyone to minister without it. No man is a minister of Jesus Christ without being a Prophet. No man can be a minister of Jesus Christ except he has the testimony of Jesus; and this is the spirit of prophecy. Whenever salvation has been administered, it has been by testimony. Men of the present time testify of heaven and hell, and have never seen either; and I will say that no man knows these things without this. (HC 3:389–90)

4 The great designs of God in relation to the salvation of the human family, are very little understood by the professedly wise and intelligent generation in which we live. (HC 4:595)

5 After this instruction, you will be responsible for your own sins; it is a desirable honor that you should so walk before our heavenly Father as to save yourselves; we are all responsible to God for the manner we improve the light and wisdom given by our Lord to enable us to save ourselves. (HC 4:606)

Salvation

2 Letter to the brethren scattered from Zion, Kirtland, 22 January 1834.

3 Discourse on the priesthood, given sometime before 8 August 1839, Commerce (Nauvoo). For a discussion on the dating of this discourse, see WJS, p. 22.

4 Editorial in the *Times and Seasons*, 15 April 1842.

5 Remarks to the Relief Society, Nauvoo, 28 April 1842.

6 There is now a day of salvation to such as repent and reform;—and they who repent not should be cast out from this society [the Relief Society]; yet we should woo them to return to God, lest they escape not the damnation of hell! (HC 5:20)

7 How oft have wise men and women sought to dictate Brother Joseph by saying, "O, if I were Brother Joseph, I would do this and that;" but if they were in Brother Joseph's shoes they would find that men or women could not be compelled into the kingdom of God, but must be dealt with in long-suffering, and at last we shall save them. (HC 5:24)

8 Salvation is nothing more nor less than to triumph over all our enemies and put them under our feet. And when we have power to put all enemies under our feet in this world, and a knowledge to triumph over all evil spirits in the world to come, then we are saved, as in the case of Jesus, who was to reign until He had put all enemies under His feet, and the last enemy was death.

Perhaps there are principles here that few men have thought of. No person can have this salvation except through a tabernacle. (HC 5:387–88)

9 Salvation means a man's being placed beyond the power of all his enemies. (HC 5:392)

10 Ordinances instituted in the heavens before the foundation of the world, in the priesthood, for the salvation of men, are not to be altered or changed. All must be saved on the same principles. (HC 5:423)

11 We are only capable of comprehending that certain things exist, which we may acquire by certain fixed principles. If men would acquire salvation, they have got to be subject, before they leave this world, to certain rules and principles, which were fixed by an unalterable decree before the world was. (HC 6:50–51)

Salvation
  6 Remarks to the Relief Society, Nauvoo, 9 June 1842.
  7 Remarks to the Relief Society, Nauvoo, 9 June 1842.
  8 Sabbath address at Yelrome (Morley's Settlement), Illinois, 14 May 1843.
  9 Items of doctrine given at Ramus, Illinois, 17 May 1843.
  10 Sabbath address, Nauvoo, 11 June 1843.
  11 Remarks upon the death of James Adams, Nauvoo, 9 October 1843.

Salvation of the Dead

1   "If the Mormon doctrine is true, what has become of all those who died since the days of the Apostles?"

All those who have not had an opportunity of hearing the Gospel, and being administered unto by an inspired man in the flesh, must have it hereafter, before they can be finally judged. (HC 3:29)

2   These men [ancient prophets] are in heaven, but their children are on the earth. Their bowels yearn over us. God sends down men for this reason. . . . All these authoritative characters will come down and join hand in hand in bringing about this work.

The Kingdom of Heaven is like a grain of mustard seed. The mustard seed is small, but bring forth a large tree, and the fowls lodge in the branches. The fowls are the angels. Thus angels come down, combine together to gather their children, and gather them. We cannot be made perfect without them, nor they without us; when these things are done, the Son of Man will descend, the Ancient of Days sit; we may come to an innumerable company of angels, have communion with and receive instructions from them. (HC 3:389)

3   I presume the doctrine of "baptism for the dead" has ere this reached your ears, and may have raised some inquiries in your minds respecting the same. I cannot in this letter give you all the information you may desire on the subject; but aside from knowledge independent of the Bible, I would say that it was certainly practiced by the ancient churches; and St. Paul endeavors to prove the doctrine of the resurrection from the same, and says, "Else what shall they do which are baptized for the dead, if the dead rise not at all? Why are they then baptized for the dead?"

I first mentioned the doctrine in public when preaching the funeral sermon of Brother Seymour Brunson: and have since then given

---

Salvation of the Dead

1   Answers to questions frequently asked the Prophet, Far West, 8 May 1838.

2   Discourse on the priesthood, given sometime before 8 August 1839, Commerce (Nauvoo). For a discussion on the dating of this discourse, see WJS, p. 22.

3   Letter to the Twelve in England, Nauvoo, 15 December 1840. The placement of this letter in HC implies that it was written in October 1840, but actually it was written on 15 December 1840 (see PWJS, p. 480).

general instructions in the Church on the subject. The Saints have the privilege of being baptized for those of their relatives who are dead, whom they believe would have embraced the Gospel, if they had been privileged with hearing it, and who have received the Gospel in the spirit, through the instrumentality of those who have been commissioned to preach to them while in prison. (HC 4:231)

4 *Minutes:* Next meeting—Joseph said the Lord said that we should build our house to his name that we might be baptized for the dead— but if we did it not we should be rejected and our dead with us and this church should not be excepted {accepted}. (WJS, pp. 62–63; standardized)

5 *Minutes:* President Joseph Smith, by request of the Twelve Apostles, gave instructions on the doctrine of baptism for the dead, which were listened to with intense interest by the large assembly. He presented baptism for the dead as the only way that men can appear as saviors on Mount Zion.

The proclamation of the first principles of the Gospel was a means of salvation to men individually; and it was the truth, not men, that saved them; but men, by actively engaging in rites of salvation substitutionally became instrumental in bringing multitudes of their kindred into the kingdom of God. . . .

There is never a time when the spirit is too old to approach God. All are within the reach of pardoning mercy, who have not committed the unpardonable sin, which hath no forgiveness, neither in this world, nor in the world to come. There is a way to release the spirits of the dead; that is by the power and authority of the Priesthood—by binding and loosing on earth. This doctrine appears glorious, inasmuch as it exhibits the greatness of divine compassion and benevolence in the extent of the plan of human salvation.

This glorious truth is well calculated to enlarge the understanding, and to sustain the soul under troubles, difficulties and distresses. For illustration, suppose the case of two men, brothers, equally intelligent, learned, virtuous and lovely, walking in uprightness and in all

---

Salvation of the Dead

4   Address at the weekly Nauvoo Lyceum, 2 February 1841. Reported in
     William P. McIntire's Minute Book, LDS Church Archives.
5   General conference address, Nauvoo, 3 October 1841.

good conscience, so far as they have been able to discern duty from the muddy stream of tradition, or from the blotted page of the book of nature.

One dies and is buried, having never heard the Gospel of reconciliation; to the other the message of salvation is sent, he hears and embraces it, and is made the heir of eternal life. Shall the one become the partaker of glory and the other be consigned to hopeless perdition? Is there no chance for his escape? Sectarianism answers "none." Such an idea is worse than atheism. . . .

This doctrine presents in a clear light the wisdom and mercy of God in preparing an ordinance for the salvation of the dead, being baptized by proxy, their names recorded in heaven and they judged according to the deeds done in the body. This doctrine was the burden of the scriptures. Those Saints who neglect it in behalf of their deceased relatives, do it at the peril of their own salvation. The dispensation of the fullness of times will bring to light the things that have been revealed in all former dispensations; also other things that have not been before revealed. He shall send Elijah, the Prophet, &c., and restore all things in Christ.

President Joseph Smith then announced: "There shall be no more baptisms for the dead, until the ordinance can be attended to in the Lord's House; and the Church shall not hold another General Conference, until they can meet in said house. *For thus saith the Lord!*" (HC 4:424–26)

6   The idea that some men form of the justice, judgment, and mercy of God, is too foolish for an intelligent man to think of: for instance, it is common for many of our orthodox preachers to suppose that if a man is not what they call converted, if he dies in that state he must remain eternally in hell without any hope. Infinite years in torment must he spend, and never, never, never have an end; and yet this eternal misery is made frequently to rest upon the merest casualty. The breaking of a shoe-string, the tearing of a coat of those officiating, or the peculiar location in which a person lives, may be the means, indirectly of his damnation, or the cause of his not being saved. I will suppose a case which is not extraordinary: Two men, who have been equally wicked, who have neglected religion, are both of them taken

---

Salvation of the Dead

6   Editorial in the *Times and Seasons*, 15 April 1842.

sick at the same time; one of them has the good fortune to be visited by a praying man, and he gets converted a few minutes before he dies; the other sends for three different praying men, a tailor, a shoemaker, and a tinman; the tinman has a handle to solder to a can, the tailor has a button-hole to work on some coat that he needed in a hurry, and the shoemaker has a patch to put on somebody's boot; they none of them can go in time, the man dies, and goes to hell: one of these is exalted to Abraham's bosom, he sits down in the presence of God and enjoys eternal, uninterrupted happiness, while the other, equally as good as he, sinks to eternal damnation, irretrievable misery and hopeless despair, because a man had a boot to mend, the button-hole of a coat to work, or a handle to solder on to a saucepan. . . .

When speaking about the blessings pertaining to the Gospel, and the consequences connected with disobedience to the requirements, we are frequently asked the question, what has become of our fathers? Will they all be damned for not obeying the Gospel, when they never heard? Certainly not. But they will possess the same privilege that we here enjoy, through the medium of the everlasting Priesthood, which not only administers on earth, but also in heaven, and the wise dispensations of the great Jehovah; hence those characters referred to by Isaiah will be visited by the Priesthood, and come out of their prison upon the same principle as those who were disobedient in the days of Noah were visited by our Savior {who possessed the everlasting Melchizedek Priesthood} and had the Gospel preached to them, by Him in prison; and in order that they might fulfill all the requisitions of God, living friends were baptized for their dead friends, and thus fulfilled the requirement of God, which says, "Except a man be born of water and of the Spirit, he cannot enter into the kingdom of God," they were baptized of course, not for themselves, but for their dead.

. . . Hence it was that so great a responsibility rested upon the generation in which our Savior lived, for, says he, "That upon you may come all the righteous blood shed upon the earth from the blood of righteous Abel unto the blood of Zacharias, son of Barachias, whom ye slew between the temple and the altar. Verily I say unto you, all these things shall come upon this generation.: (Matthew xxiii: 35, 36). Hence as they possessed greater privileges than any other generation, not only pertaining to themselves, but to their dead, their sin was greater, as they not only neglected their own salvation but that of their progenitors, and hence their blood was required at their hands.

And now as the great purposes of God are hastening to their ac-complishment, and the things spoken of in the Prophets are fulfilling, as the kingdom of God is established on the earth, and the ancient order of things restored, the Lord has manifested to us this day and privilege, and we are commanded to be baptized for our dead, thus ful-filling the words of Obadiah, when speaking of the glory of the latter-day: "And saviors shall come upon Mount Zion to judge the remnant of Esau, and the kingdom shall be the Lord's." A view of these things reconciles the Scriptures of truth, justifies the ways of God to man, places the human family upon an equal footing, and harmonizes with every principle of righteousness, justice and truth. We will conclude with the words of Peter: "For the time past of our life may suffice us to have wrought the will of the Gentiles." "For, for this cause was the Gospel preached also to them that are dead, that they might be judged according to men in the flesh, but live according to God in the spirit." (HC 4:597–99)

7 What shall I talk about to-day? I know what Brother Cahoon wants me to speak about. He wants me to speak about the coming of Elijah in the last days. I can see it in his eye. I will speak upon that subject then.

The Bible says, "I will send Elijah the Prophet before the coming of the great and dreadful day of the Lord; and he shall turn the hearts of the fathers to the children, and the hearts of the children to the fa-thers, lest I come and smite the earth with a curse."

Now, the word *turn* here should be translated *bind,* or seal. But what is the object of this important mission? or how is it to be ful-filled? The keys are to be delivered, the spirit of Elijah is to come, the Gospel to be established, the Saints of God gathered, Zion built up, and the Saints to come up as saviors on Mount Zion.

But how are they to become saviors on Mount Zion? By building their temples, erecting their baptismal fonts, and going forth and re-ceiving all the ordinances, baptisms, confirmations, washings, anoint-ings, ordinations and sealing powers upon their heads, in behalf of all their progenitors who are dead, and redeem them that they may come forth in the first resurrection and be exalted to thrones of glory with

---

Salvation of the Dead
7 Sabbath address, Nauvoo, 21 January 1844.

them; and herein is the chain that binds the hearts of the fathers to the children, and the children to the fathers, which fulfills the mission of Elijah. And I would to God that this temple was now done, that we might go into it, and go to work and improve our time, and make use of the seals while they are on earth.

The Saints have not too much time to save and redeem their dead, and gather together their living relatives, that they may be saved also, before the earth will be smitten, and the consumption decreed falls upon the world.

I would advise all the Saints to go to with their might and gather together all their living relatives to this place, that they may be sealed and saved, that they may be prepared against the day that the destroying angel goes forth; and if the whole Church should go to with all their might to save their dead, seal their posterity, and gather their living friends, and spend none of their time in behalf of the world, they would hardly get through before night would come, when no man can work; and my only trouble at the present time is concerning ourselves, that the Saints *will be divided, broken up, and scattered,* before we get our salvation secure; for there are so many fools in the world for the devil to operate upon, it gives him the advantage oftentimes.

The question is frequently asked "Can we not be saved without going through with all those ordinances, &c.?" I would answer, No, not the fullness of salvation. Jesus said, "There are many mansions in my Father's house, and I will go and prepare a place for you." *House* here named should have been translated kingdom; and any person who is exalted to the highest mansion has to abide a celestial law, and the whole law too. (HC 6:183–84)

8   The spirit, power, and calling of Elijah is, that ye have power to hold the key of the revelation, ordinances, oracles, powers and endowments of the fullness of the Melchisedeck Priesthood and of the kingdom of God on the earth; and to receive, obtain, and perform all the ordinances belonging to the kingdom of God, even unto the turning of the hearts of the fathers unto the children, and the hearts of the children unto the fathers, even those who are in heaven.

Malachi says, "I will send you Elijah the prophet before the coming of the great and dreadful day of the Lord: and he shall turn the

---

heart of the fathers to the children, and the heart of the children to their fathers, lest I come and smite the earth with a curse.". . .

In the days of Noah, God destroyed the world by a flood, and He has promised to destroy it by fire in the last days: but before it should take place, Elijah should first come and turn the hearts of the fathers to the children, &c.

Now comes the point. What is this office and work of Elijah? It is one of the greatest and most important subjects that God has revealed. He should send Elijah to seal the children to the fathers, and the fathers to the children.

Now was this merely confined to the living, to settle difficulties with families on earth? By no means. It was a far greater work. Elijah! what would you do if you were here? Would you confine your work to the living alone? No; I would refer you to the Scriptures, where the subject is manifest: that is, without us, they could not be made perfect, nor we without them; the fathers without the children, nor the children without the fathers.

I wish you to understand this subject, for it is important; and if you will receive it, this is the spirit of Elijah, that we redeem our dead, and connect ourselves with our fathers which are in heaven, and seal up our dead to come forth in the first resurrection; and here we want the power of Elijah to seal those who dwell on earth to those who dwell in heaven. This is the power of Elijah and the keys of the kingdom of Jehovah.

Let us suppose a case. Suppose the great God who dwells in heaven should reveal Himself to Father Cutler here, by the opening heavens, and tell him, I offer up a decree that whatsoever you seal on earth with your decree, I will seal it in heaven; you have the power then; can it be taken off? No. Then what you seal on earth, by the keys of Elijah, is sealed in heaven; and this is the power of Elijah, and this is the difference between the spirit and power of Elias and Elijah; for while the spirit of Elias is a forerunner, the power of Elijah is sufficient to make our calling and election sure; and the same doctrine, where we are exhorted to go on to perfection, not laying again the foundation of repentance from dead works, and of laying on of hands, resurrection of the dead, &c.

We cannot be perfect without the fathers, &c. We must have revelation from them, and we can see that the doctrine of revelation far transcends the doctrine of no revelation; for one truth revealed from heaven is worth all the sectarian notions in existence. (HC 6:251–52)

9 I want to talk more of the relation of man to God. I will open your eyes in relation to the dead. All things whatsoever God in his infinite wisdom has seen fit and proper to reveal to us, while we are dwelling in mortality, in regard to our mortal bodies, are revealed to us in the abstract, and independent of affinity of this mortal tabernacle, but are revealed to our spirits precisely as though we had no bodies at all; and those revelations which will save our spirits will save our bodies. God reveals them to us in view of no eternal dissolution of the body, or tabernacle. Hence the responsibility, the awful responsibility, that rests upon us in relation to our dead; for all the spirits who have not obeyed the Gospel in the flesh must either obey it in the spirit or be damned. Solemn thought!—dreadful thought! Is there nothing to be done—no preparation—no salvation for our fathers and friends who have died without having had the opportunity to obey the decrees of the Son of Man? Would to God that I had forty days and nights in which to tell you all! I would let you know that I am not a "fallen prophet."

What promises are made in relation to the subject of the salvation of the dead? and what kind of characters are those who can be saved, although their bodies are mouldering and decaying in the grave? When His commandments teach us, it is in view of eternity; for we are looked upon by God as though we were in eternity; God dwells in eternity, and does not view things as we do.

The greatest responsibility in this world that God has laid upon us is to seek after our dead. The apostle says, "They without us cannot be made perfect"; for it is necessary that the sealing power should be in our hands to seal our children and our dead for the fulness of the dispensation of times—a dispensation to meet the promises made by Jesus Christ before the foundation of the world for the salvation of man.

Now, I will speak of them. I will meet Paul half way. I say to you, Paul, you cannot be perfect without us. It is necessary that those who are going before and those who come after us should have salvation in common with us; and thus hath God made it obligatory upon man. Hence, God said, "I will send you Elijah the prophet before the coming of the great and dreadful day of the Lord: he shall turn the heart of the fathers to the children, and the heart of the children to their fathers, lest I come and smite the earth with a curse."

I have a declaration to make as to the provisions which God hath made to suit the conditions of man—made from before the foundation of the world. What has Jesus said? All sins, and all blasphemies, and every transgression, except one, that man can be guilty of, may be forgiven; and there is a salvation for all men, either in this world or the world to come, who have not committed the unpardonable sin, there being a provision either in this world or the world of spirits. Hence God hath made a provision that every spirit in the eternal world can be ferreted out and saved unless he has committed that unpardonable sin which cannot be remitted to him either in this world or the world of spirits. (HC 6:312–13)

10 I am going on in my progress for eternal life. It is not only necessary that you should be baptized for your dead, but you will have to go through all the ordinances for them, the same as you have gone through to save yourselves. (HC 6:365)

11 *Report of Benjamin Franklin Cummings's Recollection:* Concerning the work for the dead, he [Joseph Smith] said that in the resurrection those who had been worked for would fall at the feet of those who had done their work, kiss their feet, embrace their knees and manifest the most exquisite gratitude. We do not comprehend what a blessing to them these ordinances are. (Lundwall, comp., *The Vision*, p. 141)

Satan
See DEVIL

Saviors on Mount Zion

1 The election of the promised seed still continues, and in the last day, they shall have the Priesthood restored unto them, and they shall

---

Salvation of the Dead

Saviors on Mount Zion

be the "saviors on Mount Zion," the ministers of our God; if it were not for the remnant which was left, then might men now be as Sodom and Gomorrah. (HC 4:360)

2   *Minutes:* President Joseph Smith, by request of the Twelve Apostles, gave instructions on the doctrine of baptism for the dead, which were listened to with intense interest by the large assembly. He presented baptism for the dead as the only way that men can appear as saviors on Mount Zion.

The proclamation of the first principles of the Gospel was a means of salvation to men individually; and it was the truth, not men, that saved them; but men, by actively engaging in rites of salvation substitutionally became instrumental in bringing multitudes of their kindred into the kingdom of God. (HC 4:424–25)

3   And now as the great purposes of God are hastening to their accomplishment, and the things spoken of in the Prophets are fulfilling, as the kingdom of God is established on the earth, and the ancient order of things restored, the Lord has manifested to us this day and privilege, and we are commanded to be baptized for our dead, thus fulfilling the words of Obadiah, when speaking of the glory of the latter-day: "And saviors shall come upon Mount Zion to judge the remnant of Esau, and the kingdom shall be the Lord's." A view of these things reconciles the Scriptures of truth, justifies the ways of God to man, places the human family upon an equal footing, and harmonizes with every principle of righteousness, justice and truth. We will conclude with the words of Peter: "For the time past of our life may suffice us to have wrought the will of the Gentiles." "For, for this cause was the Gospel preached also to them that are dead, that they might be judged according to men in the flesh, but live according to God in the spirit." (HC 4:599)

4   The Bible says, "I will send you Elijah the Prophet before the coming of the great and dreadful day of the Lord; and he shall turn the hearts of the fathers to the children, and the hearts of the children to the fathers, lest I come and smite the earth with a curse."

Saviors on Mount Zion
  2 General conference address, Nauvoo, 3 October 1841.
  3 Editorial in the *Times and Seasons*, 15 April 1842.
  4 Sabbath address, Nauvoo, 21 January 1844.

Now, the word *turn* here should be translated *bind,* or seal. But what is the object of this important mission? or how is it to be fulfilled? The keys are to be delivered, the spirit of Elijah is to come, the Gospel to be established, the Saints of God gathered, Zion built up, and the Saints to come up as saviors on Mount Zion.

But how are they to become saviors on Mount Zion? By building their temples, erecting their baptismal fonts, and going forth and receiving all the ordinances, baptisms, confirmations, washings, anointings, ordinations and sealing powers upon their heads, in behalf of all their progenitors who are dead, and redeem them that they may come forth in the first resurrection and be exalted to thrones of glory with them; and herein is the chain that binds the hearts of the fathers to the children, and the children to the fathers, which fulfills the mission of Elijah. And I would to God that this temple was now done, that we might go into it, and go to work and improve our time, and make use of the seals while they are on earth. (HC 6:183–84)

5 It is not only necessary that you should be baptized for your dead, but you will have to go through all the ordinances for them, the same as you have gone through to save yourselves. There will be 144,000 saviors on Mount Zion, and with them an innumerable host that no man can number. (HC 6:365)

Scriptures

1 Much conjecture and conversation frequently occurred among the Saints, concerning the books mentioned, and referred to, in various places in the Old and New Testaments, which were now nowhere to be found. The common remark was, "They are *lost books;*" but it seems the Apostolic Church had some of these writings, as Jude mentions or quotes the Prophecy of Enoch, the seventh from Adam. To the joy of the little flock, which in all, from Colesville to Canandaigua, New York, numbered about seventy members, did the Lord reveal the following doings of olden times, from the prophecy of Enoch: [Moses 7]. (HC 1:132–33)

Saviors on Mount Zion
5   Sabbath address, Nauvoo, 12 May 1844.

Scriptures
1   Colesville, New York, December 1830.

2 We made it a rule wherever there was an opportunity, to read a chapter in the Bible, and pray; and these seasons of worship gave us great consolation. (*HC* 1:189)

3 Nothing could be more pleasing to the Saints upon the order of the kingdom of the Lord, than the light which burst upon the world through the foregoing vision [D&C 76]. Every law, every commandment, every promise, every truth, and every point touching the destiny of man, from Genesis to Revelation, where the purity of the scriptures remains unsullied by the folly of men, go to show the perfection of the theory {of different degrees of glory in the future life} and witnesses the fact that that document is a transcript from the records of the eternal world. The sublimity of the ideas; the purity of the language; the scope for action; the continued duration for completion, in order that the heirs of salvation may confess the Lord and bow the knee; the rewards for faithfulness, and the punishments for sins, are so much beyond the narrow-mindedness of men, that every honest man is constrained to explain: "*It came from God.*" (*HC* 1:252–53)

4 We have not found the Book of Jasher, nor any other of the lost books mentioned in the Bible as yet; nor will we obtain them at present. (*HC* 1:363)

5 I pray that the Lord may enable you to treasure these things in your mind, for I know that His Spirit will bear testimony to all who seek diligently after knowledge from Him. I hope you will search the Scriptures to see whether these things are not also consistent with those things which the ancient Prophets and Apostles have written. (*HC* 1:442)

6 We deem it a just principle, and it is one the force of which we believe ought to be duly considered by every individual, that all men are created equal, and that all have the privilege of thinking for themselves upon all matters relative to conscience. Consequently, then, we

---

Scriptures

2   Observation while en route from Kirtland to Missouri, June 1831.
3   The Prophet's view of the vision of the glories (D&C 76), Hiram, Ohio, 16 February 1832.
4   Letter to the brethren in Zion, Kirtland, 25 June 1833.
5   Letter to Moses C. Nickerson, written from Kirtland, 19 November 1833.
6   Letter to the brethren scattered from Zion, Kirtland, 22 January 1834.

are not disposed, had we the power, to deprive any one of exercising that free independence of mind which heaven has so graciously bestowed upon the human family as one of its choicest gifts; but we take the liberty (and this we have a right to do) of looking at this order of things a few moments, and contrasting it with the order of God as we find it in the sacred Scriptures. In this review, however, we shall present the points as we consider they were really designed by the great Giver to be understood, and the happy result arising from a performance of the requirements of heaven as revealed to every one who obeys them; and the consequence attending a false construction, a misrepresentation, or a forced meaning that was never designed in the mind of the Lord when He condescended to speak from the heavens to men for their salvation. (HC 2:6–7)

7   He that can mark the power of Omnipotence, inscribed upon the heavens, can also see God's own handwriting in the sacred volume: and he who reads it oftenest will like it best, and he who is acquainted with it, will know the hand wherever he can see it; and when once discovered, it will not only receive an acknowledgment, but an obedience to all its heavenly precepts. For a moment reflect: what could have been the purpose of our Father in giving to us a law? Was it that it might be obeyed, or disobeyed? (HC 2:14)

8   "Is not the canon of the Scriptures full?"
    If it is, there is a great defect in the book, or else it would have said so. (HC 3:30)

9   O ye Twelve! and all Saints! profit by this important *Key*—that in all your trials, troubles, temptations, afflictions, bonds, imprisonments and death, see to it . . . that you do not betray the revelations of God, whether in the Bible, Book of Mormon, or Doctrine and Covenants, or any other that ever was or ever will be given and revealed unto man in this world or that which is to come. Yea, in all your kicking and flounderings, see to it that you do not this thing, lest innocent blood be found upon your skirts, and you go down to hell. (HC 3:385)

Scriptures
   7   Letter to the brethren scattered from Zion, Kirtland, 22 January 1834.
   8   Answers to questions frequently asked the Prophet, Far West, 8 May 1838.
   9   Instructions to the Apostles and Seventies departing for missions to England, Commerce (Nauvoo), 2 July 1839.

10 Connected with the building up of the Kingdom, is the printing and circulation of the Book of Mormon, Doctrine and Covenants, hymnbook, and the new translation of the Scriptures. It is unnecessary to say anything respecting these works; those who have read them, and who have drunk of the stream of knowledge which they convey, know how to appreciate them; and although fools may have them in derision, yet they are calculated to make men wise unto salvation, and sweep away the cobwebs of superstition of ages, throw a light on the proceedings of Jehovah which have already been accomplished, and mark out the future in all its dreadful and glorious realities. Those who have tasted the benefit derived from a study of those works, will undoubtedly vie with each other in their zeal for sending them abroad throughout the world, that every son of Adam may enjoy the same privileges, and rejoice in the same truths. (HC 4:187)

11 Who is it that writes these Scriptures? Not the men of the world or mere casual observers, but the Apostles—men who knew one gift from another, and of course were capable of writing about it; if we had the testimony of the Scribes and Pharisees concerning the outpouring of the Spirit on the day of Pentecost, they would have told us that it was no gift, but that the people were "drunken with new wine," and we shall finally have to come to the same conclusion that Paul did—"No man knows the things of God but by the Spirit of God." (HC 5:30)

12 Now taking it for granted that the scriptures say what they mean, and mean what they say, we have sufficient grounds to go on and prove from the bible that the gospel has always been the same; the ordinances to fulfil its requirements, the same; and the officers to officiate, the same; and the signs and fruits resulting from the promises, the same. (*T&S* 3:904)

13 I have a key by which I understand the scriptures. I enquire, what was the question which drew out the answer, or caused Jesus to utter the parable? . . . To ascertain its meaning, we must dig up the root and ascertain what it was that drew the saying out of Jesus. (HC 5:261)

Scriptures
10 Letter to the Saints from the First Presidency, Nauvoo, 31 August 1840.
11 Editorial in the *Times and Seasons*, 15 June 1842.
12 Editorial in the *Times and Seasons*, 1 September 1842.
13 Sabbath address, Nauvoo, 29 January 1843.

14 I know the scriptures and understand them. (HC 6:314)

15 Mankind verily say that the scriptures are with them. Search the scriptures, for they testify of things that these apostates would gravely pronounce blasphemy. (HC 6:474)

Sealing

1 Until we have perfect love we are liable to fall; and when we have a testimony that our names are sealed in the Lamb's book of life, we have perfect love, and then it is impossible for false Christs to deceive us. (FWR, p. 23; standardized)

2 I then said to the Elders, As I have done so do ye; wash ye, therefore, one another's feet; and by the power of the Holy Ghost I pronounced them all clean from the blood of this generation; but if any of them should sin wilfully after they were thus cleansed, and sealed up unto eternal life, they should be given over unto the buffetings of Satan until the day of redemption. (HC 1:323–24)

3 Inasmuch as you have come up here, essaying to keep the commandments of God, I pronounce the blessings of heaven and earth upon you; and inasmuch as you will follow counsel, act wisely and do right, these blessings shall rest upon you so far as I have power with God to seal them upon you. (HC 5:354)

4 The world is reserved unto burning in the last days. He shall send Elijah the prophet, and he shall reveal the covenants of the fathers in relation to the children, and the covenants of the children in relation to the fathers.

Scriptures
  14 King Follett Discourse, Nauvoo, 7 April 1844.
  15 Sabbath address, Nauvoo, 16 June 1844.

Sealing
  1 Minutes of a conference held at Orange, Ohio, 25 October 1831.
  2 Instruction to the elders of the Church at a conference, Kirtland, 23 January 1833.
  3 Remarks to Saints newly arrived from England, Nauvoo, 13 April 1843.
  4 Remarks at the funeral of Judge Elias Higbee, Nauvoo, 13 August 1843.

Four destroying angels holding power over the four quarters of the earth until the servants of God are sealed in their foreheads, which signifies sealing the blessing upon their heads, meaning the everlasting covenant, thereby making their calling and election sure. When a seal is put upon the father and mother, it secures their posterity, so that they cannot be lost, but will be saved by virtue of the covenant of their father and mother. (HC 5:530)

5 How shall God come to the rescue of this generation? He will send Elijah the prophet. The law revealed to Moses in Horeb never was revealed to the children of Israel as a nation.

Elijah shall reveal the covenants to seal the hearts of the fathers to the children, and the children to the fathers.

The anointing and sealing is to be called, elected and made sure. (HC 5:555)

6 I would advise all the Saints to go to with their might and gather together all their living relatives to this place, that they may be sealed and saved, that they may be prepared against the day that the destroying angel goes forth; and if the whole Church should go to with all their might to save their dead, seal their posterity, and gather their living friends, and spend none of their time in behalf of the world, they would hardly get through before night would come, when no man can work; and my only trouble at the present time is concerning ourselves, that the Saints *will be divided, broken up, and scattered*, before we get our salvation secure. (HC 6:184)

7 What is this office and work of Elijah? It is one of the greatest and most important subjects that God has revealed. He should send Elijah to seal the children to the fathers, and the fathers to the children. . . .

I wish you to understand this subject, for it is important; and if you receive it, this is the spirit of Elijah, that we redeem our dead, and connect ourselves with out fathers which are in heaven, and seal up

---

Sealing

5   Sabbath address, Nauvoo, 27 August 1843.
6   Sabbath address, Nauvoo, 21 January 1844.
7   Sabbath address, Nauvoo, 10 March 1844.

our dead to come forth in the first resurrection; and here we want the power of Elijah to seal those who dwell on earth to those who dwell in heaven. This is the power of Elijah and the keys of the kingdom of Jehovah. . . .

. . . What you seal on earth, by the keys of Elijah, is sealed in heaven; and this is the power of Elijah, and this is the difference between the spirit and power of Elias and Elijah; for while the spirit of Elias is a forerunner, the power of Elijah is sufficient to make our calling and election sure; and the same doctrine, where we are exhorted to go on to perfection, not laying again the foundation of repentance from dead works, and of laying on of hands, resurrection of the dead, &c. . . .

This spirit of Elijah was manifest in the days of the Apostles, in delivering certain ones to the buffetings of Satan, that they might be saved in the day of the Lord Jesus. They were sealed by the spirit of Elijah unto the damnation of hell until the day of the Lord, or revelation of Jesus Christ. . . .

. . . According to the Scripture, if men have received the good word of God, and tasted of the powers of the world to come, if they shall fall away, it is impossible to renew them again, seeing they have crucified the Son of God afresh, and put Him to an open shame; so there is a possibility of falling away; you could not be renewed again, and the power of Elijah cannot seal against this sin, for this is a reserve made in the seals and power of the Priesthood. . . .

Again: The doctrine or sealing power of Elijah is as follows:—If you have power to seal on earth and in heaven, then we should be wise. The first thing you do, go and seal on earth your sons and daughters unto yourself, and yourself unto your fathers in eternal glory, and go ahead, and not go back, but use a little wisdom, and seal all you can, and when you get to heaven tell your Father that what you seal on earth should be sealed in heaven, according to his promise. I will walk through the gate of heaven and claim what I seal, and those that follow me and my counsel. . . .

The spirit of Elias is first, Elijah second, and Messiah last. Elias is a forerunner to prepare the way, and the spirit and power of Elijah is to come after, holding the keys of power, building the Temple to the capstone, placing the seals of the Melchisedec Priesthood upon the house of Israel, and making all things ready; then Messiah comes to His Temple, which is last of all. (HC 6:251, 252, 253, 254; *TPJS*, p. 340)

8   It is necessary that the sealing power should be in our hands to seal our children and our dead for the fulness of the dispensation of times—a dispensation to meet the promises made by Jesus Christ before the foundation of the world for the salvation of man. (*HC* 6:313)

Second Comforter

1   There are two Comforters spoken of. One is the Holy Ghost, the same as given on the day of Pentecost, and that all Saints receive after faith, repentance, and baptism. This first Comforter or Holy Ghost has no other effect than pure intelligence. It is more powerful in expanding the mind, enlightening the understanding, and storing the intellect with present knowledge, of a man who is of the literal seed of Abraham, than one that is a Gentile, though it may not have half as much visible effect upon the body; for as the Holy Ghost falls upon one of the literal seed of Abraham, it is calm and serene; and his whole soul and body are only exercised by the pure spirit of intelligence; while the effect of the Holy Ghost on a Gentile, is to purge out the old blood, and make him actually of the seed of Abraham. That man that has none of the blood of Abraham (naturally) must have a new creation by the Holy Ghost. In such a case, there may be more of a powerful effect upon the body, and visible to the eye, than upon an Israelite, while the Israelite at first might be far before the Gentile in pure intelligence.

The other Comforter spoken of is a subject of great interest, and perhaps understood by few of this generation. After a person has faith in Christ, repents of his sins, and is baptized for the remission of his sins and receives the Holy Ghost, (by the laying on of hands), which is the first Comforter, then let him continue to humble himself before God, hungering and thirsting after righteousness, and living by every word of God, and the Lord will soon say unto him, Son, thou shalt be exalted. When the Lord has thoroughly proved him, and finds that the man is determined to serve Him at all hazards, then the man will

---

Sealing

8   King Follett Discourse, Nauvoo, 7 April 1844.

Second Comforter

1   Instructions to the Twelve, Commerce (Nauvoo), 27 June 1839.

find his calling and election made sure, then it will be his privilege to receive the other Comforter, which the Lord hath promised the Saints, as is recorded in the testimony of St. John, in the 14th chapter, from the 12th to the 27th verses.

Note the 16, 17, 18, 21, 23 verses:

"16. And I will pray the Father, and He shall give you another Comforter, that he may abide with you forever;

"17. Even the Spirit of Truth; whom the world cannot receive, because it seeth him not, neither knoweth him; but ye know him; for he dwelleth with you, and shall be in you.

"18. I will not leave you comfortless: I will come to you. . . .

"21. He that hath my commandments, and keepeth them, he it is that loveth me: and he that loveth me shall be loved of my Father, and I will love him, and will manifest myself to him.

"23. If a man love me, he will keep my words: and my Father will love him, and we will come unto him, and make our abode with him."

Now what is this other Comforter? It is no more nor less than the Lord Jesus Christ Himself; and this is the sum and substance of the whole matter; that when any man obtains this last Comforter, he will have the personage of Jesus Christ to attend him, or appear unto him from time to time, and even He will manifest the Father unto him, and they will take up their abode with him, and the visions of the heavens will be opened unto him, and the Lord will teach him face to face, and he may have a perfect knowledge of the mysteries of the Kingdom of God; and this is the state and place the ancient Saints arrived at when they had such glorious visions—Isaiah, Ezekiel, John upon the Isle of Patmos, St. Paul in the three heavens, and all the Saints who held communion with the general assembly and Church of the First Born. (*HC* 3:380–81)

Second Coming

1   About 4 o'clock a.m. I was awakened by Brother Davis knocking at my door, and calling on me to arise and behold the signs in the heavens. I arose, and to my great joy, beheld the stars fall from heaven like a shower of hailstones; a literal fulfillment of the word of God, as

---

Second Coming
   1   Kirtland, 13 November 1833.

recorded in the holy Scriptures, and a sure sign that the coming of Christ is close at hand. In the midst of this shower of fire, I was led to exclaim, "How marvelous are Thy works, O Lord! I thank Thee for Thy mercy unto Thy servant; save me in Thy kingdom for Christ's sake. Amen."

The appearance of these signs varied in different sections of the country: in Zion, all heaven seemed enwrapped in splendid fireworks, as if every star in the broad expanse had been suddenly hurled from its course, and sent lawless through the wilds of ether. Some at times appeared like bright shooting meteors, with long trains of light following in their course, and in numbers resembled large drops of rain in sunshine. These seemed to vanish when they fell behind the trees, or came near the ground. Some of the long trains of light following the meteoric stars, were visible for some seconds; these streaks would curl and twist up like serpents writhing. The appearance was beautiful, grand, and sublime beyond description; and it seemed as if the artillery and fireworks of eternity were set in motion to enchant and entertain the Saints, and terrify and awe the sinners of the earth. Beautiful and terrific as was the scenery, it will not fully compare with the time when the sun shall become black like sack-cloth of hair, the moon like blood, and the stars fall to the earth—Rev. vi:13. (HC 1:439–40)

2   When I contemplate the rapidity with which the great and glorious day of the coming of the Son of Man advances, when He shall come to receive His Saints unto Himself, where they shall dwell in His presence, and be crowned with glory and immortality; when I consider that soon the heavens are to be shaken, and the earth tremble and reel to and fro; and that the heavens are to be unfolded as a scroll when it is rolled up; and that every mountain and island are to flee away, I cry out in my heart, What manner of persons ought we to be in all holy conversation and godliness! (HC 1:442)

3   How is it that these old Apostles should say so much on the subject of the coming of Christ? He certainly had once come; but Paul says, To all who love His appearing, shall be given the crown: and

---

Second Coming

2   Letter to Moses C. Nickerson, written from Kirtland, 19 November 1833.
3   Letter to the brethren scattered from Zion, Kirtland, 22 January 1834.

John says, When He shall appear, we shall be like Him; for we shall see Him as He is. Can we mistake such language as this? Do we not offer violence to our own good judgment when we deny the second coming of the Messiah? (HC 2:20)

4 We see that perilous times have truly come, and the things which we have so long expected have at last began to usher in; but when you see the fig tree begin to put forth its leaves, you may know that the summer is nigh at hand. There will be a short work on the earth. It has now commenced. I suppose there will soon be perplexity all over the earth. Do not let our hearts faint when these things come upon us, for they must come, or the word cannot be fulfilled. I know that something will soon take place to stir up this generation to see what they have been doing, and that their fathers have inherited lies and they have been led captive by the devil, to no profit; but they know not what they do. (HC 3:286)

5 We see that everything is being fulfilled; and that the time shall soon come when the Son of Man shall descend in the clouds of heaven. (HC 3:291)

6 I will prophesy that the signs of the coming of the Son of Man are already commenced. One pestilence will desolate after another. We shall soon have war and bloodshed. The moon will be turned into blood. I testify of these things, and that the coming of the Son of Man is nigh, even at your doors. If our souls and our bodies are not looking forth for the coming of the Son of Man; and after we are dead, if we are not looking forth, we shall be among those who are calling for the rocks to fall upon them.

The hearts of the children of men will have to be turned to the fathers, and the fathers to the children, living or dead, to prepare them for the coming of the Son of Man. If Elijah did not come, the whole earth would be smitten.

Second Coming

4   Letter from Liberty Jail to Mrs. Norman Bull (Buell), 15 March 1839.

5   Letter to the Saints from Liberty Jail, 20–25 March 1839.

6   Discourse on the priesthood, given sometime before 8 August 1839, Commerce (Nauvoo). For a discussion on the dating of this discourse, see *WJS*, p. 22.

There will be here and there a Stake {of Zion} for the gathering of the Saints. Some may have cried peace, but the Saints and the world will have little peace from henceforth. Let this not hinder us from going to the Stakes; for God has told us to flee, not dallying, or we shall be scattered, one here, and another there. (HC 3:390)

7   Explained concerning the coming of the Son of Man; also that it is a false idea that the Saints will escape all the judgments, whilst the wicked suffer; for all flesh is subject to suffer, and "the righteous shall hardly escape;" still many of the Saints will escape, for the just shall live by faith; yet many of the righteous shall fall a prey to disease, to pestilence, etc., by reason of the weakness of the flesh, and yet be saved in the Kingdom of God. So that it is an unhallowed principle to say that such and such have transgressed because they have been preyed upon by disease or death, for all flesh is subject to death; and the Savior has said, "Judge not, lest ye be judged." (HC 4:11)

8   There is no other way for the Saints to be saved in these last days, {than by the gathering} as the concurrent testimony of all the holy Prophets clearly proves. . . .

It is also the concurrent testimony of all the Prophets, that this gathering together of all the Saints, must take place before the Lord comes to "take vengeance upon the ungodly," and "to be glorified and admired by all those who obey the Gospel." (HC 4:272)

9   This messenger [Moroni] proclaimed himself to be an angel of God, sent to bring the joyful tidings that the covenant which God made with ancient Israel was at hand to be fulfilled, that the preparatory work for the second coming of the Messiah was speedily to commence; that the time was at hand for the Gospel in all its fullness to be preached in power, unto all nations that a people might be prepared for the Millennial reign. (HC 4:536–37)

Second Coming

7   Sabbath address, Commerce (Nauvoo), 29 September 1839.

8   Proclamation of the First Presidency, Nauvoo, 15 January 1841.

9   Letter to John Wentworth, editor of the *Chicago Democrat*, Nauvoo, 1 March 1842.

10 Seven or eight young men came to see me, part of them from the city of New York. They treated me with the greatest respect. I showed them the fallacy of Mr. Miller's *data* concerning the coming of Christ and the end of the world, or as it is commonly called, Millerism, and preached them quite a sermon; that error was in the Bible, or the translation of the Bible; that Miller was in want of correct information upon the subject, and that he was not so much to blame as the translators. I told them the prophecies must all be fulfilled; the sun must be darkened and the moon turned into blood, and many more things take place before Christ would come. (HC 5:271–72)

11 [Mr. Redding] has not seen the sign of the Son of Man, as foretold by Jesus; neither has any man, nor will any man, until after the sun shall have been darkened and the moon bathed in blood; for the Lord hath not shown me any such sign; and as the prophet saith, so it must be—"Surely the Lord God will do nothing, but He revealeth His secret unto His servants the prophets." (See Amos 3:7.) Therefore, hear this, O earth: The Lord will not come to reign over the righteous, in this world, in 1843, nor until everything for the Bridegroom is ready. (HC 5:291)

12 Were I going to prophesy, I would say the end {of the world} would not come in 1844, 5, or 6, or in forty years. There are those of the rising generation who shall not taste death till Christ comes.

I was once praying earnestly upon this subject, and a voice said unto me, "My son, if thou livest until thou art eighty-five years of age, thou shalt see the face of the Son of Man." I was left to draw my own conclusions concerning this; and I took the liberty to conclude that if I did live to that time, He would make His appearance. But I do not say whether He will make His appearance or I shall go where He is. I prophesy in the name of the Lord God, and let it be written—the Son of Man will not come in the clouds of heaven till I am eighty-five years old. Then read the 14th chapter of Revelation, 6th and 7th

---

Second Coming

10 Nauvoo, 12 February 1843. See HC 5:272 footnote for explanation concerning Millerism.

11 Letter to the editor of the *Times and Seasons*, 1 March 1843.

12 General conference address, Nauvoo, 6 April 1843.

verses—"And I saw another angel fly in the midst of heaven, having the everlasting gospel to preach unto them that dwell on the earth, and to every nation, and kindred, and tongue, and people, saying with a loud voice, Fear God and give glory to Him, for the hour of His judgment is come." And Hosea, 6th chapter, After two days, etc.,—2,520 years; which brings it to 1890. The coming of the Son of Man never will be—never can be till the judgments spoken of for this hour are poured out: which judgments are commenced. Paul says, "Ye are the children of the light, and not of the darkness, that that day should overtake you as a thief in the night." It is not the design of the Almighty to come upon the earth and crush it and grind it to powder, but he will reveal it to His servants the prophets.

Judah must return, Jerusalem must be rebuilt, and the temple, and water come out from under the temple, and the waters of the Dead Sea be healed. It will take some time to rebuild the walls of the city and the temple, &c.; and all this must be done before the Son of Man will make His appearance. There will be wars and rumors of wars, signs in the heavens above and on the earth beneath, the sun turned into darkness and the moon to blood, earthquakes in divers places, the seas heaving beyond their bounds; then will appear one grand sign of the Son of Man in heaven. But what will the world do? They will say it is a planet, a comet, &c. But the Son of Man will come as the sign of the coming of the Son of Man, which will be as the light of the morning cometh out of the east. (HC 5:336–37)

13 The inhabitants of the earth are asleep: they know not the day of their visitation. The Lord hath set the bow in the cloud for a sign that while it shall be seen, seed time and harvest, summer and winter shall not fail; but when it shall disappear, woe to that generation, for behold the end cometh quickly. (HC 5:402)

14 In the days of Noah, God destroyed the world by a flood, and He has promised to destroy it by fire in the last days: but before it should take place, Elijah should first come and turn the hearts of the fathers to the children. . . .

I have asked of the Lord concerning His coming; and while asking

---

Second Coming
   13 Sabbath address, Nauvoo, 21 May 1843.
   14 Sabbath address, Nauvoo, 10 March 1844.

the Lord, He gave a sign and said, "In the days of Noah I set a bow in the heavens as a sign and token that in any year that the bow should be seen the Lord would not come; but there should be seed time and harvest during that year: but whenever you see the bow withdrawn, it shall be a token that there shall be famine, pestilence, and great distress among the nations, and that the coming of the Messiah is not far distant."

But I will take the responsibility upon myself to prophesy in the name of the Lord, that Christ will not come this year, as Father Miller has prophesied, for we have seen the bow; and I also prophesy, in the name of the Lord, that Christ will not come in forty years; and if God ever spoke by my mouth, He will not come in that length of time. Brethren, when you go home, write this down, that it may be remembered.

Jesus Christ never did reveal to any man the precise time that He would come. Go and read the Scriptures, and you cannot find anything that specifies the exact hour He would come; and all that say so are false teachers. (HC 6:251, 254)

Secrets

1   Remember God sees the secret springs of human action, and knows the hearts of all living. . . .

It is in vain to try to hide a bad spirit from the eyes of them who are spiritual, for it will show itself in speaking and in writing, as well as in all our other conduct. It is also needless to make great pretensions when the heart is not right; the Lord will expose it to the view of His faithful Saints. (HC 1:317)

2   We hope, our brethren, that the greatest freedom and frankness will exist between you and the Bishop, not withholding from one another any information from us, but communicating with the greatest freedom, lest you should produce evils of a serious character, and the Lord become offended. (HC 1:369)

Secrets
1   Letter to William W. Phelps in Missouri, written from Kirtland, 14 January 1833. According to Dean Jessee this letter was dated 11 January (see *PWJS*, p. 262).
2   Letter to the brethren in Zion, Kirtland, 2 July 1833.

3   The reason we do not have the secrets of the Lord revealed unto us, is because we do not keep them but reveal them; we do not keep our own secrets, but reveal our difficulties to the world, even to our enemies, then how would we keep the secrets of the Lord? I can keep a secret till Doomsday. (*HC* 4:479)

4   The grand rule of heaven was that nothing should ever be done on earth without revealing the secret to his [the Lord's] servants the prophets, agreeably to Amos 3:7. (*T&S* 3:905)

Sectarianism

1   *Minutes:* There is never a time when the spirit is too old to approach God. All are within the reach of pardoning mercy, who have not committed the unpardonable sin, which hath no forgiveness, neither in this world, nor in the world to come. There is a way to release the spirits of the dead; that is by the power and authority of the Priesthood—by binding and loosing on earth. This doctrine appears glorious, inasmuch as it exhibits the greatness of divine compassion and benevolence in the extent of the plan of human salvation.

This glorious truth is well calculated to enlarge the understanding, and to sustain the soul under troubles, difficulties and distresses. For illustration, suppose the case of two men, brothers, equally intelligent, learned, virtuous and lovely, walking in uprightness and in all good conscience, so far as they have been able to discern duty from the muddy stream of tradition, or from the blotted page of the book of nature.

One dies and is buried, having never heard the Gospel of reconciliation; to the other the message of salvation is sent, he hears and embraces it, and is made the heir of eternal life. Shall the one become the partaker of glory and the other be consigned to hopeless perdition? Is there no chance for his escape? Sectarianism answers "none." Such an idea is worse than atheism. The truth shall break down and

---

Secrets
  3   Meeting of the Twelve at the Prophet's home, Nauvoo, 19 December 1841.
  4   Editorial in the *Times and Seasons*, 1 September 1842.

Sectarianism
  1   Conference address, Nauvoo, 3 October 1841.

dash in pieces all such bigoted Pharisaism; the sects shall be sifted, the honest in heart brought out, and their priests left in the midst of their corruption.

Many objections are urged against the Latter-day Saints for not admitting the validity of sectarian baptism, and for withholding fellowship from sectarian churches. Yet to do otherwise would be like putting new wine into old bottles, and putting old wine into new bottles. What! new revelations in the old churches? New revelations would knock out the bottom of their bottomless pit. New wine into old bottles! The bottles burst and the wine runs out! What! Sadducees in the new church! Old wine in new leathern bottles will leak through the pores and escape. So the Sadducee saints mock at authority, kick out of the traces, and run to the mountains of perdition, leaving the long echo of their braying behind them.

He [Joseph Smith] then referred to the {lack of} charity in the sects, in denouncing all who disagree with them in opinion, and in joining in persecuting the Saints, who believe that even such may be saved, in this world and in the world to come (murderers and apostates excepted).

This doctrine presents in a clear light the wisdom and mercy of God in preparing an ordinance for the salvation of the dead, being baptized by proxy, their names recorded in heaven and they judged according to the deeds done in the body. (HC 4:425–26)

2   They [God and Christ in the First Vision] told me that all religious denominations were believing in incorrect doctrines, and that none of them was acknowledged of God as His Church and kingdom: and I was expressly commanded "to go not after them," at the same time receiving a promise that the fullness of the Gospel should at some future time be made known unto me. (HC 4:536)

3   To say that the heathens would be damned because they did not believe the Gospel would be preposterous, and to say that the Jews would all be damned that do not believe in Jesus would be equally absurd; for "how can they believe on him of whom they have not heard, and how can they hear without a preacher, and how can he preach

Sectarianism
2   Letter to John Wentworth, editor of the *Chicago Democrat*, Nauvoo, 1 March 1842.
3   Editorial in the *Times and Seasons*, 15 April 1842.

except he be sent;" consequently neither Jew nor heathen can be culpable for rejecting the conflicting opinions of sectarianism, nor for rejecting any testimony but that which is sent of God, for as the preacher cannot preach except he be sent, so the hearer cannot believe without he hear a "sent" preacher, and cannot be condemned for what he has not heard, and being without law, will have to be judged without law. (HC 4:598)

4   The sectarian world are going to hell by hundreds, by thousands and by millions. (HC 5:554)

5   You observed, "as I have proven myself to be a philosophical divine" I must excuse you when you say that we must leave these *influences* to the mass. The meaning of "philosophical divine" may be taken in various ways. If, as the learned world apply the term, you infer that I have achieved a victory, and been strengthened by a scientific religion, as practiced by the popular sects of the age, through the aid of colleges, seminaries, Bible societies, missionary boards, financial organizations, and gospel money schemes, then you are wrong. Such a combination of men and means shows a form of godliness without the power; for is it not written, "I will destroy the wisdom of the wise." "Beware lest any man spoil you through philosophy and vain deceit, after the rudiments of the world, and not after the doctrines of Christ." (HC 6:73)

6   One truth revealed from heaven is worth all the sectarian notions in existence. (HC 6:252)

Self-Defense

1   There needs be no difficulty in relation to the revelations; for they show plainly from the face of them, that no blood is to be shed

---

Sectarianism

   4   Sabbath address, Nauvoo, 27 August 1843.
   5   Letter to James Arlington Bennett, Nauvoo, 13 November 1843.
   6   Sabbath address, Nauvoo, 10 March 1844.

Self-Defense

   1   Letter to Edward Partridge and others in Missouri, Kirtland, 30 March 1834.

except in self-defense; and that the law of God as well as man gives us a privilege. (*PWJS*, p. 319)

2 *Report of William Clayton:* He [Joseph Smith] also said that he had restrained the Saints from using violence in self-defense but from henceforth he restrained them no more. The best of feelings prevailed during the whole meeting. (*WJS*, p. 225; standardized)

3 It may be that the Saints will have to beat their ploughs into swords, for it will not do for men to sit down patiently and see their children destroyed. (*HC* 6:365)

4 If a mob annoy you, defend yourselves to the very last, and if they fall upon you with a superior force, and if you think you are not able to compete with them, retreat to Nauvoo. But we hope for better things, but remember if your enemies do fall upon you be sure and take the best and most efficient measures the emergency of the case may require. (*PWJS*, p. 591)

5 *Report of William Clayton:* He [Joseph Smith] called upon the citizens to defend the lives of their wives and children, fathers and mothers, brothers and sisters from being murdered by the mob. He urged them in strong terms not to shed innocent blood, not to act in the least on the offensive but invariably in the defensive; and if we die, die like men of God and secure a glorious resurrection. (*WJS*, p. 384; standardized)

6 There is one principle which is eternal; it is the duty of all men to protect their lives and the lives of the household, whenever necessity requires, and no power has a right to forbid it, should the last extreme arrive, but I anticipate no such extreme, but caution is the parent of safety. (*HC* 6:605)

Self-Defense
  2   Address regarding the Prophet's arrest at Dixon, Illinois, Nauvoo, 30 June 1843, as reported by William Clayton.
  3   Sabbath address, Nauvoo, 12 May 1844.
  4   Letter to John Smith, the Prophet's uncle, Nauvoo, 17 June 1844.
  5   Address to the Nauvoo Legion, 18 June 1844, as reported by William Clayton.
  6   Letter to Emma Smith from Carthage Jail, 27 June 1844.

Selfishness

1 Without virtuous principles to actuate a government all care for justice is soon lost, and the only motive which prompts it to act is ambition and selfishness. (HC 2:11)

2 Let the Saints remember that great things depend on their individual exertion, and that they are called to be co-workers with us and the Holy Spirit in accomplishing the great work of the last days; and in consideration of the extent, the blessings and glories of the same, let every selfish feeling be not only buried, but annihilated. (HC 4:230–31)

3 We are full of selfishness; the devil flatters us that we are very righteous, when we are feeding on the faults of others. (HC 5:24)

Self-Righteousness

1 Don't be limited in your views with regard to your neighbor's virtue, but beware of self-righteousness, and be limited in the estimate of your own virtues, and not think yourselves more righteous than others; you must enlarge your souls towards each other, if you would do like Jesus, and carry your fellow-creatures to Abraham's bosom. (HC 4:606)

2 Christ was condemned by the self-righteous Jews because He took sinners into His society. . . .
All the religious world is boasting of righteousness: it is the doctrine of the devil to retard the human mind, and hinder our progress, by filling us with self-righteousness. . . .

Selfishness
1 Letter to the brethren scattered from Zion, Kirtland, 22 January 1834.
2 Letter to the Twelve in England, Nauvoo, 15 December 1840. The placement of this letter in HC implies that it was written in October 1840, but actually it was written on 15 December 1840 (see PWJS, p. 480).
3 Remarks to the Relief Society, Nauvoo, 9 June 1842.

Self-Righteousness
1 Remarks to the Relief Society, Nauvoo, 28 April 1842.
2 Remarks to the Relief Society, Nauvoo, 9 June 1842.

Sisters of the society [the Relief Society], shall there be strife among you? I will not have it. You must repent, and get the love of God. Away with self-righteousness. (HC 5:24)

Service

1   Thus you see, my dear brother, the willingness of our heavenly Father to forgive sins, and restore to favor all those who are willing to humble themselves before Him, and confess their sins, and forsake them, and return to Him with full purpose of heart, acting no hypocrisy, to serve Him to the end. (HC 2:315)

2   This is one of the many instances in which I have suddenly been brought from a state of health, to the borders of the grave, and as suddenly restored, for which my heart swells with gratitude to my heavenly Father, and I feel renewedly to dedicate myself and all my powers to His service. (HC 2:493)

3   We pronounce the blessings of heaven upon the heads of the Saints who seek to serve God with undivided hearts, in the name of Jesus Christ. Amen. (HC 3:305)

4   I always feel glad to do all I can for individuals. (TWJS, p. 33)

5   The store has been filled to overflowing, and I have stood behind the counter all day, dealing out goods as steady as any clerk you ever saw, to oblige those who were compelled to go without their usual Christmas and New Year's dinners, for the want of a little sugar, molasses, raisins, &c., &c; and to please myself also, for I love to wait upon the Saints, and be a servant to all, hoping that I may be exalted in the due time of the Lord. (HC 4:492)

Service
  1   Letter to Harvey Whitlock encouraging him to return to the Church, Kirtland, 16 November 1835.
  2   Kirtland, 14 June 1837.
  3   Letter to the Saints from Liberty Jail, 20–25 March 1839.
  4   Letter to John M. Bernhisel, Nauvoo, 13 April 1841.
  5   Letter to Edward Hunter, Nauvoo, 5 January 1842.

6 Let your labors be mostly confined to those around you, in the circle of your own acquaintance, as far as knowledge is concerned, it may extend to all the world; but your administering should be confined to the circle of your immediate acquaintance. (HC 4:607)

7 I prophesied that if the council would be liberal in their proceedings, they would become rich, and spoke against the principle of pay for every little service rendered, and especially of committees having extra pay for their services. (HC 5:270)

Seventies

1 The Seventies are to constitute traveling quorums, to go into all the earth, whithersoever the Twelve Apostles shall call them. (HC 2:202)

2 If the first Seventy are all employed, and there is a call for more laborers, it will be the duty of the seven presidents of the first Seventy to call and ordain other Seventy and send them forth to labor in the vineyard, until, if needs be, they set apart seven times seventy, and even until there are one hundred and forty-four thousand thus set apart for the ministry.

The Seventy are not to attend the conferences of the Twelve, unless they are called upon or requested so to do by the Twelve. The Twelve and the Seventy have particularly to depend upon their ministry for their support, and that of their families; and they have a right, by virtue of their offices, to call upon the churches to assist them. . . .

The circumstances of the presidents of the Seventy were severally considered, relative to their traveling in the vineyard: and it was unanimously agreed that they should hold themselves in readiness to go, at the call of the Twelve, when the Lord opens the way. (HC 2:221)

Service
   6   Remarks to the Relief Society, Nauvoo, 28 April 1842.
   7   Remarks to Nauvoo City Council, 11 February 1843.

Seventies
   1   The organization of the First Quorum of Seventy in Kirtland, 28 February 1835.
   2   Minutes of a general council of the priesthood, Kirtland, 2 May 1835.

3 The Seventies are not called to serve tables, or preside over churches, to settle difficulties, but are to preach the Gospel and build them up, and set others, who do not belong to these quorums, to preside over them, who are High Priests. (HC 2:431–32)

Sign of the Son of Man

1 Sir:—Among the many signs of the times and other strange things which are continually agitating the minds of men, I notice a small speculation in the *Chicago Express,* upon the certificate of one Hyrum Redding, of Ogle county, Illinois, stating that he has seen the sign of the Son of Man as foretold in the 24th chapter of Matthew.

The slanderous allusion of a "seraglio" like the Grand Turk, which the editor applies to me, he may take to himself, for, "out of the abundance of the heart the mouth speaketh." Every honest man who has visited the city of Nauvoo since it existed, can bear record of better things, and place me in the front ranks of those who are known to do good for the sake of goodness, and show all liars, hypocrites and abominable creatures that, while vice sinks them down to darkness and woe, virtue exalts me and the Saints to light and immortality.

The editor, as well as some others, "thinks that Joe Smith has his match at last," because Mr. Redding thinks that he has seen the sign of the Son of Man. But I shall use my right, and declare that, notwithstanding Mr. Redding may have seen a wonderful appearance in the clouds one morning about sunrise (which is nothing very uncommon in the winter season,) he has not seen the sign of the Son of Man, as foretold by Jesus; neither has any man, nor will any man, until after the sun shall have been darkened and the moon bathed in blood; for the Lord hath not shown me any such sign; and as the prophet saith, so it must be—"Surely the Lord God will do nothing, but He revealeth His secret unto His servants the prophets." (See Amos 3:7.) Therefore hear this, O earth: The Lord will not come to reign over the righteous, in this world, in 1843, nor until everything for the Bridegroom is ready. (HC 5:290–91)

Seventies
3 Solemn assembly in the Kirtland Temple, 30 March 1836.

Sign of the Son of Man
1 Letter to the editor of the *Times and Seasons,* 1 March 1843.

Signs

1 Faith comes not by signs, but by hearing the word of God. (*HC* 3:379)

2 It is an eternal principle, that has existed with God from all eternity: That man who rises up to condemn others, finding fault with the Church, saying that they are out of the way, while he himself is righteous, then know assuredly, that that man is in the high road to apostasy; and if he does not repent, will apostatize, as God lives. The principle is as correct as the one that Jesus put forth in saying that he who seeketh a sign is an adulterous person; and that principle is eternal, undeviating, and firm as the pillars of heaven; for whenever you see a man seeking after a sign, you may set it down that he is an adulterous man. (*HC* 3:385)

3 The Lord cannot always be known by the thunder of His voice, by the display of His glory or by the manifestation of His power; and those that are the most anxious to see these things, are the least prepared to meet them, and were the Lord to manifest His powers as He did to the children of Israel, such characters would be the first to say, "Let not the Lord speak any more, lest we His people die." (*HC* 5:31)

4 In Mark we have these important words: Go ye into all the world, and preach the gospel to every creature. He that believeth and is baptised shall be saved, and he that believeth not shall be damned. And to show how the believers are to be known from the unbelievers, he continues and says: And these signs shall follow them that believe: in my name shall they cast out devils: they shall speak with new tongues: they shall take up serpents: and if they drink any deadly thing it shall not hurt them: they shall lay hands on the sick and they shall recover. (*T&S* 3:903)

Signs

1 Instructions to the Twelve, Commerce (Nauvoo), 27 June 1839.
2 Instructions to the Apostles and Seventies departing for missions to England, Commerce (Nauvoo), 2 July 1839.
3 Editorial in the *Times and Seasons*, 15 June 1842.
4 Editorial in the *Times and Seasons*, 1 September 1842.

5   When I was preaching in Philadelphia, a Quaker called out for a sign. I told him to be still. After the sermon, he again asked for a sign. I told the congregation the man was an adulterer; that a wicked and adulterous generation seeketh after a sign; and that the Lord had said to me in a revelation, that any man who wanted a sign was an adulterous person. "It is true," cried one, "for I caught him in the very act," which the man afterwards confessed, when he was baptized. (HC 5:268)

6   *Words of George A. Smith:* When the Church of Jesus Christ of Latter-day Saints was first founded, you could see persons rise up and ask, "What sign will you show us that we may be made to believe?" I recollect a Campbellite preacher who came to Joseph Smith, I think his name was Hayden. He came in and made himself known to Joseph, and said that he had come a considerable distance to be convinced of the truth. "Why," said he, "Mr. Smith, I want to know the truth, and when I am convinced, I will spend all my talents and time in defending and spreading the doctrines of your religion, and I will give you to understand that to convince me is equivalent to convincing all my society, amounting to several hundreds." Well, Joseph commenced laying before him the coming forth of the work, and the first principles of the Gospel, when Mr. Hayden exclaimed, "O this is not the evidence I want, the evidence that I wish to have is a notable miracle; I want to see some powerful manifestation of the power of God, I want to see a notable miracle performed; and if you perform such a one, then I will believe with all my heart and soul, and will exert all my power and all my extensive influence to convince others; and if you will not perform a miracle of this kind, then I am your worst and bitterest enemy." "Well," said Joseph, "what will you have done? Will you be struck blind, or dumb? Will you be paralyzed, or will you have one hand withered? Take your choice, choose which you please, and in the name of the Lord Jesus Christ it shall be done." "That is not the kind of miracle I want," said the preacher. "Then, sir," replied Joseph, "I can perform none, I am not going to bring any trouble upon any body else, sir, to convince you. I will tell you what you make me think of—the very first person who asked a sign of the Savior, for it is written, in the New Testament, that Satan came to the Savior in the

---

Signs
5   The Prophet's recollection of an earlier incident, Nauvoo, 9 February 1843.
6   Address by George A. Smith, Salt Lake City, 24 June 1855.

desert, when he was hungry with forty days' fasting, and said, 'If you be the Son of God, command these stones to be made bread.'" "And now," said Joseph, "the children of the devil and his servants have been asking for signs ever since; and when the people in that day continued asking him for signs to prove the truth of the Gospel which he preached, the Savior replied, 'It is a wicked and an adulterous generation that seeketh a sign,'" &c.

But the poor preacher had so much faith in the power of the Prophet that he daren't risk being struck blind, lame, dumb, or having one hand withered, or any thing of the kind. We have frequently heard men calling for signs without knowing actually what they did want. Could he not have tested the principles, and thus have ascertained the truth? But this is not the disposition of men of the religious world. (*JD* 2:326–27)

Sin

1   If men sin wilfully after they have received the knowledge of the truth, there remaineth no more sacrifice for sin, but a certain fearful looking for of judgment and fiery indignation to come, which shall devour these adversaries. For he who despised Moses' law died without mercy under two or three witnesses. Of how much more severe punishment suppose ye, shall he be thought worthy, who hath sold his brother, and denied the new and everlasting covenant by which he was sanctified, calling it an unholy thing, and doing despite to the Spirit of grace. (HC 3:232)

2   I charged the Saints not to follow the example of the adversary in accusing the brethren, and said, "If you do not accuse each other, God will not accuse you. If you have no accuser you will enter heaven, and if you will follow the revelations and instructions which God gives you through me, I will take you into heaven as my back load. If you will not accuse me, I will not accuse you. If you will throw a cloak of charity over my sins, I will over yours—for charity covereth a multitude of sins. What many people call sin is not sin; I do many things to break down superstition, and I will break it down." (HC 4:445)

Sin
1   Letter to the Church from Liberty Jail, 16 December 1838.
2   Sabbath address, Nauvoo, 7 November 1841.

3 I preached at my house, morning and evening, illustrating the nature of sin, and showing that it is not right to sin that grace may abound. (HC 4:494)

4 Don't envy the finery and fleeting show of sinners, for they are in a miserable situation; but as far as you can, have mercy on them, for in a short time God will destroy them, if they will not repent and turn unto him. (HC 4:607)

Solemn Assemblies

1 We must have all things prepared, and call our solemn assembly as the Lord has commanded us, that we may be able to accomplish His great work, and it must be done in God's own way. The house of the Lord must be prepared, and the solemn assembly called and organized in it, according to the order of the house of God; and in it we must attend to the ordinance of washing of feet. It was never intended for any but official members. It is calculated to unite our hearts, that we may be one in feeling and sentiment, and that our faith may be strong, so that Satan cannot overthrow us, nor have any power over us here.

The endowment you are so anxious about, you cannot comprehend now, nor could Gabriel explain it to the understanding of your dark minds; but strive to be prepared in your hearts, be faithful in all things, that when we meet in the solemn assembly, that is, when such as God shall name out of all the official members shall meet, we must be clean every whit. . . .

I feel disposed to speak a few words more to you, my brethren, concerning the endowment: All who are prepared, and are sufficiently pure to abide the presence of the Savior, will see Him in the solemn assembly. (HC 2:308–9, 310)

2 At eight o'clock, according to appointment, the Presidency, the Twelve, the Seventies, the High Council, the Bishops and their entire

---

Sin
  3 Sabbath address, Nauvoo, 16 January 1842.
  4 Remarks to the Relief Society, Nauvoo, 28 April 1842.

Solemn Assemblies
  1 Instructions to the Twelve, Kirtland, 12 November 1835.
  2 Solemn assembly in the Kirtland Temple, 30 March 1836.

quorums, the Elders and all the official members in this stake of Zion, amounting to about three hundred, met in the Temple of the Lord to attend to the ordinance of washing of feet. I ascended the pulpit, and remarked to the congregation that we had passed through many trials and afflictions since the organization of the Church, and that this is a year of jubilee to us, and a time of rejoicing, and that it was expedient for us to prepare bread and wine sufficient to make our hearts glad, as we should not, probably, leave this house until morning. . . .

Tubs, water, and towels were prepared, and I called the house to order, and the Presidency proceeded to wash the feet of the Twelve, pronouncing many prophecies and blessings upon them in the name of the Lord Jesus; and then the Twelve proceeded to wash the feet of the Presidents of the several quorums. The brethren began to prophesy upon each other's heads, and upon the enemies of Christ, who inhabited Jackson county, Missouri; and continued prophesying, and blessing, and sealing them with hosanna and amen, until nearly seven o'clock in the evening. . . .

I left the meeting in the charge of the Twelve, and retired about nine o'clock in the evening. The brethren continued exhorting, prophesying, and speaking in tongues until five o'clock in the morning. The Savior made His appearance to some, while angels ministered to others, and it was a Pentecost and an endowment indeed, long to be remembered, for the sound shall go forth from this place into all the world, and the occurrences of this day shall be handed down upon the pages of sacred history, to all generations; as the day of Pentecost, so shall this day be numbered and celebrated as a year of jubilee, and time of rejoicing to the Saints of the Most High God. (*HC* 2:430–31, 432–33)

3   A brief notice only was given, that a solemn assembly would be called, of the official members of the Church, on the 6th of April, for the purpose of washing, anointing, washing of feet, receiving instructions, and the further organization of the ministry. Meetings were held by the different quorums on Monday, 3rd, Tuesday, 4th, and Wednesday, 5th, to anoint such of their respective members as had not been washed and anointed, that all might be prepared for the meeting on the 6th.

Solemn Assemblies
3   Solemn assembly in the Kirtland Temple, 6 April 1837.

At an early hour on Thursday, the 6th of April, the official members assembled in the House of the Lord, when the time for the first two or three hours was spent by the different quorums in washing of feet, singing, praying, and preparing to receive instructions from the Presidency. The Presidents, together with the Seventies and their presidents, repaired to the west room in the attic story, where, for want of time the preceding evening, it became necessary to seal the anointing of those who had recently been anointed and not sealed. (HC 2:475–76)

Sons of Perdition

1   Say to the brothers Hulet and to all others, that the Lord never authorized them to say that the devil, his angels or the sons of perdition, should ever be restored; for their state of destiny was not revealed to man, is not revealed, nor ever shall be revealed, save to those who are made partakers thereof: consequently those who teach this doctrine, have not received it of the Spirit of the Lord. Truly Brother Oliver declared it to be the doctrine of the devils. We therefore command that this doctrine be taught no more in Zion. We sanction the decision of the Bishop and his council, in relation to this doctrine being a bar to communion. (HC 1:366)

2   All sins shall be forgiven, except the sin against the Holy Ghost; for Jesus will save all except the sons of perdition. What must a man do to commit the unpardonable sin? He must receive the Holy Ghost, have the heavens opened unto him, and know God, and then sin against him. After a man has sinned against the Holy Ghost, there is no repentance for him. He has got to say that the sun does not shine while he sees it; he has got to deny Jesus Christ when the heavens have been opened unto him, and to deny the plan of salvation with his eyes open to the truth of it; and from that time he begins to be an enemy. This is the case with many apostates of the Church of Jesus Christ of Latter-day Saints.

When a man begins to be an enemy to his work, he hunts me, he seeks to kill me, and never ceases to thirst for my blood. He gets the

---

Sons of Perdition

1   Letter to the brethren in Zion, Kirtland, 25 June 1833.
2   King Follett Discourse, Nauvoo, 7 April 1844.

spirit of the devil—the same spirit that they had who crucified the Lord of Life—the same spirit that sins against the Holy Ghost. . . .

. . . There have been remarks made concerning all men being redeemed from hell; but I say that those who sin against the Holy Ghost cannot be forgiven in this world or in the world to come; they shall die the second death. Those who commit the unpardonable sin are doomed to *Gnolom*—to dwell in hell, worlds without end. As they concocted scenes of bloodshed in this world, so they shall rise to that resurrection which is as the lake of fire and brimstone. Some shall rise to the everlasting burnings of God; for God dwells in everlasting burnings and some shall rise to the damnation of their own filthiness, which is as exquisite a torment as the lake of fire and brimstone. (*HC* 6:314, 317)

Sorcery

1   Having said so much upon general principles, without referring to the peculiar situation, power, and influence of magicians of Egypt, the wizards and witches of the Jews, the oracles of the heathen, their necromancers, soothsayers, and astrologers, the maniacs or those possessed of devils in the Apostles' days, we will notice, and try to detect (so far as we have the Scriptures for our aid) some few instances of the development of false spirits in more modern times, and in this our day. (*HC* 4:576)

2   The High Council, with my brother Hyrum presiding, sat on an appeal of Benjamin Hoyt, from the decision of David Evans, bishop; which was, that Brother Hoyt cease to call certain characters witches or wizards, cease to work with the divining rod, and cease burning a board or boards to heal those whom he said were bewitched. On hearing the case, the council decided to confirm the decision of Bishop Evans. (*HC* 5:311–12)

Sorcery
1   Editorial in the *Times and Seasons*, 1 April 1842.
2   Meeting of the Nauvoo high council, 25 March 1843.

Speaking

1   We met the brethren according to previous appointment, and spoke to them as the Spirit gave utterance, greatly to their gratification. (HC 1:417)

2   *Minutes:* Joseph said to D[on] C[arlos] Smith that to be free from the corruptions of the earth . . . the speaker should always speak in his natural tone of voice, and not to keep in one loud strain, but to act without affectation. (*WJS*, p. 61; standardized)

Spirit Matter

1   We . . . state that spirit is a substance; that it is material, but that it is more pure, elastic and refined matter than the body; that it existed before the body, can exist in the body; and will exist separate from the body, when the body will be mouldering in the dust; and will in the resurrection, be again united with it. (HC 4:575)

Spirits

1   The witch of Endor is a no less singular personage; clothed with a powerful agency she raised the Prophet Samuel from his grave, and he appeared before the astonished king, and revealed unto him his future destiny. Who is to tell whether this woman is of God, and a righteous woman—or whether the power she possessed was of the devil, and she

---

Speaking
  1   Westfield, New York, 10 October 1833.
  2   Lecture given at the Nauvoo Lyceum, 5 January 1841. (The lyceum met weekly at different locations in Nauvoo for several months, beginning 5 January 1841.) Recorded in William P. McIntire's Minute Book, LDS Church Archives.

Spirit Matter
  1   Editorial in the *Times and Seasons*, 1 April 1842.

Spirits
  1   Editorial in the *Times and Seasons*, 1 April 1842.

a witch as represented by the Bible? It is easy for us to say now, but if we had lived in her day, which of us could have unravelled the mystery? (HC 4:571)

2   The Turks, the Hindoos, the Jews, the Christians, the Indian; in fact all nations have been deceived, imposed upon and injured through the mischievous effects of false spirits. (HC 4:573)

3   Without attempting to describe this mysterious connection [between the spirit and the body in the resurrection], and the laws that govern the body and the spirit of man, their relationship to each other, and the design of God in relation to the human body and spirit, I would just remark, that the spirits of men are eternal, that they are governed by the same Priesthood that Abraham, Melchisedek, and the Apostles were: that they are organized according to that Priesthood which is everlasting, "without beginning of days or end of years,"—that they all move in their respective spheres, and are governed by the law of God; that when they appear upon the earth they are in a probationary state, and are preparing, if righteous, for a future and greater glory; that the spirits of good men cannot interfere with the wicked beyond their prescribed bounds, for Michael, the Archangel, dared not bring a railing accusation against the devil, but said, "The Lord rebuke thee, Satan."

It would seem also, that wicked spirits have their bounds, limits, and laws by which they are governed or controlled, and know their future destiny; hence, those that were in the maniac said to our Savior, "Art thou come to torment us before the time," and when Satan presented himself before the Lord, among the sons of God, he said that he came "from going to and fro in the earth, and from wandering up and down in it;" and he is emphatically called the prince of the power of the air; and, it is very evident that they possess a power that none but those who have the Priesthood can control, as we have before adverted to, in the case of the sons of Sceva. (HC 4:575–76)

4   The spirits of the just are exalted to a greater and more glorious work; hence they are blessed in their departure to the world of spirits. Enveloped in flaming fire, they are not far from us, and know and un-

---

Spirits
2   Editorial in the *Times and Seasons*, 1 April 1842.
3   Editorial in the *Times and Seasons*, 1 April 1842.
4   Remarks upon the death of James Adams, Nauvoo, 9 October 1843.

derstand our thoughts, feelings, and motions, and are often pained therewith. (HC 6:52)

5   When I talk to these mourners, what have they lost? Their relatives and friends are only separated from their bodies for a short season: their spirits which existed with God have left the tabernacle of clay only for a little moment, as it were; and they now exist in a place where they converse together the same as we do on the earth.

I am dwelling on the immortality of the spirit of man. Is it logical to say that the intelligence of spirits is immortal, and yet that it has a beginning? The intelligence of spirits had no beginning, neither will it have an end. That is good logic. That which has a beginning may have an end. There never was a time when there were not spirits; for they are co-equal {co-eternal} with our Father in heaven.

I want to reason more on the spirit of man; for I am dwelling on the body and spirit of man—on the subject of the dead. I take my ring from my finger and liken it unto the mind of man—the immortal part, because it had no beginning. Suppose you cut it in two; then it has a beginning and an end; but join it again, and it continues one eternal round. So with the spirit of man. As the Lord liveth, if it had a beginning, it will have an end. All the fools and learned and wise men from the beginning of creation, who say that the spirit of man had a beginning, prove that it must have an end; and if that doctrine is true, then the doctrine of annihilation would be true. But if I am right, I might with boldness proclaim from the house-tops that God never had the power to create the spirit of man at all. God himself could not create himself. (HC 6:311)

Spirit World

1   "If the Mormon doctrine is true, what has become of all those who died since the days of the Apostles?"

All those who have not had an opportunity of hearing the Gospel, and being administered unto by an inspired man in the flesh, must have it hereafter, before they can be finally judged. (HC 3:29)

Spirits
   5   King Follett Discourse, Nauvoo, 7 April 1844.

Spirit World
   1   Answers to questions frequently asked the Prophet, Far West, 8 May 1838.

2   *Words of Benjamin F. Johnson:* Then with a deep-drawn breath, as a sigh of weariness, he sank down heavily in his chair, and said, "Oh! I am so tired—so tired that I often feel to long for my day of rest. For what has there been in this life but tribulation for me? From a boy I have been persecuted by my enemies, and now even my friends are beginning to join with them, to hate and persecute me! Why should I not wish for my time of rest?"

His words and tone thrilled and shocked me, and like an arrow pierced my hopes that he would long remain with us. I said, as with a heart full of tears, "Oh! Joseph, what could we, as a people, do without you and what would become of the great latter-day work if you should leave us?"

He was touched by my emotions, and in reply he said, "Benjamin, I would not be far away from you, and if on the other side of the veil I would still be working with you, and with a power greatly increased, to roll on this kingdom." (*TK*, p. 97)

3   I will say something about the spirits in prison. There has been much said by modern divines about the words of Jesus (when on the cross) to the thief, saying, "This day shalt thou be with me in paradise." King James' translators make it out to say paradise. But what is paradise? It is a modern word: it does not answer at all to the original word that Jesus made use of. Find the original of the word paradise. You may as easily find a needle in a haymow. Here is a chance for battle, ye learned men. There is nothing in the original word in Greek from which this was taken that signifies paradise; but it was—This day thou shalt be with me in the world of spirits: then I will teach you all about it and answer your inquiries. And Peter says he went and preached to the world of spirits (spirits in prison, I Peter, 3rd chap., 19th verse), so that they who would receive it could have it answered by proxy by those who live on the earth, etc. . . .

I will criticise a little further. There has been much said about the word hell, and the sectarian world have preached much about it, describing it to be a burning lake of fire and brimstone. But what is hell? It is another modern term, and is taken from hades. I'll hunt after hades as Pat did for the woodchuck.

Spirit World
  2   Letter of Benjamin F. Johnson to George S. Gibbs, 1903. The conversation described may have occurred in March 1843.
  3   Sabbath address, Nauvoo, 11 June 1843.

Hades, the Greek, or Shaole, the Hebrew: these two significations mean a world of spirits. Hades, Shaole, paradise, spirits in prison, are all one: it is a world of spirits.

The righteous and the wicked all go to the same world of spirits until the resurrection. "I do not think so," says one. If you will go to any house any time, I will take my lexicon and prove it to you.

The great misery of departed spirits in the world of spirits, where they go after death, is to know that they have come short of the glory that others enjoy and that they might have enjoyed themselves, and they are their own accusers. "But," says one, "I believe in one universal heaven and hell, where all go, and are all alike, and equally miserable or equally happy."

What! where all are huddled together—the honorable, virtuous, and murderers, and whoremongers, when it is written that they shall be judged according to the deeds done in the body? But St. Paul informs us of three glories and three heavens. He knew a man that was caught up to the third heavens. Now, if the doctrine of the sectarian world, that there is but one heaven, is true, Paul, what do you tell that lie for, and say there are three? Jesus said unto His disciples, "In my Father's house are many mansions, if it were not so, I would have told you. I go to prepare a place for you, and I will come and receive you to myself, that where I am ye may be also." (HC 5:424–26)

4 Now, all those [who] die in the faith go to the prison of spirits to preach to the dead in body, but they are alive in the spirit; and those spirits preach to the spirits that they may live according to God in the spirit, and men do minister for them in the flesh; and angels bear the glad tidings to the spirits, and they are made happy by these means. (*WJS*, p. 370; standardized)

5 *Words of William Taylor:* He [Joseph Smith] seemed to be just as familiar with the spirit world, and as well acquainted with the other side, as he was with this world. (*TK*, p. 161)

Spirit World
4   Sabbath address, Nauvoo, 12 May 1844, as reported by George Laub.
5   Recollection of William Taylor, published in the *Young Woman's Journal*, December 1906.

6 *Words of Lucy Walker Kimball:* He [Joseph Smith] anticipated great joy in meeting his parents and friends beyond the grave. He believed that as soon as the spirit left the body we were shaking hands with and greeting our friends. (*TK*, p. 139)

Stealing

1 The occurrence of recent events makes it criminal for me to remain longer silent. The tongue of the vile yet speaks, and sends forth the poison of asps, the ears of the spoiler yet hear, and he puts forth his hands to iniquity. It has been proclaimed upon the house top and in the secret chamber, in the public walks and private circle, throughout the length and breadth of this vast continent, that stealing by the Latter-day Saints has received my approval; nay, that I have taught the doctrine, encouraged them in plunder, and led on the van—than which nothing is more foreign from my heart. I disfellowship the perpetrators of all such abominations—they are devils and not Saints, totally unfit for the society of Christians or men. It is true that some professing to be Latter-day Saints have taught such vile heresies, but all are not Israel that are of Israel; and I wish it to be distinctly understood in all coming time, that the Church, over which I have the honor of presiding, will ever set its brows like brass, and its face like steel, against all such abominable acts of villainy and crime; and to this end I append my affidavit of disavowal, taken this day before General [John C.] Bennett, that there may be no mistake hereafter as to my real sentiments, or those of the leaders of the Church, in relation to this important matter. . . .

Now it is to be hoped that none will hereafter be so reckless as to state that I, or the Church to which I belong, approve of thieving—but that all the friends of law and order will join in ferreting out thieves wherever and whenever they may be found, and assist in bringing them to that condign punishment which such infamous crimes so richly merit. (*HC* 4:461–62)

Spirit World

   6   Recollection of Lucy Walker Kimball, published in the *Woman's Exponent*, November 1910.

Stealing

   1   Affidavit dated 29 November 1841, published in the *Times and Seasons*, 1 December 1841.

2 *Minutes:* President Joseph Smith said, I think it best to continue this subject. I want the elders to make honorable proclamation abroad concerning what the feelings of the First Presidency are; for stealing has never been tolerated by them. I despise a thief. He would betray me if he could get the opportunity. I know that he would be a detriment to any cause; and if I were the biggest rogue in the world, he would steal my horse when I wanted to run away.

It has been said that some were afraid to disclose what they knew of these secret combinations; consequently I issued a proclamation, which you may read in the *Wasp,* Number 48. If any man is afraid to disclose what he knows about this gang of thieves, let him come to me and tell me the truth, and I will protect him from violence. Thieving must be stopped. (HC 5:333–34)

3 I never stole the value of a pin's head, or a picayune in my life; and when you are hungry don't steal. Come to me, and I will feed you. (HC 6:59)

Strength

1 It was clearly evident that the Lord gave us power in proportion to the work to be done, and strength according to the race set before us, and grace and help as our needs required. (HC 1:176)

2 The great and wise of ancient days have failed in all their attempts to promote eternal power, peace and happiness. Their nations have crumbled to pieces; their thrones have been cast down in their turn, and their cities, and their mightiest works of art have been annihilated; or their dilapidated towers, of time-worn monuments have left us but feeble traces of their former magnificence and ancient grandeur. They proclaim as with a voice of thunder, those imperishable truths—that man's strength is weakness, his wisdom is folly, his glory is his shame. (HC 5:62)

Stealing
2 General conference address, Nauvoo, 6 April 1843.
3 Sabbath address, Nauvoo, 15 October 1843.

Strength
1 Kirtland, 3 June 1831.
2 Editorial in the *Times and Seasons,* 15 July 1842.

Sustaining Church Leaders

1   If the Saints in Kirtland deem me unworthy of their prayers when they assemble together, and neglect to bear me up at the throne of heavenly grace, it is a strong and convincing proof to me that they have not the Spirit of God. If the revelations we have received are true, who is to lead the people? If the keys of the Kingdom have been committed to my hands, who shall open out the mysteries thereof?

As long as my brethren stand by me and encourage me, I can combat the prejudices of the world, and can bear the contumely and abuse with joy; but when my brethren stand aloof, when they begin to faint, and endeavor to retard my progress and enterprise, then I feel to mourn, but am no less determined to prosecute my task, being confident that although my earthly friends may fail, and even turn against me, yet my heavenly Father will bear me off triumphant. (HC 4:165)

2   Dear brethren, feeling desirous to carry out the purposes of God to which work we have been called; and to be co-workers with Him in this last dispensation; we feel the necessity of having the hearty cooperation of the Saints throughout this land, and upon the islands of the sea. It will be necessary for the Saints to hearken to counsel and turn their attention to the Church, the establishment of the Kingdom, and lay aside every selfish principle, everything low and groveling; and stand forward in the cause of truth, and assist to the utmost of their power, those to whom has been given the pattern and design. Like those who held up the hands of Moses, so let us hold up the hands of those who are appointed to direct the affairs of the Kingdom, so that they may be strengthened, and be enabled to prosecute their great designs, and be instrumental in effecting the great work of the last days. (HC 4:186)

3   I charged the Saints not to follow the example of the adversary in accusing the brethren, and said, "If you do not accuse each other, God will not accuse you. If you have no accuser you will enter heaven, and if you will follow the revelations and instructions which God gives

---

Sustaining Church Leaders
  1   Letter to Oliver Granger in Kirtland, sent from Nauvoo, July 1840.
  2   Letter of the First Presidency to the Church, Nauvoo, 31 August 1840.
  3   Sabbath address, Nauvoo, 7 November 1841.

you through me, I will take you into heaven as my back load. If you will not accuse me, I will not accuse you. If you will throw a cloak of charity over my sins, I will over yours—for charity covereth a multitude of sins. (HC 4:445)

4 *Report of Eliza R. Snow:* He [Joseph Smith] reproved those that were disposed to find fault with the management of the concerns of the Church, saying God had called him to lead the Church, and he would lead it right; those that undertake to interfere will be ashamed when their own folly is made manifest. . . .

If this Society [the Relief Society] listen to the counsel of the Almighty, through the heads of the Church, they shall have power to command queens in their midst. . . .

You will receive instructions through the order of the Priesthood which God has established, through the medium of those appointed to lead, guide and direct the affairs of the Church in this last dispensation. (HC 4:604, 605, 607)

5 Up to this day God had given me wisdom to save the people who took counsel. None had ever been killed who abode by my counsel. At Haun's Mill the brethren went contrary to my counsel; if they had not, their lives would have been spared. (HC 5:137)

6 The servants of the Lord are required to guard against those things that are calculated to do the most evil. The little foxes spoil the vines—little evils do the most injury to the Church. If you have evil feelings, and speak of them to one another, it has a tendency to do mischief. These things result in those evils which are calculated to cut the throats of the heads of the Church.

When I do the best I can—when I am accomplishing the greatest good, then the most evils and wicked surmisings are got up against me. I would to God that you would be wise. I now counsel you, that if you know anything calculated to disturb the peace or injure the feelings of your brother or sister, hold your tongues, and the least harm will be done. (HC 5:140)

Sustaining Church Leaders
   4   Remarks to the Relief Society, Nauvoo, 28 April 1842.
   5   Conference address, Nauvoo, 29 August 1842.
   6   Remarks to the Relief Society, Nauvoo, 31 August 1842.

7 Never, while the spirit of liberty, or the virtue of a saint, hold communion in the flesh, let us hear of those who profess to be governed by the law of God, and make their garments clean in the blood of the Lamb, shrinking from the assistance of those who bear the ark of the Lord—in the hour of danger! (*T&S* 3:903)

8 Inasmuch as you have come up here, essaying to keep the commandments of God, I pronounce the blessings of heaven and earth upon you; and inasmuch as you will follow counsel, act wisely and do right, these blessings shall rest upon you so far as I have power with God to seal them upon you. (*HC* 5:354)

9 Woe, woe be to that man or set of men who lift up their hands against God and His witness in these last days: for they shall deceive almost the very chosen ones! (*HC* 6:364)

Swearing

1 Abstain from drunkenness, and from swearing, and from all profane language. (*HC* 3:233)

2 I love that man better who swears a stream as long as my arm yet deals justice to his neighbors and mercifully deals his substance to the poor, than the long, smooth-faced hypocrite. (*HC* 5:401)

Sustaining Church Leaders
7 Editorial in the *Times and Seasons*, 1 September 1842.
8 Remarks to newly arrived Saints from England, Nauvoo, 13 April 1843.
9 Sabbath address, Nauvoo, 12 May 1844.

Swearing
1 Letter to the Church from Liberty Jail, 16 December 1838.
2 Sabbath address, Nauvoo, 21 May 1843.

Talents

1 *Minutes:* Brother Joseph Smith, Jr., was appointed to examine these brethren presenting themselves for ordination; after prayer said that he had a testimony that each had one talent and if after being ordained they should hide it God would take it from them. (*FWR*, p. 25; standardized)

2 The reflection that everyone is to receive according to his own diligence and perseverance while in the vineyard, ought to inspire everyone who is called to be a minister of these glad tidings, to so improve his talent that he may gain other talents, that when the Master sits down to take an account of the conduct of His servants, it may be said, Well done, good and faithful servant: thou hast been faithful over a few things; I will now make thee ruler over many things: enter thou into the joy of thy Lord. (*HC* 2:6)

3 Now, Brother Orson, if this Church, which is essaying to be the Church of Christ will not help us, when they can do it without sacrifice, with those blessings which God has bestowed upon them, I prophesy—I speak the truth, I lie not—God shall take away their talent, and give it to those who have no talent, and shall prevent them from ever obtaining a place of refuge, or an inheritance upon the land of Zion; therefore they may tarry, for they might as well be overtaken where they are, as to incur the displeasure of God, and fall under His wrath by the way side, as to fall into the hands of a merciless mob, where there is no God to deliver, as salt that has lost its savor, and is thenceforth good for nothing, but to be trodden under foot of men. (*HC* 2:48)

4 There are many causes of embarrassment, of a pecuniary nature now pressing upon the heads of the Church. They began poor; were needy, destitute, and were truly afflicted by their enemies; yet the

Talents
1   Minutes of a conference held at Orange, Ohio, 25 October 1831.
2   Letter to the brethren scattered from Zion, Kirtland, 22 January 1834.
3   Letter to Orson Hyde in New York State from the First Presidency, Kirtland, 7 April 1834.
4   Solemn assembly in the Kirtland Temple, 6 April 1837.

Lord commanded them to go forth and preach the Gospel, to sacrifice their time, their talents, their good name, and jeopardize their lives; and in addition to this, they were to build a house for the Lord, and prepare for the gathering of the Saints. (HC 2:478–79)

5   Everything that God gives us is lawful and right; and it is proper that we should enjoy His gifts and blessings whenever and wherever He is disposed to bestow. . . . He never will institute an ordinance or give a commandment to His people that is not calculated in its nature to promote that happiness which He has designed, and which will not end in the greatest amount of good and glory to those who become the recipients of his law and ordinances. Blessings offered, but rejected, are no longer blessings, but become like the talent hid in the earth by the wicked and slothful servant; the proffered good returns to the giver; the blessing is bestowed on those who will receive and occupy; for unto him that hath shall be given, and he shall have abundantly, but unto him that hath not or will not receive, shall be taken away that which he hath, or might have had. (HC 5:135)

Teaching

1   Let the Elders abroad be exceedingly careful upon this subject, and when they ordain a man to the holy ministry, let him be a faithful man, who is able to teach others also; that the cause of Christ suffer not. It is not the multitude of preachers that is to bring about the glorious millennium! but it is those who are "called, and chosen, and faithful." (HC 1:468)

2   And first, it becomes an Elder when he is traveling through the world, warning the inhabitants of the earth to gather together, that they may be built up an holy city unto the Lord, instead of commencing with children, or those who look up to parents or guardians to in-

---

Talents
   5   Essay on happiness, Nauvoo, 27 August 1842.

Teaching
   1   Letter to the elders of the Church, published in *The Evening and the Morning Star*, Kirtland, December 1833.
   2   Letter to the elders of the Church, Kirtland, 1 September 1835.

fluence their minds, thereby drawing them from their duties, which they rightfully owe these legal guardians, they should commence their labors with parents, or guardians; and their teachings should be such as are calculated to turn the hearts of the fathers to the children, and the hearts of the children to the fathers; and no influence should be used with children, contrary to the consent of their parents or guardians; but all such as can be persuaded in a lawful and righteous manner, and with common consent, we should feel it our duty to influence them to gather with the people of God. But otherwise let the responsibility rest upon the heads of parents or guardians, and all condemnation or consequences be upon their heads, according to the dispensation which he hath committed unto us; for God hath so ordained, that His work shall be cut short in righteousness, in the last days; therefore, first teach the parents, and then, with their consent, persuade the children to embrace the Gospel also. (HC 2:262)

3   A man of God should be endowed with wisdom, knowledge, and understanding, in order to teach and lead the people of God. (HC 5:426)

4   There has been a great difficulty in getting anything into the heads of this generation. It has been like splitting hemlock knots with a corn-dodger for a wedge, and a pumpkin for a beetle. Even the Saints are slow to understand.

I have tried for a number of years to get the minds of the Saints prepared to receive the things of God; but we frequently see some of them, after suffering all they have for the work of God, will fly to pieces like glass as soon as anything comes that is contrary to their traditions: they cannot stand the fire at all. How many will be able to abide a celestial law, and go through and receive their exaltation, I am unable to say, as many are called, but few are chosen. (HC 6:184–85)

5   The object with me is to obey and teach others to obey God in just what He tells us to do. It mattereth not whether the principle is popular or unpopular, I will always maintain a true principle, even if I stand alone in it. (HC 6:223)

Teaching
   3   Sabbath address, Nauvoo, 11 June 1843.
   4   Sabbath address, Nauvoo, 21 January 1844.
   5   Remarks following the sermon of an Episcopalian minister, Nauvoo, 21 February 1844.

6   It is my duty to teach the doctrine. I would teach it more fully—the spirit is willing but the flesh is weak. God is not willing to let me gratify you; but I must teach the Elders, and they should teach you. (HC 6:319)

7   It is my duty to teach those who err in doctrine. (*WJS*, p. 364)

8   The servants of God teach nothing but principles of eternal life, by their works ye shall know them. A good man will speak good things and holy principles, and an evil man evil things. I feel, in the name of the Lord, to rebuke all such bad principles, liars, &c., and I warn all of you to look out whom you are going after. (HC 6:366)

9   I am bold to declare I have taught all the strong doctrines publicly, and always teach stronger doctrines in public than in private. (HC 6:474)

Temper

1   I said the Lord had revealed to me that a scourge would come upon the camp in consequence of the fractious and unruly spirits that appeared among them, and they should die like sheep with the rot; still, if they would repent and humble themselves before the Lord, the scourge, in a great measure, might be turned away; but, as the Lord lives, the members of this camp will suffer for giving way to their unruly temper. (HC 2:80)

Teaching
   6   General conference address, Nauvoo, 8 April 1844.
   7   General conference address, Nauvoo, 8 April 1844, as reported by Thomas Bullock.
   8   Sabbath address, Nauvoo, 12 May 1844.
   9   Sabbath address, Nauvoo, 16 June 1844.

Temper
   1   Events of Zion's Camp somewhere between the Illinois River and Atlas, Illinois, en route to Missouri, 3 June 1834.

Temples

1 Great preparations were making to commence a house of the Lord; and notwithstanding the Church was poor, yet our unity, harmony and charity abounded to strengthen us to do the commandments of God. The building of the house of the Lord in Kirtland was a matter that continued to increase in its interest in the hearts of the brethren. (HC 1:349)

2 On the same day (July 23rd), while the brethren in Missouri were preparing to leave the county, through the violence of the mob, the corner stones of the Lord's House were laid in Kirtland, after the order of the Holy Priesthood. (HC 1:400)

3 *Minutes:* From this short letter [written by Warren A. Cowdery] we discover that the Elders failed in the outset to fill their great and important mission [to gather donations to build the temple], as they know the Lord has commanded us to build a house, in which to receive an endowment, previous to the redemption of Zion; and that Zion could not be redeemed until this takes place. (HC 2:239)

4 The order of the house of God has been, and ever will be, the same, even after Christ comes; and after the termination of the thousand years it will be the same; and we shall finally enter into the celestial Kingdom of God, and enjoy it forever. (HC 2:309)

5 I then returned to the council room in the printing office, to meet my colleagues who were appointed with myself to draft rules and regulations to be observed in the "House of the Lord," in Kirtland, built by the Church of the Latter-day Saints, in the year of our Lord 1834, which rules are as follows:

Temples
1 Kirtland, 1 June 1833.
2 Kirtland, 23 July 1833.
3 Minutes of the high council at Kirtland, 4 August 1835.
4 Instructions to the Twelve, Kirtland, 12 November 1835.
5 Kirtland, 14 January 1836.

Rules and Regulations to be Observed in the House of the Lord in Kirtland.

I. It is according to the rules and regulations of all regularly and legally organized bodies to have a president to keep order.

II. The bodies thus organized are under obligation to be in subjection to that authority.

III. When a congregation assembles in this house, it shall submit to the following rules, that due respect may be paid to the order of worship, viz.:

1st. No man shall be interrupted who is appointed to speak by the Presidency of the Church, by any disorderly person or persons in the congregation, by whispering, by laughing, by talking, by menacing gestures, by getting up and running out in a disorderly manner, or by offering indignity to the manner of worship, or the religion, or to any officer of said Church while officiating in his office, in anywise whatsoever, by any display of ill manners or ill breeding, from old or young, rich or poor, male or female, bond or free, black or white, believer or unbeliever. And if any of the above insults are offered, such measures will be taken as are lawful, to punish the aggressor or aggressors, and eject them from the house.

2nd. An insult offered to the presiding Elder of said Church shall be considered an insult to the whole body. Also, an insult offered to any of the officers of said Church, while officiating, shall be considered an insult to the whole body.

3rd. All persons are prohibited from going up the stairs in times of worship.

4th. All persons are prohibited from exploring the house, except waited upon by a person appointed for that purpose.

5th. All persons are prohibited from going into the several pulpits, except the officers who are appointed to officiate in the same.

6th. All persons are prohibited from cutting, marking or marring the inside or outside of the house with a knife, pencil, or any other instrument whatever, under pain of such penalty as the law shall inflict.

7th. All children are prohibited from assembling in the house, above or below, or any part of it, to play, or for recreation, at any time: and all parents, guardians, or masters, shall be amenable for all damage that shall accrue in consequence of their children's misconduct.

8th. All persons, whether believers or unbelievers, shall be treated with due respect by the authorities of the Church.

9th. No imposition shall be practiced upon any members of the Church, by depriving them of their rights in the house. (HC 2:368–69)

6 The assembly [in the Kirtland Temple] was then organized in the following manner, viz.: west end of the house, Presidents Frederick G. Williams, Joseph Smith, Sen., and William W. Phelps occupying the first pulpit for the Melchisedek Priesthood; Presidents Joseph Smith, Jun., Hyrum Smith, and Sidney Rigdon, the second pulpit; Presidents David Whitmer, Oliver Cowdery, and John Whitmer, the third pulpit; the fourth was occupied by the President of the High Priests' quorum and his counselors, and two choristers. The Twelve Apostles on the right, in the three highest seats. The President of the Elders, his counselors and clerk, in the seat immediately below the Twelve. The High Council of Kirtland, consisting of twelve, on the left in the three first seats. The fourth seat, and next below the High Council, was occupied by Elders Warren A. Cowdery and Warren Parrish, who served as scribes. The pulpits in the east end of the house, for the Aaronic Priesthood, were occupied as follows: The Bishop of Kirtland and his counselors, in the first pulpit; the Bishop of Zion and his counselors, in the second pulpit; the president of the Priests and his counselors, in the third pulpit: the president of the Teachers and his counselors, and one chorister, in the fourth pulpit; the High Council of Zion, consisting of twelve counselors, on the right; the president of the Deacons and his counselors, in the seat below them; the seven presidents of Seventies, on the left. The choir of singers were seated in the four corners of the room, in seats prepared for that purpose. (HC 2:411)

7 Brother George A. Smith arose and began to prophesy, when a noise was heard like the sound of a rushing mighty wind, which filled the Temple, and all the congregation simultaneously arose, being moved upon by an invisible power; many began to speak in tongues and prophesy; others saw glorious visions; and I beheld the Temple was filled with angels, which fact I declared to the congregation. The people of the neighborhood came running together (hearing an unusual sound within, and seeing a bright light like a pillar of fire resting upon the Temple), and were astonished at what was taking place. This continued until the meeting closed at eleven p.m.

The number of official members present on this occasion was four hundred and sixteen, being a greater number than ever assembled on any former occasion. (HC 2:428)

Temples
  6   Events during the dedication of the Kirtland Temple, 27 March 1836.
  7   Events during the dedication of the Kirtland Temple, 27 March 1836.

8   This day being set apart to perform again the ceremonies of the [Kirtland Temple] dedication, for the benefit of those who could not get into the house the preceding Sabbath, I repaired to the Temple at eight, a.m., in company with the Presidency, and arranged our door keepers and stewards as on the former occasion. We then opened the doors, and a large congregation entered the house, and were comfortably seated. The authorities of the Church were seated in their respective places, and the services of the day were commenced, prosecuted and terminated in the same manner as at the former dedication, and the Spirit of God rested upon the congregation, and great solemnity prevailed. (HC 2:433)

9   The corner stones of the Houses of the Lord, agreeable to the commandments of the Lord unto us, given April 26, 1838, were laid. . . .

. . . The southeast corner stone of the Lord's House in Far West, Missouri, was then laid by the presidents of the stake, assisted by twelve men. The southwest corner, by the presidents of the Elders, assisted by twelve men. The northwest corner by the Bishop, assisted by twelve men. The northeast corner by the president of the Teachers, assisted by twelve men. This house is to be one hundred and ten feet long, and eighty feet broad.

The oration was delivered by President Rigdon, at the close of which was a shout of Hosanna, and a song, composed for the occasion by Levi W. Hancock, was sung by Solomon Hancock. The most perfect order prevailed throughout the day. (HC 3:41–42)

10   Believing the time has now come, when it is necessary to erect a house of prayer, a house of order, a house for the worship of our God, where the ordinances can be attended to agreeably to His divine will, in this region of country—to accomplish which, considerable exertion must be made, and means will be required—and as the work must be hastened in righteousness, it behooves the Saints to weigh the importance of these things, in their minds, in all their bearings, and then take such steps as are necessary to carry them into operation; and arming themselves with courage, resolve to do all they can, and feel them-

---

Temples
   8   The dedication ceremony was performed again for those not able to attend the first session, Kirtland, 31 March 1836.
   9   Far West, 4 July 1838.
   10   Letter to the Saints from the First Presidency, Nauvoo, 31 August 1840.

selves as much interested as though the whole labor depended on themselves alone. By so doing they will emulate the glorious deeds of the fathers, and secure the blessings of heaven upon themselves and their posterity to the latest generation.

To those who feel thus interested, and can assist in this great work, we say, let them come to this place; by so doing they will . . . assist in the rolling on of the Kingdom. (HC 4:186)

11 The Temple of the Lord is in process of erection here, where the Saints will come to worship the God of their fathers, according to the order of His house and the powers of the Holy Priesthood, and will be so constructed as to enable all the functions of the Priesthood to be duly exercised, and where instructions from the Most High will be received, and from this place go forth to distant lands. Let us then concentrate all our powers, under the provisions of our *magna charta* granted by the Illinois legislature, at the "City of Nauvoo" and surrounding country, and strive to emulate the action of the ancient covenant fathers and patriarchs, in those things which are of such vast importance to this and every succeeding generation. (HC 4:269)

12 In order to erect the Temple of the Lord, great exertions will be required on the part of the Saints, so that they may build a house which shall be accepted by the Almighty, and in which His power and glory shall be manifested. Therefore let those who can freely make a sacrifice of their time, their talents, and their property, for the prosperity of the kingdom, and for the love they have to the cause of truth, bid adieu to their homes and pleasant places of abode, and unite with us in the great work of the last days, and share in the tribulation, that they may ultimately share in the glory and triumph. (HC 4:273)

13 If the strict order of the Priesthood were carried out in the building of Temples, the first stone would be laid at the south-east corner, by the First Presidency of the Church. The south-west corner should be laid next. The third, or north-west corner next; and the fourth, or north-east corner last. The First Presidency should lay the south-east

---

Temples

11 Proclamation of the First Presidency, Nauvoo, 15 January 1841.

12 Proclamation of the First Presidency, Nauvoo, 15 January 1841.

13 Principles outlined in conjunction with the laying of the cornerstones of the Nauvoo Temple, 6 April 1841.

corner stone and dictate who are the proper persons to lay the other corner stones.

If a Temple is built at a distance, and the First Presidency are not present, then the Quorum of the Twelve Apostles are the persons to dictate the order for that Temple; and in the absence of the Twelve Apostles, then the Presidency of the Stake will lay the south-east corner stone; the Melchisedec Priesthood laying the corner stones on the east side of the Temple, and the Lesser Priesthood those on the west side. (HC 4:331)

14 The Church is not fully organized, in its proper order, and cannot be, until the Temple is completed, where places will be provided for the administration of the ordinances of the Priesthood. (HC 4:603)

15 I preached in the grove, on the keys of the kingdom, charity, &c. The keys are certain signs and words by which false spirits and personages may be detected from true, which cannot be revealed to the Elders till the Temple is completed. The rich can only get them in the Temple, the poor may get them on the mountain top as did Moses. The rich cannot be saved without charity, giving to feed the poor when and how God requires, as well as building. There are signs in heaven, earth and hell; the Elders must know them all, to be endowed with power, to finish their work and prevent imposition. The devil knows many signs, but does not know the sign of the Son of Man, or Jesus. No one can truly say he knows God until he has handled something, and this can only be in the holiest of holies. (HC 4:608)

16 I spent the day in the upper part of the store, that is in my private office . . . and in my general business office, or lodge room . . . in council with General James Adams, of Springfield, Patriarch Hyrum Smith, Bishops Newel K. Whitney and George Miller, and President Brigham Young and Elders Heber C. Kimball and Willard Richards, instructing them in the principles and order of the Priesthood, attending to washings, anointings, endowments and the communication of keys pertaining to the Aaronic Priesthood, and so on to the highest order of the Melchisedek Priesthood, setting forth the order pertain-

Temples
  14 Remarks to the Relief Society, Nauvoo, 28 April 1842.
  15 Sabbath address, Nauvoo, 1 May 1842.
  16 First temple endowment given in this dispensation, Nauvoo, 4 May 1842.

ing to the Ancient of Days, and all those plans and principles by which any one is enabled to secure the fullness of those blessings which have been prepared for the Church of the First Born, and come up and abide in the presence of the Eloheim in the eternal worlds. In this council was instituted the ancient order of things for the first time in these last days. And the communications I made to this council were of things spiritual, and to be received only by the spiritual minded: and there was nothing made known to these men but what will be made known to all the Saints of the last days, so soon as they are prepared to receive, and a proper place is prepared to communicate them, even to the weakest of the Saints; therefore let the Saints be diligent in building the Temple, and all houses which they have been, or shall hereafter be, commanded of God to build; and wait their time with patience in all meekness, faith, perseverance unto the end, knowing assuredly that all these things referred to in this council are always governed by the principle of revelation. (HC 5:1–2)

17 The architectural designs of the Temple at Jerusalem, together with its ornaments and beauty, were given of God. (HC 5:63)

18 It is for the same purpose that God gathers together His people in the last days, to build unto the Lord a house to prepare them for the ordinances and endowments, washings and anointings, etc. One of the ordinances of the house of the Lord is baptism for the dead. God decreed before the foundation of the world that that ordinance should be administered in a font prepared for that purpose in the house of the Lord. "This is only your opinion, sir," says the sectarian.

If a man gets a fullness of the priesthood of God, he has to get it in the same way that Jesus Christ obtained it, and that was by keeping all the commandments and obeying all the ordinances of the house of the Lord. . . .

These things are revealed in the most holy place in a Temple prepared for that purpose. Many of the sects cry out, "Oh, I have the testimony of Jesus; I have the spirit of God: but away with Joe Smith; he says he is a prophet; but there are to be no prophets or revelators in the last days." Stop, sir! The Revelator says that the testimony of Jesus is the spirit of prophecy; so by your own mouth you are condemned.

Temples
17 Editorial in the *Times and Seasons*, 15 July 1842.
18 Sabbath address, Nauvoo, 11 June 1843.

But to the text. Why gather the people together in this place? For the same purpose that Jesus wanted to gather the Jews—to receive the ordinances, the blessings, and the glories that God has in store for His Saints.

I will now ask this assembly and all the Saints if you will now build this house and receive the ordinances and blessings which God has in store for you; or will you not build unto the Lord this house, and let Him pass by and bestow these blessings upon another people? (HC 5:424, 427)

19 The 2nd Priesthood is Patriarchal authority. Go to and finish the temple, and God will fill it with power, and you will then receive more knowledge concerning this priesthood. (HC 5:555)

20 Some say it is better to give to the poor than to build the Temple. The building of the Temple has sustained the poor who were driven from Missouri, and kept them from starving; and it has been the best means for this object which could be devised.

Oh, all ye rich men of the Latter-day Saints from abroad, I would invite you to bring up some of your money—your gold, your silver, and your precious things, and give to the Temple. We want iron, steel, spades, and quarrying and mechanical tools. (HC 6:58–59)

21 The declaration this morning is, that as soon as the Temple and baptismal font are prepared, we calculate to give the Elders of Israel their washings and anointings, and attend to those last and more impressive ordinances, without which we cannot obtain celestial thrones. But there must be a holy place prepared for that purpose. There was a proclamation made during the time that the foundation of the Temple was laid to that effect, and there are provisions made until the work is completed, so that men may receive their endowments and be made kings and priests unto the Most High God, having nothing to do with temporal things, but their whole time will be taken up with things pertaining to the house of God. There must, however, be a place built expressly for that purpose, and for men to be baptized for their dead. It must be built in this the central place; for every man who wishes to save his father, mother, brothers, sisters and friends, must go through all the ordinances for each one of them separately, the same as for himself, from baptism to ordination, washings and anointings, and receive all the keys and powers of the Priesthood, the same as for himself. . . .

The Lord has an established law in relation to the matter: there must be a particular spot for the salvation of our dead. I verily believe there will be a place, and hence men who want to save their dead can come and bring their families, do their work by being baptized and attending to the other ordinances for their dead, and then may go back again to live and wait till they go to receive their reward. (HC 6:319)

Temporal Matters

1   As God governed Abraham, Isaac and Jacob as families, and the children of Israel as a nation; so we, as a Church, must be under His guidance if we are prospered, preserved and sustained. Our only confidence can be in God; our only wisdom obtained from Him: and He alone must be our protector and safeguard, spiritually and temporally, or we fall. (HC 5:65)

2   In the first place, where a crowd is flocking from all parts of the world, of different minds, religions, &c., there will be some who do not live up to the commandments; there will be some designing characters who would turn you aside and lead you astray. You may meet speculators who would get away your property; therefore it is necessary that we should have an order here, and when emigrants arrive, instruct them concerning these things. If the heads of the Church have laid the foundation of this place, and have had the trouble of doing what has been done, are they not better qualified to tell you how to lay out your money than those who have had no interest in the work whatever?

Some start {in faith} on the revelations to come here. Before they arrive, they get turned away, or meet with speculators who get their money for land with bad titles, and lose all their property; then they

---

Temporal Matters
1   Editorial in the *Times and Seasons*, 15 July 1842.
2   Remarks to Saints newly arrived from England, Nauvoo, 13 April 1843.

come and make their complaints to us, when it is too late to do anything for them. The object of this meeting is to tell you these things; and then, if you will pursue the same course, you must bear the consequences of your own folly. (*HC* 5:355)

Temptation

1   Those who resisted the Spirit of God, would be liable to be led into temptation, and then the association of heaven would be withdrawn from those who refused to be made partakers of such great glory. God would not exert any compulsory means, and the devil could not. (*HC* 4:358)

Ten Tribes
See Lost Tribes of Israel

Testimony

1   You remember the testimony which I bore in the name of the Lord Jesus, concerning the great work which He has brought forth in the last days. You know my manner of communication, how that in weakness and simplicity, I declared to you what the Lord had brought forth by the ministering of His holy angels to me for this generation. I pray that the Lord may enable you to treasure these things in your mind, for I know that His Spirit will bear testimony to all who seek diligently after knowledge from Him. I hope you will search the Scriptures to see whether these things are not also consistent with those things which the ancient Prophets and Apostles have written. (*HC* 1:442)

2   When the Lord's anointed go forth to proclaim the word, bearing testimony to this generation, if they receive it they shall be blessed; but if not, the judgments of God will follow close upon them, until

---

Temptation
   1   Sabbath address, Nauvoo, 16 May 1841.

Testimony
   1   Letter to Moses C. Nickerson, written from Kirtland, 19 November 1833.
   2   Remarks made during the dedication of the Kirtland Temple, 27 March 1836.

that city or that house which rejects them, shall be left desolate. (*HC* 2:418–19)

3   Know assuredly, dear brethren, that it is for the testimony of Jesus that we are in bonds and in prison. But we say unto you, that we consider that our condition is better (notwithstanding our sufferings) than that of those who have persecuted us, and smitten us, and borne false witness against us. (*HC* 3:226)

4   Faith comes by hearing the word of God, through the testimony of the servants of God; that testimony is always attended by the Spirit of prophecy and revelation. (*HC* 3:379)

5   No man can be a minister of Jesus Christ except he has the testimony of Jesus; and this is the spirit of prophecy. Whenever salvation has been administered, it has been by testimony. Men of the present time testify of heaven and hell, and have never seen either; and I will say that no man knows these things without this. (*HC* 3:389–90)

6   And as the new commandment given anciently was *to love one another*, even so the works of the Saints at home and abroad will bear its own testimony whether *they love the brethren*. (*HC* 6:69)

7   *History Entry:* During the evening the Patriarch Hyrum Smith read and commented upon extracts from the Book of Mormon, on the imprisonments and deliverance of the servants of God for the Gospel's sake. Joseph bore a powerful testimony to the guards of the divine authenticity of the Book of Mormon, the restoration of the Gospel, the administration of angels, and that the kingdom of God was again established upon the earth, for the sake of which he was then incarcerated in that prison, and not because he had violated any law of God or man. (*HC* 6:600)

Testimony
   3   Letter to the Church from Liberty Jail, 16 December 1838.
   4   Instructions to the Twelve, Commerce (Nauvoo), 27 June 1839.
   5   Discourse on the priesthood, given sometime before 8 August 1839, Commerce (Nauvoo). For a discussion on the dating of this discourse, see *WJS*, p. 22.
   6   Letter to the Saints encouraging them to patronize the Church newspaper, published in the *Times and Seasons*, 1 November 1843.
   7   Carthage Jail, 26 June 1844.

Theocracy

1   When the children of Israel were chosen with Moses at their head, they were to be a peculiar people, among whom God should place His name; their motto was: "The Lord is our lawgiver; the Lord is our Judge; the Lord is our King, and He shall reign over us." While in this state they might truly say, "Happy is that people, whose God is the Lord." Their government was a theocracy; they had God to make their laws, and men chosen by Him to administer them; He was their God, and they were His people. Moses received the word of the Lord from God Himself; he was the mouth of God to Aaron, and Aaron taught the people, in both civil and ecclesiastical affairs; they were both one, there was no distinction; so will it be when the purposes of God shall be accomplished; when "the Lord shall be King over the whole earth," and "Jerusalem His throne." "The law shall go forth from Zion, and the word of the Lord from Jerusalem." (HC 5:64)

Tithing

1   On the evening of the 29th of November, I united in prayer with Brother Oliver [Cowdery] for the continuance of blessings. After giving thanks for the relief which the Lord had lately sent us by opening the hearts of the brethren from the east, to loan us $430; after commencing and rejoicing before the Lord on this occasion, we agreed to enter into the following covenant with the Lord, viz.:

That if the Lord will prosper us in our business and open the way before us that we may obtain means to pay our debts; that we be not troubled nor brought into disrepute before the world, nor His people; after that, of all that He shall give unto us, we will give a tenth to be bestowed upon the poor in His Church, or as He shall command; and that we will be faithful over that which He has entrusted to our care, that we may obtain much; and that our children after us shall remember to observe this sacred and holy covenant; and that our children, and our children's children, may know of the same, we have subscribed our names with our own hands. (HC 2:174–75)

Theocracy
   1   Editorial in the *Times and Seasons*, 15 July 1842.

Tithing
   1   Kirtland, 29 November 1834.

2   While the busy multitudes have thus been engaged in their several vocations performing their daily labor, and working one-tenth of their time, others have not been less forward in bringing in their tithings and consecrations for the same great object. Never since the foundation of this Church was laid, have we seen manifested a greater willingness to comply with the requisitions of Jehovah, a more ardent desire to do the will of God, more strenuous exertions used, or greater sacrifices made than there have been since the Lord said, "Let the Temple be built by the tithing of my people." It seemed as though the spirit of enterprise, philanthropy and obedience rested simultaneously upon old and young, and brethren and sisters, boys and girls, and even strangers, who were not in the Church, united with an unprecedented liberality in the accomplishment of this great work; nor could the widow, in many instances, be prevented, out of her scanty pittance from throwing in her two mites. (*HC* 4:609)

3   Let them who are owing tithing pay it up. (*WJS*, p. 212)

4   *Clerk's Report:* Brother Wilkie now feels anxious to do right in all things, and especially to pay his tithing to the full. President Joseph showed him the principles of consecration and the means whereby he might realize the fullness of the blessings of the celestial kingdom; and as an evidence that he desired to do right, he paid over to the Trustee-in-Trust the sum of three hundred dollars in gold and silver for the benefit of the Temple, and which is now recorded on consecration.

He also signified his intention of paying more as soon as he could get matters properly arranged. The president then pronounced a blessing upon him and his companion, that they should have the blessing of God to attend them in their basket and in their store—that they should have the blessing of health and salvation and long life, inasmuch as they would continue to walk in obedience to the commandments of God. (*HC* 6:265)

Tithing
  2   Editorial in the *Times and Seasons*, 2 May 1842.
  3   Sabbath address, Nauvoo, 11 June 1843, as reported by Willard Richards.
  4   Instruction and blessing for John Wilkie, Nauvoo, 15 March 1844.

Titles

1 *Minutes:* After assembling, we received a rebuke for our former low, uncultivated, and disrespectful manner of communication and salutation with and unto each other, by the voice of the Spirit, saying unto us: "Verily, condemnation resteth upon you, who are appointed to lead my Church, and to be saviors of men; and also upon the Church; and there must needs be a repentance and a reformation among you in all things, in your ensamples before the Church and before the world, in all your manners, habits, and customs, and salutations one toward another; rendering unto every man the respect due the office, calling, and priesthood whereunto I, the Lord, have appointed and ordained you. Amen."

It is only necessary to say, relative to the foregoing reproof and instruction, that though it was given in sharpness, it occasioned gladness and joy, and we were willing to repent and reform in every particular, according to the instruction given. It is also proper to remark that after the reproof was given, we all confessed, voluntarily, that such had been the manifestations of the Spirit a long time since, in consequence of which the rebuke came with greater sharpness. (*PJS* 1:22; standardized)

Tolerance

See JUDGING, PREJUDICE, RELIGIOUS FREEDOM AND TOLERANCE

Tongue

1 *Report of Eliza R. Snow:* [President Joseph Smith] said . . . to put a double watch over the tongue: no organized body can exist without this at all. . . .

Titles
  1 The Prophet assembled with Oliver Cowdery, Sidney Rigdon, and Frederick G. Williams to ordain Oliver Cowdery to the office of Assistant President of the Church, 5 December 1834.

Tongue
  1 Remarks to the Relief Society, Nauvoo, 26 May 1842.

. . . The tongue is an unruly member—hold your tongues about things of no moment—a little tale will set the world on fire. At this time, the truth on the guilty should not be told openly, strange as this may seem, yet this is policy. We must use precaution in bringing sinners to justice, lest in exposing these heinous sins we draw the indignation of a Gentile world upon us (and, to their imagination, justly too). . . .

. . . All things contrary to the will of God, should be cast from us, but don't do more hurt than good, with your tongues—be pure in heart. (HC 5:20)

2   I now counsel you, that if you know anything calculated to disturb the peace or injure the feelings of your brother or sister, hold your tongues, and the least harm will be done. (HC 5:140)

3   The pagans, Roman Catholics, Methodists and Baptists shall have place in Nauvoo—only they must be ground in Joe Smith's mill. I have been in their mill. I was ground in Ohio and York States, in a Presbyterian smut machine, and the last machine was in Missouri; and the last of all, I have been through the Illinois smut machine; and those who come here must go through my smut machine, and that is my tongue. (HC 5:287)

Tongues, Gift of

1   *Words of Heber C. Kimball:* In September, 1832, Brothers Brigham and Joseph Young and myself went to Kirtland, Ohio. We saw Brother Joseph Smith and had a glorious time, during which Brother Brigham spoke in tongues, this being the first time Joseph had heard the gift. The Prophet rose up and testified that it was from God. The gift then fell upon him, and he spoke in tongues himself. (*TK*, p. 36)

Tongue
  2   Remarks to the Relief Society, Nauvoo, 31 August 1842.
  3   Address at the temple site in Nauvoo, 21 February 1843.

Tongues, Gift of
  1   Recollection of Heber C. Kimball, quoted by Helen Mar Whitney in the *Woman's Exponent*, (1 August 1880). The date of this incident in which Brigham Young and the Prophet spoke in tongues is thought to be about November 1832.

2 As to the gift of tongues, all we can say is, that in this place, we have received it as the ancients did: we wish you, however, to be careful lest in this you be deceived. Guard against evils which may arise from any accounts given by women, or otherwise; be careful in all things lest any root of bitterness spring up among you, and thereby many be defiled. Satan will no doubt trouble you about the gift of tongues, unless you are careful; you cannot watch him too closely, nor pray too much. May the Lord give you wisdom in all things. (HC 1:369)

3 *Minutes:* President Joseph Smith then gave an explanation of the gift of tongues, that it was particularly instituted for the preaching of the Gospel to other nations and languages, but it was not given for the government of the Church. (HC 2:162)

4 Tongues were given for the purpose of preaching among those whose language is not understood; as on the day of Pentecost, etc., and it is not necessary for tongues to be taught to the Church particularly, for any man that has the Holy Ghost, can speak of the things of God in his own tongue as well as to speak in another; for faith comes not by signs, but by hearing the word of God. (HC 3:379)

5 Speak not in the gift of tongues without understanding it, or without interpretation. The devil can speak in tongues; the adversary will come with his work; he can tempt all classes; can speak in English or Dutch. Let no one speak in tongues unless he interpret, except by the consent of the one who is placed to preside; then he may discern or interpret, or another may. (HC 3:392)

6 We have also had brethren and sisters who have had the gift of tongues falsely; they would speak in a muttering unnatural voice, and their bodies be distorted like the Irvingites before alluded to; whereas, there is nothing unnatural in the Spirit of God. (HC 4:580)

Tongues, Gift of
2   Letter to the brethren in Zion, Kirtland, 2 July 1833.
3   Minutes of a conference of elders at New Portage, Ohio, 8 September 1834.
4   Instructions to the Twelve, Commerce (Nauvoo), 27 June 1839.
5   Discourse on the priesthood, given sometime before 8 August 1839, Commerce (Nauvoo). For a discussion on the dating of this discourse, see *WJS*, p. 22.
6   Editorial in the *Times and Seasons*, 1 April 1842.

7   If you have a matter to reveal, let it be in your own tongue; do not indulge too much in the exercise of the gift of tongues, or the devil will take advantage of the innocent and unwary. You may speak in tongues for your own comfort, but I lay this down for a rule, that if anything is taught by the gift of tongues, it is not to be received for doctrine. (HC 4:607)

8   The gift of tongues is the smallest gift perhaps of the whole, and yet it is one that is the most sought after. . . .
     Be not so curious about tongues, do not speak in tongues except there be an interpreter present; the ultimate design of tongues is to speak to foreigners, and if persons are very anxious to display their intelligence, let them speak to such in their own tongues. The gifts of God are all useful in their place, but when they are applied to that which God does not intend, they prove an injury, a snare and a curse instead of a blessing. (HC 5:30, 31–32)

Traditions

1   It is very difficult for us to communicate to the churches all that God has revealed to us, in consequence of tradition. (HC 2:52)

2   This glorious truth [salvation for the dead] is well calculated to enlarge the understanding, and to sustain the soul under troubles, difficulties and distresses. For illustration, suppose the case of two men, brothers, equally intelligent, learned, virtuous and lovely, walking in uprightness and in all good conscience, so far as they have been able to discern duty from the muddy stream of tradition, or from the blotted page of the book of nature.
     One dies and is buried, having never heard the Gospel of reconciliation; to the other the message of salvation is sent, he hears and embraces it, and is made the heir of eternal life. Shall the one become the partaker of glory and the other be consigned to hopeless perdition?

Tongues, Gift of
   7   Remarks to the Relief Society, Nauvoo, 28 April 1842.
   8   Editorial in the *Times and Seasons*, 15 June 1842.

Traditions
   1   Conference of the elders of the Church, Norton, Ohio, 21 April 1834.
   2   General conference address, Nauvoo, 3 October 1841.

Is there no chance for his escape? Sectarianism answers "none." Such an idea is worse than atheism. The truth shall break down and dash in pieces all such bigoted Pharisaism; the sects shall be sifted, the honest in heart brought out, and their priests left in the midst of their corruption. (HC 4:425–26)

3   We believe in it {this gift of the Holy Ghost} in all its fullness, and power, and greatness, and glory; but whilst we do this, we believe in it rationally, consistently, and scripturally, and not according to the wild vagaries, foolish notions and traditions of men. (HC 5:27)

4   To become a joint heir of the heirship of the Son, one must put away all his false traditions. (HC 5:554)

5   I have tried for a number of years to get the minds of the Saints prepared to receive the things of God; but we frequently see some of them, after suffering all they have for the work of God, will fly to pieces like glass as soon as anything comes that is contrary to their traditions: they cannot stand the fire at all. How many will be able to abide a celestial law, and go through and receive their exaltation, I am unable to say, as many are called, but few are chosen. (HC 6:185)

Traitors

1   Renegade "Mormon" dissenters are running through the world and spreading various foul and libelous reports against us, thinking thereby to gain the friendship of the world, because they know that we are not of the world, and that the world hates us; therefore they {the world} make a tool of these fellows {the dissenters}; and by them try to do all the injury they can, and after that they hate them worse than they do us, because they find them to be base traitors and sycophants.

Traditions
   3   Editorial in the *Times and Seasons*, 15 June 1842.
   4   Sabbath address, Nauvoo, 27 August 1843.
   5   Sabbath address, Nauvoo, 21 January 1844.

Traitors
   1   Letter to the Church from Liberty Jail, 16 December 1838.

Such characters God hates; we cannot love them. The world hates them, and we sometimes think that the devil ought to be ashamed of them. (HC 3:230)

2   My life is more in danger from some little dough-head of a fool in this city than from all my numerous and inveterate enemies abroad. I am exposed to far greater danger from traitors among ourselves than from enemies without, although my life has been sought for many years by the civil and military authorities, priests, and people of Missouri; and if I can escape from the ungrateful treachery of assassins, I can live as Caesar might have lived, were it not for a right-hand Brutus. I have had pretended friends betray me. All the enemies upon the face of the earth may roar and exert all their power to bring about my death, but they can accomplish nothing, unless some who are among us and enjoy our society, have been with us in our councils, participated in our confidence, taken us by the hand, called us brother, saluted us with a kiss, join with our enemies, turn our virtues into faults, and, by falsehood and deceit, stir up their wrath and indignation against us, and bring their united vengeance upon our heads. All the hue-and-cry of the chief priests and elders against the Savior, could not bring down the wrath of the Jewish nation upon His head, and thereby cause the crucifixion of the Son of God, until Judas said unto them, "Whomsoever I shall kiss, he is the man; hold him fast." Judas was one of the Twelve Apostles, even their treasurer, and dipt with their Master in the dish, and through his treachery, the crucifixion was brought about; and *we have a Judas in our midst.* (HC 6:152)

3   I despise the man who will betray you with a kiss. (HC 6:238)

4   I testify again, as the Lord lives, God never will acknowledge any traitors or apostates. (HC 6:478)

Traitors
  2   Address to the Nauvoo Police, 29 December 1843.
  3   Remarks at meeting at temple in Nauvoo, 7 March 1844.
  4   Sabbath address, Nauvoo, 16 June 1844.

Translated Beings

1   Now the doctrine of translation is a power which belongs to this Priesthood. There are many things which belong to the powers of the Priesthood and the keys thereof, that have been kept hid from before the foundation of the world; they are hid from the wise and prudent to be revealed in the last times.

Many have supposed that the doctrine of translation was a doctrine whereby men were taken immediately into the presence of God, and into an eternal fullness, but this is a mistaken idea. Their place of habitation is that of the terrestrial order, and a place prepared for such characters He held in reserve to be ministering angels unto many planets, and who as yet have not entered into so great a fullness as those who are resurrected from the dead. "Others were tortured, not accepting deliverance, that they might obtain a better resurrection." (See Heb. 11th chap., part of the 35th verse.)

Now it was evident that there was a better resurrection, or else God would not have revealed it unto Paul. Wherein, then, can it be said a better resurrection. This distinction is made between the doctrine of the actual resurrection and translation: translation obtains deliverance from the tortures and sufferings of the body, but their existence will prolong as to the labors and toils of the ministry, before they can enter into so great a rest and glory.

On the other hand, those who were tortured, not accepting deliverance, received an immediate rest from their labors. "And I heard a voice from heaven, saying, Blessed are the dead who die in the Lord, for from henceforth they do rest from their labors and their works do follow them." (See Revelation, 14th chap., 13th verse).

They rest from their labors for a long time, and yet their work is held in reserve for them, that they are permitted to do the same work, after they receive a resurrection for their bodies. But we shall leave this subject and the subject of the terrestrial bodies for another time, in order to treat upon them more fully. (HC 4:209–10)

2   Translated bodies cannot enter into rest until they have undergone a change equivalent to death. Translated bodies are designed for future missions. (HC 4:425)

Translated Beings
1   Article on priesthood read at general conference, Nauvoo, 5 October 1840.
2   General conference address, Nauvoo, 3 October 1841.

3   He [the Lord] selected Enoch, whom He directed, and gave His law unto, and to the people who were with him; and when the world in general would not obey the commands of God, after walking with God, he translated Enoch and his church, and the Priesthood or government of heaven was taken away. (HC 5:64)

Translation of Records

1   Through the medium of the Urim and Thummim I translated the record [the Book of Mormon] by the gift and power of God. (HC 4:537)

2   The *boldness of my plans and measures* can readily be tested by the touchstone of all schemes, systems, projects, and adventures—*truth;* for truth is a matter of fact; and the fact is, that by the power of God I translated the Book of Mormon from hieroglyphics, the knowledge of which was lost to the world, in which wonderful event I stood alone, an unlearned youth, to combat the worldly wisdom and multiplied ignorance of eighteen centuries, with a new revelation, which (if they would receive the everlasting Gospel,) would open the eyes of more than eight hundred millions of people, and make "plain the old paths," wherein if a man walk in all the ordinances of God blameless, he shall inherit eternal life. (HC 6:74)

Trials

1   He [Ezra Booth] went up to Missouri as a companion of Elder Morley; but when he actually learned that faith, humility, patience, and tribulation go before blessing, and that God brings low before He exalts; that instead of the "Savior's granting him power to smite men and make them believe," (as he said he wanted God to do in his own

---

Translated Beings
3   Editorial in the *Times and Seasons*, 15 July 1842.

Translation of Records
1   Letter to John Wentworth, editor of the *Chicago Democrat*, Nauvoo, 1 March 1842.
2   Letter to James Arlington Bennett, Nauvoo, 13 November 1843.

Trials
1   Hiram, Ohio, September 1831.

case)—when he found he must become all things to all men, that he might peradventure save some; and that, too, by all diligence, by perils by sea and land, as was the case in the days of Jesus—then he was disappointed. (*HC* 1:216)

2   There is no safety only in the arm of Jehovah. None else can deliver and he will not deliver unless we do prove ourselves faithful to him in the severest trouble, for he that will have his robes washed in the blood of the Lamb must come up through great tribulation, even the greatest of all affliction. (*PWJS*, p. 285; standardized)

3   God has suffered it [expulsion from Jackson County, Missouri] not for your sins but that he might prepare you for a greater work, that you might be prepared for the endowment from on high. (*PWJS*, p. 286; standardized)

4   We know not what we shall be called to pass through before Zion is delivered and established; therefore, we have great need to live near to God, and always be in strict obedience to all His commandments, that we may have a conscience void of offense toward God and man. . . .

The inhabitants of this county threaten our destruction, and we know not how soon they may be permitted to follow the example of the Missourians; but our trust is in God, and we are determined, His grace assisting us, to maintain the cause and hold out faithful unto the end, that we may be crowned with crowns of celestial glory, and enter into the rest that is prepared for the children of God. (*HC* 1:450)

5   I would remind you of a certain clause . . . which says, that after *much* tribulation cometh the blessing. . . .

. . . When I contemplate upon all things that have been manifested, I am aware that I ought not to murmur, and do not murmur, only in this, that those who are innocent are compelled to suffer for

---

Trials
   2   Letter to William W. Phelps and others following mob destruction of the
        Saints' property in Missouri, Kirtland, 18 August 1833.
   3   Letter to William W. Phelps and others following mob destruction of the
        Saints' property in Missouri, Kirtland, 18 August 1833.
   4   Letter to the brethren in Missouri, Kirtland, 5 December 1833.
   5   Letter to the exiled Saints in Missouri, Kirtland, 10 December 1833.

the iniquities of the guilty; and I cannot account for this, only on this wise, that the saying of the Savior has not been strictly observed: "If thy right eye offend thee, pluck it out, and cast it from thee; or if thy right arm offend thee, cut it off, and cast it from thee." Now the fact is, if any of the members of our body is disordered, the rest of our body will be affected with it, and then all are brought into bondage together; and yet, notwithstanding all this, it is with difficulty that I can restrain my feelings when I know that you, my brethren, with whom I have had so many happy hours—sitting, as it were, in heavenly places in Christ Jesus; and also, having the witness which I feel, and ever have felt, of the purity of your motives—are cast out, and are as strangers and pilgrims on the earth, exposed to hunger, cold, nakedness, peril, sword—I say when I contemplate this, it is with difficulty that I can keep from complaining and murmuring against this dispensation; but I am sensible that this is not right, and may God grant that notwithstanding your great afflictions and sufferings, there may not anything separate us from the love of Christ. (HC 1:453, 454)

6 We have all been children, and are too much so at the present time; but we hope in the Lord that we may grow in grace and be prepared for all things which the bosom of futurity may disclose unto us. Time is rapidly rolling on, and the prophecies must be fulfilled. The days of tribulation are fast approaching, and the time to test the fidelity of the Saints has come. Rumor with her ten thousand tongues is diffusing her uncertain sounds in almost every ear; but in these times of sore trial, let the Saints be patient and see the salvation of God. Those who cannot endure persecution, and stand in the day of affliction, cannot stand in the day when the Son of God shall burst the veil, and appear in all the glory of His Father, with all the holy angels. (HC 1:468)

7 *Minutes:* [Joseph] then gave a relation of some of the circumstances attending us while journeying to Zion—our trials, sufferings; and said God had not designed all this for nothing, but He had it in remembrance yet. (HC 2:182)

Trials

    6 Letter to the elders of the Church, published in *The Evening and the Morning Star*, Kirtland, December 1833.

    7 Minutes of the meeting at which members of the first Quorum of the Twelve Apostles in this dispensation were chosen and ordained, Kirtland, 14 February 1835.

8   Brethren, some of you are angry with me, because you did not fight in Missouri; but let me tell you, God did not want you to fight. He could not organize His kingdom with twelve men to open the Gospel door to the nations of the earth, and with seventy men under their direction to follow their tracks, unless He took them from a body of men who had offered their lives, and who had made as great a sacrifice as did Abraham. Now the Lord has got His Twelve and His Seventy, and there will be other quorums of Seventies called, who will make the sacrifice, and those who have not made their sacrifices and their offerings now, will make them hereafter. (*HC* 2:182)

9   *Words of Daniel Tyler:* When Joseph arose and addressed the congregation, he spoke of his many troubles, and said he often wondered why it was that he should have so much trouble in the house of his friends, and he wept as though his heart would break. Finally he said, "The Lord once told me that if at any time I got into deep trouble and could see no way out of it, if I would prophesy in His name, he would fulfill my words." He then said, "I prophesy in the name of the Lord that those who have thought I was in transgression shall have a testimony this night that I am clear and stand approved before the Lord."

The next Sabbath his brother William and several others made humble confessions before the public. (*TK*, p. 52)

10   And I know that the cloud will burst, and Satan's kingdom be laid in ruins, with all his black designs; and that the Saints will come forth like gold seven times tried in the fire, being made perfect through sufferings and temptations, and that the blessings of heaven and earth will be multiplied upon their heads; which may God grant for Christ's sake. Amen. (*HC* 2:353)

11   We believe that that God who seeth us in this solitary place, will hear our prayers, and reward you openly. (*HC* 3:226)

Trials

  8   Address to the elders given soon after the calling of the First Quorum of Seventy (the first such quorum in this dispensation), as reported by Joseph Young in his "History of the Organization of the Seventies," Kirtland, February 1835.

  9   Daniel Tyler's recollection of a meeting in Kirtland, published in the *Juvenile Instructor*, 15 February 1892.

10   Kirtland, 1 January 1836.

11   Letter to the Church from Liberty Jail, 16 December 1838.

12 My heart bleeds continually when I contemplate the distress of the Church. O, that I could be with them! I would not shrink at toil and hardship to render them comfort and consolation. . . . Trials will only give us the knowledge necessary to understand the minds of the ancients. For my part, I think I never could have felt as I now do, if I had not suffered the wrongs that I have suffered. All things shall work together for good to them that love God. (HC 3:286)

13 And now, beloved brethren, we say unto you, that inasmuch as God hath said that He would have a tried people, that He would purge them as gold, now we think that this time He has chosen His own crucible, wherein we have been tried; and we think if we get through with any degree of safety, and shall have kept the faith, that it will be a sign to this generation, altogether sufficient to leave them without excuse; and we think also, it will be a trial of our faith equal to that of Abraham, and that the ancients will not have whereof to boast over us in the day of judgment, as being called to pass through heavier afflictions; that we may hold an even weight in the balance with them; but now, after having suffered so great sacrifice and having passed through so great a season of sorrow, we trust that a ram may be caught in the thicket speedily, to relieve the sons and daughters of Abraham from their great anxiety, and to light up the lamp of salvation upon their countenances, that they may hold on now, after having gone so far unto everlasting life. (HC 3:294–95)

14 At that time [Second Coming] the hearts of the widows and fatherless shall be comforted, and every tear shall be wiped from their faces. The trials they have had to pass through shall work together for their good, and prepare them for the society of those who have come up out of great tribulation, and have washed their robes and made them white in the blood of the Lamb.

Marvel not, then, if you are persecuted; but remember the words of the Savior: "The servant is not above his Lord; if they have persecuted me, they will persecute you also;" and that all the afflictions through which the Saints have to pass, are the fulfillment of the words of the Prophets which have spoken since the world began. (HC 3:330–31)

Trials

12 Letter from Liberty Jail to Mrs. Norman Bull (Buell), 15 March 1839.

13 Letter to the Saints from Liberty Jail, 20–25 March 1839.

14 Reflections on Missouri persecutions and confinement in Liberty Jail, Quincy, Illinois, 22 April 1839.

15 Having confidence in the power, wisdom, and love of God, the Saints have been enabled to go forward through the most adverse circumstances, and frequently, when to all human appearances, nothing but death presented itself, and destruction inevitable, has the power of God been manifest, His glory revealed, and deliverance effected; and the Saints, like the children of Israel, who came out of the land of Egypt, and through the Red Sea, have sung an anthem of praise to his holy name. This has not only been the case in former days, but in our days, and within a few months, have we seen this fully verified. (HC 4:185)

16 We contemplate a people who have embraced a system of religion, unpopular, and the adherence to which has brought upon them repeated persecutions. A people who, for their love to God, and attachment to His cause, have suffered hunger, nakedness, perils, and almost every privation. A people who, for the sake of their religion, have had to mourn the premature death of parents, husbands, wives, and children. A people, who have preferred death to slavery and hypocrisy, and have honorably maintained their characters, and stood firm and immovable, in times that have tried men's souls. Stand fast, ye Saints of God, hold on a little while longer, and the storm of life will be past, and you will be rewarded by that God whose servants you are, and who will duly appreciate all your toils and afflictions for Christ's sake and the Gospel's. Your names will be handed down to posterity as Saints of God and virtuous men. (HC 4:337)

17 We intend to struggle with all our misfortunes in life, and shoulder them up handsomely, like men. (HC 4:432)

18 All difficulties which might and would cross our way must be surmounted. Though the soul be tried, the heart faint, and the hands hang down, we must not retrace our steps; there must be decision of character, aside from sympathy. (HC 4:570)

Trials

    15 Letter to the Saints from the First Presidency, Nauvoo, 31 August 1840.

    16 Report of the First Presidency at general conference, Nauvoo, 7 April 1841.

    17 Letter to Smith Tuttle, Nauvoo, 9 October 1841.

    18 Remarks to the Relief Society, Nauvoo, 30 March 1842.

19 It is my meditation all the day, and more than my meat and drink, to know how I shall make the Saints of God comprehend the visions that roll like an overflowing surge before my mind.

Oh! how I would delight to bring before you things which you never thought of! But poverty and the cares of the world prevent. But I am glad I have the privilege of communicating to you some things which, if grasped closely, will be a help to you when earthquakes bellow, the clouds gather, the lightnings flash, and the storms are ready to burst upon you like peals of thunder. Lay hold of these things and let not your knees or joints tremble, nor your hearts faint; and then what can earthquakes, wars and tornadoes do? Nothing. All your losses will be made up to you in the resurrection, provided you continue faithful. By the vision of the Almighty I have seen it. (HC 5:362)

20 Men have to suffer that they may come upon Mount Zion and be exalted above the heavens. (HC 5:556)

21 *Words of John Taylor:* I heard the Prophet Joseph say, in speaking to the Twelve on one occasion: "You will have all kinds of trials to pass through. And it is quite as necessary for you to be tried as it was for Abraham and other men of God, and (said he) God will feel after you, and He will take hold of you and wrench your very heart strings, and if you cannot stand it you will not be fit for an inheritance in the Celestial Kingdom of God." (JD 24:197)

22 *Words of John Taylor:* I heard Joseph Smith say—and I presume Brother Snow heard him also—in preaching to the Twelve in Nauvoo, that the Lord would get hold of their heart strings and wrench them, and that they would have to be tried as Abraham was tried. Well, some of the Twelve could not stand it. They faltered and fell by the way. It was not everybody that could stand what Abraham stood. And Joseph said that if God had known any other way whereby he could have touched Abraham's feelings more acutely and more keenly he would have done so. (JD 24:264)

Trials

19 Remarks upon the death of Lorenzo D. Barnes, Nauvoo, 16 April 1843.
20 Sabbath address, Nauvoo, 27 August 1843.
21 Address by John Taylor, Salt Lake City, Utah, 18 June 1883.
22 Address by John Taylor, Parowan, Utah, 24 June 1883.

Truth

1   Truth, remember, is hard and severe against all iniquity and wickedness. (*HC* 1:326)

2   Righteousness and truth are to sweep the earth as with a flood. And now, I ask, how righteousness and truth are going to sweep the earth as with a flood? I will answer. Men and angels are to be co-workers in bringing to pass this great work, and Zion is to be prepared, even a new Jerusalem, for the elect that are to be gathered from the four quarters of the earth, and to be established an holy city, for the tabernacle of the Lord shall be with them. . . .

   And again—hear ye the parable of the sower. Men are in the habit, when the truth is exhibited by the servants of God, of saying, All is mystery; they have spoken in parables, and, therefore, are not to be understood. It is true they have eyes to see, and see not, but none are so blind as those who will not see; and, although the Savior spoke this to such characters, yet unto His disciples he expounded it plainly; and we have reason to be truly humble before the God of our fathers, that He hath left these things on record for us, so plain, that notwithstanding the exertions and combined influence of the priests of Baal, they have not power to blind our eyes, and darken our understanding, if we will but open our eyes, and read with candor, for a moment.

   But listen to the explanation of the parable of the Sower: "When any one heareth the word of the Kingdom, and understandeth it not, then cometh the wicked one, and catcheth away that which was sown in his heart." Now mark the expression—that which was sown in his heart. This is he which receiveth seed by the way side. Men who have no principle of righteousness in themselves, and whose hearts are full of iniquity, and have no desire for the principles of truth, do not understand the word of truth when they hear it. The devil taketh away the word of truth out of their hearts, because there is no desire for righteousness in them. "But he that receiveth seed in stony places, the same is he that heareth the word, and anon, with joy receiveth it; yet hath he not root in himself, but dureth for a while: for when tribula-

---

Truth
   1   Letter to N. E. Seaton (N. C. Saxton), a newspaper editor in Rochester, N.Y., Kirtland, 12 February 1833.
   2   Letter to the elders of the Church, Kirtland, 1 September 1835.

tion or persecution ariseth because of the word, by and by, he is offended. He also that receiveth seed among the thorns, is he that heareth the word; and the care of this world, and the deceitfulness of riches choke the word, and he becometh unfruitful. But he that received seed into the good ground is he that heareth the word, and understandeth it, which also beareth fruit, and bringeth forth, some an hundred fold, some sixty, and some thirty." Thus the Savior Himself explains unto His disciples the parable which He put forth, and left no mystery or darkness upon the minds of those who firmly believe on His words.

We draw the conclusion, then, that the very reason why the multitude, of the world, as they were designated by the Savior, did not receive an explanation upon His parables, was because of unbelief. To you, He says, (speaking to His disciples,) it is given to know the mysteries of the Kingdom of God. And why? Because of the faith and confidence they had in Him. This parable was spoken to demonstrate the effects that are produced by the preaching of the word; and we believe that it has an allusion directly, to the commencement, or the setting up of the Kingdom in that age; therefore we shall continue to trace His sayings concerning this Kingdom from that time forth, even unto the end of the world. (HC 2:260, 266–67)

3   I have learned by experience that the enemy of truth does not slumber, nor cease his exertions to bias the minds of communities against the servants of the Lord, by stirring up the indignation of men upon all matters of importance or interest. (HC 2:437)

4   When a lying spirit is abroad it is difficult for truth to be understood. (HC 2:512)

5   We believe in . . . the final triumph of truth. (HC 3:30)

6   Truth is "Mormonism." God is the author of it. He is our shield. It is by Him we received our birth. (HC 3:297)

Truth
3   Letter on abolition published in the *Messenger and Advocate*, April 1836.
4   Kirtland, 10 September 1837.
5   Answers to questions frequently asked the Prophet, Far West, 8 May 1838.
6   Letter to the Saints from Liberty Jail, 20–25 March 1839.

7 The doctrine of the Latter-day Saints is truth. . . . Now, sir, you may think that it is a broad assertion that it is truth; but sir, the first and fundamental principle of our holy religion is that we believe that we have a right to embrace all and every item of truth, without limitation or without being circumscribed or prohibited by the creeds or superstitious notions of men. (*PWJS*, p. 420; standardized)

8 Time and experience will teach us more and more how easily falsehood gains credence with mankind in general, rather than the truth; but especially in taking into consideration the plan of salvation. The plain simple order of the Gospel of Jesus Christ never has been discerned or acknowledged as the truth, except by a few—among whom were "not many wise men after the flesh, not many mighty, not many noble;" whilst the majority have contented themselves with their own private opinions, or have adopted those of others, according to their address, their philosophy, their formula, their policy, or their fineness may have attracted their attention, or pleased their taste. But, sir, of all the other criterions whereby we may judge of the vanity of these things, one will be always found true, namely, that we will always find such characters glorying in their own wisdom and their own works; whilst the humble Saint gives all the glory to God the Father, and to His Son Jesus Christ, whose yoke is easy and whose burden is light, and who told His disciples that unless they became like little children they could not enter the Kingdom of Heaven. (*HC* 4:8)

9 Prejudice, with its attendant train of evil, is giving way before the force of truth, whose benign rays are penetrating the nations afar off. (*HC* 4:336)

10 The Standard of Truth has been erected; no unhallowed hand can stop the work from progressing; persecutions may rage, mobs may combine, armies may assemble, calumny may defame, but the truth of God will go forth boldly, nobly, and independent, till it has penetrated

Truth

7 Letter to Isaac Galland, written while the Prophet was imprisoned in Liberty Jail, 22 March 1839.
8 Letter to Isaac Galland, Commerce (Nauvoo), 11 September 1839.
9 Report of the First Presidency at general conference, Nauvoo, 7 April 1841.
10 Letter to John Wentworth, editor of the *Chicago Democrat*, Nauvoo, 1 March 1842.

every continent, visited every clime, swept every country, and sounded in every ear, till the purposes of God shall be accomplished, and the Great Jehovah shall say the work is done. (*HC* 4:540)

11 The great and wise of ancient days have failed in all their attempts to promote eternal power, peace and happiness. Their nations have crumbled to pieces; their thrones have been cast down in their turn, and their cities, and their mightiest works of art have been annihilated; or their dilapidated towers, of time-worn monuments have left us but feeble traces of their former magnificence and ancient grandeur. They proclaim as with a voice of thunder, those imperishable truths—that man's strength is weakness, his wisdom is folly, his glory is his shame. (*HC* 5:62)

12 We don't ask any people to throw away any good they have got; we only ask them to come and get more. What if all the world should embrace this Gospel? They would then see eye to eye, and the blessings of God would be poured out upon the people, which is the desire of my whole soul. (*HC* 5:259)

13 One of the grand fundamental principles of "Mormonism" is to receive truth, let it come from whence it may.

. . . If by the principles of truth I succeed in uniting men of all denominations in the bonds of love, shall I not have attained a good object?

If I esteem mankind to be in error, shall I bear them down? No. I will lift them up, and in their own way too, if I cannot persuade them my way is better; and I will not seek to compel any man to believe as I do, only by the force of reasoning, for truth will cut its own way. (*HC* 5:499)

14 Have the Presbyterians any truth? Yes. Have the Baptists, Methodists, &c., any truth? Yes. They all have a little truth mixed with error. We should gather all the good and true principles in the world and treasure them up, or we shall not come out true "Mormons." (*HC* 5:517)

Truth

11 Editorial in the *Times and Seasons*, 15 July 1842.
12 Sabbath address, Nauvoo, 22 January 1843.
13 Sabbath address, Nauvoo, 9 July 1843.
14 Sabbath address, Nauvoo, 23 July 1843.

15 Truth carries its own influence and recommends itself. (*WJS*, p. 237; standardized)

16 I assure the Saints that truth, in reference to these matters, can and may be known through the revelations of God in the way of His ordinances, and in answer to prayer. . . .

. . . Wherever light shone, it stirred up darkness. Truth and error, good and evil cannot be reconciled. (*HC* 6:51)

17 I cannot believe in any of the creeds of the different denominations, because they all have some things in them I cannot subscribe to, though all of them have some truth. I want to come up into the presence of God, and learn all things; but the creeds set up stakes, and say, "Hitherto shalt thou come, and no further;" which I cannot subscribe to. (*HC* 6:57)

18 The *boldness of my plans and measures* can readily be tested by the touchstone of all schemes, systems, projects, and adventures—*truth*. (*HC* 6:74)

19 One truth revealed from heaven is worth all the sectarian notions in existence. (*HC* 6:252)

20 In relation to the power over the minds of mankind which I hold, I would say, It is in consequence of the power of truth in the doctrines which I have been an instrument in the hands of God of presenting unto them, and not because of any compulsion on my part. I wish to ask if ever I got any of it unfairly? if I have not reproved you in the gate? I ask, Did I ever exercise any compulsion over any man? Did I not give him the liberty of disbelieving any doctrine I have preached, if he saw fit? Why do not my enemies strike a blow at the doctrine? They cannot do it: it is truth, and I defy all men to upset it. (*HC* 6:273)

Truth
   15 Sabbath address, Nauvoo, 6 August 1843, as reported by Levi Richards.
   16 Remarks upon the death of James Adams, Nauvoo, 9 October 1843.
   17 Sabbath address, Nauvoo, 15 October 1843.
   18 Letter to James Arlington Bennett, Nauvoo, 13 November 1843.
   19 Sabbath address, Nauvoo, 10 March 1844.
   20 Sabbath address, Nauvoo, 24 March 1844.

21 I do not calculate or intend to please your ears with superfluity of words or oratory, or with much learning; but I calculate {intend} to edify you with the simple truths from heaven. (HC 6:303)

22 If you don't believe me, it will not make the truth without effect. (HC 6:310)

23 I told him I obtained power on the principles of truth and virtue, which would last when I was dead and gone. (HC 6:343)

24 When facts are proved, truth and innocence will prevail at last. . . . . . . If the doctrine that I preach is true, the tree must be good. . . . . . . I mean to live and proclaim the truth as long as I can. (HC 6:408, 410)

25 Study the Bible, and as many of our books as you can get; pray to the Father in the name of Jesus Christ, have faith in the promises made to the fathers, and your mind will be guided to the truth. (HC 6:459)

26 I want to stick to my text, to show that when men open their lips against these truths they do not injure me, but injure themselves. To the law and to the testimony, for these principles are poured out all over the scriptures. When things that are of the greatest importance are passed over by weak-minded men without even a thought, I want to see truth in all its bearings and hug it to my bosom. I believe all that God ever revealed, and I never hear of a man being damned for believing too much; but they are damned for unbelief. (HC 6:477)

Truth

21 King Follett Discourse, Nauvoo, 7 April 1844.
22 King Follett Discourse, Nauvoo, 7 April 1844.
23 Answer to a brother who worked for the *St. Louis Gazette* and asked about the Prophet's source of power, Nauvoo, 25 April 1844.
24 Sabbath address, Nauvoo, 26 May 1844.
25 Letter to Washington Tucker, Nauvoo, 12 June 1844.
26 Sabbath address, Nauvoo, 16 June 1844.

United States

1   I arrived safely at Nauvoo, after a wearisome journey, through alternate snow and mud, having witnessed many vexatious movements in government officers, whose sole object should be the peace and prosperity and happiness of the whole people; but instead of this, I discovered that popular clamor and personal aggrandizement were the ruling principles of those in authority; and my heart faints within me when I see, by the visions of the Almighty, the end of this nation, if she continues to disregard the cries and petitions of her virtuous citizens, as she has done, and is now doing. (HC 4:89)

2   Our nation, which possesses greater resources than any other, is rent, from center to circumference, with party strife, political intrigues, and sectional interest; our counselors are panic stricken, our legislators are astonished, and our senators are confounded, our merchants are paralyzed, our tradesmen are disheartened, our mechanics out of employ, our farmers distressed, and our poor crying for bread, our banks are broken, our credit ruined, and our states overwhelmed in debt, yet we are, and have been in peace.
    . . . With all our evils we are better situated than any other nation. (HC 5:62)

3   In the United States the people are the government, and their united voice is the only sovereign that should rule, the only power that should be obeyed, and the only gentlemen that should be honored at home and abroad, on the land and on the sea. Wherefore, were I the president of the United States, by the voice of a virtuous people, I would honor the old paths of the venerated fathers of freedom; I would walk in the tracks of the illustrious patriots who carried the ark of the Government upon their shoulders with an eye single to the glory of the people. (HC 6:208)

United States
  1   Nauvoo, 4 March 1840.
  2   Editorial in the *Times and Seasons*, 15 July 1842.
  3   A pamphlet containing the Prophet's political platform, entitled *Views of the Powers and Policy of the Government of the United States*, Nauvoo, 7 February 1844.

Unity

1 And the spirit of confession and forgiveness was mutual among us all, and we convenanted with each other, in the sight of God, and the holy angels, and the brethren, to strive thenceforward to build each other up in righteousness in all things, and not listen to evil reports concerning each other; but, like brothers indeed, go to each other, with our grievances, in the spirit of meekness, and be reconciled, and thereby promote our happiness, and the happiness of the family, and, in short, the happiness and well-being of all. (HC 2:353)

2 The Saints at this time are in union; and peace and love prevail throughout; in a word, heaven smiles upon the Saints in Caldwell. (HC 3:11)

3 I stated to the meeting, that the time had come when it was necessary that we should have a weekly newspaper, to unite the people, and give the news of the day. (HC 3:56)

4 In order to conduct the affairs of the Kingdom in righteousness, it is all important that the most perfect harmony, kind feeling, good understanding, and confidence should exist in the hearts of all the brethren; and that true charity, love one towards another, should characterize all their proceedings. If there are any uncharitable feelings, any lack of confidence, then pride, arrogance and envy will soon be manifested; confusion must inevitably prevail, and the authorities of the Church set at naught; and under such circumstances, Kirtland cannot rise and free herself from the captivity in which she is held, and become a place of safety for the Saints, nor can the blessings of Jehovah rest upon her. . . .

. . . I hope that even in Kirtland there are some who do not make a man an offender for a word, but are disposed to stand forth in defense of righteousness and truth, and attend to every duty enjoined upon them; and who will have wisdom to direct them against any

---

Unity
  1 Kirtland, 1 January 1836.
  2 Letter to Church leaders at Kirtland, written from Far West, Missouri, 29 March 1838.
  3 Far West, Missouri, 6 August 1838.
  4 Letter to Oliver Granger in Kirtland, sent from Nauvoo, July 1840.

movement or influence calculated to bring confusion and discord into the camp of Israel, and to discern between the spirit of truth and the spirit of error. (HC 4:165–66)

5   We are glad indeed to know that there is such a spirit of union existing throughout the churches, at home and abroad, on this continent, as well as on the islands of the sea; for by this principle, and by a concentration of action, shall we be able to carry into effect the purposes of our God. (HC 4:213)

6   Unity is strength. "How pleasing it is for brethren to dwell together in unity!" Let the Saints of the Most High ever cultivate this principle, and the most glorious blessings must result, not only to them individually, but to the whole Church—the order of the kingdom will be maintained, its officers respected, and its requirements readily and cheerfully obeyed. (HC 4:227)

7   *Minutes:* The greatest unanimity prevailed; business was conducted with the most perfect harmony and good feelings, and the assembly dispersed with new confidence in the great work of the last days. (HC 4:429)

8   All must act in concert, or nothing can be done, and should move according to the ancient Priesthood. (HC 4:570)

9   When the brethren, as in this instance, show a unity of purpose and design, and all put their shoulder to the wheel, our care, labor, toil and anxiety is materially diminished, our yoke is made easy and our burden is light.

The cause of God is one common cause, in which the Saints are alike all interested; we are all members of the one common body, and

---

Unity

5   Report of the First Presidency at general conference, Nauvoo, 5 October 1840.

6   Letter to the Twelve in England, Nauvoo, 15 December 1840. The placement of this letter in HC implies that it was written in October 1840, but actually it was written on 15 December 1840 (see *PWJS*, p. 480).

7   Minutes of general conference, Nauvoo, 5 October 1841.

8   Remarks to the Relief Society, Nauvoo, 30 March 1842.

9   Editorial in the *Times and Seasons*, 2 May 1842.

all partake of the same spirit, and are baptized into one baptism and possess alike the same glorious hope. The advancement of the cause of God and the building up of Zion is as much one man's business as another's. The only difference is, that one is called to fulfill one duty, and another another duty; "but if one member suffers, all the members suffer with it, and if one member is honored all the rest rejoice with it, and the eye cannot say to the ear, I have no need of thee, nor the head to the foot, I have no need of thee;" party feelings, separate interests, exclusive designs should be lost sight of in the one common cause, in the interest of the whole. (HC 4:609)

10 If one member suffer all feel it; by union of feeling we obtain power with God. (HC 5:23)

11 Now, let me say once for all, like the Psalmist of old, "How good and how pleasant it is for brethren to dwell together in unity." "As the precious ointment upon the head that ran down upon Aaron's beard, that went down to the skirts of his garments, as the dew of Hermon that descended upon the mountains of Zion," is such unity; "for there the Lord commanded the blessing, even life for evermore!" Unity is power; and when the brethren as one man sustain the *Times and Seasons*, they sustain me, by giving a spread to the revelations, faith, works, history and progress of the Church. (HC 6:70)

12 I want to read the text to you myself—"I am agreed with the Father and the Father is agreed with me, and we are agreed as one." The Greek shows that it should be agreed. "Father, I pray for them which Thou hast given me out of the world, and not for those alone, but for them also which shall believe on me through their word, that they all may be agreed, as Thou, Father, art with me, and I with Thee, that they also may be agreed with us," and all come to dwell in unity, and in all the glory and everlasting burnings of the Gods; and then we shall see as we are seen, and be as our God and He as His Father. (HC 6:476)

Unity
10 Remarks to the Relief Society, Nauvoo, 9 June 1842.
11 Letter to the Saints encouraging them to patronize the Church newspaper, published in the *Times and Seasons*, 1 November 1843.
12 Sabbath address, Nauvoo, 16 June 1844.

Unpardonable Sin
See also SONS OF PERDITION

1   There is never a time when the spirit is too old to approach God. All are within the reach of pardoning mercy, who have not committed the unpardonable sin, which hath no forgiveness, neither in this world, nor in the world to come. (HC 4:425)

2   Our Savior says, that all manner of sin and blasphemy shall be forgiven men wherewith they shall blaspheme; but the blasphemy against the Holy Ghost shall not be forgiven, neither in this world, nor in the world to come, evidently showing that there are sins which may be forgiven in the world to come, although the sin of blasphemy {against the Holy Ghost} cannot be forgiven. (HC 4:596)

3   The unpardonable sin is to shed innocent blood, or be accessory thereto. All other sins will be visited with judgment in the flesh, and the spirit being delivered to the buffetings of Satan until the day of the Lord Jesus. (HC 5:391–92)

4   A man cannot commit the unpardonable sin after the dissolution of the body. . . .
    . . . I warn you against all evil characters who sin against the Holy Ghost; for there is no redemption for them in this world nor in the world to come. . . .
    . . . There have been remarks made concerning all men being redeemed from hell; but I say that those who sin against the Holy Ghost cannot be forgiven in this world or in the world to come; they shall die the second death. Those who commit the unpardonable sin are doomed to *Gnolom*—to dwell in hell, worlds without end. As they concocted scenes of bloodshed in this world, so they shall rise to that resurrection which is as the lake of fire and brimstone. Some shall rise to the everlasting burnings of God; for God dwells in everlasting burn-

---

Unpardonable Sin
  1   General conference address, Nauvoo, 3 October 1841.
  2   Editorial in the *Times and Seasons*, 15 April 1842.
  3   Instruction given to a few Saints at the home of Benjamin F. Johnson, Ramus, Illinois, 16 May 1843.
  4   King Follett Discourse, Nauvoo, 7 April 1844.

ings and some shall rise to the damnation of their own filthiness, which is as exquisite a torment as the lake of fire and brimstone. (*HC* 6:314, 315, 317)

Urim and Thummim

1   With the records [Book of Mormon plates] was found a curious instrument, which the ancients called "Urim and Thummim," which consisted of two transparent stones set in the rim of a bow fastened to a breast plate. Through the medium of the Urim and Thummim I translated the record by the gift and power of God. (*HC* 4:537)

2   While at dinner, I remarked to my family and friends present, that when the earth was sanctified and became like a sea of glass, it would be one great urim and thummim, and the Saints could look in it and see as they are seen. (*HC* 5:279)

Vanity

1   All are subjected to vanity while they travel through the crooked paths and difficulties which surround them. Where is the man that is free from vanity? None ever were perfect but Jesus; and why was He perfect? Because He was the Son of God, and had the fullness of the Spirit, and greater power than any man. But notwithstanding their vanity, men look forward with hope (because they are "subjected in hope") to the time of their deliverance. (*HC* 4:358–59)

Urim and Thummim
1   Letter to John Wentworth, editor of the *Chicago Democrat*, Nauvoo, 1 March 1842.
2   Nauvoo, 18 February 1843.

Vanity
1   Sabbath address, Nauvoo, 16 May 1841.

Veil

1   It is the privilege of every elder to speak of the things of God, &c.; and could we all come together with one heart and one mind in perfect faith the veil might as well be rent today as next week, or any other time, and if we will but cleanse ourselves and covenant before God, to serve him, it is our privilege to have an assurance that God will protect us at all times. (*FWR*, p. 20; standardized)

2   From the foregoing [JST, Genesis 1:27–31; 2:18–22, 25–27] we learn man's situation at his first creation, the knowledge with which he was endowed, and the high and exalted station in which he was placed—lord or governor of all things on earth, and at the same time enjoying communion and intercourse with his Maker, without a veil to separate between. (*LF* 2:12)

3   Though our first parents were driven out of the garden of Eden, and were even separated from the presence of God by a veil, they still retained a knowledge of his existence, and that sufficiently to move them to call upon him. And further, . . . no sooner was the plan of redemption revealed to man, and he began to call upon God, than the Holy Spirit was given, bearing record of the Father and Son. (*LF* 2:25)

4   The word of the Lord is precious; and when we read that the vail spread over all nations will be destroyed, and the pure in heart see God, and reign with Him a thousand years on earth, we want all honest men to have a chance to gather and build up a city of righteous-

---

Veil
1   Minutes of a conference held at Orange, Ohio, 25 October 1831.
2   Lectures on Faith, delivered to a school of the elders, Kirtland, December 1834. Although the Lectures on Faith were not written only by Joseph Smith, he reviewed them carefully and prepared them for publication (see Larry E. Dahl and Charles D. Tate, Jr., eds., *The Lectures on Faith in Historical Perspective*, p. 10).
3   Lectures on Faith, delivered to a school of the elders, Kirtland, December 1834. Although the Lectures on Faith were not written only by Joseph Smith, he reviewed them carefully and prepared them for publication (see Larry E. Dahl and Charles D. Tate, Jr., eds., *The Lectures on Faith in Historical Perspective*, p. 10).
4   Meeting of the high council at Kirtland, 6 January 1836.

ness, where even upon the bells of the horses shall be written *Holiness to the Lord*. (HC 2:358)

5   Achan {see Joshua vii} must be brought to light, iniquity must be purged out from the midst of the Saints; then the veil will be rent, and the blessings of heaven will flow down—they will roll down like the Mississippi river. (HC 4:605)

6   When you climb up a ladder, you must begin at the bottom, and ascend step by step, until you arrive at the top; and so it is with the principles of the gospel—you must begin at the first, and go on until you learn all the principles of exaltation. But it will be a great while after you have passed through the veil before you will have learned them. It is not all to be comprehended in this world; it will be a great work to learn our salvation and exaltation even beyond the grave. (HC 6:306–7)

Virtue

1   Certainly, then, those two classes of men [virtuous and wicked] could not hold the reins of the same government at the same time in peace; for internal jars, broils, and discords would rack it to the center, were such a form of government to exist under such a system. The virtuous could not enjoy peace in the constant and unceasing schemes and evil plans of the wicked; neither could the wicked have enjoyment in the constant perseverance of the righteous to do justly. That there must be an agreement in this government, or it could not stand, must be admitted by all. Should the king convey the reins into the hands of the rebellious the government must soon fall; for every government, from the creation to the present, when it ceased to be virtuous, and failed to execute justice, sooner or later has been overthrown. And without virtuous principles to actuate a government all care for justice is soon lost, and the only motive which prompts it to act is ambition and selfishness. (HC 2:10–11)

Veil
5   Remarks to the Relief Society, Nauvoo, 28 April 1842.
6   King Follet Discourse, Nauvoo, 7 April 1844.

Virtue
1   Letter to the brethren scattered from Zion, Kirtland, 22 January 1834.

2   Now for a man to consecrate his property, wife and children, to the Lord, is nothing more nor less than to feed the hungry, clothe the naked, visit the widow and fatherless, the sick and afflicted, and do all he can to administer to their relief in their afflictions, and for him and his house to serve the Lord. In order to do this, he and all his house must be virtuous, and must shun the very appearance of evil. (HC 3:231)

3   We think that truth, honor, virtue and innocence will eventually come out triumphant. (HC 3:292)

4   Therefore we beseech of you, brethren, that you bear with those who do not feel themselves more worthy than yourselves, while we exhort one another to a reformation with one and all, both old and young, teachers and taught, both high and low, rich and poor, bond and free, male and female; let honesty, and sobriety, and candor, and solemnity, and virtue, and pureness, and meekness, and simplicity crown our heads in every place; and in fine, become as little children, without malice, guile or hypocrisy. (HC 3:296)

5   Brother Hyrum and the Twelve present bore testimony that they had never heard me teach any principles but those of the strictest virtue, either in public or private. (HC 4:582–83)

6   *Report of Eliza R. Snow:* He [Joseph Smith] said . . . if you do right, there is no danger of your going too fast.

He said he did not care how fast we run in the path of virtue; resist evil, and there is no danger. (HC 4:605)

7   *Report of Eliza R. Snow:* He [Joseph Smith] said . . . there is now a day of salvation to such as repent and reform;—and they who repent not should be cast out from this society [the Relief Society]; yet we should woo them to return to God, lest they escape not the damna-

---

Virtue
  2   Letter to the Church from Liberty Jail, 16 December 1838.
  3   Letter to the Saints from Liberty Jail, 20–25 March 1839.
  4   Letter to the Saints from Liberty Jail, 20–25 March 1839.
  5   Nauvoo, 6 April 1842.
  6   Remarks to the Relief Society, Nauvoo, 28 April 1842.
  7   Remarks to the Relief Society, Nauvoo, 26 May 1842.

tion of hell! Where there is a mountain top, there is also a valley—we should act in all things on a proper medium to every immortal spirit. Notwithstanding the unworthy are among us, the virtuous should not, from self importance, grieve and oppress needlessly, those unfortunate ones—even these should be encouraged to hereafter live to be honored by this society, who are the best portions of the community. Said he had two things to recommend to the members of this society, to put a double watch over the tongue: no organized body can exist without this at all. All organized bodies have their peculiar evils, weaknesses and difficulties, the object is to make those not so good reform and return to the path of virtue that they may be numbered with the good, and even hold the keys of power, which will influence to virtue and goodness—should chasten and reprove, and keep it all in silence, not even mention them again; then you will be established in power, virtue, and holiness, and the wrath of God will be turned away. (HC 5:20)

8   *Report of Eliza R. Snow:* [Joseph Smith] said it is no matter how fast the society [Relief Society] increases, if all the members are virtuous; that we must be as particular with regard to the character of members now, as when the society was first started; that sometimes persons wish to crowd themselves into a society of this kind when they do not intend to pursue the ways of purity and righteousness, as if the society would be a shelter to them in their iniquity. (HC 5:23)

9   Every honest man who has visited the city of Nauvoo since it existed, can bear record of better things, and place me in the front ranks of those who are known to do good for the sake of goodness, and show all liars, hypocrites and abominable creatures that, while vice sinks them down to darkness and woe, virtue exalts me and the Saints to light and immortality. (HC 5:290–91)

10 With the smiling prospects around us at present, success seems certain; and, with the blessings of Jehovah, we shall reap the reward of virtue and goodness. I go for the good of the world; and if all honest men would do so, mean men would be scarce. (HC 6:55–56)

Virtue

   8   Remarks to the Relief Society, Nauvoo, 9 June 1842.
   9   Letter to the editor of the *Times and Seasons*, 1 March 1843.
   10 Letter to Horace R. Hotchkiss, Nauvoo, 12 October 1843.

11 The whole earth shall bear me witness that I, like the towering rock in the midst of the ocean, which has withstood the mighty surges of the warring waves for centuries, *am impregnable*, and am a faithful friend to virtue, and a fearless foe to vice,—no odds whether the former was sold as a pearl in Asia or hid as a gem in America, and the latter dazzles in palaces or glimmers among the tombs.

I combat the errors of ages; I meet the violence of mobs; I cope with illegal proceedings from executive authority; I cut the gordian knot of powers, and I solve mathematical problems of universities, *with truth—diamond truth; and God is my "right hand man."*

And to close, let me say in the name of Jesus Christ to you, and to presidents, emperors, kings, queens, governors, rulers, nobles, and men in authority everywhere, Do the works of righteousness, execute justice and judgment in the earth, that God may bless you and her inhabitants; and

> The laurel that grows on the top of the mountain
>   Shall green for your fame while the sun sheds a ray;
> And the lily that blows by the side of the fountain
>   Will bloom for your virtue till earth melts away.
>   (HC 6:78)

12 Where is the virtue of our forefathers? and where is the sacred honor of freemen!

. . . Must we, because we believe in enjoying the constitutional privilege and right of worshiping Almighty God according to the dictates of our own consciences, and because we believe in repentance, and baptism for the remission of sins, the gift of the Holy Ghost by the laying on of hands, the resurrection of the dead, the millennium, the day of judgment, and the Book of Mormon as the history of the aborigines of this continent,—must we be expelled from the institutions of our country, the rights of citizenship and the graves of our friends and brethren, and the Government lock the gate of humanity and shut the door of redress against us? If so, farewell freedom! adieu to personal safety! and let the red hot wrath of an offended God purify the nation of such sinks of corruption; for that realm is hurrying to ruin where vice has the power to expel virtue. (HC 6:91, 92)

Virtue

  11 Letter to James Arlington Bennett, Nauvoo, 13 November 1843.

  12 Letter to the "Green Mountain Boys" in Vermont, appealing for their support, Nauvoo, 29 November 1843.

13 With the strictest scrutiny publish the facts, whether a particle of law has been evaded or broken: virtue and innocence need no artificial covering. (*HC* 6:218)

14 Truth, virtue, and honor, combined with energy and industry, pave the way to exaltation, glory and bliss. (*HC* 6:425)

15 Sir:—We understand that you have been cut off from the Church of Jesus Christ of Latter-day Saints; and feeling an ardent desire for the salvation of the souls of men, we take pleasure in feeling after you; and therefore would, in the sincerity of men of God, advise you to be rebaptized by Elder Nickerson, one of the servants of God, that you may again receive the sweet influences of the Holy Ghost, and enjoy the fellowship of the Saints.

    The law of God requires it, and you cannot be too good. Patience is heavenly, obedience is noble, forgiveness is merciful, and exaltation is godly; and he that holds out faithful to the end shall in no wise lose his reward. A good man will endure all things to honor Christ, and even dispose of the whole world, and all in it, to save his soul. Grace for grace is a heavenly decree, and union is power where wisdom guides. (*HC* 6:427)

Visions

1 Nothing could be more pleasing to the Saints upon the order of the kingdom of the Lord, than the light which burst upon the world through the foregoing vision [D&C 76]. Every law, every commandment, every promise, every truth, and every point touching the destiny

---

Virtue
> 13 A pamphlet containing the Prophet's political platform, entitled *Views of the Powers and Policy of the Government of the United States*, Nauvoo, 7 February 1844.
> 14 Letter to Joel Hamilton Walker, Nauvoo, 1 June 1844.
> 15 Letter of the Prophet and Hyrum Smith to Mr. Tewkesbury (Abijah R. Tewksbury), Nauvoo, 4 June 1844, seeking to restore him to fellowship.

Visions
> 1 The Prophet's view of the vision of the glories (D&C 76), Hiram, Ohio, 16 February 1832.

of man, from Genesis to Revelation, where the purity of the scriptures remains unsullied by the folly of men, go to show the perfection of the theory {of different degrees of glory in the future life} and witnesses the fact that that document is a transcript from the records of the eternal world. The sublimity of the ideas; the purity of the language; the scope for action; the continued duration for completion, in order that the heirs of salvation may confess the Lord and bow the knee; the rewards for faithfulness, and the punishments for sins, are so much beyond the narrow-mindedness of men, that every honest man is constrained to exclaim: "*It came from God.*" (HC 1:252–53)

2 I then observed to the brethren, that it was time to retire. We accordingly closed our interview and returned home at about two o'clock in the morning, and the Spirit and visions of God attended me through the night. (HC 2:383)

3 During this night the visions of the future were opened to my understanding; when I saw the ways and means and near approach of my escape from imprisonment. (HC 3:316)

4 We may look for angels and receive their ministrations, but we are to try the spirits and prove them, for it is often the case that men make a mistake in regard to these things. God has so ordained that when He has communicated, no vision is to be taken but what you see by the seeing of the eye, or what you hear by the hearing of the ear. When you see a vision, pray for the interpretation; if you get not this, shut it up; there must be certainty in this matter. An open vision will manifest that which is important. Lying spirits are going forth in the earth. There will be great manifestations of spirits, both false and true. (HC 3:391–92)

Visions

  2 Statement after spending the evening in the Kirtland Temple with the Twelve and Presidency of the Seventy performing anointings and blessings, 22 January 1836.

  3 Liberty Jail, 11 April 1839.

  4 Discourse on the priesthood, given sometime before 8 August 1839, Commerce (Nauvoo). For a discussion on the dating of this discourse, see *WJS*, p. 22.

5 Would you think it strange if I relate what I have seen in vision in relation to this interesting theme? Those who have died in Jesus Christ may expect to enter into all that fruition of joy when they come forth, which they possessed or anticipated here.

So plain was the vision, that I actually saw men, before they had ascended from the tomb, as though they were getting up slowly. They took each other by the hand and said to each other, "My father, my son, my mother, my daughter, my brother, my sister." And when the voice calls for the dead to arise, suppose I am laid by the side of my father, what would be the first joy of my heart? To meet my father, my mother, my brother, my sister; and when they are by my side, I embrace them and they me.

It is my meditation all the day, and more than my meat and drink, to know how I shall make the Saints of God comprehend the visions that roll like an overflowing surge before my mind. (HC 5:361–62)

6 Could you gaze into heaven five minutes, you would know more than you would by reading all that ever was written on the subject. (HC 6:50)

7 In the afternoon, Elder William Weeks (whom I had employed as architect of the Temple,) came in for instruction. I instructed him in relation to the circular windows designed to light the offices in the dead work of the arch between stories. He said that round windows in the broad side of a building were a violation of all the known rules of architecture, and contended that they should be semicircular—that the building was too low for round windows. I told him I would have the circles, if he had to make the Temple ten feet higher than it was originally calculated; that one light at the center of each circular window would be sufficient to light the whole room; that when the whole building was thus illuminated, the effect would be remarkably grand. "I wish you to carry out *my* designs. I have seen in vision the splendid appearance of that building illuminated, and will have it built according to the pattern shown me." (HC 6:196–97)

Visions
5 Remarks upon the death of Lorenzo D. Barnes, Nauvoo, 16 April 1843.
6 Remarks upon the death of James Adams, Nauvoo, 9 October 1843.
7 Nauvoo, 5 February 1844.

War

1   To take possession by conquest or the shedding of blood is entirely foreign to our feelings. The shedding of blood we shall not be guilty of, until all just and honorable means among men prove insufficient to restore peace. (HC 2:122)

2   Preserve peace with all men, if possible. (HC 2:455)

3   We think, gentlemen, that we have pursued the subject far enough, and we here express to you, as we have in a letter accompanying this to our friends, our decided disapprobation to the idea of shedding blood, if any other course can be followed to avoid it; in which case, and which alone, we have urged upon our friends to desist, only in extreme cases of self defense; and in this case not to give the offense or provoke their fellow men to acts of violence, which we have no doubt they will observe as they ever have done; for you may rest assured, gentlemen, that we would be the last to advise our friends to shed the blood of men or commit one act to endanger the public peace. . . .

   . . . Be they [the Saints removing from Clay County] where they will we have this gratifying reflection, that they have never been the first, in an unjust manner, to violate the laws, injure their fellow men, or disturb the tranquility and peace under which any part of our country has heretofore reposed. (HC 2:459–60)

Washing of Feet

1   On the 23rd of January, we again assembled in conference; when, after much speaking, singing, praying, and praising God, all in tongues, we proceeded to the washing of feet (according to the practice

---

War
   1   Statement of the intent of Zion's Camp, Clay County, Missouri, 22 June 1834.
   2   Letter to the brethren in Missouri, Kirtland, 25 July 1836.
   3   Letter to John Thornton and others, Kirtland, 25 July 1836.

Washing of Feet
   1   Instruction to the elders of the Church at a conference, Kirtland, 23 January 1833.

recorded in the 13th chapter of John's Gospel), as commanded of the Lord. Each Elder washed his own feet first, after which I girded myself with a towel and washed the feet of all of them, wiping them with the towel with which I was girded. Among the number, my father presented himself, but before I washed his feet, I asked of him a father's blessing, which he granted by laying his hands upon my head, in the name of Jesus Christ, and declaring that I should continue in the Priest's office until Christ comes. At the close of the scene, Brother Frederick G. Williams, being moved upon by the Holy Ghost, washed my feet in token of his fixed determination to be with me in suffering, or in journeying, in life or in death, and to be continually on my right hand; in which I accepted him in the name of the Lord.

I then said to the Elders, As I have done so do ye; wash ye, therefore, one another's feet; and by the power of the Holy Ghost I pronounced them all clean from the blood of this generation; but if any of them should sin wilfully after they were thus cleansed, and sealed up unto eternal life, they should be given over unto the buffetings of Satan until the day of redemption. (HC 1:323–24)

2   The item to which I wish the more particularly to call your attention to-night, is the ordinance of washing of feet. This we have not done as yet, but it is necessary now, as much as it was in the days of the Savior; and we must have a place prepared, that we may attend to this ordinance aside from the world.

. . . We must have all things prepared, and call our solemn assembly as the Lord has commanded us, that we may be able to accomplish His great work, and it must be done in God's own way. The house of the Lord must be prepared, and the solemn assembly called and organized in it, according to the order of the house of God; and in it we must attend to the ordinance of washing of feet. It was never intended for any but official members. It is calculated to unite our hearts, that we may be one in feeling and sentiment, and that our faith may be strong, so that Satan cannot overthrow us, nor have any power over us here. (HC 2:308–9)

3   *Clerk's Report:* Tuesday, 29. . . . The word of the Lord came, through President Joseph Smith, Jun., that those who had entered the

---

Washing of Feet
2   Instructions to the Twelve, Kirtland, 12 November 1835.
3   Solemn assembly in the Kirtland Temple, 29–30 March 1836.

holy place, must not leave the house until morning, but send for such things as were necessary, and, also, during our stay, we must cleanse our feet and partake of the Sacrament that we might be made holy before Him, and thereby be qualified to officiate in our calling, upon the morrow, in washing the feet of the Elders.

Accordingly we proceeded to cleanse our faces and our feet, and then proceeded to wash one another's feet. President Sidney Rigdon first washed President Joseph Smith, Junior's feet, and then, in turn, was washed by him; after which President Rigdon washed President Joseph Smith, Sen., and Hyrum Smith. President Joseph Smith, Jun., washed President Frederick G. Williams, and then President Hyrum Smith washed President David Whitmer's and President Oliver Cowdery's feet. Then President David Whitmer washed President William W. Phelps' feet, and in turn President Phelps washed President John Whitmer's feet. The Bishops and their Counselors were then washed, after which we partook of the bread and wine. The Holy Spirit rested down upon us, and we continued in the Lord's House all night, prophesying and giving glory to God.

Wednesday, 30.—At eight o'clock, according to appointment, the Presidency, the Twelve, the Seventies, the High Council, the Bishops and their entire quorums, the Elders and all the official members in this stake of Zion, amounting to about three hundred, met in the Temple of the Lord to attend to the ordinance of washing of feet. . . .

Tubs, water, and towels were prepared, and I called the house to order, and the Presidency proceeded to wash the feet of the Twelve, pronouncing many prophecies and blessings upon them in the name of the Lord Jesus; and then the Twelve proceeded to wash the feet of the Presidents of the several quorums. The brethren began to prophesy upon each other's heads, and upon the enemies of Christ, who inhabited Jackson county, Missouri; and continued prophesying, and blessing, and sealing them with hosanna and amen, until nearly seven o'clock in the evening. (HC 2:430, 431)

4   At an early hour on Thursday, the 6th of April, the official members assembled in the House of the Lord, when the time for the first two or three hours was spent by the different quorums in washing of feet, singing, praying, and preparing to receive instructions from the Presidency. (HC 2:475–76)

Washing of Feet
   4   Solemn assembly in the Kirtland Temple, 6 April 1837.

Welfare
See also POOR

1   He [John P. Greene] is fully authorized to receive donations by the liberality of the Saints for the assistance of the poor among us, who have been persecuted and driven from their homes in the State of Missouri. . . . We beseech the brethren, in the name of the Lord Jesus, to receive this brother in behalf of the poor with readiness, and to abound unto him in a liberal manner; for "inasmuch as ye have done it unto the least of these, ye have done it unto me." (HC 3:347, 348)

2   The Church passed a resolution that the Twelve proceed on their mission as soon as possible, and that the Saints provide for their families during their absence. (HC 4:5)

3   *Minutes:* The President made some observations respecting the pecuniary affairs of the Church, and requested the brethren to step forward, and assist in liquidating the debts on the town plot, so that the poor might have an inheritance. (HC 4:106)

4   No industrious man need suffer in this land. The claims of the poor on us are such that we have claim on your good feelings, for your money to help the poor; and the Church debts also have their demands to save the credit of the Church. This credit has been obtained to help the poor and keep them from starvation, &c. Those who purchase Church land and pay for it, this shall be their sacrifice.

Men of considerable means who were robbed of everything in the state of Missouri, are laboring in this city for a morsel of bread; and there are those who must have starved, but for the providence of God through me. We can beat all our competitors in lands, price and everything; we have the highest prices and best lands, and do the most good with the money we get. Our system is a real smut machine, a bolting machine; and all the shorts, bran and smut runs away, and all the flour remains with us. Suppose I sell you land for ten dollars an

---

Welfare
1   John P. Greene's letter of appointment to collect funds for the assistance of the poor among the Saints, Commerce (Nauvoo), 6 May 1839.
2   Commerce (Nauvoo), 4 August 1839.
3   Minutes of general conference, Nauvoo, 7 April 1840.
4   Remarks to Saints newly arrived from England, Nauvoo, 13 April 1843.

acre, and I gave three, four or five dollars per acre; then some persons may cry out, "You are speculating." Yes. I will tell how: I buy other lands and give them to the widow and the fatherless. (HC 5:356)

5   Some say it is better to give to the poor than build the Temple. The building of the Temple has sustained the poor who were driven from Missouri, and kept them from starving; and it has been the best means for this object which could be devised. (HC 6:58)

Wickedness

1   Have not the pride, high-mindedness, and unbelief of the Gentiles, provoked the Holy One of Israel to withdraw His Holy Spirit from them, and send forth His judgments to scourge them for their wickedness? This is certainly the case. (HC 1:314)

2   The law of heaven is presented to man, and as such guarantees to all who obey it a reward far beyond any earthly consideration; though it does not promise that the believer in every age should be exempt from the afflictions and troubles arising from different sources in consequence of the acts of wicked men on earth. (HC 2:7)

3   The Church is in its infancy, and if you take this rash step [of plucking up the tares], you will destroy the wheat, or the Church, with the tares; therefore it is better to let them grow together until the harvest, or the end of the world, which means the destruction of the wicked, which is not yet fulfilled. . . .
     . . . The end of the world is the destruction of the wicked, the harvest and the end of the world have an allusion directly to the human family in the last days, instead of the earth, as many have imagined; and that which shall precede the coming of the Son of Man, and the restitution of all things spoken of by the mouth of all the holy prophets since the world began; and the angels are to have something

Welfare
   5   Sabbath address, Nauvoo, 15 October 1843.

Wickedness
   1   Letter to N. E. Seaton (N. C. Saxton), a newspaper editor in Rochester, N.Y., Kirtland, 4 January 1833.
   2   Letter to the brethren scattered from Zion, Kirtland, 22 January 1834.
   3   Letter to the elders of the Church, Kirtland, 1 September 1835.

to do in this great work, for they are the reapers. As, therefore, the tares are gathered and burned in the fire, so shall it be in the end of the world; that is, as the servants of God go forth warning the nations, both priests and people, and as they harden their hearts and reject the light of truth, these first being delivered over to the buffetings of Satan, and the law and the testimony being closed up, as it was in the case of the Jews, they are left in darkness, and delivered over unto the day of burning; thus being bound up by their creeds, and their bands being made strong by their priests, are prepared for the fulfillment of the saying of the Savior—"The Son of Man shall send forth His angels, and gather out of His Kingdom all things that offend, and them which do iniquity, and shall cast them into a furnace of fire, there shall be wailing and gnashing of teeth." We understand that the work of gathering together of the wheat into barns, or garners, is to take place while the tares are being bound over, and preparing for the day of burning; that after the day of burnings, the righteous shall shine forth like the sun, in the Kingdom of their Father. Who hath ears to hear, let him hear. (HC 2:267, 271)

4 And we rejoice that the time is at hand, when the wicked who will not repent will be swept from the earth as with a besom of destruction, and the earth become an inheritance of the poor and the meek. (HC 2:324)

5 Therefore, dearly beloved brethren, we are the more ready and willing to lay claim to your fellowship and love. For our circumstances are calculated to awaken our spirits to a sacred remembrance of everything, and we think that yours are also, and that nothing therefore can separate us from the love of God and fellowship one with another; and that every species of wickedness and cruelty practiced upon us will only tend to bind our hearts together and seal them together in love. (HC 3:290)

6 It is for us to be righteous, that we may be wise and understand; for none of the wicked shall understand; but the wise shall understand, and they that turn many to righteousness shall shine as the stars for ever and ever. (HC 5:65)

Wickedness
  4 Kirtland, 2 December 1835.
  5 Letter to the Saints from Liberty Jail, 20–25 March 1839.
  6 Editorial in the *Times and Seasons*, 15 July 1842.

7 Instead of arraigning [John C. Bennett's] character before you, suffice it to say that his own conduct, wherever he goes, will be sufficient to recommend him to an enlightened public, whether for a bad man or a good one. (*HC* 5:157)

8 There is no pain so awful as that of suspense. This is the punishment of the wicked; their doubt, anxiety and suspense cause weeping, wailing and gnashing of teeth. (*HC* 5:340)

9 The inhabitants of this continent anciently were so constituted, and were so determined and persevering, either in righteousness or wickedness, that God visited them immediately either with great judgments or blessings. (*HC* 5:390)

10 What can be the matter with these men? Is it that the wicked flee when no man pursueth, that hit pigeons always flutter, that drowning men catch at straws? (*HC* 6:170)

Will

1 The man who willeth to do well, we should extol his virtues, and speak not of his faults behind his back. A man who wilfully turneth away from his friend without a cause, is not easily forgiven. (*HC* 1:444)

2 God requires the will of His creatures to be swallowed up in His will. (*HC* 2:342)

Wickedness
7 Letter to James Arlington Bennett, Nauvoo, 8 September 1842.
8 General conference address, Nauvoo, 8 April 1843.
9 Sabbath address at Yelrome (Morley's Settlement), Illinois, 14 May 1843.
10 Remarks to the city council meeting where William Law and William Marks expressed fear that their lives were in jeopardy, Nauvoo, 5 January 1844.

Will
1 Kirtland, 19 November 1833.
2 Letter to William Smith, the Prophet's brother, Kirtland, 18 December 1835.

3   As a Church and a people it behooves us to be wise, and to seek to know the will of God, and then be willing to do it. (HC 5:65)

Wisdom

1   About this time my brother Samuel H. Smith came to visit us. We informed him of what the Lord was about to do for the children of men, and began to reason with him out of the Bible. We also showed him that part of the work [the Book of Mormon] which we had translated, and labored to persuade him concerning the Gospel of Jesus Christ, which was now about to be revealed in its fulness. He was not, however, very easily persuaded of these things, but after much inquiry and explanation he retired to the woods, in order that by secret and fervent prayer he might obtain of a merciful God, wisdom to enable him to judge for himself. (HC 1:44)

2   I have his [the Lord's] immutable covenant that this [the redemption of Zion] shall be the case, but God is pleased to keep it hid from mine eyes the means how exactly the thing will be done. . . . Never at any time have I felt as I now feel that pure love and for you, my brethren, the warmth and zeal for your safety that we can scarcely hold our spirits; but wisdom, I trust, will keep us from madness and desperation, and the power of the gospel will enable us to stand and bear with patience the great affliction that is falling upon us on all sides. (*PWJS*, p. 285; standardized)

3   We have reason to believe that many things were introduced among the Saints before God had signified the times; and notwithstanding the principles and plans may have been good, yet aspiring men, or in other words, men who had not the substance of godliness about them, perhaps undertook to handle edged tools. Children, you know, are fond of tools, while they are not yet able to use them.

Will
3   Editorial in the *Times and Seasons*, 15 July 1842.

Wisdom
1   Harmony, Pennsylvania, May 1829.
2   Letter to William W. Phelps and others following mob destruction of the Saints' property in Missouri, Kirtland, 18 August 1833.
3   Letter to the Saints from Liberty Jail, 20–25 March 1839.

Time and experience, however, are the only safe remedies against such evils. There are many teachers, but, perhaps, not many fathers. There are times coming when God will signify many things which are expedient for the well-being of the Saints; but the times have not yet come, but will come, as fast as there can be found place and reception for them. (HC 3:301–2)

4   Steer clear of making the Church appear as either supporting or opposing you in your politics lest such a course may have a tendency to bring about persecution on the Church, where a little wisdom and caution may avoid it. (HC 3:367)

5   Why will not man learn wisdom by precept at this late age of the world, when we have such a cloud of witnesses and examples before us, and not be obliged to learn by sad experience everything we know? Must the new ones that are chosen to fill the places of those that are fallen, of the quorum of the Twelve, begin to exalt themselves, until they exalt themselves so high that they will soon tumble over and have a great fall, and go wallowing through the mud and mire and darkness, Judas like, to the buffetings of Satan, as several of the quorum have done, or will they learn wisdom and be wise? O God! Give them wisdom, and keep them humble, I pray. (HC 3:384)

6   There are many things of much importance, on which you ask counsel, but which I think you will be perfectly able to decide upon, as you are more conversant with the peculiar circumstances than I am; and I feel great confidence in your united wisdom; therefore you will excuse me for not entering into detail. If I should see anything that is wrong, I would take the privilege of making known my mind to you, and pointing out the evil. (HC 4:228–29)

7   I contend that if one man cannot understand these things but by the Spirit of God, ten thousand men cannot; it is alike out of the

---

Wisdom

   4   Letter to Lyman Wight, Commerce (Nauvoo), 27 May 1839.
   5   Instructions to the Twelve and Seventies departing for missions to England, Commerce (Nauvoo), 2 July 1839.
   6   Letter to the Twelve in England, Nauvoo, 15 December 1840. The placement of this letter in *HC* implies that it was written in October 1840, but actually it was written on 15 December 1840 (see *PWJS*, p. 480).
   7   Editorial in the *Times and Seasons*, 1 April 1842.

reach of the wisdom of the learned, the tongue of the eloquent, the power of the mighty. And we shall at last have to come to this conclusion, whatever we may think of revelation, that without it we can neither know nor understand anything of God, or the devil; and however unwilling the world may be to acknowledge this principle, it is evident from the multifarious creeds and notions concerning this matter that they understand nothing of this principle, and it is equally as plain that without a divine communication they must remain in ignorance. (HC 4:574)

8   Emma having arrived at Yelrome, last night from Quincy, with the carriage, we rode home together. On our way, we stopped a short time at Brother Perry's. Brothers George A. Smith and Wilford Woodruff rode in my buggy. I was asked if the horse would stand without tying. I answered, "Yes: but never trust property to the mercy or judgment of a horse." (HC 5:390)

9   A man of God should be endowed with wisdom, knowledge, and understanding, in order to teach and lead the people of God. (HC 5:426)

10   You observed, "as I have proven myself to be a philosophical divine" I must excuse you when you say that we must leave these *influences* to the mass. The meaning of "philosophical divine" may be taken in various ways. If, as the learned world apply the term, you infer that I have achieved a victory, and been strengthened by a scientific religion, as practiced by the popular sects of the age, through the aid of colleges, seminaries, Bible societies, missionary boards, financial organizations, and gospel money schemes, then you are wrong. Such a combination of men and means shows a form of godliness without the power; for is it not written, "I will destroy the wisdom of the wise." "Beware lest any man spoil you through philosophy and vain deceit, after the rudiments of the world, and not after the doctrines of Christ." But if the inference is that by more love, more light, more virtue, and more truth from the Lord, I have succeeded as a man of God, then you reason truly, though the weight of the sentiment is lost, when the *"influence is left to the mass."*. . .

Wisdom
  8   The Prophet returning to Nauvoo from Yelrome, 15 May 1843.
  9   Sabbath address, Nauvoo, 11 June 1843.
  10   Letter to James Arlington Bennett, Nauvoo, 13 November 1843.

. . . Truth is mighty and must prevail, and . . . one man empowered from Jehovah has more influence with the children of the kingdom than eight hundred millions led by the precepts of men. God exalts the humble, and debases the haughty. (HC 6:73–74)

Witnessing

1   To find ourselves engaged in the very same order of things as observed by the holy Apostles of old; to realize the importance and solemnity of such proceedings; and to witness and feel with our own natural senses, the like glorious manifestations of the powers of the Priesthood, the gifts and blessings of the Holy Ghost, and the goodness and condescension of a merciful God unto such as obey the everlasting Gospel of our Lord Jesus Christ, combined to create within us sensations of rapturous gratitude, and inspire us with fresh zeal and energy in the cause of truth. (HC 1:85–86)

2   We (the apostles) are His witnesses of these things, and so is the Holy Ghost, whom God had given to them that obey Him (see Acts v). So that after the testimony of the Scriptures on this point, the assurance is given by the Holy Ghost, bearing witness to those who obey Him, that Christ Himself has assuredly risen from the dead; and if He has risen from the dead, He will, by His power, bring all men to stand before Him. (HC 2:19)

3   "And another parable spake He unto them. The Kingdom of Heaven is like unto leaven which a woman took and hid in three measures of meal till the whole was leavened." It may be understood that the Church of the Latter-day Saints has taken its rise from a little leaven that was put into three witnesses. Behold, how much this is like the parable! It is fast leavening the lump, and will soon leaven the whole. (HC 2:270)

4   Everlasting covenant was made between three personages before the organization of this earth, and relates to their dispensation of

---

Witnessing
  1   First conference of the Church, Fayette, New York, 9 June 1830.
  2   Letter to the brethren scattered from Zion, Kirtland, 22 January 1834.
  3   Letter to the elders of the Church, Kirtland, 1 September 1835.
  4   Nauvoo, 1841. Manuscript history, LDS Church Archives.

things to men on the earth; these personages, according to Abraham's record, are called God the first, the Creator; God the second, the Redeemer; and God the third, the witness or Testator. (*TPJS*, p. 190)

5   The Lord makes manifest to me many things, which it is not wisdom for me to make public, until others can witness the proof of them. (HC 4:607–8)

6   I have one remark to make respecting the baptism for the dead to suffice for the time being, until I have opportunity to discuss the subject at great length—all persons baptized for the dead must have a recorder present, that he may be an eyewitness to record and testify of the truth and validity of his record. It will be necessary, in the Grand Council, that these things be testified to by competent witnesses. Therefore let the recording and witnessing of baptisms for the dead be carefully attended to from this time forth. If there is any lack, it may be at the expense of our friends; they may not come forth. (HC 5:141)

7   One thing more in order to prove the work as we proceed. It is necessary to have witnesses, two or three of whose testimonies, according to the laws or rules of God and man, are sufficient to establish any one point. (HC 6:76)

8   The whole earth shall bear me witness that I, like the towering rock in the midst of the ocean, which has withstood the mighty surges of the warring waves for centuries, *am impregnable,* and am a faithful friend to virtue, and a fearless foe to vice,—no odds whether the former was sold as a pearl in Asia or hid as a gem in America, and the latter dazzles in palaces or glimmers among the tombs.

I combat the errors of ages; I meet the violence of mobs; I cope with illegal proceedings from executive authority; I cut the gordian knot of powers, and I solve mathematical problems of universities, *with truth—diamond truth; and God is my "right hand man."* (HC 6:78)

9   I shall read the 24th chapter of Matthew, and give it a literal

---

Witnessing

5   Nauvoo, 29 April 1842.
6   Remarks to the Relief Society, Nauvoo, 31 August 1842.
7   Letter to James Arlington Bennett, Nauvoo, 13 November 1843.
8   Letter to James Arlington Bennett, Nauvoo, 13 November 1843.
9   Sabbath address, Nauvoo, 12 May 1844.

rendering and reading; and when it is rightly understood, it will be edifying. {He then read and translated it from the German}.

I thought the very oddity of its rendering would be edifying anyhow—"*And it will preached be, the Gospel of the kingdom, in the whole world, to a witness over all people: and then will the end come.*" I will now read it in German {which he did, and many Germans who were present said he translated it correctly}.

The Savior said when these tribulations should take place, it should be committed to a man who should be a witness over the whole world: the keys of knowledge, power and revelations should be revealed to a witness who should hold the testimony to the world. It has always been my province to dig up hidden mysteries—new things—for my hearers. Just at the time when some men think that I have no right to the keys of the Priesthood—just at that time I have the greatest right. The Germans are an exalted people. The old German translators are the most correct—most honest of any of the translators; and therefore I get testimony to bear me out in the revelations that I have preached for the last fourteen years. The old German, Latin, Greek and Hebrew translations all say it is true: they cannot be impeached, and therefore I am in good company.

All the testimony is that the Lord in the last days would commit the keys of the priesthood to a witness over all people. Has the Gospel of the kingdom commenced in the last days? And will God take it from the man until He takes him Himself? I have read it precisely as the words flowed from the lips of Jesus Christ. John the Revelator saw an angel flying through the midst of heaven, having the everlasting Gospel to preach unto them that dwell on the earth.

The scripture is ready to be fulfilled when great wars, famines, pestilence, great distress, judgments, &c., are ready to be poured out on the inhabitants of the earth. John saw the angel having the holy priesthood, who should preach the everlasting Gospel to all nations. God had an angel—a special messenger—ordained and prepared for that purpose in the last days. Woe, woe be to that man or set of men who lift up their hands against God and His witness in these last days: for they shall deceive almost the very chosen ones! (HC 6:363–64)

Word of Wisdom

1 *Minutes:* After the Councilors had spoken, the President proceeded to give the decision:

No official member in this Church is worthy to hold an office, after having the Word of Wisdom properly taught him, and he, the official member, neglecting to comply with or obey it; which decision the Council confirmed by vote. (HC 2:35)

2 *Minutes:* Resolved unanimously, that we will not fellowship any ordained member who will not, or does not, observe the Word of Wisdom according to its literal reading. (HC 2:482)

3 This was the first public conference of the Church in England, and at this conference the Word of Wisdom was first publicly taught in that country. (HC 2:529)

4 *Minutes:* President Joseph Smith, Jun., made a few remarks on the Word of Wisdom, giving the reason of its coming forth, saying it should be observed. (HC 3:15)

5 [Several brethren] were ordained elders, with this express injunction, that they quit the use of tobacco and keep the Word of Wisdom. (HC 5:349)

Words

1 Were we capable of laying any thing before you as a just comparison, we would cheerfully do it; but in this our ability fails, and we are

---

Word of Wisdom
1 Minutes of a high council meeting, Kirtland, 20 February 1834.
2 Meeting at Far West, Missouri, May 1837. Although Joseph was not present at this meeting, the action was taken by the presidency of the Church in Missouri and was included in the official history of the Church.
3 History entry referring to a Church meeting held in England on 25 December 1837.
4 Minutes of conference, Far West, Missouri, 7 April 1838.
5 Special conference of elders, Nauvoo, 10 April 1843.

Words
1 Letter to the brethren scattered from Zion, Kirtland, 22 January 1834.

inclined to think that man is unable, without assistance beyond what has been given to those before, of expressing in words the greatness of this important subject [the power and glory of god]. (HC 2:14)

2   And again, outward appearance is not always a criterion by which to judge our fellow man; but the lips betray the haughty and overbearing imaginations of the heart; by his words and his deeds let him be judged. Flattery also is a deadly poison. (HC 3:295)

3   Words and language are inadequate to express the gratitude that I owe to God for having given me so honorable a parentage. (HC 5:126)

4   I do not calculate or intend to please your ears with superfluity of words or oratory, or with much learning; but I calculate {intend} to edify you with the simple truths from heaven. (HC 6:303)

Works

1   If the "intelligent" inhabitants of Hancock county want peace, want to abide by the Governor's advice, want to have a character at home, and really mean to follow the Savior's golden rule, "To do unto others as they would wish others to do unto them," they will be still now, and let their own works praise them in the gates of justice and in the eyes of the surrounding world. (HC 6:219)

2   The best men bring forth the best works. (HC 6:315)

3   The servants of God teach nothing but principles of eternal life, by their works ye shall know them. A good man will speak good things and holy principles, and an evil man evil things. (HC 6:366)

Words
  2   Letter to the Saints from Liberty Jail, 20–25 March 1839.
  3   Nauvoo, 22 August 1842.
  4   King Follett Discourse, Nauvoo, 7 April 1844.

Works
  1   Article entitled "Pacific Innuendo," Nauvoo, 17 February 1844.
  2   King Follett Discourse, Nauvoo, 7 April 1844.
  3   Sabbath address, Nauvoo, 12 May 1844.

World

1 Who but those who can see the awful precipice upon which the world of mankind stands in this generation, can labor in the vineyard of the Lord without feeling a sense of the world's deplorable situation? (HC 2:5)

2 We again remark here—for we find that the very principle upon which the disciples were accounted blessed, was because they were permitted to see with their eyes and hear with their ears—that the condemnation which rested upon the multitude that received not His saying, was because they were not willing to see with their eyes, and hear with their ears; not because they could not, and were not privileged to see and hear, but because their hearts were full of iniquity and abominations; "as your fathers did, so do ye." The prophet, foreseeing that they would thus harden their hearts, plainly declared it; and herein is the condemnation of the world; that light hath come into the world, and men choose darkness rather than light, because their deeds are evil. (HC 2:266)

3 The end of the world is the destruction of the wicked, the harvest and the end of the world have an allusion directly to the human family in the last days, instead of the earth, as many have imagined; and that which shall precede the coming of the Son of Man, and the restitution of all things spoken of by the mouth of all the holy prophets since the world began. (HC 2:271)

4 I stood alone, an unlearned youth, to combat the worldly wisdom and multiplied ignorance of eighteen centuries, with a new revelation, which (if they would receive the everlasting Gospel,) would open the eyes of more than eight hundred millions of people, and make "plain the old paths," wherein if a man walk in all the ordinances of God blameless, he shall inherit eternal life. (HC 6:74)

World
1 Letter to the brethren scattered from Zion, Kirtland, 22 January 1834.
2 Letter to the elders of the Church, Kirtland, 1 September 1835.
3 Letter to the elders of the Church, Kirtland, 1 September 1835.
4 Letter to James Arlington Bennett, Nauvoo, 13 November 1843.

Worship

1   When about fourteen years of age, I began to reflect upon the importance of being prepared for a future state, and upon inquiring {about} the plan of salvation, I found that there was a great clash in religious sentiment; if I went to one society they referred me to one plan, and another to another; each one pointing to his own particular creed as the *summum bonum* of perfection. Considering that all could not be right, and that God could not be the author of so much confusion, I determined to investigate the subject more fully, believing that if God had a Church it would not be split up into factions, and that if He taught one society to worship one way, and administer in one set of ordinances, He would not teach another, principles which were diametrically opposed. (HC 4:536)

2   We can only live by worshiping our God; all must do it for themselves; none can do it for another. (HC 5:24)

Worthiness

1   May God enable us to perform our vows and covenants with each other, in all fidelity and righteousness before Him, that our influence may be felt among the nations of the earth, in mighty power, even to rend the kingdoms of darkness asunder, and triumph over priestcraft and spiritual wickedness in high places, and break in pieces all kingdoms that are opposed to the kingdom of Christ, and spread the light and truth of the everlasting Gospel from the rivers to the ends of the earth. (HC 2:375)

Worship
1   Letter to John Wentworth, editor of the *Chicago Democrat*, Nauvoo, 1 March 1842.
2   Remarks to the Relief Society, Nauvoo, 9 June 1842.

Worthiness
1   Instructions to the Twelve, Kirtland, 16 January 1836.

Zeal

1   When we arrived, some of the young Elders were about engaging in a debate on the subject of miracles. The question—"Was it, or was it not, the design of Christ to establish His Gospel by miracles?" After an interesting debate of three hours or more, during which time much talent was displayed, it was decided, by the President of the debate, in the negative, which was a righteous decision.

I discovered in this debate, much warmth displayed, too much zeal for mastery, too much of that enthusiasm that characterizes a lawyer at the bar, who is determined to defend his cause, right or wrong. I therefore availed myself of this favorable opportunity to drop a few words upon this subject, by way of advice, that they might improve their minds and cultivate their powers of intellect in a proper manner, that they might not incur the displeasure of heaven; that they should handle sacred things very sacredly, and with due deference to the opinions of others, and with an eye single to the glory of God. (HC 2:317–18)

2   Many already have been ordained, who ought not to hold official stations in the Church, because they dishonor themselves and the Church, and bring persecution swiftly upon us, in consequence of their zeal without knowledge. (HC 2:394)

3   Our name will be handed down to future ages; our children will rise up and call us blessed; and generations yet unborn will dwell with peculiar delight upon the scenes that we have passed through, the privations that we have endured; the untiring zeal that we have manifested; the all but insurmountable difficulties that we have overcome in laying the foundation of a work that brought about the glory and blessing which they will realize; a work that God and angels have contemplated with delight for generations past; that fired the souls of the ancient patriarchs and prophets; a work that is destined to bring about the destruction of the powers of darkness, the renovation of the earth, the glory of God, and the salvation of the human family. (HC 4:610)

Zeal
1   Counsel given to a few Saints in Father Smith's home, Kirtland, 18 November 1835.
2   Remarks at a meeting of several priesthood quorums in the schoolroom of the Kirtland Temple, 12 February 1836.
3   Editorial in the *Times and Seasons*, Nauvoo, 2 May 1842.

4 There is another error which opens a door for the adversary to enter. As females possess refined feelings and sensitiveness, they are also subject to overmuch zeal, which must ever prove dangerous, and cause them to be rigid in a religious capacity—{they} should be armed with mercy, notwithstanding the iniquity among us. (HC 5:19)

5 I do not think to mention the particulars of the history of that sacred night, which shall forever be remembered by me; but the names of the faithful are what I wish to record in this place. These I have met in prosperity, and they were my friends; and I now meet them in adversity, and they are still my warmer friends. These love the God that I serve; they love the truths that I promulgate; they love those virtuous, and those holy doctrines that I cherish in my bosom with the warmest feelings of my heart, and with that zeal which cannot be denied. (HC 5:108)

Zion

1 Our reflections were many, coming as we had from a highly cultivated state of society in the east, and standing now upon the confines or western limits of the United States, and looking into the vast wilderness of those that sat in darkness; how natural it was to observe the degradation, leanness of intellect, ferocity, and jealousy of a people that were nearly a century behind the times, and to feel for those who roamed about without the benefit of civilization, refinement, or religion; yea, and exclaim in the language of the Prophets: "When will the wilderness blossom as the rose? When will Zion be built up in her glory, and where will Thy temple stand, unto which all nations shall come in the last days?" Our anxiety was soon relieved by receiving the following: [D&C 57]. (HC 1:189)

Zeal
  4 Remarks to the Relief Society, Nauvoo, 26 May 1842.
  5 Reflections on those who were faithful to the Prophet in Nauvoo, 16 August 1842.

Zion
  1 Jackson County, Missouri, 20 July 1831.

2 On the second day of August, I assisted the Colesville branch of the Church to lay the first log, for a house, as a foundation of Zion in Kaw township, twelve miles west of Independence. The log was carried and placed by twelve men, in honor of the twelve tribes of Israel. At the same time, through prayer, the land of Zion was consecrated and dedicated by Elder Sidney Rigdon for the gathering of the Saints. (HC 1:196)

3 The season is mild and delightful nearly three quarters of the year, and as the land of Zion, situated at about equal distances from the Atlantic and Pacific oceans, as well as from the Alleghany and Rocky mountains, in the thirty-ninth degree of north latitude, and between the sixteenth and seventeenth degrees of west longitude, it bids fair—when the curse is taken from the land—to become one of the most blessed places on the globe. The winters are milder than the Atlantic states of the same parallel of latitude, and the weather is more agreeable; so that were the virtues of the inhabitants only equal to the blessings of the Lord which He permits to crown the industry of those inhabitants, there would be a measure of the good things of life for the benefit of the Saints, full, pressed down, and running over, even an hundred-fold. The disadvantages here, as in all new countries are self-evident—lack of mills and schools; together with the natural privations and inconveniences which the hand of industry, the refinement of society, and the polish of science, overcome.

But all these impediments vanish when it is recollected what the Prophets have said concerning Zion in the last days; how the glory of Lebanon is to come upon her; the fir tree, the pine tree, and the box tree together, to beautify the place of His sanctuary, that He may make the place of His feet glorious. Where for brass, He will bring gold; and for iron, He will bring silver; and for wood, brass; and for stones, iron; and where the feast of fat things will be given to the just; yea, when the splendor of the Lord is brought to our consideration for the good of His people, the calculations of men and the vain glory of the world vanish, and we exclaim, "Out of Zion the perfection of beauty, God hath shined." (HC 1:198)

Zion
  2 Dedication of Zion, Kaw Township, Missouri, 2 August 1831.
  3 Dedication of Zion, Kaw Township, Missouri, 2 August 1831.

4   The city of Zion spoken of by David, in the one hundred and second Psalm, will be built upon the land of America, "And the ransomed of the Lord shall return, and come to Zion with songs and everlasting joy upon their heads" (Isaiah xxxv:10); and then they will be delivered from the overflowing scourge that shall pass through the land. But Judah shall obtain deliverance at Jerusalem. See Joel ii:32; Isaiah xxvi:20 and 21; Jeremiah xxxi:12; Psalm 1:5; Ezekiel xxxiv:11, 12 and 13. These are testimonies that the Good Shepherd will put forth His own sheep, and lead them out from all nations where they have been scattered in a cloudy and dark day, to Zion, and to Jerusalem; besides many more testimonies which might be brought. (*HC* 1:315)

5   The Lord will have a place whence His word will go forth, in these last days, in purity; for if Zion will not purify herself, so as to be approved of in all things, in His sight, He will seek another people; for His work will go on until Israel is gathered, and they who will not hear His voice, must expect to feel His wrath. Let me say unto you, seek to purify yourselves, and also all the inhabitants of Zion, lest the Lord's anger be kindled to fierceness. Repent, repent, is the voice of God to Zion; and strange as it may appear, yet it is true, mankind will persist in self-justification until all their iniquity is exposed, and their character past being redeemed, and that which is treasured up in their hearts be exposed to the gaze of mankind. I say to you (and what I say to you I say to all,) hear the warning voice of God, lest Zion fall, and the Lord swear in His wrath the inhabitants of Zion shall not enter into His rest.

The brethren in Kirtland pray for you unceasingly, for, knowing the terrors of the Lord, they greatly fear for you. You will see that the Lord commanded us, in Kirtland, to build a house of God, and establish a school for the Prophets, this is the word of the Lord to us, and we must, yea, the Lord helping us, we will obey: as on conditions of our obedience He has promised us great things; yea, even a visit from the heavens to honor us with His own presence. We greatly fear before the Lord lest we should fail of this great honor, which our Master

---

Zion

    4   Letter to N. E. Seaton (N. C. Saxton) a newspaper editor in Rochester, New York, Kirtland, 4 January 1833.

    5   Letter to William W. Phelps in Missouri, written from Kirtland, 14 January 1833. According to Dean Jessee this letter was dated 11 January (see *PWJS*, p. 262).

proposes to confer on us; we are seeking for humility and great faith lest we be ashamed in His presence. Our hearts are greatly grieved at the spirit which is breathed both in your letter and that of Brother Gilbert's, the very spirit which is wasting the strength of Zion like a pestilence; and if it is not detected and driven from you, it will ripen Zion for the threatened judgments of God. Remember God sees the secret springs of human action, and knows the hearts of all living.

. . . All we can say by way of conclusion is, if the fountain of our tears be not dried up, we will still weep for Zion. This from your brother who trembles for Zion, and for the wrath of heaven, which awaits her if she repent not.

{Signed} Joseph Smith, Jun.

P.S.—I am not in the habit of crying peace, when there is no peace; and, knowing the threatened judgments of God, I say, Wo unto them who are at ease in Zion; fearfulness will speedily lay hold of the hypocrite. (HC 1:316–17)

6 I feel to say, O Lord, let Zion be comforted, let her waste places be built up and established an hundred fold; let Thy Saints come unto Zion out of every nation; let her be exalted to the third heavens, and let Thy judgment be sent forth unto victory; and after this great tribulation, let Thy blessing fall upon Thy people, and let Thy handmaid live till her soul shall be satisfied in beholding the glory of Zion; for notwithstanding her present affliction, she shall yet arise and put on her beautiful garments, and be the joy and glory of the whole earth. (HC 1:408)

7 You will recollect that the Lord has said, that Zion should not be removed out of her place; therefore the land should not be sold, but be held by the Saints, until the Lord in His wisdom shall open a way for your return; and until that time, if you can purchase a tract of land in Clay county for present emergencies, it is right you should do so, if you can do it, and not sell your land in Jackson county. (HC 1:451)

8 I cannot learn from any communication by the Spirit to me, that Zion has forfeited her claim to a celestial crown, notwithstanding the

Zion
6 Letter to Vienna Jacques, Kirtland, 4 September 1833.
7 Letter to the brethren in Missouri, Kirtland, 5 December 1833.
8 Letter to the exiled Saints in Missouri, Kirtland, 10 December 1833.

Lord has caused her to be thus afflicted, except it may be some individuals, who have walked in disobedience, and forsaken the new covenant; all such will be made manifest by their works in due time. I have always expected that Zion would suffer some affliction, from what I could learn from the commandments which have been given. But I would remind you of a certain clause in one which says, that after *much* tribulation cometh the blessing. By this, and also others, and also one received of late, I know that Zion, in the due time of the Lord, will be redeemed; but how many will be the days of her purification, tribulation, and affliction, the Lord has kept hid from my eyes; and when I inquire concerning this subject, the voice of the Lord is: Be still, and know that I am God! all those who suffer for my name shall reign with me, and he that layeth down his life for my sake shall find it again.

Now, there are two things of which I am ignorant; and the Lord will not show them unto me, perhaps for a wise purpose in Himself—I mean in some respects—and they are these: Why God has suffered so great a calamity to come upon Zion, and what the great moving cause of this great affliction is; and again, by what means He will return her back to her inheritance, with songs of everlasting joy upon her head. These two things, brethren, are in part kept back that they are not plainly shown unto me; but there are some things that are plainly manifest which have incurred the displeasure of the Almighty. (HC 1:453–54)

9   And so long as unrighteous acts are suffered in the Church, it cannot be sanctified, neither can Zion be redeemed. (HC 2:146)

10 Now the Lord wants the tares and wheat to grow together: for Zion must be redeemed with judgment, and her converts with righteousness. Every Elder that can, after providing for his family (if he has any) and paying his debts, must go forth and clear his skirts from the blood of this generation. While they are in that region instead of trying members for transgressions, or offenses, let every one labor to prepare himself for the vineyard, sparing a little time to comfort the mourners; to bind up the broken-hearted; to reclaim the backslider; to bring back the wanderer; to re-invite into the kingdom such as have

Zion
9 Letter written from Kirtland to the high council in Zion, 16 August 1834.
10 Letter to the Saints in Missouri published in the *Messenger and Advocate*, June 1835.

been cut off, by encouraging them to lay to while the day lasts, and work righteousness, and, with one heart and one mind, prepare to help redeem Zion, that goodly land of promise, where the willing and the obedient shall be blessed. (HC 2:229)

11 They [the brethren traveling as missionaries] pray our heavenly Father that you may be very prayerful, very humble, and very charitable; working diligently, spiritually and temporally for the redemption of Zion, that the pure in heart may return with songs of everlasting joy to build up her waste places, and meet the Lord when He comes in His glory. (HC 2:230)

12 All the officers in the land of Clay County, Missouri, belonging to the Church, are more or less in transgression, because they have not enjoyed the Spirit of God sufficiently to be able to comprehend their duties respecting themselves and the welfare of Zion; thereby having been left to act in a manner that is detrimental to the interest, and also a hindrance to the redemption of Zion. (HC 2:230)

13 I received, by a heavenly vision, a commandment in June following, to take my journey to the western boundaries of the State of Missouri, and there designate the very spot which was to be the central place for the commencement of the gathering together of those who embrace the fullness of the everlasting Gospel. Accordingly I undertook the journey, with certain ones of my brethren, and after a long and tedious journey, suffering many privations and hardships, arrived in Jackson County, Missouri, and after viewing the country, seeking diligently at the hand of God, He manifested Himself unto us, and designated, to me and others, the very spot upon which He designed to commence the work of the gathering, and the upbuilding of an "holy city," which should be called Zion—Zion, because it is a place of righteousness, and all who build thereon are to worship the true and living God, and all believe in one doctrine, even the doctrine of our Lord and Savior Jesus Christ. . . .

Zion
11 Letter to the Saints in Missouri published in the *Messenger and Advocate*, June 1835.
12 Letter to Hezekiah Peck, a Church leader in Missouri, 31 August 1835. The date of this letter is given in *PWJS*, p. 345.
13 Letter to the elders of the Church, Kirtland, 1 September 1835.

First, I shall begin by quoting from the prophecy of Enoch, speaking of the last days: "Righteousness will I send down out of heaven, and truth will I send forth out of the earth, to bear testimony of mine Only Begotten, His resurrection from the dead (this resurrection I understand to be the corporeal body); yea, and also the resurrection of all men; righteousness and truth will I cause to sweep the earth as with a flood, to gather out mine own elect from the four quarters of the earth, unto a place which I shall prepare, a holy city, that my people may gird up their loins, and be looking forth for the time of my coming, for there shall be my tabernacle, and it shall be called Zion, a new Jerusalem" [see Moses 7:62].

Now I understand by this quotation, that God clearly manifested to Enoch the redemption which He prepared, by offering the Messiah as a Lamb slain from before the foundation of the world; and by virtue of the same, the glorious resurrection of the Savior, and the resurrection of all the human family, even a resurrection of their corporeal bodies, is brought to pass; and also righteousness and truth are to sweep the earth as with a flood. And now, I ask, how righteousness and truth are going to sweep the earth as with a flood? I will answer. Men and angels are to be co-workers in bringing to pass this great work, and Zion is to be prepared, even a new Jerusalem, for the elect that are to be gathered from the four quarters of the earth, and to be established an holy city, for the tabernacle of the Lord shall be with them. (HC 2:254, 260)

14 In speaking of the gathering, we mean to be understood as speaking of it according to scripture, the gathering of the elect of the Lord out of every nation on earth, and bringing them to the place of the Lord of Hosts, when the city of righteousness shall be built, and where the people shall be of one heart and one mind, when the Savior comes; yea, where the people shall walk with God like Enoch, and be free from sin. The word of the Lord is precious; and when we read that the veil spread over all nations will be destroyed, and the pure in heart see God, and reign with Him a thousand years on earth, we want all honest men to have a chance to gather and build up a city of righteousness, where even upon the bells of the horses shall be written *Holiness to the Lord*. (HC 2:357–58)

Zion
14 Meeting of the high council at Kirtland, 6 January 1836.

15 I also beheld the redemption of Zion, and many things which the tongue of man cannot describe in full. (HC 2:381)

16 Be honest one with another, for it seems that some have come short of these things, and some have been uncharitable, and have manifested greediness because of their debts towards those who have been persecuted and dragged about with chains without cause, and imprisoned. Such characters God hates—and they shall have their turn of sorrow in the rolling of the great wheel, for it rolleth and none can hinder. Zion shall yet live, though she seem to be dead. (HC 3:233)

17 We ought to have the building up of Zion as our greatest object. When wars come, we shall have to flee to Zion. . . .
    . . . The time is soon coming, when no man will have any peace but in Zion and her stakes. (HC 3:390, 391)

18 I now deliver it as a prophecy, if the inhabitants of this state, with the people of the surrounding country, will turn unto the Lord with all their hearts, ten years will not roll round before the kings and queens of the earth will come unto Zion, and pay their respects to the leaders of this people; they shall come with their millions, and shall contribute of their abundance for the relief of the poor, and the building up and beautifying of Zion. (HC 4:605–6)

19 The advancement of the cause of God and the building up of Zion is as much one man's business as another's. The only difference is, that one is called to fulfill one duty, and another another duty; "but if one member suffers, all the members suffer with it, and if one member is honored all the rest rejoice with it, and the eye cannot say to the ear, I have no need of thee, nor the head to the foot, I have no need of thee;" party feelings, separate interests, exclusive designs should be lost sight of in the one common cause, in the interest of the whole.

Zion
   15 Vision in the Kirtland Temple, 21 January 1836.
   16 Letter to the Church from Liberty Jail, 16 December 1838.
   17 Discourse on the priesthood, given sometime before 8 August 1839, Commerce (Nauvoo). For a discussion on the dating of this discourse, see *WJS*, p. 22.
   18 Remarks to the Relief Society, Nauvoo, 28 April 1842.
   19 Editorial in the *Times and Seasons*, 2 May 1842.

The building up of Zion is a cause that has interested the people of God in every age; it is a theme upon which prophets, priests and kings have dwelt with peculiar delight; they have looked forward with joyful anticipation to the day in which we live; and fired with heavenly and joyful anticipations they have sung and written and prophesied of this our day; but they died without the sight; we are the favored people that God has made choice of to bring about the Latter-day glory; it is left for us to see, participate in and help to roll forward the Latter-day glory, "the dispensation of the fullness of times, when God will gather together all things that are in heaven, and all things that are upon the earth, even in one," when the Saints of God will be gathered in one from every nation, and kindred, and people, and tongue, when the Jews will be gathered together into one, the wicked will also be gathered together to be destroyed, as spoken of by the prophets; the Spirit of God will also dwell with His people, and be withdrawn from the rest of the nations, and all things whether in heaven or on earth will be in one, even in Christ. The heavenly Priesthood will unite with the earthly, to bring about those great purposes; and whilst we are thus united in one common cause, to roll forth the kingdom of God, the heavenly Priesthood are not idle spectators, the Spirit of God will be showered down from above, and it will dwell in our midst. The blessings of the Most High will rest upon our tabernacles, and our name will be handed down to future ages; our children will rise up and call us blessed; and generations yet unborn will dwell with peculiar delight upon the scenes that we have passed through, the privations that we have endured; the untiring zeal that we have manifested; the all but insurmountable difficulties that we have overcome in laying the foundation of a work that brought about the glory and blessing which they will realize; a work that God and angels have contemplated with delight for generations past; that fired the souls of the ancient patriarchs and prophets; a work that is destined to bring about the destruction of the powers of darkness, the renovation of the earth, the glory of God, and the salvation of the human family. (HC 4:609–10)

20 Moses received the word of the Lord from God Himself; he was the mouth of God to Aaron, and Aaron taught the people, in both

civil and ecclesiastical affairs; they were both one, there was no distinction; so will it be when the purposes of God shall be accomplished: when "the Lord shall be King over the whole earth," and "Jerusalem His throne." "The law shall go forth from Zion, and the word of the Lord from Jerusalem." (HC 5:64)

21 In regard to the building up of Zion, it has to be done by the counsel of Jehovah, by the revelations of heaven; and we should feel to say, "if the Lord go not with us, carry us not up hence." We would say to the Saints that come here, we have laid the foundation for the gathering of God's people to this place, and they expect that when the Saints do come, they will be under the counsel that God has appointed. The Twelve are set apart to counsel the Saints pertaining to this matter; and we expect that those who come here will send before them their wise men according to revelation; or if not practicable, be subject to the counsel that God has given, or they cannot receive an inheritance among the Saints, or be considered as God's people, and they will be dealt with as transgressors of the laws of God. We are trying here to gird up our loins, and purge from our midst the workers of iniquity; and we hope that when our brethren arrive from abroad, they will assist us to roll forth this good work, and to accomplish this great design, that "Zion may be built up in righteousness; and all nations flock to her standard;" that as God's people, under His direction, and obedient to His law, we may grow up in righteousness and truth; that when His purposes shall be accomplished, we may receive an inheritance among those that are sanctified. (HC 5:65–66)

22 I want to make a proclamation to the Elders. I wanted you to stay, in order that I might make this proclamation. You know very well that the Lord has led this Church by revelation. I have another revelation in relation to economy in the Church—a great, grand, and glorious revelation. I shall not be able to dwell as largely upon it now as at some other time; but I will give you the first principles. You know there has been great discussion in relation to Zion—where it is, and where the gathering of the dispensation is, and which I am now going to tell you. The prophets have spoken and written upon it; but I will

Zion
21 Editorial in the *Times and Seasons*, 15 July 1842.
22 General conference address, Nauvoo, 8 April 1844.

make a proclamation that will cover a broader ground. *The whole of America is Zion itself from north to south, and is described by the Prophets, who declare that it is the Zion where the mountain of the Lord should be, and that it should be in the center of the land.* When Elders shall take up and examine the old prophecies in the Bible, they will see it. (HC 6:318–19)

Zion's Camp

1   While we were refreshing ourselves and teams about the middle of the day {June 3rd}, I got up on a wagon wheel, called the people together, and said that I would deliver a prophecy. After giving the brethren much good advice, exhorting them to faithfulness and humility, I said the Lord had revealed to me that a scourge would come upon the camp in consequence of the fractious and unruly spirits that appeared among them, and they should die like sheep with the rot; still, if they would repent and humble themselves before the Lord, the scourge, in a great measure, might be turned away; but, as the Lord lives, the members of this camp will suffer for giving way to their unruly temper. (HC 2:80)

Zion's Camp
  1   Events of Zion's Camp somewhere between the Illinois River and Atlas, Illinois, en route to Missouri, 3 June 1834.

Bibliography

Andrus, Hyrum L. *Joseph Smith, the Man and the Seer.* Salt Lake City: Deseret Book Co., 1960.

Andrus, Hyrum L., and Helen Mae Andrus, comps. *They Knew the Prophet.* Salt Lake City: Bookcraft, 1974.

Backman, Milton V., Jr. *Joseph Smith's First Vision: Confirming Evidences and Contemporary Accounts.* 2d ed., rev. and enl. Salt Lake City: Bookcraft, 1980.

Bitton, Davis, and Gary L. Bunker. "Phrenology Among the Mormons." *Dialogue* 9 (Spring 1974): 43–61.

Brigham Young University (BYU) Studies (Provo, Utah). 1959–present.

Burton, Alma P., comp. and arr. *Discourses of the Prophet Joseph Smith.* Salt Lake City: Deseret Book Co., 1965.

Cannon, Donald Q., comp. *The Wisdom of Joseph Smith.* Orem, Utah: Grandin Book Co., 1983.

Cannon, Donald Q., and Lyndon W. Cook, eds. *Far West Record: Minutes of The Church of Jesus Christ of Latter-day Saints, 1830–1844.* Salt Lake City: Deseret Book Co., 1983.

Cannon, Donald Q., and Larry E. Dahl. *The Prophet Joseph Smith's King Follett Discourse: A Six-Column Comparison of Original Notes and Amalgamations.* Provo, Utah: Religious Studies Center, Brigham Young University, 1983.

Conkling, J. Christopher. *A Joseph Smith Chronology.* Salt Lake City: Deseret Book Co., 1979.

Dahl, Larry E., and Charles D. Tate, Jr., eds. *The Lectures on Faith in Historical Perspective.* Provo, Utah: Religious Studies Center, Brigham Young University, 1990.

Derr, Jill Mulvay, Janath Russell Cannon, and Maureen Ursenbach Beecher. *Women of Covenant: The Story of Relief Society.* Salt Lake City: Deseret Book Co., 1992.

Deseret News Weekly (Salt Lake City, Utah). 1850–1897.

Dibble, Philo. "Philo Dibble's Narrative." In *Early Scenes in Church History*, pp. 74–96. Salt Lake City: Juvenile Instructor Office, 1882. *Early Scenes in*

Church History was reprinted as part of the 4-vols.-in-1 publication *Four Faith-Promoting Classics*. Salt Lake City: Bookcraft, 1968.

Elders' Journal (Kirtland, Ohio, and Far West, Mo.). 1837–1838.

The Evening and the Morning Star (Independence, Mo., and Kirtland, Ohio). 1832–1834.

Gates, Susa Young. *History of the Young Ladies MIA*. Salt Lake City: Deseret News, 1911.

Improvement Era (Salt Lake City, Utah). 1897–1970.

Jarvis, Zora Smith, comp. *Ancestry, Biography, and Family of George A. Smith*. Provo, Utah: Brigham Young University Press, 1962.

Johnson, Benjamin F. *My Life's Review*. Mesa, Ariz.: 21st Century Printing, 1992.

Journal of Discourses. 26 vols. London: Latter-day Saints' Book Depot, 1854–1886.

Juvenile Instructor (Salt Lake City, Utah). 1866–1929.

Kimball, Stanley B. *Heber C. Kimball: Mormon Patriarch and Pioneer*. Urbana and Chicago, Ill.: University of Illinois Press, 1981.

Latter Day Saints' Messenger and Advocate (Kirtland, Ohio). 1834–1837.

Latter-day Saints' Millennial Star (Manchester, Liverpool, and London, England). 1840–1970.

Lundwall, N. B., comp. *The Vision*. Salt Lake City: Bookcraft, n.d.

Madsen, Truman G. *Joseph Smith the Prophet*. Salt Lake City: Bookcraft, 1989.

———., ed. *Concordance of Doctrinal Statements of Joseph Smith*. Salt Lake City: I.E.S. Publishing, 1985.

McConkie, Joseph Fielding, and Robert L. Millet. *Joseph Smith, the Choice Seer*. Salt Lake City: Bookcraft, 1996.

Nauvoo Neighbor (Nauvoo, Ill.). 1843–1845.

Pratt, Parley P. *Autobiography of Parley P. Pratt*. Edited by Parley P. Pratt, Jr. Classics in Mormon Literature. Salt Lake City: Deseret Book Co., 1985.

Smith, Joseph. *An American Prophet's Record: The Diaries and Journals of Joseph Smith*. Edited by Scott H. Faulring. Salt Lake City: Signature Books, 1987.

———. *History of The Church of Jesus Christ of Latter-day Saints*. Edited by B. H. Roberts. 2d ed., rev. 7 vols. Salt Lake City: The Church of Jesus Christ of Latter-day Saints, 1932–51.

———. *Lectures on Faith*. Salt Lake City: Deseret Book Co., 1985.

————. *The Papers of Joseph Smith.* Edited by Dean C. Jessee. 2 vols. Salt Lake City: Deseret Book Co., 1989, 1992.

————. *The Personal Writings of Joseph Smith.* Compiled and edited by Dean C. Jessee. Salt Lake City: Deseret Book Co., 1984.

————. *Scriptural Teachings of the Prophet Joseph Smith.* Selected by Joseph Fielding Smith. Scriptural annotations and introduction by Richard C. Galbraith. Salt Lake City: Deseret Book Co., 1993.

————. *Teachings of the Prophet Joseph Smith.* Selected by Joseph Fielding Smith. Salt Lake City: Deseret Book Co., 1938.

————. *The Words of Joseph Smith.* Compiled and edited by Andrew F. Ehat and Lyndon W. Cook. Provo, Utah: Religious Studies Center, Brigham Young University, 1980.

Smith, Joseph F. *Gospel Doctrine: Selections from the Sermons and Writings of Joseph F. Smith.* Salt Lake City: Deseret Book Co., 1939.

Smith, Lucy Mack. *History of Joseph Smith by His Mother.* Edited by Preston Nibley. Salt Lake City: Bookcraft, 1954.

Times and Seasons (Nauvoo, Ill.). 1839–1846.

Walker, Rodney W., and Noel C. Stevenson, comps. *Ancestry and Descendants of John Walker.* Kaysville, Utah: The John Walker Family Organization, 1953.

Whitney, Orson F. *Life of Heber C. Kimball.* Collector's Edition. Salt Lake City: Bookcraft, 1992.

Woman's Exponent (Salt Lake City, Utah). 1872–1914.

Woodruff, Wilford. *Wilford Woodruff's Journal, 1833–1898.* Typescript. 9 vols. Edited by Scott G. Kenney. Midvale, Utah: Signature Books, 1983–85.

Young Woman's Journal (Salt Lake City, Utah). 1889–1929.

Index

place next to, 50, 53; washing of feet by, 637–39

First principles, 74–75, 242, 249–51, 303, 391, 432. *See also* Baptism; Faith; Gift of the Holy Ghost; Repentance

First Vision, 252–69, 627

Flattery, 269, 716

Flood, 180, 203, 476, 624

Follett, King, 437–38, 561

Fools, 70, 269

Fordham, Elijah, 26–27

Foreordination, 238, 270; of Christ, 345, 347. *See also* Premortality

Forgiveness: and murderers, 438; merciful, 463, 699; of others, 271–73, 514; of sins, 270–73, 292, 297, 360, 389, 494, 609; of sins of Joseph Smith, 254, 255, 264; through confession, 503

Fornication, 29

Foxes, evils compared to, 125, 226, 649

Freedom, 273–74; American, 465; of conscience, 137–38; religious, 144–45, 306, 497. *See also* Liberty

Friends, 560, 720

Friendship, 110, 274–76, 316, 421, 422; must arise from love, 110, 344, 406

— G —

Gabriel (Noah), 19

Garden of Eden, 237, 277, 410, 694

Gates, Susa Young, words of, 436

Gathering, 162, 183, 196, 277–84, 488, 652–63; by angels, 35, 279, 601; for sealing, 177, 210, 284, 605, 611; laws of priesthood predicated upon, 498; necessary to bring about glories of last dis-

pensation, 554; object of, to build temples, 283, 459; of Jews, 196, 277, 282–83; of Lamanites, 336; of Saints from among wicked, 215, 381, 430; of wheat, 707; place of, in Missouri, 433; promise of, 195, 431; to little stone mentioned by Daniel, 154; to Missouri, 281, 433; to Nauvoo, 330; to New Jerusalem, 446; to receive temple ordinances, 661–62; to Zion, 278, 722–23, 725–29; Zion consecrated for, 721

General conference, 284

Gentiles, 86, 329, 367, 461, 462, 551; effect of Holy Ghost on, 82, 323; fulness of, 277; Saints gathered out from, 278, 285; Twelve to preach among, 45, 285

Gift of the Holy Ghost, 75, 103, 152, 202, 275, 285–88, 425, 712; belief in, 55, 250, 698; by laying on of hands, 121, 124, 285, 315, 458; knowledge through, 355, 495, 553; manifestations of, 286–87, 574; through repentance, 479; through baptism, 64–67, 285–87, 458, 479. *See also* Holy Ghost

Gift of tongues. *See* Tongues, gift of

Gifts of the Spirit, 289–90, 346; belief in, 55, 250, 287; discerning of spirits through, 194; through faith, 235–37, 399. *See also* names of individual gifts

Gilbert, Algernon S., 445

God, 142, 197, 290–97; Abel conversed with, 1–2; Abraham conversed with, 470; Adam conversed with, 19; Adam in image of, 22; an exalted man, 295, 324; appearance to Joseph Smith,

About the Editors

Larry E. Dahl is a professor of Church History and Doctrine and serves as an associate dean of Religious Education at Brigham Young University. He received a bachelor's degree in education from the University of Alberta, followed by a master's degree in religious education and a doctorate in education administration from BYU. His background with the Church Educational System has included many teaching and administrative positions. He is coauthor of *Follow the Living Prophets*, and coeditor of *The Capstone of Our Religion: Insights into the Doctrine and Covenants* and *The Lectures on Faith in Historical Perspective*. He has also written many articles for professional and religious publications. He is married to Roberta Erickson Dahl, and the couple have nine children.

Donald Q. Cannon is a professor of Church History and Doctrine and also serves as an associate dean of Religious Education at Brigham Young University. He received bachelor's and master's degrees in history from the University of Utah and a doctorate in history from Clark University. He has taught U.S. history, Church history, the Doctrine and Covenants, and several other courses. He has authored or edited several articles and books on Latter-day Saint Church history, including *Far West Record: Minutes of The Church of Jesus Christ of Latter-day Saints, 1830–1844* and *Historical Atlas of Mormonism*. He is married to JoAnn McGinnis Cannon, and they are the parents of six children.

ISBN 1-57008-311-8
SKU 3395239
$27.95